Modern Employment Law

Modern Employment Law covers all aspects relating to the employment relationship between employer and employee at both individual and collective levels. All chapters are absorbing and exact, with nuanced topics such as unfair dismissal, discrimination and trade union law being explored from several different angles. Pedagogical features such as Thinking Points and Further Reading sections enable students to consolidate and extend their knowledge.

Though primarily aimed at LLB students, this book offers a wide-ranging, accurate, authoritative, contemporary and readable guide to modern employment law for all students of the subject, at both undergraduate and postgraduate level.

Although a collaborative effort, each author focused on specific areas of employment law. Ann Lyon examined the statutory rights of employees including topics such as redundancy, unfair dismissal and discrimination, and equal pay issues. Charles Barrow had primary responsibility for the introduction, the majority of the contract of employment chapters and the collective aspects of employment law.

Charles Barrow, BSc (Econ), LLM (LSE), Cert Ed, Barrister-at-Law, is Senior Lecturer at the Brighton Business School, University of Brighton.

Ann Lyon, BA(Hons) History, MA Medieval Studies, York, MPhil Archaeology, Durham, is Senior Lecturer at the School of Law, Criminology and Government (Faculty of Business), University of Plymouth.

Modern Employment Law

Charles Barrow and Ann Lyon

Routledge
Taylor & Francis Group
LONDON AND NEW YORK

First published 2018
by Routledge
2 Park Square, Milton Park, Abingdon, Oxon OX14 4RN

and by Routledge
711 Third Avenue, New York, NY 10017

Routledge is an imprint of the Taylor & Francis Group, an informa business

British Library Cataloguing in Publication Data
A catalogue record for this book is available from the British Library

Library of Congress Cataloging in Publication Data
Names: Barrow, Charles, author. | Lyon, Ann, 1959- author.
Title: Modern employment law / Charles Barrow and Ann Lyon.
Description: Abingdon, Oxon ; New York, NY : Routledge, 2018. | Includes bibliographical references and index.
Identifiers: LCCN 2017060830| ISBN 9781138887763 (hbk) | ISBN 9781138887879 (pbk) | ISBN 9781317499275 (epub) | ISBN 9781317499268 (mobipocket)
Subjects: LCSH: Labor laws and legislation—England.
Classification: LCC KD3009 .B37 2018 | DDC 344.4201—dc23
LC record available at https://lccn.loc.gov/2017060830

ISBN: 9781138887763 (hbk)
ISBN: 9781138887879 (pbk)
ISBN: 9781315713861 (ebk)

Typeset in Joanna
by Florence Production Ltd, Stoodleigh, Devon, UK

Contents

Table of cases

F

G

I

J

N

O

S

V

W

X

Y

Z

Table of legislation

Statutes

F

G

H

I

U

W

Statutory instruments

C

D

E

European Union

International conventions

Chapter 1

Introduction, historical overview and the institutions of employment law

Chapter contents

1.1 Overview

This chapter considers the historical background to the development of modern employment law and examines the operation of the institutions of employment law that advise on employment issues or adjudicate on and settle employment disputes.

- From the middle ages to the industrial revolution the state controlled the employment relationship through legislation that regulated wages and criminalised workers who left employment or who agitated for higher pay.
- Skilled workers were able to protect their position through the guilds or through self-help groups set up to petition Parliament or JPs to set higher wages. But direct action was criminalised as a common law conspiracy.
- A feature of the industrial revolution was further conflict with the property-owning classes and the state. The Combination Acts of 1799 and 1800 further criminalised workers' organisations.
- Government during the mid-period of the Victorian era did pass social legislation to limit the worst excesses of the factory system but it was not until unions obtained freedom to organise after the passage of the Conspiracy and Protection of Property Act 1875 that some workers gained the benefits of union representation.
- Employers were able to use the new common law civil liabilities developed by the judiciary to limit union influence at the workplace. It was not until 1906 that industrial action to enforce collective bargaining became lawful.
- The modern contract of employment developed from the late nineteenth century onwards with the abolition of criminal controls over employees; replaced by the regulation of the employment relationship by judicial enforcement of contractual obligations.
- After 1906 trade union representation and collective bargaining became an accepted aspect of the employment relationship. The fledging 'voluntarist' system of industrial relations now developed, based on the non-intervention of the law in industrial disputes and on free collective bargaining between the parties.
- In the 1960s the economy deteriorated, and in order to solve the issue of increased industrial action, the Conservative government introduced the Industrial Relations Act 1971 – which reversed 'voluntarism' by introducing legal controls over trade union activity.
- On the election of a new Labour government in 1974 legislative initiatives were introduced to support collective bargaining. On the fall of the government in 1979 many of these provisions were repealed. The new Conservative regimes (in power from 1979 until 1997) followed a legal strategy that limited and regulated trade union activity and looked to reduce individual rights where possible.
- The New Labour government from 1997 introduced new rights at the collective and individual level, including the right to recognition and new unfair dismissal and 'family friendly' rights.
- The coalition government, formed in 2010, undertook a review of individual employment law resulting in reforms to unfair dismissal procedure introduced by the Enterprise and Regulatory Reform Act 2013.
- The Conservative administration, elected in May 2015, has introduced far reaching additional regulation of trade unions through the Trade Union Act 2016.
- A number of specialist institutions exist in this field. The Certification Officer plays an important part in regulating trade unions; ensuring that unions follow their rule book and that the numerous statutory rules that apply to unions are complied with. The Advisory, Conciliation and Arbitration Service's (ACAS) role is to promote the improvement of industrial relations by engaging in the conciliation of disputes at the collective and individual level and to arbitrate on disputes where the parties have agreed. The Central Arbitration Committee's (CAC) main

function is to oversee, administer and determine a recognition application under the Employment Relations Act 1999.

- The vast majority of employment disputes start in the employment tribunal. They were originally intended to provide for a system of quick informal dispute resolution. The complexity of current law has meant that they operate more like employment courts. Appeals from an employment tribunal proceed to the Employment Appeal Tribunal (EAT).

1.2 Employment law – introduction

Employment law regulates the individual relationship between employers and workers and the collective relationship between employers, workers and trade unions. These legal relationships are governed by a variety of sources including the contract of employment individually agreed by the employer and employee (or by a trade union with the employer on the employee's behalf through the mechanism of the collective agreement) and by a wealth of domestic statutory provisions, case law and European Union initiatives that, over the last 30 years, have transformed the nature of the subject.

To better understand the interrelationship between the different sources of law and the contemporary structure of employment law it is helpful to be aware of the historical perspective. Historical perspective also assists us in understanding the political and industrial dynamic that has informed the development of modern employment law; particularly employment protection legislation introduced to soften the often-one-sided common law 'contract of service'. Historically, the employment relationship at the individual level was based on the rights of the 'master' over his 'servant'; limited, by late Victorian times, by the power of collective bargaining where the worker was a member of a trade union recognised by the employer. Thus, much of the early emphasis of the law concerns the fight for the legality of trade unions – the institutions that were striving to actively protect employees at the workplace through collective bargaining and direct representation.

Partly due to the influence of the trade union movement, who preferred to protect their members through industrial strength and collective bargaining rather than by parliamentary intervention, the state did not legislate to secure workers' interests at the individual level in any substantial way until the mid-1960s. It was from this period that the pace of legal intervention in the employment relationship quickened. Modern employment law, as we identify it today, developed at speed after the United Kingdom's accession to the European Community (as was) in 1972; with domestic statutes and European initiatives overlaying the common law with a myriad of regulatory provisions at the individual and collective level. It is these individual and collective employment law provisions – that regulate the contemporary employment relationship – which this book intends to subject to detailed legal analysis.

1.3 Employment law – a historical overview

1.3.1 From the Middle Ages to the Industrial Revolution

Prior to the enormous changes to the economy that occurred with the onset of the Industrial Revolution in the late eighteenth and early nineteenth centuries, the British economy was predominantly agrarian, serviced by a vast pool of unskilled labour. The unskilled labourers were serfs – owned and controlled by their masters. The few skilled workers were known as journeymen, who traditionally plied their trades travelling around the local district. They were members of a craft association or guild and were employed by a master craftsman after serving a lengthy apprenticeship. The 'contract of employment' as known today did not exist – rather, the relationship between the two parties was described as between 'master' and 'servant' with punitive laws regulating the activities of the 'servant'.

The advent of the Black Death in the fourteenth century decimated the working population and the resulting shortage of labour triggered demands for higher wages from both the skilled and the unskilled. The response of the state to this unwanted development was the passage of legislation (the Statute of Labourers 1349 and 1351) that regulated wages and criminalised workers who agitated for higher pay or left their work without permission.

The Tudor and Stuart eras were marked by ever increasing regulation of the economy with the imposition of further wage and price controls through the Statute of Artificers 1563. This Act gave local JPs the authority to fix the wages of both skilled and unskilled labour and, like previous regulatory statutes it was an offence to break an agreement with the employer. Under this legislation, wage fixing for the skilled worker became a form of minimum wage – exceeded where masters could be persuaded, through the power of the guild system or by labour scarcity, to improve the established wage. For the agricultural labourer, however, wage fixing underlined their subservient status as, with no skill to sell, there was usually little need for employers to enhance the pay above the very low subsistence rates set by JPs.[1]

However, over time, the power of the guilds to fix wages and other conditions of work and to protect the customs of the trade was seriously weakened by the extensive regulation of the economy. It was because of the failure of the guilds to adjust to the new conditions of production and to protect the interests of journeymen against the iniquities of wage fixing that groups of journeymen initiated self-help groups that eventually evolved into the first forms of trade unions.

Locally based associations of journeymen had previously existed for recreational and social purposes. The failure of wage fixing to secure acceptable living standards transformed these associations, in the late seventeenth and early eighteenth centuries, into societies and clubs for the provision of mutual insurance benefits against sickness, unemployment, old age and death. These self-help groups were the forerunners of what later became known as 'friendly societies' and spread widely across the country throughout the eighteenth and nineteenth centuries. The more permanent social clubs or friendly societies were transformed into pressure groups to petition Parliament or local JPs to act on their powers of wage fixing. Where these groups agitated for improved pay and conditions the courts declared their actions unlawful as a criminal common law conspiracy,[2] and Parliament proscribed their activities with a series of statutes targeted at specific trades.[3]

An important factor in the development of trade associations during the latter part of the eighteenth century was the response by skilled workers to the changing economic conditions. As the control economy of the seventeenth and early eighteenth centuries was discredited by the new ideas of economic laissez-faire, wage fixing declined and lapsed into disuse, eventually being formally discontinued in 1813. This breakdown of wage fixing, combined with the disintegration of the guild system, meant that skilled workers, when they were dissatisfied with their wages, increasingly directed their demands for redress to employers rather than relying on the system of petitioning Parliament or JPs.

The skilled worker, in adjusting to the new economic realities created by the system of industrial production (with increased specialisation and new methods of machine based work), soon recognised that their bargaining strength was heightened when workers acted in consort.

1 The use of the criminal law to enforce workers' obligations was reinforced by similar legislation in 1747 and 1758.
2 *R v Journeyman Tailors of Cambridge* [1721] 8 Mod Rep 10.
3 For example, in 1747 Parliament made it an offence to leave work unfinished and permitted employers to withhold wages and prosecute servants for any 'ill-behaviour'.

Consequently, despite residual illegality and hostile employers, by the beginning of the nineteenth century a form of organised craft unionism had grown out of the original journeymen trade associations and societies.

1.3.2 The Industrial Revolution

A feature of the early years of the Industrial Revolution was the rise in the demand for both unskilled and skilled labour as the economy grew. The demand for unskilled labour was satisfied by the movement of agrarian labourers to the industrial centres, creating an urban working class. The demand for skilled labour encouraged local autonomous trade associations to take advantage of these economic conditions to flex their newly acquired influence. However, to the owners of capital, combinations of workers were a threat to the profitability of the factories and trade: to the property-owning classes, they were agents of revolution and a threat to political stability. Parliament reacted to the continuing spread of trade unionism by passing the Combination Acts of 1799 and 1800 – criminalising workers' organisations in all trades or occupations by imposing a penalty of 3 months' imprisonment for those who interfered with an employer's business or the employment of workers.

As direct union activities were proscribed, the only alternative for the new workers in the mills and factories was to follow the path beaten by the older craft associations, by either banding together lawfully for the purposes of mutual welfare through friendly societies, or by organising unlawfully in secret in order to avoid suppression from the authorities and victimisation from employers. It was for organising in secret that five agricultural labourers in Dorset, known as the Tolpuddle Martyrs, were prosecuted and sentenced in 1834 to 7 years' transportation to Australia under the Unlawful Oaths Act 1797, which made it an offence to swear unlawful oaths for seditious purposes.

Employers and opponents of trade unions also had other weapons to suppress organised labour. The Master and Servants Act 1823 provided that a servant who was absent from their job before the expiry of their contract committed a criminal offence punishable by 3 months' imprisonment. It was thus unlawful for a servant to pressurise an employer to improve wages and conditions as each individual worker who followed a strike call was personally open to prosecution. Paradoxically, it was at this time that the state initiated the first forms of social legislation to regulate the worst aspects of the early Victorian factory system. The Factories Act 1844 restricted the working hours of women and children in the textile industry, and the Mines Regulation Act 1842 barred women and children from working underground. Parliament was, however, wary of interfering with the employment conditions of adult males and it was not until the end of the century with the passage of the Factories and Workshop Act 1895 that rudimentary health and safety regulation for adult males at the workplace was introduced.

When faced with hostile employers and the trade depression of 1837–1842 (which caused large scale unemployment, a severe loss of union membership and an inevitable weakening of union organisation), workers organisations declined in number and influence. It was not until the end of the trade depression, with the Victorian economy reaching its peak in the 1850s, that skilled artisans vital to the industrial economy revived trade unionism and spawned the birth of a new generation of strong but cautious unions described by the Webbs as the 'new model unions'.[4]

These new unions, based on the old and new skills essential to the economy, were a rather elitist grouping, noted for their 'moderation' in negotiations with employers and belief in the

4 Webb & Webb, 1926, p. 216. The foundation in 1851 of the Amalgamated Society of Engineers is regarded as a landmark in trade union history, as the forerunner of other 'new model unions' organised around the skilled trades essential to the Victorian economy.

provision of friendly benefits. Where possible, they avoided conflict with employers and courted contact with government to win legal reforms on industrial safety and other matters relevant to their membership.

1.3.3 The fight for legality, the rise of collective bargaining and the development of the modern employment contract

Although 'new unionism' spread widely in the skilled trades, many employers remained hostile to broader trade unionism and applied the existing criminal law to limit the organisation of unskilled factory workers. The Combination Act 1825 had given unions a bare legality but, when unions attempted to pursue their objects of improving pay and conditions, they offended against the penal provisions of the Act. To threaten or to take strike action, to boycott non-union labour or picket peacefully were all illegal.

Some of the harshness of the Combination Act was mitigated by the Molestation of Workmen Act 1859. It was lawful under this Act to attempt to secure changes in wages or hours, 'peaceably and in a reasonable manner, and without threats or intimidation to persuade others to cease or abstain from work'. Yet the courts initially responded to this limited protection by interpreting 'threats or intimidation' quite widely[5] and in 1867 despite opposition from unions, a new Master and Servant Act was passed which criminalised certain misconduct at the workplace such as 'neglecting work' in breach of contract.[6]

A further serious setback to trade unions was the decision in *Hornby v Close*[7] that unions were unlawful associations at civil law – union rules could not be enforced as they were in 'restraint of trade'. The Trade Union Act 1871 overturned the *Hornby v Close* decision and provided unions with an immunity from the civil and criminal consequences of the doctrine of restraint of trade and provided unions with a form of legal status. However, another statute – the Criminal Law Amendment Act 1871 – was less favourable to trade unions. This Act repealed the Unlawful Oaths Act 1797 and parts of the Combination Act 1825, but it retained some of the penal sections of the 1825 Act, further imposed other criminal liabilities and failed to deal with the problem of common law criminal conspiracy, revived from time to time by the courts.[8]

The response of the trade union movement to the inadequacies of the Criminal Law Amendment Act 1871 and the judiciary's revival of common law conspiracy was to establish a Parliamentary Committee of the Trades Union Congress (TUC) to vigorously campaign for the repeal of these criminal restrictions. In 1875 the Criminal Law Amendment Act and the remainder of the provisions of the Combination Acts were all repealed, to be replaced by the Conspiracy and Protection of Property Act 1875. This provided an immunity from criminal liability for common law conspiracy where a union was acting in furtherance of a trade dispute and legalised peaceful picketing by providing that mere attendance at a place for the purpose of peacefully communicating information was lawful. Additionally, at the individual level, the Employers and Workman Act 1875 repealed the magistrates' jurisdiction under the Master and Servant Act to punish an individual for breach of contract.

---

5 See *R v Druitt* (1867) 10 Cox CC 592 0 – to give 'black looks' was classified as intimidatory conduct under the Act.

6 The Master and Servant Acts of the nineteenth century were applied selectively and were not enforced against professional or 'higher status' employees – those employees outside of the scope of these Acts had a relationship with their employers more in keeping with a modern contractual model. For lower-level unskilled employees who were defined as 'servants', their behaviour was heavily controlled by this legislation.

7 [1867] LR 2B 155.

8 See *R v Bunn* [1872] 12 Cox CC 316.

It is from this time that the modern contract of employment developed as a mechanism to regulate relations between the individual and their employer. The master-servant model of the eighteenth and nineteenth centuries – where the employer's power of control and direction over the lower class 'servant' employee supported by criminal sanctions – was now being slowly eroded. The abolition of the Master and Servants Acts removing criminal sanctions for breach of contract was an important step, although it did not totally eradicate state control over the contractual relationship.[9] By the early twentieth century the employment relationship based on the contractual model of agreed obligations became more entrenched with the courts now developing implied terms in the contract and enforcing the bilateral express obligations contained in the contract.[10]

With much of the criminal law neutralised, and with trade unions gaining an element of legality by the passage of the Trade Union Act 1871, unskilled workers were now free to initiate organising activity unfettered by the law. This growth of unionism was not, however, without its problems as judicial hostility now resurfaced. The courts responded to the concerns of employers by developing a series of civil liabilities enforceable by way of injunctions and damages claims. The judges developed and refined trade union liability in tort. For example, in *Temperton v Russell*,[11] the tort of inducing breach of contract was applied to the circumstances of an industrial dispute. The House of Lords held that, when a union calls on its members to take strike action, it is committing the tort by persuading members to unlawfully break their contracts of employment.[12] In *Quinn v Leathem*,[13] the House of Lords held that, when industrial action was threatened or occurred, unions as a combination of workers act unlawfully as a civil conspiracy.

As a result of union disquiet over these decisions a Royal Commission on Trade Disputes was set up in 1903 to examine the legal position of trade unions during industrial conflict. The reforming 1906 Liberal government, influenced by their supporters in the union movement, took account of many of the proposals from the TUC, which were enacted in the Trade Disputes Act 1906. This Act forms the basis of the present structure of industrial action law, providing the unions with a liberty to strike by granting trade unions an immunity from certain actions in tort, providing the action is taken 'in contemplation or furtherance of a trade dispute'. This pattern of protection has remained until today, although as will be seen in Chapter 20, these immunities have often been under judicial attack.[14]

It was from the late nineteenth century to 1914 that the system of industrial relations that lasted for much of the twentieth century was developed. By the time of the First World War, the enactment of the Trade Union Act 1871, the Trade Disputes Act 1906 and the Trade Union Act 1913 had removed criminal liabilities, mitigated the worst effects of the civil liabilities, and thereby had temporarily halted statutory and judicial interference in union industrial, political and internal affairs. The legitimacy of union action in the pursuit of recognition and collective bargaining was recognised and the system of 'voluntarism' or 'collective laissez-faire' had now emerged, based on the non-intervention of the law in industrial disputes and on free collective bargaining unhindered by legal constraints.

---

9 For example, section 3(3) of the Employers and Workmen Act 1875 permitted courts to grant an order of specific performance to enforce contractual obligations against employees in breach of contract.

10 See as examples, *Parkin v South Hetton Coal Co* (1907) 98 LT 162; *Hanley v Pease Partners* [1915] 1 KB 698; *Devonald v Rosser & Sons Ltd* [1906] 2 KB 728.

11 [1893] 2 QB 545.

12 In the landmark decision of *Taff Vale Railway Co v ASRS* [1901] AC 426, the House of Lords declared that trade unions themselves possessed sufficient legal status to be held liable in their own name for inducing breach of contract.

13 [1901] AC 495.

14 The courts in this period also attempted to interfere with the political activities of trade unions by declaring (in *Osborne v ASRS* [1910] AC 87) that it was unlawful for trade unions to apply their funds for political purposes as it was contrary to their objects contained in the Trade Union Act 1871. Parliament reversed this decision in the Trade Union Act 1913.

During this period union influence played a part in the passage of many social and industrial reforms – such as the Workers Compensation Act 1906, Old Age Pensions Act 1908, Coal Mines (Eight Hours) Act 1908 and National Insurance Act 1911. Furthermore, the impact of collective bargaining was recognised by the House of Commons Fair Wages Resolutions of 1891 and 1909, which introduced the notion of the State as a 'model' employer. These resolutions required employers who contracted with government departments to observe minimum standards of pay for their employees equivalent to that 'commonly' recognised in the relevant industry. In those industries where workers were denied union representation and so were without proper bargaining structures, the Trade Boards Act 1909 set up machinery to determine guaranteed minimum wages.

This fledgling 'voluntarist' or 'non-interventionist' policy was, however, put under pressure by the inexorable rise of union influence in the early years of the twentieth century. As trade unions grew in strength, recognition disputes escalated. The response of the government to these developments was to establish the Whitley Committee in 1917 with the remit to advise on securing improvements in industrial relations. The main thrust of the Committee's recommendations was that the role of government was to support ordered collective bargaining by creating the means for union and employer to meet and negotiate, and to provide machinery to facilitate settlement of industrial disputes. Accordingly, the Industrial Courts Act 1919 granted the Ministry of Labour authority to assist in the settlement of disputes by conciliation, voluntary arbitration or special inquiry. The Act also set up the Industrial Court – a permanent court of arbitration. Also stemming from the Whitley Committee proposals was a new Trade Boards Act, which was passed in 1918. This Act permitted the Minister of Labour to establish a Trade Board in any industry where there was no collective bargaining, with the authority to set minimum wages in the relevant trade. Even after the general strike of 1926, voluntary structures for the settlement of strikes remained in place and the promotion of national bargaining remained a focus of industrial policy throughout the 1930s.

1.3.4 The years of 'voluntarism': 1945–1979

The Second World War years were characterised by the imposition of legal regulation justified on the grounds of wartime necessity. The Conditions of Employment and National Arbitration Order (SI 1940/1305) gave legal force to collective agreements enforceable via an award of the National Arbitration Tribunal. Where employers refused to negotiate or renegotiate a new collective agreement, the Order enforced the 'recognised terms and conditions of employment' pertaining to the industry.

In the post-war period provisions that supplemented and supported collective bargaining were developed. The Wages Councils Act 1945 renamed the Trade Boards and expanded their authority to determine additional terms and conditions of service for employees apart from pay, and to examine other industrial matters such as training issues. The Fair Wages Resolution was revised in 1946, extending its application to sub-contractors and incorporating collectively negotiated industry-wide standards into government contracts.

For almost a decade from the early 1950s, a degree of consensus existed between the political parties on industrial policy and employment protection issues. There was broad acceptance of the role of trade unions within a system of collective bargaining unhampered by state intervention. Significant pieces of employment legislation were introduced in this period – the Contracts of Employment Act 1963 provided that all employees were entitled to a minimum period of notice and a written statement of terms and conditions of employment, and the Redundancy Payments Act 1965 guaranteed a minimum level of compensation for dismissal on grounds of redundancy.

As the economic position in the late 1950s changed, wage inflation became a matter of grave concern to successive governments in the 1960s, both Labour and Conservative, who believed that trade union bargaining was responsible for initiating inflationary wage-price spirals. The failure of a voluntary strategy of wage restraint led to a non-statutory pay policy imposed in the public sector in 1961. In 1962, the first Incomes Policy was formally put into place to control collective bargaining between employer and union by imposing pay norms in certain industries. The Labour government, elected in 1964, introduced greater management of the economy by creating a National Board for Prices and Incomes with powers to recommend pay freezes in a particular industry. An even more comprehensive regulation of prices and incomes was put into place by the Prices and Incomes Act 1966, setting specific upper limits to wage increases. Conflict soon arose between these economic policies, based on counter-inflationary incomes policies to limit pay increases, and the free operation of the collective bargaining process.

The response of the Labour government to the deteriorating industrial situation was to set up a Royal Commission[15] to examine the industrial relations framework. The Commission (known as the Donovan Commission after Lord Donovan, the Commission's chairman) emphasised that industrial conflict was merely a symptom of the underlying problems of ineffective collective bargaining procedures in industry. The Donovan Commission recommended a strengthening of central bargaining and argued that the law should be used to foster and encourage this model of collective bargaining. Most radically the Commission proposed that legal support for collective bargaining was required, such as a union right to recognition and consultation and to information for collective bargaining purposes.

Before any recommendations of the Donovan Commission could be fully implemented, the Labour government was defeated at the 1970 general election. The new Conservative government introduced a radical new approach to the organisation of industrial relations, building on ideas imported from the United States. This approach was based on the legal regulation of industrial relations by the provision of legally enforceable rights and obligations for employers and workers. These ideas were embodied into the Industrial Relations Act 1971. The Act introduced the notion of legally binding collective agreements fixed for a set period and the regulation of industrial action. Ballots before industrial action were introduced. In certain circumstances a compulsory 'cooling off' period of 28 days had to be observed before the action could continue. Although the Act provided for certain additional individual rights – such as the right to claim the new remedy of unfair dismissal – to trade unions the Industrial Relations Act was an unacceptable restriction on their hard-won autonomy from legal intervention. Consequently, the experiment collapsed amongst industrial chaos far worse than the strife it was designed to cure.

The Labour administration elected in 1974 repealed the Industrial Relations Act (apart from provisions protecting against unfair dismissal) and set about introducing a comprehensive package of legal measures (through the Trade Union and Labour Relations Act 1974 and the Employment Protection Act 1975) to encourage and underpin collective bargaining. The Advisory, Conciliation and Arbitration Service (ACAS) was created with a brief to promote the improvement of industrial relations by encouraging the extension of collective bargaining and to advise on the improvement and reform of bargaining procedures within industries. The Central Arbitration Committee (CAC) replaced the National Arbitration Board set up in 1971, itself the replacement for the Industrial Court established in 1919. Industrial tribunals were given additional jurisdiction and more powers and a new specialist appeal court, the Employment Appeal Tribunal, was created.

There was enhanced legal support for collective bargaining by strengthening trade union organisation through rights for members and officials to engage in trade union activities. Collective 'props' to bargaining were introduced which provided unions with rights to recognition, consultation on issues such as collective redundancies and information for bargaining purposes. Furthermore, a 'floor of (individual) rights' (such as maternity pay and guaranteed pay on lay-off) was provided by the Employment Protection Act 1975 via the incorporation of statutory implied

---

15 The Royal Commission on Trade Unions and Employers Associations, Cmnd 3623, 1968.

terms into the individual employment contract. The Terms and Conditions of Employment Act 1959 was replaced by Schedule 11 to the Employment Protection Act 1975, which introduced procedures for imposing collectively agreed minimum terms on employers within a particular industry. It was also during this period that legislation was brought forward to tackle sex and race discrimination – the Equal Pay Act 1970, the Race Relations Act 1976 and the Sex Discrimination Act 1975 were passed.

The *quid pro quo* for the provision of these employment benefits was union co-operation in the drive to conquer inflation by the moderation of their wage demands – this became known as the Social Contract. However, by the late 1970s the Social Contract had broken down, particularly in the public sector, which did not benefit from the productivity deals. The Labour pay policy was this time challenged, not by the unofficial wildcat strikes of the 1960s, but by co-ordinated national action. Industrial action in the winter of 1978–1979, the so-called 'winter of discontent', ushered in the General Election of 1979 and the Thatcher-led Conservative government.

1.3.5 The Conservative administrations: 1979–1997

In the 1980s and 1990s, consecutive Conservative administrations followed a legal strategy that limited trade union rights and regulated their activities whilst promoting labour market flexibility by deregulating in the area of the individual employment relationship – resulting in profound changes in the relationship between workers and their employer.

At the collective level the Conservatives introduced a series of statutes that, incrementally, over the years, has had a major impact on trade union behaviour and activity. The first legislative intervention – the Employment Act 1980 – repealed the existing statutory recognition procedure, introduced curbs on picketing and secondary action and restricted the individual's right to claim unfair dismissal. In 1982 the Employment Act restricted lawful industrial action by narrowing the definition of a trade dispute, severely limited the operation of the closed shop and removed the immunity trade unions enjoyed from actions in tort. The Trade Union Act 1984 concerned itself with the internal administration of a trade union. It enforced compulsory elections for union executive committee positions and the use of ballots prior to a union establishing a political fund or engaging in industrial action.

Emboldened by success in facing down the miners' strike of 1984–1985, and by the 1987 landslide victory, the administration quickened the pace of reform. The Employment Act 1988 further intervened in unions' internal affairs by introducing additional balloting rules, the right for individual members to sue their union where it was acting unlawfully and regulation of a union's financial affairs. The Employment Act 1990 abolished the closed shop completely by making it unlawful to refuse to employ a person on the grounds of non-membership of a union, outlawed all secondary action and limited the rights strikers had to claim unfair dismissal. The final major statute of this period on collective labour law was the Trade Union Reform and Employment Rights Act 1993, which introduced further compulsory procedural requirements prior to calling strike action and additional regulation of the internal financial affairs of trade unions.[16]

At the individual level the Conservatives attempted to limit workers' statutory rights but were often frustrated by developments at the European level, with specific rights being created through European Community initiatives.[17] Where there was a lack of European protection the government

---

16 All collective labour law was consolidated in 1992 into the Trade Union and Labour Relations (Consolidation) Act.

17 For example, the Acquired Rights Directive forced the government in 1981 to introduce the TUPE Regulations (SI 1981 No 1794) giving employees rights on takeovers and mergers of undertakings, and the Equal Pay Directive spawned the Equal Pay (Amendment) Regulations (SI 1983 No 1794) which gave women the right to claim equal pay when their work was of 'equal value'.

revoked a number of the individual provisions created by the previous Labour regime. The repeal of Schedule 11 in 1980 had struck the first blow against the 'fair wages' policy in poorly unionised industries. The Fair Wages Resolution was rescinded in 1983. This was followed in 1986 by the Wages Act, which curtailed their powers by removing protection for anyone over 21; with full abolition being finally achieved in 1993. The 1989 Employment Act further reduced individual rights by exempting small employers from aspects of unfair dismissal law. However, one landmark piece of legislation, the Disability Discrimination Act 1995, demonstrated that a more expansive approach was taken towards discrimination issues. It was also in the early part of the 1990s that the government had to respond to further European Directives extending individual rights. Thus, by 1993 there was legislation on issues such as maternity pay and leave, extending protection on a transfer of undertakings and redundancy and to a written statement of terms and conditions – with all individual employment law provisions consolidated in 1996 into the Employment Rights Act.

1.3.6 The Labour governments: 1997–2010

On the replacement of the Conservative government after the victory of the Labour Party in the General Election of May 1997 the New Labour administration's flagship initiative on employment and trade union law – outlined in the White Paper *Fairness at Work*,[18] and contained in the subsequent Employment Relations Act 1999 – saw the introduction of new rights at the individual and collective level, although not the repeal of the vast majority of the recent trade union reforms. At the collective level the Employment Relations Act introduced, *inter alia*, the right for trade unions to claim recognition after a successful ballot of the designated workforce and protection for those dismissed during an industrial dispute. The 1999 Act also included individual employment provisions, reducing the qualification period for claiming unfair dismissal or redundancy, introducing new maternity and paternity rights and providing the powers for government to transpose new EU Directives. Other important legal developments introduced at an early stage in the first Parliament included the National Minimum Wage Act 1998, the Working Time Regulations 1998 (passed to implement the 1993 EU Working Time Directive, which limits hours of work for many workers and regulates annual leave and rest break entitlements) and the Public Interest Disclosure Act 1998 (which protects 'whistleblowers' for making disclosures in the public interest).

The Employment Act 2002 further implemented the 'family friendly' aspects of Labour policies, providing better parental and maternity entitlements and the right to request flexible working, rights further developed in the Work and Families Act 2006. The 2004 Employment Relations Act included both individual and collective provisions. Amendments were made to the recognition procedures; measures were introduced to simplify the law on industrial action ballots and extend protection for those who have been dismissed for engaging in lawful industrial action. The operation of some individual rights was enhanced, such as improving the national minimum wage enforcement procedure and certain unfair dismissal provisions. The Employment Act 2008 concerned itself with streamlining tribunal procedural issues and further developing the enforcement procedure for the national minimum wage.

European developments continued to influence the landscape of both individual and collective rights. At the collective level the Information and Consultation Directive 2002 led to the Information and Consultation of Employees Regulations 2004, requiring employers to set up information and consultation mechanisms with the workforce. A new Acquired Rights Directive, introduced by the Transfer of Undertakings (Protection of Employment) Regulations 2006, further reformed the

18 Cmnd 3968, 1998.

protection employees are entitled to on mergers of enterprises. A number of European Directives (on discrimination against part-time workers and fixed term employees) were transposed in early 2000.[19] The law on discrimination was overhauled by the EU Equal Treatment Framework Directive, resulting in additional domestic provisions on religious, sexual orientation and age discrimination, and amendments to existing laws on equal pay, and race, sex and disability discrimination. One of the final acts of the Labour administration before the 2010 election was the introduction of the Equality Act, which received the royal assent in October 2010. This is both a consolidating Act, bringing all the discrimination grounds into one statute, and one that refines and extends protection.

1.3.7 The Liberal Democrat/Conservative coalition government: 2010–2015

The new government, elected in spring 2010, made it clear there were no plans to repeal the restrictive trade union law. On the contrary, as a consequence of public sector strike action in response to coalition economic pressures, both the Secretary of State for Business, Innovation and Skills[20] and the Cabinet Secretary,[21] amongst others, warned that the government was minded to further regulate trade union industrial activities.

At the individual level the main focus of employment policy had been to reduce the 'burden on businesses'. Thus, in order to cut 'red tape', deregulate the labour market and stimulate the economy, the government announced a departmental review of individual employment law rights soon after taking office. The review considered changes to redundancy rights, unfair dismissal and discrimination compensation, employment tribunal procedure, and flexible working and parental leave provisions. The review resulted in the passage of the Enterprise and Regulatory Reform Act 2013, which has introduced, amongst other changes to employment law, amendments to unfair dismissal protection – with the qualification period to be able to claim increasing from 1 year to 2 years,[22] and procedural changes permitting employment tribunal judges to sit alone on all unfair dismissal cases.[23]

Additionally, the Act has introduced provisions enforcing compulsory conciliation before tribunal claims are entitled to be lodged and has granted powers to tribunals to introduce financial penalties on employers who have breached individual rights. Employment tribunal procedure has been streamlined, with tribunals permitted to engage in paper adjudication in certain circumstances. Controversially the Act also introduced a deposit system of employment tribunal fees for applicants, with a sliding scale, starting at £250 for the simplest claims. In 2017 the trade union, Unison, successfully challenged the fees regime as indirectly discriminatory. The fee requirements had an adverse impact on women, as the fees for discrimination claims were substantially higher than for other claims in employment tribunals.[24]

1.3.8 The Conservative government: 2015–

On the return of a majority Conservative administration in the May 2015 election the government introduced legislation further regulating trade union activity. The Trade Union Act 2016 introduced

19 Part-time Workers (Prevention of Less Favourable Treatment) Regulations (SI 2000/1551); Fixed Term Employees (Prevention of Less Favourable Treatment) Regulations (SI 2002/2034)).

20 Speech at the GMB annual conference, *Guardian*, 6 June 2011.

21 Interview in *The Telegraph*, 26 November 2011.

22 Unfair Dismissal (Variation of Qualifying Period) Order (SI 2012/989).

23 The Employment Tribunal Act 1996 (Tribunal Composition) Order (SI 2012 /988).

24 *R (on the application of UNISON) v Lord Chancellor* [2017] UKSC 51.

new restrictions on industrial action through additional constraints on picketing, and imposed further balloting requirements on trade unions prior to industrial action. The Act introduced threshold tests that must be met – otherwise industrial action will be unlawful. At least 50 per cent of the membership must participate in the ballot and (for strikes in the public sector) there is a requirement that 40 per cent of those entitled to vote (not those who have voted) must vote 'yes' for the ballot to be effective. The Act also further regulated union political funds and facility time, and increased the powers of the Certification Officer to investigate trade union behaviour.

A major development of some importance was, of course, the result of the referendum on the withdrawal of the United Kingdom from the European Union. A significant amount of United Kingdom employment law emanates from the European Union. Thus, the on-going Brexit negotiations may well have significant consequences for employment rights in the near future. At the time of writing there is no clear understanding of how the Brexit process will unfold.

1.4 The institutions of employment law

Where employment disputes arise, either at the collective or individual level, specialised courts have a role to play in determining the outcome. Additionally, as we have seen from our historical review, governments have been concerned to encourage settlement of disputes at the collective and individual level without recourse to legal action. The institutions below play a role in the adjudication, conciliation and arbitration of disputes.

1.4.1 The Certification Officer

The Certification Officer is an independent official, appointed by government, who plays an important role in the area of internal trade union law. The office of Certification Officer has a lengthy historical pedigree. The original forerunner to the Certification Officer was the Registrar of Friendly Societies who administered the registration of unions under the Trade Union Act 1871. This was abolished by the Industrial Relations Act 1971, and replaced by a system of registration administered by a Registrar of Trade Unions.

After the repeal of the Industrial Relations Act in 1975, the Registrar of Trade Unions was replaced by the office of the Certification Officer created by the Employment Protection Act 1975. The Certification Officer is appointed by the Secretary of State for Business, Energy and Industrial Strategy and is financed and staffed by the Advisory, Conciliation and Arbitration Service (ACAS), although formally independent of both ACAS and government.

Under the Employment Protection Act 1975, the duties of the Certification Officer were limited to supervising trade union compliance with the statutory requirements outlined in the Trade Union and Labour Relations Act 1974, and with administering the list of trade unions and certifying their independence. As the statutory regulation of trade unions increased during the 1980s and early 1990s, the administrative role of the Certification Officer has been supplemented by an expansion in supervisory and judicial functions relating to internal and external trade union activity.[25] The role of the Certification Officer has been further expanded by the Trade Union Act 2016 – equipping the Certification Officer with enlarged powers to investigate and take enforcement

25 The rationale for the expansion of the Certification Officers role by the Employment Relations Act 1999 (as set out in the White Paper *Fairness at Work*, Cmnd 3968, 1998) was that by giving this responsibility to the Certification Officer trade union members would be able to secure their rights more easily and effectively without the cost and delay associated with court proceedings.

action against trade unions for breaches of their statutory duties. It should, however, be noted that, as of December 2017, not all of these powers are in force.

The main responsibilities of the Certification Officer have been consolidated into the Trade Union and Labour Relations (Consolidation) Act (TULR(C)A) 1992, and now include:

a) maintaining a list of trade unions and employers' associations and certifying the independence of trade unions who are on this list and who apply for a certificate of independence;
b) seeing that unions keep appropriate accounts and comply with the statutory provisions governing union accounting and superannuation matters;
c) ensuring compliance with statutory procedures relating to the setting up and operation of union political funds and approving political fund ballot rules;
d) ensuring the observance of the statutory rules concerning union mergers and transfer of engagements;
e) hearing complaints over the handling of secret ballots for union elections, over the conduct of merger ballots and for breaches of the political fund rules;
f) hearing complaints over the failure of a union to compile and maintain a register of members' names and addresses;
g) hearing and investigating complaints about alleged financial malpractice; and
h) investigating and adjudicating on alleged trade union breaches of the rule book.

Part Three of the Transparency of Lobbying, Non-Party Campaigning and Trade Union Administration Act 2014 has (amongst other changes to trade union law) built upon the existing duty in s. 24 TULR(C)A 1992 (for a trade union to ensure that its register of members is accurate and up-to-date), by requiring unions to supply an Annual Audit Certificate. Unions with more than 10,000 members must appoint an external 'Assurer' to certify that the union systems are satisfactory for the purposes of meeting the requirements of s. 24.

1.4.1.1 Jurisdiction for breach of statutory rights

Where a union member's right to inspect union accounts (s. 30 of the TULR(C)A 1992) is violated, s. 31 of the TULR(C)A 1992 provides that the Certification Officer has jurisdiction (in conjunction with the court) to adjudicate on breaches of this right.[26] The Certification Officer should determine the application within 6 months, is entitled to make 'enquiries as he thinks fit', and give both parties the opportunity to be heard.[27] Where the Certification Officer finds the claim well founded, an order may be made (enforceable in the same way as a court order) to ensure enforcement of the right – to inspect the accounts, to be accompanied by an accountant and to be supplied with extracts or copies of the accounts.[28]

Section 72A TULR(C)A 1992 gives the Certification Officer jurisdiction (as an alternative, not as an addition to court proceedings) over complaints of a breach of the statutory rules on the use of general funds for political objects. Similar procedural requirements as outlined above apply – although here the application is for a declaration, and reasons for the decision must be given. Where the union intends to remedy the breach, the declaration must specify the steps the union needs to take to do so. The Certification Officer also has the authority to issue any necessary order, and both declarations and orders are enforceable as if made by the court.[29]

---

26 An applicant cannot however apply to both the court and certification officer (s. 31(6)(7)).
27 Section 31(2A)(2C).
28 Section 31(2B).
29 Section 72A(4)(5)(7).

1.4.1.2 Additional jurisdiction over breaches of union rules

The Employment Relations Act 1999 (creating ss. 108A–108C of the TULR(C)A 1992) introduces additional powers for the Certification Officer to investigate certain breaches of union rules; previously, the only remedy was a common-law action in the civil courts. A member of a trade union has the right to apply to the Certification Officer if there has been a breach or threatened breach of a trade union's rules (including the rules of any branch or section) relating to any of the matters set out in s. 108A(2) of the TULR(C)A 1992. The matters are:

a) the appointment or election of a person to, or the removal of a person from, any office;
b) disciplinary proceedings by the union (including expulsion);
c) the balloting of members on any issue other than industrial action;
d) the constitution or proceedings of any executive committee or of any decision-making meeting; and
e) such other matters as may be specified in an order made by the Secretary of State.

The applicant must be a member of the union, or have been a member at the time of the alleged or threatened breach and the application must be made within a 6-month time limit from the date of the breach or the conclusion of the internal complaint procedure.[30] Once an application has been made to the Certification Officer, the applicant may not complain to the court on the same matter.[31] The Certification Officer may refuse to accept an application unless satisfied that the applicant has taken all reasonable steps to resolve the claim by the use of any existing union internal complaints procedure.[32] On the acceptance of the complaint, the Certification Officer has powers to initiate enquiries regarding the claim, must provide the applicant and the trade union with an opportunity to be heard and must give reasons for his decision to make or refuse the declaration asked for.[33]

Where a declaration is made, the Certification Officer may also make an enforcement order, imposing on the union one or more of the following requirements:

a) To take such steps to remedy the breach, or withdraw the threat of a breach, as may be specified in the order.
b) To abstain from such acts as may be so specified with a view to securing that a breach or threat of the same or a similar kind does not occur in the future.

Where an order imposes a requirement on the union, as in (a) above, the order must specify the period within which the union must comply with the requirement of the order, and any union member is entitled to enforce an enforcement order, not just the original applicant.[34]

1.4.1.3 Enforcement procedure

The enforcement mechanism provides for binding orders (enforceable as an order of the court) to be granted where:

a) a union has failed to maintain the register of members;
b) a union permits an officer (having offended against certain provisions of the TULR(C)A 1992) to hold union office contrary to the statute;

30 Section 108A(3)(6)(7).
31 Section 108A(14)(15).
32 Section 108B(1).
33 Section 108B(2).
34 Section 108B(7).

c) a union has failed to comply with the statutory requirements to hold a balloted election for union office; or
d) a union has failed to comply with the statutory requirements to hold ballots on political resolutions or failed to comply with ballot rules.

Where there is an application to the Certification Officer for an order to force the union to comply with the relevant provision, that individual cannot then apply to the court (and vice versa, should the application be first made to the court). However, a different person is not barred from applying to the Certification Officer or court on the same issue, although when considering the new application, the Certification Officer or court should have regard to any previous decisions or deliberations on the matter.

The procedure to obtain and enforce an order under this jurisdiction is complex and detailed. On an application, the Certification Officer should make such enquiries as he thinks are necessary, and must give the applicant and trade union the opportunity to be heard. A declaration may then be made, specifying the trade union's failure, and giving reasons for the decision. Unless the Certification Officer deems it inappropriate, an enforcement order (enforceable by any member of the union) may now be made ordering the union to remedy the failure (such as to hold a ballot in accordance with political ballot rules or an election ballot in accordance with the statutory requirements), or to abstain from future acts so the failure is not repeated. A declaration or enforcement order is to be treated as if granted by a court. Rights of appeal proceed to the Employment Appeal Tribunal (on points of law) from the Certification Officer's decisions.

1.4.1.4 Conclusions

The Certification Officer's annual reports are a source of information on the type of complaints received. The reports confirm that trade unions broadly comply with the regulatory framework. For example, in the 2013/2014 annual report it was disclosed that there were 569 enquiries that resulted in 28 complaints under the legislation with, after investigation, the Certification Officer making two enforcement orders. The most recent Certification Officer report, 2016/2017 confirms this, with a very low number of complaints being upheld against trade unions.

The additional powers and new enforcement procedure provided for the Certification Officer in the Trade Union Act 2016 may well see a change in this trend. To date, only a handful of sections of the 2016 Act have been implemented that impact on the work of the Certification Officer. Section 11 (amending s. 84 TULR(C)A 1992) holds that where a trade union sets up a new political fund then all members of the union must give express consent to making contributions to the political fund and have the right to cancel their contribution at any time. A new s. 84A TULR(C)A 1992 requires a trade union to send detailed information on this right to all members, with the Certification Officer having the duty to monitor compliance and hear complaints about its operation. Section 12 (introducing a new s. 32ZB TULR(C)A 1992) adds a requirement for unions to include details of their political expenditure in their annual returns. Section 7 (introducing a new s. 32ZA TULR(C)A 1992) requires a trade union to include details of any industrial action (taken in the reporting period) in its annual return to the Certification Officer – including confirmation that the relevant ballot thresholds have been met.

When fully implemented, the Trade Union Act will significantly affect the role and work of the Certification Officer. The Certification Officer will have the power to investigate and determine breaches of statutory provisions without a complaint from a member and will be given increased penalty and enforcement powers. In his 2015/2016 Annual Report the Certification Officer identified some concerns about these significant changes. In particular, he warned that permitting complaints to be made by members of the public might expose unions to complaints made for industrial, political or other reasons.[35] Furthermore, the changes in the 2016 Act allow the Certification Officer to be investigator, prosecutor and adjudicator of complaints, raising issues as to whether the powers may violate Article 6 of the European Convention on the right to a fair trial.[36]

❖ THINKING POINT

Why do you think the Certification Officer's regulatory and enforcement functions have increased so markedly over the last 25 years? Are there any other voluntary bodies regulated to this extent? If not, why not?

1.4.2 The Advisory, Conciliation and Arbitration Service (ACAS)

ACAS is funded by the Department for Business, Energy and Industrial Strategy and is a non-departmental public body. ACAS was originally established by the Employment Protection Act 1975 as a single unifying agency to take over the responsibilities of conciliation and aspects of arbitration previously held by the Department of Employment and the Commission on Industrial Relations. ACAS was also charged under the Employment Protection Act with the broader remit, previously undertaken by the Commission on Industrial Relations, of 'promoting the improvement of industrial relations, and in particular of encouraging the extension of collective bargaining and the development and where necessary, reform of collective bargaining machinery'.

This requirement to promote and encourage the extension of collective bargaining was looked on unfavourably by the Conservative government and this was repealed by the Trade Union Reform and Employment Rights Act 1993. Instead there was a reaffirmation of ACAS's conciliation and arbitration duties in s. 209 of the TULR(C)A 1992. This section stated that the duty of ACAS was now 'to promote the improvement of industrial relations, in particular, by exercising its functions in relation to the settlement of trade disputes (by conciliation and arbitration)'.

In the employment White Paper, *Fairness at Work*,[37] ACAS's advisory mediation and dispute resolution functions were identified as being of particular relevance to modern day industrial relations. ACAS was seen as a proponent and facilitator of the 'partnership at work' principle that was the main focus of New Labour's employment policy. In order to enhance ACAS's role in dispute prevention, s. 26 of the Employment Relations Act 1999 repeals much of the wording that was introduced in 1993, leaving the statutory terms of reference of ACAS now to be solely 'to promote the improvement of industrial relations'.[38]

1.4.2.1 Conciliation

ACAS engages in both collective and individual conciliation. For a number of years ACAS has offered a system of voluntary individual conciliation for unfair dismissal claims prior to employment tribunal proceedings being initiated. The conciliation officer allocated to the case contacts the parties after the claim has been submitted to ascertain whether a settlement is possible – but participation is not compulsory, either party can decline to co-operate with the process. In order

35 Certification Officer's Annual Report, 2015/2016, p. 3.
36 For a detailed analysis of the reforms introduced by the Trade Union Act 2016, see Cavalier & Arthur, 2016.
37 Cm 3968, 1998.
38 Section 209 TULR(C)A 1992.

to further encourage earlier settlement of claims the Employment Act 2008 introduced an ACAS-led voluntary 'pre-claim conciliation' service before the application is processed. As a consequence of the success of this more proactive conciliation system the government in 2013 (via provisions in the Enterprise and Regulatory Reform Act[39]) has introduced a compulsory intervention process run by ACAS for nearly all workplace disputes, known as 'Early Conciliation'. All claimants are required to engage with the conciliation process before presenting a tribunal claim. A tribunal claim will only be considered once a Certificate has been issued by ACAS confirming conciliation on the dispute has been attempted and failed. The aim behind this process (where ACAS resolves the claim without tribunal involvement) is clearly to lessen the burden on tribunals and subsequently save on the costs of tribunals.

The procedures concerning collective conciliation are contained in ss. 210 and 211 of the TULR(C)A 1992. Where one or both parties to a 'trade dispute' request the assistance of the services of ACAS, an officer of ACAS may be appointed to offer assistance to the parties 'with a view to bringing about a settlement'. The parties are encouraged by the ACAS conciliator to settle the dispute using their own agreed procedure. Intervention by a conciliator will not normally happen until these procedures have been exhausted. Often a referral to ACAS is written into collectively agreed dispute procedures as a final stage after the effort to resolve the dispute internally has failed.

The success of the conciliation of collective trade disputes is dependent on the parties' willingness to accept the good offices of ACAS and to submit in good faith to the process. Statistical evidence suggests that both sides of industry frequently have recourse to ACAS and are satisfied with this aspect of ACAS's work.[40]

1.4.2.2 Arbitration and mediation

Voluntary arbitration is the process where a dispute has been referred to an arbitrator for settlement with the consent of both parties. Usually, the parties accept the binding nature of the arbitrator's award. Dispute mediation occurs where the parties have agreed to refer the issues in dispute to a mediator, but they have not necessarily agreed to accept the mediator's findings, although the mediator's recommendations may form the basis of a settlement. Unlike conciliation, the mediator takes an active role, putting forward possible solutions, which are considered by both sides.

ACAS has a brief under s. 212 of the TULR(C)A 1992 to administer the arbitration process where there is a dispute between union and employer. ACAS does not provide arbitrators directly from its staff but, on the request of one of the parties and with the consent of both, will appoint an independent person from a panel it maintains or refer the dispute to the Central Arbitration Committee. ACAS should normally recommend arbitration only after internal disputes procedures and conciliation have failed. An arbitrator has sole authority on matters of procedure and will usually take written and oral evidence before making an award. The decision of an arbitrator is not legally binding, although it is unusual for the parties to refuse to accept an award as they have explicitly consented to the process and ACAS policy is to strongly advise the parties, before the arbitration process is initiated, that adherence to an award is expected.

Similarly, with the movement to formal conciliation clauses in collective agreements, there has been a growth in standing arbitration clauses in disputes procedures. Here, the parties, on exhaustion of negotiation, will refer the matter to a nominated arbitrator. This is private arbitration, rather than arbitration under the TULR(C)A 1992, and so the Arbitration Act 1950 is not excluded. A feature of this form of arbitration is that the parties do not put a bargaining case to the arbitrator but both make a final submission. The arbitrator then must choose between the two submissions.

---

39 Section 7, inserting new ss. 18A and 18B into the Employment Tribunal Act 1996.

40 In 2016 ACAS received 923 collective conciliation requests of which over 90 per cent were settled. ACAS *Annual Report*, 2016–2017, p. 34.

Despite such developments, in general terms, arbitration has become less popular with both unions and employers. For unions, it compromises the autonomy of the bargaining process. For employers, it compromises the right to manage, to impose change on employees. Consequently, requests for ACAS arbitration and dispute mediation have been consistently declining since the 1970s, from an average of 300 in that decade to an average of 200 in the 1980s, falling to 170 in the early 1990s. By 2016 ACAS reported fewer than 20 references to arbitration.[41]

ACAS has also introduced a voluntary arbitration dispute resolution scheme for individuals who claim unfair dismissal.[42] However, as an arbitration award is binding with no right of appeal, the evidence is there is a very low take up of this scheme.

1.4.2.3 Advisory services

ACAS has the authority to act in a general advisory role on matters of industrial relations and employment policies. Of particular importance over the last decade has been the development of advisory mediation – a process of dispute prevention whereby organisations can identify and resolve problems at work and address underlying difficulties affecting the employment relationship. This role has expanded over the last two decades, in part due to economic changes and industrial policies. Industrial reorganisation caused by the privatisation of public sector organisations, mergers and the development of new industries have all contributed to the restructuring of collective bargaining with an emphasis on decentralised bargaining arrangements. This has been a serious cause of conflict between employers and unions. ACAS, through the setting up of advisory joint councils, has advised and encouraged consultation, both before the changes in collective bargaining are formalised and during the implementation of any changes. ACAS also has the authority to conduct wide-ranging investigations into any question of industrial relations, which may include an inquiry into a particular industrial dispute.[43] The successful conclusion of an inquiry is dependent upon the voluntary co-operation of the parties, as ACAS has no powers of compulsion.

ACAS is also empowered to issue Codes of Practice, after consultation with interested parties, on the statutory provisions regarding the disclosure of information for collective bargaining purposes, disciplinary practices in employment and time off for trade union members and officials. These Codes are designed to provide practical guidance on how detailed legislative provisions should be applied, and provide examples of good practice. Once submitted to the Secretary of State and approved, the Code is laid before Parliament and brought into force through a statutory instrument. The Codes do have a significant legal status. They are admissible in evidence in tribunal or arbitrational proceedings, and any provision of the Code that is relevant to an issue arising in proceedings must be taken into account in determining that question.[44]

The Secretary of State has also had the power to issue Codes of Practice since 1980 'for the purposes of promoting the improvement of industrial relations'. Under this authority two Codes have been issued: on picketing in 1980 (revised in 1992 and 2017) and on the closed shop in 1983 (revoked in 1991). Further statutory authority to publish Codes of Practice for the purposes of promoting appropriate practices in the conduct of trade union ballots and elections was provided by the Employment Act 1988. Like the ACAS Codes, they are intended to contain practical advice on how to apply the relatively complex and detailed legislation and can be used as evidence of good practice.[45]

41 ACAS *Annual Report* 2016–2017, p. 37.

42 S. 7 Employment Rights (Dispute Resolution) Act 1998.

43 Section 214 TULR(C)A1992.

44 Furthermore, s. 3 Employment Act 2008 now provides that if a tribunal finds that a party before it has unreasonably failed to comply with the ACAS Code of Practice on Disciplinary and Grievance Procedures (revised in 2009), it may increase or decrease compensation by up to 25 per cent.

45 Section 207(3) TULR(C)A 1992 specifies that these Codes are admissible before tribunals and before a court.

1.4.3 The Central Arbitration Committee

The Central Arbitration Committee (CAC) was established as a separate body within ACAS by the Employment Protection Act 1975, inheriting many of the duties formerly exercised by the Industrial Arbitration Board. The CAC's original jurisdiction was extensive. The CAC had the responsibility to adjudicate on recognition disputes where the employer had refused to comply with a decision of ACAS to recommend recognition. If the CAC subsequently ordered recognition, and the employer refused to comply, the CAC could award the workers involved in the dispute improved terms and conditions of employment. The recognition provisions of the Employment Protection Act 1975 were repealed by the Employment Act 1980.

Another major function of the CAC was to consider applications by unions under Schedule 11 of the Employment Protection Act. Under Schedule 11 if, in the absence of agreement, an employer was failing to observe terms and conditions that were generally applicable in the relevant trade or industry, the CAC had the authority to make an award. Schedule 11 operated in a similar manner to the Fair Wages Resolution, whereby government contractors had to pay wages of a comparable level to that generally accepted in the relevant industry. The Schedule 11 formula was repealed in 1980 and the Fair Wages Resolution was rescinded in 1983. The focus of the CAC's remaining work was then on voluntary arbitration in collective disputes and on the adjudication of complaints where employers have failed to disclose information to recognised unions as required by ss. 181–185 of the TULR(C)A 1992.

The Employment Relations Act 1999 substantially altered, and expanded the CAC's role. The CAC now has the primary responsibility to oversee, administer and determine a recognition application under Schedule 1A to the 1999 Act – to decide the appropriate bargaining unit, and whether the union enjoys an appropriate level of support, to arrange the secret ballot, through to the award of recognition. In order to better administer the complex recognition procedure, the CAC decision-making powers have been streamlined and the appointment system has been restructured.

Section 25 of the 1999 Act amended s. 263 of the TULR(C)A 1992 (which deals with proceedings before the CAC) and inserted a new s. 263A. This section states that when discharging its functions under the recognition (and de-recognition) scheme, the CAC shall consist of a panel of three appointed by the chairman of the CAC. This must include the chairman or deputy chairman and one representative of each side of the industry. If the panel cannot reach a unanimous decision, but a majority of the panel agree (that is, two out of three), it is their opinion that decides the case. Otherwise, if there is no majority at all (that is, all three have different opinions) then the chairman of the panel has the authority to decide the issue.

The 1999 Act also introduced minor alterations to the appointment process to the CAC. Section 24 amends s. 260 of the TULR(C)A 1992 by substituting two new subsections. Previously, ACAS had an input into appointments to the CAC, with members appointed from a list submitted by ACAS. The new provisions leave the choice of appointments (of chairman, deputy chairman and members) solely to the Secretary of State, after consultation with ACAS. The only proviso is that all must be experienced in industrial relations as an employer or employee representative. The reasoning behind this change was to ensure the Secretary of State had a wider group of members to choose from than had previously been the case (as ACAS nominations have tended to be from its own panel of arbitrators).

The CAC continues to adjudicate on complaints relating to the failure of employers to disclose information for the purpose of collective bargaining. Other areas of jurisdiction include determining applications under the Transnational Information and Consultation of Employees Regulations[46]

46 SI 1999/3323.

(implementing the European Works Council Directive) regarding disputes over the establishment and constitution of works councils. Additionally, the CAC has become responsible for applications under the national regulations on employee rights to information and consultation,[47] and on the employee involvement provisions of the European Public Limited Company Regulations[48] and the European Co-operative Societies Regulations.[49]

1.4.4 The Equality and Human Rights Commission

The Equality and Human Rights Commission was established by the Equality Act 2006 and is funded by the department for Culture, Media and Sport. The Commission took over the role of the three former Commissions (Commission for Racial Equality, Equal Opportunities Commission and Disability Rights Commission), and now has the general responsibility for the promotion and enforcement of equality, human rights and non-discrimination laws across the United Kingdom. The Commission's paramount duties include: to uphold the rights of individuals and tackle instances of discrimination; to ensure that equality issues and human rights are considered by government, employers and society; to provide information, guidance and advice on discrimination; and to act directly to enforce legislation.[50]

In order to execute these responsibilities, the Equality Act provides that the Commission has 'standing' in order to apply for judicial review against public authorities and to intervene in court proceedings.[51] Under s. 31 of the Equality Act the Commission has the authority to assess public authorities' compliance with their positive equality responsibilities and to issue 'compliance notices' if the public authority is in breach of its duty. Furthermore, where the Commission has received a complaint against an employer or there is other evidence of unlawful discrimination it may carry out an investigation and initiate prosecutions or enter into binding agreements with the employer to ensure the discriminatory practice is eliminated. These agreements are enforceable by injunctive relief. At the individual level, under s. 28, the Commission may provide legal assistance to victims of discrimination and human rights violations to initiate court action.

1.4.5 The employment courts

The vast majority of cases concerning employment disputes at work are dealt with at an employment tribunal. These tribunals were originally introduced in 1964 by the Industrial Training Act (with a very limited jurisdiction relating to the adjudication of disputes over employers training levies), with the aim of providing quick informal resolution of disputes. The Donovan report noted in 1968 that tribunals provided an inexpensive, informal and quick system of justice and recommended an extension of their jurisdiction to cover all statutory and contractual claims by employees.[52] Consequently, over the years, the jurisdiction of tribunals has grown substantially.

Employment tribunals now have jurisdiction encompassing not just statutory claims under unfair dismissal and discrimination legislation, but also wrongful dismissal actions at common law and other actions on termination of the employment contract up to a damages limit of £25,000.[53]

47 The Information and Consultation of Employees Regulations (SI 2004/3426).

48 SI 2009/2401.

49 SI 2006/2059.

50 Equality and Human Rights Commission *Annual Report* 2016–2017, p. 6.

51 Section 30 Equality Act 2006.

52 The Royal Commission on Trade Union and Employers Associations, Cmnd 3623, 1968, para. 578.

53 The majority of wrongful dismissal or other claims stemming from the contract of employment are heard in the County Court or High Court. Actions against trade unions in relation to industrial action are heard in the High Court.

In the modern era, however, it is arguable that the original aims of the tribunal system have been compromised by the increasing complexity of common law principles, modern employment protection legislation and associated tribunal procedure.

There is no legal aid for tribunal cases and, as claimants often conduct their cases personally, costs are not normally awarded against either side. However, the tribunal system has been a victim of its own success with the number of applicants rising year on year.[54] Consequently, government policy has been to reduce the strain on tribunal resources and the public exchequer. In order to reduce the numbers of cases heard, in 2001 a procedural rule was introduced where costs may be awarded if the party or their representative acted unreasonably or 'the bringing or conducting of the proceedings had been misconceived'. This introduced the possibility of the applicant being penalised for bringing a weak case, although the evidence is that this power is rarely exercised by the tribunal. However, as the decade went on, further reforms were introduced to reduce claims and save resources. The 2004 rules of procedure introduced the possibility of a wasted costs order against paid representatives who needlessly wasted tribunal time. More recently (and controversially) the Enterprise and Regulatory Reform Act 2013 has introduced compulsory conciliation prior to the filing of a claim and the charging of fees (up to £250) on applicants who wish to initiate a claim and further charges of up to £930 on those who wish to proceed to a hearing. As noted earlier, the Supreme Court has struck down these provisions as indirectly discriminatory.[55]

An employment tribunal[56] consists of three members – a legally qualified chair and two lay members with experience of employment on each side of the industry. The lay members are intended to use their employment experience to assist the tribunal to come to a decision on the facts. In response to the rise in tribunal applications, and in order to reduce the pressure on tribunal resources certain claims, such as breach of contract proceedings or unfair dismissal cases, may now be heard by a single chair (known as an employment judge since 2007) sitting alone.[57]

An appeal from a decision of an employment tribunal lies to the Employment Appeal Tribunal (EAT). The EAT is chaired by a High Court or Circuit judge, although lay members may sit to represent both sides of the industry.[58] An appeal from an employment tribunal is solely on a point of law. Thus, the appellant must show that the tribunal erred on a point of law – defined as a wrongful interpretation and application of the law, or the tribunal's decision was so perverse that it was clear that no reasonable tribunal properly directed to the issues of law could have come to that conclusion.[59] The EAT is empowered on appeal to substitute its own decision for that of the first instance tribunal, but if the EAT re-considered existing facts during its review the EAT will normally remit the case to the ET for a re-examination in the light of the EAT's clarification of the law. The EAT is not bound by its own previous decisions and appeals from the EAT lie to the Court of Appeal.

---

54 In 2001 there were 71,821 applications – which had increased to 186,300 by 2011. By 2014 applications had fallen to 40,948, partly as a consequence of the introduction of application fees. ACAS *Annual Report* 2013–2014, p. 26.

55 *R (on the application of UNISON) v Lord Chancellor* [2017] UKSC 51.

56 Known previously, before 1998, as industrial tribunals.

57 S. 4 Employment Tribunals Act 1996.

58 The default constitution of the EAT is that the judge sits alone in all cases unless he or she directs that lay members should sit as well.

59 *Yeboah v Crofton* [2002] IRLR 634.

1.5 Further reading

Cavalier & Arthur, 'A discussion of the Certification Officer Reforms' (2016) 45 *Industrial Law Journal* 263.

Hodge, 'The curious history of trade union law' (1989) *Denning Law Journal* 92.

Lewis, 'The historical development of labour law' (1976) 14 *British Journal of Industrial Relations* 1.

Mumford, 'Arbitration and ACAS in Britain: a historical perspective' (1996) 34 *British Journal of Industrial Relations* 287.

O'Cinneide, 'The Commission for Equality and Human Rights: a new institution for new and uncertain times' (2007) 36 *Industrial Law Journal* 141.

Orth, *Combination and Conspiracy: A Legal History of Trade Unionism*, Oxford: Oxford University Press, 1991.

Pelling, *A History of British Trade Unionism*, 1993.

Sanders, 'Part 1 of the Employment Act 2008: "better" dispute resolution?' (2009) 38 *Industrial Law Journal* 30.

Webb & Webb, *The History of Trade Unionism*, London: Longmans, Green and Co., 1926.

Chapter 2

The contract of employment

Chapter contents

2.1 Overview

This chapter considers the formation and content of the contract of employment and the sources of express terms.

- Express terms may derive from a variety of sources – including express oral statements made in an interview or written promises contained in a letter of appointment.
- A written agreement that attempts to exclude any external evidence of an alternative agreement is not always legally effective. An 'entire agreement' clause can exclude reference to other sources of terms of the contract.
- A statutory statement of written particulars must be given to every employee within 2 months of starting work. This is *prima facie* good evidence of the contract but can be contradicted by alternative evidence of agreement provided by the employee.
- An employer must issue a new statutory statement if the employer wishes to amend details of the provisions. Change and variation of contractual terms via a statutory statement still requires employee assent. Therefore, a unilateral change of terms by an employer is not a valid variation.
- On starting work an employee may be given a works booklet or referred to a notice board for information on workplace issues. As rules regulating how an employee should behave at work they are not normally terms of the contract unless it was clear that agreement was sought and received by the employer.
- Collective agreements (agreements between a union and employer) have an important impact on the contract of employment. If incorporated expressly or impliedly then clauses relevant to the individual can become part of the contract of employment.
- Express incorporation comes about by a clear and unambiguous reference to the collective agreement in a written document agreed by both parties. The statutory statement is the most useful mechanism for this purpose.
- Where express incorporation has not occurred then the collective agreement can still be effective if it is impliedly incorporated. The courts look for an intention of both parties that they would be bound by the collective agreement. Intention can be derived from knowledge of the provisions of the agreement and subsequent acceptance by conduct. One method of incorporation is custom and practice if the agreement has been followed without fail over a number of years.
- Not all provisions of a collective agreement are apt for incorporation. Only substantive matters of relevance to an individual employee can be incorporated – such as pay, hours of work, place of work, etc. Matters of collective interest – such as recognition of a union by an employer or dispute resolution procedure, are not incorporated into an individual's contract of employment.
- Once terms are incorporated by a collective agreement neither party can vary or change these terms without agreement.

2.2 Introduction

The basic structure of the relationship between employer and employee is governed by the contract of employment that comprises both express and implied terms. The agreed rights and responsibilities of the parties outlined in the contract of employment are supplemented by, and often subject to, statutory provisions. Thus, a purely contractual approach to the determination of employment matters, such as disputes at the workplace, would be misleading. However, the contract of employment as a legal construct cannot be ignored as terms voluntarily agreed by the parties and terms implied by law have a significant role to play in the regulation of the relationship between the employer and employee regarding issues, such as wrongful and constructive dismissal, restriction of competition, and protection of confidential information and common law rights to health and safety, amongst others. The formation of the employment contract and the sources and content of express terms is the subject of this chapter. The role of implied terms is considered in Chapter 3.

2.3 Formation of the contract of employment

The contract of employment is formed in accordance with the ordinary common law rules of contract. Consequently, an offer, acceptance, consideration and intention to create legal relations are all required. It is generally accepted that promises made in a business environment during a recruitment process are intended to have legal effect. Consideration exists as part of the bargain – one party promises to provide remuneration for the other's labour. Both parties must also have the capacity to enter into the contract, which must not have illegal purposes. Minors under the age of 18 are unable to formally enter into an employment contract. However, a contract entered into before 18 is *prima facie* binding if it is of overall benefit to the minor – for example, contracts of apprenticeship common to the industry in question. A contract that is tainted with illegality is unenforceable by either party – for example, a contract that has the purpose of defrauding HM Revenue and Customs.[1]

Where conditional offers are made, such as offers subject to satisfactory written references, the contract is not normally formally concluded until the circumstances are fulfilled. Thus, if the applicant is subsequently refused the position he or she cannot sue for a contractual breach as there is no contract existing. The case law indicates that the appropriate test for ascertaining whether the condition has been satisfied is not an objective test of whether the employer has acted reasonably in deciding that the condition has not been met – but is a subjective test based on whether the employer believed the condition has been satisfied. In *Wishart v NACAB*[2] the employer refused the applicant a job on the basis that the offer was made subject to 'satisfactory' references that the employer deemed to be unsatisfactory when they were received. The Court of Appeal applied a subjective analysis and refused to enforce the conditional job offer, withdrawn in good faith, as there was no employment relationship – no contract to sue under. The employer has explicitly reserved the right to make up his own mind based on his own views after scrutiny of the references.

❖ THINKING POINT

Do you think different principles could apply where employment is conditional on a satisfactory medical report?

2.4 Express terms – the content of the contract

A recruitment process will usually involve advertising, job interviews, possible negotiations and the offer and acceptance of a post. An advert is usually considered to be an invitation to treat: an

1 See, as examples, *Napier v National Business Agency* [1951] 2 All ER 264; *Corby v Morrison* [1980] ICR 564 and *Hewcastle v Ahmed* [1991] IRLR 473.

2 [1990] IRLR 393.

invitation to the potential employee to apply for the post on terms and conditions to be determined by negotiation or pre-established by the potential employer. However, an advert may contain statements of fact (such as the length of the contract or actual salary). These statements could be regarded as an inducement to enter into a contract and, if false, could be deemed to be an actionable misrepresentation or even to be an actual part of the contract.[3]

The interview process may also result in valid terms and conditions being created. If an employer makes a formal offer of the job during an interview, statements or promises made during the interview process may constitute actual express oral terms or be used in the interpretation of express written terms, as occurred in *Hawker Siddeley Ltd v Rump*.[4] A situation of uncertainty, where oral representations made at interview or elsewhere may override a written document, is unsatisfactory and it is generally of importance that both parties are aware what terms are contractually binding.[5] A clearly written document provided at the completion of negotiations that contradicts or amends any oral representations may override them. It is also possible to avoid this problem by inserting into the written document an 'entire agreement' clause. This was the case in *White v Bristol Rugby Club Ltd*[6] where the operative clause in this contract provided that:

> Each party to this agreement now acknowledge that this agreement contains the whole agreement between the parties and that they have not relied upon oral or written representations made to them by other persons, its employees or agents.

The employee attempted to rely on an oral representation made to him during the interview process that limited the damages he would have to pay on his breach of contract. The court accepted that an oral representation to this effect had been made to him – however, the written contract in its entirety was binding specifically because of the 'entire agreement' clause contained in the contract stating that the document represented the sole content of the contract – thus excluding any collateral terms outside of this specific written agreement.[7]

An additional issue that arises is to what extent are unilateral variation clauses contained in a letter of appointment valid? In *Norman v Audit Office*[8] the clause in the letter of appointment provided that leave arrangements could be amended unilaterally by the employer. The EAT held that the usual rules of construction apply. If the clause giving the employer this power is clear and unambiguous and incorporated into the contract by consent, then it has contractual force and is thus enforceable.

2.5 Express terms – the statutory statement of written particulars of employment

As we have already seen in the introduction, express terms in a contract of employment may derive from a variety of sources. It is not always the case that all such terms can be found by reference to

3 See, as an example, *Financial Techniques Ltd v Hughes* [1981] IRLR 32.
4 [1979] IRLR 425.
5 See *Prometric v Cunliffe* [2016] IRLR 776, where the court held that general conversations about pay and conditions can certainly form part of the contractual agreement, but that good evidence of a specific agreement is required to substantiate the employee's claim.
6 [2002] IRLR 204.
7 See also *RNLI v Bushaway* [2005] IRLR 674, where the court noted that such clauses should be construed strictly, and so where the clause was drafted ambiguously and did not cover the facts in question it was unenforceable.
8 [2015] IRLR 634.

one single written document entitled 'The contract of employment'. It may be that there are several sources of express terms, some of which may conflict – terms may stem from a job advert where, for example, hours of work are clearly stated, or where a job description is included in a letter of appointment, or oral terms may be offered in a job interview that differs from the terms in a document received by the employee. Which term is binding depends on an analysis of what has been agreed by reference to the intention of the parties – which itself depends on the evidence submitted.

As a matter of policy, statute has intervened in order to ensure a degree of certainty with the requirement that employers must provide a statutory statement of written particulars of employment. The required content of the statutory statement is outlined in Part 1 of the Employment Rights Act 1996 (first contained in the Contracts of Employment Act 1963, as amended by the Trade Union Reform and Employment Rights Act 1993, so as to comply with the EEC Directive 1991/533/EEC on an employer's obligation to inform employees of their employment conditions).

Under section 1 of the Employment Rights Act 1996, within 2 months of starting employment all employees must be issued with a statutory statement of written particulars of employment. This statement must provide details of:

- the names of the employer and employee;
- the date employment began (and will finish, if temporary employment) and the date continuous employment commences;
- pay (or the method of calculating pay), intervals of pay (e.g. weekly, monthly), hours of work, details relating to entitlement to holidays and holiday pay (if any), sick pay arrangements (if any) and any incapacity for work arrangements;
- the notice period required on both sides to terminate the contract;
- any details regarding pension rights;
- job title or short description of the work the employee is employed to do;
- expected length of the contract where the contract is not expected to be permanent;
- place of work, or if employee is required to work at various places, an indication of this; and
- any collective agreements which affect the terms and conditions of employment.

Section 2 provides that an employee may be referred to another document (e.g. staff handbook) for details relating to time off for incapacity, sick pay, pensions and to a collective agreement or the statutory requirements for provisions on notice periods. Additionally, s. 3 of the Employment Rights Act 1996, as amended by the Employment Act 2002, establishes that the statement should specifically include information about disciplinary rules and procedures applicable to the employee which may be contained in a reasonably accessible document. The information must also specify which individual within the organisation is responsible for dealing with grievance or disciplinary issues. In essence, this ensures that all stages of the minimum statutory disciplinary and dismissal procedures are set out in the written statement.

The Employment Act 2002 also added a new s. 7A to the Employment Rights Act 1996 – providing for further opportunities for alternative documents to act as a statutory statement. Where a letter of appointment or other written document contains all the information required by ss. 1–3 and is given within the 2-month timescale, that will discharge the requirement of providing a written statement of terms.

2.5.1 What is the legal significance of the written employment particulars?

It is important to understand that the relevant statutory provisions do not require the employer to provide a written contract of employment – but merely a written statement that may represent the agreement between the parties. Thus, the statutory statement is not necessarily a contractual document. The case law demonstrates that, although it is good evidence of what the parties have agreed, it is not necessarily the only evidence. It is the employer's view of the agreement, and the employee may challenge the statement (where the employee has contradictory evidence) on the basis that it is not a true record. Rebutting evidence may well show that what was actually agreed is found by reference to another document. In *Robertson and Jackson v British Gas Corpn*[9] the employee had originally received a written letter of appointment with details of a bonus scheme that was applicable to him. The statutory statement failed to refer to this matter. On the question of whether there was a term on bonus payments the employee successfully argued that the statutory statement did not accurately reflect what was agreed at the beginning of employment.

The courts thus recognise that the statutory statement is merely strong *prima facie* evidence of what is contained in the contract of employment – but is not the contract *per se*. In *System Floors Ltd v Daniel*[10] the Employment Appeal Tribunal (EAT) held that the signing of a mere receipt acknowledging that the statement had been received did not indicate employee approval of the contents of the statement and so wasn't the only evidence of the terms of the contract. The operative principles in this area were outlined by Browne Wilkinson J when he said

> In the absence of an acknowledgement by the parties that the statement itself is a contract and that the terms are correct . . . the statutory statement does not itself constitute a contract in writing. In the present case, all the employee did was to sign an acknowledgment that he has received the statement. In no sense did he sign it as a contract or acknowledge the accuracy of the terms in it.[11]

However, where the employee has clearly accepted the content of the statutory statement it is contractually binding. In *Gascol Conversions v Mercer*[12] the employee signed a statutory statement underneath the words 'I confirm receipt of a new contract of employment which sets out my terms and conditions of employment'. This indicated the employee's full agreement with its contents and so is therefore the sole evidence of the contract and its terms.

2.5.2 What happens if a statement is not provided or some of the mandatory terms are missing?

Under section 11 of the Employment Rights Act 1996 a complaint that the statement has not been given, or that it did not contain all the relevant particulars, proceeds to an employment tribunal. Section 12 states that the tribunal has the power to determine what particulars ought to have been provided or to amend particulars. However, the tribunal's function is to only determine what has already been agreed, not to impose terms that the court thinks they should have agreed.[13] The Court of Appeal affirmed this approach in *Eagland v British Telecom*,[14] where it held that a tribunal should only exercise their power to determine the provisions after examining the evidence, on the basis of what the parties have agreed impliedly or expressly by conduct or otherwise, and if necessary, to amend the statement so that it reflects that agreement.[15] Furthermore, tribunals do not have the

---

9 [1983] ICR 351, noted by Leighton (1983) 12 ILJ 115.
10 [1982] ICR 54.
11 Ibid. p. 58.
12 [1974] IRLR 155.
13 See *Brown v Stuart, Scott and Co Ltd* [1981] ICR 166.
14 [1992] IRLR 323. See also *Southern Cross Healthcare Co Ltd v Perkins* [2011] IRLR 247.
15 See *Hilton v Shiner Ltd* [2001] IRLR 728 as an example of the tribunal implying terms by reference to examining the conduct of the parties.

authority to interpret agreed provisions already in the written statement. That is a matter for the civil courts in their jurisdiction to interpret and enforce the contract.[16]

Where the tribunal finds in favour of the employee, s. 38 of the Employment Act 2002 provides that compensation of between 2 and 4 weeks' pay may be awarded for the failure to provide written particulars. However, this claim only arises where the failure to provide an accurate statutory statement is connected to another statutory claim, such as unfair dismissal.[17] It is also automatically unfair to dismiss an employee for asserting this statutory right to receive a written statement of employment particulars or for making a subsequent complaint under s. 11 of the Employment Rights Act 1996.

❖ THINKING POINT

If the employee does not receive a statutory statement of written particulars or any other written document does that mean that no terms of the employment contract exist?

2.6 Change and the statutory statement

Section 4 of the Employment Rights Act 1996 states that changes to a written statement must be notified to an employee within 1 month of the change in question unless the employee is re-employed within 6 months of ending an earlier employment and the same terms and conditions apply. An employee may be directed to a reasonably accessible document or collective agreement for the details of any changes in conditions relating to sickness, pension rights and disciplinary provisions. This does not mean that an amendment communicated to the employee is automatically effective as a valid change to the contract of employment. The change is only effective if it is agreed with the employee. Thus, a unilateral change is not a valid amendment to contractual terms as consent is required from the employee.[18]

A different, if related issue, is where an employer argues that change has come about through developing circumstances. For example, in *Horrigan v Lewisham Borough Council*[19] Horrigan's express contractual requirement was to work for 40 hours. On request he also performed an extra one hour's overtime on a voluntary basis for a substantial period of time. The court was clear that his hours of work had not automatically changed as a consequence of his behaviour. Developing circumstance did not impact on his contract of employment – where express terms of the contract are clear a mere change in job practice undertaken by the employee is not evidence of implied acceptance.

However, developing circumstance may be of relevance where there is no express agreement on a particular term. Changes in job practice during employment, without objection by the employee, can be taken as evidence of what the parties have agreed on that issue, and that the change has been impliedly accepted by the employee. Yet, in *Jones v Associated Tunnelling*[20] the

16 See *Construction Board Training Board v Leighton* [1978] IRLR 60.
17 For a critical evaluation of the value of this right, see Mogridge, 1981.
18 As an example, see *Security and Facilities Ltd v Hayes* [2001] IRLR 81.
19 [1978] ICR 15.
20 [1981] IRLR 477.

EAT cautioned against a too literal and harsh application of this approach. Jones had received a new statutory statement that contained a new mobility clause that the employer attempted to enforce some years later. The EAT stated that the mere issuing of a new statutory statement did not mean he was bound by it without evidence of actual agreement with its contents. Evidence of consent may be implied where the employee continues in the job and the new particulars have a practical impact on the employee's position – such as a change in hours or pay, or related terms.[21] Where there is a unilateral variation of an existing term that has no practical effect on the employee it would be wrong to imply consent merely from a failure to object to the new clause.[22]

2.7 Works rules/company handbooks as express terms

On joining an employer an employee may be issued with a company handbook or referred to a company notice board for information relating to workplace issues. The question arises whether such statements in a company handbook or pinned up on a notice board have contractual force or are they merely instructions on how the employee should do his or her job – such as rules regulating conduct and behaviour at work? If such matters are defined as mere rules of work imposed by management then they can be altered unilaterally; if express terms, then technically, any changes must be agreed with the employee.[23] If the material is brought to an employee's attention at the commencement of employment for specific agreement then the parties may have intended them to have contractual effect and consequently they are binding on both parties. In *Keeley v Fosroc International Ltd*[24] clear and unambiguous provisions for enhanced redundancy pay contained in a staff handbook formed part of the employee's contractual terms as they had been incorporated by direct reference via an earlier written document.[25]

However, in general terms, rules relating to policy or conduct at work are usually perceived as not incorporated into a contract of employment as it is within the employer's legal discretion to issue reasonable orders and it is not normally the employer's intention that these rules should have contractual force. Therefore, as instructions, they are subject to unilateral variation. In *Dryden v Greater Glasgow Health Board*[26] the introduction of a non-smoking policy was not a contractual amendment – a mere change of policy on health and safety grounds governing behaviour at the workplace. Likewise, in *Wandsworth LBC v D'Silva*[27] the code of practice that informed staff of changes in reporting illness could be unilaterally altered as sickness policy was not a term that required agreement.[28]

---

21 As an example, see *FW Farnworth v Lacy* [2012] EWHC 2820.

22 See also *Aparau v Iceland Frozen Foods Ltd* [1996] IRLR 119; *Harlow v Artemis International Corpn* [2008] IRLR 629.

23 For example, in *Department of Transport v Sparks* [2016] IRLR 643, an absence policy contained in a departmental handbook was deemed to have contractual force and therefore could not be unilaterally amended.

24 [2006] IRLR 961.

25 For further examples, see *Taylor v Secretary of State for Scotland* [2000] IRLR 502 and *Attril v Dresdner Kleinwort Ltd* [2011] IRLR 613. Note that, in a heavily criticised decision (*Bateman v ASDA Stores Ltd* [2010] IRLR 370), the EAT held that a clause in a company handbook that permitted unilateral change justified the imposition of amended contractual terms as the employees had essentially given permission in advance for the employer's actions.

26 [1992] IRLR 469.

27 [1998] IRLR 502.

28 An employer's 'handbook' or 'code of practice' may now be a reference to a specific file on the employer's intranet site. Contractual status will still be dependent on an analysis of the rules discussed above.

2.8 Collective agreements as express terms

Where trade unions are recognised, employers will often engage in collective bargaining on a variety of matters relevant to the employees' terms and conditions of work, such as pay, hours of work, holiday entitlement, place of work, amongst others. A collective agreement is often a formal document signed by both union and employer. However, this is not always the case – a collective agreement can come about through an informal process (such as an exchange of letters) so long as there is a mutual intention on the part of both parties to enter into a bargain.[29]

Collective agreements are not ordinarily legally binding between employer and trade union (s. 179 of the Trade Union Labour Relations (Consolidation) Act 1992), but if they are translated into a contractual relationship between employer and employee, then they do have legal force as express terms of the contract. To assume contractual validity the agreement must be incorporated into the contract of employment expressly or impliedly and the relevant clauses of the collective agreement must be capable of being legally binding between the employer and the employee.

2.9 Collective agreements – express incorporation

The most effective way for the collective agreement to be incorporated is for the employment contract to refer expressly to the relevant agreement. The reference should be clear and unambiguous. For example, in *Robertson and Jackson v British Gas Co Ltd*[30] the appropriate contract read 'The provision of the agreement of the National Joint Council . . . relating to remuneration and increments will apply to you'. This was sufficient to incorporate the terms of an incentive bonus scheme negotiated between union and employer into the contract of employment. The form of incorporation may give advance authority to the union to negotiate subsequent agreements. So, in *NCB v Galley*,[31] miners' written contracts specified that wages were regulated by the 'national agreements for the time being in force'. The particular agreement in force at the time required Galley to work overtime. Galley argued that, since there was nothing specific in his contract referring to the need to work overtime, he had not agreed to it and so it was not a valid term of his contract. The High Court held on the interpretation of the phrase 'for the time being in force' that Galley had expressly agreed in advance to his wages being determined in this manner. The provision in the renegotiated collective agreement on compulsory overtime had become a valid term of Galley's employment contract without it having to be specifically written into his contract.[32]

2.9.1 Express incorporation – the role of the statutory statement

The most useful mechanism for express incorporation is often the written particulars of employment or statutory statement that, as we've seen earlier, every employer is bound to supply to any new employee. Prior to the changes introduced by the Trade Union Reform and Employment Rights Act 1993 it was permissible for details on most of these matters to be notified to an employee by reference to another document – i.e. a collective agreement. An express clause of this nature (stating, for example, 'your terms and conditions are determined by the current collective

---

29 See *Burke v Royal Liverpool University Hospital NHS Trust* [1997] ICR 730 and *Edinburgh Council v Brown* [1999] IRLR 208.
30 [1983] ICR 357.
31 [1958] 1 WLR 18.
32 See also *Toucher v General Motors Scotland Ltd* [1981] IRLR 55.

agreement') would ordinarily incorporate the terms of the agreement into the individual's contract of employment. However, as we saw earlier, the majority of particulars and any subsequent alterations must now be explicitly provided in a full written statement.

Where the provisions of a collective agreement are fully reproduced in the written particulars of employment, there should be little doubt of their incorporation as part of the individual contract. If, in practice, some employers fail to adhere to the new statutory requirements and refer (as previously permitted) to the collective agreement in name only, that does not necessarily mean that the collective agreement has no effect at the individual level. As the content of the contract is a matter of common law, the express reference will probably still have contractual effect (as we saw earlier in *Robertson and Jackson v British Gas*[33]) even though the employer has acted contrary to statutory provisions.

2.10 Collective agreements – implied incorporation

If the collective agreement is not expressly incorporated through the statutory statement or through any specific written contract, it is still possible for the agreement to have legal effect as express terms if the agreement is impliedly incorporated into the contract of employment. In strict legal terms, the courts look for an agreement between the parties that the collective bargain is binding. They consider whether the facts indicate that the employer and employee intended that the relevant part of the collective agreement should be part of the employment contract. Intention can be derived from knowledge of the provisions of the agreement and subsequent conduct. However, problems have arisen over the level of knowledge of the collective agreement and the appropriate conduct necessary to establish intention.

Many industrial relations commentators support the notion that industrial common sense demands that, since a national level collective agreement provides a well-accepted standard throughout a particular industry, this is automatically part of a contract of employment on the basis of industrial custom and practice. The celebrated industrial relations lawyer, Kahn-Freund, characterised this process as 'crystallised custom'.[34] The provisions of the collective agreement are tacitly embodied into the contract of employment by the unexpressed assumptions of the parties – an unchallenged consensus between them. There is no requirement for any particular level of knowledge or positive affirmative response as both parties passively expect that the terms of the employment contract are governed by the existing collective agreement.

There is, however, limited direct legal authority for this view. When deciding whether to incorporate a collective agreement on the basis of custom and practice, the courts have preferred to apply explicit legal criteria. The custom must be a well-known and accepted practice of a particular industry or trade. In *Duke v Reliance Systems Ltd*[35] the Court of Appeal restated the test that a collective agreement would need to be 'clear, certain and notorious' before it could be incorporated on the basis of custom. Clarity and certainty may be present but the concept of notoriety requires both a level of knowledge of the agreement and adherence to it for a substantial period. Collective agreements that follow the criteria will be incorporated. For example, in *McLea v Essex Lines*[36] the terms of a well-established, and therefore well known, collective agreement were incorporated into the contracts of merchant seamen, since evidence was available that it had been followed in the

33 [1983] ICR 351.
34 Kahn-Freund, *Labour and the Law*, 1983.
35 [1982] IRLR 347.
36 [1933] 45 LLR 254.

past for a number of years. A more recent example occurred in *Henry v London General Transport Services Ltd*,[37] where a collective agreement consistently followed over a number of years by both parties was held by the Court of Appeal as 'reasonable, certain and notorious' and thus incorporated through custom and practice.

Even though 'crystallised custom' as a basis for automatic incorporation has had little legal support, it still has some residual legal importance. This was illustrated by the decision in *Howman and Son v Blyth*.[38] A national agreement on sick pay was not formally incorporated, expressly or impliedly, but since there was a gap in the contract it was necessary to imply a term on sick pay. The clauses in a non-incorporated collective agreement were, therefore, used as a guide in determining on what terms sick pay should be implied.

It is apparent that the mere existence of a collective agreement does not mean that it is incorporated through industrial relations practice. However, the fact that both parties have universally observed the agreement at the workplace is evidence of implied agreement; for example, incorporation is readily implied where wage rates have always been fixed by reference to a collective agreement without protest. This presumption of incorporation can be countered where a new collective agreement has been negotiated and the individual worker objects to the new provisions. This is clearly illustrated by *Singh v British Steel Corporation*.[39] Singh had previously been a union member and had adhered to all previous collective agreements. After a disagreement, he left the union before a new shift system had been negotiated introducing new hours of work. Singh refused to work the new shift, arguing that his express terms of employment were unaffected by the newly negotiated collective agreement since it was not expressly incorporated into his contract. The Court of Appeal accepted the argument that, as he had formally rejected the new agreement, any change was a unilateral variation that he was not bound to accept. Although Singh had knowledge of the new agreement there was no evidence that he agreed to it. Any previous implied acceptance through acquiescence was no longer relevant since he had expressly renounced the agreement.

Evidence of acceptance of the new or changed collective agreement does, of course, serve as a basis for implying incorporation of the new agreement. In *Joel v Cammell Laird Ship-repairers Ltd*[40] the collective agreement introduced job flexibility with a consequent increase in pay. Joel refused to change his work practices, yet did accept the related pay rise. His conduct clearly was good evidence to the court that he had, in reality, accepted the contents of the collective agreement.

On the basis of an analysis of these cases, it can be said that the extent of the worker's knowledge of the collective agreement and conduct in response to it play a major part in determining whether a collective agreement is impliedly incorporated. The greater the knowledge and subsequent conduct the more likely the agreement is impliedly incorporated.

2.11 Collective agreements – incorporation by way of agency

In *Heatons Transport Ltd v TGWU*[41] the House of Lords cautiously seemed to have approved the principle that trade union members automatically authorise the results of negotiations by union officials on the basis that the union acts as the members' agent. This has not been regarded as an attractive solution to the problem of the incorporation of collective agreements due to the anomalies it would

37 [2002] IRLR 472.
38 [1983] ICR 416.
39 [1974] IRLR 131.
40 [1969] ITR 206.
41 [1973] AC 15.

create. As only union members would be bound, non-union employees could opt out of collective agreements. Thus, some workers would be able to enforce and have enforced against them, terms and conditions of employment that did not apply to others. In *Burton Group Ltd v Smith*[42] the EAT dismissed the notion of an agency relationship arising solely by virtue of union membership. Any agency relationship must derive from the particular facts of the case and does not arise automatically from the relationship of union and member.

However, union membership may well be relevant when determining whether a collective agreement has been impliedly incorporated on the basis of the principles of implied acceptance. It may be assumed by the court that as a matter of evidence, if the employee is a union member, then he or she has greater knowledge of union negotiations than non-members and so mere acquiescence is sufficient to establish incorporation. In *Nelson v The Post Office*[43] the employee was bound by the collective agreement despite his objections to a particular clause after the agreement had been finalised. The fact that he was a member of the relevant union indicated to the court that he had intended to be bound by the agreement. Union membership was also specifically referred to in *Gray Dunn v Edwards*[44] as a pertinent and major factor in determining intention. Edwards had been disciplined under an agreed disciplinary code. On the question whether this code had been incorporated as an express term into his employment contract, Lord McDonald stated, 'where employers negotiate a detailed agreement with a recognised union, they are entitled to assume all employees who are members of the union know of and are bound by its provisions'.[45]

In conclusion, if the agreement has been expressly incorporated, then it is of direct legal effect. The employee may later attempt to refute the incorporation clause but this would not be of any consequence. Union membership or non-membership is also of no relevance here as the employee has formally pledged acceptance of incorporation. If express incorporation is absent, then the courts look for some deemed acceptance. The degree of evidence required for these purposes is variable, but actual or assumed knowledge of the agreement and subsequent behaviour would be sufficient. There seems to be little clear and unequivocal support for the notion of automatic incorporation *via* 'crystallised custom'.

❖ THINKING POINT

Would a collective agreement be impliedly incorporated where a union member, who had previously followed the terms of a collective agreement, resigned their membership and expressly rejected the agreement between union and employer?

2.12 Collective agreements – incorporation of individual clauses

Not all provisions of a collective agreement are suitable for incorporation into an individual's contract of employment as an express term. For a clause to be capable of incorporation, it must

42 [1977] IRLR 351.
43 [1978] IRLR 548.
44 [1980] IRLR 23.
45 Ibid. p. 28.

specifically relate to a substantive issue, an issue relevant to an individual's terms and conditions of employment and not be vague or imprecise.[46] There also must be an intention of both parties that it should be binding.

Matters of industrial policy or procedural matters of concern only to the union, rather than the individual worker, are not capable of incorporation. This is clearly demonstrated in the cases dealing with the withdrawal of recognition from unions. In *Gallagher v The Post Office*[47] it was argued that the relevant clause in the collective agreement guaranteeing recognition for the relevant union was incorporated into the union members' contracts of employment. Brightman J held, however, that as the content of this clause was a matter of interest only between the union and the employer it was not a substantive term suitable for incorporation into the employment contract and for enforcement as a breach of contract against the employer.

A similar decision was made by the High Court in *NCB v NUM*.[48] The National Union of Mineworkers (NUM) had been given exclusive recognition for collective bargaining purposes by virtue of s. 46 of the Coal Nationalisation Act 1945. The Coal Board unilaterally terminated the provision so as to include the new Union of Democratic Mineworkers (UDM) as a negotiating partner. Scott J applied the decision in *Gallagher* that recognition rights contained in a collective agreement are procedural collective matters only and so are not appropriate for incorporation into an individual contract of employment. This is not to say, however, that trade union support agreements are always deemed to be procedural matters. The Court of Appeal has accepted that it was arguable that a sufficiently clear and specific collective agreement that provided workplace facilities for trade union officials is capable of incorporation into the individual contract of a particular shop steward.[49]

The distinction between individual matters that are appropriate for incorporation and procedural matters that are not can at times be a relatively fine one. This can be illustrated by contrasting the decisions in *British Leyland v McQuilken*[50] and *Marley v Forward Trust Group*.[51] In *McQuilken*, a collective agreement was negotiated on redundancy issues. This was not capable of incorporation since it was interpreted by the court as a long-term policy statement about how redundancies should be handled if they occur. Thus, as a procedural matter of concern only to the union and employer, this was not suitable for incorporation as an express term into individual contracts. By contrast, in *Marley* the agreement between union and employer contained a detailed plan of action following redundancy. Clauses outlined that employees should be given the opportunity to take on new posts for a six-month trial period and that their redundancy rights were not affected if, after the six-month period, they did not wish to continue in the trial post. Unlike the case in *McQuilken*, the agreement was specific enough and would sufficiently affect the individual to make it appropriate for incorporation into an employment contract. In addition, there was evidence that the parties intended that it should be incorporated.

In *Alexander v Standard Telephones (No 2)*[52] Hobhouse J regarded the inference of contractual intent as central to the decision on whether a clause is apt for incorporation. Here, the collective agreement was a long and discursive document that included clauses on redundancy procedure. These clauses outlined a selection procedure that included calling for volunteers first, followed, if necessary, by selection based on the 'last in, first out' criteria. When redundancies were required, the employer

---

46 See *Lee v GEC Telecommunications* [1993] IRLR 383.
47 [1970] 3 All ER 712.
48 [1986] IRLR 439.
49 See *NUPE v City and Hackney AHA* [1985] IRLR 252.
50 [1978] IRLR 245.
51 [1986] IRLR 369, noted by MacLean (1987) 16 ILJ 59.
52 [1991] IRLR 286.

refuted the agreement. Hobhouse J concluded that the agreement as a whole was predominantly on industrial issues and so of collective interest only. Although the redundancy clauses were more specific, there was nothing to suggest that these clauses should be treated any differently from the rest of the agreement, essentially because there was no evidence to suggest the parties intended them to be binding. The court in *Kaur v MG Rover Group*[53] followed this approach – although the collective agreement included a precise statement that there would be no compulsory redundancies, the overall content of the agreement predominantly related to procedural issues and without specific evidence of intention the provisions were not apt for incorporation.[54]

❖ THINKING POINT

Do you think 'no strike' clauses in a collective agreement are capable of incorporation into an individual contract of employment?

2.13 Collective agreements – conflicting agreements

Where there are different levels of bargaining, there is always the possibility of a clash between local and national agreements. The question then to be considered is which express term has primacy where two or more terms of opposing collective agreements are contradictory. The few cases directly on this point have tended to suggest that national agreements have precedence. In *Loman v Merseyside Transport*[55] Lord Parker CJ in the Divisional Court said both 'in law and common sense', where conflict arises between local and national provisions and there is no evidence which has priority, the national agreement should be followed in preference to a local agreement. The Master of the Rolls, Lord Denning, essentially concurred in that view in *Gascol Conversions Ltd v Mercer*[56] – unless there is evidence to the contrary, a national agreement should take precedence. In *Barnett v NCB*[57] the EAT felt that this was too simplistic an approach to the problem. The crucial issue to consider is the intention of the parties. If the local agreement was made after the national agreement (as a supplement or addition to it), then the parties might reasonably expect that matters in the local agreement, which depart from the nationally agreed terms, would have priority over the national agreement.[58] Alternatively, it could be argued that since the local agreement is usually more immediate there is a presumption that this has priority, whether negotiated before or after a national agreement, unless there is a clear inference from the evidence that the intention of the parties was for the national agreement to take precedence.

---

53 [2005] IRLR 40.

54 More recently, note the two Court of Appeal cases – *George v Ministry of Justice* [2013] EWCA 324 and *Malone v British Airways* [2011] IRLR 32 – where it was intimated in both cases that when assessing the intention of the parties (in order to ascertain whether a provision was 'apt' for incorporation), an employer could not have intended a clause to be individually enforceable where it would have a substantially negative impact on the employer's business. For further analysis of these cases, see Barrow, 2014.

55 [1968] 3 ITR 108.

56 [1974] IRLR 155.

57 [1978] ICR 1102.

58 See also *Donelan v Kerby Construction Ltd* [1983] IRLR 91.

2.14 Collective agreements – variation and change

Since relevant clauses of a collective agreement, once incorporated, form part of an individual's employment contract, change is governed by the traditional common law rules that emphasise the need for mutual consent. Thus, it is a breach of contract for an employer to vary or revoke the collective agreement without consent of the employee, or for the employee to refute a new collective agreement negotiated between union and employer. The consent of the employee is automatic if there is a valid variation clause contained in a binding statutory statement or other written document (such as in *NCB v Galley*,[59] considered earlier). In that situation, the employee is, in advance, expressly agreeing to be bound by the changes to the collective agreement. Such clauses usually presuppose that any variation has been agreed between employer and union, although it is possible for an express clause to be agreed which permits a unilateral change by an employer.[60]

Where there has been no express incorporation of the collective agreement, but implied incorporation only, any new collective agreement negotiated with the relevant union will normally be binding on the employee in the same way as the previous agreement was. Although, as we saw earlier in *Singh v British Steel Corporation*,[61] where an agreement is only impliedly incorporated there is greater scope for an employee to reject the new collective agreement.

Where an employer attempts unilaterally to withdraw from the collective agreement, without the consent of the union or employee, such abrogation has no effect on the individual contract of employment. Termination of the collective agreement does not alter the terms of the individual contract that are already incorporated from the collective agreement. In *Miller v Hamworthy Engineering*[62] the collective agreement providing for a guaranteed weekly wage was ignored by the employer who instituted a 3-day week due to a loss of orders. As there was no evidence that the employee or union had consented to the change, the employer was in breach of the employment contract and employees were able to recover their loss of wages. A similar situation arose in *Burroughs Machines Ltd v Timmoney*.[63] The employers' federation negotiated a collective agreement establishing a level of work and guaranteed pay within the industry. Contained in the collective agreement was a provision that guaranteed pay could be suspended during any industrial action. Two years after having resigned from the federation, the employer, relying on the collective agreement, refused to provide guaranteed pay during a period of industrial action. It was held that the fact of resignation from the employers' federation had no effect on the contractual position between employer and employees. The agreement had been incorporated at the time of membership – the employer leaving the negotiating forum did not affect this incorporation.[64]

In *Lee v GEC Telecommunications Ltd*[65] the employer argued that by issuing a new statutory statement of employment particulars, which did not refer to the previously incorporated collective agreement, any employee who did not formally object to the changes in the statement had consented to the variation. The EAT regarded a failure of the relevant employees to respond as insufficient evidence of consent to the change in terms of employment. As the imposed change was a unilateral variation, it was not legally effective at the individual level and the employer remained bound by the incorporated terms of the collective agreement.[66] In the course of the judgment, the EAT indicated

---

59 [1958] 1 WLR 16.

60 See *Airlie v Edinburgh DC* [1996] IRLR 516.

61 [1974] IRLR 131.

62 [1986] IRLR 461.

63 [1977] IRLR 404.

64 See also *Gibbons v Associated British Ports* [1985] IRLR 376.

65 [1993] IRLR 383.

66 See also *Davies v Hotpoint Ltd* [1994] IRLR 538.

that, in the absence of agreement with the appropriate trade union or of a clause in the collective agreement permitting unilateral variation, express (rather than implied) consent of an individual employee to a variation of terms of employment derived from a collective agreement would be valid.

2.15 Further reading

Barrow, 'Collective agreements and the contract of employment: determining the intention of the parties or denying legitimate expectations' (2014) 23 *Nottingham Law Journal* 145.
Dunville & Leighton, 'From statement to contract' (1977) 6 *Industrial Law Journal* 133.
Hepple, 'Restructing employment rights' (1986) 15 *Industrial Law Journal* 69.
Honeyball, 'Employment law and the primacy of contract' (1989) 18 *Industrial Law Journal* 97.
Honeyball & Pearce, 'Contract, employment and the contract of employment' (2006) 35 *Industrial Law Journal* 30.
Kenner, 'Statement or contract' (1999) 28 *Industrial Law Journal* 205.
Lewis, 'Collective agreements: the Kahn-Freund legacy' (1979) 42 *Modern Law Review* 613.
Mogride, 'Giving a written particulars of employment – a valueless exercise?' (1981) *New Law Journal* 1250.
Pitt, 'Further and better particulars' (1994) 144 *New Law Journal* 84.
Reynolds & Hendy, 'Reserving the right to change terms and conditions: how far can an employee go?' (2012) 41 *Industrial Law Journal* 79.
Rideout, 'The contract of employment' (1966) *Current Legal Problems* 111.
Underwood, 'Collective bargaining and the law' (2006) 8 *Employment Law Journal* 3.
Wilson, 'Contract and prerogative: a reconsideration of the legal enforcement of collective agreements' (1984) 13 *Industrial Law Journal* 1.

Chapter 3

Implied duties in the contract of employment

Chapter contents

3.1 Overview

This chapter looks at the terms which the common law implies into employment contracts. They differ from 'ordinary' implied terms in that they apply to *all* employment contracts and form part of the contract irrespective of the actual or presumed intention of the parties. They were developed by the common law before statutory employment rights came into being on any scale, and were initially created in order to protect the employee. However, certain implied duties are owed by the employee to his employer.

3.2 Introduction

We have already seen that the courts have power under the concept of implied terms to impose terms on the parties where the contract is silent. This power applies on a contract-specific basis. As such, the courts are implying terms into one individual contract only, not into every contract. By contrast, the common law has decided over the years that some terms are so important that they should be included in *every* contract. If the parties have omitted them the courts will insert the necessary provision. These terms are often known as implied duties to distinguish them from the implied terms considered earlier, although judges in decided cases (and writers in textbooks!) frequently do not make the distinction clear.
In recent years, statute law has moved further than the concept of implied duties in giving employees minimum rights which cannot normally be contracted out from. However, implied duties in particular remain highly relevant:

- when disputes occur during the subsistence of the contract;
- in deciding whether in the circumstances the employee has been unfairly dismissed under the statutory provisions.

Frequently, an employee will claim that the employer has ordered him to do something which is not within his contractual duties. *Prima facie*, this would constitute a breach of the contract. However, the employee is under an implied duty to obey the reasonable and lawful orders of his employer, which are not restricted to matters specified in his job description. The employee claims that the order concerned is not a reasonable order, and, in the alternative, that the employer is acting in breach of the implied duty of mutual respect. The employee resigns, and claims unfair dismissal on the basis that the employer's action constitutes constructive dismissal. In order to succeed, he will first be required to satisfy the Employment Tribunal that the employer was guilty of a breach of contract, which was sufficiently serious to entitle him to terminate the contract without notice. This includes breach of an implied duty. Note that constructive dismissal does not require that the employer has acted unreasonably, rather that he has acted in fundamental breach of contract. If the employee clears this hurdle, the statutory provisions relating to unfair dismissal in ERA 1996 will apply, and the tribunal will no longer be concerned with questions dealing directly with the terms of the contract.

3.3 Personal nature of the contract

Implied duties are imposed during the currency of a contract and limit the way in which either side exercises its rights. This is unusual in contract law, where, generally speaking, the common law leaves the contractual terms and their enforcement to the parties who negotiated them.

At its most basic level, an employment contract is a personal one, whereby the two parties agree to provide services for one another; the employee agrees to work, the employer to pay him for that work. The requirement to serve in person is central to the employment contract. A contract cannot constitute an employment contract if the worker is able to delegate his duties to another.

The courts cannot force the parties to continue with the contract should they no longer wish to do so, in contrast to other types of contract, which are enforceable by means of orders for specific performance. The Trade Union and Labour Relations (Consolidation) Act 1992 s. 236 provides that no court by order of specific performance shall compel the parties to continue the contract, and, likewise, no court shall order an injunction to prevent a breach or threatened breach of contract by an individual employee, if either order would have the effect of compelling an employee to work or to attend a place for the purpose of doing work.

In *Whitwood Chemical Company v Hardman* ([1891] 2 Ch 416) a manager's contract contained a clause that he agreed to devote the whole of his time to company business. He intended to work for a rival company in his spare time and the employer sought specific performance of the clause. It was held that the action did not lie.

Likewise, if an injunction will have the effect of specific performance, in that it will compel the parties to continue the contract, it will not be granted. In *City & Hackney Health Authority v NUPE* [1985] IRLR 252 a shop steward obtained an injunction to restrain his employers from preventing him from entering the premises when he was suspended. The employers appealed and the Court of Appeal lifted the injunction. To allow it to stand would have forced the employers to allow the employee to attend the place of work and so have the effect of an order for specific performance.

However, case law shows that the court will, on the application of the employee, compel the parties to continue the contract where the employer is ignoring the employee's contractual rights and preventing him from pursuing a remedy provided by the contract itself, or where, in the circumstances, damages would be an inadequate remedy.

The courts only exercise this power in exceptional circumstances, and in the great majority of situations it will decide that the better remedy is damages for breach of contract. Further, an injunction will normally only be granted in order to preserve the existence of the employment relationship, not to require the employer to allow the employee to work. Any injunction will only be granted for a limited period.

The leading case in this area is *Hill v CA Parsons & Co. Ltd* [1972] Ch 305, where an employee refused to join the workplace union at a time when there was a closed shop in existence and the employer gave him one month's notice of dismissal. The court held that, given his position as a senior engineer, the employee was entitled to six months' notice and granted him an injunction restraining the employers from treating the contract as terminated until after that date. However, the court conceded that there were the following exceptional circumstances:

- There was no loss of confidence between the parties and the employer had dismissed the employee solely because of union pressure.
- The employee had been continuously employed for 35 years. He had two years to go before retirement and dismissal would affect his pension entitlement.
- The Industrial Relations Act 1971, creating the concept of unfair dismissal was due to come into force six months after the dismissal, and, if given six months' notice, he would be able to make a claim of unfair dismissal, which, in all the circumstances, was likely to succeed.

From decided cases the normal remedy for the dismissed employee is damages, only if damages are in all the circumstances inadequate will an order to continue the contract be granted. Moreover, it should be noted that in all but one of the cases where an injunction has been granted, it is only for the contract to continue for a relatively short space of time. The cases show that the court may compel the employer to continue the contract where:

- the employer, in the circumstances, is seeking to deprive the employee of a remedy available under the contract, and/or an opportunity to put his case against dismissal. In *Robb v London Borough of Hammersmith and Fulham* ([1991] IRLR 72) Morland J held that an industrial tribunal was not a suitable alternative forum for adjudicating on matters as complex as the Plaintiff's capabilities in relation to interest swaps;
- damages would be an inadequate remedy; and
- there has been no loss of confidence in the employee.

Wadcock v London Borough of Brent ([1990] IRLR 223, QBD) represents an exception to all these, though it has yet to be followed in any reported decision. The Plaintiff had been employed as a social worker since 1975. The employer re-organised the work so that its social workers were appointed to one of three specialist teams. The Plaintiff refused to indicate his preference and was placed, against his wishes, in the special needs team. He refused to work in the new team from the due date of 21 November, but on 7 December attached himself to the special needs team although he remained uncooperative. On 8 December, he was dismissed with 12 weeks' notice. He sought an injunction pending trial of his application for a declaration that the council's demand that he work in the special needs team was unlawful. Although he was prepared to work in that team until trial, the council rejected the proposal on the basis of the breakdown of mutual trust and confidence. The High Court granted the injunction.

Mervyn Davies J said:

> [I]t seems to me quite impossible to conclude that if an injunction is made in the terms sought . . . there will arise a 'workable situation' as that phrase is used above. On the other hand, there is no doubt that Mr Wadcock is a competent social worker and would be well able to work in special needs if he were minded to obey the orders of his team leader and superiors . . . As a separate point, I have in mind that Mr Wadcock *may* have been deprived of the protection of the disciplinary procedure.

In these circumstances, I propose to make an order embracing these provisions:

a) On Mr Wadcock undertaking henceforth to work in accordance with the orders, instructions and wishes expressed orally or in writing by his team leader for the time being or by any other member of the Social Services Department having authority over him, Brent are to allow Mr Wadcock, pending trial, to work for them in special needs at the usual rate of pay;
b) I will retain this matter pending trial and give Brent leave to apply on two days' notice to revoke this order should Mr Wadcock's undertaking be breached in any respect. If Mr Wadcock is not prepared to give that undertaking unreservedly, there will be no order on the motion.

This decision can be criticised on several grounds:

- Mr Wadcock was dismissed with the notice he was entitled to, for which he was paid, and there is nothing in the reported facts of the case to indicate that the employer was seeking to prevent him from utilising a contractual disciplinary procedure.
- Mr Wadcock had the opportunity to bring a claim for unfair dismissal in the Employment Tribunal.
- It is difficult to see how the employer could have maintained trust and confidence in Mr Wadcock, given that he refused to co-operate with what was, on the face of it, a reasonable reorganisation of working practices. In any case, the reasonableness of the reorganisation would be considered by the Tribunal in unfair dismissal proceedings.

- It is also difficult to see why the employee should be required to allow Mr Wadcock to work, given that previous precedents only enabled the contract to continue in being (and thus the employee was entitled to be paid). What would Mr Wadcock have lost by not working?

3.4 Implied duties of the employer

3.4.1 Is there a duty to provide work?

The expression 'the right to work' is frequently heard, but, legally speaking, there is, *prima facie*, no such thing. The starting point was summed up neatly by Asquith J in *Collier v Sunday Referee Publishing Co. Ltd* [1940] 2 KB 647, 'Provided I pay my cook her wages regularly, she cannot complain if I choose to take some or all of my meals out'.

As with many things, however, this principle is subject to many exceptions, developed on a case-by-case basis. Lord Denning MR seemed at one time anxious to establish that there was a right to work. In *Nagle v Fielden* ([1966] 2 QB 633) a woman argued that the rule of the Jockey Club which prevented a woman from holding a racehorse trainer's licence prevented her from earning a living. This rule was held to be in restraint of trade and void. However, it should be noted that although this decision allowed the Plaintiff to operate as a trainer, it did not require that she be provided with work. It was up to owners to decide whether to send their horses to her stable.

In *Langston v Chrysler United Kingdom* ([1974] 1 All ER 980) Lord Denning MR declared *obiter*, 'We have repeatedly said in this court that a man has a right to work which the courts will protect . . . I would not wish to state the decided view, but merely state the argument'. However, despite the enthusiasm of Lord Denning the courts have been reluctant to establish a general right to work, as distinct from the well-established right to be paid for being available to work. However, the courts have recognised a more limited duty to *provide* work in certain types of case.

This can first be seen in *Turner v Sawdon* ([1901] 2 KB 728), where two exceptions to the general rule were suggested *obiter*:

- when the employee must perform work in order to be paid;
- when the contract specifically provides that he be given work.

Case law has since developed further along these lines. The decision in *Herbert Clayton & Jack Waller Ltd v Oliver* [1930] AC 209 recognises that a man does not necessarily work for pay alone. The employee had been contracted to play the lead in a play, but was subsequently given a lesser part at the same salary. The employer was held to be in breach of contract as the nature of the work was as important as the salary in terms of the publicity the employee needed in order to maintain his acting career.

Devonald v Rosser & Sons ([1906] 2 KB 728) established a duty to provide work where work is needed to enable the employee to earn the wage. This covers the situation of those on piecework (paid according to what they produce) or employed on a commission-only basis, where the failure to provide work means that the employee receives no pay. However, this will only apply if the commission or piecework is the *only* way of earning. In *Devonald*, the employee was a foreman in a tinplate works and paid on piecework rates. His contract provided that he could be dismissed on 28 days' notice if there was no work. When the employer announced that the works would close down in two weeks' time, the court held that the Plaintiff was entitled to be paid for his contractual 28 days' notice.

However, this principle only applies in circumstances where the employee will only be paid when he is working. It is common in the financial services sector for employees to receive a small salary and obtain the great bulk of their income from commission on products sold. Provided the employer paid the salary there would be no requirement to provide work.

Dicta in *Langston* suggest that if the nature of the job is such that the employee needs the work to develop or maintain his skills, the employer would be in breach of contract if he failed to provide it. This would certainly cover the situation of apprentices or trainees – an obvious example is that under SRA rules, a firm employing trainee solicitors must provide them with sufficient work and variety of work to enable them to develop their professional abilities to a point where they are of a suitable standard to be admitted as solicitors – and may extend further.

Later cases seem willing to accept that *Turner v Sawdon* did not lay down a definitive list. In *Pedersen v London Borough of Camden* [1981] ICR 674 it was suggested that it may be a breach of contract to deprive an employee of a substantial proportion of his job, so entitling him to resign and claim constructive dismissal, on the basis that a man does not work for pay alone. This relies on the earlier case of *Breach v Epsylon Industries Ltd* [1976] IRLR 180, where the employer moved a large part of his operation to Canada, leaving the employee with little to do. On appeal to the EAT, Phillips J said *obiter* that *Turner v Sawdon* envisaged exceptions to the general principle, but the case was old and in more modern times there may be facts on which it is easier to imply that there is an implied obligation to provide work.

A more recent case is *William Hill Organisation v Tucker* [1998] IRLR 313. This involved a senior employer working for one of the two companies in Great Britain licensed to offer 'spread betting', which is where the public bet, not on a single event (which horse will win the Grand National?) but on a 'spread' of events (how many points will England score in the Six Nations Rugby Championship?). The employee was entitled to six months' notice, and when he resigned in order to take up a post with the rival company, his employer informed him that they did not require him to work during the notice period – so-called 'garden leave' – and sought an injunction to prevent him from working for any other organisation until the notice expired. Spread betting is a fast-developing area of work, one in which an employee needs to work to maintain his skills and keep up to date – six months out would greatly reduce the Claimant's value to the rival company. The court ruled that in order for an employer to prevent his employee from working for another employer during his period of paid notice, there must be an express term in the contract of employment permitting this. Only then will the court grant an injunction in favour of the employer. There was no such express term in Mr Tucker's contract, so he was free to begin working for the rival company.

A different conclusion was reached in *SG & R Valuation Service v Boudrais* ([2008] EWHC 1340 (QB)), which can clearly be distinguished on its facts. Two employees of a finance company gave three months' notice of resignation in order to join a competitor. Almost immediately, the employer began to uncover evidence of wrongdoing, particularly in relation to misuse of confidential information. The employer asked them to stay on garden leave for their notice period, although there was no contractual provision covering this. The employees then resigned with immediate effect, claiming a repudiatory breach of contract. The employers sought an injunction to place the employees on garden leave for the balance of the notice period.

The court held that:

- Given the nature of their work and the fact that bonuses formed a substantial part of their remuneration, the employees had an implied right to work.
- However, this right was subject to the qualification that the employee must not have demonstrated, by a breach of contract or implied duty, that they were **not** ready or willing to work.
- Where there was such a breach which constituted wrongdoing and by reason of which the employee would potentially profit, then there was no obligation to provide work.

- The court held that the pair had a right to work, but their behaviour (in particular, the specific hostility shown towards the company) had demonstrated that they were not ready and willing to work in accordance with their employment contracts.
- As such, the company was entitled to place them on garden leave and the court granted an injunction under which the employees remained subject to their contractual and other duties for the three-month notice period.

Note that *Boudrais* extends the circumstances in which the employer is under a duty to provide work from those where the employee must work in order to obtain *any* remuneration to those where bonuses form a substantial element in the total remuneration.

3.4.2 Duty to pay the employee

Although there is no duty on the employer to provide work, his duty to pay the employee is fundamental to the bargain. The employee makes himself available to provide the employer with personal services, and the employer pays him accordingly. If this duty is persistently broken the employee is entitled to sue for a repudiatory breach of contract, or to resign and claim constructive dismissal. Normally the contract will state the amount of pay that the employee is entitled to receive, either from individual negotiation between the parties, or from a collective agreement. If the contract is silent the law will imply that *reasonable remuneration* should be paid. The court will then assess the value of the employee's services on an action for *quantum meruit* – what the service is worth.

3.4.2.1 National Minimum Wage

The amount of pay which a worker is entitled to receive is now subject to the National Minimum Wage, which is couched in terms of a minimum hourly rate. From April 2018, this is £7.83 for eligible workers aged over 25 ('National Living Wage'), £7.38 for those aged 21–24, £5.90 where the worker is aged 18–20 and £4.20 for workers aged 16–17. An 'apprentice rate' of £3.70 applies to apprentices aged under 19 or in the first year of their apprenticeships. The Low Pay Commission recommends that the NMW should apply to the employee's gross standard pay. This excludes premium payments for overtime and shift work, and benefits such as company cars and private health insurance. If the employer provides accommodation, only the first £7.00 per day counts towards the National Minimum Wage. 'Accommodation' includes not only rent, but utility bills and laundry.

Note that the National Minimum Wage applies to 'workers' rather than only to employees.

The definition of working time for the purpose of calculating the worker's hourly rate is based on the definition used in the EC Working Time Directive (No 93/104), that is, any period when a worker is working at his employer's disposal and carrying out his duties. The NMW should also be payable when a worker is required to be at his place of work even if no work is available. If workers are required to sleep on the premises, the NMW should apply when they are awake and required to be available for work. The hourly rate should be determined by calculating the average pay over the normal pay period, and that average hourly rate should not be below the NMW.

Most case law on the NMW concerns the issue of whether a person is an eligible employee, and what constitutes time when he is working. Most of the problem areas concern employees who are in some way on call.

3.4.2.2 Itemised pay statement

By ERA s. 8 every employee who works for eight hours per week or more is entitled to an itemised pay statement at or before each payment of salary, which must state:

- gross and net amount of pay;
- amount of any variable or fixed deductions and purpose for which those deductions are made.

3.4.2.3 Deductions from pay

The Truck Acts 1831–1840 were passed in order to require employers to pay their employees in cash, different Acts covering different industries. Previously, unscrupulous factory owners frequently paid employees in tokens which could only be used at shops owned by the employers, and which provided poor quality foodstuffs and other basics at inflated prices.

The Wages Act 1986 was brought in to remedy deficiencies in the Truck Acts. In particular, it covered all employees, rather than those in specified industries. Given that there had been major societal changes since the 1830s, such that increasing numbers of employees had bank accounts and could be paid through them, the duty to pay employees in cash was abolished. A by-product of this development was the virtual disappearance of a form of robbery known as the 'wages snatch'. In order to pay their workforce in cash, employers needed to obtain large quantities of cash – several thousand pounds in small-denomination notes – from banks on a regular day each week, and criminal gangs would ambush the vans carrying the cash on their routes from bank to workplace.

The provisions of the 1986 Act now constitute ERA 1996 ss. 13–14. These have far-reaching consequences for many contractual terms in that there must be a statutory or contractual right to deduct from pay before any such deductions can lawfully be made. This has implications should an employer wish to impose a disciplinary sanction such as suspension without pay, demotion or a deduction for bad workmanship. Under *Robertson v Blackstone Franks Investment Management Ltd* [1998] IRLR 376, these provisions also apply to those employed on a commission-only basis and described in their contracts as 'self-employed', as long as they fall within the definition of 'worker' in ERA s. 230(1).

By ERA s. 13(1) an employer may not make a deduction from the wages of an employee unless the deduction is:

- required or authorised by statute (e.g. PAYE or some occupational pension contributions); or
- required or authorised by a provision in the contract of employment which has been given to the employee or notified to the employee previously in writing; or
- agreed to by the employee in writing before the making of the deduction.

However, the wording of the contractual provision or agreement must be precise, and will be narrowly interpreted. *Potter v Hunt Contracts Ltd* ([1992] IDS Brief 461) is an example. When the employee joined Hunts, he had to repay the cost of an HGV course to his previous employer. Hunts agreed to give him a loan for this purpose under an agreement which provided that if he left within 24 months 'you shall be required to return the fee, less any repayments made'. When the employee left within 24 months he received no pay, because the sum owed exceeded his pay. The EAT held that the employer had no right to *deduct*, but only to *receive* repayment from him (presumably they would have to sue him for the sum due).

Tobacco and Confectionery Ltd v Williamson [1993] ICR 371 establishes that where the employer relies on an agreement in writing to deduct, the agreement must not only pre-date the deduction, but also the event giving rise to the deduction. The employee was manager of a store where large stock deficiencies were found in December 1988 and again in February 1989. In March 1989, he signed a document empowering the employer to deduct £3,500 from his pay at £20 per week. In May 1989, there was a further deficiency and the employer dismissed him, withholding his pay in reliance on the March document. S. 13(6) states that any agreement by the employee to deduct shall not operate to authorise any deduction before the agreement was signed. The EAT held that this meant that the agreement had to pre-date not only the deduction, but the event which led to the deduction, so that deductions in respect of the deficiencies prior to the March agreement were unlawful.

❖ THINKING POINT

Why does the law take such a narrow approach? Bear in mind that a lot of agreements to deduct cover non-controversial and non-punitive matters, such as pension contributions and payment for workplace car parking.

1996 Act s. 14 then sets out a list of exceptions to the requirement for authority to deduct. S. 13(1) does not apply to deductions in respect of the following:

- overpayment of wages or expenses;
- disciplinary proceedings held by virtue of any statutory provision;
- a statutory requirement to deduct from wages to pay over to a public authority;
- payments agreed to by the employee which are to be made over by the employer to a third party;
- a strike or other industrial action in which the employee took part;
- the satisfaction of a court or tribunal order requiring the employee to pay something to the employer.

These exceptions do not give the employer a right to deduct such payments, but merely mean that such deductions do not infringe s. 13(1). The deduction may still be unlawful for other reasons. For example, recovering an overpayment of wages is within s. 14, but in some circumstances the employer may have lost the right to claim the overpayment back.

In *Avon CC v Howlett* [1983] IRLR 171 the employee was a teacher who had been regularly overpaid while off sick. The overpayment totalled £1,007, which the Council sought to reclaim by deductions from salary. The Court of Appeal held that when the money was accompanied by an express or implied representation that the recipient was to treat it as his own, the employer is prevented from recovering. Here, the employee, without any idea that the overpayment had been made, or that the Council would seek repayment, had changed his position so that repayment would be inequitable. The overpayment was due to a mistake of fact on the part of the Council, which had failed to realise that the employee had been off sick for more than six months, so that he was only entitled to half pay for his continuing absence, and the employee had spent the money, believing it to be his. There is, however, a hint in the judgment that the result could have been different had the employee not spent the money.

❖ THINKING POINT

Given that the employee was off work for over six months, and the sick pay provisions of his contract were presumably easily ascertainable, did the court give him the benefit of considerable doubt?

Case law on deductions, which is copious, mainly concerns two issues:

- Is the deduction made from 'wages'?
- Is there contractual authority to make the deduction?

One obvious problem area is that provisions may have been added to contracts or removed from them in a haphazard fashion over a long period. Further, employers may seek to reorganise and rationalise, and then face claims from the workforce that the change gives rise to an unlawful deduction. This can also happen as a result of attempts to equalise pay between men and women.

Morgan v Greater Glasgow Health Board [2012] UKEATS/0044/11/BI provides a convenient example of the complexity of this area. Dr Morgan was a hospital doctor in the course of specialist training to become a consultant. As is commonplace, he worked under a contract which provided for a 'rotation' between different posts under the same health authority in order to gain the necessary professional experience. His pay package comprised a basic salary, together with a non-pensionable supplement in respect of out-of-hours working. The issue in the case was whether the halving of the supplement when he moved to a different placement in the rotation constituted an unlawful deduction. On the basis of the contractual terms, the EAT concluded that there was no unlawful deduction in reducing the supplement to reflect a reduction in out-of-hours working.

Note that a demotion will normally involve a reduction in pay, and therefore must be authorised by the contract.

3.4.2.4 What are 'wages'?

ERA s. 27 lists payments which can be regarded as 'wages'. In particular, s. 27(1)(a) refers to 'any fee, bonus, commission, holiday pay or other emolument referable to his employment, whether payable under his contract or otherwise'. A number of cases since the Wages Act 1986 was passed have discussed whether pay in lieu of notice constitutes wages for this purpose.

A payment in lieu of notice is commonly made when a person leaves a job. Rather than being required to work out his notice, the person is given pay for the requisite notice period, whether at the time of the dismissal or resignation or at the normal pay points during the notice period. For obvious reasons, payments in lieu of notice are often made when an employee is dismissed or resigns 'under a cloud'.

Delaney v Staples (trading as De Montfort Recruitment) [1992] IRLR 191. The Claimant was dismissed without a payment in lieu of notice. She claimed that this represented an unlawful deduction, and that the Employment Tribunal therefore had jurisdiction to hear her claim. The underlying issue was whether a payment in lieu constituted 'wages'. If it did not, the Claimant's claim was in contract, and jurisdiction lay only with the County Court. In the House of Lords, Lord Browne-Wilkinson distinguished between four different types of payment in lieu of notice:

1) 'Garden leave', where the employer gives proper notice of termination to his employee, tells him that he need not work during the notice period and gives him the pay attributable to the notice period as a lump sum. The employment continues until the end of the notice period and the lump sum is simply an advance payment of wages, thus the payment constitutes 'wages' for the purpose of s. 7 (now s. 27).
2) The contract provides expressly that the employment may be terminated either by notice or summarily by a sum in lieu of notice. In such a case the employer who dismisses an employee summarily is not in breach of contract provided he makes the payment in lieu. The payment in lieu is not 'wages' since it is not a payment in respect of work to be done, although the employer would be in breach of contract if he failed to make the payment.
3) At the end of the employment, the employer and employee agree that the contract is to terminate forthwith on payment of a sum in lieu of notice. Again, the employer is not in breach of contract by dismissing summarily, and the payment in lieu is not wages since it is not remuneration for work done during the continuance of the employment, although an employer who failed to make the payment would be in breach of contract.
4) Without the agreement of the employee, the employer summarily dismisses the employee and tenders a payment in lieu of proper notice. The employer is in breach of contract by terminating

> the employment without proper notice (unless there is a breach of contract by the employee which justifies summary dismissal), but the summary dismissal is effective in ending the employment relationship, whether or not it unilaterally discharges the contract of employment. Since the employment relationship is at an end, no further services are to be rendered by the employee under the contract and it follows that the payment in lieu of notice does not constitute wages.

On this basis, only the first type of payment in lieu constitutes wages. In that case, the payment came within the fourth category, and therefore the Claimant had to take her case against the employer to the County Court. This issue – at any rate in relation to jurisdiction – has been largely resolved since *Delaney v Staples* by the extension of Tribunal jurisdiction to cover breach of contract claims worth a maximum of £25,000, provided employment has terminated.

Further problems have arisen in relation to whether a payment which is stated to be *ex gratia* can be wages for the purpose of the Act.

In *Kent Management Services Ltd v Butterfield* [1992] ICR 272 the employee complained that on his dismissal the employer refused to pay him outstanding commission. The employers argued that commission and bonus schemes were discretionary and *ex gratia* because a document attached to his letter of appointment stated that such payments would not be made in exceptional circumstances such as bankruptcy. As such payments were discretionary they could not be contractual. The EAT considered the definition of wages in s. 27(1)(a). Wood P said that such schemes must be fairly common and that while they were in being the anticipation of both parties must be that in normal circumstances commission, etc. would be paid. Here, no exceptional circumstances existed to prevent payment, and therefore the expectation of both parties must have been that commission would be paid. As such, the commission was wages and thus there had been an unlawful deduction.

'Wages' is a term interpreted widely, on the basis that it is widely drawn in ERA s. 27, but whether the contract authorises the deduction at issue depends very much on the court's interpretation (usually narrow) of the specific contractual term. Since all case law thus turns on the precise wording of the contractual provisions, examples are numerous.

Hayes v Securities and Facilities Division ([2000] *The Times*, 26 April, CA) dealt with the change in an overnight subsistence allowance from £62.50 in London and £60 elsewhere to a single flat rate of £50. On a true construction of the contractual term, the scheme provided for a fixed-rate entitlement subject to defined exceptions. There was no provision in the contract for unilateral variation of the allowance, and therefore the employer acted in breach of contract in reducing it without the agreement of the employees.

In *Cantor Fitzgerald International v Callaghan* [1999] EWCA Civ 622 the Court of Appeal made it clear that in a contract of employment the contractual arrangements for pay between employer and employee were of crucial importance. The deliberate and determined refusal by an employer to honour an agreement, thus diminishing the value to the employee of an agreed salary package, amounted to a repudiatory breach.

The employees were members of a team of brokers employed by Cantor on its Belgian government securities desk. Their contracts with Cantor made provision for payment to each of them of four-year forgivable loans of £60,000, which included arrangements to exclude any prospect of tax liability being incurred by the employees. As a result of subsequent changes to tax legislation, each employee became liable to tax on the imputed benefit of the interest-free element of the loans. Cantor refused to do anything about this. In 1997 the employees handed in a joint notice of termination, intending to start work with Cantor's rivals. For the purposes of the appeal, the employees claimed that their contracts had been repudiated on the ground, *inter alia*, that Cantor had wrongly failed or refused to comply with agreed salary arrangements.

According to Judge LJ, the question of whether non-payment of agreed wages or interference by an employer with a salary package was or was not fundamental to the continued existence of the contract of employment, depended on a critical distinction between an employer's *failure to pay, or his delay in paying agreed remuneration*, on the one hand, and his *deliberate refusal* to do so. Although a failure or delay constituted a breach of contract, that might represent no more than a temporary fault in the employer's technology, an accounting error or mistake, or illness, or unexpected events. If so, it would be open to the court to conclude that the breach did not go to the root of the contract. On the other hand, if the failure or delay in payment was repeated and persistent, perhaps also unexplained, then the court might be driven to conclude that the breach or breaches were indeed repudiatory.

Where, however, an employer unilaterally reduced his employee's pay or diminished the value of his salary package, the entire foundation for the contract of employment was undermined. Therefore, an emphatic denial by the employer of his obligation to pay the agreed salary, or a determined resolution not to comply with his contractual obligations in relation to pay and remuneration would normally be regarded as repudiatory.

Judge LJ stated that it was doubtful the concept of *de minimis* had any relevance in this field. If the amount at stake was very small, and the circumstances justifying a minimal reduction were explained to the employee, then the likelihood was that he would be prepared to accept new terms by way of mutual variation of the original contract. However, an apparently slight change imposed on a reluctant employee by economic pressure exercised by the employer should not be confused with consensual variation, and in such circumstances an employee would be entitled to treat the contract as being discharged by the employer's breach.

Here, in the context of the overall salary package the amount at issue was not very great. However, the refusal to pay was deliberate and determined, motivated by a desire to pressurise the employees into harder work. The decision wholly undermined the contract of employment and constituted a repudiatory breach.

❖ THINKING POINT

On the basis of Judge LJ's dicta, there will not be a repudiatory breach of contract if the employer is delayed in paying his workforce because of a wages snatch, or the more modern problem of a computer glitch at the bank. But what if these are not simply one-off occurrences, but happen several times over a period of months? Would it make any difference if the problems are not caused by third parties (criminals or the bank's computer), but the employer's own financial difficulties? Bear in mind that delays in paying them are often the first intimation employees have that their employer is in serious financial difficulty.

3.4.2.5 Payment during sickness

There is no presumption that the employee will be paid by his employer while he is sick. Although an employee may be entitled to statutory sick pay, this will only give a statutory level of payment. Since 1 April 2018 SSP is paid at £92.05 per week (for a maximum of 28 weeks), where the employee is earning at least £116 per week. It is therefore important to establish whether there is a term in the contract providing for payment of normal or reduced pay during sickness. Such a term may be express or implied.

Mears v Safecar Security ([1982] IRLR 183) establishes that before the court will imply a term into the contract that the employee will be paid during sickness, there must be evidence that the parties intended this to be the case. The employee was off ill for six months. During that time, he did not ask for pay, nor did he send in medical certificates. When he asked his colleagues about sick pay they told him it was not available and had never been paid in the past. The Court of Appeal held that as there was no express term in his contract relating to sick pay it was necessary to see whether there was an implied term. To see whether there was an implied term the court had to look at the conduct of the parties. Given that the employer had never paid sick pay in the past, and that the conduct of the employee indicated that he did not expect to receive sick pay, no term could be implied.

3.4.2.6 Pay during layoffs or short time working

The general rule at common law is that the employer must pay his employees who are available for work even if no work can be provided for them. If there is an interruption in the provision of work the employee is still entitled to be paid (*Devonald v Rosser & Sons*). However, if the failure to provide work is totally outside the employer's control, it appears that the courts will imply a term that employees are not entitled to be paid.

Browning v Crumlin Valley Collieries [1926] 1 KB 522 involved a serious land fault in a colliery. The owners closed the pit down until repairs had been carried out. The miners sued for loss of pay during the closure. It was held that the failure to provide work was totally outside the employer's control, and, as such, the implied term that the employees were entitled to payment would not apply.

It should be noted that if the employer finds it merely difficult, but not impossible, to provide work, the general principle will apply.

Unlike most implied duties, this may be ousted by an express term to the contrary (*Hulme v Ferranti Ltd* [1918] 2 KB 426). However, the law will restrict the employer's exercise of such a contractual right. Under *A Dakri & Co. Ltd v Tiffen* ([1981] IRLR 57) such a right can only be exercised for a reasonable length of time, and after such a time has elapsed the employee is entitled to treat the non-payment as a repudiatory breach and may, if he has sufficient continuity of employment, sue for constructive dismissal.

3.4.3 Duties in relation to references

It must be said that there is no duty to provide references, unless there is a specific term in the contract to this effect. It is well established that the employer owes a duty of care in tort to the *recipient* of a reference, but does he owe such a duty to the *subject*?

Spring v Guardian Assurance Co ([1994] 3 All ER 129) established that a duty to the subject of the reference did exist in the tort of negligence. The Plaintiff had worked for the Defendant company and left to sell insurance policies on behalf of another insurance company. As required by financial services regulation body, LAUTRO, the Defendant company provided a reference, which doubted, *inter alia*, the Plaintiff's honesty and selling tactics. Although the writer of the reference honestly believed the information given in the reference to be true, on the facts he had been negligent because he had failed to investigate the reasons for the Plaintiff's poor performance; in particular, that he had sold unsuitable policies because of inadequate training rather than any dishonest intention.

The majority in the House of Lords held that the writer of a reference owed a duty to the subject of that reference, as well as the recipient, to take reasonable care, on the basis that the damage caused by a negligently prepared reference is reasonably foreseeable, there was sufficient proximity between the parties and that it was fair and reasonable to impose such a duty. It was argued by the Defendants that the imposition of such a duty would deter employers from providing references, but that was not considered a serious enough risk to make it improper to impose such a duty.

The case is interesting for a number of reasons, not least because the court is allowing a person to recover in respect of loss which, arguably, is purely economic – failure to obtain another job. The Plaintiff could not bring an action in respect of libel or malicious falsehood because the writer of the reference honestly believed the facts given were true.

Hassan v Sandwell & West Birmingham Hospital NHS Trust [2006] EWHC 2407 (QB) is worth reading as an example of the way the courts consider whether a reference is fair and accurate or not. Dr Hassan had come to Britain from Pakistan in 1993 and, as is commonplace, had been granted limited registration to practise here on the basis of participating in an official Overseas Doctors' Training Scheme. He alleged that references provided by two consultants in 1997, which were couched in rather guarded terms, made assertions that were untrue, unfair and inaccurate, and had prevented him from obtaining work as a doctor in Britain.

3.4.4 Duty of trust and confidence

This is frequently termed the implied duty of mutual respect, and is among the most significant of the implied duties, being frequently relied on as the basis of a claim of constructive dismissal.

At the beginning of the Industrial Revolution the employment relationship was seen as one of servitude and this was reflected in the names the law chose for the parties to the relationship. For many years, the law thought of the employment relationship as being that of master and servant rather than employer and employee, and many old cases reflect this judicial attitude to the relationship. *Turner v Mason* ([1845] M & W 112) is perhaps the classic example, where it was held that an employer was entitled to sack a domestic servant who had, in breach of a contractual provision requiring her to be on duty 24 hours a day, taken a day off to visit her dying mother.

The law has moved on with changes in society since then, and now imposes a duty on the employer to treat the employee with respect (*Donovan v Invicta Airways* [1970] 1 Lloyd's Rep 486). Conduct such as telling an experienced employee before his subordinates that he is incapable of doing the job has been found to be a breach (*Courtaulds Northern Textiles Ltd v Andrew* [1979] IRLR 84), as has describing a senior officer as wholly unsuitable for promotion without any evidence to support that finding (*Post Office v Roberts* [1980] IRLR 515).

Case law in this area is, however, very fact-specific, and care needs to be taken when applying a principle drawn from one case to a different factual situation. *Bliss v South East Thames Regional Health Authority* [1987] ICR 700 provides a good example. A hospital consultant was suspended for a lengthy period as a result of a dispute with a colleague. Eventually, the Health Authority informed him that they would permit him to return to work on condition he first underwent a psychiatric examination. He resigned and claimed constructive dismissal. The Court of Appeal concluded that there had been a repudiatory breach of the duty of trust and confidence and thus a constructive dismissal. However, this decision was very much predicated on there being no evidence that the Plaintiff was suffering from any form of mental instability and thus no need for a psychiatric examination.

Bliss is an important case, but unusual on its facts. *Prima facie* an employer cannot require an employee to undergo a medical examination, as to do so would lead to a trespass to the person. However, a professionally drawn-up contract will normally include a provision to require the employee to undergo a medical examination in defined circumstances (typically after a set period of absence through sickness). Further, it is likely that refusal to undergo a medical examination without good reason would constitute refusal to obey a lawful and reasonable order (see below).

French v Barclays Bank plc ([1998] IRLR 646, CA) involves a subtler and more complex situation. The Claimant was a bank manager and the terms of his contract included a mobility clause. In order to ensure that employees did not suffer any loss through compliance with the mobility clause, the contract also made provision for payment of removal expenses, and, subject to certain conditions, financial assistance through an interest-free bridging loan when the sale and purchase of property was involved. The employee was required to transfer from Oxfordshire to Essex, and in order to enable him to buy a new house before selling the old one, the bank agreed to give him an interest-free bridging loan of £190,000. With that sum, and a further mortgage loan of £46,795, the employee paid off his existing mortgage and purchased a house in Essex for £208,000. The old house was offered for sale at £195,000, by agreement between the parties, but the housing market then collapsed and the house was valued by estate agents at £150,000. At this point the bank offered the employee either:

- that the bank would buy the house for £150,000 with the employee being responsible for the shortfall; or
- paying interest on the loan of £190,000 once it had been outstanding for 12 months.

Under protest, the employee sold the house to the bank for £147,500, and, in order to repay the balance of the bridging loan, accepted an arrangement which involved increased borrowing and selling the bank a proportion of the equity in his new house. He subsequently brought an action against the bank for breach of contract.

The Court of Appeal held that the bank was in breach of the implied duty in the employee's contract not to undermine the mutual trust and confidence between them when they changed to his detriment the terms of the bridging loan, which had been granted to assist him in relocating at their behest. To seek to invoke a change of policy or a change in the terms on which loans are made, which have been applied to other employees over many years and appeared in the staff handbook at the time the loan was made, was conduct on the part of the employer likely to destroy mutual trust and confidence.

Here, the employee had been asked to move and an interest-free loan had been sanctioned to enable him to do so. His expectation was that the bank would not wish him to suffer financial loss by virtue of the relocation, and, as long as he continued to market the house at the original valuation, that the loan would remain interest-free. He was then given the alternative of agreeing to take substantially less for the house than the agreed valuation, or paying interest on the loan, which he could not afford. Anything more calculated to destroy mutual trust and confidence would be hard to imagine.

This case can be contrasted with *University of Nottingham v Eyett* ([1998] *The Times* 3 December, Ch.D). Under the rules of the university's pension scheme, the employee was entitled, with the university's consent, to take early retirement without actuarial reduction on reaching the age of 60. Early in 1994, he enquired of the university what his pension entitlement would be if he retired on 31 July 1994, his 60th birthday. He was informed that his pension would be calculated by reference to his average salary for the years 1991, 1992 and 1993, and was quoted a figure of £4,937.67. The employee duly retired on 31 July. What he had not realised, and so not enquired about, was that had he chosen to retire on the earliest possible date after 31 July, his pension would have been calculated by reference to his salary for 1992, 1993 and 1994, producing the figure of £5,118, an increase of £170 per annum. The employee alleged that the university had been in breach of an implied duty in failing to inform him of this prior to his retirement. It was not disputed that the university would have been perfectly willing to allow him to retire after 31 July 1994 had he wished to do so.

The Court of Appeal held that the implied duty of good faith in an employment contract did not include a positive obligation on an employer to advise that the way in which an employee proposed to exercise his pension rights might not be to his financial advantage. Hart LJ said that the decided cases in which a breach of the implied duty had been established all involved deliberate conduct on the part of the employer. Moreover, the terms in which the implied duty had been expressed had consistently been in the negative form of prohibiting conduct calculated or likely to produce destructive or damaging consequences, rather than as positively enjoining conduct which would avoid such consequences. Nevertheless, he did not think that the principle underlying the implied duty of mutual trust and confidence necessarily excluded the possibility that it might have a positive rather than a purely negative content.

In the specific area of giving advice to employees on their pension rights, the furthest the courts had gone in recognising such a default obligation was in *Scally v Southern Health and Social Services Board*, where the term implied was a duty to take reasonable steps to bring the existence of a valuable right to the attention of the employee. This provided no support for the employee here, who undoubtedly knew of the existence of his early retirement rights. In addition, the authorities on the duties of pension fund holders to give advice to beneficiaries did not encourage the imposition of such an obligation on them.

Quite simply, the employee had asked too narrow a question.

The case of *Bank of Credit and Commerce International (in compulsory liquidation) v Ali* ([1999] 30 June, Ch.D) raises a different possibility, that an employer could be liable to an ex-employee in damages for his breach of the duty.

BCCI was an international bank founded in 1972, with headquarters in London and Karachi. Much of its business involved the Middle East. The Bank came under suspicion several times over the years in relation to its business practices, and eventually collapsed in 1991. Subsequent investigations established that long after the Bank had become insolvent, the directors had continued to trade (thereby operating illegally) and had actively encouraged employees with no knowledge of the situation to tout for business. A number of former employees then argued that the 'taint' of having worked in good faith for a fraudulent employer prevented them from obtaining further employment in the financial services industry. BCCI had thus been in breach of the duty of trust and confidence and was liable to them in damages in respect of their inability to secure suitable employment.

The Chancery Division concluded that in order to constitute the carrying on of an unlawful business so as to amount to a breach of the implied duty of trust and confidence, it was necessary to show that the employer's conduct was such that the employee could not reasonably be expected to tolerate it a moment longer after he had discovered it, and could walk out of his job without prior notice. Thus, the test was whether there had been a repudiatory breach of contract such as to give rise to a constructive dismissal. Lightman J found that this test was satisfied, giving the Plaintiff a potential remedy for wrongful or unfair dismissal. However, he did not find the necessary causal link between the breach of the duty and the post-employment losses to make an award of damages.

Morrow v Safeway Stores plc ([2001] EAT/0275/00, EAT) is a most important case, as it establishes that *any* breach of the implied duty of trust and confidence constitutes a repudiatory breach of contract, entitling the employee to resign and claim constructive dismissal. The employee was a bakery supervisor, and claimed that over a period of some months she had been subjected to harassment and unreasonable pressure from her superiors over the way in which she did her work, in particular over her repeated failure to ensure that there was sufficient stock on the shelves at any one time, and that she had received no support from those who worked under her. During this period, the employer became increasingly concerned that Mrs Morrow had been promoted beyond her ability.

On 20 August 1999, when the store was offering a 'two bloomers for the price of one' promotion in the bakery, things came to a head. Soon after the store opened, the manager, Mr Walsh, found that there were no bloomers at all on the shelves and that the employee was making no attempt to produce extra. He gave her a severe telling-off, in front of both colleagues and customers, which included the words, 'if you cannot do the job that I pay you to do, then I will get someone who can', and gave her two hours to sort things out. He returned two hours later to find that little had improved, and told the employee off again. She became distressed, began to apply for other jobs and on 10 September resigned, claiming to have been constructively and unfairly dismissed. The employer alleged that she had merely resigned.

The Tribunal held that the manager's action in telling the employee off in public certainly amounted to a breach of the implied duty of trust and confidence. However, not every breach of that duty was a repudiatory breach, and that in all the circumstances of this case there was no repudiatory breach.

On appeal the EAT took the view that the Tribunal had been in error to separate the content of the reprimand, which they thought not unreasonable in the circumstances, from the fact that it took place in public, and so misdirected themselves. In the view of Mr Recorder Cox, who gave the judgment, any breach of the implied duty of trust and confidence was, on the recent authorities, a repudiatory breach. The appeal was therefore allowed, though not to the extent of the EAT ruling that there had been a constructive dismissal. The matter was referred for a re-hearing.

As yet, this approach has not been confirmed by the Court of Appeal, but seems to be generally accepted.

❖ THINKING POINT

Is it fair that something said by a superior in a moment of exasperation, which may be understandable in the circumstances, should give rise to a constructive dismissal if the employee chooses to resign?

In the subsequent case of *Mayer v BBC* ([2004] UKEAT 0010_04_1009) the EAT arguably took an unduly narrow approach to the duty of trust and confidence. Mr Mayer presented the BBC South-East TV news programme *South-East Tonight* and was employed on a one-year contract, which was extended by six months in April 2002. As the end of his contract approached, he made management aware of an unhappy atmosphere in the newsroom, which he attributed primarily to the Managing Editor and one of the Assistant Editors, who lived together. There were other problems, including resources. In June 2002, it was decided that Mr Mayer's contract would not be renewed when it expired in October. He was informed of this on 25 June and it was agreed then that he would not return after going on leave in July but would be paid until the end of October. The incident on which Mr Mayer based his claim of constructive dismissal took place on the afternoon of 26 June.

First, Mr Mayer spoke to the Managing Editor,

> who expressed concerns about his enthusiasm and commitment, and the BBC, he said, wanted presenters who would be more supportive, and then just before the programme was due to go on air that evening, [the Director of Regions] spoke to him because she was concerned that news of his departure was leaking out. She said that the station wanted presenters who were more supportive of management and she said that the viewing figures were terrible and she considered that it was the Appellant's fault. She also said there had been criticism about his style of presenting, although he had not been notified of any criticism prior to this. He asked to see evidence of the poor ratings, but Mrs Ellis did not think that that was appropriate. He was so upset by this conversation that he decided not to present the evening show.

Mr Mayer told the Tribunal he felt 'shattered and completely undermined by the events on this particular day, and he felt that any remaining trust or confidence in his management had been destroyed'.

According to the Court of Appeal, issues of workplace conduct and their gravity were matters for the Tribunal to consider. In this case, the Tribunal considered that the BBC was entitled to question Mr Mayer's style of presentation and viewing figures. Such matters were properly capable of being raised between a presenter and a manager, albeit at a more appropriate time and in a less peremptory manner than here. The Tribunal had adopted the correct balance. Although the BBC erred in its presentation and timing, its conduct did not go to the root of the contract.

❖ THINKING POINT

Do you think the conclusion might have been different had the presenter been Miss Mayer rather than Mr Mayer?

3.4.4.1 What is the effect of a repudiatory breach on the contract of employment?

Under ordinary Contact Law a repudiatory breach entitles the other party to terminate the contract if he so decides. If the other party is the employee, and he decides to end the contract by resigning, then *prima facie* he will be left with a claim in damages only (usually for payment in lieu of the notice he would have received had the contract been honoured). If he has two years' continuous employment he will be protected by the unfair dismissal legislation and able to bring a claim in respect of constructive dismissal. If it is the employee who commits the repudiatory breach, then the termination of the contract is treated as a dismissal. However, it would seem from case law that the repudiatory breach will not normally end the contract until it is taken as doing so by the innocent party; if the breach is rectified before the resignation the contract will continue as normal.

This point can be seen in *Norwest Holst Group Administration v Harrison* ([1985] IRLR 240). The employee worked for the employer in a post which included a directorship, his contract being renewed every year. On 14 June, he was told that he was being transferred to a new post which did not include a directorship. He replied in a letter headed 'without prejudice' that he assumed that his contract had been terminated and asked for a meeting to discuss matters amicably. This meeting was held on 24 June, at which he was offered his original post plus directorship. He purported to accept the original repudiatory breach and claimed unfair dismissal. It was held that there had been no dismissal. A repudiatory breach terminates the contract only when it is unequivocally accepted as such by the innocent party. Since the employee's letter was headed 'without prejudice', his acceptance was not unequivocal, and the employer could therefore rectify the breach up to the time of any unequivocal acceptance, and this he had done. The employee had simply resigned.

3.5 Implied duties of the employee

3.5.1 Duty to obey reasonable and lawful orders

This is the most fundamental duty of the employee. Within the employment contract the employee gives consideration by providing his services in the manner required by the employer, just as the employer gives consideration by paying him. Since this duty is fundamental, it follows that should the employee refuse to obey a legitimate order the employer is entitled at common law to dismiss without notice. By refusing to obey orders, the employee is essentially stating that he does not wish to be bound by the contractual terms any longer and is thus committing a repudiatory breach. The classic example is a strike. The employer, subject to the statutory unfair dismissal provisions, is entitled to accept the strike as a breach which terminates the contract. See Chapter 20 for legislation and case law relating to industrial action.

In *Laws v London Chronicle* [1959] 1 WLR 698, Lord Evershed MR said:

> Wilful disobedience of a lawful and reasonable order shows a disregard . . . of a condition essential to the contract of service, namely the condition that the servant must obey the proper orders of the master, and that unless he does so the relationship is, so to speak, struck at fundamentally.

However, this duty is subject to a very important caveat. It is not to obey *all* orders of the employer, but only those that are *reasonable* and *lawful*. Further, the duty is to obey *orders* and not requests. To establish whether the duty has been breached, it is necessary to ask first whether the order is reasonable. This generally means asking whether the order is within the contractual obligations of the employee. Most reasonable orders are also lawful, but there are exceptions.

Very often the order will be in relation to the employee's job. The starting point is therefore what the contract states to be the employee's job duties. A refusal to perform such duties will usually be a breach of contract. However, the courts recognise that the employee must be prepared to be flexible and may decide that his duties are wider than those expressly listed in the contract. Certainly, an employee will be expected to perform duties which are reasonably incidental to his main job duties. *Sim v Rotherham BC* shows that the courts may imply duties into particular types of contracts. They will also expect the employee to adapt to new methods of carrying out his duties (*Cresswell v Board of Inland Revenue*).

Some employers try to foresee any eventual problems by including a 'flexibility' clause in the contract. This is essentially a broad clause requiring the employee to perform any task ordered by the employer. Taken to their logical conclusion, these clauses could mean that the employee can legitimately be asked to do anything. Such an interpretation has important consequences in relation to redundancy, since the employer could argue that the employee could be redeployed in any role in any location covered by a mobility clause, and therefore is not entitled to a redundancy payment.

Haden v Cowan ([1983] ICR 1) was a case involving redundancy. The employer argued that the employee was not redundant because it was possible to move him to an alternative post within the scope of his very general job description, which was effectively a flexibility clause. However, the Court of Appeal limited the application of flexibility clauses by holding that such clauses had to refer back to the employee's main job duties.

In addition to orders relating to the job itself, there may be other areas where the employee refuses to obey, most often in the decided cases mobility requirements. Again, the starting point is the contract, bearing in mind that the courts may imply a term if they believe that would have been the parties' intention.

In *Courtaulds Northern Spinning v Sibson* ([1988] IRLR 305) the employee was asked to transfer to another site which was within easy travelling distance of home. The contract was silent as to mobility between sites, but the employee had worked on that site in the past. The Court of Appeal held that on the basis of his past conduct there was an implied term in the contract requiring him to move sites if ordered to do so, and refusal to move was a breach of contract.

Case law since then has strongly suggested that an implied term as to mobility is not created merely because the employee has moved without protest in the past (*Jones v Associated Tunnelling*), although in that case the nature of the employer's operation, involving a number of relatively short-term contracts at pits across a fairly small area, made it appropriate to imply a mobility clause into the contract. In addition, there may be circumstances in which an instruction to move may be held a lawful and reasonable order, even in the absence of an express or implied mobility clause.

Certainly, refusal to move where there is an express mobility clause will normally be a breach of contract on the face of it, as will refusal to work contractually binding overtime. However, the courts may decide that an employee is fairly dismissed even though what he is refusing to do is outside the ambit of his contract, demonstrating that the tests of breach of contract under the common law and unfair dismissal under statute are quite different.

A good example is *Horrigan v Lewisham LBC* ([1978] ICR 15). The employee was a driver working for the council social services department whose job included taking elderly people to a day centre each morning and returning them in the evening. He was contracted to work until 4.30pm but in practice rarely finished work until later. He was paid overtime rates for working after 4.40pm but there was no contractual requirement for him to work overtime. After ten years of working overtime, the employee began to work only his contractual hours and was eventually dismissed. His dismissal was held to be fair given the difficulties the employer would face in not knowing from day-to-day whether the employee would be available to complete the round.

Therefore, while the contract is the starting point, the courts interpret the word 'reasonable' in a flexible way and this can mean that the employee may be required to do duties which are not within his contract. However, this works both ways, and there have been situations where the courts have decided that even though the order is within the contractual authority of the employer, it is still unreasonable and the employee is not in breach of contract in refusing to obey it.

The classic example is that of *Ottoman Bank Ltd v Chakarian* ([1930] AC 277, PC), the facts of which arose in 1922, during the revolution and civil war which brought the fall of the Ottoman sultanate and the coming to power of Kemal Ataturk. The employer, a bank based in Cyprus, ordered the employee to stay at the bank's branch in Constantinople (now Istanbul). The employee was an Armenian, a member of a Christian minority subjected to genocide by the Ottoman authorities from 1916 onwards. He had escaped the genocide, but argued that his life was in immediate danger in Constantinople, as in 1919, when working elsewhere in Turkey, he had been sentenced to death by the Kemalist forces which had now taken the city. When his superiors ignored his requests for an immediate transfer to any bank branch outside Turkey, he escaped from Constantinople on board a ship bound for Athens. He then made his way to Cyprus and reported to the bank's headquarters. The employee was summarily dismissed and brought an action for wrongful dismissal. It was held that although the order was within the employer's contractual rights, and therefore lawful, it was not in these very unusual circumstances a reasonable order, and the employee was entitled to refuse to obey it. The Privy Council accepted that Mr Chakarian was in real and imminent danger of his life as long as he remained in Constantinople, and that by being prepared to work at any branch outside Turkey he was fulfilling his contractual duties towards the bank. He was therefore entitled to recover damages for wrongful dismissal.

This case can usefully be contrasted with *Bouzourou v Ottoman Bank* ([1930] AC 271, PC) decided by the same panel on the same day. Here the Privy Council made it clear that an order by an employer to his employee to remain in the place of his employment is lawful unless it involves an *immediate* threat of danger by violence or disease. A Turkish Christian employee of the same bank was posted from Constantinople to a branch at Mersina, a small town in a distant part of Asia Minor. He refused to go on two grounds:

- Mersina was not within the geographical area of his employment, which under his contract was confined to Constantinople and its suburbs.
- The order was unreasonable in view of his inability to speak Turkish, and the hostility of the Turkish civil authorities in the area towards Christians.

The Privy Council held

1) On the proper construction of the employee's contract, he could be required to work anywhere in Turkey.

2) Since the employee did not allege any danger to his life stemming from the move to Mersina, the order was a reasonable one, and the employer was entitled to dismiss him for his refusal to comply.

The reasoning from these two cases was applied in more recent times in *Walmsley v Udec Refrigeration Ltd* ([1972] IRLR 80). During the worst period of the Northern Ireland Troubles, with terrorist bombs and shootings a weekly, if not daily occurrence across the province, the employee was instructed to move from the UK mainland to Wexford in the Irish Republic. He refused, claiming that Wexford was an IRA stronghold, and was dismissed. The Tribunal said that there was no evidence that Wexford was so dangerous as to justify a refusal to work there; at the time, there had been no significant terrorist activity in the Irish Republic. However, the EAT added *obiter* that had the employee been ordered to move to Belfast, the position might have been different.

❖ THINKING POINT

Given that on the existing case law the employee must show that he is in danger of his life before a lawful order ceases to be reasonable, is the bar not set too high? For example, the Zika virus, which causes birth defects, is widespread in parts of Latin America. Could a pregnant woman argue that being required to visit, say, Mexico, is not a reasonable order?

In addition to the requirement that the order be reasonable, it must also be lawful, and the employee can legitimately refuse to obey an order requiring him to act illegally. This distinction can be seen in *Morrish v Henlys (Folkestone) Ltd* ([1973] IRLR 610). An employee was dismissed when he refused to obey an order to falsify the account books at the garage where he worked. His dismissal was held to be unfair as he was not in breach of contract by refusing to comply with an unlawful order.

Farrant v The Woodroffe School ([1998] IRLR 176, EAT) involves variation of express terms. However, it would seem that it was also not a reasonable order for the employer to require the employee to move out of one department entirely, although a change in the balance of time he spent in the two departments would probably have been lawful.

3.5.2 Duty of co-operation

The law has always required that an employee should serve his employer faithfully and act in a loyal manner. More specific duties have evolved out of this proposition. The idea, however, that an employee should always co-operate with his employer was first expounded in detail by the Court of Appeal as recently as 1972, in *Secretary of State for Employment v ASLEF (No.2)* [1972] ICR 19.

Under the Industrial Relations Act 1971 the Secretary of State could seek a court order to require a union to hold a ballot of its membership where there was 'irregular industrial action short of a strike'. ASLEF (Amalgamated Society of Locomotive Engineers and Firemen – the train drivers' union) was conducting a work to rule, under which the drivers refused to perform any duties outside the strict letter of their contracts. In particularly, they refused to move trains to and from their depots at the beginning and end of the working day. Within a few days, this brought the railway system to a virtual standstill. ASLEF argued that the drivers were not acting in breach of contract, and thus no 'industrial action short of a strike'. All the judges in the Court of Appeal held that the employees were in breach of contract. Lord Denning MR said that if the employee takes steps wilfully to disrupt his employer's undertaking he would be in breach of contract. Buckley LJ said that there was an implied term in all contracts that the employee should serve his employer faithfully and promote the employer's commercial interests.

It has been argued that *British Telecom v Ticehurst* ([1992] IRLR 219) limited the scope of this duty to managers and other senior employees, on the basis that they were in a position to influence others to act against the employer's interests. The union instituted a series of one-day strikes and also a withdrawal of goodwill – i.e. refusing to do more than the bare minimum required under their contracts. BT wrote to all employees to say that if they did not comply fully with the terms of their contracts they would be considered to be taking industrial action and sent home without pay until they were prepared to work normally. The employee, who was both a manager and a union official, took part in the strikes and when she returned to work refused to sign an undertaking that she would work normally in the future.

As a result, she was sent home and subsequently sued for pay deducted for the days she had not been at work. At first instance, it was held that BT were not entitled to deduct pay as she had been ready, willing and able to work. The Court of Appeal held, however, that she had demonstrated that if she returned to work she would withdraw her goodwill, which amounted to breach of the implied term that she would serve her employer faithfully. It was necessary to imply such a term into a manager's contract because managers oversee other employees and must therefore exercise judgement and discretion when they give orders. Managers were bound to exercise their discretion to further the employer's interests, and as the employee had indicated that she would withdraw her goodwill, she could not be promoting the employer's interest. The employer was entitled not to accept her part-performance of her duties and to deduct pay.

It may be argued that this decision confines the duty of co-operation to managers. However, the Court of Appeal was dealing with an employee who was a manager, and *ASLEF* remains good law.

3.5.3 Duty not to accept bribes or secret commission

The employee should only accept rewards from his employer, and is under an implied duty not to accept payment from another source, even if the payment does not influence him in the performance of his duties. The basis of this duty is that the employee must serve his employer faithfully, and in his employer's interests, and it is inconsistent with this duty that he should receive payment from another source for doing his job.

The starting point is *Boston Deep Sea Fishing and Ice Co. v Ansell* ([1888] 39 Ch.D 339), where the employee was accepting payment for placing orders with a supplier, and at the same time receiving dividends from shares he owned in another supplier. His dismissal was held to be justified by his breach of duty.

Breach of this duty is considered by the courts to be so serious that it will normally justify summary dismissal. However, the payment must be secret, so that the duty is not broken if the employer knows about the payment and accepts it. For example, it is accepted in some jobs that employees will receive tips – restaurant staff are the obvious example.

This duty is easy to state, but in practice it may be difficult to enforce. Many employers will receive presents from customers or suppliers, and will often receive free meals and drinks. There is now a large 'hospitality' industry providing just such inducements. Technically, a breach of contract may have occurred, but in reality, the majority of employers would not pursue a remedy against the employee. In practice, many employers provide employees with guidance on what is and what is not acceptable. For example, it is accepted in many solicitors' firms that a client will give a bottle of wine or box of chocolates to the solicitor who deals with their house purchase, but there are specific Practice Rules dealing with the situation where a client bequeaths money to a solicitor by will (the solicitor must ensure that the client is independently advised). Should an employee then step out of line, he will be in breach of contract.

Neary and Neary v Dean of Westminster ([1999] IRLR 288) attracted huge publicity, as Dr Neary was organist and choirmaster of Westminster Abbey, and a leading figure in church music. In particular, the Abbey choir made regular recordings and gave concerts elsewhere. Further, because of the unusual legal position of Westminster Abbey, which is a 'royal peculiar' – a church under the direct authority of the monarch – the Nearys sought legal redress following his dismissal by petitioning the Queen. After Dr Neary was appointed in 1988, his wife became part-time secretary of the music department and concert secretary. In addition to his salary, Dr Neary was entitled to fees for certain performances. Lay vicars (adult choristers paid a salary) were also entitled to additional fees for taking part in the same events.

From 1991, when Mrs Neary was appointed concert secretary, all arrangements for outside events involving the Abbey choir were handled by the Nearys. The financial aspects were dealt with by the Abbey finance department, who received the fees paid by the outside bodies and dispersed them to the lay vicars as gross payments on which Schedule D income tax was due. However, in April 1994, the Inland Revenue informed the Abbey that such fees must be taxed at source under Schedule E and made subject to National Insurance deductions. Thereafter, following some discussion with the Abbey finance department as to how Schedule D status could be preserved for the lay vicars, Dr Neary arranged with the outside bodies for the fees to be paid into a separate bank account, operated by Mrs Neary, who would then pay the lay vicars. Mrs Neary subsequently formed a company for this purpose (Neary Music Ltd), and operated a bank account in the company's name.

Between April 1994 and December 1996, Mrs Neary received 'fixing fees' from outside bodies in relation to events in which the Abbey choir had taken part, amounting to some £11,900. She also received a dividend from the company in lieu of fixing fees for 1997. Where an event resulted in a surplus after payment of costs, that surplus was retained in the Neary Music bank account, along with any interest earned on fees before they were disbursed to the lay vicars.

The Abbey authorities were not aware of the new system for paying lay vicars until March 1998. Following a disciplinary hearing, on 22 April both Nearys were summarily dismissed for gross misconduct, although there was no suggestion that they had acted dishonestly in taking fixing fees and retaining surpluses, which were the main charges against them.

Dr Neary maintained that he thought he had been given approval for the new scheme, that he and his wife were acting in the best interests of the lay vicars, and that any money Mrs Neary received reflected only the work she had done in connection with the events concerned. He petitioned the Queen as Visitor to the Abbey, requesting resolution of the dispute between himself and the Dean. Lord Jauncey of Tullichettle was appointed by the Queen to determine that petition, and also to arbitrate on Mrs Neary's dispute with the Dean.

Dr and Mrs Neary accepted the following propositions:

1) The Abbey was a collegiate body where trust between individuals was most important;
2) The highest standards of integrity were expected of its officers and staff;
3) In carrying out their duties it was important not to conduct themselves in a way that would undermine the trust and confidence which had to exist between fellow officers;
4) They were obliged to carry out their duties in a spirit of openness befitting a religious foundation; and
5) They should not make a secret profit from their positions.

The Court held that the conduct of the Nearys in taking fixing fees from external promoters and retaining surpluses amounted to gross misconduct justifying their summary dismissal.

Conduct amounting to gross misconduct justifying summary dismissal must so undermine the trust and confidence which is inherent in the particular contract of employment, that the employer should no longer be required to retain that employee in his employment. Whether particular misconduct justifies summary dismissal is a question of fact. The character of the institutional employer, the role played by the employer in that institution and the degree of trust reposed in that employee must all be considered in determining the extent of the duty of trust and the seriousness of the breach. It cannot be accepted that when financial wrongdoing is alleged, nothing short of deliberate dishonesty or deceit will constitute gross misconduct.

Here, the Nearys used their positions to run a business which made secret profits over a prolonged period. Contrary to the spirit of openness which they accepted was required, they failed entirely to inform the Abbey authorities of what they were doing, even though they had ample opportunities for doing so and no good reason for not doing so. That conduct was such as to fatally undermine the relationship of trust and confidence which should have subsisted between them and the Abbey.

❖ THINKING POINT

Would the decision have been different had it not been for the special character of Westminster Abbey as a religious institution?

The circumstances where this duty applies may be quite subtle, as in *Nottingham University v Fishel* ([2000] *The Times*, 31 March, QBD). The Defendant, a consultant embryologist, was employed full-time by the university as Scientific Director of its infertility clinic. In breach of his contract of employment, he undertook outside work at private clinics for payment, without formal consent from the University. He also received fees for sending embryologists trained by him and employed by the University to work under supervision at those clinics. The University was not aware of this work, but the court found that it contributed significantly to the research and development of the University clinic, and did not prejudice its work.

Therefore, no loss resulted from the Defendant's failure to obtain the University's consent for these activities, so no damages could be awarded. The University could not say that it was entitled to damages on the basis that if it been made aware by the Defendant of the opportunity to do this work, it would have done the work itself. This was because an employee was not bound as a general principle to inform his employer if and when he was doing outside work in breach of his contract; in any event, it could not have done the work without the Defendant's co-operation.

Within a contract of employment, an employee's fiduciary duty not to pursue his own interests where he was duty bound to advance the interests of his employer arose only where there was a specific contractual provision under which the employee had to act solely in the interests of his employer. An employee was not bound as a general principle to inform his employer if he was doing outside work in breach of his contract.

In determining whether a fiduciary duty arose in the context of an employment relationship, it was necessary to identify the particular duties undertaken by the employee, and to ask whether in all the circumstances he has placed himself in a position where he must act solely in the interests of his employer. Care had to be taken in employment cases not automatically to equate the duties of good faith and loyalty, or trust and confidence, with fiduciary duties.

In this case, the Defendant was not under a specific contractual duty to secure for the University the work he undertook abroad, so a fiduciary duty did not arise. An employee did not in general promise to give his employer the benefit of every opportunity falling within the scope of its business. However, the Defendant breached his specific fiduciary duty to direct the embryologists to work in the interests of the University, by accepting work for them and directing them abroad to the benefit of his own financial interests. The University was therefore entitled to an account of the profits he made in this way, minus an allowance for the payments he made to the embryologists.

By contrast, in *PMC Holdings Ltd v Smith QBD* (Burton J) 23/4/2002 an employee who had an interest in another company was held liable to his employer in damages for breach of his implied duties of good faith and fidelity, and liable to give an account of profits or pay equitable compensation for breach of fiduciary duty in respect of transactions arranged by him that benefited him and the company in which he had an interest.

The Defendant was employed by PMC. He was also, unknown to PMC, a director and 50 per cent shareholder in another company, ISC. PMC claimed that the Defendant had been in breach of his contact of employment in that he had breached the implied duties of good faith and fidelity, and that he had breached fiduciary duties.

In his role as director of ISC, the Defendant had caused contracts to be entered into between PMC and ISC and between ISC and customers and suppliers of PMC. The Defendant argued that there was an oral agreement with PMC that he was free to undertake consultancy work in the chemical industry but PMC denied that such an agreement existed. PMC sought damages for breach of contract and an account of profits, or alternatively equitable compensation, for breach of fiduciary duty.

The court applied the principles in *Fishel*. The Defendant had held a senior position with PMC and was held to be a fiduciary to PMC in respect of his placing, negotiating and approving sales and purchases to and from ISC, and in causing ISC to be paid substantial consultancy fees for export advice which fell within his remit. The Defendant had not disclosed his full involvement with ISC and his implied duties and fiduciary position prohibited him from holding the position as director and shareholder of ISC, or, at the very least, he had a duty to disclose that position to PMC and not to mislead PMC. He had a duty to disclose all transactions or contracts between ISC and PMC and between ISC and PMC's customers and suppliers. Even if the oral agreement alleged by the Defendant had existed, it would not have overcome the breaches of duty by him. Insofar as ISC had received money from the transactions in question, knowing that it involved the Defendant being in breach of duty, ISC had procured and assisted in that breach of duty. PMC was therefore entitled to damages for breach of contract to be assessed against the Defendant and ISC, and a declaration that the Defendant was liable to account for profits (or, at PMC's option, to pay equitable compensation) on the grounds of breach of fiduciary duty in respect of the transactions in question.

3.5.4 Duty not to disclose confidential information

The law recognises that if the employee divulges confidential information he has acquired during the course of his employment, this may harm the employer's interests. The duty not to disclose such information applies not only during the currency of the relationship, but may also continue after the relationship has ended. However, this is another area in which the law must operate a difficult balancing act, as enterprise may be unduly limited if employees are prevented from using knowledge and experience gained under one employer when working for a second, or, in particular, in going into business on their own account.

The leading case in this area is *Faccenda Chicken v Fowler* ([1987] Ch 117). The employee left a firm to set up a business in competition. He recruited a number of his ex-employer's staff and most of his customers were former customers of the ex-employer. The ex-employer sued for damages in respect of misuse of sales information relating to prices and customers. The Court of Appeal dismissed the claim and laid down that as a matter of principle the duty of an employee once he has left his employment is more restricted than that which applies during the currency of his employment. The court distinguished between two types of confidential information:

a) Information of a highly confidential nature, which should be treated as if it were a trade secret. The employee can be restrained from revealing such information even after the relationship has ended;
b) Information which is confidential, so that it would be a breach of duty to disclose it while in employment, but not a breach to disclose it once the relationship has ended. An employer who wishes to protect himself after the relationship has ended must insert a restraint covenant in the contract to bind the employer once he has left. Where there is no such covenant, the court must consider the following:
   - nature of the employment;
   - nature of the information;
   - whether the information concerned can be isolated from other information which the employee is free to use; and
   - whether the employer impressed on the employee the need for confidentiality.

Here, the employer was held not to be protected after the employment relationship had ended.

In many cases, it may be difficult to distinguish between the two types of information, but the judgment in *Faccenda Chicken* means that the duty will not normally protect the employer in relation to ex-employees. In the few successful cases, a clear breach has occurred during the currency of the relationship. In *Robb v Green* ([1895] 2 QB 315) a manager copied his employer's customer list before leaving his employment, then set up in competition and solicited the customers on the list. The employer was successful in obtaining an injunction against him. Otherwise, case law shows the courts to be reluctant to intervene.

Although the duty may be restricted in relation to ex-employees, the only restriction in relation to existing employees is that the information must be confidential. This begs the question of what information is regarded as confidential. It includes information which the law allows the employer to protect by means of a restrictive covenant, which means any information which the law regards as the employer's property. This includes trade secrets, secret processes and customer lists. However, there may be other information which the employer regards as confidential and which, if divulged, could injure the employer's business.

The court in *Marshall (Thomas) (Exports) Ltd v Guinle* ([1979] Ch 227) identified certain factors which should be considered in deciding whether information is confidential and in need of protection:

a) The owner of the information must reasonably believe that the release of the information would benefit a competitor or cause harm to himself;
b) The owner must reasonably believe that the information is confidential and not already public knowledge; and
c) The information must be judged bearing in mind the practice of the particular trade or industry.

On this basis, it is irrelevant that the item disclosed is simple or could be discovered with a little research by the person to whom the information is disclosed. One problem which exists in determining whether the employee is in breach of duty, is separating out confidential information from the skills the employee has learnt during his employment and which he is entitled to use for the benefit of his new employer. For example, if the employee has learnt a process during his employment, is that a skill he has acquired or confidential information?

Printers and Finishers Ltd v Holloway ([1964] 3 All ER 731) involved an ex-employee with knowledge of the employer's flock printing process, skill in using a flock printing plant, plus information from documents acquired from his ex-employer. His ex-employer was only successful in obtaining an injunction relating to the information in the documents. The other information was skill he had acquired in the course of his employment, which he could use for the benefit of another employer. Here, the dividing line was clear-cut, but in many cases it will not be.

There is one exception when the duty not to disclose confidential information does not apply. This is where the information must be disclosed by law, or it is in the public interest that the information should become known. This exception was established in *Initial Services Ltd v Putterill* ([1968] 1 QB 396), where an ex-employee gave details of restrictive trade practices operated by his ex-employer to a newspaper. Such practices were in breach of the Restrictive Trade Practices Act 1968, and it was held that the disclosure was not in breach of the employee's duty as the information should be divulged in the public interest.

Likewise, employers are required to divulge information under certain statutes such as the Health and Safety at Work Act, and to do so will not be a breach of the duty to the employer.

This area of common law is now affected by the 'whistleblowing' provisions inserted into the Employment Rights Act (Part IVA, ss. 43A–L and s. 47B) by the Public Interest Disclosure Act 1998. These do not create a duty to report wrongdoing by the employer, but do provide protection from unfair dismissal for an employee who makes such a report.

S. 47B provides:

(1) A worker has the right not to be subjected to any detriment by any act, or any deliberate failure to act, by his employer done on the ground that the worker has made a protected disclosure.
(1A) A worker ('W') has the right not to be subjected to any detriment by any act, or any deliberate failure to act, done
  (a) by another worker of W's employer in the course of that other worker's employment, or
  (b) by an agent of W's employer with the employer's authority, on the ground that W has made a protected disclosure.
(1B) Where a worker is subjected to detriment by anything done as mentioned in subsection (1A), that thing is treated as also done by the worker's employer.
(1C) For the purposes of subsection (1B), it is immaterial whether the thing is done with the knowledge or approval of the worker's employer.
(1D) In proceedings against W's employer in respect of anything alleged to have been done as mentioned in subsection (1A)(a), it is a defence for the employer to show that the employer took all reasonable steps to prevent the other worker
  (a) from doing that thing, or
  (b) from doing anything of that description.
(1E) A worker or agent of W's employer is not liable by reason of subsection (1A) for doing something that subjects W to detriment if
  (a) the worker or agent does that thing in reliance on a statement by the employer that doing it does not contravene this Act, and
  (b) it is reasonable for the worker or agent to rely on the statement.

But this does not prevent the employer from being liable by reason of subsection (1B).

S. 43A defines a protected disclosure as a 'qualifying disclosure' under s. 43B, which provides:

(1) In this Part a 'qualifying disclosure' means any disclosure of information which, in the reasonable belief of the worker making the disclosure, is made in the public interest and tends to show one or more of the following:

(a) that a criminal offence has been committed, is being committed or is likely to be committed,
(b) that a person has failed, is failing or is likely to fail to comply with any legal obligation to which he is subject,
(c) that a miscarriage of justice has occurred, is occurring or is likely to occur,
(d) that the health or safety of any individual has been, is being or is likely to be endangered,
(e) that the environment has been, is being or is likely to be damaged, or
(f) that information tending to show any matter falling within any one of the preceding paragraphs has been, is being or is likely to be deliberately concealed.

(2) For the purposes of subsection (1), it is immaterial whether the relevant failure occurred, occurs or would occur in the United Kingdom or elsewhere, and whether the law applying to it is that of the United Kingdom or of any other country or territory.
(3) A disclosure of information is not a qualifying disclosure if the person making the disclosure commits an offence by making it.
(4) A disclosure of information in respect of which a claim to legal professional privilege (or, in Scotland, to confidentiality as between client and professional legal adviser) could be maintained in legal proceedings is not a qualifying disclosure if it is made by a person to whom the information had been disclosed in the course of obtaining legal advice.
(5) In this Part 'the relevant failure', in relation to a qualifying disclosure, means the matter falling within paragraphs (a) to (f) of subsection (1).

Such a disclosure is protected if made to a person in one of the following categories (ss. 43C–F):

- The employer
- A 'prescribed person' under the Public Interest Disclosure (Prescribed Persons) Order 1999, that is:
  - Health and Safety Executive
  - Data Protection Registrar
  - Trades Union Certification Officer
  - Environment Agency
  - Secretary of State for Trade and Industry
- In the course of seeking legal advice
- Ministers of the Crown
- Persons appointed for this purpose by the Secretary of State

Underlying these categories is an intention to enable employees and other workers to make protected disclosures primarily to their employers and, where available, their professional bodies. It was also the intention at the time the legislation came into force to encourage employers to create their own internal procedures for employees to raise matters of concern. Where possible, the employee should raise his concerns with a person in one of these categories. Only where this is not possible, or the employee has tried this and failed, do provisions covering disclosure to other bodies, such as newspapers, come into effect.

43G Disclosure in other cases.

(1) A qualifying disclosure is made in accordance with this section if:
(a) The worker reasonably believes that the information disclosed, and any allegation contained in it, are substantially true,
(b) He does not make the disclosure for purposes of personal gain,
(c) Any of the conditions in subsection (2) is met, and
(d) In all the circumstances of the case, it is reasonable for him to make the disclosure.

(2) The conditions referred to in subsection (1)(d) are:
   (a) That, at the time he makes the disclosure, the worker reasonably believes that he will be subjected to a detriment by his employer if he makes a disclosure to his employer or in accordance with section 43F [to a prescribed person],
   (b) That, in a case where no person is prescribed for the purposes of section 43F in relation to the relevant failure, the worker reasonably believes that it is likely that evidence relating to the relevant failure will be concealed or destroyed if he makes a disclosure to his employer, or
   (c) That the worker has previously made a disclosure of substantially the same information:
      (i) to his employer, or
      (ii) in accordance with section 43F.

(3) In determining for the purposes of subsection (1)(e) whether it is reasonable for the worker to make the disclosure, regard shall be had, in particular, to:
   (a) The identity of the person to whom the disclosure is made,
   (b) The seriousness of the relevant failure,
   (c) Whether the relevant failure is continuing or is likely to occur in the future,
   (d) Whether the disclosure is made in breach of a duty of confidentiality owed by the employer to any other person,
   (e) In a case falling within subsection (2)(c)(i) or (ii), any action which the employer or the person to whom the previous disclosure in accordance with section 43F was made has taken or might reasonably be expected to have taken as a result of the previous disclosure, and
   (f) In a case falling within subsection (2)(c)(i), whether in making the disclosure to the employer the worker complied with any procedure whose use by him was authorised by the employer.

(4) For the purposes of this section a subsequent disclosure may be regarded as a disclosure of substantially the same information as that disclosed by a previous disclosure as mentioned in subsection (2)(c) even though the subsequent disclosure extends to information about action taken or not taken by any person as a result of the previous disclosure.

S. 43J(1) then provides that any contractual provision imposing a duty of confidentiality on the employer is void insofar as it applies to protected disclosures.

Unsurprisingly, the bulk of the case law turns on the issue of whether an employee has made a protected disclosure, i.e. the disclosure comes within the scope of s.43B and is made to a person within ss.43C-F.

3.6 Further reading

Anon, 'No need to imply temporary mobility clause: *Luke v Stoke on Trent City Council*: Court of Appeal' (2007) 838 *IDS Employment Law Brief* 5.

Brodie, 'Health and safety, trust and confidence and Barber v Somerset County Council: some further questions' (2004) 33(3) *Industrial Law Journal* 261.

Brodie, 'Mutual trust and confidence: catalysts, constraints and commonality' (2008) 37(4) *Industrial Law Journal* 329.

Irving, 'The role and development of mutual trust and confidence as an implied term of the contract of employment' (2008) 13(1) *Coventry Law Journal* 22.

Chapter 4

Termination of the contract of employment

Chapter contents

4.1 Overview

This chapter examines the ways a contract of employment can be terminated. It considers the issue of when a dismissal occurs and the implications of dismissal, including the remedy of wrongful dismissal.

- Resignation is where the employee voluntarily gives notice to the employer, permitted under the contract, to terminate the contract of employment. It must be a voluntary act; any undue pressure by the employer will invalidate the resignation.
- Termination of the contract may also occur where the parties formally agree to end the contract. Such agreements must be consensual and courts will scrutinise formal termination agreements to ascertain that they are genuine.
- A contract of employment may also be terminated by operation of law. For example, the doctrine of frustration may apply where the performance of the contract has become impossible or radically different due to an event that is no fault of either party, such a long-term sickness or imprisonment of the employee.
- The statutory definition of dismissal includes circumstances where the contract is terminated by the employer, where the contract is not renewed, or where the employee terminates the contract due to the employer's behaviour (constructive dismissal).
- Express dismissal occurs where the employer informs the employee that the contract is at an end. Words used must be communicated to the employee and be clear and unequivocal.
- Constructive dismissal occurs where the employer violates an important term of the contract, such as a failure to pay wages or a unilateral change in contractual terms. A breach of the implied duty of 'trust and confidence' is often cited to justify the employee arguing that he or she has been constructively dismissed.
- Summary dismissal is immediate dismissal without the correct notice being given. This can be justified if the employee has committed an act of 'gross misconduct'.
- Wrongful dismissal is not a way a contract is terminated but a remedy – a claim that the employer was in breach of contract in dismissing the employee. This may occur where the employer fails to give the employee the correct amount of notice or the employer has terminated a fixed term contract that does not have a notice period. The employer then becomes liable to pay damages reflecting all the losses the employee has sustained from the breach.
- Damages recoverable include wages and other benefits earned or accrued during the specific extent of the notice period. There are circumstances where an injunction may be granted to continue the contract.

4.2 Termination not involving dismissal

4.2.1 By resignation

Resignation is a voluntary act by an employee and is where the employee gives proper notice to the employer that he or she is leaving employment. Where an employee, however, is prevailed upon to resign by pressure, that is not a valid resignation but rather, in practice, a dismissal. As Brightman J stated in *East Sussex County Council v Walker*[1]

1 [1972] ITR 280.

> if an employee is told she is no longer required in her employment and is expressly invited to resign, a court of law is entitled to come to the conclusion that, as a matter of common sense, the employee was dismissed.

It is a matter of fact whether the circumstances indicate there was a genuinely voluntary decision by the claimant. In *Martin v MBS Fastening Ltd*[2] the claimant informed his employer that he was being prosecuted for drunk driving. When he was told that that there would be an inquiry and it could end in dismissal he resigned. The claimant later changed his mind but was refused re-instatement and so consequently made an application for unfair dismissal. The Court of Appeal held that there were no grounds to intervene in the tribunal's conclusion that there had not been a dismissal in law. The tribunal's decision that the degree of pressure applied was not sufficient to induce the employee's resignation was commensurate with the evidence submitted.

Even a formal threat to dismiss may not necessarily result in a subsequent resignation being set aside by the court. In *Sheffield v Oxford Controls Co Ltd*[3] a dispute arose between the applicant and his employer resulting in the applicant receiving a letter threatening dismissal if he did not resign. Later, after negotiation, an agreement was signed setting out the financial terms for his resignation. The applicant then claimed he had been unfairly dismissal. The EAT held that the applicant had not been dismissed as he had clearly agreed to terminate his employment on mutually acceptable terms. The threat of dismissal was not a sufficiently causative factor in the applicant's decision to resign; rather, he had willingly resigned because of the satisfactory terms that were offered to him to do so. By contrast, if the circumstances are such that it is clear the employer had instigated the employee's decision to leave employment then it is unlikely the employee's resignation could be said to be truly voluntary. This occurred in *Caledonian Mining Co Ltd v Bassett*[4] where the defendant company wrote to all employees informing them that a number of jobs would be lost to redundancy. The redundant employees were interviewed for other work with the company but eventually it was arranged for them to find future work with other employers. Subsequently the claimants terminated their employment with the defendants and claimed a redundancy payment. It was argued by the employer that as the applicants had resigned to take other jobs they had not been dismissed and so were not able to make a redundancy claim. The EAT concluded that in these circumstances – where the employers had caused the employees to leave employment and the employers purpose in finding the applicants other employment was to avoid having to make redundancy payments – resignation was not the reason for the termination of the contract of employment, the applicants had been dismissed.[5]

There may well be circumstances where the employee does not formally write a letter of resignation but purports to resign, for example, in a fit of anger or during a heated interview. The courts have concluded that where an employee unambiguously resigns, by actions or words, with immediate effect, an employer is entitled to assume them as genuine and treat them as such by accepting the repudiation of the contract immediately.[6] However, in cases where the words are spoken or the actions are taken under pressure, and in the heat of the moment, an employer should allow a reasonable period of time to elapse before accepting a resignation at face value. During this period facts may emerge which cast doubt upon whether the resignation was truly intended to be taken seriously.[7] Although an employer is not under a duty to investigate the circumstances of such

---

2 [1983] IRLR 198.

3 [1979] IRLR 133.

4 [1987] IRLR 165.

5 See also *Allders International Ltd v Parkin* [1981] IRLR 68; *Jones v Mid-Glamorgan County Council* [1997] IRLR 685.

6 *Sothern v Franks Charsley & Co* [1981] IRLR 278.

7 *Kwik Fit UK v Lineham* [1992] IRLR 156.

a 'resignation', it may be prudent to do so to ascertain whether the employee possessed the appropriate intention to resign.[8] Furthermore, where an employee informs their employer that they merely *intend* to resign that should not be taken by the employer as an actual formal notice of resignation – a mere indication of an intention to resign does not amount to an unequivocal actual resignation.[9]

In some situations, an employer may argue that an employee has 'resigned by conduct' or have 'constructively resigned' because of their behaviour. In *London Transport Executive v Clarke*[10] the applicant had been refused time off work to visit family abroad but went ahead without permission. On his return, he was denied entry to the workplace and his pay was stopped. His employers argued that he had not been dismissed, but by leaving without permission he had left of his own accord and effectively resigned. A majority of the Court of Appeal held that the employee's contract of employment had not been terminated by his own conduct in absenting himself from work without permission. Where an employee has engaged in a repudiatory breach of contract the contract is not terminated automatically, but is dependent on the employer responding to the breach. Although an employer will normally terminate the employee's contract by formal written means – here, acceptance of the repudiatory breach and subsequent termination of contract by the employer occurred impliedly when the employee was refused permission to return to work.

❖ THINKING POINT

What would have been the practical consequences if the courts had found that an employee's fundamental breach of contract could by itself terminate the contract?

4.2.2 By subsequent agreement

The parties to an employment contract may agree to terminate the contract in circumstances that do not involve a formal resignation. Where there is genuine consensual agreement such a termination will not be a dismissal. As termination by mutual agreement favours the employer (as there will be no statutory requirement to pay redundancy or unfair dismissal compensation), the courts will scrutinise such agreements to ensure the agreement was genuine. For example, in *McAlwane v Boughton Estates*[11] the employee was given notice of termination of employment by his employer. A week before the expiry of the notice the employee asked, and was given permission, to leave immediately in order to start a new job. The employer then argued that as the employee had himself requested permission to leave before the expiry of notice this was now a case of an agreed termination of the contract rather than a dismissal. The court was unimpressed by this argument and held that that this was not a consensual termination, but merely an agreed variation of notice; consequently, the dismissal remained effective.

8 Note that in *Barclay v City of Glasgow District Council* [1983] IRLR 313, the court held that an oral resignation by an employee who had serious learning difficulties should not be treated as a notice of termination. Employers are expected to take account of the special circumstances of each employee when determining whether the 'resignation' was a conscious and rational decision. See also the Court of Appeal's decision in *Sovereign House Security Services Ltd v Savage* [1989] IRLR 115.

9 *Ely v Y.K.K. Fasteners Ltd* [1994] ICR 164.

10 [1981] IRLR 166.

11 [1973] ICR 470.

The courts will also scrutinise formal termination agreements to ensure that the employee agreed to the terms with full knowledge of the implications. This issue arose in *Igbo v Johnson Matthey Ltd.*[12] Mrs Igbo had requested, and had been given, extended unpaid leave to visit relatives in Nigeria. Before she left she signed a holiday agreement which stated, *inter alia*, 'you have agreed to return to work on 28.9.83. If you fail to do this your contract of employment will automatically terminate on that date'. Although Mrs Igbo returned to the UK before the due date she did not report for work as she was unwell. Her employers claimed that as she had failed to comply with the agreement her employment was terminated in accordance with the terms of the contract. The Court of Appeal commented that if such an agreement could bring a contract to an end it would be possible, for example, for an employer to insert a clause in an employment contract stating that lateness for work would be treated as a reason for automatic termination, thereby excluding any unfair dismissal claim in such circumstances. Therefore, the Court held that such termination agreements offend against s. 140 of the Employment Protection (Consolidation) Act 1978 (now s. 203(1) of the Employment Rights Act 1996) which holds that any term in a contract which purports to limit or exclude rights (e.g. to unfair dismissal) provided by the statute is void and unenforceable.

❖ THINKING POINT

Would it have made any difference if Mrs Igbo had received a financial or other inducement to sign the document?

Cases of agreed early retirement and voluntary redundancy may well be treated as valid examples of consensual termination if there has been no coercion by the employer and the employee has received independent advice and consideration for the agreement. This was the position in *Humber & Birch v University of Liverpool*,[13] where the two employees volunteered for premature retirement and received enhanced retirement payments after consultation with their trade union. The claimants argued that they had been dismissed as it was the employer who had formally terminated their contracts. To the Court of Appeal this was a genuine agreement (not imposed as in *Igbo* above) facilitated by the financial benefit provided to the employees. Employment had been terminated by the employee's offer to retire, accepted by the university. Consequently, this was a case of termination by mutual agreement, not dismissal.[14]

Occasionally mutual termination agreements may be made after a disciplinary process. In order to forestall a dismissal an employee may well accept a negotiated financial settlement to leave employment. In these circumstances, any agreement will be a valid and enforceable termination agreement. As Wood J stated in *Logan Saltan v Durham County Council*,[15]

> in the resolution of . . . disputes, it is in the best interests of all concerned that a contract made without duress, for good consideration, preferably after proper and sufficient advice, and which

---

12 [1986] IRLR 215.

13 [1985] IRLR 165.

14 See also *Tracey v Zest Equipment Co Ltd* [1982] IRLR 268; *Morley v C.T. Morley Ltd* [1985] ICR 499; *Scott v Coalite Fuels Ltd* [1988] IRLR 131; *Hilton Hotels Ltd v Kaissi* [1994] IRLR 270 & *Crees v Royal London Insurance* [1997] IRLR 85.

15 [1989] IRLR 99.

> has the effect of terminating a contract of employment by mutual agreement (whether at once or on some future date) should be effective between the contracting parties, in which case there will not have been a dismissal.

This, however, should be distinguished from the position where an employee has been dismissed and the financial settlement is negotiated after the dismissal. In such circumstances the mere acceptance of financial severance terms does not make the termination by mutual agreement as there is no genuine choice to be made by the employee – it is a unilateral termination by the employer on specific terms.[16]

4.2.3 The doctrine of frustration

As employment is regulated by the law of contract, the doctrine of frustration may apply in certain circumstances. This doctrine applies where performance of the contract has become impossible or performance would be radically different through an event that is no fault of either party. The consequence of frustration is that the contract will be terminated automatically – there is no need for an employer to inform the employee or take any other steps. As the contract of employment is terminated immediately there is no pay or other obligations enforceable after the date of frustration and no statutory or common law claims based on dismissal can be made. The two main areas where frustration may apply due to long term absence are illness and imprisonment.

4.2.3.1 Frustration by absence through illness

In the employment context, a possible frustrating event is the non-availability of the employee due to illness. In one of the earlier employment cases on this doctrine the High Court held that a contract between an opera singer and the defendant theatre had been frustrated by her illness where she had been unable to perform for three months – the performance of the contract was sufficiently radically different from envisaged at the time the contract was agreed.[17] A similar outcome occurred in *Condor v Barron Knights Ltd*,[18] where the drummer in a band was unable to perform on the number of nights specified in the contract due to his illness. As it was unlikely he would be able to return to execute his duties under the contract his illness was a sufficiently serious event to frustrate the execution of the contract.

In both the examples above the contracts under consideration were of a temporary fixed term nature where it was highly unlikely the employees would return and perform their duties under the contract. The question of whether the doctrine applies to contracts of employment of indefinite length was considered in *Marshall v Harland Woolf*[19] where Sir John Donaldson in the National Industrial Relations Court proceeded on the basis that the doctrine did apply to these contracts but that the courts need to be cautious of applying a too liberal interpretation of the principles of frustration. Here the applicant had been absent for 18 months but the medical evidence was that the employee might well recover and resume work. As further performance of the employee's obligations was not impossible or radically different from that undertaken under his contract the relationship had not been terminated by frustration.

Further guidance on the factors to consider when adjudicating on frustration was provided by Phillips J in *Egg Stores Ltd v Leibovici*:[20]

---

16 *Sandhu v Jan de Rijk Transport* [2007] IRLR 519.
17 *Poussard v Spiers* [1876] 1 QB 410.
18 [1966] 1 WLR 87.
19 [1972] ICR 101.
20 [1976] IRLR 376, 378.

> if an event such as an accident or illness occurs, the course and outcome of which is uncertain, . . . there will have been frustration of the contract if the time arrives when, looking back, one can say that at some point matters had gone on so long, and the prospects for future employment were so poor, that it was no longer practical to regard the contract as still subsisting. Among the matters to be taken into account in such a case in reaching a decision are these:
>
> 1) the length of the previous employment;
> 2) how long it had been expected that the employment would continue;
> 3) the nature of the job;
> 4) the nature, length and effect of the illness or disabling event;
> 5) the need of the employer for the work to be done, and the need for a replacement to do it;
> 6) the risk to the employer of acquiring obligations in respect of redundancy payments or compensation for unfair dismissal to the replacement employee;
> 7) whether wages have continued to be paid;
> 8) the acts and the statements of the employer in relation to the employment, including the dismissal of, or failure to dismiss, the employee; and
> 9) whether in all these circumstances a reasonable employer could have expected to wait any longer.

These criteria were re-affirmed by the Court of Appeal in *Notcutt v Universal Equipment Co*[21] where an employee had suffered a heart attack and was unlikely to return to work. Dillon LJ could see no reason why the doctrine could not apply as

> the coronary which left the complainant unable to work again was an unexpected occurrence which made his performance of the contractual obligations to work impossible and brought about such a change in the significance of the mutual obligations that the contract if performed would be a different thing than that contracted for.

Furthermore, the Court of Appeal also held that previous authority in *Harman v Flexible Lamps Ltd*[22] that the doctrine did not apply in cases of long term employment (as it conflicts with statutory protection for unfair dismissal), could not be sustained. Subsequently, however, the EAT has cautioned that the courts should be wary of allowing the doctrine to apply too readily where, on the face of it, redundancy occurs or where there is evidence that in reality a dismissal by reason of disability has occurred. In these circumstances an employer may argue that a contract has been frustrated to avoid redundancy or unfair dismissal compensation. Thus, courts need to pay proper consideration to the factors outlined by Phillips J in *Leibovici* – in particular, whether there is a prospect of recovery and return to employment.[23] Furthermore, where there are provisions in the contract specifically to provide for an occurrence of long term sickness it is more difficult for an employer to argue that the incapacity is an unforeseen event.[24]

Since the introduction of the Disability Discrimination Act 1995 (now subsumed into the Equality Act 2010), long term incapacity due to sickness may satisfy the definition of 'disability' under the statute. In those circumstances, it has been held by the EAT that even if the contract has

21 [1986] IRLR 218.

22 [1980] IRLR 418.

23 The EAT in *Watson v Williams Luxury Coaches Ltd* [1990] IRLR 164 also noted that if the employer has caused the injury which results in the employee being off work, the employer cannot rely on the doctrine of frustration as they are at fault in creating the frustrating event.

24 *Villella v MFI Furniture Stores* [1999] IRLR 468.

been technically frustrated by reference to the common-law doctrine, that does not preclude the application of the anti-discrimination employment protection provisions of the Equality Act 2010.[25] An employer may thus find that an employee's contract is *prima facie* frustrated (due to long term sickness), but specific employment rights still apply.

4.2.3.2 Frustration by imprisonment

A contract of employment may also be frustrated by imprisonment. A sufficiently long sentence (unforeseen at the time the contract was made) will result in an employee unable to perform his or her obligations under the contract, so frustrating the contract.[26] Although the event (the criminal sentence) may be unforeseen at the start of employment a question arises as to whether the event was without the fault of either party – a necessary component of the doctrine. In *Norris v Southampton City Council*[27] the EAT considered that where there is fault, such as where the contract cannot be performed due to the employee's own conduct in committing a criminal offence, then the doctrine of frustration cannot arise.

However, the Court of Appeal has subsequently disagreed with this view in *FC Shepherd & Co Ltd v Jerrom*[28] where it was held that the imposition of a custodial sentence on an employee was capable in law of frustrating a contract of employment even though performance of the contract had been rendered impossible by an act that was the fault of one of the parties. The principle that the frustrating act must have occurred without the fault of either of the parties is to ensure that the party against whom frustration is asserted cannot rely on his own misconduct to avoid the legal consequences of his actions. Otherwise, to permit an employee to improve his position by asserting that an event which would otherwise bring about a discharge by frustration did not do so because it was caused by his own fault would per Lord Justice Mustill,

> be an affront to common sense and an infringement of what Diplock LJ in *Hongkong Fir Shipping Co v Kawasaki Kischen Kaisha* described as 'the fundamental legal and moral rule that a man should not be allowed to take advantage of his own wrong'.[29]

❖ THINKING POINT

Considering the effect of the doctrine of frustration on the remedy of unfair dismissal and redundancy, should it be excluded by statute as an operative reason for the termination of an employment contract?

4.3 Termination by dismissal

The statutory definition of dismissal is contained in s. 95(1) Employment Rights Act 1996 and provides that an employee can be treated as dismissed by his employer if the contract under which

25 *Warner v Armfield Retail & Leisure Ltd* [2014] Eq LR 122.

26 *Hare v Murphy Brothers* [1974] ICR 603.

27 [1982] IRLR 141.

28 [1986] IRLR 358.

29 Note that Lord Justice Balcombe, in a concurring opinion, argued from the position (agreeing with Lord Denning in *Hare v Murphy Brothers*) that it was not the actual crime that caused the frustrating event but the imposition of the sentence by the court, which was independent of the 'fault' of the claimant. This had also been the position of the EAT in earlier decisions in *Harrington v Kent County Council* [1980] IRLR 353 and *Chakki v United Yeast Co* [1982] ICR 141.

he is employed is terminated (with or without notice) by the employer; where a limited-term contract expires or otherwise terminates without being renewed or where the employee terminates the contract with or without notice, because of the employer's repudiatory conduct.

4.3.1 Express dismissal with or without notice

Under s. 95(1)(a) dismissal occurs where the employer informs the employee that his or her contract of employment is at an end.[30] There are no legal formalities required (although by s. 92 ERA 1996 the employee is entitled to receive a written statement of the reason for dismissal) so termination may be in writing or by oral means. Whatever method is applied the employer must ensure that the words used are clear and unequivocal with an intention to bring employment to an end. For example, in *Futty v D&D Brekkes Ltd*[31] the applicant often engaged in abusive 'banter' with fellow workers and his supervisors. During one bantering session, the exchanges became more acrimonious and the applicant was told, by his supervisor, 'If you don't like the job, fuck off'. The applicant took the supervisor at his word and left the premises, later claiming he was unfairly dismissed. The tribunal held that the meaning of these words had to be considered against the background of the custom and practice of the trade and the circumstances of the job. Here, where the use of 'industrial' language and light hearted conflict was common, the words did not necessarily mean the applicant was dismissed. Instead, the words amounted to general criticism and an exhortation to the applicant to take a 'cooling down' break from work.

In *J&J Stern v Simpson*[32] the Court of Appeal re-iterated that where an employer acts in the 'heat of the moment' to reprimand an employee (and does not necessarily intend to bring the contract to an end) it is not a dismissal in law unless the words used can be clearly construed, in the context of the facts, that a dismissal has taken place. If there is some ambiguity, a further test – of whether a reasonable employee in all the circumstances of the case would have understood that the words spoken were clearly intended to terminate the contract – should be applied.[33]

❖ THINKING POINT

Could the behaviour of the employer in *Futty* have amounted to a breach of the implied term of trust and confidence and thus have resulted in a constructive dismissal of the employee?

A threat of dismissal sometime in the future is not a dismissal, as a contract can only be terminated where there is a known date for termination or where circumstances are such that the date of termination can be ascertained. So, it is not a dismissal if an employer merely issues a warning that he or she may be dismissed in the future, although a threat of dismissal at a particular future date can be a dismissal.[34]

---

30 It is crucial that the employer informs the employee by word or deed, expressly or impliedly that the relationship is at an end – *Sandle v Adecco UK Ltd* [2016] IRLR 941.

31 [1974] IRLR 130.

32 [1983] IRLR 52.

33 See *Tanner v D.T. Kean Ltd* [1978] IRLR 110.

34 *Haseltine Lake & Co v Dowler* [1981] IRLR 25. See also *Doble v Firestone Tyre Co Ltd* [1981] IRLR 300 & *Tunnel Holdings Ltd v Woolf* [1976] ICR 307.

It may also be an express dismissal where an employer introduces a fundamental change in employment terms without obtaining an employee's consent. This was the case in *Alcan Extrusions v Yates*[35] where a new shift system was imposed which worsened the terms and conditions of employment. Yates informed the employer that he would only work the new shift system under protest and would reserve the right to claim unfair dismissal. Subsequently he put in an application for unfair dismissal while continuing to work under protest. It was held by the EAT that this could constitute an express dismissal with Judge Smith QC commenting that

> where an employer unilaterally imposes radically different terms of employment . . . there is a dismissal under (s. 95(1)(a)) if, on an objective construction of the relevant letters or other conduct on the part of the employer, there is a removal or withdrawal of the old contract.

It is important to note the significance of identifying a unilateral change of contract as an express dismissal rather than a repudiatory breach for the purposes of constructive dismissal (see 4.3.3). The logic of this is that in a situation where a contract has been imposed on an employee, he or she may claim the right of unfair dismissal although still technically employed – so long the 'acceptance' of the changes was under protest and so without prejudice to his or her statutory rights.[36]

4.3.2 Dismissal through expiry of a limited term contract

Most contracts of employment are of indefinite length determinable by notice. However, a significant number of employees may be employed on contracts that are time limited (fixed term contracts) or limited by some other means – such as so-called 'task' or 'purpose' contracts, where the contract ends on the completion of the assignment or the happening of an event. Although at common law such 'limited term' contracts are discharged by performance, the Employment Rights Act 1996 s. 95(1)(b) states that expiry or non-renewal of such a contract is a dismissal, thus allowing employees the right to claim unfair dismissal. Prior to 1 October 2002 this provision only applied to those employees working under a fixed term contract, not a 'task' contract. It is still the case that the vast majority of contracts that fall foul of this section are fixed term contracts although the scope of what determines a 'fixed term' contract has been the subject of some judicial disagreement.

In *Dixon v BBC*[37] the employee was employed as a porter under a series of fixed term contracts that were determinable by one week's notice. When the final contract expired, the BBC failed to renew it and Dixon claimed he had been unfairly dismissed. The BBC argued that where a contract includes a term providing for notice of termination it cannot be a 'fixed term contract' for the purposes of the Act. It was held by the Court of Appeal that Dixon had been dismissed within the meaning of (s. 95(1)(b)) when his fixed term contract had not been renewed, even though the contract included a term that it could be determined by one week's notice within that period. To decide otherwise would, per Lord Denning 'mean that an employer could always evade the Act by inserting a simple clause 'determinable by one week's notice'. That can never have been the intention of the legislature at all'. The Court of Appeal, in coming to this conclusion, directly contradicted the decision of a differently constituted Court of Appeal in *BBC v Ioannou*[38] that if a notice clause is included in a contract it is not a 'fixed term' contract for the purposes of the statute.

---

35 [1996] IRLR 327.

36 See also *Hogg v Dover College* [1990] ICR 39.

37 [1978] IRLR 114.

38 [1975]ICR 267.

The decision in Dixon was justified by a finding that the Ioannou judgment was given *per incuriam*, as the court had failed to consider the true intention behind the legislation.[39]

In *Wiltshire County Council v NATHFE and Guy*[40] the applicant had been employed as a part time teacher for several years at a college in Wiltshire to teach on specified courses for a specified number of hours – with the contracts terminating at the end of the academic year when the courses she taught on finished. At the beginning of the academic year for 1977 her appointment was not renewed and she claimed this amounted to a non-renewal of a fixed term contract and that she had been dismissed in law. Her employer argued that the circumstances of her engagement amounted to a contract for specified work – when the courses ended her contract was discharged by performance. The Court of Appeal held that this was a fixed term contract within the meaning of the statute. A fixed term contract has a defined beginning and a defined end and, as the applicant was employed for the academic session ending on the last day of the summer term, it was known when the contract would cease and so it did have a defined or determinable end. However, in *obiter* comments the Court of Appeal did accept the argument that if it had been shown that it was a contract to perform a specified task – to teach certain courses the length of which were not known when the contract was made – she would not have been employed for a fixed term.

This was the distinction made by the EAT in *Brown v Knowsley BC*[41] where the employee was offered and accepted a contract which stipulated, *inter alia*, that 'The appointment will last only as long as sufficient funds are provided by either the Manpower Services Commission or by other sponsors to fund it'. On the failure of the College to attract sufficient funding for the relevant courses, the contract terminated in accordance with the clause above. The EAT's view was that the employee had not been employed on a fixed term contract but on a contract for a specific purpose. When that specific purpose was completed or came to an end the contract was discharged by performance. Thus, in such circumstances there was no dismissal within the meaning of the statutory definition that applied at the time.[42]

As noted earlier, in 2002, this loophole was closed by regulations that introduced into the Employment Rights Act 1996 a wide definition of 'limited term' contracts.[43] Statute now defines 'limited term' contracts where employment is not intended to be permanent and provision has been made in the contract for it to terminate on a 'limiting event'.[44] The limiting event is defined as expiry of a fixed term contract or the performance of a specific task or the occurrence or non-occurrence of an event.[45]

4.3.3 Constructive dismissal

A constructive dismissal occurs where an employee terminates the contract by reason of the employer's conduct. This doctrine is designed to protect the employee where the employer commits a sufficiently serious breach of contract – such as reducing pay or increasing hours unilaterally. In these circumstances the employee is entitled to treat him or herself as discharged from any further performance of the contract. Constructive dismissal is thus a device to enable the employee to take

39 Also on fixed term contracts and the exclusion of employment rights, see *Housing Services v Cragg* [1997] IRLR 380; *Bhatt v Chelsea & Westminster HealthCare NHS Trust* [1997] IRLR 660; *Allen v National Australia Group Ltd* [2004] IRLR 847.

40 [1980] IRLR 198.

41 [1986] IRLR 102.

42 For further historical cases on the discharge of a 'task contract' by performance, see *Ryan v Shipboard Maintenance Ltd* [1980] IRLR 16; *Ironmonger v Movefield Ltd* [1988] IRLR 461; *Crees v Royal London Insurance* [1997] IRLR 85.

43 Fixed Term (Prevention of Less Favourable Treatment) Regulations 2002.

44 ERA 1996 s. 235(2A).

45 ERA 1996 s. 235(2B).

the initiative, leave employment and then claim a remedy such as wrongful or unfair dismissal. The leading case on this doctrine is *Western Excavating Ltd v Sharp*[46] where the Court of Appeal held that that an employee is not entitled to claim constructive dismissal merely on an allegation the employer has engaged in 'unreasonable behaviour'. The conduct of the employer must be such that a repudiatory breach of contract has occurred – the employer must have been guilty of conduct which is a significant breach going to the root of the contract of employment, or which shows that the employer no longer intends to be bound by one or more of the essential terms of the contract.[47] It is not necessary for the employer to act with the intention of causing the employee to leave, but if such intention exists, it is material to the question of whether repudiatory conduct has occurred.[48]

Certain express terms are so fundamental that a repudiatory breach is automatically assumed – such as a failure to pay agreed wages,[49] unilateral change in job content and contractual terms,[50] unjustified demotion or suspension[51] or unreasonable enforcement of a mobility clause.[52] Additionally, implied terms of the contract are relevant in determining whether a constructive dismissal has come about. The development of the implied term of 'trust and confidence' (where the employer has acted unreasonably and arbitrarily) has played an important role in determining a constructive dismissal. For example, in *Courtaulds Ltd v Andrew*[53] the employer had severely criticised the applicant without good reason in earshot of other staff and customers. To the EAT this was conduct which destroyed the relationship of trust and confidence between the parties, which is essential for the contract to be performed effectively. As a fundamental breach that goes to the root of the contract this justified the employee to claim he had been constructively dismissed.[54] A similar decision was reached in *Lewis v Motorworld Garages Ltd*.[55] Lewis had been demoted from his position as sales manager. Consequently, he lost his office, was given a smaller company car and a salary increase was withheld from him. After numerous incidents of senior management criticising his work the applicant left his job and claimed that he had been constructively dismissed. The Court of Appeal held that the conduct of the employer must be viewed objectively and the intention of the employer was irrelevant. Taken together, the employer's conduct could cumulatively amount to a breach of the implied obligation of trust and confidence. There had been a course of conduct which cumulatively undermined the position of the employee and was of sufficient gravity to justify the appellant in claiming that he had been constructively dismissed.[56]

In *Bracebridge Engineering Ltd v Darby*[57] the applicant had been sexually harassed and assaulted by two fellow employees at work. Believing that her complaint had not been taken seriously by her employers, she resigned and claimed unfair dismissal and sex discrimination. Given that the applicant had suffered shock and trauma as a consequence of the incident and that the incident had not been treated with the gravity it deserved, the tribunal was correct to conclude that the implied

---

46 [1978] QB 761.

47 The EAT in *Greenaway Harrison Ltd v Wiles* [1994] IRLR 380 have also held that a threat to terminate the contract may be sufficient to constitute a repudiatory breach of contract. Otherwise if this was not the case, per Judge Hague QC, 'an employer who wished to make a fundamental alteration to the contract of employment could avoid the effect of (s. 95(1)(c)) simply by making a threat of notice of termination'. See also *Kerry Foods Ltd v Lynch* [2005] IRLR 680.

48 *Grewals v Koo Sen Lin* [2016] IRLR 638.

49 *Hill Ltd v Mooney* [1981] IRLR 258; *Reid v Camphill Engravers* [1990] IRLR 268.

50 *Millbrook Ltd v McIntosh* [1981] IRLR 309; *Aparau v Iceland Frozen Foods* [1996] IRLR 119.

51 *McNeil v Charles Grimm Ltd* [1984] IRLR 179.

52 *United Bank v Akhatar* [1989] IRLR 507; *White v Reflecting Roadstuds Ltd* [1991] IRLR 331.

53 [1979] IRLR 84.

54 See also *Hilton Hotels (UK) Ltd v Protopapa* [1990] IRLR 316.

55 [1985] IRLR 465.

56 See also *Omijalu v Waltham Forest BC* [2005] ICR 481; *Gibbs v Leeds Utd Football Club Ltd* [2016] IRLR 493.

57 [1990] IRLR 3.

term of mutual trust and confidence had been violated and that the employee was entitled to resign and treat herself as being constructively dismissed.[58]

Although there is not a strict requirement for an employee to inform the employer that, due to the employers repudiatory conduct, they regarded the contract as at an end, it is inevitably more difficult to substantiate a claim of constructive dismissal where the employee has not communicated this, either by words or conduct.[59] Furthermore, it is important for the employee to leave in response to the breach, demonstrating that he or she has elected to accept the repudiation and end the contract. If the employee delays leaving employment the court may determine that the employee has 'waived' the breach and affirmed the contract[60] – although the courts have recognised that there may be valid reasons why an employee may delay and work for a short period 'under protest'.[61]

4.4 Summary dismissal

Summary dismissal is immediate dismissal without the correct notice being given. In the majority of contracts of employment there is an explicit term detailing notice provisions – where either party may bring the contract to an end after the appropriate notice has been given. If, however, a notice period is not explicitly stated in the contract a 'reasonable period' is implied in the contract. The general rule is that more senior the employee the longer the implied notice period.[62] However, there is a statutory minimum period of notice that all employees are entitled to receive.[63] Under s. 86(1) Employment Rights Act 1996 employers must give a week's notice for those employees with more than a month but fewer than two years' service and an additional week per year of service up to 12 years of service. Thus, a minimum of 12 weeks' notice must be provided for employment of over 12 years. Details of the relevant notice period must be included in the written particulars of employment provided to all employees.[64]

Ordinarily a summary dismissal amounts to a wrongful dismissal which entitles the employee to claim damages (see p. 83). If the reason for the dismissal is due to a repudiatory fundamental breach of a condition by the employee, immediate termination (without reference to the notice provision) of the contract of employment is legally justified. The employer's right of summary dismissal arises from the terms of the contract, express or implied. If there is an express term detailing the circumstances when an employer is entitled to summarily dismiss an employee then the reason for the dismissal must come within this definition outlined in the term.[65] Even where there is not a violation of an express term, summary dismissal may still be a justifiable dismissal at common law where the employee has violated an important implied term of the contract sufficient for it to be a repudiatory breach of contract.

An example of a repudiatory breach is demonstrated in *Laws v London Chronicle Ltd*[66] where the claimant was dismissed on the spot for refusing to follow an order given by the managing director to remain at a meeting. The claimant argued that her minor act of disobedience had not justified

---

58 For further examples of an employer acting officiously and insensitively towards an employee that has constituted a repudiatory breach of the implied term of trust and confidence, see *Isle of Wight Tourist Board v Coombes* [1976] IRLR 413; *Post Office v Roberts* [1980] ICR 347; *Woods v WM Car Services* [1981] IRLR 347; *Warnes v Cheriton Oddfellows Social Club* [1993] IRLR 58.

59 *Weathersfield Ltd v Sargent* [1999] IRLR 94; *Edwards v Surrey Police* [1999] IRLR 456.

60 *Robinson v Tescom Corpn* [2008] IRLR 408.

61 *Jones v F. Sirl & Sons* [1997] IRLR 493.

62 See *Hill v CA Parsons Co Ltd* [1971] 3 All ER 1345; *Reda v Flag Ltd* [2002] UKPC 38.

63 Subject to the dismissal being a justifiable summary dismissal – ERA 1996 s. 86(6).

64 ERA 1996 s. 1(4)(e).

65 *Dietman v LB of Brent* [1988] IRLR 299.

66 [1959] 1 WLR 698.

the defendant's actions and that, as she had not received due notice of dismissal, this amounted to a wrongful dismissal in breach of contract. The Court of Appeal held that wilful disobedience of a lawful and reasonable order can be a repudiatory breach of contract, but this single act of disobedience was not wilful nor particularly grave or serious to amount to a repudiatory act that justified a summary dismissal. Consequently, the plaintiff was entitled to damages for wrongful dismissal, i.e. for dismissal in breach of contract.[67] By contrast, in *Pepper v Webb*[68] the claimant refused to follow a lawful order after a number of heated arguments with his employer. Here the summary dismissal was lawful as the employee had repudiated the contract of employment by his wilful refusal to obey a lawful and reasonable order which, in combination with the other incidents of disobedience and insolence, amounted to a repudiation of a fundamental term of the contract.[69]

❖ THINKING POINT

Would it be a repudiatory breach if the employee genuinely believed (mistakenly) that the work which he had been instructed to do did not fall within his contract and so refused to co-operate with the employer?

Actions amounting to gross misconduct will be a repudiatory breach as they offend against the implied term of trust and confidence inherent in every contract of employment – this is conduct that undermines an employer's trust and confidence in the employee to such an extent that the employer can no longer be expected to continue the employee's employment. In *Sinclair v Neighbour*[70] the manager of a betting shop was summarily dismissed when he borrowed money openly from the till replacing it with an IOU for the same sum. He had every intention of returning the cash but he knew the practice was forbidden. The Court of Appeal held that his summary dismissal was justified. Although the claimant may not have been openly dishonest, he was guilty of a gross breach of good faith when he took money from the till knowing that such misconduct was specifically forbidden by the employer. In such circumstances this was a breach of the mutual trust and confidence obligation to serve your employer faithfully that must exist between the parties and was behaviour incompatible with his employment. As the working relationship was now seriously damaged, the employee's action amounted to a repudiatory breach of contract justifying the decision of the employer to dismiss summarily. Other examples of gross misconduct justifying summary dismissal include: using an unauthorised password in order to enter or attempt to enter a computer known to contain information to which he is not entitled[71]; disclosure of confidential information[72]; downloading pornography[73]; sending obscene images in the internal post[74]; and taking fees from clients for your own benefit without the employer's knowledge.[75] It has also been

---

67 See also *Wilson v Racher* [1974] ICR 428, where there had also been an argument between employer and employee over employment duties – however, the one-off use of abusive language by the employee did not amount to a fundamental breach of contract and the immediate summary dismissal was not justifiable.

68 [1969] 2 All ER 216.

69 See also *Blyth v The Scottish Liberal Club* [1983] IRLR 245.

70 [1967] 2 QB 279.

71 *Denco v Joinson Ltd* [1991] IRLR 63.

72 *Farnan v Sunderland Football Club Ltd* [2016] IRLR 185.

73 *Thomas v Hillingdon Borough Council* [2002] All ER 202.

74 *Williams v Leeds United Football Club* [2015] IRLR 383.

75 *Neary v Dean of Westminster* [1999] IRLR 288.

determined that in certain circumstances gross negligence can amount to gross misconduct justifying summary dismissal.[76]

Summary dismissal must follow closely on the act which allegedly justifies the action, since delay amounts to waiver of the breach and the right to dismiss will be lost, leaving only a remedy for damages against the employee. In such a situation employers rarely sue their employees (as there is little obvious financial loss) but could, for example, withhold wages to recover any specific loss if this is provided for in the contract.

4.5 Wrongful dismissal

Wrongful dismissal is not a way a contract is terminated but is a remedy – a claim that the employer was in breach of contract in dismissing the employee. This may occur where the employer fails to give the employee the proper amount of notice that is required under the contract or where the employer has terminated a fixed term contract that does not have a notice period. The employer then becomes liable to pay damages reflecting all the losses the employee has sustained from the breach.

4.5.1 Damages

Damages are limited to those specific losses arising out of the breach of contract.[77] The principle in assessing contractual damages is to put the party into the position if the contract had been performed. As a contract of employment has an express or implied notice period the contract can be lawfully terminated by the employer giving the correct notice. Damages recoverable will, therefore, only be the wages and other benefits that would have been earned or accrued during this specific period. For most employees, this would not be an amount that would sufficiently compensate them for losing their job. For those employees, the statutory remedy of unfair dismissal may be more lucrative (considered in Chapters 7–9). However, for higher paid employees with long notice periods or those with fixed term contracts without a notice period (like premiership football managers), a wrongful dismissal claim may well be profitable as there is no ceiling on this contractual claim.[78] Apart from salary a claim may include the loss of pension benefits[79] and share options,[80] private health cover,[81] commission and bonuses[82] due during the notice period, but not if the benefits are discretionary under the contract.[83]

The courts have long denied employees compensation for the physical or mental effects of a wrongful dismissal. In *Bliss v South East Thames Health Authority*[84] Dillon LJ re-iterated the general principle outlined in *Addis v Gramophone Record Co*[85] that where damages fall to be assessed for breach

76 *Adesokan v Sainsburys Supermarkets* [2017] IRLR 346.

77 Note that, as discussed at p. 81, if an employee is summarily dismissed as a result of gross misconduct a claim for wrongful dismissal cannot be brought as the employer is justified in dismissing the employee.

78 For example, in *Clark v BET plc* [1997] IRLR 348 the employee was a finance director with a notice entitlement of three years who was dismissed within months of employment. Damages for unjustified summary dismissal was calculated to amount to approximately £2.5 million.

79 *Silvey v Pendragon plc* [2001] IRLR 665.

80 *Mallone v BPB Industries plc* [2002] IRLR 452.

81 *Adin v Sedco Forex* [1997] IRLR 280.

82 *Clark v Nomura International plc* [2000] IRLR 766.

83 *Lavarack v Woods of Colchester* [1967] 1 QB 278.

84 [1985] IRLR 308.

85 [1909] AC 488.

of contract rather than for tort it is not permissible to award general damages for frustration, anxiety or mental distress, injured feelings or general anger caused by the breach.[86] It may be the case, however, that dismissal has made it more difficult for the employee to obtain alternative employment. In these circumstances, so-called 'stigma' damages were awarded in *Malik v BCCI*.[87] Here, ex-employees of a failed Bank claimed damages in respect of injury to their reputation and future employment prospects caused by the bank operating in a dishonest and corrupt manner. The House of Lords upheld the claim on the basis that the employer's conduct was a serious breach of the implied term of mutual trust and confidence present in every employment contract. Here the damages awarded were not for injury to feelings for the way the dismissal occurred or for stress or anxiety, but for future financial loss resulting from damage to the employees' reputation.

However, this approach has now been doubted in a number of subsequent cases. In *Johnson v Unisys Ltd*[88] the scope of 'stigma' damages was limited to an action on breach of contract during employment – not when the contract was terminated. Once a dismissal has occurred the implied term (relied upon in *Malik*) has been extinguished, therefore it is not possible for a claimant to substantiate such a claim on this basis. The decision in *Johnson* was affirmed in *Edwards v Chesterfield NHS*[89] where a majority of the Supreme Court held that 'stigma' damages are only recoverable where they flow from a breach of contract (which can be of an express or implied term) during employment, not from a wrongful dismissal. In coming to this conclusion, the Supreme Court took account that to allow stigma damages would side-step the statutory scheme for the regulation of dismissals (the right to claim damages for unfair dismissal) and it would be undesirable for the common law to evolve in order to permit damages for the manner of dismissal – an issue the statutory provisions regulate.[90]

Damages may also be available in specific circumstances for the loss of statutory rights – such as the opportunity to make a claim for unfair dismissal[91] or redundancy.[92] This may occur where an employer has failed to follow a contractual disciplinary procedure and, consequently, employment has been cut short by a number of weeks. If the procedure had been followed employment would have been extended to provide the employee with sufficient continuous employment to initiate a statutory claim for redundancy pay or unfair dismissal compensation.[93]

An employee in normal circumstances is under a duty to mitigate loss. Therefore, the dismissed employee should make efforts to seek new employment. If the employee fails to take active steps to find alternative employment the court may deduct an amount the employee might reasonably have earned during the period up to the trial. However, the employee is only obliged to take reasonable steps and therefore is expected only to seek similar employment.[94] If the employee does find employment before the end of the notice period, the new salary must be taken into account in calculating the actual loss to the employee. In order to avoid a double benefit, damages are also reduced by the amount of social security benefits received and by any unfair dismissal compensation awarded for loss of earnings. Since the measure of damages is based on the amount of lost wages,

86 The principle was upheld in *French v Barclays Bank plc* [1998] IRLR 646.

87 [1997] IRLR 462.

88 [2003] 1 AC 518.

89 [2011] UKSC 58.

90 The Supreme Court (on the same grounds) also rejected the argument that stigma damages should be available on breach of an express contractual term (as opposed to an implied term) on dismissal.

91 *Raspin v United News Shops Ltd* [1999] IRLR 9, but in *Harper v Virgin Net Ltd* [2004] IRLR 390 the Court of Appeal doubted this decision as a consequence of developments in *Johnson v Unisys* [2001] IRLR 279.

92 *Jenvey v Australian Broadcasting Corpn* [2002] IRLR 520.

93 However, note that if there is a right in the contract for the employer to make a payment in lieu of notice, the date of termination of the contract is the date of payment, not the date notice runs out – *Morran v Glasgow Council of Tenants Association* [1998] IRLR 67.

94 *Yetton v Eastwoods Froy* [1967] 1 WLR 104; *Wilding v BT plc* [2002] IRLR 524.

the court will deduct the correct level of tax that is appropriate. However, benefits received under private insurance schemes are not deducted, nor are any retirement pension payments.[95]

Where a wrongful dismissal claim is successful the employee is discharged from all contractual obligations – including compliance with restraint of trade clauses. This is the case even where the clause was expressed to come into effect where the contract was terminated 'for whatever reason'.[96]

4.5.2 Payment in lieu of notice

It is common practice for an employer not to require an employee to work out their notice period and to pay an amount in lieu of notice (equivalent to the amount of pay that would have been earned in this period).[97] This payment is usually regarded as a *prima facie* measure of damages for wrongful dismissal – unless otherwise specified as a debt in the contract (see below). In these circumstances, a claim for wrongful dismissal would be futile as the employer has paid in advance for the lost wages – although a wrongful dismissal action may still be taken where the employer has failed to compensate the employee fully for the loss of their job – such as where there are ancillary benefits (such as pension rights) under the contract that have accrued over that period.[98] However, if the payment compensates the employee appropriately and all financial benefits that would have been due during the notice period had been provided, then a wrongful dismissal claim would fail – as the employee has essentially been put into the same position as he would have been if notice had been given.

However, if there is a specific contractual right to a payment in lieu of notice, it is a debt under the contract, not compensation for wrongful dismissal. The Court of Appeal has therefore held in *Abrahams v Performing Rights Society*[99] that the mitigation principle does not apply where the payment in lieu is a contractual right. Abrahams had been entitled to a payment in lieu of two years' salary where he was dismissed without the correct notice period having applied. The Court of Appeal held that as this was not an action for damages – he was entitled to the payment in lieu in full without regard to whether he had attempted to mitigate his loss. This decision was followed in *Cerebrus Software Ltd v Rowley*[100] where the Court of Appeal made it clear that there should not be any 'set-off' in a damages action against any sums to which an employee is contractually entitled.

The general rule is that where a payment in lieu of notice has been given, the date of the termination of the contract will be the date wages in lieu are paid (not the end of the notice period). Therefore, where an employer makes a payment in lieu under the contract an employee does not have the right to work out the notice period as the contract has been terminated.[101] This principle is also important in determining statutory rights (where there is a minimum qualifying period of continuous employment) and certain rights under the contract (such as when a bonus payment should be made). Furthermore, the Supreme Court in *Geys v Société Générale, London Branch*[102] (*Geys*) has held that payment in lieu of notice provisions are subject to an implied term that termination only takes place once the payment has actually been made, and that the employee has received notice that the payment has been made in exercise of this specific contractual right. The Supreme Court

95 *Hopkins v Norcross Ltd* [1994] IRLR 18.
96 *Briggs v Oates* [1990] IRLR 472.
97 ERA 1996 s. 86 (3)(6) establishes that the right to receive the statutory minimum period of notice may be waived in order to accept a payment in lieu of notice.
98 *Silvey v Pendragon* [2001] IRLR 685.
99 [1995] IRLR 486.
100 [2001] IRLR 160.
101 *Marshall (Cambridge) Ltd v Hamblin* [1994] IRLR 260.
102 [2012] UKSC 63.

in *Geys* has also advised that if an employer wishes to exercise a contractual payment in lieu provision, the employer ought to explicitly make clear that the clause has been activated to ensure no confusion as to why a payment has been made.

If there is a specific payment in lieu of notice term in the contract, dismissal is lawful and therefore any restraint of trade clause is still valid.[103] However, if there is an unjustified summary dismissal and the employer offers a payment in lieu of notice, the employer remains in breach of contract and the payment in lieu can (as noted earlier) be treated as a form of damages for the wrongful dismissal – and will usually extinguish any wrongful dismissal claim. As an unlawful termination, however, any restraint of trade clause will be invalid. An employment contract may also specify a specific sum (unrelated to a payment in lieu) is payable on termination of contract – so long it is not so extravagant to be deemed to be a penalty clause in the contract such a clause is enforceable.[104]

❖ THINKING POINT

Do you think an employee should be entitled to a contractual payment in lieu of notice where the contractual terms specify it will be withdrawn if the employee has committed a repudiatory breach of contract?

4.5.3 Effect of the employer's breach of contract

In the employment context it has been argued that an unjustified summary dismissal (a repudiatory breach of contract) by the employer results in an automatic termination of the contract as it destroys the whole basis of the relationship – which must be one based on mutual trust and confidence.[105] However, this approach has been criticised as an unnecessary departure from the traditional rule in contract that it is for the innocent party to either choose to ignore the breach and 'elect' to continue the contract, or to 'accept' it and terminate the contract. In practice the problem is often of purely academic interest as when an employee is dismissed he or she normally exits the workplace – which is ample evidence that the employee has 'accepted' the repudiatory breach by the employer.

There are circumstances, however, where the question is of some importance – such as whether an employee is entitled to a bonus which is based on employment at a specific date, or where there is an issue of unpaid wages where the employee works for a period beyond the date of the repudiatory breach. For example, in *Rigby v Ferado Ltd*[106] the employee had continued to work after the employer had unilaterally reduced his wages. The Court of Appeal's view was that the employee was still entitled to claim damages for the unpaid contractual wages as an unaccepted repudiation did not discharge the contract. As the contract was clearly not at an end – there having been no express or implied acceptance of the breach – the employee was entitled to claim damages for the loss of wages.[107]

103 *Dixon v Stenor Ltd* [1973] IRLR 28.

104 *Murray v Leisureplay Ltd* [2005] IRLR 946.

105 *Sanders v Ernest Neale Ltd* [1974] ICR 565; *Gunton v London Borough of Richmond Upon Thames* [1980] IRLR 321.

106 [1987] IRLR 516.

107 See also *Boyo v Lambeth London Borough Council* [1995] IRLR 50.

The Supreme Court has now definitively considered the issue in *Geys*[108] where the specific date of termination of the contract of employment was of significance in determining whether the employee was entitled to a substantial bonus payment. The Supreme Court ruled that in all circumstances the 'elective' theory applies. Where an employer dismisses an employee without providing an employee the correct contractual period of notice, the employee has a choice of either accepting the breach (impliedly or expressly) and bringing the contract to an end or affirming the contract so that it continues until the end of the contractual notice period (along with any contractual entitlements which accrue during this period).

This decision highlights the importance for employers of including a payment in lieu of notice provision in the employment contract. This gives the employer a contractual right to terminate the contract of employment immediately, thus there is no danger of the employer being exposed to the risk of the employee refusing to accept the termination and therefore keeping the employment relationship active.

4.5.4 Enforcement of the contract through specific performance or injunction

It is not possible for an employee to obtain an order of specific performance to compel their employer to re-instate their employment as s. 236 TULR(C)A 1992 provides that no court may compel an employee to do any work or attend any place to do work.[109] As an employer cannot enforce a contract of employment there is no reciprocal rights for the employee to do so – which offends against the doctrine of mutuality. There are circumstances, however, where an interlocutory injunction may be granted in order to prevent a dismissal taking place – to stop an employer who is in the process of committing a repudiatory breach of contract that could result in dismissal. For example, in *Peace v City of Edinburgh Council*[110] the employer was prevented from introducing a new disciplinary procedure that was in breach of the employee's contract. The court was not prohibiting the employer from using the sanction of dismissal but merely enforcing the agreed original procedure prior to dismissal (which had the effect of prolonging the employee's employment for a number of weeks).

In order for a court to grant an injunction to restrain a purported dismissal, a number of older cases have established that the court can only intervene where a degree of mutual trust and confidence still exists between the parties. Without such a relationship between the parties the employment relationship is irretrievably damaged and the court is unable to act. Thus, where the dispute between the parties is of a minor nature or the dismissal is unrelated to any specific conflict at the workplace (such as a redundancy dismissal),[111] then the court may grant an injunction where the employer has acted in breach of contract. For example, in *Robb v London Borough of Hammersmith and Fulham*[112] the issue of trust and confidence was not of such importance as the employee had been suspended prior to dismissal and so was not engaged in employment duties at the time of the request to restrain dismissal.

In *Powell v London Borough of Brent*[113] the issue concerned a unilateral variation of the employee's contract after a flawed promotion process. An injunction to restrain the breach and enforce the contract was granted as the employment relationship has not been irretrievably destroyed.

---

108 n 102.

109 Enshrining in statute the common-law rule deriving from *De Francesco v Barnum* [1890] 45 Ch 430, that to permit the enforcement of a contract of employment would be tantamount to condoning forced labour.

110 [1999] IRLR 417.

111 *Anderson v Pringle of Scotland* [1998] IRLR 64.

112 [1991] IRLR 72.

113 [1988] 1 Ch 176.

There had been no attempt by either side to terminate the contract and it was clear both sides retained confidence in the relationship. In *Wadcock v London Borough of Brent*[114] the High Court thought that a more appropriate question to ask was whether the parties could still effectively work together, rather than focus exclusively on the implied term of 'trust and confidence'.[115]

Rules against enforcement of an employment contract do not prevent the court enforcing an agreement by way of restrictive covenants not to compete with the employer during or after employment – even though this indirectly pressurises the employee to remain in the present employment.[116] However, a restrictive covenant that is structured to compel employment by not permitting any employment for a period after termination of employment will not be enforced.[117]

In certain limited circumstances where the individual is employed as an 'office holder', where employment is governed by a statutory scheme, a court may declare the dismissal as invalid where the employer's actions are contrary to natural justice (the right to be heard by an unbiased tribunal, to receive proper notice of the charges, to speak in response to the charge and a right of appeal),[118] or the dismissal was *ultra vires* the statute (for example, there is a breach of the procedure for dismissal outlined in the legislation creating the employment).[119] In this way the contract is indirectly enforced through these administrative law principles. What is clear is that the mere fact the employee is employed in the public sector is not the test for determining whether the applicant has protected status under statute. In *R v East Berks Health Authority ex p Walsh*[120] the Court of Appeal rejected the claim as the case did not raise sufficient issues of public law – the nature of the complaint concerned exclusively matters of contract and so there were no relevant issues of public law.[121]

4.6 Further reading

Aitken, 'Elective or automatic termination of a contract of employment?' (2013) 129 *Law Quarterly Review* 335.

Barmes, 'The continuing conceptual crisis in the common law of the contract of employment' (2004) *Modern Law Review* 435.

Bogg, 'Express disciplinary procedures in the contract of employment: Parliamentary intention and the Supreme Court' (2015) 131 *Law Quarterly Review* 15.

Brodie, 'Protecting dignity in the workplace: the vitality of mutual trust and confidence' (2004) 33 *Industrial Law Journal* 349.

Burrows, 'What is the effect of a repudiatory breach of a contract of employment' (2013) 42 *Industrial Law Journal* 281.

Cabrelli & Zahn, 'The elective and automatic theories of termination at common law: resolving the conundrum' (2012) 41 *Industrial Law Journal* 346.

Ewing, 'Remedies for breach of the employment contract' (1993) 52 *Cambridge Law Journal* 405.

Goulding, 'Injunctions and contracts of employment' (1990) 19 *Industrial Law Journal* 98.

McColgan, 'Remedies for breach of employment contracts' (1992) *21 Industrial Law Journal* 58.

Sedley, 'Public law and contractual entitlement' (1994) 23 *Industrial Law Journal* 201.

114 [1990] IRLR 223.

115 For further examples of the application of injunctive relief, see *Irani v Southampton & South West Hampshire Health Authority* [1985] IRLR 203; *Dietman v Brent London Borough Council* [1988] IRLR 299; *Jones v Gwent County Council* [1992] IRLR 521; *West London Mental Health Trust v Chabra* [2013] UKSC 80.

116 *Warner Bros Inc v Nelson* [1937] 1 KB 209.

117 *Page One Records Ltd v Britton* [1967] I WLR 157.

118 *Ridge v Baldwin* [1964] AC 40; *Malloch v Aberdeen Corpn* [1971] 1278.

119 *Vine v National Dock Labour Board* [1957] AC 488.

120 [1984] IRLR 278.

121 Full guidelines of when administrative law remedies are available for public sector employees were set out by Woolf LJ in *McClaren v Home Office* [1990] IRLR 338.

Chapter 5

Transfer of undertakings

Chapter contents

5.1 Overview

- At common law, if the identity of one of the parties to the employment contract changes, that contract terminates. This has serious implications for the employee if the identity of his employer changes, for example, as the result of a takeover by another company. In that situation, the new employer has complete discretion on whether to offer employment to his predecessor's employees. If he chooses to offer employment, he then has complete discretion over the terms and conditions of that employment. Further, the employee who chooses to work for the new employer loses all his continuous employment with the original employer, and with it the opportunity to claim unfair dismissal or a redundancy payment until he has spent two years with the new employer.
- Since the 1970s, statute (now the Employment Rights Act 1996 s. 218) has recognised the injustice caused to employees who find themselves in this situation, and provides for the contract of employment to transfer automatically to the new employer in defined circumstances, with no effect on continuity of employment, so that service with the original and new employers is treated as one for the purpose of claiming employment rights linked to length of service.
- EU Law goes further and provides not only that employment transfers automatically in the event of change in the identity of the employer, but on the existing employees' contractual terms and conditions. The two relevant EU Directives have been implemented into UK law as the Transfer of Undertakings (Protection of Employment) Regulations 1981 and 2006 (the TUPE Regulations, or, simply, TUPE).
- The TUPE Regulations 2006 apply to 'relevant transfers', defined sufficiently broadly to cover the great majority of transfers, including the contracting-out and contracting-back of public sector functions. Where there is a relevant transfer, the employees transfer automatically from the transferor employer to the transferee at the point the transfer takes effect, with their continuity of employment and terms and conditions of employment intact, except for pension provisions. Liability to the employees in respect of matters arising before the transfer but not yet concluded also transfers. Any dismissal arising from the transfer or a matter linked to the transfer is automatically unfair unless a limited range of exceptions apply. Even in the latter case, a dismissal may still be unfair under the ordinary law of unfair dismissal.
- Problems arise largely because of the provisions preventing change to terms and conditions rather than the protection from dismissal. How long must elapse before the transferee can change the terms of conditions of transferred employees – for example, to match those of existing employees – without liability under TUPE, remains an open question.

5.2 Background

It is far from uncommon for employees to move between employers, for reasons which typically include career development, higher pay, or improved quality of life outside work. In doing so, the employee begins a fresh contract of employment on new terms and conditions and his continuity 'clock' is reset to zero. Such changes normally occur of the employee's own volition. The new contractual terms and temporary loss of eligibility to claim unfair dismissal or a redundancy payment are factors which he accepts as a necessary consequence of his decision to move, and part of the balancing exercise underlying that decision.

However, what if the employee remains in the same job, but the identity of his employer changes? This may occur for a variety of reasons, the most obvious being that the company he works for is taken over by another. Or that company splits into two or more different companies.

❖ EXAMPLE

Plymouth Compass Ltd is a long-established company producing marine navigational instruments. In recent years, the company has been steadily losing money as a result of the development of satellite navigation systems. The directors have now agreed a sale of Plymouth Compass to Chichester Yachts Ltd. The contract agreed between the two companies includes the sale of various tangible assets, such as premises, equipment, work-in-progress and future orders. Plymouth Compass, however, cannot sell its 27 employees – that would be tantamount to slavery. What is their position?

At common law, employment contracts with Plymouth Compass terminate when the transfer takes effect. If Chichester Yachts wishes to take on the Plymouth Compass employees, it must engage them on fresh contracts. There is no obligation on Chichester Yachts to engage those employees, and it has complete freedom to negotiate their terms and conditions of employment under the new contracts. If it does not wish to employ them, it has no obligations towards them.

Either situation has serious implications for the Plymouth Compass employees. Even if they are re-employed and continue working in the same job, the change in the identity of the employer means that the continuity clock is reset to zero. They therefore lose important forms of employment protection – the right to redundancy payments and the right to claim unfair dismissal – until they have remained with Chichester Yachts for two years. Even then, the loss of their previous service will considerably reduce the redundancy payments and Basic Awards for unfair dismissal that they may be entitled to. Further, the new contracts with Chichester Yachts may be on considerably less favourable terms, in relation, say, to pay, duties and hours.

This is not the case if the company is subject to a change in its shareholding. In that situation, the company, as a legal person separate from its shareholders, retains its original identity, and the contracts of the employees are unaffected.

Alternatively, employees may work for a business which operates as a partnership. A firm of solicitors is the most obvious example. At common law, and in the absence of a partnership deed providing for the continuation of the partnership, any change in the partners – for example, the retirement of a partner or the appointment of a new partner – dissolves the existing partnership and brings the employees' contracts to an end. The new partnership may choose whether to re-employ the workforce on the same or differing terms. Similarly, if a sole trader dies, responsibility for his business passes to the executors or administrators of his estate. Again, the contracts of employment terminate. In both cases the employees will lose all employment protection rights based on continuous service, and the new employer may choose not to re-employ them, or to re-employ them on less favourable terms.

Legislation has sought to provide some protection for employees in situations where the identity of the employer changes, although successive governments have recognised that a balance needs to be struck between preserving the rights of employees, and avoiding a situation where organisations are discouraged from taking over other businesses, often businesses in financial trouble.

Purely UK measures, now contained in the Employment Rights Act 1996, simply preserve continuity of employment. The Transfer of Undertakings (Protection of Employment) Regulations, implementing EU Directives, go much further, and may protect an employee from changes to his contractual terms and conditions. Though two sources of protection exist, they overlap, and the majority of changes in the identity of the employer will be covered by both.

5.3 Protection under the Employment Rights Act 1996

Continuity will be preserved in circumstances where:

- a trade, business or undertaking is transferred (s. 218(2));
- a body corporate is substituted for another body corporate by statute (s. 218(3));
- an employer dies and the employee is retained by his personal representatives or trustees (s. 218(4));
- there is a change of partners, personal representatives or trustees (s. 218(5)); or
- the employee is taken on by an associated employer of his employer (s. 218(6)).

S. 218(2) applies only where a business is transferred as a 'going concern', i.e. where a business is sold and continues to trade under its old name despite the change of ownership. Such sales will usually include a transfer of 'goodwill', i.e. the purchaser buys not only the business, but its reputation and customer base. The transfer will then include restrictive covenants to prevent the vendor from trading under the same or a similar name.

❖ EXAMPLE

H.L. Matthews & Son is a long-established butchers' business in Bidford. George Matthews, grandson of the founder, who operates the business as a sole trader, is now approaching 70 and has decided to retire. He negotiates a sale of the business with Peter, under which the sale includes the name and goodwill of the business as well as the assets (the premises and equipment). George also covenants not to set up another butchers' business in the locality, and, in particular, not to trade under the name of Matthews. As the business is thus transferred as a going concern, George's three staff continue their employment under Peter, and there is no break in their continuity of employment, which runs from when they began working for George.

In *Woodhouse v Peter Brotherhood Ltd* [1972] 2 QB 520, the employee had worked for some 14 years for Crossleys, at a plant which was taken over by the Respondent company, which kept on the staff and utilised the plant and machinery. However, Crossleys did not sell its name or goodwill, and in fact carried on its business independently at another factory. Six years later the claimant was made redundant. The Court of Appeal held that the sale had been a sale of assets rather than a sale of the business as a going concern, so that s. 218(2) did not apply. Therefore, the claimant only had six years' service for the purpose of calculating his redundancy payment.

There was a similar finding in *Melon v Hector Powe Ltd* [1981] ICR 43, where the new employers finished off the work of the old employers before starting their own business, in the same premises and using the transferred assets.

How different must the new business be to prevent s. 218(2) from operating? This is a question for the Tribunal. For s. 218(2) to operate, the business and physical assets must be transferred to the new employer, along with the goodwill.

As a limited company is a legal person in its own right, separate from its shareholders, there is no transfer for the purposes of the legislation where there is a change of share ownership alone. In the UK, the majority of changes in the ownership of businesses take place via share transfers.

S. 218(4) is important where individuals are employed by sole traders. If a sole trader dies, the personal representatives of his estate have power to run the business on behalf of the beneficiaries until the estate is wound up. Under s. 218(3) the employee's continuity of employment is maintained during this period. The transfer of the business to the beneficiary under the will or to a new owner by the personal representatives may fall within s. 218(2) depending on the exact circumstances.

S. 218(5) is relatively rarely engaged. At common law, if a business is conducted as a partnership and there is a change in the identity of the partners, then the original partnership is dissolved and a new partnership created. This issue is dealt with in most professionally drawn partnership deeds, which provide that a change of partners does not dissolve the partnership.

Issues involving s. 218 have become much less common since the first TUPE Regulations came into force.

5.4 EU legislation

5.4.1 Overview

EU employment legislation is designed both to protect employees and to promote free movement of labour by harmonising national employment measures. The European Acquired Rights Directive 77/187, now reissued in amended form as Directive 2001/23/EC (known as the Acquired Rights Directive or Business Transfers Directive), was intended to ensure that the employees of a business were not adversely affected by a change in the identity of the employer, and to put them in the same position as if a sale of the business had been carried out by means of a share transfer. Therefore:

- On the sale of a business all employees are automatically transferred to the new owner on their existing contractual terms and conditions.
- If either the transferor or transferee dismisses employees in order to avoid the application of the above, those dismissals are ineffective.

The term 'undertaking' is used in the Directives to cover a range of legal forms for businesses, not all of which exist in each Member State, and is capable of including public sector bodies, as well as, in the British context, companies and partnerships.

5.4.2 The 1977 Directive

The original Directive provided:

> **Article 3**
>
> The transferor's rights and obligations arising from a contract of employment or from an employment relationship existing on the date of a transfer shall, by reason of such transfer, be transferred to the transferee.
>
> **Article 4**
>
> 1) The transfer of the undertaking, business or part of the undertaking or business shall not in itself constitute grounds for dismissal by the transferor or transferee. This provision

shall not stand in the way of dismissals that may take place for economic, technical or organisational reasons entailing changes in the workforce.

2) If the contract of employment or the employment relationship is terminated because the transfer involves a substantial change in working conditions to the detriment of the employee, the employer shall be regarded as having been responsible for the termination of the contract of employment or the employment relationship.

In the United Kingdom, the Directive was implemented via the Transfer of Undertakings (Protection of Employment) Regulations 1981, which came into force early in 1982.

Regulation 4 defined a 'relevant transfer' for the purpose of the Regulations, i.e. a transfer under which the employees would be entitled to the protection.

5.4.3 The 2001 Directive

The 2001 Directive preserved these principles, but broadened their application. In particular, the 1977 Directive and the original UK TUPE Regulations only applied to transfers of 'commercial undertakings', so excluding large numbers of people employed, for example, on functions originally carried out by local authorities in-house, but were then contracted out to other organisations. Further, the 2001 Directive is much more specific on what is protected.

Article 1

1.

(a) This Directive shall apply to any transfer of an undertaking, business, or part of an undertaking or business to another employer as a result of a legal transfer or merger.

(b) Subject to subparagraph (a) and the following provisions of this Article, *there is a transfer within the meaning of this Directive where there is a transfer of an economic entity which retains its identity, meaning an organised grouping of resources which has the objective of pursuing an economic activity, whether or not that activity is central or ancillary.*

(c) *This Directive shall apply to public and private undertakings engaged in economic activities whether or not they are operating for gain.* An administrative reorganisation of public administrative authorities, or the transfer of administrative functions between public administrative authorities, is not a transfer within the meaning of this Directive.

5.5 The 1981 Regulations

5.5.1 Provisions

Regulation 3 defined a transfer covered by the Regulations ('a relevant transfer'): 'These Regulations apply to a transfer from one person to another of an undertaking situated immediately before the transfer in the United Kingdom, or a part of one which is so situated'.

Note that the concept of a relevant transfer included the sale of an insolvent company by a receiver or administrator appointed by the company (though not one appointed by the court).

Regulation 5 provided:

(1) A relevant transfer shall not operate to terminate the contract of employment of any person employed by the transferor in the undertaking or part transferred but any such contract which would otherwise have been terminated by the transfer shall have effect after the transfer as if initially made between the person so employed and the transferee.

(2) On the completion of a relevant transfer

a) All the transferor's rights, powers, duties and liabilities under or in connection with any such contract, shall be transferred by virtue of this Regulation to the transferee; and
b) Anything done before the transfer is completed by or in relation to the transferor in respect of that contract or a person employed in that undertaking or part shall be deemed to have been done by or in relation to the transferee.

(3) Any reference in paragraph (1) or (2) above to a person employed in an undertaking or part of one transferred by a relevant transfer is a reference to a person so employed immediately before the transfer;
(4) [Excludes criminal liability from the effect of the above provisions.]
(5) Paragraph (1) above is without prejudice to the right of an employee arising apart from these Regulations to terminate his contract of employment without notice if a substantial change is made in his working conditions to his detriment; but no such right shall arise by reason only that, under that paragraph, the identity of his employer changes, unless the employee shows that, in all the circumstances, the change is a significant change and is to his detriment.

Therefore,

- all employees employed by the transferor 'immediately before' the completion of the transfer transferred to the transferee under their existing contractual terms; and
- all outstanding liabilities of the transferor in respect of the employees or their contracts, other than criminal liabilities, transferred to the transferee.

It is important to note that nowhere in Regulation 5, or in the underlying Directive, was there any limitation of time after which the contracts of the transferred employees could be changed. This created obvious difficulties for the transferee, who might well wish to

- make more efficient use of the transferred employees in order to return an ailing business to profitability;
- harmonise the terms and conditions of the transferred employees with his existing employees, whether at that establishment or elsewhere.

Regulation 8 provided:

(1) Where either before or after a relevant transfer, any employee of the transferor or transferee is dismissed, that employee shall be treated for the purpose of [ERA 1996 Part X] as unfairly dismissed if the transfer or a reason connected with it is the reason or principal reason for the dismissal.
(2) Where an economic, technical or organisational reason entailing changes in the workforce of either the transferor or transferee before or after a relevant transfer is the reason or principal reason for dismissing an employee
   (a) Paragraph (1) shall not apply to his dismissal, but
   (b) Without prejudice to the application of [ERA 1996 s. 98(4)] (test of fair dismissal) the dismissal shall be for the purposes of [ERA1996 s. 98(1)] (substantial reason for dismissal) be regarded as having been for a substantial reason of a kind such as to justify the dismissal of an employee holding the position which the employee held.

This meant

- a dismissal because of the transfer or for a reason connected with it was automatically unfair unless the employer could demonstrate an economic, technical or organisational reason ('ETO reason') for changes in the workforce. This entitled the dismissed employee to compensation for unfair dismissal, including a Compensatory Award based on his actual financial loss arising from the dismissal, rather than the lower level of a statutory redundancy payment;

- if an ETO reason applied, the fairness or otherwise of the dismissal would be determined on the basis of the ordinary law of unfair dismissal.

5.5.2 A relevant transfer

All this potentially created considerable additional burdens and costs for transferees. Therefore, a body of case law developed in which both transferors and transferees sought to argue that the transfer they had entered into was not a 'relevant transfer' for the purposes of the Regulations, so that the protection accorded to employees by the Regulations did not apply. In particular, a transferor and transferee would agree that the transferor would dismiss the employees shortly before the transfer took effect – as little as one hour before – and then argue that the employees were not employed 'immediately before' the transfer for the purposes of Regulation 5(3). In *Secretary of State for Employment v Spence* [1986] ICR 651 the Court of Appeal took a very literal view of the expression 'immediately before' and concluded that a gap of 1–2 hours was sufficient to put an employee outside the protection of the Regulations. Clearly this offered considerable scope to employers wishing to evade the effect of the Regulations.

This was the issue in *Litster v Forth Dry Dock & Engineering Co. Ltd* [1989] ICR 341 HL. The company went into receivership, and carried on trading for some months prior to a sale. The receivers dismissed the workforce about an hour before the sale took effect at the request of the purchasers. Some of the employees were re-engaged by the purchasers, but others were not, and 12 of these claimed unfair dismissal as against both the receivers and the purchasers. The purchasers argued that the dismissed employees were not employed immediately before the transfer as required by r. 5(3). The House of Lords rejected this argument, holding that the phrase 'immediately before' the transfer must be given a purposive interpretation in order to give effect to the Acquired Rights Directive.

Per Lord Templeman:

> The result of Article 4(1) is that the new owner intending to dismiss the workers cannot achieve his purpose by asking the old owner to dismiss the workers prior to the transfer taking place. Any such dismissal, whether by the old owner or the new owner, would be inconsistent with the object of protecting the rights of the workers and is prohibited by Article 4(1).
>
> The result of Regulation 8(1) is the same as Article 4(1), namely, that if the new owner wishes to dismiss the workers he cannot achieve his purpose either by procuring the old owner to dismiss the worker, prior to the transfer taking place, or by himself dismissing the workers after the date of the transfer.
>
> The appellants were dismissed at 3.30pm on 6 February by Forth Dry Dock, and the business was transferred to Forth Estuary at 4.30pm on the same day. . . Thus, it is said, . . . the workforce of Forth Dry Dock . . . were not employed 'immediately before the transfer' . . . and therefore Regulation 5(1) did not transfer any liability for the workforce from Forth Dry Dock to Forth Estuary. The argument is inconsistent with the Directive.

Lord Templeman cited the ECJ case of *P Bork International A/S v Foreningen af Arbeidsledere I Danmark* (Case 101/87) [1989] IRLR 41 as authority for the requirement to give a purposive construction to the Regulations, and went on:

> In the present case . . . it seems to me . . . that [Regulation] 5(3) . . . was not intended and ought not to be construed so as to limit the operation of Regulation 5 to persons employed immediately

> before the transfer in point of time. Regulation 5(3) must be construed on the footing that it applies to a person employed immediately before the transfer or who would have been so employed if he had not been dismissed before the transfer for a reason connected with the transfer. It would, of course, still be open for a new owner to show that the employee had been dismissed for 'an economical, technical or organisational reason entailing changes in the workforce' [Regulation 8(2)], but no such reason could be advanced in the present case where there was no complaint against the workers, they were not redundant, and there were no relevant reasons entailing changes in the workforce.

What, then, is the legal effect of dismissals made in breach of the directive? Under some continental legal systems, such dismissals are void, or voidable, so that the employees concerned would simply transfer to the employment of the transferee under their existing terms and conditions, as if the purported dismissals had never taken place. Under the law of England and Wales, however, this reasoning does not apply.

The issue was considered by the House of Lords in the conjoined cases of *Wilson v St Helens Borough Council* and *British Fuels Ltd v Baxendale* [1999] 2 AC 52. In *Wilson*, responsibility for a group of state schools was transferred from the county council to St Helens Borough Council. In *Wilson*, teachers at one of the schools were dismissed by the County Council for redundancy but immediately afterwards accepted employment with the Borough Council. If the dismissals had been effective in terminating their employment, the teachers would have been able to claim unfair dismissal against both councils, but would not have the benefit of their original contracts of employment in working for the Borough Council. The Lords concluded that the dismissals were effective.

Lord Slynn said:

> The overriding emphasis in the European Court's judgment is that the existing rights of employees are to be safeguarded if there is a transfer. That means no more and no less than that the employee can look to the transferee to perform those obligations which the employee could have enforced against the transferor. The employer, be he transferor or transferee, cannot use the transfer as a justification for dismissal, but if he does dismiss it is a question for national law as to what those rights are. . . . In English law, there would as a rule be no order for specific performance. The claim would be for damages for wrongful dismissal or statutory rights, including, it is true, reinstatement and re-engagement where applicable. It may be that in other countries an order for specific performance could be obtained under the appropriate domestic law and that on this approach different results would be achieved in different Member States. That I do not find surprising or shocking. The Directive is to 'approximate' the laws of the Member States. Its purpose is to 'safeguard' rights on a transfer. The 'rights' of an employee must depend on national rules of the law of contract or of legislation. There is no Community law of contract common to Member States, nor is there a common system or remedies. The object and purpose of the Directive is to ensure that in all Member States that an employee has against the transferee the rights and remedies which he would have had against the original employer. To that extent it reduces the differences which may exist in the event of a change of employers as to the enforcement by employees of existing rights. They must all provide for enforcement against the transferee of rights existing against the transferor at the time of the transfer. It seems to me that the Court [ECJ] has clearly recognised that the precise rights to be transferred depend on national law. But neither the Regulations nor the Directive nor the jurisprudence of the Court create a Community right to continue in employment which does not exist under national law.
>
> It is said that this is not an adequate remedy because some employees do not have statutory rights – e.g. those in the United Kingdom who have not been employed for a qualifying

period – but that is inherent in the differences which exist in the laws of the Member States and seems to me to derive from the wording and limited purpose of the Directive.

Thus, where there is a transfer of an undertaking and the transferee actually takes on the employee the contract of employment is automatically transferred so that, in the absence of a permissible variation [i.e. for an ETO reason], the terms of the initial contract go with the employee, who though he may refuse to go, cannot as a matter of public policy, waive the rights which the Directive and the Regulations confer upon him. When the transferee does not take on the employees who are dismissed on transfer the dismissal is not a nullity, though the contractual rights formerly available against the transferor remain intact against the transferee. For the latter purpose, an employee dismissed prior to the transfer in breach of article 4(1), i.e. on the basis of the transfer, is to be treated as still in the employment of the transferor at the date of transfer.

[. . .]

The Court has said that the employees' rights are safeguarded by 'enabling them to remain in employment with the new employer on the terms and conditions agreed with the transferor' (*Bork*) or by 'making it possible for them to continue to work for the new employer on the same conditions as those agreed with the transferor' (*Katsikas v Konstantinidis* [1993] ECR I-6577 ECJ). . . . The emphasis is on the same terms and conditions applying if the employment is continued. I do not read, however, any of these expressions as meaning that the transferee is bound actually to take on an employee who has been dismissed, whether because of the transfer or for independent reasons, and to give him the same work that he had before. They mean that if he does take the employee he takes him on the terms of employment with the transferor. . . . If the transferee does not take the employee because the latter has already been dismissed by the transferor, or because he himself dismisses the employee on the transfer, then he must meet all of the transferor's contractual and statutory obligations, unless:

a. The employee objects to being employed by the transferee, or
b. The sole or the principal reason for the dismissal is an economic, technical or organisational reason entailing changes in the workforce, when the employee is not to be treated as unfairly dismissed and when for the purposes of [ERA 1996] the employee is to be regarded as having been dismissed for a substantial reason justifying the dismissal as fair.

What does all this mean?

a) A dismissal by the transferor prior to the transfer or by the transferee at the time of the transfer or later because of the transfer or for a reason connected with the transfer is effective – the employee is dismissed.
b) If the employee is retained in employment, the relationship is governed by the contract as formed with the transferor.
c) If the employee is dismissed, he is automatically unfairly dismissed, and his remedy lies against the transferee, who has accepted the business subject to all liabilities (other than criminal liability) vis-à-vis the employees, unless he can establish the existence of an ETO reason entailing changes in the workforce. In that situation, there will be 'some other substantial reason' operating as a potentially fair reason for dismissal, but the dismissal may still be unfair on the basis that it was not reasonable to dismiss this employee for this reason, or on procedural grounds.

5.6 The 2006 Regulations

5.6.1 Relevant transfers under the 2006 Regulations

The 2006 Regulations give an entirely different definition of 'relevant transfer', designed not only to cover the transfer of an entire business or an identifiable part of a business, but a group of workers. The context for this is the practice in the public sector, particularly among local authorities, of contracting out particular functions, often low-skilled but requiring large numbers of workers, such as canteen services or rubbish collections, to the private sector. Other functions might be high-skilled but relatively low in volume, such as certain types of legal work. Indeed, the Thatcher government of the 1980s introduced compulsory competitive tendering for a range of local authority functions. This was replaced under the Local Government Act 1999 by a system known as 'best value', whereby local authorities were placed under a duty to secure economic, efficient and effective services. This regime remains in force and encourages contracting out where this appears to the authority to achieve 'best value'. Under compulsory competitive tendering, the organisation winning the tender would frequently agree to take on the local authority employees previously carrying out the relevant work, but on less favourable terms and conditions, arguing that they could only make a profit from the arrangement by paying the employees less.

Initially, the 1981 Regulations only applied to undertakings which were 'commercial enterprises', a category which, clearly, did not normally cover public sector organisations or their functions. A series of court decisions rejected this limitation, but much uncertainty remained. The 2006 Regulations, following the amended Directive of 2001, attempted to provide an all-encompassing definition of a relevant transfer, which, *inter alia*, encompassed contracting out (and, indeed, situations where local authorities, having earlier contracted out a service, now contracted it back in).

3.—

(1) These Regulations apply to—

(a) a transfer of an undertaking, business or part of an undertaking or business situated immediately before the transfer in the United Kingdom to another person where there is a transfer of an economic entity which retains its identity;

(b) a service provision change, that is a situation in which—

(i) activities cease to be carried out by a person ('a client') on his own behalf and are carried out instead by another person on the client's behalf ('a contractor');

(ii) activities cease to be carried out by a contractor on a client's behalf (whether or not those activities had previously been carried out by the client on his own behalf) and are carried out instead by another person ('a subsequent contractor') on the client's behalf; or

(iii) activities cease to be carried out by a contractor or a subsequent contractor on a client's behalf (whether or not those activities had previously been carried out by the client on his own behalf) and are carried out instead by the client on his own behalf, and in which the conditions set out in paragraph (3) are satisfied.

(2) In this regulation 'economic entity' means an organised grouping of resources which has the objective of pursuing an economic activity, whether or not that activity is central or ancillary.

(3) The conditions referred to in paragraph (1)(b) are that—

(a) immediately before the service provision change—

(i) there is an organised grouping of employees situated in Great Britain which has as its principal purpose the carrying out of the activities concerned on behalf of the client;

(ii) the client intends that the activities will, following the service provision change, be carried out by the transferee other than in connection with a single specific event or task of short-term duration; and

(iii) the activities concerned do not consist wholly or mainly of the supply of goods for the client's use.

(4) Subject to paragraph (1), these Regulations apply to—

(a) public and private undertakings engaged in economic activities whether or not they are operating for gain;

(b) a transfer or service provision change howsoever effected notwithstanding—

(i) that the transfer of an undertaking, business or part of an undertaking or business is governed or effected by the law of a country or territory outside the United Kingdom or that the service provision change is governed or effected by the law of a country or territory outside Great Britain;

(ii) that the employment of persons employed in the undertaking, business or part transferred or, in the case of a service provision change, persons employed in the organised grouping of employees, is governed by any such law;

(c) a transfer of an undertaking, business or part of an undertaking or business (which may also be a service provision change) where persons employed in the undertaking, business or part transferred ordinarily work outside the United Kingdom.

(5) An administrative reorganisation of public administrative authorities or the transfer of administrative functions between public administrative authorities is not a relevant transfer.

(6) A relevant transfer—

(a) may be effected by a series of two or more transactions; and

(b) may take place whether or not any property is transferred to the transferee by the transferor.

This is a much more complex, but much more all-encompassing definition. The intention underlying the definition is that the great majority of transfers should be considered relevant transfers, so that employees benefit from the protection of the Regulations. In order for a transfer to fall within the definition, there needs to be either:

- the transfer of an *economic entity* which *retains its identity*; or
- a *service provision change*.

Each must be considered in turn.

5.6.1.1 An economic entity which retains its identity

An 'economic entity' is defined in Regulation 3(2) as 'an organised grouping of resources which has as its objective the pursuing of an economic activity, whether that activity is central or ancillary'. 'Resources' need mean no more than 'manpower', i.e. an organised grouping of workers assigned to a particular economic activity; by r. 3(6)(b) there is no requirement for the grouping to have any tangible assets, such as premises or equipment. Since the activity need not be central to the operations of the organisation, the definition is clearly capable of covering the contracting out of ancillary services such as cleaning and catering, as well as the more obvious transfers of entire businesses, whatever their legal form.

The recent case of *Ceva Freight (UK) Ltd v Seawell Ltd* [2013] provides some guidance as to what will qualify as a relevant transfer under the 'economic entity' test. Mr Moffat was employed by Ceva Freight (UK) Ltd, a freight-forwarding and management-logistics company. Its workforce was organised into two groups, one dealing with 'inbound' goods, the other with 'outbound' goods.

Mr Moffat and seven others worked on the outbound division. Of these eight, five, including Mr Moffat, worked on the Seawell Ltd contract. Mr Moffat spent 100 per cent of his time working on the Seawell contract; other members of the outbound team spent 10–30 per cent of their time on this work.

In late 2009, Seawell decided to bring the work that had been carried out on its behalf by Ceva back in-house. Ceva asserted that Mr Moffat transferred to Seawell by operation of the 2006 Regulations. This was disputed by Seawell. Mr Moffat claimed unfair dismissal against both Ceva and Seawell.

There was no dispute as to whether the activities had transferred. Therefore, the key issue for the tribunal was to ascertain whether Mr Moffat had transferred pursuant to reg. 3(3). Was there an organised grouping of employees that had as its principal purpose the carrying out of the activities concerned on behalf of Seawell?

At first instance, the employment tribunal concluded that, as the definition of an 'organised grouping of employees' includes a single employee and Mr Moffat's role had the principal purpose of carrying out the relevant activities, he had transferred. Seawell was therefore liable for unfair dismissal.

On Seawell's appeal, the EAT overturned the tribunal's decision, finding that the tribunal had applied the wrong test. It decided that, although the Regulations specify that a single employee can be an organised grouping, this does not mean that an employee who spends 100 per cent of his time on work for a particular client necessarily constitutes an organised grouping. As arrangements were not deliberately made for Mr Moffat to work on the Seawell contract and he did not perform the entirety of the Seawell activities on his own, there was no organised grouping. As a result, he had not transferred to Seawell.

Ceva appealed to the Scottish Court of Session, which followed the EAT decision in *Eddie Stobart Ltd v Moreman* [2012] IRLR 356 EAT, and emphasised that the concept of an 'organised grouping' suggests an element of deliberate organisation of employees that has as its principal purpose the carrying-out of the relevant activities. In the *Ceva* case, the activities were organised by reference to the type of service being provided (inbound and outbound service), not according to the identity of the client. Although Mr Moffat spent all his time on the Seawell contract, other employees also worked on behalf of Seawell. As the outbound team in which Mr Moffat worked did not amount to an organised grouping that had as its principal purpose the carrying out of activities for Seawell – it was not organised as a 'Seawell team' doing wholly or mainly Seawell work – Mr Moffat's individual 100 per cent-time commitment to working on the Seawell contract was irrelevant.

In addressing Ceva's argument that an organised grouping can include a single employee, the Court of Session held that that definition was not relevant to this type of case, but to cases where the activities in question can be, and are, carried out by a single individual. The examples that the Court of Session gave were those of a cleaner working for one single client or a firm of solicitors providing a single solicitor to advise full-time a client such as an insurance claims handler. Indeed, the Court of Session noted that 'where the activities are carried out by a plurality of employees, the reference in the definition to a single employee does not in our view, warrant disaggregation of that group of employees'.

This case reinforces that when considering whether employees will transfer pursuant to the Regulations, it is not enough to consider the activities that they carry out. It is also imperative to consider whether the employees have been deliberately organised according to the requirements of the client. Where an individual spends all his time working for a particular client, it should not automatically be assumed that he or she will transfer to that client on a service provision change.

Under reg. 4(1) it is those employees who are *assigned to* the transferred economic entity who are transferred. What constitutes 'assigned to' is a question of fact for the Tribunal, and is to be decided on the basis, not on the terms of the contract, but of the employee's function (*Botzen v Rotterdamsche Droogdok Maatschaapij* [1985] ECR 519, ECJ). It is important to note that the test of whether an individual employee is assigned to the part of the business being transferred does not require him to work exclusively for that part (*Buchanan-Smith v Schleicher & Co International Ltd* [1996] ICR 547).

5.6.1.2 Service provision change

This category seems to have been created specifically to deal with 'outsourcing' of work by public bodies, though it applies to both public and private bodies and, to judge from *Ceva*, may overlap to some degree with the concept of 'economic entity'. The Regulations state specifically that a service provision change embraces not only the original contracting-out of a service, but a change of contractor and contracting back in at the end of a period of contracting out.

The issue of whether a change in contractors constituted a service provision change within the Regulations was considered in *Clearsprings Management v Ankers* [2009] UKEAT/0054/08. This decision shows that there may not be a relevant transfer if a service provision is transferred to a number of different employers. In 2000 the National Asylum Seekers Service awarded five-year contracts to a number of organisations to provide advice services for asylum seekers on a regional basis. Clearsprings was one of four organisations contracted to provide advice services in the North-West. As the 5-year term expired, a new tendering exercise took place. Clearsprings was not awarded a further contract, and its functions were divided between the other three service providers. Clearsprings's employees were allocated randomly between those three.

The EAT held that there was a service provision change. However, they followed *Kimberley Group Housing v Hambley* [2008] ICR 1030 in concluding that the transfer fell outside the Regulations, on the basis that, although a transfer could fall within the Regulations where a service formerly provided by one organisation was split between several, there could be instances where the service became so fragmented that there could not be a 'relevant transfer'. A factor that influenced the EAT was that there was no apparent pattern in allocating the asylum seekers between the organisations.

5.6.2 Protection for employees under the 2006 Regulations

Despite the issues thrown up by cases such as *Ceva* and *Clearsprings*, it is relatively rarely that the applicability of the Regulations will be challenged in a transfer situation. On the basis that the great majority of transfers will be relevant transfers, so that the employees enjoy the protection accorded by the Regulations, we must consider the nature and extent of that protection.

Where there is a relevant transfer:

- those employed by the transferor at the time of the transfer automatically transfer to the employment of the transferee with no break in their continuity of employment and with the terms and conditions of their employment intact. Collective agreements are also transferred intact, as is trade union recognition. However, this protection only applies to employees who were transferred at the time of the transfer, not to those who may have joined the transferee since.
- any dismissal of an employee because of the transfer or for 'a reason connected with the transfer' is automatically unfair, unless the employer can establish an 'economic, technical or organisational reason entailing changes in the workforce' ('ETO reason').
- all outstanding liabilities of the transferor towards the employees transfer to the transferee, along with all future liabilities.
- if the transferee wishes to alter the terms and conditions of employment of the transferred employees, he must demonstrate an ETO reason for doing so, except in the case of pension provision (see below for details).

Since transfer is automatic, the individual employee need do nothing. What, however, is the individual employee's position if he does not wish to be transferred? Given that the employee's terms and conditions of employment are preserved where there is a relevant transfer, an outright refusal to transfer is likely to be a rare event.

Until 1993, a relevant transfer resulted in the automatic transfer of *all* the employees concerned from the transferor to the transferee. However, reg. 4(7) now provides that if the employee objects to the transfer *before the transfer takes effect* the contract terminates without a dismissal. This provision is hardly to the employee's benefit as he is not then entitled to claim unfair dismissal or to receive a redundancy payment.

'Objects' is construed narrowly, to mean an active refusal to be transferred, rather than mere reluctance. The employee in *Hay v George Hanson (Building Contractors) Ltd* [1996] ICR 427 was a joiner working for a local council which contracted out work to various building contractors. Mr Hay first attempted to find other work with the council, then tried to negotiate a redundancy package with the council after the transfer had taken effect. The council sought to argue that he had objected to the transfer within what is now reg. 4(7), and, consequently, that his contract had terminated without a dismissal. The EAT found in favour of the employee, concluding that although he had sought to avoid being transferred, he had not refused as such, so that reg. 4(7) did not apply. In the unreported case of *Ladies Health and Fitness Clubs Ltd v Eastmond* the EAT took a similar approach, though they referred back to the Tribunal the issue of whether the claimants' objections to the transfer and petition against the transfer to a particular company were sufficient to constitute a refusal to transfer. However, it would seem that a refusal may be express or implied by conduct. Further, the EAT ruled that neither transferor nor transferee is under any duty to warn the employee concerned of the consequences of any refusal to transfer. This being so, an employee who is unhappy about any transfer would be well-advised to accept it for the time being and start looking for another job!

5.6.2.1 Protection against dismissal

Unless the employer can establish an ETO reason entailing changes in the workforce, any dismissal of an employee who is protected by the Regulations by reason of the transfer itself, or a reason connected with the transfer, is automatically unfair. If an ETO reason applies, neither the transferor nor transferee may dismiss with impunity, since the ordinary law of unfair dismissal will still apply. As yet there is no case law on the difference, if any, between an ETO reason and a potentially fair reason for dismissal under ERA 1996 s. 98. Even if the two coincide, the transferee must demonstrate that he (or the transferor) acted reasonably in dismissing the individual employees for that reason, and that a fair procedure was followed. 'Fair procedure' in such circumstances, will doubtless include discussion with trade unions or other employee representatives where there is no recognised trade union.

A dismissal falling within reg. 7 is effective – i.e. the employee is dismissed (*Litster v Forth Dry Dock & Engineering Co. Ltd* [1989] ICR 341). It is not a nullity. However, the dismissed employee becomes entitled to compensation.

Not infrequently, the transferor disposes of the business or part of the business because it is not profitable or insufficiently profitable. The transferee believes he can 'turn the business around' by reducing its manpower and making other changes, or by combining it with his existing operations and, again, reducing its manpower. Can the employer do this without the dismissals being deemed to be 'for a reason connected with the transfer' and thus automatically unfair?

The Regulations provide that a dismissal connected with the transfer will not be automatically unfair if the employer can show that it is for an 'economic, technical or organisational reason entailing changes in the workforce' (although it could still be 'ordinarily' unfair). What does this mean? Neither the Regulations nor the underlying Directive define economic, technical or organisational ('ETO') reasons, although some 1981 guidance issued by the Thatcher government in respect of the privatisation of nationalised industries gave the following examples:

- An economic reason might apply where demand for the employer's product has fallen to such an extent that profitability could not be sustained unless staff were dismissed.
- A technical reason might apply where the transferee intends to use new technology and not all the transferred staff have the necessary skills.
- An organisational reason might apply where the transferee operates at a different site from the transferor and it is not practicable to relocate all the transferred staff.

Case law shows that the 'ETO' reason must be the direct cause of the dismissal for the employer to be able to rely on it in order to avoid a finding of automatic unfair dismissal. In *Berriman v Delabole Slate* [1985] ICR 546 the connection was indirect in that the employee resigned and claimed constructive dismissal after the transferee altered the terms and conditions of the transferred employees to bring them into line with those of his existing employees. The Court of Appeal held that the dismissal was not for an ETO reason and was therefore automatically unfair.

On that basis, if the transferee makes changes to terms and conditions in order to make the business profitable, as is frequently the case, and employees then resign and claim constructive dismissal, the employer cannot rely on the protection of the Regulations and the dismissals will be automatically unfair, even though, if there were no transfer, the employer might well be able to rely on 'some other substantial reason' under the ordinary law of unfair dismissal. Even if the employer can demonstrate an ETO reason for the dismissals, the ordinary law of unfair dismissal will still apply. In particular, if the ETO reason amounts to redundancy, the dismissed employees will be entitled to redundancy payments based on the length of their service with both transferor and transferee.

Under the Regulations, it is the transferee who is liable for dismissals, irrespective of whether they were carried out by the transferor or transferee.

5.6.2.2 Changes to contractual terms following the transfer

This is a problem area for two reasons:

- Although the Regulations allow the employer to make contractual changes where an ETO reason applies, there is no case law on what constitutes an ETO reason for this purpose.
- The protection of the Regulations applies in relation to contractual changes arising from the transfer or for a reason connected with the transfer. Logically, changes will no longer be for these reasons once a certain time has passed after the transfer, but there is no case law setting out the minimum time which must elapse for this purpose.

❖ THINKING POINT

Should there be a time limit after which the employer may make changes in the terms and conditions of the transferred employees? We may draw a comparison with the situation where an employee is moved to a different job, at a lower salary, in the organisation as an alternative to redundancy, but retains his previous salary for a limited period.

Under reg. 4(4)–(5), a variation in the employee's contract is void if either:

a) the reason for it is the transfer itself; or
b) the reason is connected with the transfer and is not an ETO reason entailing changes in the workforce.

However, the employer and employee may agree a variation:

a) for an ETO reason; or
b) for a reason unconnected with the transfer.

The formula seems strange, as, if the parties agree to a variation, why should this only be effective if an ETO reason applies or if the reason is unconnected with the transfer?

If some substantial change is made to the employee's working conditions which is to the employee's *material detriment*, then reg. 4(9) preserves his right to resign and claim constructive dismissal. Inevitably, this raises issues of what is a substantial change and when is it to the employee's detriment.

Importantly, a change which is within the employee's existing contract may found a claim based on constructive dismissal. That was the case in *Barnetts Solicitors v Royden* [2009] EAT. Twenty-three employees working at the Birkenhead office of a firm of solicitors with offices in Liverpool resigned *en masse* rather than work for transferees who wished them to work at offices in Southport, Manchester or Bradford, relying on an existing mobility clause in their contracts. In the case of the employees required to move to Southport, it was held that there was a substantial change in working conditions which was to the employees' material detriment because of the increased cost of travelling. The journey from Birkenhead to Southport by road is approximately 40 minutes and involves the Mersey Tunnel and going through the centre of Liverpool (about one hour by train, including a change). Importantly, the test is a practical one, not a contractual one, so that the employees could claim constructive dismissal despite a mobility clause. On the basis of *Berriman*, the employer could not then rely on an ETO reason to avoid a finding of automatic unfair dismissal.

Such decisions beg the question of how much time must elapse before the transferee may alter the terms and conditions of transferred employees (perhaps to bring them into line with the rest of his workforce, or making changes affecting the entire workforce), without falling foul of the Regulations. Perhaps inevitably, the position is unclear. So far, case law has produced nothing specific on this issue. In *British Fuels v Baxendale* [1998] IRLR 706, Lord Slynn said *obiter* that there was nothing in what is now reg. 4 to restrict its effect to the time of the transfer itself. He accepted that there would come a time when there would no longer be a link between the transfer and a variation, but went on to say that if a case turned on that point he would refer the matter to the ECJ.

Clearly this creates a difficulty for the transferee, who may have very good reasons for wishing to change the transferred employees' terms and conditions, particularly if he wishes to avoid difficulties between the transferred employees and his original employees, who may well be on different and less favourable terms – a perfect recipe for tensions in the workplace! It also creates difficulties for solicitors advising the employer. The best which can be suggested is that the transferee should endeavour to reach agreement with the employees about any variation, and otherwise hope that those who do resign and claim constructive dismissal on the basis of a variation are few in number, so that the cost of any unfair dismissal compensation is outweighed by the benefits accruing from the changes.

Case law under the Equal Pay Act established that the preservation of higher pay rates arising from a TUPE transport could be relied on as a defence in an equal pay claim. In *Nelson v Carillion Services Ltd* [2003] IRLR 428, CA, Carillion had taken over a contract to provide specified services at Chelsea and Westminster Hospital with effect from 1 April 1997. By the Regulations, Carillion was under a duty to maintain the existing pay scales and conditions of employment of some 300 transferred employees. These included six waiters in the private wing of the hospital, four male and two female, who were paid £5.78 per hour, received a food allowance of £2.50 per day and were entitled to double time on bank holidays. Some 15 months later, Carillion took on two more waiters, one the Applicant, who were paid £5.00 per hour (above the National Minimum Wage then applicable) and were not entitled either to the food allowance or double time on bank holidays. These were Carillion's standard terms and conditions. By 2000 the Applicant's pay had risen to £5.22 per hour and that of Mr d'Silva, the only remaining transferee, and whom she chose as comparator, to £6.38 per hour. It was accepted that the two were doing like work, but Carillion argued that the TUPE requirements constituted a genuine material difference.

The Applicant alleged indirect discrimination, following *Enderby*, on the basis that of the five men employed, four (80 per cent) could comply with the condition of being covered by TUPE, as against two out of three women (66.7 per cent). Thus, a considerably smaller proportion of women than men could comply. The Tribunal ruled that the pool – eight people – was too small to be statistically reliable. The EAT upheld their decision.

The Applicant then argued before the Court of Appeal that the Tribunal had erred in placing the burden of proof of establishing indirect discrimination on her. Following *Enderby*, the court stated that the burden of proving sex discrimination lay initially on the employee. To shift the burden to the employer, the employee must establish that the measure at issue had, in practice, an adverse impact on substantially more members of one sex than the other, or, where the system lacked transparency, must establish, in relation to a relatively large group of employees, that average pay for women was lower than for men. It was therefore for the Applicant to establish 'an appreciable difference in pay' by 'significant statistics', after which the burden of proof shifted to the employer to show that the difference was not based on sex. SDA s. 63A, recently introduced and dealing with a change in the burden of proof, did not change that, nor was the position different when the claim involved the Equal Pay Act. It was not sufficient for the employee merely to advance 'a credible suggestion' that there was a disparate impact between the sexes. Since the Tribunal had found as a fact that the pool was too small to be statistically reliable, the Claimant had not discharged the burden of proof, and the maintenance of the transferred employees' pay and conditions under TUPE could be relied on as a defence to an equal pay claim. That being said, had indirect discrimination arisen, the employer would have had to demonstrate objective justification for maintaining the pay differential. It may then be argued that an employer should be able to rely on his duty under TUPE for this purpose, as otherwise he will be between the Devil and the deep blue sea of two incompatible pieces of legislation.

5.6.2.3 Pension provision and TUPE

All employees whose continuity of employment is preserved by a relevant transfer are transferred with their terms and conditions of employment unchanged, except for pension entitlements.

Reg. 10 has the effect of excluding almost anything to do with occupational pensions from the automatic transfer provisions, though it does not cover early retirement schemes used as alternatives to redundancy. Given the 'pensions time bomb' arising from the vast increase in life expectation since most occupational pension schemes were set up, it is not surprising that they are exempted from the general provisions of the Regulations, as the government sought to balance the protection of employees and the economic burden on employers.

Some protection for pension rights is given by the Transfer of Employment (Pension Protection) Regulations 2005. Where employees who are transferred were members of an occupational pension scheme before the transfer, the transferee is under a duty to provide them with *a* pension scheme. However, this scheme need not be equivalent to the transferor's scheme, as the transferee is free to choose the form of the scheme, provided it meets certain requirements set out in the Pensions Act 2004 ss. 257–258. Thus, the transferee could replace a final salary scheme with a much less favourable 'money purchase' scheme, and/or may reduce the employer's contributions to the scheme, although where the transferor was making contributions to an occupational scheme or a stakeholder scheme the 2004 Act prevents the transferee from abandoning employer's contributions altogether. 2006 Regulations reg. 10(4) creates an exception to the general principle that transferred employees may claim constructive dismissal on the basis of 'substantial' contractual changes in that no claim for constructive dismissal may lie when the change at issue involves pension rights.

5.7 Further reading

Kastrinou, Shah & Gough, 'Corporate rescue in the UK and the effect of the TUPE' (2011) 32(5) *Company Lawyer* 131.

Omambala & Motraghi, 'The implications of Brexit for TUPE in the area of public procurement' (2017) 1 *Public Procurement Law Review* 62.

Strathdee, '*TUPE and pensions auto-enrolment – mix and match, or no change? (Legislative Comment)*' (2014) 119(Feb) *Employment Law Bulletin* 6.

Wynn-Evans, 'TUPE and mothballs: Crystal Palace FC Limited and Another v Kavanagh and Others (Case Comment)' (2014) 43(2) *Industrial Law Journal* 185.

Chapter 6

Part-time and fixed-term employees

Chapter contents

6.1 Overview

This chapter deals with the specific protection which legislation provides for employees on part-time or fixed-term contracts. Unlike most areas of employment law, this protection derives entirely from legislation, and is in turn derives from EU Law.

6.2 Introduction

The traditional approach to employment law assumes that employees work full-time – seven to eight hours per day over a five-day working week, possibly with overtime, and are employed on 'permanent' contracts, which have no inbuilt termination date and last until one or other party chooses to give notice.

A considerable proportion of employees, however, work part-time under a variety of contractual arrangements, or on contracts stated at the outset to last for fixed terms. In some cases, an employee's contract may be both part-time *and* for a fixed term.

Increasingly, professional people of both sexes, on good salaries, most obviously doctors, choose to work part-time for purposes of work-life balance. However, part-time work is often regarded as mainly an option for women with domestic commitments, and is frequently low-status and badly paid.

Fixed-term contracts, whether full-time or part-time, tend to be found in two widely differing circumstances:

- Where funding for a particular project comes from a source external to the employer, and is only guaranteed for a set period. This is often the case for academics doing post-doctoral research at an early stage in their careers.
- High-status employees in posts such as Chief Constables and university vice-chancellors are often appointed for five-year fixed-terms, usually without provision for the employer to give notice.

Specific legal protection for part-time and fixed-term employees is derived from two EU Directives, and is much more limited than that available under the Equality Act. In particular, the legislation only protects against direct discrimination. Therefore, a part-time employee cannot argue that a requirement for particular experience in order to go on a training course is indirectly discriminatory on the grounds that it would be more difficult for part-timers to gain; he would only be able to bring a claim if the employer required *full-time* experience. Further, the employer has a defence of justification – unusual in relation to direct discrimination. The expression used in the legislation is 'justified on objective grounds', whereas the Equality Act uses 'a proportionate means of achieving a legitimate aim'. It remains to be seen whether the same test will be applied in practice.

Unlike discrimination under the Equality Act, the claimant is also not entitled to compensation for injury to feelings, but only in respect of actual financial loss. It should be noted, however, that many part-time or fixed-term employees will also be able to rely on protected characteristics under the Equality Act.

6.3 Protection for part-time employees

This is derived from the Part-Time Workers (Prevention of Less Favourable Treatment) Regulations 2000 (SI 2000/1551), which implement the EU Part-time Work Directive 97/81/EC.

Reg. 2 defines full-time and part-time workers as follows:

(1) A worker is a full-time worker for the purpose of these Regulations if he is paid wholly or in part by reference to the time he works and, having regard to the custom and practice of the employer in relation to workers employed by the worker's employer under the same type of contract, is identifiable as a full-time worker.
(2) A worker is a part-time worker for the purpose of these Regulations if he is paid wholly or in part by reference to the time he works and, having regard to the custom and practice of the employer in relation to workers employed by the worker's employer under the same type of contract, is not identifiable as a full-time worker.

Therefore, a part-time worker is a person who is not a full-time worker. By regs. 3–4 the protection accorded by the Regulations to part-time workers is accorded to those who move from full-time to part-time work.

Reg. 5 then sets out the protection accorded to part-time workers.

(1) A part-time worker has the right not to be treated by his employer less favourably than the employer treats a comparable full-time worker—
   a. as regards the terms of his contract; or
   b. by being subjected to any other detriment by any act, or deliberate failure to act, of his employer.
(2) The right conferred by paragraph (1) applies only if—
   a. the treatment is on the grounds that the worker is a part-time worker, and
   b. the treatment is not justified on objective grounds.
(3) In determining whether a part-time worker has been treated less favourably than a comparable full-time worker the pro rata principle shall be applied unless it is inappropriate.
(4) A part-time worker paid at a lower rate for overtime worked by him in a period than a comparable full-time worker is or would be paid for overtime worked by him in the same period shall not, for that reason, be regarded as treated less favourably than the comparable full-time worker where, or to the extent that, the total number of hours worked by the part-time worker in the period, including overtime, does not exceed the number of hours the comparable full-time worker is required to work in the period, disregarding absences from work and overtime.

In order to establish less favourable treatment, reg. 5 requires a comparison between the treatment of the part-time employee and a comparable full-time worker, as defined in reg. 2(4):

(5) A full-time worker is a comparable full-time worker in relation to a part-time worker if, at the time when the treatment that is alleged to be less favourable to the part-time worker takes place—
   (a) both workers are—
      (i) employed by the same employer under the same type of contract, and
      (ii) engaged in the same or broadly similar work having regard, where relevant, to whether they have a similar level of qualification, skills and experience; and
   (b) the full-time worker works or is based at the same establishment as the part-time worker or, where there is no full-time worker working or based at that establishment who satisfies the requirements of sub-paragraph (a), works or is based at a different establishment and satisfies those requirements.

This definition is similar to that of a comparator for equal pay purposes under the Equality Act. In particular, it is not possible to use a hypothetical comparator. The same issue thus arises as in equal pay claims, that in a workplace where the great majority of workers are part-time (often low-paid women) it may be impossible for a potential claimant to find a comparable full-time worker.

Early case law under these provisions largely concerned access to occupational pension schemes, which were previously often restricted to full-timers. This battle has now been won, in part through changes to pension legislation, and the volume of cases under the Regulations has been much reduced.

A good example is *Matthews v Kent & Medway Towns Fire Authority* [2006] UKHL 8, HL, although the final conclusion is not reported, as the case was simply referred back to the original Tribunal. This was a case brought by retained firefighters, who undergo similar training to full-time firefighters and make themselves available to be called out in emergencies in a similar fashion to lifeboat crews, with the difference that retained firefighters are paid. In many rural areas, there is insufficient work to justify employing full-time firefighters, and stations are therefore manned by retained firefighters. The issue was whether they were entitled to join the pension scheme provided for full-time firefighters. Since a pension is in law a species of pay, the question for the courts was whether they were 'engaged in the same or broadly similar work' and so entitled to the same pay on a pro rata basis.

The issues were:

(1) whether the retained firefighters were employed under the same type of contract as their chosen full-time comparators within the meaning of reg. 2(3) and reg. 2(4)(a)(i) of the Regulations, and
(2) if they were, whether the retained and full-time firefighters were engaged in the same or broadly similar work, having regard to whether they had a similar level of qualification, skill and experience within the meaning of reg. 2(4)(a)(ii). The Employment Tribunal, the Employment Appeal Tribunal found against them on both questions and the Court of Appeal found against them on the second question.

The House of Lords held on a 3:2 majority:

(1) The wording of reg. 2(4)(a)(ii) identified the matters to be inquired into. The Tribunal had to look at the work that both the full-time worker and the part-time worker were engaged in and ask whether it was the same work or was broadly similar. That question had to be directed to the *whole of the work* that the two kinds of worker were actually engaged in. The Tribunal had failed to ask itself whether the differing levels of skills, qualifications and experience showed that they were each contributing something different to that work. The Tribunal treated the fact that there were differences in the levels of skills and experience as an additional factor leading to the conclusion that comparability could not be established, without assessing the extent to which those differences affected the work that the two different kinds of worker were actually engaged in. That defect in its reasoning amounted to a misdirection on a point of law.
(2) The Tribunal had not given sufficient weight to the extent to which the work on which both groups of firefighters were engaged *was* the same work. The Tribunal's conclusion that the job of the full-time firefighter was a fuller, wider, job than that of the retained firefighter was not the end of the exercise. It still had to address the question posed by the statute which was whether, notwithstanding the fact that the job of the full-time firefighter was a fuller and wider job, the work on which both groups were engaged could nevertheless be described as broadly similar. Accordingly, it was not open to the Tribunal to conclude that the work of the full

time firefighter was not comparable with that of the retained firefighter. The case should be remitted to the Tribunal for reconsideration of whether the retained and full-time firefighters were engaged in the same or broadly similar work.

Otherwise, the main issue in decided case law relates to bank holidays, and whether a part-time worker who would not be required to work on the day of a bank holiday in any event, because he does not work on Mondays, is nevertheless entitled to equivalent time off. In *McMenemy v Business Capita Services Ltd* ([2007] IRLR 400) an employee who worked on Wednesdays, Thursdays and Fridays argued that he had been less favourably treated than his comparator because he had not been given time off in lieu of a bank holiday. The Inner House of the Court of Session concluded that he had not been less favourably treated because of his part-time status. The reason for the treatment was the fact he did not work on Mondays, and a full-time employee whose working week did not include Mondays would have been treated in exactly the same fashion. Nevertheless, the Chartered Institute of Personnel and Development does recommend that part-time employees be given equivalent time off.

6.4 Protection for fixed-term employees

As in the case of part-time employees, protection for employees on fixed-term contracts is available under Regulations which implement an EU Directive. The Fixed-Term Employees (Prevention of Less Favourable Treatment) Regulations 2002 (SI 2002/2034) give effect to the Fixed-Term Work Directive 1999 (99/70/EC). Again, the Regulations prohibit direct discrimination only, and do not provide for compensation in respect of injury to feelings. However, the Regulations (reg. 8) do provide that a person who works continuously for four years or more on a series of fixed-term contracts – at least two such contracts – is to be treated in law as a permanent employee with the same contractual terms. This is important for employees such as academics, who may frequently be employed for lengthy periods under successive fixed-term contracts. Reg. 8 does provide a defence for the employer of objective justification, but there is currently no case law to demonstrate how this is applied. Reg. 4(1) does provide explicitly that the defence is made out if the fixed-term employee's overall contractual terms are 'at least as favourable' as those of the comparator. This is a clear difference from the equal pay provisions of the Equality Act, where the comparison must be done on a term-by-term basis, leading at times to the claimant achieving a markedly more favourable pay package than the comparator.

Like the Part-Time Regulations, the Fixed-Term Employees Regulations make it unlawful to treat a fixed-term employee less favourably than a comparable permanent employee except when such treatment is objectively justified.

3.—

(1) A fixed-term employee has the right not to be treated by his employer less favourably than the employer treats a comparable permanent employee—
  (a) as regards the terms of his contract; or
  (b) by being subjected to any other detriment by any act, or deliberate failure to act, of his employer.

(2) Subject to paragraphs (3) and (4), the right conferred by paragraph (1) includes in particular the right of the fixed-term employee in question not to be treated less favourably than the employer treats a comparable permanent employee in relation to—
  (a) any period of service qualification relating to any particular condition of service,
  (b) the opportunity to receive training, or
  (c) the opportunity to secure any permanent position in the establishment.

(3) The right conferred by paragraph (1) applies only if—
  (a) the treatment is on the ground that the employee is a fixed-term employee, and
  (b) the treatment is not justified on objective grounds.
(4) Paragraph (3)(b) is subject to regulation 4.
(5) In determining whether a fixed-term employee has been treated less favourably than a comparable permanent employee, the pro rata principle shall be applied unless it is inappropriate.
(6) In order to ensure that an employee is able to exercise the right conferred by paragraph (1) as described in paragraph (2)(c) the employee has the right to be informed by his employer of available vacancies in the establishment.
(7) For the purposes of paragraph (6) an employee is 'informed by his employer' only if the vacancy is contained in an advertisement which the employee has a reasonable opportunity of reading in the course of his employment or the employee is given reasonable notification of the vacancy in some other way.

A comparable permanent employee is then defined in reg. 2:

(1) For the purposes of these Regulations, an employee is a comparable permanent employee in relation to a fixed-term employee if, at the time when the treatment that is alleged to be less favourable to the fixed-term employee takes place,
  (a) both employees are—
    (i) employed by the same employer, and
    (ii) engaged in the same or broadly similar work having regard, where relevant, to whether they have a similar level of qualification and skills; and
  (b) the permanent employee works or is based at the same establishment as the fixed-term employee or, where there is no comparable permanent employee working or based at that establishment who satisfies the requirements of sub-paragraph (a), works or is based at a different establishment and satisfies those requirements.
(2) For the purposes of paragraph (1), an employee is not a comparable permanent employee if his employment has ceased.

Therefore, the fixed-term employee must be employed at the same time as the comparator, and cannot rely on a hypothetical comparator.

As is the case with the Part-Time Workers Regulations, there is currently very little reported case law to demonstrate the way in which these provisions are applied. *Department for Work and Pensions v Webley* [2004] EWCA Civ 1745 establishes on a very literal reading of the Regulations that a dismissal is not less favourable treatment in a situation where the employer had adopted a practice of dismissing temporary employees after 51 weeks of employment, on the basis that their fixed-terms had expired, in order to prevent them from gaining sufficient continuity to claim unfair dismissal (at the time one year). It should be noted that under ERA s. 95(1)(b) the expiry and non-renewal of a fixed-term contract constitutes a dismissal for the purposes of claiming unfair dismissal or a redundancy payment. However, this does not assist the employee who is dismissed in this fashion before achieving the requisite continuity of employment. Clearly this is a loophole capable of abuse by unscrupulous employers.

❖ THINKING POINT

Helen is working as an office administrator on a one-year fixed-term contract to cover a permanent employee's absence on maternity leave. Three months before the end of the fixed-term, she applies to go on a week's advanced course on Microsoft Excel. Her application is rejected on the grounds that the employer will not be able to recoup the cost via the benefit of her increased skills before the fixed-term expires.

Can the employer argue that this decision is justified on objective grounds? Would your answer be any different if there was a strong possibility of Helen's contract being extended for a further three months?

❖ THINKING POINT

Do you think that this protection for part-time and fixed-term employees is likely to disappear as a result of Brexit?

6.5 Further reading

Busby, 'The Part-Time Workers (Prevention of Less Favourable Treatment) Regulations 2000: righting a wrong or out of proportion?' (2001) Jul *Journal of Business Law* 344.

Koukiadaki, 'Case law developments in the area of fixed-term work' (2009) 38(1) *Industrial Law Journal* 89.

McColgan, 'The Fixed-Term Employees (Prevention of Less Favourable Treatment) Regulations 2002: fiddling while Rome burns?' (2003) 32(3) *Industrial Law Journal* 194.

Meves, 'Fixed-term employees: myths and misunderstandings' (2011) 18(3) *Employment Lawyers Association Briefing* 6.

Chapter 7

Unfair dismissal 1

Chapter contents

7.1 Overview

This chapter deals with the claimant's eligibility to claim unfair dismissal – what he must prove in order to bring his claim. It also looks at the procedure involved, in particularly the time limit for making a claim.

A claim of unfair dismissal is brought in the Employment Tribunal by the former employee. Essentially, any claim involves two stages:

1. The burden is on the claimant to comply with the necessary procedural requirements and to prove the following eligibility criteria if in issue:
   - status as employee;
   - completion of two years' continuous employment ending with the effective date of termination of the contract;
   - fact of dismissal;
   - not an 'excluded employee'.
2. The employer must then show:
   - dismissal was for a potentially fair reason;
   - dismissal was reasonable in the circumstances;
   - a fair procedure was followed in dismissing the claimant.

7.2 Introduction

The concept of unfair dismissal was introduced into UK law by the Industrial Relations Act 1971, primarily as a means of reducing the high incidence of strikes which was a feature of that era. The provisions relating to unfair dismissal were the only parts of the 1971 Act to survive when the Labour Party returned to power in 1974. The present statutory provisions are found in the Employment Rights Act 1996.

In the late 1960s there were numerous strikes, particularly in major industries and public services. A considerable proportion were 'wildcat' strikes, called without warning by shop stewards in a particular workplace as a protest dismissals, particularly summary dismissals. The concept of unfair dismissal was created in order to provide employees with a realistic form of redress against dismissal and so reduce the incidence of wildcat strikes.

The common law has always provided inadequate remedies in respect of dismissals – if the employer complies with the relevant notice provisions in the contract, the employee has no protection against arbitrary dismissal. Unfair dismissal was intended to give protection against the harshness of the common law. However, the rights available in unfair dismissal only apply to those who satisfy the qualifying criteria to make a claim. In essence, this means that all employees have the minimal protection of the common law and a proportion of employees have the additional protection of statutory unfair dismissal provisions.

Created by statute, unfair dismissal bears no relation to a common-law breach of contract claim and thus a dismissal may be *lawful*, in that the contract has been complied with, but still *unfair*. Conversely, a dismissal may be unlawful, in that a breach of contract has occurred, but not unfair according to the statute – *Farrant v The Woodroffe School* is an example of the latter.

Unfair dismissal does not look for breach of contract on the part of the employer but breach of the statute. The remedies which lie against the employer are not remedies which rely on a contractual claim, but rather recognise that the dismissed employee has a property right in his job. This means that the tribunal should consider the remedies available under the statute in the following order:

- reinstatement (giving the employee back his job);
- re-engagement (re-employing him in a comparable alternative job);
- financial compensation, based on his age, length of service and, to some extent, actual loss.

It has already been noted that not all workers can rely on the protection of the statute.

- Only employees are protected, not the self-employed. ERA s. 230(1) defines an employee as an individual who works under a contract of employment, and a contract of employment as a contract of service or apprenticeship, whether express or implied, oral or in writing. Effectively, this definition follows the common law.
- Employees must generally have been continuously employed for two years prior to dismissal in order to qualify for statutory protection, although there are certain exceptions where no continuity is required (automatic unfair dismissal).
- The decision in *R v Secretary of State for Employment ex p EOC* [1994] 1 All ER 910 led to the introduction of the Employment Protection (Part-Time Employees) Regulations 1995, which abolished any distinction between full-time and part-time employees based on hours of work, so that all employees qualified for protection after the same period of continuous employment.
- Certain classes of employee are excluded from the legislation. Employees of the Crown are probably the most numerous group, since this includes police and civil servants.
- If the employee shows that he has the required continuity and that he is not an excluded employee, he must then show that he has been dismissed. He must also present his claim to the tribunal within three months of the effective date of termination of his employment, unless the tribunal feels that it was not reasonably practicable for him to present his claim within that period (ERA s. 111(2)).

Once the employee has surmounted these hurdles, the issues are as follows:

- whether the reason for dismissal falls within one of the potentially fair reasons set out in the statute;
- whether the employer acted fairly in dismissing for that reason – did the employer act reasonably in the way he handled the dismissal, and was dismissal an appropriate sanction in all the circumstances?

Any unfair dismissal case therefore divides itself into the following elements:

- Has the employee the required continuity?
- Is the employee a member of a class excluded from the statute?
- Has the employee been dismissed?
- Has the employer a potentially fair reason for dismissing the employee?
- Was the decision to dismiss a reasonable one in all the circumstances?
- Did the employer follow a fair procedure in the events leading to the dismissal?

7.3 Continuity of employment

At present many employment protection rights require a period of 'continuous employment' before the right may be claimed. In most cases of unfair dismissal, the minimum period is two years.

Continuity of employment is defined in ERA ss. 212–218. The aim of the statutory provisions is to exclude the common-law rule that a change of terms means a new contract comes into force.

The effect of such a rule would be that every time the employee received a pay rise, for example, a new contract would come into being and the old contract cease to exist. Equally, if a person moved to a different job within the same organisation, the old contract would come to an end. S. 212(1) therefore bases eligibility on the length of *employment* with a particular employer rather than the length of the *contract*.

This was made clear in *Wood v York City Council* [1978] IRLR 228, where the employee had a variety of jobs within the City Council for three years and then took up a post with the Council's York Festival office. When he was made redundant after a further year, it was held that he had sufficient continuity to claim redundancy pay.

If there is a break in employment of less than a week, then, by virtue of ERA s. 212, there is no loss of continuity. In *Carrington v Harwich Dock Co. Ltd.* ([1998] *The Times* 31 August) an employee resigned from his employment on Friday 5 April 1996 and was re-employed by the same employer from the following Monday, 8 April, in the next financial year. This was done by agreement with the employer in order that a previous period of high earnings was factored into his pension entitlement. On 19 August 1996, he was dismissed.

ERA 1996 s. 212 provides:

> (1) Any *week* during the whole or part of which an employee's relations are governed by a contract of employment counts in computing the employee's period of [continuous] employment.

The court concluded that a week ended on a Saturday and that employment was presumed continuous unless the contrary was established. It was not generally possible to contract out of continuous employment. Since he was employed in two successive weeks, the employee was held to have been continuously employed.

The situation in *Welton v Deluxe Retail Ltd (t/a Madhouse)* ([2012] UKEAT 0266_12_2111) was more complicated and the gap was longer. Mr Welton worked at a store in Sheffield that closed down, and his employment was terminated on 23 February 2010. The working week ended on 27 February 2010. On 1 March, during what would have been his next working week, he agreed to accept employment with the same employer in Blackpool, with the first working day falling in the following week, on 8 March 2010. A few months later, his employment terminated. He brought a claim for unfair dismissal.

At a pre-hearing review, the employment judge had to determine whether Mr Welton had sufficient continuity of service to bring the unfair dismissal claim. If his employment in Blackpool was continuous with his employment in Sheffield, he had sufficient service to bring the claim; if his employment was interrupted, he did not have sufficient continuity of service. The judge found there was no continuity of employment.

Mr Welton appealed to the Employment Appeal Tribunal (EAT). Three points arose:

- Is an agreement made in one week to start work the following week a contract of employment that, under part XIV of the Employments Right Act 1996, means that there is no break in continuity because a contract of employment is deemed to have been in place for the whole of the week of dismissal and the week of re-engagement?
- Alternatively, was there a temporary cessation of work (see below) to which s. 212 of the Employment Rights Act 1996 applied to preserve continuity?
- Finally, was the judge right to regard an 'arrangement' in s. 212(3) of the Employment Rights Act 1996 (which preserves continuity during any period in which the employee is absent, but by arrangement or custom is regarded as continuing in employment), as one that cannot be made retrospectively? There was conflicting EAT authority on this point.

The EAT concluded:

- there was a contract of employment in place from 1 March, notwithstanding that work had yet to be performed under it;
- the absence was on account of a cessation of work, and could be regarded only as temporary;
- however, on the third issue, the employment judge was right that an arrangement could not be entered retrospectively so as to confer continuity.

On that basis, any week in which there is a contract of employment governing the relationship will count towards the period of continuous employment, even if it was only for one of the days of that week. A week is defined as 'a week ending with Saturday'.

If an employee terminates his or her employment on a Monday and recommences the following Tuesday, there has not been a gap of the requisite 'week ending with Saturday' to break continuity. It is necessary to consider carefully whether there was any interval lasting from Sunday to Saturday that did not count towards continuous employment. A contract of employment can exist even where there is no performance.

In this case, the EAT held that an employee's service under two contracts of employment with the same employer was continuous, even though he did not start work under the second contract until more than a week after the end of the first contract. The EAT found that the second contract of employment had been created when the employee accepted the job offer, which meant that there was not a week's gap between the two contracts.

In the particular circumstances of this case, continuity of employment was preserved where a new contract was entered into within the same working week that the previous contract terminated, even where the employee did not commence working under the new contract until a later date.

Continuity starts when the contractual employment starts, not the actual employment (*General of the Salvation Army v Dewsbury* ([1984] IRLR 222)), and will normally continue until employment comes to an end. This is important because employment with another organisation can on occasion be counted into continuous employment – the statutory statement states when an employee's continuous employment begins. Certain breaks in the period of employment will not stop the continuity (see below) and will be counted in the final computation. Other breaks will not stop the continuity running but will be discounted in the final computation.

7.3.1 Effect of illegality on continuity

Continuity stops altogether when the contract involves an illegal act, although the tribunal has discretion whether to apply this rule in individual cases. If continuity is broken, a new period starts when the illegality ceases.

In *Hyland v J.H. Barker (North-West) Ltd* ([1985] IRLR 403) a lorry driver who had been employed for 16 years received a tax-free lodging allowance for one month in the 12 months prior to his dismissal. It was held that he did not have the continuity to claim unfair dismissal because the illegality wiped out the period when the contract was legal and continuity started from scratch once the illegality ceased.

This draconian approach was limited in *Hewcastle Catering Ltd v Ahmed* ([1992] ICR 626), where the employers devised a scheme to avoid paying VAT and gave the employees instructions which were intended to facilitate the scheme. The court held that the contract was only unenforceable if the employee was a knowing and willing participant in the illegality *and* stood to benefit from it. Here the employees did not receive any direct benefit from the scheme, and the court accepted evidence that pressure had been put on them to participate. It was a further factor that the court considered it contrary to public policy to deny them compensation when the employers had dismissed them, because they gave evidence for the prosecution in criminal proceedings brought by Customs and Excise (the case arose before the current 'whistleblowing' legislation, contained in the Public Interest Disclosure Act 1998).

The *Hewcastle* approach was followed in *Beauvale Furnishing Ltd v Chapman* ([2000] EAT/79/00, EAT), without any definite conclusion, since the matter was, rather surprisingly, referred back to the original tribunal on issues of fact. The employers offered the employee employment as a director in the late summer of 1995. He responded by letter on 6 September 1995, stating:

> Because of my particular financial situation which is slightly unique, I could not be a director of the company and would not like my wages known to the Inland Revenue generally. I would have to be a consultant to the company for at least the next two years. I could put together a package that was realistic but would be tailored to fit my situation. For disclosure purposes I will discuss only if this is acceptable. We are the only people who need know.

In February 1996 the employee began employment, ostensibly as a consultant but in fact as an employee. Thereafter, he presented invoices to the employer for 'Sales/Marketing Consultancy', and was paid gross at a rate of £3,333.00 per month. On the face of it this arrangement continued until June 1997, when for the first time he received a payslip, and tax and National Insurance were deducted at source. Up to this point, the employee, having declared himself to the Contribution Agency as being self-employed, paid tax based on an estimate of 'business profits' at £4,000 per annum for the tax year 1995–1996 and £1,000 per annum for the year 1996–1997.

The EAT found that the employee was

> at the beginning of his service in receipt of legal aid and states that he was concerned that formal employment would have caused a suspension of such aid, and this was the reason why he wished to begin his association with the company with a self-employed label. . . . He requested that his status be changed to that of an employee as early as May 1996. This was soon after his litigation had been concluded.

The EAT found that on the face of the documents the employee had not conducted his tax affairs properly; he had failed to make tax returns and had not paid tax or National Insurance based on his full income. Clearly, the employee was postponing or avoiding the payment of substantial amounts of tax. Contrary to the Tribunal's findings, there was clear evidence that the employee did not 'pay his proper tax liability throughout his association with the Respondent'. Nevertheless, the EAT sent the matter back to the Tribunal, in case evidence could be adduced to show that the employee had not set out to defraud the Revenue.

7.3.2 Weeks which do not break continuity and count towards the final computation

These provisions envisage situations in which the employee will not be at work, but his continuity will continue and the time be counted towards the total period of continuous employment (s. 212(3)):

- incapability due to sickness or injury (up to 26 weeks);
- temporary cessation of work;
- absence due to an arrangement or custom;
- absence due to pregnancy or childbirth.

The first and last are self-explanatory, but the other two require some explanation, and, indeed, can be said to overlap, as an 'arrangement' may be made between the parties when there is no work for the employee.

A temporary cessation of work envisages situations where, not due to the fault of the employee, work is not available for him. It is work for the particular employee which must have temporarily ceased and not work in the factory itself (*Fitzgerald v Hall, Russell & Co Ltd* [1970] AC 984). This provision will only operate if the cessation of work is temporary, and this begs the question of how long is temporary? The aim of the section was to protect workers in particular industries where lay-offs are common, but the effect has in practice been much wider, as is seen in *Ford v Warwickshire County Council* [1983] 2 AC 71.

Mrs Ford was a teacher who was employed by the Council under a series of consecutive short-term contracts, each for one academic year (September to July), for a total of eight years. There was, therefore, a gap between the end of each contract and the beginning of the next. The House of Lords held that EPCA 1978 Sch..13, para. 9(1)(b) (now ERA s. 213(3)(b)) could apply, so as to preserve her continuity of employment and allow her claim for unfair dismissal and a redundancy payment to be heard. The fact that the cessation of work was foreseeable and happened at the same time each year did not prevent it from falling within the statutory provision.

The EAT took a contrary view on the facts of *Reed v Royal Highland & Agricultural Society of Scotland* ([2002] EATS/0020/02). There the Applicant worked for the Society from 1994 to 2001 for some four months each year on the organisation of the Royal Highland Show. For the rest of the year she worked on her own account on a self-employed basis. The Tribunal concluded that she was not employed continuously, but merely on a series of contracts for 4–5 months at a time. It was stretching things too far to hold that the eight months between periods of work amounted to a temporary cessation of work, or absence due to an arrangement or custom, since there was no obligation to return.

The EAT took the view that s. 212 was intended to prevent an existing contract from being brought to an end in certain specific circumstances when there was no work being done. It could not apply when there was no contract. Here, according to the EAT, the contract terminated each year when work on the Show came to an end, although there was an informal understanding that the Applicant would be re-engaged the following year.

Although the EAT has stated that a strict mathematical approach is wrong (*Flack v Kodak Ltd* [1986] IRLR 255), it has also taken the common-sense approach that it would not be possible to call a cessation temporary when the periods of lay off were longer than the periods of working (*Berwick Salmon Fisheries Co Ltd v Rutherford* [1991] IRLR 203).

In *Lloyds Bank Ltd v Secretary of State for Employment* [1979] IRLR 41 an employee worked one week on, one week off for five years. When she became pregnant, the employer paid her statutory maternity pay and sought to recover from the Maternity Fund. It was held that she had been continuously employed for five years and the employer was entitled to recover.

The most common example under this provision is that of secondment to another employer or where the employee is allowed unpaid time off for personal reasons. Continuing to pay the employee is strong evidence that there is an arrangement that continuity should continue.

If an employee is absent because of pregnancy, in addition to the maternity leave to which she is entitled and which will count towards continuity in any event, she may count a further 26 weeks towards continuity of service (s. 212(4)). Therefore, should she take time off before her maternity leave begins, up to 26 weeks will count for continuity purposes.

Additionally, if a person is reinstated or re-engaged after an unfair dismissal or redundancy, he may count the period between the dismissal and his reinstatement or re-engagement towards his continuity (s. 219).

7.3.3 Weeks which do not break continuity, but which do not count in the final computation

a) Any period during which an employee is on strike or locked out by his employer (s. 216);
b) Periods spent in the Armed Forces (s. 217). In addition, the provisions of the Reserve Forces (Protection of Employment) Act 1986 and Defence Reform Act 2014 require a person's job to be kept open for him should he be called up for full-time military service.

Should the employee not fall within the above, any break in employment will break the continuity period and a new period will begin when the employment restarts.

7.4 Change of employer

Under the common law, only service with the same employer is counted for continuity purposes. This means that if the employee changes his job, the continuity he acquired with his old employer is ignored and a new period commences with the start of his new employment. This is also the situation where his employer transfers his business to another employer. Again, the employer has changed and continuity is broken. This can be hard on an employee who, due to matters entirely outside his control, may lose years of continuous service and with it a great deal of statutory protection. However, successive governments have recognised that a balance needs to be struck between preserving the rights of employees and avoiding a situation where organisations are discouraged from taking over other businesses, often businesses in financial trouble.

Protection for employees comes from two sources:

- ERA 1996 s. 218; and
- Transfer of Undertakings (Protection of Employment) Regulations 2006.

While two sources exist, it should be noted that the Act and Regulations in fact overlap and a transfer will often be covered by both.

7.4.1 Employment Rights Act 1996

Continuity will be preserved in the following circumstances:

- a trade, business or undertaking is transferred (s. 218(2));
- a body corporate is substituted for another body corporate by statute (s. 218(3));
- an employer dies and the employee is retained by his personal representatives or trustees (s. 218(4));
- there is a change of partners, personal representatives or trustees (s. 218(5)); or
- the employee is taken on by an associated employer of his employer (s. 218(6)).

For s. 218(2) to apply, the business must be transferred as a 'going concern'. If only the assets are transferred, the business is not transferred as a going concern. This is seen in *Woodhouse v Peter Brotherhood Ltd* [1972] 2 QB 520. The Applicant had worked for some 14 years for Crossleys, at a plant which was taken over by the Respondent company, which kept on the staff and utilised the plant and machinery. However, Crossleys did not sell its name or goodwill, and in fact carried on its business independently at another factory. Six years later the Applicant was made redundant, and the Court of Appeal held that the sale had been a sale of assets rather than a sale of the business as a going concern, and therefore the Applicant only had six years' service for the purpose of calculating his redundancy payment.

How different the new business must be to prevent s. 218(2) from operating is a question for the Tribunal. For s. 218(2) to operate, the business and physical assets must be transferred to the new employer, along with the goodwill.

7.4.2 Transfer of Undertakings (Protection of Employment) Regulations 2006

These were brought in to give effect to EC Directive 2001/23 and extend the protection given to employees by the TUPE Regulations 1981. The effect of the 2006 Regulations is that where there is a 'relevant transfer' of the business, the employees are transferred from the original employer to the successor with full continuity of employment and under their existing terms and conditions except in relation to pension entitlements. 'Relevant transfer' is defined such that it will be a rare transfer which does not fall within the Regulations. In particular, the Regulations deal with loop-holes in earlier legislation which became apparent in relation to contracting out by local authorities of various functions. See Chapter 5 for further information.

7.5 Effective date of termination of employment

For the purpose of both unfair dismissal and redundancy it is necessary to know the exact date the employment relationship came to an end, for two reasons:

- In order to calculate the period of continuous employment.
- Because the time the dismissed employee has to present his claim is limited in the case of unfair dismissal to three months from the effective date of termination, and in the case of redundancy to six months.

The effective date of termination is defined in ERA 1996 s. 97(1) and (4) as:

- If the contract is terminated by notice on either side, the date that notice expires, whether it is the proper length of notice or not.
- If the contract is terminated without notice, the date on which the termination takes effect.
- If a fixed term contract expires without being renewed, the date on which it expires.
- If the employee gives counter-notice which is shorter than the employer's notice, the date on which the counter-notice expires.

The only significant problems arise where the contract is terminated without notice.

a) The employer may summarily dismiss the employee in order to prevent him from acquiring the continuity to claim unfair dismissal – i.e. just before he accumulates two years' continuous employment. Though this decision clearly creates an opportunity for the unscrupulous employer to evade a potential claim for unfair dismissal, in *Stapp v Shaftesbury Society* [1982] IRLR 326 the Court of Appeal confirmed that the actual date of termination is the effective date of termination.
b) If the employee accepts payment in lieu of notice, then again the date of termination is the date the employee leaves rather than the date the notice would have expired, unless there is some ambiguity, as where the employee is given written notice, but agrees verbally to accept payment in lieu (*Robert Cort v Charman* [1981] IRLR 437).

7.6 Excluded employees

The legislation excludes certain employees from protection from unfair dismissal. As has already been seen, the employee must normally have the requisite continuity of employment in order to make a claim. Unless the reason for dismissal is one for which no continuity is required, employees with less than the requisite continuity will not be protected. In addition, certain classes of employee are statutorily excluded. The main areas of exclusion are:

7.6.1 Where the parties have agreed to use the arbitration scheme operated by ACAS

Normally, an employee cannot sign away his rights to compensation for unfair dismissal or redundancy, and any agreement which purports to exclude such rights is void by virtue of ERA 1996 s. 203. There are two exceptions to s. 203:

1) Under s. 203(2)(e) where a claim has been made and an officer of ACAS has promoted an agreement between the parties and the employee accepts that agreement in full settlement of his claim. The normal procedure is for both parties to sign an ACAS Form COT3.
2) Under s. 203(2)(f) an employee may enter into a compromise agreement which is legally binding provided that:
   - the agreement is in writing;
   - the agreement relates to the particular complaint;
   - the employee has received independent legal advice from a qualified lawyer (not necessarily a solicitor);
   - the adviser has an insurance policy in force covering the risk of loss to the employee;
   - the agreement identifies the adviser; and
   - the agreement states that the conditions regulating compromise agreements under the Act are satisfied

Both situations are far from uncommon, as the majority of claims are settled (with or without ACAS involvement) before they reach the Tribunal. Settlement agreements frequently include 'gagging clauses' to prevent either party revealing the terms of the settlement. The requirement that the employee receive legal advice is intended to protect both parties, the employee from having an unfair settlement forced on him, the employer from having an ex-employee accept a settlement and then make a further Tribunal claim on the same facts.

7.6.2 An employee who falls within a class of excluded persons

Most of these exclusions have been gradually whittled away, but police officers remain an excluded class by virtue of s. 200. Provisions excluding members of the Armed Forces are contained in s. 192, and may be amended by Order in Council, although there is no sign of this being done.

❖ THINKING POINT

Why should members of the Armed Forces and police officers be excluded from claiming unfair dismissal?

7.6.3 An employee dismissed under a procedure which has been certified by the Secretary of State as a substitute for the statutory provisions (s. 203(2)(b)–(c) and s. 110 and s. 157)

These provisions allow employers and trade unions to create their own procedures by agreement, but have rarely been used.

As a consequence of the Employment Equality (Age) Regulations 2006 there is no longer an upper age limit for claiming unfair dismissal.

7.7 Has there been a dismissal?

In order to claim unfair dismissal, the employee must show that he has been dismissed. For the purposes of unfair dismissal there is a statutory definition of dismissal which is contained in ERA 1996 s. 95. This states that dismissal will occur in the following three situations:

a) **Employer terminating with or without notice**
This is the classic termination at common law. It is the employer who ends the relationship and the question of whether the dismissal is wrongful or not is irrelevant to the issue of fairness. Thus, a lawful dismissal may be unfair and a wrongful dismissal may be fair. All the situations discussed previously which constitute a dismissal at common law are dismissals under s. 95.

b) **Fixed term contract which expires and is not renewed**
s. 95(1)(b) states specifically that this is a dismissal.

c) **Constructive dismissal (s. 95(1)(c))**
This third category is the one which creates the most difficulties. The concept of constructive dismissal involves the common-law situation of a repudiatory breach by the employer which forces the employee to resign. On the face of it this is a resignation rather than a dismissal. However, the law is aware that this construction can leave an employee with little protection against an unscrupulous employer who makes life so difficult as to force them out, and therefore statute regards this as a dismissal. It must be the breach by the employer which caused the employee to resign, however, and not some other reason (*Jones v F Sirl & Son (Furnishers) Ltd* [1997] IRLR 493). Further, the employer's conduct must involve a breach of contract and not mere unreasonableness (*Western Excavating v Sharp* [1978] ICR 221).

The following points should be noted:

1) The concept of constructive dismissal normally only protects those employees with the requisite continuity to claim unfair dismissal. Until the employee has been employed by that employer for two years any resignation by the employee for whatever reason will be treated as a resignation only (although in some cases the facts constituting a constructive dismissal may give rise to a claim in discrimination, for which no continuity is required).
2) Statute has created the concept of a constructive dismissal but has chosen not to create the corollary – a constructive resignation. Therefore, if the employee commits a repudiatory breach and the employer chooses to end the relationship, there is a dismissal, since it is the employer who has chosen to end the contract, although the reasons for the dismissal will be relevant when the tribunal considers the issue of fairness.

7.8 Time limit for claims

Under ERA 1996 s. 111 the normal time limit for making an unfair dismissal claim is three months from the effective date of termination of the contract (normally the last day the employee worked, or the date the notice given expired).

This is now done by submitting an online Form ET to the Court Service before midnight on the day the time limit expires. What this means is that the Court Service must actually receive the ET1 by midnight on the day *before* the three-month anniversary – if the effective date of termination was 1 May, the form must reach the tribunal on or before 31 July.

The tribunal has discretion under s. 111 to extend the time limit for such further period as it considers reasonable if it was not reasonably practicable for the application to be submitted within the normal limit. In practice, the tribunals take a strict view of the three-month limit. For example, an extension will not be granted where the delay is due to the employee making use of his employer's internal appeal procedure, or because of mistaken advice from a solicitor or the Citizen's Advice Bureau.

In *Marks & Spencer plc v William-Ryan* ([2005] IRLR 562) the Court of Appeal held that the tribunal had been entitled to find that it had been reasonably practicable for the employee to present her claim within the time, when the employer and the Citizen's Advice Bureau had mistakenly advised her that she must go through the appeal procedure before she could make a claim.

In another decided case, it was held that where the employee's solicitor had missed the deadline, the proper remedy was a claim in negligence. This was applicable where the solicitor had submitted the form online 90 seconds late! If the employee relied on mistaken advice, then tribunals are of the view that the proper remedy is an action for negligence against the advisor (the Citizen's Advice Bureau, like solicitors, are required to have professional indemnity insurance).

7.8.1 Early conciliation

The situation is now slightly complicated by the new statutory requirement that a claimant submit an Early Conciliation Form to ACAS before submitting the ET1. The Government's intention in imposing this requirement is to encourage the parties to settle employment disputes without recourse to full tribunal proceedings. When the form has been submitted, an Early Conciliation Period begins, during which ACAS contacts both parties and encourages them to make use of their free conciliation service, though there is no requirement that the parties actually use it. During the Early Conciliation Period, the time-limit clock is stopped, giving the claimant time to submit an ET1 to begin formal tribunal proceedings if either one or other party refuses conciliation or no settlement is reached.

If no agreement is reached through Early Conciliation, ACAS will issue a certificate, which the claimant must submit with his ET1. The time-limit clock restarts when the certificate is issued.

❖ THINKING POINT

Is there any point to early conciliation if the parties are not required to use it?

7.9 Further reading

Cabrelli, 'Liability and remedies for breach of the contract of employment at common law: some recent developments' (2016) 45(2) *Industrial Law Journal* 207.
Morris & Fredman, 'Civil servants: a contract of employment?' (1988) Spring *Public Law* 58.
Wynn & Leighton, 'Will the real employer please stand up? agencies, client companies and the employment status of the temporary agency worker' (2006) 35(3) *Industrial Law Journal* 301.

Chapter 8

Unfair dismissal 2

Chapter contents

8.1 Overview

This chapter considers the reasons by which the employer may fairly dismiss an employee, although it is important to note that establishing a fair reason is only the first step, as the employer must then show that it was reasonable to dismiss this employee for this reason, and that he followed a fair procedure in dismissing.

8.2 Introduction

Once the employee has established his eligibility to claim, the burden of proof shifts to the employer. Until the Industrial Relations Act 1971 created the concept of unfair dismissal, the law took no account of the employer's reasons for dismissing his employee, nor, unless there was a failure to follow contractual procedures, the procedure by which he did so.

ERA s. 98 provides:

(1) In determining for the purposes of this Part whether the dismissal of an employee is fair or unfair, it is for the employer to show—
   (a) the reason (or, if more than one, the principal reason) for the dismissal, and
   (b) that it is either a reason falling within subsection (2) or some other substantial reason of a kind such as to justify the dismissal of an employee holding the position which the employee held.
(2) A reason falls within this subsection if it—
   (a) relates to the capability or qualifications of the employee for performing work of the kind which he was employed by the employer to do,
   (b) relates to the conduct of the employee,
   (c) is that the employee was redundant, or
   (d) is that the employee could not continue to work in the position which he held without contravention (either on his part or on that of his employer) of a duty or restriction imposed by or under an enactment.
(3) In subsection (2)(a)—
   (a) 'capability', in relation to an employee, means his capability assessed by reference to skill, aptitude, health or any other physical or mental quality, and
   (b) 'qualifications', in relation to an employee, means any degree, diploma or other academic, technical or professional qualification relevant to the position which he held.
(4) Where the employer has fulfilled the requirements of subsection (1), the determination of the question whether the dismissal is fair or unfair (having regard to the reason shown by the employer)—
   (a) depends on whether in the circumstances (including the size and administrative resources of the employer's undertaking) the employer acted reasonably or unreasonably in treating it as a sufficient reason for dismissing the employee, and
   (b) shall be determined in accordance with equity and the substantial merits of the case.

Therefore, the employer must first satisfy the Tribunal that, on the balance of probabilities, he dismissed the claimant for one of the following reasons:

a) incapability or absence of qualifications required for the position held;
b) misconduct;
c) redundancy;
d) statutory restriction preventing the employment of the claimant in that position;
e) 'some other substantial reason' justifying the dismissal.

Second, the employer must show that it was reasonable to dismiss *that* claimant for *that* reason. This requirement has two elements, which will here be considered separately.

8.3 Potentially fair reasons for dismissal

8.3.1 Standard of proof

By the decision in *British Home Stores v Burchell* ([1978] IRLR 379), the employer must show that he had a genuine belief, based on reasonable grounds and at the time of the dismissal, that the facts he relied on in dismissing the claimant were true. This means that:

- The employer cannot rely on matters which only emerge after the dismissal (*Devis & Sons Ltd v Atkins* [1977] IRLR 314). This is opposite to the position at common law seen in *Ridgeway v Hungerford Market* ([1835] 3 Ad & El 516).
- The facts relied on by the employer do not actually have to be true, but in order to establish a genuine belief in their truth, based on reasonable grounds, the employer must have conducted a thorough investigation with an open mind. On the basis of *Farrant v The Woodroffe School* ([1998] IRLR 176, EAT), the employer may rely on a mistaken belief, provided it is reasonable – in that case the employer had consulted the local education authority personnel department, and been informed that the claimant could properly be dismissed on grounds of breach of contract.

❖ THINKING POINT

Christopher worked for a company as a financial controller, and was dismissed last week after an argument with one of the managers. His work has been handed over to James. As James was going through the paperwork he had inherited, he discovered that Christopher had been placing large online bets on horseracing from one of the company's accounts, for which he was responsible.

What can the company do about this?

Although in theory the employer does not have to prove that he acted as would a reasonable employer (see below), in practice reasonableness and the reason for the dismissal are closely linked. In particular, an employer who has not investigated thoroughly will find it hard to prove that he genuinely and reasonably believed a proper reason to exist. Case law shows that the tribunals place particular emphasis on the need for a full investigation before dismissal.

8.3.2 Capability or qualifications s. 98(2)(a)

8.3.2.1 Capability

Capability is defined as 'capability assessed by reference to skill, aptitude, health, or any other physical or mental quality' (s. 98(3)(a)). It is essentially concerned with incapability to carry out the job the employee is employed to do. It has two elements:

- Inherent incapability – the employee has never had the necessary capability.
- Acquired incapability – a formerly capable employee has ceased to be so, most frequently for medical reasons.

8.3.2.1.1 Inherent incapability

Inherent incapability involves failure to reach acceptable standards for whatever reason. Case law makes it clear that the employer must communicate the required standard to the employee and give him a proper opportunity to reach it.

Davison v Kent Meters Ltd ([1975] IRLR 145) involved an employee who was moved from one part of the factory to another, and was shortly afterwards dismissed for assembling 500 components wrongly. She said that she was merely following the instructions laid down by the foreman. The foreman in fact gave evidence that he had never shown her how to assemble the components. Not surprisingly it was held that the dismissal was unfair.

Aptitude includes the situation where the employee is unsuited to the particular job because of a facet of his character – a diffident individual is unlikely to be a success in sales! It can also cover aptitude tests, although it will be unfair if the employer dismisses before the employee has exhausted all the attempts allowed (*Blackman v Post Office* [1974] IRLR 46).

The Tribunal will look to see whether the employee knew that he was failing to achieve the correct standards or whether he was left in ignorance. Just as it will be unfair not to make the employee aware of the standards, it will be unfair not to warn him that his standards are not reaching an acceptable level. As Donaldson J pointed out in *Winterhalter Gastronom v Webb* [1973] IRLR 120, 'Many do not know that they are capable of jumping the five-bar gate until the bull is close behind them'. In most cases dismissal for incapability will only be fair if there is a period of inability, with evidence of warnings and of the employee's lack of improvement.

Alidair v Taylor ([1978] IRLR 82) suggests that a one-off failure may give rise to a fair dismissal if the consequences are sufficiently serious, actually or potentially. There, an airline pilot was dismissed after a bad landing in daylight and in good weather. The landing caused some damage to the aircraft although no one was injured. However, this is an old case, and the position may well no longer be clear-cut.

❖ THINKING POINT

On the facts of that case, what could Alidair have done as an alternative to dismissal?

8.3.2.1.2 Ill-health

Ill-health, whether short- or long-term, comes within the general umbrella of incapability, as it causes the employee to be incapable of carrying out his work, either completely or to a satisfactory standard, and whether temporarily or permanently. Clearly, no amount of training or warnings will get a genuinely ill employee fit again. But how far is the employer expected to 'carry' an employee who is frequently off work and/or off for long periods? Difficulties also arise where there is suspicion on the part of the employer that the employee is malingering. If this suspicion is well-founded, a dismissal on the basis of misconduct may well not be unfair, but the employer must satisfy the Tribunal that he had investigated the matter thoroughly and that the medical evidence did not point to genuine illness. Certainly, if there is a difference of opinion as to the employee's state of health, the employer must obtain further information (see *Harris v Nottinghamshire CC* [2000] EAT/308/00).

This area may overlap with the disability provisions of the Equality Act, which affect the position if the employee's condition falls within the concept of disability. Asthma is an obvious example of a condition which may lead to frequent short-term absences and is also a disability. Case law makes it clear that a dismissal for absence arising from disability will not necessarily be unfair, as the employer may be able to show that it is justified, but the burden of proof is high.

Generally speaking, in situations of sickness which does not constitute a disability, the starting point is the cause of the sickness. If the sickness is caused by the working conditions then the employer is expected to take steps to alleviate the conditions or provide alternative employment, and only if neither of these is possible or effective will a dismissal be fair.

However, in *Royal Bank of Scotland v McAdie* (EAT 29/11/2006) the employer was not precluded from fairly dismissing an employee on the grounds of incapacity where its conduct was at least partly responsible for that employee's inability to work.

Mrs McAdie complained to her manager about her temporary transfer to another branch, and was called to a meeting to discuss it. A dispute followed about the accuracy of the notes of the meeting. Mrs McAdie also alleged that during a telephone conversation the manager spoke to her in an authoritarian way and failed to deal with her concerns. She wrote to the manager again, but he failed to deal with her concerns to her satisfaction.

Mrs McAdie then went off sick due to work-related stress and instigated the bank's internal grievance procedure. The bank found that there had been no inappropriate behaviour by the manager, and offered her a return to work in a different role or location. An occupational health doctor found that, although Mrs McAdie was medically fit, she was unable to work due to the continued ill-feeling between herself and the bank. Eventually. Mrs McAdie was dismissed on grounds of ill health.

The Employment Tribunal concluded that she was dismissed on the potentially fair ground of capability, but that the bank was responsible for causing her ill health by failing to deal with her concerns properly. The Tribunal held that no reasonable employer would have dismissed her in those circumstances, as no reasonable employer would have found themselves in those circumstances to begin with, and that the dismissal was therefore unfair.

The EAT considered that the relevant question was whether it was reasonable for the bank to dismiss Mrs McAdie in light of the circumstances present on the date that it did, not whether the bank should have found itself in those circumstances to begin with. The medical evidence was unequivocal that she was unfit for work and that there was no prospect of recovery. The fact that the bank was responsible for Mrs McAdie's ill health did not preclude it from effecting a fair dismissal. Employees who had been injured as a result of a breach of duty by their employers were entitled to compensation in the ordinary courts. Both the medical evidence and Mrs McAdie suggested that there was no possibility of the employment continuing, and in those circumstances there was no alternative but for the bank to dismiss her.

Where illness is *not* caused by working conditions, the law distinguishes between persistent short-term illness and a single long-term illness.

Frequent short-term illness The approach of the Employment Tribunal is neatly summed up in *International Sports Company Ltd v Thompson* ([1980] IRLR 340, EAT). The Claimant was absent for about 25 per cent of the last 18 months of her employment, for a variety of reasons, including dizzy spells, anxiety and nerves, bronchitis, virus infections, cystitis, housemaid's knee, dyspepsia and flatulence. According to the EAT:

> Paraphrasing words used by Kilner Brown J in giving the judgment of the EAT in *Post Office v Jones* [1977] IRLR 422, there are circumstances in which a reasonable employer is entitled to say 'Enough is enough' [. . .]
>
> [The employers] were concerned with the impact of an unacceptable level of intermittent absences due to unconnected minor ailments. In such a case, it would be placing too heavy a

> burden on an employer to require him to carry out formal medical investigations and, even if he did, such an investigation would rarely be fruitful because of the transient nature of the employee's symptoms and complaints. . . . What is required in our judgment is firstly, that there should be a fair review by the employer of the attendance record and the reason for it, and, secondly, appropriate warnings after the employee has been given an opportunity to make representations. If then there is no adequate improvement in the attendance record, it is likely that in most cases the employer would be justified in treating the persistent absences as sufficient reason for dismissing the employee.

On that basis the employer must first consider whether there may be an underlying cause for the employee's absences. If there is not, the employer must:

- hear the employee's representations about the reasons for his absence;
- inform the employee of the standard of attendance that is required in the future, and warn of the consequences should he fail to meet that standard; and
- give the employee adequate time and support to improve.

In practice, many employers have an absence policy in several stages, which must all be completed before the absentee employee may be dismissed. Here is an example:

❖ EXAMPLE

If you have a high number of short term absences a sickness absence alert will be triggered, and your manager will arrange to meet with you to discuss your absences. Support will be provided to help you attend work regularly based on individual need, and this will include reasonable adjustments and/or redeployment.

Where there is evidence of a pattern to your absence or there are an unreasonable number of days absent, the short-term absence process will be followed. You will have the right to be accompanied by a Trade Union representative, or work colleague at all stages:

(a) Your manager will arrange a first absence review meeting to talk to you about the reasons for your absence. The purpose of the meeting is to talk to you about how your attendance can be improved, what support you might need, such as an Occupational Health referral, and to set some objectives to help you to improve your attendance at work.
(b) You may be referred to Occupational Health to see if you have an underlying medical condition before improvement objectives are set.
(c) In some situations your manager may ask you to get a fit note from your GP for all future absences, which the University will pay for if you get a receipt.
(d) If you don't meet the objectives set at the first meeting, your manager will arrange a second absence review meeting with an Employee Relations Specialist. After this meeting, you may be given a written warning about how you must improve your attendance at work, timescale for review, and what will happen if there are more absences.
(e) If there is no improvement in your attendance, the improvement is not enough, or you do not come into work regularly, your manager will arrange a hearing which could mean you are dismissed.
(f) If a decision is made to dismiss you, you can appeal against the dismissal and you will be told how to do this in a letter or email.

❖ THINKING POINT

Is this sufficiently clear to demonstrate to employees the standard of attendance which is required? Could a dismissed employee argue that it allows the employer to impose arbitrary requirements that he cannot realistically achieve?

Long-Term Illness The situation and procedure are different in relation to long-term sickness. It is possible that the nature and length of the illness may frustrate the contract, in which case issues of fairness are irrelevant as there has been no dismissal. Frustration is rare in practice (see Chapter 4). Where the illness does not frustrate the contract, the Tribunal will look for sympathetic treatment by the employer, including consultation with the employee.

A condition which causes long periods off work may well constitute a disability for the purposes of the Equality Act – a physical or mental impairment which has a substantial and long-term effect on a person's ability to carry out normal day-to-day activities. 'Long-term' is defined as 'more than 12 months'. Case law shows that individual absences need not themselves last more than 12 months, thus a condition which involves relapses will suffice for this purpose.

The starting point is evidence. Reliance on medical certificates is unlikely to suffice, so that consultation with the employee's doctor and an occupational health doctor or an independent specialist is normally essential. The employee's doctor cannot give information to an employer without the employee's consent, and by the Access to Medical Reports Act 1988 the employee is entitled to see any report prepared by his doctor and to veto its transmission to his employer. Further, an employer does not have an automatic right to require his employees to undergo a medical examination (*Bliss v SE Thames RHA* [1987] ICR 700). There needs to be express provision in the contract. However, in appropriate circumstances a requirement to undergo a medical examination is likely to be a lawful and reasonable order, and if the employee refuses to be examined the tribunal may well find any subsequent dismissal fair.

Once the medical evidence has been obtained, the employer should consult with his employee, and consider possible alternatives to dismissal, most obviously suitable alternative work.

In *Michell v Arkwood Plastics (Engineering) Ltd* ([1993] ICR 471) the EAT considered whether an employee off work for a lengthy period was under a duty to keep the employer informed of developments in his condition. The Claimant was absent from work from May 1990 after breaking his leg. For four months, apart from sick notes, he did not communicate with the employer. On 27 September, the employer wrote to ask when he would be fit to return to work. He saw his doctor and replied on 5 October, stating that he did not know when he would return as he was due to see a consultant. A week later he was dismissed. The Tribunal held the dismissal fair on the basis that an employee was under a duty to keep his employer informed as to his condition. The EAT held that there was no such duty, that the employer should have ascertained the true health position before dismissing on the grounds of sickness, and should also have considered the possibility of the employee returning to work on light duties until he was fully recovered.

❖ THINKING POINT

Does this place an unfair burden on the employer, given that an unscrupulous employee may want to keep quiet about his true condition?

On the issue of whether a dismissal on the basis of a lengthy absence through illness or injury is fair or unfair, the starting point was cogently expressed by Phillips J as President of the EAT in *Spencer v Paragon Wallpapers Ltd* ([1977] ICR 301):

> Every case depends on its own circumstances. The basic question which has to be determined in every case is whether, in all the circumstances, the employer can be expected to wait any longer and, if so, how much longer? Every case will be different, depending upon the circumstances.

Relevant circumstances included:

- the nature of the illness;
- the likely length of the continuing absence;
- the employer's need to have that employee's work done.

Although many illnesses resulting in long-term absence constitute disabilities, the employer is not precluded from dismissing in such circumstances. The issue there is whether the dismissal was justified, i.e. was it possible, by means of reasonable adjustments, to keep the disabled employee at work? Ultimately, however, case law on both disability discrimination and unfair dismissal demonstrates that a point may be reached at which an employer is entitled to say, 'enough is enough'.

The recent case of *O'Brien v Bolton St Catherine's Academy* ([2017] EWCA Civ 145) turns on information received by the employer between the dismissal and the internal appeal hearing. It should be noted that the Claimant was off work for over a year and at the time of the dismissal there was nothing to suggest that she was likely to return to work within the foreseeable future.

The Claimant, a teacher, was signed off work with stress on 9 December 2011, some nine months after being assaulted by a pupil. After more than a year of continuous absence, and procrastination over providing information requested by the employer, at an incapacity meeting on 28 January 2013 she was dismissed with effect from 31 January. At the internal appeal, on 10 April, she argued that she was now fit to return to work, and so the dismissal should be rescinded. The Tribunal found in her favour, but the EAT upheld the employer's appeal. Underhill LJ, giving the judgment of the Court of Appeal, approached the fairness of the dismissal and the issue of justification of unfavourable treatment for reasons relating to disability, i.e. that it was a proportionate means of achieving a legitimate aim, as follows:

> 1) The issue of justification had to be considered not only at the date of the original decision to dismiss, but also as at the date of the failure of the Claimant's appeal against that decision.
>
> As a matter of substance, her dismissal was the product of the combination of the original decision and the failure of her appeal, and it is that composite decision that requires to be justified. This is well recognised in the context of unfair dismissal – see *Taylor v OCS Group Ltd* [2006] EWCA Civ 702, [2006] ICR 1602, . . . and it must equally be the case in the discrimination context. The appeal procedure expressly contemplated that one of the grounds for allowing an appeal might be 'the coming to light of new information'. I suspect that that language may be primarily directed at cases of dismissal for misconduct and at situations where information 'comes to light' which was not, or not readily, available, at the initial hearing. But it is also apt to cover a case of medical incapacity where the position has changed between the hearings as a result of developments in the condition itself or the progress of treatment [. . .]
>
> We are here concerned with the specific case of an employee who deploys on the appeal evidence of changes in her medical condition and prognosis since the date of the initial hearing. A different approach may well be appropriate where what the employee is seeking is a second

bite of the cherry as regards material that was available, still more as regards material that was deployed, at the first hearing [. . .]

My conclusion on this issue is important. The Appellant's case that her dismissal could not be justified on the basis of the material before the original medical incapacity panel seems to me to be very weak. She had been off work for over a year, and there was no evidence that she would be fit to return in the foreseeable future if at all. But the position had changed by the time of the appeal hearing. There was now evidence, albeit not unproblematic, that she was fit to return to work at once. In my view this appeal turns on whether it was open to the ET to reach the conclusion that it was unjustifiable for the appeal panel to confirm the dismissal of the Appellant (at that point) in the light of that evidence.

2) In reaching their decision that the school had not established that dismissal was a proportionate means of achieving a legitimate aim, the Tribunal relied heavily on the failure of the school to provide clear evidence of problems created by the Claimant's lengthy absence. Counsel for the school argued that the Tribunal had been wrong to require detailed evidence, but the Court of Appeal rejected this argument, concluding that the Tribunal's approach did not involve perversity.

Underhill LJ went on:

I think I should say that even if it had been open to the school to advance a perversity argument on this point I doubt if I would have accepted it. By the time of the appeal hearing the Appellant was claiming that she was fit. It is true that the Tribunal accepted that the panel might reasonably have required a further examination before accepting that . . . but, even if that took a little time to arrange, the available evidence suggested that – to put it no higher – she might well be fit to return in the near future. In those circumstances the question of the impact of the Appellant's continuing absence on the school was thrown into sharp focus: even if her absence over the previous 15 months had caused real difficulties, as I would for myself be very willing to accept without detailed evidence, that harm was already done, and if the school had in fact managed to cope adequately with those difficulties it might be expected it to cope a little longer. It is clear . . . that that is how the Tribunal was approaching the question. I find it hard to say that the Tribunal was perverse in wanting more evidence about the school's ability to put up with the Appellant's absence for that short further period.

Underhill LJ then concluded that it was not proportionate to its legitimate aim for the school to have upheld the original dismissal rather than to have waited the short period necessary to gather its own evidence as to whether the Claimant was actually fit to return to work, even though the Claimant's own evidence was somewhat unsatisfactory.

By a 2:1 majority, the Court of Appeal concluded that the Claimant had been both discriminated against for a reason related to disability and unfairly dismissed.

The case can fairly be regarded as near the borderline because of the length of the Appellant's absence and the unsatisfactory nature of the evidence about when she might be fit to return. But the essential point is that by the time of the appeal hearing there was some evidence, albeit not wholly satisfactory, that she was now fit to return; and in my view it was open to the Tribunal to hold that it was disproportionate/unreasonable for the school to disregard that evidence without at least a further assessment by its own occupational health advisers.

A dissenting judgment was, however, given by Davies LJ, as follows:

The appellant had been a long-serving Head of Department at the school. Her sustained and continuing absence from the school was bound to cause it significant and ongoing detriment.

I regard it as unreal – as did the Employment Appeal Tribunal – to think that specific further detailed evidence was required to be lodged by the school before the appeal panel (which included experienced school governors) to that effect. It was obvious. The appellant, through her representative, did not even raise any challenge before the appeal panel to there being an adverse impact on the school by reason of her continuing absence.

During the period of her sustained absence, the appellant had, for whatever reason, been to a degree unco-operative. It was wholly unsurprising, at all events, that the school felt frustrated by her non-co-operation, notwithstanding all its own efforts. The school's position as to the effect of the appellant's continued absence after all these months was in any event explained by Mr Hopkinson in evidence at the incapacity hearing in January 2013. I consider, as I understand Underhill LJ to accept, that the written decision of 29 January 2013, which included a finding that no prognosis indicated that a return to work was likely in the near future, was justified.

The question then is whether circumstances changed such that the decision of the appeal panel, following the hearing of 10 April 2013, was unjustified. The appellant never herself sought an adjournment of that hearing in order to put in further medical evidence. I find it rather odd that the appeal panel is now in effect to be criticised for not adjourning the matter 'for a little longer' to make further checks when the appellant herself, through her representative, had wished to proceed. Further, through her union representative she accepted at the hearing that the focus was primarily on the validity of the previous panel decision. It is true that, very late in the day, the appellant had produced further limited materials relating to her medical condition at the appeal hearing. In my view they were demonstrably half-baked. It is said that the fresh evidence was 'not entirely satisfactory'. In my view, it was more than that: it was entirely unsatisfactory. At all events the appeal panel, which considered it, could properly so conclude. Self-evidently the pro forma note of the GP as to fitness to work was cursory and evidenced no real engagement whatsoever with the psychological issues of the appellant or (for instance) her prospective reaction if she came into contact with her pupil assailant or there were a recurrence of some trigger event. The letter of Mrs Welden [the therapist whom the appellant had consulted in February] was dated some months earlier and pre-dated the proposed course of treatment. It was cautious and equivocal. Nothing updated thereafter was put in by her of the actual effect of the recommended treatment, assuming it – or some of it – had in the meantime taken place as proposed. The appellant's own assertions of current fitness to return thus could, in such circumstances, properly be discounted – as they were – by the appeal panel in the absence of proper corroborating evidence.

Governors of schools do not have an easy task. Of course they have to comply with prescribed procedures. Of course, on behalf of the employers, they have to comply with employment law and process. But it lends no service to their role if they are to be tripped up by tribunals by a process of, in effect, second guessing. In my view, the decision which the appeal panel reached on the evidence presented to it and as appraised by it not only was within the range of reasonable responses open to it but also was proportionate and objectively justified.

Underhill LJ cautions against a broad brush approach. I do understand that. But this decision of the appeal panel in my view was a proper one. I consider that the decision of the Employment Tribunal was, with respect, unacceptably purist. It in effect substituted its own view for that of the appeal panel without, in my opinion, sufficient cause. Moreover, it did so in circumstances where its reasoning was tainted by the unrealistic requirement for more specific evidence as to the ongoing detriment to the school occasioned by continued absence of the appellant. It thereby erred in law.

How much longer was the school to wait? The Employment Tribunal does not say. It could not say. I can just about see some prima facia attraction, in the abstract, in the argument that a 'little longer' might be considered appropriate, given the time already elapsed, had the

> appellant been asserting on a properly evidenced basis that she was now (or almost) fit to return to work. . . . But the point is not just whether the panel *could* have adjourned further; it is whether it *should* have done. Given the wholly unsatisfactory nature of the further evidence, such as it was, produced by the appellant at the last minute at the appeal hearing, given the course the appeal hearing took and given the whole history of this protracted saga that assertion could properly be treated with scepticism by the appeal panel and rejected as a reason for giving the appellant yet more time. It thus could perfectly properly be concluded, some 17 months on since the appellant first went off sick, that enough was enough here. It goes too far, in my opinion, to say that the decision of the appeal panel on this was unreasonable or unjustified.

As a matter of law, the Court of Appeal also concluded that the test of justification in respect of a dismissal for a disability-related reason was the same as that of reasonableness in unfair dismissal.

❖ THINKING POINT

On the facts of this case, was Davies LJ being cynical or realistic? How long should an employer be expected to wait in cases of lengthy illness?

8.3.2.1.3 Qualifications

Qualifications are defined in s. 98(3)(b) as any degree, diploma or other technical or professional qualification *relevant to the position which the employee held.*

An employee's lack of qualifications for a particular position is argued relatively seldom by employers, although there is a potential overlap with two other potentially fair reasons for dismissal. One is statutory restriction, where the absence of a particular qualification makes it illegal to employ the individual in a particular post. Most obviously, this covers persons employed as drivers who do not have the necessary driving licence, either at all or for that particular class of vehicle. It is also, for example, unlawful to employ a person as a doctor who is not on the Medical Register maintained by the General Medical Council. The other is misconduct, which is applicable where a person claims falsely to have a particular qualification.

❖ EXAMPLE

On completion of a solicitor's training contract, there is an administrative process to be completed before a person can be formally 'admitted as a solicitor' and entered on the Roll of Solicitors. During the intervening period, typically one to two months, it frequently happens that an individual moves between firms and starts work as a newly qualified solicitor, in the expectation that he will shortly be admitted. Christine undertook a part-time training contract at the same time as doing the Legal Practice Course by distance learning. She completed the training contract and accepted a post as a newly qualified solicitor although she still had to resit one of the LPC exams. The firm she joined did not take up her references, but subsequently discovered that Christine would not be in a position to be admitted as a solicitor for at least another six months. The firm summarily dismissed Christine for gross misconduct. As she did not have two years' continuous employment, she could not claim unfair dismissal.

Where there is no issue of either statutory restriction or dishonesty, case law shows that possession of the relevant qualification must be a contractual requirement in order for a dismissal to be fair.

In *Litster v Thom & Sons Ltd* ([1975] IRLR 47) the employee was employed as a fitter/driver. He was required to hold an HGV licence if he drove heavy goods vehicles, but he failed the necessary test. He continued in employment as a fitter, for which his contract did not require a licence. After a disagreement with his employer he was told that if he did not obtain an HGV licence he would be sacked. He tried again, failed, and was dismissed. His dismissal was held to be unfair.

However, the requirement to hold the particular qualification may be implied into the contract (*Tayside Regional Council v McIntosh* [1982] IRLR 272).

❖ THINKING POINT

Both these cases are old. Is the Tribunal likely to take a different approach today?

8.3.3 Conduct (s. 98(2)(b))

Conduct, or, more accurately, misconduct, is one of the most common reasons for dismissal, along with incapability through illness and 'some other substantial reason'. Yet again it is up to the employer to provide evidence that the reason exists and therefore an investigation is essential. In relation to this reason in particular, the procedure used by the employer will be closely scrutinised by the tribunal, especially the extent to which the employer's procedure complies with or adopts the principles of the ACAS Code of Practice on Disciplinary Powers and Procedures. The Code and the employer's procedures will be discussed in Chapter 9 when looking at aspects of reasonableness.

While the statute lays down no guidelines as to the type or seriousness of misconduct that may justify dismissal, some principles seem to have emerged from the cases:

- The conduct does not have to be gross, only substantial in relation to the circumstances of the case, so that relatively minor acts may, in some circumstances, justify dismissal.
- The conduct does not have to be blameworthy. In *Jury v EEC Quarries Ltd* [1980] EAT 241/80 the employee, a Class 3 HGV driver, refused to train as a Class 2 driver when all Class 3 vehicles went out of service, and was dismissed. It was held that his dismissal was fair although the Tribunal stated that he was not to blame.

If the employer has a number of suspects and, after an investigation, he cannot discover which of them is guilty, it appears that it is fair to dismiss them all. This is the decision of the Court of Appeal in *Monie v Coral Racing Ltd* ([1981] ICR 109), and was applied to the dismissal of four employees in *Parr v Whitbread plc t/a Threshers Wine Merchants* ([1990] IRLR 39). It is very clear, however, that the employer must demonstrate that he has narrowed the group down to include *only* those who could have done it, and his investigation must show how he has discounted other possible suspects.

❖ THINKING POINT

How will an employer ensure this?

Looking simply at the reason for dismissal at the moment, by an analysis of the cases we can establish the type of misconduct which constitutes a potentially fair reason for dismissal. This may include misconduct outside employment as well as within.

8.3.3.1 Misconduct inside employment

8.3.3.1.1 Absenteeism and lateness

As a starting point, absenteeism and lateness are not gross misconduct and therefore the employer cannot fairly dismiss for a first offence. The employer must warn his employee, investigate the reasons for the absenteeism or lateness (if any), and give an opportunity to improve before dismissing. Note that there is an overlap with frequent short-term illness, and with disability discrimination should there be an underlying cause for the illnesses – asthma is probably the most obvious example.

Lynock v Serial Packaging Ltd ([1988] IRLR 510) provides a useful though non-exhaustive list of factors to be taken into account when absence is due to frequent short-term illnesses:

- the nature of the illness;
- the likelihood of its recurring;
- the length of the various absences and the spells of good health in between;
- the employer's need to have that work done by that employee; and
- the impact of the absences on other employees.

In *Wilkes v Fortes (Sussex) Ltd* IRRR, the EAT placed emphasis on the size of the firm in deciding whether it would be fair to dismiss an employee who is off work intermittently for sickness reasons – clearly, in a large firm it will be easier to cover for a particular person's absence than in a small organisation.

❖ THINKING POINT

Is the large organisation/small organisation dichotomy over-simplistic? What if the person concerned works in a small and specialist department within a large organisation, or carries out a highly specialist function, such as a university lecturer?

8.3.3.1.2 Disloyalty

The employee owes a duty of loyalty to his employer and, should he act disloyally, he will be in breach of contract. Disloyalty may take a number of forms. The employee may disclose confidential information to an unauthorised person, he may be working for his employer's competitor in his spare time, or actually conducting a rival business. In all those situations, provided the employer has evidence that the employee is guilty, dismissal, in some cases instant dismissal, will be justified.

8.3.3.1.3 Disobedience

Another duty in the employment contract is that the employee shall obey the reasonable and lawful orders of his employer, and thus, refusal to do so is a breach of contract and misconduct. It has further been demonstrated that not all orders are necessarily reasonable even where they are within the employee's contract, and, likewise, that some orders will be deemed reasonable even though they go beyond the employee's duties. What is a reasonable order is very often a question of fact for the tribunal, looking at the circumstances of the individual case. In any case of dismissal for disobedience, therefore, the tribunal will look to see whether the order is lawful and reasonable and whether the employee had valid grounds for refusing to comply with it.

Breach of workplace rules may amount to disobedience even where they are not contractual, although just because the rules state that certain conduct will lead to dismissal it does not follow that the dismissal will be fair. In *Laws Stores Ltd v Oliphant* ([1978] IRLR 251) it was held unfair to dismiss an employee with eight years' service for till irregularities even though the works rules stated that till irregularities constituted gross misconduct. This was supported by the Court of Session in *Ladbroke Racing Ltd v Arnott* ([1983] IRLR 154), and has been followed in many cases since.

8.3.3.1.4 Dishonesty

Although dishonesty is frequently a criminal matter, the employer does not have to produce evidence that establishes beyond a reasonable doubt that the employee is guilty, but, as with all the other reasons, that he has a genuine belief in the employee's guilt. A criminal conviction is normally considered sufficient evidence that the allegations are true. However, the fact that the employee is charged with an offence is not sufficient to establish a genuine belief without investigation by the employer (*Scottish Special Housing Association v Cooke and others* ([1979] IRLR 264).

A major problem in this area is that the employer needs to investigate to discover the evidence he needs to establish his reason, but often the police are also investigating, and the employee will be instructed by his solicitor to say nothing during the employer's investigation. It appears that if the employer has enough evidence without the employee's statement to come to a reasonable belief, the dismissal will be fair even if the employee is subsequently acquitted of criminal charges (*Harris and Shepherd v Courage* [1981] IRLR 153). That being said, many employers await the outcome of criminal proceedings before moving towards dismissal. The same is true when an employee is charged with a criminal offence in respect of wrongdoing outside employment.

The following recent cases are first instance, but are useful in demonstrating the importance of thorough investigations and establishing clear evidence of dishonesty.

In *Patel v Sainsbury's Supermarkets Ltd* ET/2401414/10 the Claimant was employed as a customer services assistant at Sainsbury's Bolton store. He was entitled to a colleague discount card, which entitled him to up to 15 per cent on purchases from the company. There were strict rules governing the use of discount cards, breach of which could result in disciplinary action. The rules stated that:

- purchases using the card must be for the use of the cardholder or his or her immediate household, unless the purchase is a gift;
- goods purchased must not be resold; and
- bulk purchases must be authorised.

On 10 November 2009, the store took part in a national promotion of *Call of Duty: Modern Warfare* 2. The company had negotiated a deal that allowed it to sell the game for a discounted price for a limited period. Customers were limited to one copy each, and the game sold out extremely quickly.

The company operated an electronic purchase review system called Eagle Eye to detect unusual or suspicious transactions. On 12 November 2009, the store was informed that three members of staff, including Mr Patel, had used their discount cards in suspicious transactions related to the game promotion. Mr Patel had bought at least 11 copies of the game in several transactions over 10 and 11 November. The company regarded these transactions as a bulk purchase, where there was no authorisation and the opportunity for resale existed. On 13 November, the deputy store manager held an investigation meeting with Mr Patel regarding potential misuse of his discount card. Mr Patel stated that, with regard to the purchase of numerous copies of the game on 11 November 2009, he was shopping with his mother and had been asked by his brothers and cousins – whom he said lived in the same house – to pick up copies of the game for them. His explanation for the number of transactions was that further requests were made during the day. The deputy manager decided to give Mr Patel the benefit of the doubt.

Over the following weekend, the deputy manager was troubled by Mr Patel's statement that his brothers and cousins lived in the same household. CCTV footage showed that Mr Patel had used different tills for his purchases, and that, of the final two transactions on 11 November 2009, one was made by him and one immediately after by his mother, which suggested a deliberate attempt to buy a large number of copies of the game in contravention of the bulk purchasing rules.

At a second investigation meeting, on 20 November, Mr Patel said that the reason for the different transactions was that he was receiving requests throughout the day, although he no longer maintained that his relatives lived at his home. Mr Howarth suspected that Mr Patel had misused his discount card and tried to conceal it, with a view to reselling the games at a profit.

A disciplinary hearing took place on 27 November. It was clarified at the meeting, and accepted by Mr Patel, that he had bought 11 copies of the game. His explanation was that they were bought as presents for his relatives for the Hindu religious festival, Diwali, which he said took place on 29 October. He said that it had not been possible to arrange a family party until 14 November. The disciplinary officer confirmed independently that it had taken place on 17 October. Mr Patel stated that only one of the purchases, other than the one for himself, was for household members.

The disciplinary officer concluded that Mr Patel had deliberately breached the discount card rules, and dismissed him for gross misconduct. Mr Patel's appeal against dismissal failed, the appeal officer being unable to accept that he had bought 11 identical games as presents. Mr Patel claimed unfair dismissal.

The tribunal found that the investigation evidence showed that Mr Patel was familiar with the discount card rules, as well as showing what appeared to have been a careful and calculated attempt by him to disguise his multiple purchases by buying the games in five different transactions over day days, using his mother on one occasion, using different payment methods, and visiting different tills. Based on this evidence, the tribunal found that the disciplinary officer had reasonable grounds for his belief in Mr Patel's alleged misconduct. The company's investigation was also reasonable, and the tribunal noted that there had been two investigation meetings prior to the disciplinary hearing. Regarding the sanction imposed, the tribunal found that misconduct such as Mr Patel's would reasonably cause an employer to lose confidence in an employee, despite his or her previously good work record. The tribunal held that Mr Patel had been fairly dismissed.

In *Price v NSL Ltd NIIT/01827/10* the employer did not have absolute proof that the employee had committed misconduct, but carried out a thorough investigation that showed that it was highly likely that he had. Mr Price was employed as a traffic warden from November 2006 until April 2010 in Newtownards, Northern Ireland. The company alleged that Mr Price had falsified company records on five occasions from January–March 2010. It alleged that, on these five occasions, Mr Price was staying inside during inclement weather at times when his recording device and pocket-book records showed that he was out on patrol.

The company's suspicions were aroused when a manager, Mr Goddard, noticed that the entries in Mr Price's recording device and pocket book, although consistent with each other, were inconsistent with his observations as to when Mr Price was entering and leaving the company's base. The company accepted that the times of the entries in the recording device were accurate, because the device recorded the time when entries were made and these times could not be altered. However, the company's case against Mr Price was that he was not at the locations where he claimed he was when he made the entries, but indoors to escape bad weather. On becoming suspicious, Mr Goddard began to observe Mr Price when he entered the front of the building, although he could not see the rear exit from where he was. Mr Goddard gathered information on five occasions when Mr Price had entered but not left the building by the front entrance, even though the record on the device said that he was out on patrol.

Mr Price was suspended two days after the fifth incident, pending a disciplinary investigation. On the same date, Mr Price attended an investigatory interview, which was conducted by Mr Goddard. A second investigatory interview took place a few weeks later after Mr Goddard had carried out what the tribunal later described as an 'exhaustive' investigation. At the subsequent disciplinary hearing, Mr Price's main argument was that he had a habit of leaving the premises using the rear exit. The disciplinary officer, decided that Mr Price should be dismissed for gross misconduct. This decision was upheld in the disciplinary appeal hearing, which was conducted by another manager.

The tribunal found that the company had carried out as much investigation into the matter as was reasonable in the circumstances. That investigation had led the company to have a reasonable suspicion of Mr Price's guilt. First, Mr Price never provided the company with any convincing explanations for his decision to enter by the front door, but leave by a back, fire door, on each occasion. Second, if Mr Price had exited the premises by the back entrance, he would have begun or resumed his patrols in Mill Street, a street that, on several relevant occasions, he did not record passing through, either electronically or on paper. Third, during each relevant period, Mr Price did not issue any parking tickets. Fourth, on some of the relevant occasions, Mr Price recorded himself as being in streets some distance from the base, at times very close to the times at which he was seen by Mr Goddard to be entering or leaving it.

The tribunal concluded with a reminder that it was not its job to decide whether Mr Price was guilty of the relevant misconduct. Its decision-making role was confined to the question of whether, in arriving at its conclusion that Mr Price was indeed guilty of the misconduct, the company acted within the 'range of reasonable responses'. It held that the company had dismissed Mr Price fairly.

8.3.3.1.5 Violence and fighting

The employer must gather all the evidence available before he can establish this as a reason. Interviewing only one or two witnesses will be insufficient. Again, many employers will class fighting as gross misconduct within the works rules, but, as in other areas, rigid enforcement of rules without taking all the circumstances into account will render a dismissal unfair. Issues such as the status of the employees, where the fight took place, provocation and past record should all be considered.

8.3.3.2 Conduct outside employment

As a starting point, conduct outside employment hours has nothing to do with the employer and he cannot therefore discipline his employee for this reason. Obviously, in some cases loss of professional registration will make it impossible to employ a person in a particular capacity, and may well be a fair reason for dismissal – though the employer may be expected to consider alternative work, particularly if the loss of registration is temporary rather than permanent.

In some circumstances the conduct may reflect on the employer-employee relationship in such a way that the employer loses all trust and confidence in his employee. Therefore, dismissal may be fair if the employer can show that the misconduct outside the working hours has a direct effect on the employment relationship. A conviction for theft in a person whose job involves responsibility for other people's money is an obvious example.

❖ THINKING POINT

Mary is a financial manager for a small company, and has also been treasurer of her local church for the past 15 years. When a new vicar – a former accountant – takes over the parish, he goes through the accounts in detail and discovers that Mary has for years been quietly drawing money from church funds for her own use. The police are called; Mary eventually pleads guilty to fraud and receives a suspended sentence.

Is it fair for the employer to dismiss Mary on the basis of this conviction?

Clearly, if a lorry driver is banned from driving it will be fair to dismiss him if there is no alternative work he can do. But where that example is self-explanatory, others are not. It appears from case law that if the conduct is such that it makes the employee unsuitable for his job or unacceptable to other employees, or could cause potential harm to his employer's business, dismissal will be fair.

In *Gardiner v Newport Borough Council* ([1974] IRLR 262) a lecturer dealing with 16- to 18-year-old boys was convicted of gross indecency with another man in a public lavatory. His dismissal was held fair. Such a decision might seem surprising in today's moral climate. Nevertheless, in *X v Y* ([2003] EAT/0765/02/TM) the EAT upheld the dismissal of a probation officer, who worked with 16 to 25 year olds, after he was formally cautioned for gross indecency in a public lavatory (at a motorway service station). Here it was important that the employee was expected to act as a role model for young men, and that he himself accepted that his offence was relevant to his employment. The EAT, asked to consider the effect of ECHR Art. 8, considered that the 'right to respect for private life' did not apply as the offence had taken place in a public place.

Bradshaw v Rugby Portland Cement Ltd ([1972] IRLR 46) is a case which might well be decided differently today. The employee, who worked in a quarry, was dismissed following a conviction for incest with his teenage daughter and his being sentenced to probation. The dismissal was held to be unfair. His conduct had no bearing on his work and there was no evidence that his colleagues found him unacceptable to work with.

Post Office v Liddiard ([2001] EWCA Civ 940) is not a satisfactory precedent, as it was decided during a brief period when a different test of the reasonableness of a dismissal was in use (see Chapter 9). In 1998, during riots involving English football hooligans attending the World Cup, the Respondent was arrested and convicted in France of offences amounting to football hooliganism. He was sentenced to 40 days' imprisonment. There was widespread condemnation by the Prime Minister and the press of those involved in the violence. The Respondent was identified in a national newspaper as being a Post Office employee. He was subsequently dismissed and issued proceedings claiming unfair dismissal.

The Employment Tribunal took into account the fact that the Respondent had had an excellent employment record, the incident for which he had been convicted in France had no relation to his employment, and that he was employed within the Post Office and not in contact with the public. The Tribunal also took into account the fact that the proceedings in France had a number of anomalies, that the Respondent's manager who dismissed him admitted that he had been influenced by the press involvement, that the Respondent had no previous convictions, and, although convicted, had denied the offences. On those grounds, the Tribunal found that the Respondent had been unfairly dismissed.

The Court of Appeal held that the central issue that the Tribunal should have addressed was whether it was reasonable for the Respondent to have been dismissed for reasons that amounted to gross misconduct which brought the Post Office into disrepute. That question was not addressed by the Tribunal and accordingly, the Tribunal's determination could not stand.

Foster v Brighton & Hove City Council ([2005] UKEAT/0737/04/ILB) involved a care worker whose work involved visiting vulnerable old people at home. She was summarily dismissed after her employer concluded that she had been actively involved in a benefit fraud by her husband over a nine-year period (they falsely claimed to be living apart and that the children were living with the husband), and that this gross misconduct was compounded by her lying about the matter when it was investigated. The Tribunal concluded that she had been unfairly dismissed on the basis that the employer's investigation had been inadequate, but that the employee's conduct was such that no financial award should be made. The EAT quashed the decision on the basis that the Tribunal's approach to the issues was fundamentally flawed, but left open the issue of whether this form of misconduct could be a fair reason for dismissal.

Myers v Metropolitan Police Authority (ET/3202331/2010 and ET/3200046/2010) is a more recent first instance case, where a civilian police worker unsuccessfully claimed unfair dismissal and disability discrimination after she lost her job for a dangerous driving conviction.

From 2001, Ms Myers worked as a civilian detention officer with the Metropolitan Police Authority. In December 2003, she had to cut free a prisoner who had tried to hang himself. Ms Myers was traumatised and suffered a series of mental-health problems after the incident. From July 2004, she was employed in a series of administrative roles that required very little contact with the public. Ms Myers was diagnosed with bipolar disorder in 2006 and the police force was aware of this from at least January 2007.

In June 2008, Ms Myers was involved in a road-traffic accident that resulted in her being arrested and charged with dangerous driving, assault with intent to resist arrest and failure to stop after a road accident. The day after the accident, she was sectioned under the Mental Health Act 1983 and spent four months in hospital.

In early 2009, Ms Myers appeared at Snaresbrook Crown Court. She pleaded guilty to dangerous driving and was sentenced to:

- forty weeks' imprisonment, suspended for two years;
- a two-year supervision order requiring her to undergo mental-health treatment; and
- a driving disqualification for 21 months, with a requirement to take a driving test after that period before she could go back on the road.

The Metropolitan Police Authority has a policy that any member of staff who is convicted, cautioned or given a formal warning for a serious traffic offence must go in front of a conviction board to show cause why he or she should not be dismissed. Ms Myers attended her hearing in March 2009. An occupational-health adviser gave evidence based on a consultant psychiatrist's report that Ms Myers would be unable to return to reliable employment with the Metropolitan Police Authority and that to remain in employment with it would pose a serious risk to her health. The Tribunal subsequently found that the decision to dismiss was based on a combination of the occupational health evidence and the seriousness of the conviction.

In July 2009, Ms Myers's appeal resulted in the police force offering to reduce the penalty to a formal reprimand without an appeal hearing. Surprisingly, Ms Myers turned this offer down. The tribunal later surmised that this decision was taken because Ms Myers thought that there had been a complete breakdown in her relationship with the police force.

The Metropolitan Police Authority offered to rehear Ms Myers's case from scratch and the new hearing took place in October 2009. Its decision was that Ms Myers should be dismissed because of the seriousness of the incident. The rationale noted that Ms Myers's conviction related to an incident that took place on a busy road, she repeatedly failed to stop for the police, drove through red traffic lights and went down the road the wrong way. Four police officers were injured in the incident. Despite Ms Myers's health problems being put forward in mitigation, Chief Superintendent Bending concluded that her conduct 'fell significantly below the standard expected' of her. Ms Myers did not appeal this decision, but later claimed disability discrimination and unfair dismissal.

The Employment Tribunal rejected Ms Myers's claims of direct disability discrimination and disability-related discrimination, brought in relation to the original decision to dismiss. The Tribunal concluded that there could not be direct disability discrimination because it was established that Ms Myers was not dismissed because of her disability and the same decision would have been made against a non-disabled employee whose actions were the same. The Tribunal also rejected Ms Myers's unfair dismissal claim. The claimant was dismissed because her actions had fallen below the standards expected of her. The principal reason for dismissal was therefore conduct, albeit conduct that occurred outside the workplace.

According to the tribunal, in procedural terms, the dismissal might have been unfair if the decision had stopped at the outcome of the conviction board's original hearing. That hearing had concentrated too much on the occupational health advice on Ms Myers's fitness for work and not enough on her conviction, which was ultimately the reason why she was at risk of dismissal. However, these procedural defects were later rectified, bringing the dismissal within the band of reasonable responses.

The Employment Tribunal concluded that there were powerful mitigating factors, especially Ms Myers's long service and the link between the suicide incident in December 2003 and Ms Myers's subsequent mental-health problems, which had led to the behaviour that resulted in her arrest while driving. There was no evidence of 'external' reputational damage to the police service, given the length of time between her conviction and the hearing that ultimately resulted in her dismissal. The tribunal noted that there had not been negative publicity, as the press had not picked up on the story.

However, the Employment Tribunal's conclusion was that the sanction of dismissal was within the range of reasonable responses because:

- the conviction was for a serious offence, especially when compared with the less grave driving offences that normally came before the conviction board;
- it was common for police workers to be dismissed for less serious driving convictions outside work;
- the claimant had been given a stiff penalty by the Crown Court, including a suspended prison sentence; and
- the potential reputational damage could be 'internal' as well as external, with other members of staff (i.e. the injured officers) being part of a 'very frightening' incident.

8.3.4 Redundancy (s. 98(1)(c))

See also Chapter 10.

Redundancy is the third potentially fair reason which may be pleaded by the employer. If the employee claims a redundancy payment, there is a presumption that the dismissal was due to redundancy (ERA s. 163(2)) but this will not apply if the employee claims unfair dismissal (*Midland Foot Comfort Centre v Moppett* [1983] All ER 294). In such a case, the employer must show that redundancy was the reason for the dismissal. Even if redundancy is the reason, if the employee shows that he was selected for redundancy for a reason which is automatically unfair, or that there was a lack of warning or consultation, he will succeed in a claim for unfair dismissal.

To establish the reason, the employer must show that a redundancy situation exists within the statutory definition contained in ERA s. 139(1). For present purposes it is sufficient to state that this means that the employer must show that either:

- he is ceasing business or moving his place of business; or
- that work of the particular kind that the employee was employed to do has ceased or diminished, or is expected to cease or diminish.

8.3.4.1 Automatically unfair selection for redundancy

However, even though the reason may exist, there will be an unfair dismissal if the employee can show that he falls within the provisions making the redundancy automatically unfair contained in ERA s. 105(1) and the Trade Union and Labour Relations (Consolidation) Act 1992 s. 153. If so, the normal continuity period does not apply (ERA s. 108), nor does the normal age limit (ERA s. 109).

ERA s. 105(1) provides that there is an unfair dismissal where the circumstances constituting the redundancy applied equally to one or more other employees in the same undertaking who held positions similar to that held by the dismissed employee and who have not been dismissed by the employer, *and* the reason for selection was one of the following:

- pregnancy or childbirth or the exercise of maternity rights;
- the carrying out of health and safety duties;
- the employee is a shop or betting shop worker who refused to work on Sundays; or
- the employee was selected for asserting a statutory right.

The 1992 Act s. 153 provides that selection for redundancy is unfair if made for a reason specified in s. 152, that is membership or non-membership of an independent trade union or participation in the activities of an independent trade union at the appropriate time. 'Participation', however, excludes taking part in a strike or other industrial action (see Chapter 20).

All the above provisions show that there are three stages involved in arguing an automatically unfair reason for selection:

- the employees must be in the same undertaking;
- similar employees must have been retained; and
- selection must have been on the basis of one of the reasons given above.

8.3.4.1.1 The same undertaking

The meaning of undertaking is not clear, but it is probably wider than an establishment at a particular location and could mean the whole of the employer's business if run in a unified way. A common management will be a relevant factor, but flexibility of labour and different skills could also affect the decision. Thus, departments could be considered in isolation from one another in some circumstances.

8.3.4.1.2 Simarly placed employees

At least one other employee must be retained in a similar position to that of the dismissed employee. The tribunal will look at the type of work as well as the status of the employee, his skills and the terms and conditions of employment (*Simpson v Roneo Ltd* [1972] IRLR 5). If others are capable of doing the work of the redundant employee, they will only be in similar positions if they have covered the work in the past or there is a great deal of interchange of labour at the workplace (*Dorrell v Engineering Developments Ltd* [1975] IRLR 234).

8.3.4.1.3 Automatically unfair reason

The employee must show that the reason for selection is one of the four mentioned above. If that is the case, then the selection for redundancy is unfair – there is no need to consider any other matters.

8.3.5 Statutory Restriction (s. 98(1)(d))

The penultimate potentially fair reason is that the employee could no longer continue to work in the position which he held without contravention by himself or his employer of a duty or restriction imposed by or under any enactment.

The statutory restriction may be general – a prohibition on the individual doing any type of work – or specific. The latter is much more common, though there is an important area of general restriction under the immigration legislation.

In *Hounslow LBC v Klusova* ([2007] EWCA Civ 1127) the employer's genuine but mistaken belief that to continue employment would contravene statute was held sufficient to give rise to a fair dismissal. The employee came to Britain from Russia in 1996 and remained on a series of student visas until 2000, when she was granted leave to remain for four years. After this expired she was *prima facie* forbidden by virtue of the Asylum and Immigration Act 1996 s. 8 to work in the United Kingdom. However, as she had applied for extension of her leave to remain before the original term expired she was entitled to continue to work until her application was decided. The Court of Appeal found that the employer's belief that she was not entitled to work (they had made inquiries of the Home Office and been given to understand that she was not entitled to work until the determination of her request for extension of leave to remain) constituted a potentially fair reason for dismissal. However, on the facts the dismissal was unfair as there had been no consultation with the employee.

If the statutory provision is specific it must relate to the work the employee was actually employed to do. Thus, if an employee is employed solely or substantially to drive, he may be fairly dismissed should he be disqualified from driving, as in *Appleyard v Smith (Hull) Ltd* ([1972] IRLR 19). There, a mechanic in a small garage was banned from driving. A substantial part of his job was road testing vehicles and during his ban his employer could not find him sufficient work which did not involve driving. His dismissal was held to be fair.

An employer must show, however, that the prohibited part of the employee's duties constituted a significant part of his job and that the employer considered whether he could continue to employ him until the disqualification ceased. *Mathieson v W.J. Noble & Son Ltd* ([1972] IRLR 76) is an example. A travelling salesman was disqualified from driving and arranged for a driver to drive him for the period of his ban. The employer dismissed him without seeing whether this arrangement would work and it was held that the dismissal was unfair.

8.3.6 Some other substantial reason (ERA s. 98(1)(b))

This is somewhat of a 'catch-all' category, given that almost anything not covered by the first four reasons may potentially fall under this heading. While case law shows that a variety of different situations will fall within s. 98(1)(b), the most common is where the employee refuses to comply with a reasonable reorganisation.

This is the situation where the employer is changing the terms of the employee's contract and thus is in breach, and the employee refuses to accept the change. It should be stressed that the fact that the employee is entitled under common law to refuse to accept the change has no bearing on the fairness or otherwise of the dismissal and in many cases the needs of the business will be overriding.

In *RS Components v Irwin* ([1973] IRLR 239) the employer was losing business because his sales staff were leaving and working for competitors. The employer unilaterally imposed restrictive covenants on the existing salesmen and the employee was dismissed when he refused to accept the change in his contractual terms. It was held that his dismissal was fair.

A dismissal arising from a change in terms is more likely to be held fair if:

- all or many of the other employees have agreed to the change (*Robinson v Flitwick Frames Ltd* [1975] IRLR 261);
- the union has agreed to the change (*Bowater Containers v McCormack* [1980] IRLR 50); or
- the change is trivial (*Baverstock v Horsley Smith & Co* (COIT 910/112)).

In *British Association for Service to the Elderly v Lawton* ([2008] EAT 6/6/2008) the Employee had been employed by a charity for five years. The employer found itself in a financially precarious situation and decided to restructure the terms and conditions of its employee contracts. It sought to impose a single standard on employees that reflected the minimum statutory obligations. In those circumstances, the employee would no longer be able to claim as generous a benefit package as she had in the past. The staff raised a grievance which was never determined, and they were sent letters asking them to agree to the new terms of employment or face dismissal. The employee wrote a personal letter of grievance to the employer, but her concerns was not addressed. She was subsequently dismissed when she refused to comply with the new terms. The employment tribunal considered that she had been unfairly dismissed.

The employer submitted on appeal that:

- It had been reasonable to dismiss the employee, having regard to her conduct in refusing to listen to or accept its arguments, and in taking a part-time job elsewhere without informing the Employer that she had done so.
- The tribunal failed to take into account the fact that it was in a financially precarious position and that, in those circumstances, it had been perfectly reasonable for it to have dismissed the employee for failing to comply with the new terms, which it had implemented in order to survive.

The EAT held:

(1) At no time had the employer put forward misconduct as a reason for the dismissal. In any event, the employer had not known that the employee was working elsewhere whilst working for it, so this could not have been a reason for her dismissal.
(2) The tribunal had plainly considered the employer's financial situation and had had it well in mind in reaching its decision. Whilst the factual result which emerged from the judgment was one which the employer found difficult to accept, it disclosed no error of law amounting to perversity.

Whilst reorganisation is the most common situation constituting some other substantial reason, the tribunals do accept others.

In *Farr v Hoveringham Gravels Ltd* ([1972] IRLR 104) it was held fair to dismiss an employee on 24-hour call-out when he moved to a house 40 miles from the workplace.

In *Foot v Eastern Counties Timber Co. Ltd* [1972] IRLR 83 the employee was dismissed when it was discovered that she was married to an employee of a rival firm. Again, the dismissal was held fair.

❖ THINKING POINT

Foot was decided before the Sex Discrimination Act 1975 came into force. Would that have made any difference to the decision?

Another potential fair reason is pressure from third parties – when other employees refuse to work with a colleague (*Treganowan v Robert Knee & Co* [1975] IRLR 247), or customers put pressure on the employer. However, cases which support this are old.

In *Dobie v Burns International Security Services (UK) Ltd* ([1984] ICR 812) the employee was employed by a company providing the security service at Liverpool Airport as a security officer. Following two incidents for which he was not to blame the airport authorities refused to have him working there. The employer offered him alternative work at a lower rate of pay which he refused and he was dismissed. The Court of Appeal held the dismissal to be fair.

In one situation, however, pressure put upon the employer must be ignored for the purposes of determining whether a dismissal is fair or not. This is where the pressure is brought by a union in the form of the threat of a strike or other industrial action (ERA 1996 s. 107). Further, by 1992 Act s. 160, either the employer or employee may join the union as a party to the unfair dismissal proceedings and the tribunal may apportion any compensation to be paid between the employer and the union so that, ultimately, the union may be required to pay the whole of the compensation.

8.4 Further reading

Barnard & Merrett, 'Winners and losers: Edwards and the unfair law of dismissal (Case Comment)' (2013) 72(2) *Cambridge Law Journal* 313.

Brodtkorb, 'Employee misconduct and UK unfair dismissal law: does the range of reasonable responses test require reform?' (2010) 52(6) *International Journal of Law & Management* 429.

Mantouvalou & Collins, 'Private life and dismissal (Case Comment)' (2009) 38(1) *Industrial Law Journal* 133.

Thornton, 'The Shoesmith dismissal' (2010) 160(7418) *New Law Journal* 726.

Chapter 9

Unfair dismissal 3

Chapter contents

9.1 Overview

For the employer, establishing a potentially fair reason for dismissal is only the first stage in satisfying the Tribunal that the dismissal was not unfair. It is still necessary to demonstrate that it was reasonable to dismiss this employee for this reason and that a fair procedure was followed. This chapter therefore looks at these two elements, together with the remedies available for unfair dismissal.

9.2 The concept of reasonableness

ERA 1996 s. 98(4) states:

> Where the employer has fulfilled the requirements of subsection (1) . . . the determination of the question whether the dismissal was fair or unfair, having regard to the reasons shown by the employer, shall depend on whether in the circumstances (including the size and administrative resources of the employer's undertaking) the employer acted reasonably or unreasonably in treating it as sufficient reason for dismissing the employer; and that question shall be determined in accordance with equity and the substantial merits of the case.

Having a potentially fair reason to dismiss is thus only the first step. The employer must also show the tribunal that he acted reasonably in dismissing the employee for that reason. Essentially, this has two aspects. The employer must show that he:

- made thorough investigations to establish the facts prior to dismissal; and
- acted in a manner consistent with earlier cases, and consistent with the seriousness of the employee's 'offence'.

In *Iceland Frozen Foods v Jones* ([1983] ICR 17) Browne-Wilkinson J set out a five-stage approach which tribunals should adopt:

1) The starting point should always be the words of [s. 98(4)] themselves.
2) In applying the section an industrial tribunal must consider the reasonableness of the employer's conduct, not simply whether they [the members of the tribunal] consider the dismissal to be fair.
3) In judging the reasonableness of the employer's conduct the industrial tribunal must not substitute its own decision as to what was the right course to adopt for that employer.
4) In many, though not all, cases there is a band of reasonable responses to the employee's conduct within which one employer might reasonably take one view, another quite reasonably take another.
5) The function of an industrial tribunal, as an industrial jury, is to determine whether in the particular circumstances of each case the decision to dismiss the employee fell within the band of reasonable responses which a reasonable employer might have adopted.

The concept of a 'band of reasonable responses' to the situation is at the heart of any unfair dismissal case. It might be assumed that this allows employers considerable latitude and that only the most unreasonable dismissals will be judged to be unfair. Although this might have been the case when the unfair dismissal legislation first came into force, it is no longer. It is fair to say that many, if not the majority, of successful unfair dismissal claims succeed on the basis of procedural failure, but, given the facts of cases arising over the past ten years or so, it appears that employers are much slower to dismiss than they used to be, and likely to wait until they have very clear grounds for dismissal.

Iceland Frozen Foods makes it clear that the Tribunal should not apply their own view of what was reasonable in substitution for that of the employer. This was restated by the Court of Appeal in *HSBC Bank Ltd v Madden* [2000] EWCA Civ 330, which also deals in detail with the requirements of a proper investigation – in this case into the alleged misappropriation by a bank employee of customers' credit cards (see below).

> The reason for Mr Madden's dismissal related to his conduct within the meaning of s. 96(2)(b) . . , that is, the Bank's reasonable belief that he had been involved in the misappropriation of debit cards and that that had led to an irretrievable breakdown of trust between the Bank and Mr Madden. In holding that the dismissal of Mr Madden for that reason was unreasonable the Tribunal erred in law in substituting itself as employer in place of the Bank in assessing the quality and weight of the evidence. Instead, it should have asked itself whether, by the standards of a reasonable employer, the Bank had established reasonable grounds for its belief that Mr Madden had been guilty of misconduct and whether the Bank's investigation into the matter had been reasonable in the circumstances.

In practice, arguments put forward in appeal from Tribunal decisions frequently involve claims that the Tribunal has substituted its own decision for that of the employer, rather than considering whether the employer's decision was within the range of reasonable responses.

S. 98(4) speaks of the tribunal deciding whether the employer acted reasonably in treating the reason as sufficient reason to justify dismissal 'in accordance with equity and the substantial merits of the case'. In practice, this means that the tribunal will look at two aspects when considering reasonableness:

- the actual fairness of the decision – was dismissal within the range of reasonable responses for this type of conduct?
- procedural fairness – did the employer use a fair procedure before the employee's eventual dismissal?

In practice, the two strands are very much interlinked.

9.2.1 Fairness of the decision

It has been noted already that the decision of the employer must be within the band of reasonable responses a reasonable employer would choose, but this begs the question, what is a reasonable employer, and what does he take into account in making his decision? The tribunal will look at a variety of factors such as:

- How has the employer treated such cases in the past?
- Has he taken the employee's past work record into account?
- Has he taken the employee's length of service into account?
- Has he considered alternatives to dismissal in appropriate circumstances?

9.2.1.1 Consistency

An employee must know where the goal posts are and know what penalty he can expect to receive for certain conduct. If the employer is inconsistent in the way he applies his sanctions, the employee cannot know where he stands. This may in itself render a dismissal unfair. This creates difficulties for an employer who has treated certain conduct leniently in the past and then decides to raise his standards. There is also a tension between the requirement for consistency and the requirement to take the employee's history into account (see below).

In *Post Office v Fennell* [1981] IRLR 221 an employee was summarily dismissed after assaulting a colleague in the staff canteen. He argued that other workers who had committed the same offence in the past had not been dismissed. The Court of Appeal held his dismissal was unfair.

However, in *Hadjioannou v Coral Casinos Ltd* [1981] IRLR 352 the EAT limited the operation of *Fennell* by saying that consistency was only relevant where employees had been *misled* into thinking that certain conduct would be overlooked or that dismissal would not be the sanction.

It was established *Wilcox v Humphrey & Glasgow Ltd* ([1975] IRLR 211) that before deciding to dismiss, the employer should consider *truly* comparable cases which he knew about or ought reasonably to have known about.

However, according to *Paul v East Surrey District Health Authority* ([1995] IRLR 305), if the employer considers the cases not to be comparable, the tribunal cannot substitute its own decision for that of the employer.

❖ THINKING POINT

Does this open the door to an employer relying on hair-splitting comparison exercises to avoid liability?

9.2.1.2 Past work record and length of service

In misconduct cases in particular, failure to take account of the employee's past record and length of service may render a dismissal unfair. There is some overlap with the requirement for consistency.

In *Johnson Matthey Metals Ltd v Harding* ([1978] IRLR 248) the employee, who had been employed for 15 years with an unblemished record, was dismissed when a colleague's watch, which had gone missing some time before, was found in his possession. The EAT held that the dismissal was unfair given the length of his previous good service.

❖ THINKING POINT

Given that the facts involved theft from a colleague, was the EAT over-generous here?

Sherrier v Ford Motor Company ([1976] IRLR 146) involved two employees who were caught fighting. Despite an investigation by the employer, the instigator could not be established. One employee had a 15-year unblemished record and the employer suspended him for six days without pay. Sherrier, on the other hand, had been employed for two years and had six disciplinary offences on his record. The employer dismissed him, and this dismissal was held to be fair.

❖ THINKING POINT

How can this case be reconciled with the requirement for consistency?

In *Enterprise Liverpool v Bauress* ([2006] EAT 0645/05) two joiners, both of whom had recently finished their apprenticeships, used the employer's van and materials to moonlight during working hours. They were caught doing work on their own account at a time when they should have been doing an urgent job for the employer. The Tribunal found their dismissals to be unfair on the basis that a previous employee guilty of the same misconduct had not been dismissed, although compensation was reduced by 75 per cent for contributory conduct. On the employer's appeal the EAT noted two major differences between these employees' case and the earlier one and considered that it fell within the band of reasonable responses to regard these as distinguishing features:

- the previous employee had admitted his guilt, while these two had initially lied about their activities;
- the previous employee had 30 years' service.

9.2.1.3 Alternative employment

In some cases a reasonable employer will look to see if there is alternative work for the employee to do, particularly in the case of illness or redundancy, although the principle can be applied to almost any situation bar serious misconduct. For example, an employee may have been over-promoted and demotion back to their original grade is a possibility (*Hall v Lodge* IRRR (LIB) 76). However, a tribunal will not expect an employer to demote a person who is clearly incompetent at any level.

On the other hand, in the case of illness, a tribunal will expect an employer to consider alternative employment and failure to do so may well render the dismissal unlawful. The main authority for this is *Todd v North Eastern Electricity Board* ([1975] IRLR 60), although that case is now old, and was decided at a time when 'overmanning' was commonplace, especially in manual occupations.

In relation to redundancy, the ERA 1996 envisages alternative work being offered. S. 138 allows the employee a trial period in the new employment without loss of redundancy compensation should it prove unsuitable. Refusing to allow a redundant employee a trial period where alternative employment is offered is unfair dismissal (*Elliot v Richard Stump Ltd* [1987] IRLR 215).

9.3 Procedural requirements

In some ways, meeting procedural requirements is the most important aspect of avoiding successful claims for unfair dismissal. The problem is that case law tends to leave procedural requirements rather vague. However, the procedure created by the Employment Act 2002, and in force from 2004 until 5 April 2009, makes a useful starting point.

9.3.1 Employment Act 2002 procedure

From 1 October 2004, the provisions of the Employment Act 2002, brought into force by the Employment Act 2002 (Dispute Resolution) Regulations 2004, made it a mandatory requirement for employers to meet minimum procedural standards. otherwise the dismissal would be automatically unfair. These were abolished with effect from 6 April 2009. The Government's purpose in promoting this scheme was the laudable one of reducing claims to employment tribunals by minimising claims based on procedural grounds alone. However, the tribunals were swamped with claims based on highly technical procedural points.

However, even though the statutory procedures have now been repealed by the Employment Act 2008, a dismissal may still be unfair on the basis that the procedure followed was not fair in the circumstances. In those circumstances a tribunal has discretion to increase any compensation awarded by up to 25 per cent if the employer has failed to comply with 'any Code of Practice', in particular the ACAS Code of Practice on Discipline and Grievance Procedures, published under Trade Union and Labour Relations (Consolidation) Act 1992 s. 199 and regularly updated.

Overall, a fair procedure requires that:

a) the employee be given sufficient time and information to be able to prepare for the hearing at which dismissal will be considered;
b) the employee must be given an oral hearing, with the opportunity to call witnesses and to hear the witnesses against him. He is also entitled to be accompanied to that hearing by a colleague or trade union officials, but not a lawyer other than in special circumstances (see below);
c) where a decision is taken to dismiss, the employee must be given reasons for the decision, and a proper opportunity to appeal.

9.3.1.1 Standard dismissal procedure

This applied to:

a) all dismissals except constructive dismissals, some collective dismissals (e.g. large-scale redundancies, for which there are already detailed procedural requirements), some gross misconduct dismissals (which may be dealt with by summary dismissal), and dismissals for reasons outside the parties' control. The word 'dismissals' was used of the last category, but, legally speaking, these are frustrations;
b) all disciplinary action except oral and written warnings and suspension on full pay.

There were three stages to this procedure:

1) The employer must provide the employee with a written statement setting out the reasons why dismissal or disciplinary action is being considered, and setting a date and time for the hearing of the matter. This statement (normally in the form of a letter) should also state that the employee is entitled to be accompanied at the hearing by a colleague or union official. The notice of the hearing should be sufficient to allow the employee time to prepare properly.
2) The hearing must be at a reasonable time and in a convenient location. Reasonable steps must be taken to ensure that any disabled person involved can participate fully. The employee must be given a proper opportunity to put his case.
3) Following the hearing, the employer should write to the employee to inform him of the decision and the reasons for it, and giving a date and time for an appeal hearing. If possible, the appeal should be heard by a different person from the initial decision-maker, and, again, the employee must be given a proper opportunity to put his case. He is also entitled to be accompanied.

9.3.1.2 Modified dismissal procedure

This could be used in 'exceptional' cases involving gross misconduct where summary dismissal was justified. In such cases, there were only two stages to the procedure:

1) written statement;
2) appeal.

9.3.2. Fair procedures

Vauxhall Motors Ltd v Ghafoor ([1993] ICR 370) makes it clear that following the employer's own procedure will not prevent a finding of unfair dismissal where there is an inherent unfairness in that procedure. The employee was dismissed for fighting. Under the disciplinary procedure agreed with the union, he could only appeal against his dismissal with the consent of the union convenor, who refused consent in this case. The EAT held that this constituted procedural unfairness since the right to appeal is the right of every individual and should not be taken away without the individual's express consent. The fact that the employee was a union member did not mean he had given this consent.

In any unfair dismissal case the Tribunal will require the employer to have conducted a thorough investigation, followed by a fair disciplinary hearing and an appeal. Under early case law, failure to follow a fair procedure would not render the dismissal unfair if the employer could show that even if a fair procedure had been followed the employee would have been dismissed anyway, so that the breach of procedure had made no difference to the employee (*British Labour Pump Co. Ltd v Byrne* [1979] IRLR 94).

In *Polkey v A.E. Dayton Services Ltd* ([1987] IRLR 503) the employee was one of four van drivers employed by the Respondent company. As part of a reorganisation, it was decided to replace the four drivers with two van salesmen and a sales representative. Only one of the drivers was considered suitable for transfer to the new duties and, accordingly, the other three were made redundant. The first the Applicant knew of the situation was when he was called into the branch manager's office and told that he was being made redundant. He was immediately driven home by one of the other drivers, who was himself dismissed on his return. The EAT and Court of Appeal upheld the dismissal as fair, despite the failure of the employer to consult with the redundant employees, since such consultation would have made no difference to the result. The House of Lords deemed the 'no difference' rule derived from *British Labour Pump* to be a misinterpretation of s. 98(4), on the basis that the rule concentrated on the unfairness of the decision to the employee rather than, as the section required, the reasonableness of the employer's action.

The *British Labour Pump Principle* was restored by the Employment Act 2002 and consequent regulations, so that a dismissal would not be unfair on the grounds of failure to follow a 'fair' procedure if following a fair procedure would have made no difference, provided the requirements of the 2002 Act were complied with. However, the 2008 Act restored the *Polkey* position, which pertains today.

9.3.2.1 Investigation

It has already been seen that the employer must have a genuine belief, based on reasonable grounds after a reasonable investigation, that the employee has committed the offence. Thus, the employer must gather all the relevant evidence so that he can make a reasoned and fair decision. If, for example, the employee has been caught fighting, the employer should investigate:

- who started the fight?
- was there any provocation?
- was it a subordinate who started a fight against a superior, or vice versa?
- was the fight in potentially dangerous circumstances?
- was it in work time on work premises, etc.?

All these factors will be relevant and the employer cannot discover the answers without a full investigation, involving the questioning of everybody who saw the fight.

In misconduct cases, it has traditionally been usual for the employer to suspend the suspect with pay pending the outcome of the investigation. This is, *inter alia*, in order to prevent the suspect from influencing witnesses – the terms of a suspension usually include a prohibition on contacting colleagues. However, case law makes it clear that suspension should not be used routinely in such cases, and that the employer should always consider whether it is possible to carry out a proper investigation while the employee continues to work. In some cases, indeed, an unnecessary suspension has been held to give rise to a constructive dismissal.

In *Camden & Islington Mental Health and Social Care Trust v Atkinson* ([2007] UKEAT 0058_07_2008) the Claimant was an experienced mental health nurse, and one of a number of nurses at a mental hospital against whom allegations were made of mistreatment of patients. The allegations made against the Claimant were relatively minor, that she had locked a patient out of the ward because he was smoking, and remarked that another needed a bath. Under the Trust's disciplinary policy, a meeting was held at which the decision was made to suspend all the employees who had been named in the abuse allegations, at which the Claimant was entitled to be accompanied by a trade union official, a representative of her professional body or a friend, but was not accompanied. On that basis, the suspension was in breach of contract, and, further, destroyed the relationship of trust and confidence between the parties. The Tribunal said:

> We regard this as an unreasonable exercise of the right to suspend. The unreasonableness was to give no regard to the allegations the Claimant faced and to weigh their seriousness in the overall picture. It was compounded by the unjustifiable decision to deny her representation at the suspension meeting. When we turn to the detail of the two grounds of criticism, the decision to suspend can itself be seen to be unreasonable, such that we conclude that there was lacking any reasonable or proper cause to suspend her. The 'bath' allegation was relatively slight and she gave an answer at the suspension meeting that, as far as we can tell, was complete. . . . The lock-out allegation amounted, potentially, to involvement in an unjustified practice. It was, however, a practice that had been carried out for 11 years and had the imprimatur (again, as far as we can judge) of the next two levels of management above the Claimant. The decision not to suspend [another named nurse], because he no longer worked with patients, only serves to heighten our disquiet that the Claimant was suspended at all. We also know that the Respondent failed to consider the most obvious option to suspension. This was to ensure that the Claimant abandoned the policy there and then. We see from the subsequent interview that she had no difficulty in accepting the advice that the policy was 'illegal', using her term. It was not, we conclude, necessary to suspend her for the better protection of patients. The reality, rather, is that she was suspended because all the Daleham employees complained about by name were suspended.

❖ THINKING POINT

If the suspect continues to work, how can the employer ensure that he cannot interfere with witnesses?

Although the employer should normally conduct as thorough an investigation as possible, this may not be possible where the conduct at issue is a criminal offence and the police are also investigating. In that case the employee will often remain silent on the advice of his solicitor and therefore the employer will not be able to ascertain his version of events. Case law establishes that as long as the employer has enough evidence to form a reasonable belief in the employee's guilt, and has given the suspect a proper opportunity to put his case, the dismissal will be fair.

9.3.2.2 Hearing

The principles of a fair hearing are as follows:

a) The employee must know the case against him in order to enable him to answer the complaint (*Hutchins v British Railways Board* IRLR 303). Since the aim of this rule is to enable him to prepare his case, he should be informed of the case against him sufficiently far in advance of the hearing to enable him to prepare adequately. It was also held in *A v Company B Ltd* [1997] IRLR 405 that an employee must not only know the allegations against him, but also the identity of his accuser.
b) The employee must have the opportunity to put his side of the case. The employer should listen to his side of the story and allow him to explain his conduct or put forward mitigating circumstances.

In *Clarke v Trimoco Motor Group Ltd* ([1993] IRLR 148) the Claimant, who worked in a petrol station, and another employee were accused by a customer of billing for petrol which had not been put in customers' lorries. During the investigation Clarke denied fraud but admitted that he had post-dated some fuel vouchers at the request of drivers. He was given a written warning by the employers, and also told that further action might be taken if the police came up with new evidence. During the police investigation two drivers confessed to fraud and implicated Clarke. All three were charged with criminal offences. The employers then suspended Clarke pending the outcome of the court case. After the case was adjourned twice, but before it was heard, Clarke was dismissed for the original offence of altering the fuel vouchers. The tribunal found that the real reason for the dismissal was the suspicion of fraud, although this was not the reason given, and the dismissal was fair because he knew this was the reason. Further, the employer had not acted unfairly in failing to give Clarke an opportunity to answer the allegation of fraud as he could have raised it via the grievance procedure between his suspension and dismissal.

The EAT, however, found the dismissal to be unfair, although they agreed with the tribunal that Clarke knew the real reason for his dismissal, holding that the fact that he could have used the grievance procedure was no excuse for not allowing him to answer the allegations of fraud.

c) The employee must be allowed representation at the hearing. Statute now provides that an employee is always entitled to be accompanied at a disciplinary hearing by a union official or colleague. There is no general entitlement to legal representation, but such a right may arise where the employee is at risk of losing the opportunity to practise a particular profession altogether.

In *R (On the Application of G) v X School* ([2010] EWCA 1) the Claimant, a male teaching assistant at X School, was alleged to have kissed a 15-year-old boy on work experience. Although the allegation, if true, could have amounted to a criminal offence, no criminal proceedings were pursued. The governors conducted an internal investigation and disciplinary hearing, and dismissed G for abuse of trust.

As a result of the governors reporting their decision to the authorities, as required by law, G's name could be added to a statutory register, which would prevent him from working with children in the future. He applied for a judicial review of the governors' decisions not to allow him legal representation at the disciplinary hearing or the appeal hearing (which had been postponed pending the outcome of the judicial review). He contended that the governors' decisions violated his rights under Article 6 of the European Convention on Human Rights. G's case was successful in the High Court, but the governors appealed this decision to the Court of Appeal.

The Court of Appeal held that if the purpose of a hearing is to determine an individual's civil rights or criminal charges against that individual, Article 6 provides a right to a fair hearing.

Article 6 was engaged in this case because G's disciplinary hearing was going to determine his civil rights (i.e. to practise as a teaching assistant), as the outcome of the hearing would inevitably have a substantial influence or effect on G's right to practise his profession. The governors were required to notify their decision to the authority administrating the register, now the Independent Safeguarding Authority (ISA). Although the ISA is an autonomous body, it would not necessarily conduct its own investigation or hold an oral hearing with cross examination. It was likely, therefore, that the governors' decision at the original disciplinary hearing would influence the ISA's decision as to whether to include G on the register and, as a result, whether G would be able to practise his profession in future.

The Court of Appeal went on to decide that the right to a fair hearing under Article 6 includes a right to legal representation where the issue to be determined is sufficiently serious to warrant it, as it was in this case.

d) The hearing should be unbiased; that is, the employer should approach the hearing with an open mind and not prejudge the issue.

In *Moyes v Hylton WMC* ([1986] IRLR 482) two witnesses to an alleged act of sexual harassment also conducted the investigation; one chaired the disciplinary hearing which decided to dismiss the employee. Not surprisingly, it was held that the dismissal was unfair.

e) The employee should be informed of his right to appeal to a higher level of management who have not been involved in the previous decision to dismiss. Should the employee fail to exercise his right to appeal he will not have failed to mitigate his loss and it will not contribute to the finding of the tribunal in any way (*William Muir (Bond 9) Ltd v Lamb* [1985] IRLR 95). On the other hand, refusing to allow the employee to exercise a contractual right of appeal will almost always render a dismissal unfair (*West Midlands Co-operative Society v Tipton* [1986] IRLR 112). In addition, the court may place an injunction on the employer to prevent the contract from being treated as terminated until the appeal has taken place (*Jones v Lee and Guilding* [1980 IRLR 67).

9.3.2.3 Appeals

The Tribunal will expect the employer to have provided a means of appeal against the original decision to dismiss. All the principles which apply to a fair hearing also apply on appeal, together with two further points:

- Given the rule against bias, the same individuals cannot take part in both the disciplinary hearing and the appeal, though case law makes exceptions in the case of very small organisations, where there are simply not enough senior employees for this purpose.
- Given that the employee must know the case against him, it follows that the appeal cannot endorse the original decision to dismiss for a different reason. In *Monie v Coral Racing Ltd* ([1981] ICR 109) the employee was dismissed for theft, but the appeal panel did not feel there was sufficient evidence to support the allegation. Instead, it confirmed the dismissal on the grounds that the employee concerned failed to report thefts by fellow employees. The dismissal was ruled unlawful by the EAT.

Appeals may take different forms. Some involve a complete rehearing of the case, while others simply involve a paper review. *Whitbread & Co plc v Mills* ([1988] IRLR 501) demonstrates that an appeal hearing which is a total re-hearing of the case, may rectify previous breaches of a fair procedure at the disciplinary hearing stage, so that overall the dismissal is not unfair. This is logical, since the requirement of a proper procedure is that the employee has a proper opportunity to put his case against dismissal.

9.3.3 Case law on procedure

This section deals with procedural issues specific to the various potentially fair reasons for dismissal.

9.3.3.1 Capability and qualifications

9.3.3.1.1 Inadequate work

The starting point for the employer is to consider whether this is deliberate incapability – laziness or deliberate negligence – or inherent incapability. The first is really misconduct and the employer is entitled to treat it as such. Where the reason appears to be inherent incapability the tribunal will normally look for three stages in the employer's procedure:

- investigation;
- reasonable opportunity to improve;
- warnings.

In addition, the employer should consider the possibility of alternative employment where appropriate.

Investigation Instant dismissal without an investigation will almost always be unfair. When the employee is the subject of an investigation, he should be told the scope of that investigation and the facts and matters alleged against him.

Davison v Kent Meters Ltd ([1975] IRLR 145) was a case where the employee was dismissed after assembling 500 components incorrectly, having never been trained to do so. Although the dismissal was held unfair on substantive grounds, the EAT noted that a proper investigation would have revealed the absence of training.

Reasonable opportunity to improve If, after the investigation, the employer can detect no reason for the incapability, such as lack of training, a failure to allow the employee opportunity to improve will often render a dismissal unfair (*Mansfield Hosiery Mills Ltd v Bromley* [1977] IRLR 301).

Warnings Normally the employer should warn the employee before dismissal, but early cases suggest that failure to do so may not invariably render the dismissal unfair. In *Lowndes v Specialist Heavy Engineering Ltd* ([1977] ICR 30) the employee was dismissed after five serious and expensive mistakes. He was not warned and was given no opportunity to make representations. His dismissal was held not unfair, but the case is now 40 years old and the precedent might well not be followed today.

9.3.3.1.2 Sickness or injury

Case law shows that tribunals will pay particular attention to the provision of warnings and opportunities for the employee's attendance to improve. Further, the employer must obtain sufficient medical information to be able to make an informed decision. In the recent case of *O'Brien v Bolton St Catherine's Academy* ([2017] EWCA Civ 145) the Claimant's dismissal was held unfair by a 2:1 majority in the Court of Appeal because the employer did not allow time to make further inquiries after the Claimant argued that she was now fit to return to work at once.

Ward v Secretary of State for Work & Pensions ([2013] UKEAT/0271/12/JOJ) makes a useful example of a case where an employee with a lengthy history of illness was found not to have been unfairly dismissed. In addition, except for a claim of failure to make reasonable adjustments which was accepted, his claims under the disability discrimination legislation were also rejected, both at first instance and by the EAT. The Claimant had worked in Jobcentres since 1994 and developed Irritable Bowel Syndrome (IBS) in or around 2000. It was accepted that from then on he was a disabled person. Between May 2001 and January 2009, the employer obtained seven Occupational Health reports, and on the basis of these made various adjustments to enable the claimant to continue to work. In particular, since his IBS was a greater problem in the mornings, they allowed him to begin work at 9.30am, with no client meetings before 11.30am, and until 2007 they disregarded absences which were caused by IBS. In the course of 2007, however, the employer became concerned about high levels of sickness absence in the organisation and 'tightened up' its procedures.

The employer had two sickness absence procedures. One, covering absences longer than 28 days, was used in relation to the Claimant's ten-month absence in 2006–2007. The other, known as the Irregular Attendance Process, was used in respect of repeated short-term absences, and operated as follows:

a) When a 'consideration point' was reached – normally eight days' absence in a rolling 12-month period – the employee was given a warning, and could be put on a Review Period of six months, during which his attendance had to reach a set level.
b) If the employee did not meet the required standard during the Review Period, the manager moved to a 'consider dismissal' stage. If he did meet the required standard, then his attendance would be monitored for a further 'backsliding period'. Again, if the attendance fell below standard during the 'backsliding period' the manager moved on to the 'consider dismissal' stage.
c) At the 'consider dismissal' stage the manager must refer the issue to an 'independent decision maker', who is responsible for deciding whether the employee should be dismissed or demoted or, in the alternative, that the period of attendance monitoring should continue.

The issue in *Ward* was whether the employer should have granted a more generous consideration point because of the Claimant's IBS. From 2007 a dispute developed as to whether the Claimant had been granted a consideration point of 18 days' absence, as he claimed, or 13 days' absence, as the employer argued. The Claimant's attendance did not improve, despite continuing adjustments, and on 11 August 2009 a decision was taken to dismiss him on grounds of unsatisfactory attendance.

The Employment Tribunal said:

> The Claimant was dismissed for capability reasons which is a potentially fair reason under section 98(1)(2) [sic] of the Employment Rights Act 1996. We are satisfied that this has been shown to us by the Respondent. We then have to consider whether the dismissal is fair for the purpose of section 98(4). The key to fairness in such cases is a fair procedure. Such a procedure requires, in particular,
>
> (i) Consultation with the employee;
> (ii) A thorough investigation of the medical situation and the reason for the absences;
> (iii) Consideration of other options.

We have set out in our findings the details of the various consultation procedures and appeals which the Respondent went through. Whilst the Claimant argues with the decisions reached in those matters he does not argue about their inherent fairness. His views were certainly consulted at every stage of the procedure, even though they were not accepted. There was a fair procedure with various stages provided in it. There was a general allowance of eight days for sickness absence, which the Respondents had increased [by] five days in the case of the Claimant. He was therefore given every opportunity of showing that he could attend work on a regular basis. In connection with unfair dismissal we had to disregard the provisions for Disability Discrimination Act. These we have considered separately but they are immaterial for the purposes of unfair dismissal.

The Respondent's Occupational Health department regularly assessed the Claimant and produced reports with which the Claimant did not essentially take issue. There was no doubt that the Respondent knew about the Claimant's IBS and the reasons for its absences. Indeed it is noteworthy that they tolerated absences in excess of what they had agreed when taking into account his long term absences.

Consideration was given to alternative employment. He was moved from his position from managing counter staff to being a disability adviser, a job which he accepted was compatible with his difficulties. Other adjustments were also made as set out above. None of these procedures have any element of unfairness[. . .]

We have also been asked to consider whether there was a general bias against the Claimant. . . . It is certain that the Respondent had decided to take a more stringent line on absence. There is nothing unfair in that, and it is a duty of management to manage such absences. The ultimate tool in such management is the threat of dismissal and, eventually, if there should be no improvement, actual dismissal. We have had to judge the conduct of those actually managing the process with the Claimant. We have found no bias in them against the Claimant.

Taking all these matters into account we have come to the conclusion that there was no unfairness in the Claimant's dismissal. He was dismissed for exceeding, by some way, the permitted levels of absence which were, in themselves, quite generous. A fair and proportionate procedure had taken place over a period of two years. The Claimant's attendance had not improved. In the circumstances we find that the Claimant's dismissal was not unfair and his complaint is accordingly dismissed.

9.3.3.2 Conduct

The employer may have his own disciplinary procedures instead of applying the ACAS Code on Discipline and Grievance Procedures, but these must be equivalent to those contained in the Code. An employer's code will normally set out:

- rules, including matters regarded as gross misconduct justifying summary dismissal;
- procedures;
- sanctions.

9.3.3.2.1 Rules

Disciplinary rules will either be part of the employer's disciplinary procedures or contained in a separate document, or, nowadays, may be found on the employer's internal website.

The following is a non-exhaustive list of matters regarded by a university as gross misconduct.

- Stealing from the university, members of staff, students or the public.
- Misuse or unauthorised possession of the assets, funds, equipment or property of the university, staff, students or visitors.
- Fraud, including any deliberate attempt to defraud the university, staff, students or other people or organisations in the course of your duties and responsibilities.
- Corruption, including accepting money, goods, favours or excessive hospitality from people outside the university in return for carrying out acts or services which are not in line with our interests.
- Deliberately falsifying or misrepresenting records or claims made.
- Serious harassment or bullying.
- Discriminating against or harassing another person because of their sex, sexual orientation, race, disability, age, religion or belief.

- Physical violence towards other members of staff, students or visitors.
- Deliberately damaging property belonging to the university, staff, students or visitors.
- Serious negligence or breaking safety rules which could cause unacceptable loss, damage or injury.
- Not keeping to our policies, procedures, regulations or rules.
- Being seriously incapable of doing your work, for example, because you have been drinking alcohol or taking illegal drugs or other substances.
- Serious acts of insubordination, including refusing to follow a reasonable instruction.
- Serious misuse of our property, facilities or name.
- Doing or failing to do something which might damage our operations or which seriously damages our reputation.
- Inappropriate use of information technology, the internet or social media, including posts or online content, including emails, for example racist, sexist, pornographic or homophobic material, that is or could be offensive or harmful to employees, students, or our reputation.
- Unauthorised use of, or release of, commercially sensitive or confidential information relating to the university.

Case law shows that it is essential that the rules are both unambiguous and available for access by the employee.

In *Brooks and Son v Skinner* ([1984] IRLR 379) the employer agreed with the union that any employee who, as a result of over-indulgence at the Christmas party, failed to turn up for work the next day would be dismissed. This agreement was not communicated to the employees and Skinner was dismissed when he failed to turn up. It was held that the dismissal was unfair as he could not have realised, without being told, that such conduct would lead to dismissal.

This begs the question, however, of the extent to which the employer must communicate obvious rules, i.e. that theft is gross misconduct.

In *CA Parsons & Co Ltd v McLoughlin* ([1978] IRLR 65) a dismissal for fighting was fair even though it was not included in the employer's rules as gross misconduct because everyone would know that such conduct would be looked upon gravely by management. However, the fight took place on the factory floor close to machinery, so that the risk was held obvious to the reasonable employee. Not every instance is as obvious.

Henderson v Hackney LBC ([2010] UKEAT/0072/09/JOJ) involved a very modern issue. A woman teacher at a school for 'vulnerable' girls downloaded internet porn and sent examples to colleagues. Although the school had no internet policy which stated specifically that viewing porn at work was a disciplinary offence, the dismissal was held not to be unfair. The Tribunal paid particular regard to the nature of the work.

❖ THINKING POINT

There was no evidence that the teacher's pupils had seen any of the porn. Should that make a difference to the Tribunal's decision?

In addition to adequate communication of the rule, it is essential that the employee understands that what is being communicated is a standard to which he must conform. Vague and badly drafted rules which could be misunderstood by an employee may again lead to a finding of unfair dismissal. Even if the rule has been adequately made known to the employee and has been broken, the employer may still be acting unreasonably in dismissing if the rule breached has no relevance to the employment.

In *Talbot v Hugh M Fulton Ltd* ([1975] IRLR 52) a male delicatessen employee was dismissed for having long hair, contrary to company rules. It was held that the rules did not define what was meant by long hair, and in any event, there were no safety or hygiene grounds to justify such a rule. The dismissal was unfair. The facts of the case occurred before the Sex Discrimination Act came into force, such a rule would now be sexually discriminatory unless it was justified on the grounds of safety or hygiene and analogous standards were laid down for women.

The Claimant in *Lock v Cardiff Railway Company Ltd* ([1998] IRLR 358) was employed as a train conductor, and was dismissed as a result of an incident in which he required a teenage boy (aged 16 but looking older) to leave the train at an intermediate station because he had no valid ticket and no money to pay the excess fare. The boy was left in a strange area with no means of getting home.

Following a disciplinary hearing at which the Applicant conceded that he had made a mistake, the employers concluded that he had shown a lack of judgement in the exercise of his discretion as a train conductor as to how to deal with a passenger in this situation, which amounted to misconduct justifying dismissal. The employer's disciplinary code set out a number of potential disciplinary offences and a range of possible sanctions. It did not, however, specify which offences would be regarded as gross misconduct justifying dismissal for a single breach.

The EAT held that:

1) The tribunal's finding that the employers had acted reasonably in dismissing the Applicant for a one-off act of misjudgement was perverse. Since the employee had never been told that he would be dismissed for a one-off act of that sort, no reasonable tribunal properly conducting itself could have concluded that dismissal was a fair penalty.
2) The tribunal had also misdirected itself in law in failing to have regard to the provisions of the ACAS Code. Even where the Code is not expressly referred to by the parties, tribunals should always use it as a guide as to what is good sound industrial relations practice. Accordingly, the tribunal should have considered whether the Code had been complied with in this case. Had it done so, it would have found that the employers had failed to meet the Code's requirements by not specifying those offences which would be regarded as gross misconduct justifying dismissal for a first offence.

It would appear from the facts of this case that the Claimant had failed to follow clear written instructions as to how to deal with such a situation, and was also under a final warning at the time of the incident, although the internal appeal considered only the specific incident. Although the EAT considered that the dismissal was unfair, they also regarded the Applicant as culpable, and that there should be a reduction in compensation.

9.3.3.2.2 Sanctions

The employer will normally have a range of sanctions he may impose for misconduct, dismissal being the ultimate sanction. The variety of the employer's sanctions will be an important consideration for the tribunal in deciding whether the decision to dismiss is a fair one and whether the 'punishment fits the crime'. Imposing too harsh a sanction short of dismissal may itself be a repudiatory breach of contract, justifying the employee in resigning and claiming constructive dismissal.

Warnings Apart from gross misconduct, an employee should receive a warning before being dismissed. The ACAS Code recommends three warnings before dismissal; the first verbal, the second written and a final written, although these are simply guidelines, and much will depend on the circumstances of the case and the type of misconduct. It may well be unreasonable to depart from that sequence in relation to, for example, an employee being five minutes late on one occasion; but it would not be unreasonable in a case of serious misconduct to circumvent the earlier stages of the procedure and go straight to a final warning. The ACAS Code further urges that, apart from gross misconduct, no one should be dismissed for a first offence, and recommends that warnings should only remain on an employee's record for a set period (usually six to 12 months).

Fines or deductions The employer must have contractual authority or obtain the employee's written consent in order to make any deduction from pay.

Suspension without pay It follows that if deductions from pay without contractual authority or the employee's written consent form a breach of ERA 1996 and a potential constructive dismissal, so does suspension without pay.

Demotion Given that the employee is employed in a certain capacity to perform certain duties, any alteration in either, without his consent, is a fundamental breach by the employer and again a potential constructive dismissal. The same is true if the employer imposes a disciplinary transfer on the employee. However, such a constructive dismissal is not necessarily unfair.

In *Hall v Lodge* (IRRR (LIB) 76) an employee was promoted from supervisor to manager. It soon became clear that she had been over-promoted and was unable to do the manager's job. The employer therefore offered her another supervisor's job at a different branch at her old salary. She refused, resigned and claimed constructive dismissal. The EAT held that although there had been a constructive dismissal, in the circumstances that dismissal was fair.

However, where the demotion etc. is out of proportion to the misconduct, even where there is a contractual right to demote, the excessiveness of the employer's action is likely to render the (constructive) dismissal unfair.

9.3.3.3 Statutory restriction

There are no specific procedural issues involved when dismissing for this reason. The fairness of the dismissal will turn on the fairness of the decision - for example whether the employer has fully considered alternative employment, rather than the procedure adopted.

9.3.3.4 Redundancy

By contrast, a fair procedure is an important aspect of establishing that a dismissal for redundancy is not unfair. Further details can be found in the Chapter 10.

A redundancy will be automatically unfair if the employee is selected for redundancy by reason of his trade union membership/non-membership or activities (Trade Union and Labour Relations (Consolidation) Act 1992) or if he is selected for a reason specified in ERA 1996 s. 105. Even where those statutory provisions are not infringed, a redundancy may still be unfair if the employer has not acted reasonably. In particular, the tribunal will look at the unit of selection used, the criteria chosen for selection, the reasonableness of the procedure, and the efforts made to find alternative employment.

9.3.3.4.1 Unfair unit of selection

The employer should define his pool of employees in a reasonable manner before using his selection criteria. If the union have agreed the selection unit it is more likely to be held that this unit was reasonable.

9.3.3.4.2 Unfair selection criteria

The selection criteria should be objective and not subjective. Criteria such as 'employees who in the opinion of management will keep the company viable' were considered in *Williams v Compair*

Maxam Ltd [1982] IRLR 83 (EAT) to be too heavily reliant on individual opinion. 'Last in, first out' is a traditional starting point and a selection based on this is unlikely to be held unfair. However, this has now been superseded by a 'matrix' approach using a number of criteria such as experience, skill, attendance, etc. Another approach which is used by some employers is to require those employees who wish to remain to apply for the jobs available and to operate a selection procedure analogous to recruitment. The employer must ensure that any criteria he adopts are not discriminatory. It has already been noted that giving full-time employees priority for retention is indirect discrimination, and including attendance as a criterion may discriminate against disabled employees.

9.3.3.4.3 Reasonable procedure

Williams v Compair Maxam laid down guidelines for a fair procedure where there is a recognised trade union. Although the guidelines only apply where there is such a union and may be inappropriate in a small business (*Simpson & Son (Motors) v Reid and Findlater* [1983] IRLR 401), some of the principles are appropriate to any business.

1) The employer should give as much warning as possible of the impending redundancies to the union and employees concerned;
2) the employer should seek the agreement of the union regarding selection criteria, and the best means of achieving the necessary result, causing as little hardship and unfairness as possible;
3) the employer should consider any representation made by the union as to the selection;
4) the employer should consider whether, instead of dismissing the employee, he could offer alternative employment.

Warning and consultation Consultation is required whether the employee is a member of a recognised union or not. *Hough v Leyland DAF* ([1991] IRLR 194) establishes that failing to consult with the employee, despite consulting with the employee's union, renders a redundancy unfair. Collective and individual consultation are both required; where there is no recognised union, the employer must arrange for employee representatives to be elected for this purpose.

Consultation requires positive action on the part of the employer. Merely informing the employees of impending redundancies and telling them the selection criteria is not consultation (*Rowell v Hubbard Group Services Ltd* [1995] IRLR 195). The employer is under a duty to consult with all the relevant employees even if they are on fixed-term contracts (*University of Glasgow v Donaldson and McNally* [1995] IDS Brief 543).

Statutory requirements apply where 30 or more employees are to be made redundant, including minimum periods for consultation.

Alternative employment The employer should consider whether there is alternative employment he can offer the employee concerned, although he is under no duty to create vacancies.

9.3.4 Some other substantial reason

As with statutory restrictions, there are few, if any, procedural issues in relation to this. The only relevant issue is in relation to pressure from third parties, where the employer must show that he has adequately investigated and has sufficient evidence on which to base his decision.

9.4 Automatically unfair reasons for dismissal

In certain cases of dismissal, the issue of reasonableness is irrelevant, as a dismissal for certain specified reasons is automatically unfair. These reasons are all creations of statute, and generally apply where the employee concerned was dismissed for utilising or seeking to utilise the relevant statutory right. In such cases, all that is necessary is that the employee show a causal link between the assertion of the statutory right and the dismissal. Further, no minimum continuity of employment is required in respect of automatically unfair dismissal claims.

9.4.1 Pregnancy (ERA s. 99)

A dismissal for pregnancy or a reason connected with pregnancy is automatically unfair. However, there must be a causal link between the dismissal and the pregnancy or exercise of maternity rights. Therefore, if the employee can no longer do the job she is employed to do, or it would be a breach of a statutory provision to keep employing her, the dismissal will not be automatically unfair, but on the basis of the reasonableness test the tribunal may still find the dismissal to be unfair – where, for example, there is alternative work she could do. Where a woman is selected for redundancy because of pregnancy, this is a dismissal for pregnancy and not redundancy as such (*Brown v Stockton on Tees BC* [1988] IRLR 263 and ERA s. 105). This category does not apply where the employee does not know of the pregnancy (*Ramdoolar v Bycity Ltd* [2005] ICR 368).

9.4.2 Parental leave/time off for dependants

The Employment Relations Act 1999 added two further automatically unfair reasons for dismissal to ERA 1996 s. 96. These are where an employee is dismissed for exercising the rights to parental leave contained in the Maternity and Parental Leave Regulations 1999, or the right to reasonable time off to deal with dependants under ERA 1996 s. 57A.

9.4.3 Spent convictions

The Rehabilitation of Offenders Act 1974 was enacted to ensure that those who had been convicted of a criminal offence and had genuinely tried to rehabilitate themselves should not be handicapped by having to disclose their past record. Under the Act, certain rehabilitation periods are laid down, at the end of which the conviction is deemed to be spent. The rehabilitation period depends on the seriousness of the offence and the penalty imposed, and, generally, once a conviction is spent the employee does not have to reveal it. For employment purposes, s. 4(3)(b) states that a spent conviction or failure to disclose such conviction shall not be grounds for dismissing or excluding a person from any office, profession, occupation or employment, or for prejudicing him in any way in any occupation or employment.

The rehabilitation period runs from the date of conviction, not the expiry of the sentence. The periods of imprisonment which are relevant are the sentence imposed, not the time actually served. Certain professions are exempt from the Act by the Rehabilitation of Offenders (Exceptions) Order 1975, including solicitors, accountants, and nurses.

The Act provides no remedy if a person is refused a job because of a spent conviction, nor if he is discriminated against by reason of such conviction. However, once a person has become an employee a dismissal for a spent conviction is unfair.

9.4.4 Trade union membership or activities

By Trade Union and Labour Relations (Consolidation) Act 1992 s. 152(1) a dismissal is automatically unfair if the reason for the dismissal was that the employee:

a) was, or proposed to become, a member of an independent trade union;
b) had taken, or proposed to take, part in the activities of an independent trade union at an appropriate time; or

c) was not a member of any trade union, or of a particular trade union, or one of a number of particular trade unions, or had refused, or proposed to refuse, to become or remain a member.

The protection in respect of taking part in trade union 'activities' at an 'appropriate time' begs two questions:

1) What are trade union 'activities'?
2) What constitutes an 'appropriate' time?

'Activities' are given their normal meaning so that union meetings, recruitment, etc., are all union activities. By s. 152(2) 'appropriate time' means outside working hours or within working hours in accordance with arrangements made with the consent of the employer. In *Marley Tile Co Ltd v Shaw* ([1980] ICR 72) a union meeting during working hours was not held with the consent of the employer where he merely remained silent when informed that the meeting was going to take place.

It should be noted that striking or other industrial action are not trade union activities for the purpose of this section.

9.4.5 Dismissal in connection with recognition or derecognition

The Employment Relations Act 1999 introduced Sch. A1 into TULR(C)A 1992. This provides procedures for the recognition and derecognition of unions in the workplace. Para. 156 protects a worker against suffering a detriment for action taken in respect of recognition or derecognition, and para. 161 renders the dismissal of an employee in such circumstances unfair, unless the actions of the employee are unreasonable actions or omissions.

9.4.6 Dismissal in health and safety cases

By 1996 Act s. 100, a dismissal will be automatically unfair if the reason for dismissal was that:

a) the employee was a health and safety representative and performed or proposed to perform any of the functions of such;
b) there is no such representative and the employee brought to his employer's attention circumstances which the employee reasonably believed were harmful or potentially harmful to his health and safety;
c) in circumstances of danger which he reasonably believed to be imminent and which he could not avert he left or proposed to leave his work place, or refused to return to his workplace while the danger continued;
d) in circumstances of danger he reasonably believed to be imminent he took or proposed to take steps to prevent himself and others from danger.

Such a dismissal will not be unfair if the employer can demonstrate that it was or would be negligent for the employee to take those steps to the extent that a reasonable employer would have dismissed him.

Selection for redundancy for any of these reasons is again deemed to be selection for an inadmissible reason, and no continuity is required in order to claim unfair dismissal on these grounds.

9.4.7 Dismissal on the grounds of assertion of a statutory right

1996 Act s. 104 applies where an employee has brought proceedings to enforce a relevant statutory right or alleged that the employer had infringed his relevant statutory rights. This is akin to victimisation under the Equality Act, but applies where the employee has brought proceedings under other legislation.

Relevant statutory rights for this purpose are any rights conferred where the remedy for infringement is a complaint to an employment tribunal (ERA 1996) and union activities and time off rights conferred by the 1992 Act. It is irrelevant for this purpose whether the employee has the right in question or not, and whether it has in fact been infringed, provided the allegation or proceedings were made in good faith.

Again, selection for redundancy for this reason is automatically unfair dismissal and no continuity is required.

9.4.8 Dismissal on the grounds that the employee is an employee representative

Dismissal is automatically unfair if the reason for the dismissal was that the representative performed or proposed to perform any functions or activities as a representative or candidate for the office of representative (s. 103).

9.4.9 Shop workers and betting workers

By s. 101 it is automatic unfair dismissal to dismiss a shop worker or betting worker who has opted out of Sunday working within the meaning of ERA s. 41 (applies to shop workers whose continuous employment commenced prior to 26 August 1994 and betting workers whose continuous employment began before 2 January 1995, when the Sunday Trading Act 1994 came into force, and to others who have opted out of Sunday working by giving three months' notice in writing, once that notice has expired), where the reason for dismissal is the employee's refusal to work on Sundays. Note that this *only* applies to shop and betting workers.

❖ THINKING POINT

Why should this provision only apply to shop and betting workers?

9.4.10 Dismissal of a trustee of an occupational pension scheme

By s. 102 it is an automatic unfair dismissal to dismiss a trustee of an occupational pension scheme where the reason for dismissal is that he performs or proposes to perform any of his functions as a trustee.

9.4.11 Dismissal for making a protected disclosure

By s. 103A it is automatic unfair dismissal to dismiss an employee for making a protected disclosure under the Public Interest Disclosure Act 1998.

9.5 Remedies for unfair dismissal

A claim for unfair dismissal must normally be presented within three months of the effective date of termination of the contract. By ERA s. 111(2)(b) the tribunal may hear complaints out of time if it is satisfied that it was not reasonably practicable to present the complaint in time.

Should the applicant be successful in his claim, there are a number of remedies the tribunal may award:

9.5.1 Reinstatement

Reinstatement is an order that the employer shall treat the employee in all respects as if he had not been dismissed, and must include all the benefits payable in the period since his dismissal, including seniority and pensions (ERA s. 114(2)). In exercising its discretion to make an order for reinstatement, the tribunal must have regard to:

a) the wishes of the complainant;
b) whether it is reasonably practicable for the employer to comply with the order;
c) if there is contributory conduct, whether it is just to make the order.

While reinstatement is rarely ordered, if the tribunal does exercise its discretion, failure to comply with a reinstatement order will lead to an additional award (see below).

9.5.2 Re-engagement

If the tribunal declines to order reinstatement it must then consider re-engagement. Such an order means that the employee is returned to a comparable job rather than his original job, although the job must be as favourable as the old (s. 115(2)). In deciding whether to exercise its discretion, the tribunal takes into account similar factors to those relating to reinstatement. The tribunal cannot order the employer to provide a job which is more favourable (*Rank Xerox Ltd v Stryczek* [1995] IRLR 568).

9.5.3 Financial compensation

Orders for reinstatement or re-engagement are made in fewer than 5 per cent of cases, and therefore the main remedy for unfair dismissal is financial compensation. Compensation comes under a number of headings.

9.5.3.1 Basic award

This compensates the employee for the loss of his job and is calculated in the same way as redundancy pay, being based on the employee's age, length of service and gross weekly pay, as follows:

a) service below the age of 22: half a week's pay per completed year of service;
b) service between 22 and 40: one week's pay per year of service;
c) service over the age of 41: one and a half weeks' pay per year of service (s. 119(2)).

Pay is subject to a statutory maximum, increased annually in line with inflation, and service to a statutory maximum of 20 years. The basic award may also be reduced for:

a) conduct (whether it contributed to the dismissal or not);
b) unreasonable refusal of an offer of reinstatement;
c) any redundancy pay received;
d) any *ex gratia* payments.

Soros v Davison ([1994] IRLR 264) establishes that a tribunal cannot reduce compensation on the grounds of conduct after the dismissal, although this prohibition does not apply where conduct occurring before the dismissal was only discovered after the dismissal.

9.5.3.2 Compensatory award

This award is intended to compensate the employee for the loss he has suffered as a result of the dismissal (s. 123(1)). Again, it is subjected to a statutory maximum, set annually, or 12 months' net pay, whichever is the less. Unlike the basic award, the compensatory award is based on net pay. This is entirely logical, since it is intended to compensate the claimant for the actual loss flowing from his dismissal. While the award should reflect the employee's loss, it must also be just and equitable in the circumstances.

The tribunal will consider a number of factors when assessing compensation under this heading, such as:

- immediate loss of earnings (the tribunal will calculate the loss between the date of dismissal and the date of the hearing, less any benefits received);
- future loss of earnings (tribunal will estimate how long the employee is likely to remain unemployed – the employee is under a duty to mitigate his loss);
- loss of fringe benefits;
- loss of pension rights;
- expenses in looking for work;
- loss of employment protection – usually a standard sum representing a week's pay for basic award purposes;
- manner of dismissal.

9.5.3.3 Additional award

The tribunal may make an additional award where the employer has ignored an order for reinstatement or re-engagement, or the dismissal was discriminatory.

An additional award is within the range of 26–52 weeks' pay, but the upper limit does not apply where the reason for dismissal was on health and safety grounds, because the employee is a trustee of an occupational pension scheme, or the employee is an employee representative (s. 117(4)).

9.6 Further reading

Wynn-Evans, 'Harsh but fair – the "range of reasonable responses" test and the "substitution mindset" revisited: *Newbound v Thames Water Utilities Ltd*' (2015) 44(4) *Industrial Law Journal* 566.

Chapter 10

Redundancy

Chapter contents

10.1 Overview

This chapter considers redundancy, which is a potentially fair reason for dismissal under ERA s. 98. It differs from other potentially fair reasons, in that a redundant employee is normally entitled to financial recompense in the form of a payment calculated in the same way as the basic award for unfair dismissal. The main issues relating to redundancy are procedural, relating to the selection of employees and consultation with them prior to redundancy, and the chapter therefore concentrates on these.

10.2 Introduction

The statutory concept of redundancy covers the situation where a person's job ceases to exist, either because the employer's business closes down, or it closes down in a particular location, or the employer has reduced need for staff, whether generally or of a particular kind.

The origins of the statutory scheme go back to 1964, but it was extended to cover all areas of civilian employment by the Industrial Relations Act 1971, when it was accepted by the government that traditional large-scale employers such as heavy industry were in urgent need of modernisation and frequently heavily 'overmanned', partly as a result of the restrictive practices of trade unions. Modernisation, including the introduction of computer technology for many routine jobs, would lead to reduced demand for employees. The provision of automatic statutory payments to employees who were made redundant, and so found themselves jobless for reasons wholly outside their control and without any personal fault, was intended to recognise the personal 'stake' a person has in his job and to provide a cushion against the financial effects of job loss, even when a person found another job immediately.

❖ EXAMPLE

It is 1986. West Devon Yachts is a firm building luxury yachts based in Plymouth. In common with most shipbuilding and engineering companies, it has a large staff of draughtsmen whose job it is to produce detailed technical drawings of components at the design stage. Recently, the company has had a reduction in orders, and Francis Drake, the managing director, has decided to make savings. A new computer-aided design package is available, which can do much of the work currently done by the draughtsmen. Mr Drake decides to purchase the package, train eight of the draughtsmen to use it, and make the rest redundant. This will save a substantial amount in salaries over the next few years, which will outweigh the initial cost of the package and the redundancy payments.

Cresswell v Board of Inland Revenue ([1984] ICR 508) establishes that an employer can be required to adapt to new ways of doing his existing job, so the introduction of new technology, and consequent redundancy for a proportion of the workforce, does not involve a breach of contract, as long as any necessary training is provided. That case involved employees in tax offices who were responsible for calculating individuals' PAYE tax codes each year and sending out this information to taxpayers and their employers.

Redundancy is a potentially fair reason for dismissal under ERA 1996 s. 98(1), but differs from the other potentially fair reasons in that if the dismissal is due to redundancy the employee is automatically entitled to a redundancy payment, calculated according to the same formula as the basic award in unfair dismissal, even if he obtains another job immediately.

Redundancy payments are available under the statutory scheme to all except the following:

- workers who are not 'employees' (ERA 1996 s. 135);
- employees working under an illegal contract;
- employees with fewer than *two* years' service (s. 155) *after* age 18 (s. 211(2));
- 'excluded employees' such as members of the Armed Forces.

A person over the age of 65 is not precluded from claiming a redundancy payment since the abolition of the default retirement age on 1 October 2011.

Case law shows that courts and tribunals normally accept without argument the employer's assertion that a redundancy situation exists. However, the employee concerned may still be unfairly dismissed, either because he was selected for redundancy for an improper reason, or because the employer failed to follow a fair procedure. This is so in the latter case even if dismissal for redundancy was inevitable (*Polkey v AE Dayton Services Ltd* [1987] UKHL 8).

10.3 What is a redundancy situation?

ERA 1996 s. 139(1) defines redundancy as follows:

> An employee who is dismissed shall be taken to be dismissed by reason of redundancy if the dismissal is wholly or mainly attributable to
>
> a) the fact that his employer has ceased (or intends to cease)
>   (i) to carry on the business for the purposes of which the employee was employed by him; or
>   (ii) to carry on that business in the place where the employee was so employed; or
>
> b) the fact that the requirements of that business
>   (i) for employees to carry out work of a particular kind; or
>   (ii) for employees to carry out work of a particular kind in the place where the employee was employed by the employer have ceased or diminished or are expected to cease or diminish.

Therefore, redundancy is where either the need for employees in the employer's business, either generally or at a specific location, has ceased or diminished, or the need for employees of a particular type, again either generally or at a particular location, has ceased or diminished.

Under ERA s. 163(2) there is a presumption that an employee who claims a redundancy payment is redundant. This is rebuttable by the employer. It is unusual for the employer to contest entitlement to a redundancy payment, but he may argue that the employee has in fact departed for some other reason, or has unreasonably refused an offer of suitable alternative employment.

What if the employer argues that the workforce has brought about the redundancy situation? The obvious example is where the employer seeks to impose contractual changes to save money, the workforce goes on strike and the employer argues that this exacerbates the financial problems to such an extent that the business is forced to close down.

In *Saunders v Ernest A. Neale Ltd* ([1974] IRLR 236) the employees conducted a work to rule, and were sacked by the employer. The factory then closed down and the employees claimed redundancy payments. It was held that they were not redundant; it was the work to rule which had led to the dismissals and then to the factory closing down. However, Sir John Donaldson P was careful to confine this decision to the facts of the case.

> We should like to take this opportunity of exorcising the ghost of 'self-induced redundancy'. It can certainly occur, but as such it has no legal significance. Interruption of service due to industrial action can cause customers to look to competitors or to turn to substitute materials or services. This can lead to a diminution in the requirements of the business to carry out work of a particular kind and to workers being dismissed. But the mere fact that the employees' action created the redundancy situation does not disentitle them to a redundancy payment. The entitlement depends on the words of the statute, and there is no room for any general consideration of whether it is equitable that the employee should receive a payment.

The ultimate issue is whether the *requirement of the business for employees* has ceased or diminished. It matters not whether there is the same amount of *work* to be done, if it can be done by fewer employees. Further, there is nothing to prevent the employer from making his *employees* redundant and having the work done by *self-employed* individuals. This is something that happens quite frequently in the public sector – senior managers are made redundant with large contractual pay-offs, and within a short time are working for the same organisation as 'consultants'! If the employee is replaced, even by an employee of a different type, then there cannot be a redundancy – as in the early case of *Vaux Breweries v Ward* [1968] ITR 385, where the employer decided to replace barmaids with bunny girls in the hope of attracting a trendier clientele.

In practice, arguments over redundancy situations turn on whether a particular employee is dismissed for redundancy, rather than whether there is actually a reduced need for employees. This most often arises when the employer operates from more than one site, the employer reduces numbers at a particular site and invokes a contractual mobility clause to move employees elsewhere. Frequently, an employee may prefer to be dismissed with a redundancy payment than be required to move elsewhere, however short-sighted this may appear to the outsider. *Jones v Associated Tunnelling* ([1981] IRLR 477) is an example where the employer successfully argued that a mobility clause should be implied into the contract so that an employee who refused to move to an alternative site within reasonable travelling distance of home was not entitled to a redundancy payment.

10.4 The business closes down

This situation does not usually raise any issues. If a business closes down entirely it no longer has need for *any* employees. All employees, therefore, are redundant and those who come within the statutory scheme are entitled to redundancy payments. If the business closes down because of insolvency, then the redundancy payments are payable from the fund maintained by the Secretary of State for Work and Pensions if the assets of the business are insufficient to meet them.

10.5 'The requirement for employees to do work of a particular kind has ceased or diminished'

Where the business does not close down, but the employer concludes that a portion of the workforce needs to be made redundant, the situation is a good deal more complicated, as the following issues then arise:

- If suitable work is available at other locations, can the employer insist on moving otherwise redundant employees there?
- What is 'work of a particular kind'?
- If the requirement for employees has diminished rather than ceased altogether, how should the employees to be made redundant be selected?
- What procedural requirements must be satisfied when making employees redundant?

10.5.1 Moving to other locations

ERA s. 139(1)(a)(ii) provides that there is a redundancy situation when the requirement for employees to do work of the particular kind that the individual was employed to do, at the place he was employed to do it has ceased. On the ordinary and natural meaning of the words used, if the employer is able to move the employee elsewhere, then he is not redundant. If the employee refuses such a post, he then disentitles himself to a redundancy payment. Early case law suggested that if there was a mobility clause in the employee's contract, the employer could rely on it without restriction, as in *Jones v Associated Tunnelling*.

More recent case law considers not only the strict wording of the mobility clause, but the way it has been operated prior to the alleged redundancy situation. In *High Table Ltd v Horst* ([1997] IRLR 513) the Applicants were waitresses employed by a company which provided catering services for businesses in the City of London and elsewhere. The employer's staff handbook, which was incorporated into their contracts, provided that:

> Your place of work is as stated in your letter of appointment which acts as part of your terms and conditions. However, given the nature of our business, it is sometimes necessary to transfer staff on a temporary or permanent basis to another location. Whenever possible, this will be within reasonable daily travelling distance of your existing place of work.

In practice, the Applicants had all worked at Hill Samuel's offices from 10am–4pm for a number of years. In 1993 Hill Samuel cut its catering budget, and the employer responded with a reorganisation which meant that in future waitresses would have to work longer hours. The Applicants were dismissed and claimed unfair dismissal. The employer argued that they were redundant. Though this argument was upheld, the Court of Appeal rejected the view that 'the place where the employee was so employed' embraced any place where the employee *could* be employed under the terms of his contract.

The issue was considered by the Court of Appeal in *Home Office v Evans* ([2007] EWCA Civ 1089. The employees were immigration officers employed on a 'mobile grade' in the civil service, which meant that they could be required to move anywhere within Great Britain. They worked at Waterloo International when it was the British terminus for the Eurostar service. When immigration controls were no longer required there, the Home Office wished to move the employees concerned to Heathrow Airport, where they had previously worked, rather than instigate their contractual redundancy procedure. The employees argued that they could not be required to move, and subsequently resigned and claimed to have been constructively dismissed.

At first instance the tribunal concluded that there was, in fact, a redundancy situation, and that the employer had failed to apply their contractual redundancy procedure. The employer's attempt to use the mobility clause to evade the requirements of the redundancy procedure was a fundamental breach of contract. On that basis, the Claimants had been constructively and unfairly dismissed. The EAT upheld that decision.

In the Court of Appeal Mummery LJ held that the EAT had been mistaken in interpreting *Curling v Securicor* ([1992] IRLR 549)

> as authority for the proposition that the employer is not legally entitled to invoke a mobility clause when a redundancy situation might arise or has arisen on the closure of part of a business. In my judgment, *Curling* is a case in which the employer was not entitled to rely on the mobility obligations at the hearing in the tribunal, as it had already implemented the redundancy procedure, in which the employees had participated, and had not sought to rely on the contractual mobility obligations until the hearing, by which time the tribunal considered that it was too late to raise a new point. In this case there is no question of the Home Office dodging from one contractual procedure to another, having left it too late to invoke the mobility

> obligations, or having waived its right to invoke them. From the time of its staff announcement of the decision to close the WIT the Home Office made it clear to the Claimants that it was invoking the mobility obligations and would be following that procedure, not the redundancy procedure, which it consistently did.

On that basis, there was no redundancy situation, and therefore it was not necessary to apply the contractual redundancy procedure.

The critical point in *Curling* was that it was only when the matter reached the Employment Tribunal that the employer argued that, because of the mobility clause, there was no redundancy situation at all.

On the basis of *Home Office v Evans*, if there is a mobility clause in the contract and sufficient alternative employment elsewhere for employees who are no longer needed at a particular location, the employer may rely on that mobility clause to avoid redundancies altogether. However, on the basis of cases such as *United Bank v Akhtar* ([1989] IRLR 80) and *Meade-Hill v the British Council* ([1995] IRLR 478, CA), the employer cannot enforce a mobility clause without regard to the circumstances of the individual employee. There was no consideration of whether it was reasonable to require those individuals to move from Waterloo station to Heathrow Airport, a distance of some 19 miles by road, and at least 45 minutes by public transport. Surprisingly, perhaps, this issue has not arisen in any other case which has reached the Court of Appeal.

10.5.2 Reduction in working hours

What if there is a reduction in the amount of work to be done, but the employer takes the view that there need be no redundancies if the relevant employees accept shorter hours? This was considered in *Packman v Fauchon* ([2012] UKEAT/0017/12/LA). The Claimant was the employer's bookkeeper, at a time when there was a considerable diminution in work for her due to a reduction in turnover and the introduction of new accounting software. The employer offered her part-time hours, which she refused, as she was contractually entitled to work the hours she was working, and the employer dismissed her. The issue for the EAT was whether there could only be a redundancy situation where there had to be a reduction in the *number* of employees, or whether it was sufficient that there was a reduction in the amount of work to be done by the same number of employees, and hence a reduction in their working hours. The EAT decided that the latter applied, saying that in terms of the number of full-time equivalent employees there was a reduction in the need for employees to do the work.

10.5.3 Work of a particular kind

A reduction in the need for employees to do work of a particular kind may result from a diminution in work, more efficient use of manpower so that fewer employees are needed to do the same amount of work, or the introduction of new technology. Usually, the employer does not seek to get rid of all the employees doing a particular type of work, so that there are *selective redundancies*. This raises the issue of the proper pool from which the selection for redundancies should be made. Put simply, if the employer wishes to make three cooks redundant, should the selection be made only from among those actually working as cooks at that time, or from the (larger) group of all those whose contracts could require them to work as cooks?

Some cases apply a 'job function' test, looking at whether there has been a diminution in the requirement for employees to do the work the employee is doing at the material time. An alternative approach, which has been followed in some cases, is whether there has been a diminution in the requirement for employees to do work of *any* kind which the employee can be required to perform under his contract.

In *Murray v Foyle Meats Ltd* ([1999] ICR 827) the employee worked in a slaughterhouse and his contract described him as a 'meat plant operative'. In practice, he worked in the main slaughter hall on one of two 'killing lines'. The employer decided to close down one killing line and reduce the workforce accordingly. The issue was whether the selection should have been made only from among the slaughter hall personnel, or from the entire manual workforce, all of whom were 'meat plant operatives'. The House of Lords ruled that the proper approach for a Tribunal was to consider:

- Was the employee dismissed?
- If so, had the requirements of the employer's business for employees to carry out work of a particular kind ceased or diminished, or were they expected to cease or diminish?
- If so, was the employee's dismissal caused wholly or mainly by this state of affairs?

If this approach is followed it would seem to make precise arguments over 'work of a particular kind' superfluous, as it concentrates on the redundant employee as an individual – why has *he* been dismissed?

10.6 Dismissal

By virtue of ERA 1996 s. 136 'dismissal' has the same meaning as in unfair dismissal, i.e. unilateral termination by employer, expiry and non-renewal of fixed-term contract or constructive dismissal. This seems straightforward, but special problems arise in relation to redundancy because it can frequently be argued that an employee has left voluntarily and so is not entitled to a redundancy payment. For example,

- volunteers for redundancy;
- early retirements;
- employees anticipating redundancy and leaving for another job (the employer warning of impending redundancies does *not* amount to dismissal);
- resignation because of a lay-off or short-time working; or
- rejection of alternative job during trial period.

Voluntary redundancy or early retirement may frequently result in a much better financial package than is available under the statutory scheme, and there may in such cases be a public policy reason for not allowing the employee to recover a statutory redundancy payment as well. Such cases are likely to be seen by the courts as terminations *by agreement* or resignations, so that there is no dismissal and therefore no entitlement to a redundancy payment.

10.6.1 Anticipation of redundancy

It not infrequently happens that an employee, knowing that redundancies are 'in the air', actively looks for another job and obtains one. Can he obtain a redundancy payment? ERA 1996 s. 136(3) provides that such an employee is entitled to a redundancy payment if:

a) he was under actual notice of dismissal for redundancy at the time of his resignation, and not simply reacting to a preliminary warning;
b) he gives written notice of resignation sufficiently close to the original termination date that the remaining period of employment is less than the contractual notice he is entitled to.

Whether these requirements are met is a question of fact in individual cases.

10.6.2 Rejection of alternative job

The employer is under a duty to consider whether an employee who would otherwise be made redundant can be given 'suitable alternative employment' elsewhere in the organisation (see below). Under ERA 1996 s. 141, an employer may make an offer of employment which is identical to the original job in all respects (only applicable where the employer realises that the employee's job is not redundant after all!), or some different job which is suitable for the employee. In either case, the employer must give the employee a trial period of four weeks in the new job. Before beginning the new job, during this trial period, or at the end of it, he may reject the new job and elect to be treated as dismissed for the purpose of receiving a redundancy payment. In such a case, he is entitled to a redundancy payment unless his rejection of the new job is *unreasonable* (see below).

10.7 Redundancy procedure

This is a complex area which has generated much case law. Failure to follow fair procedures makes a dismissal for redundancy unfair even if redundancy is inevitable (*Polkey v AE Dayton Services* [1987] UKHL 8).

Essentially, there are two issues:

- selection of employees for redundancy; and
- collective and individual consultation.

In *Williams v Compair Maxam* [1982] ICR 156 the EAT set out principles to be followed by an employer in implementing redundancies, where there is a recognized trade union:

1) the employer will seek to give as much warning as possible of impending redundancies so as to enable the union and those employees who may be affected to take early steps to inform themselves of the relevant facts, consider possible alternative solutions and, if necessary, find alternative employment in the undertaking or elsewhere;
2) the employer will take steps in collaboration with the union to avoid dismissals altogether;
3) the employer should consult the union as to the best means by which the desired management can be achieved fairly and with as little hardship to the employees as possible;
4) whether an agreement as to the criteria for selection has been reached with the union, the employer should seek to establish criteria which as far as possible do not depend on the subjective opinion of the person making the selection, but can be objectively checked against such things as attendance record, efficiency in the job, experience or length of service;
5) the employer should seek to ensure that the selection is made fairly in accordance with the criteria established and consider any representations any union may make;
6) the employer will consider whether it is possible to offer employees alternative employment instead of making them redundant.

10.7.1 Selection of employees for redundancy

10.7.1.1 The unit of selection

If the business is closing down in its entirety there is no issue of the unit of selection, as all the employees will be made redundant. There may be no major difficulty if all employees of a particular type are to be made redundant – perhaps on the basis that technical advances have made their skills obsolete. However, if there are to be selective redundancies in the sense that *fewer* employees are required in order to carry out a particular kind of work, then there will be an issue of which employees should be made redundant and which retained, and which 'unit of selection' they should be chosen from.

The employer is between the Devil and the deep blue sea in defining the unit of selection! If it is defined narrowly – confined, say, to those actually working as cooks – then the redundant employees can argue that it should have been defined more widely, and that if it had been they themselves might well not have been selected for redundancy. If the group is defined more widely – all kitchen workers, say – some employees may argue that the work they were actually doing remains to be done, so that they themselves were not really redundant at all.

On the basis of *Safeway Stores plc v Burrell* [1997] ICR 523, the employer is free to define the unit of selection in the way that best suits the business, provided the issue is considered carefully and decided on a logical basis.

Situations where the employer may need to take particular care in defining the unit of selection include:

- where people with similar skills or doing similar jobs are employed in different departments; should the employer treat each group separately or together?
- where people doing similar jobs are employed on different grades; again, should the different groups be treated separately or together?

The case law does not give any definitive answer; what the employer needs to show is that he has considered the issue logically and carefully, and to have considered suggestions made by the employee representatives.

10.7.1.2 Method of selection

This is the most controversial single area of law and practice relating to redundancy, and that most likely to lead to claims of unfair dismissal.

Traditionally, trade unions have favoured 'last-in-first-out' (LIFO) as the basis of selection, thus favouring long-service employees over newcomers. However, this may infringe the age discrimination legislation, and in any case is inefficient from the employer's point of view. Case law makes it clear that LIFO is not regarded as the sole fair method of selection, but that the method employed must be based on objective criteria and non-discriminatory. For example, a system which favoured full-time over part-time employees would be held indirectly discriminatory against women, or one which favoured employees prepared to work on any day of the week might be regarded as indirectly discriminatory on grounds of religion or belief, though in either case the employer could argue justification (see Chapter 11).

Nowadays, it is usual for an employer not to select on the basis of a single criterion, but to have a series of criteria, which may or may not be weighted, and allocate points to each, producing a total score for each employee. At least some of the criteria should involve matters which are capable of objective measurement, so that selection or non-selection is not simply based on the subjective views of a particular person. Such criteria could include:

- length of service;
- experience in that particular job;
- qualifications;
- attendance record.

Those matters which are automatically unfair reasons for dismissal are also automatically unfair reasons for selection for redundancy. These include:

- trade union membership or activities;
- pregnancy, childbirth or taking maternity leave.

In designing a matrix the employer should:

- seek agreement with employee representatives;
- include some criteria which involve objective measurement;
- ensure that those applying the matrix are clearly aware of what they should be doing, and that measurements of things such as time off ill are done accurately;
- be careful of factors such as 'attitude', which may appear to give scope for personal prejudice; and
- have regard to disability discrimination legislation, given that a disability may affect attendance, output, etc. However, the duty is not to treat a disabled person *more favourably* than a non-disabled person, but not to treat him *unfavourably*. Case law shows that using criteria such as attendance record and flexibility in job duties is not necessarily unlawful discrimination, as the employer may be able to prove justification.

10.7.1.3 Consultation

Statute and case law require the employer to consult with both employee representatives and individuals at risk of redundancy as part of a fair procedure.

10.7.1.3.1 Consultation with employee representatives

Under Trade Union and Labour Relations (Consolidation) Act 1992 (TULRCA) s. 188, the employer is under a duty to consult employee representatives where 20 or more dismissals for redundancy are proposed. This must take place at least 30 days before the first of the dismissals takes effect (45 days if there are to be more than 100 redundancies). Where negotiation of terms and conditions of employment normally takes place with a trade union, consultation must be with union representatives. In such circumstances the tribunal is likely to expect the employer to consult union representatives even if fewer than 20 redundancies are involved and so the statutory duty does not apply. If there is no recognized union and the statutory duty to consult applies, the employer must make arrangements for employee representatives to be elected. Again, if the statutory duty does not apply, the tribunal is likely to expect the employer to consult with elected employee representatives.

What is meant by consultation, and what should the consultation be about? TULRCA defines 'consultation' as an attempt to reach agreement with the representatives, and common law, in other contexts, as involving a genuine invitation to discussion, with a *receptive mind*. Matters to be considered include:

- avoiding dismissals altogether;
- reducing the number of dismissals;
- mitigating the effect of dismissals;
- methods of selection.

If, following an application to the tribunal, it is found that the employer has failed to consult as required, the tribunal is under a duty under TULRCA s. 189(2) to make a declaration to that effect. The tribunal may also make a protective award, which has the effect of keeping the redundant employees in employment – and being paid – for a defined period of up to 90 days.

An individual employee may argue that a failure to comply with the requirements for collective consultation makes his dismissal for redundancy unfair.

10.7.1.3.2 Individual consultation

Having decided which employees should be selected for redundancy, the employer now comes under a duty to consult with them. This duty goes well beyond merely informing them of their forthcoming redundancy and when it will take effect. Employees are entitled to be consulted individually *before* being issued with redundancy notices. When the Employment Act 2002 was in force, the statutory dismissal procedure applied to dismissal for redundancy. As in 'ordinary' dismissals, it may be advisable for employers to follow the three-stage procedure:

1) the employer must set out the reasons for redundancy in writing and invite the employee to a meeting;
2) a meeting must be held;
3) the employee must be given the opportunity to appeal against the dismissal.

Matters to be covered in the meeting should include:

a) explanation of why the job the employee is doing is to be affected by redundancy;
b) explanation of why this employee is at risk of selection for redundancy, including the matrix;
c) time for the employee and his representative to consider the matter and express their views, in particular on the assessment and the possibility of alternative employment;
d) consideration any views put forward, and alternatives to redundancy for this employee.

It is important to note that both consultation with employee representatives and individual consultation are essential parts of a fair redundancy procedure – one is not a substitute for the other! In practice, lack of individual consultation is frequently alleged in cases involving large companies – consultation with unions tends to be seen as sufficient – and lack of collective consultation in small organisations, not least because there may well be no recognised trade union and the managers may not realise that collective consultation is still necessary. In the latter case, employee representatives need to be elected specifically for this purpose.

10.7.1.4 Alternative work

Two factors make it important for the employer actively to consider whether there is suitable alternative work the employee under threat of redundancy could do:

1) if the employee unreasonably refuses an offer of suitable alternative work, he loses entitlement to a redundancy payment;
2) it is part of a fair procedure for the employer to consider alternatives to redundancy, both at the collective and individual level. Failure to do so may make dismissal unfair.

For the offer of alternative work to be capable of ending entitlement to a redundancy payment, the offer must be made before the old job ends and the new job must start no later than four weeks after the old job ends. What constitutes suitable alternative work is a matter for the objective judgment of the tribunal, based not only on the pay and conditions, but on such matters as the level of skill involved. Whether the employee then unreasonably refuses a suitable offer is, however, a subjective test, as seen from the standpoint of the employee concerned, so, for example, such matters as travelling time and availability of public transport would become relevant factors.

An example, to do with the nature of the work itself, can be found in *Readman v Devon Primary Care Trust* ([2011] UKEAT 0116_11_0112). Mrs Readman had worked in community nursing from 1985, latterly in charge of community and district nursing in Teignmouth and Dawlish, Devon. As a result of a reorganization, her post was abolished, and she was thus at risk of redundancy. The employer offered her a post on the same grade at Teignmouth Hospital, which she did not accept. Subsequently, she accepted a community nursing post in Canada and emigrated there with her family. The employer argued that as Mrs Readman had refused an offer of suitable alternative employment, she was not entitled to a redundancy payment.

Following previous precedents, the Tribunal considered first whether, objectively, Mrs Readman had received an offer of suitable alternative employment, and concluded that she had:

> The Tribunal pointed out that the offer was identical to the current role in status, pay, professional lead and nursing management responsibilities. They commented that it only differed in that it was no longer community based but was in a hospital setting. They then went on to describe that hospital setting, to which we have already referred, namely that she already had her office at the hospital. It was a small, 12 bed community hospital. She knew many of the staff, the GPs, the procedures and the layout of the hospital. The Tribunal acknowledged that it was true that she would be supervising the care of patients in that hospital rather than in their homes, but commented that her skill set was transferable. It commented that she would need to learn, or to re-familiarise herself with certain procedures, but that none of these would require any extensive training or separate qualification and could be acquired easily with peer mentoring or assistance. In that respect, they were reflecting the evidence which the Appellant had given in the course of cross-examination.

The EAT considered that the Tribunal had approached the first question in an entirely proper fashion, and emphasised that it was not its own role to reopen the issue simply because it might not agree with the Tribunal's conclusion. However, the Tribunal had not considered the subjective issue of whether Mrs Readman was justified in refusing the offer.

> In our judgment, the reason for the Appellant refusing the job had nothing to do with the question whether she could be easily retrained in certain of the basic administration skills – required for somebody working as a Hospital Matron, rather than someone working as a Matron in the community – her evidence before the Tribunal was very clear that she would have no difficulty performing that retraining. Her main objection was the fact that she had taken a considered decision in 1985 to move away from working and delivering nursing in a hospital setting, in favour of delivering her nursing skills in a community setting.
>
> She had continued in that setting for some 23 years. . . . The Tribunal accepted that and made findings of fact, that the emphasis would now be on being a Matron in a hospital setting, as opposed to in a community setting.
>
> In our judgment, that desire not to work in a hospital setting, in the particular circumstances of this Appellant, did provide her with a sound and justifiable reason for turning the offer down. The fact that she may have had in the background an idea that she would like to go to Canada, and the fact that she might prefer to have the redundancy money, rather than to work in a hospital setting, whilst no doubt they were to some extent influences on her, were plainly not the main reason for her refusal, which was set out in her letter of 26 August and repeated on more than one occasion thereafter.

That being so, Mrs Readman was entitled to a redundancy payment, as she had not refused the offer unreasonably. However, it might be argued that the facts of this case were 'close to the line'. In other cases on this issue, the reasons for refusing an offer of alternative employment considered by the Tribunal to be suitable have largely involved matters separate from the nature of the job itself, such as travelling time. Here there is the contradiction that the job was, by its nature, 'suitable', yet, because of its nature, and despite a considerable overlap with her previous role, Mrs Readman was entitled to refuse it.

❖ THINKING POINT

Were the EAT rather over-generous to Mrs Readman, in assuming that she had not already decided to move to Canada when she refused the hospital job?

10.8 Redundancy payments

An employee dismissed by reason of redundancy is automatically entitled to a redundancy payment, irrespective of whether he finds another job immediately. The redundancy payment is calculated in the same way as the basic award for unfair dismissal, that is:

Service × Week's pay × Age factor

- Service – *completed* years of continuous employment, subject to maximum of 20
- Week's pay – gross pay, subject to statutory maximum, increased each year, currently £508
- Age factor
  - For service over the age of 41, age factor equals 1.5
  - For service between 22 and 40, age factor equals 1
  - For service below the age of 22, age factor equals 0.5

This is (currently) not affected by the Employment Equality (Age) Regulations 2006, or the Equality Act 2010.

The maximum possible statutory redundancy payment, representing 20 years' service over the age of 41, is therefore:

20 × 508 × 1.5 = £15,240.

The amount of a statutory redundancy payment is not normally disputed. However, many employers are prepared to pay much larger sums, based, for example, on the employee's actual pay rather than the statutory figure, and a considerable volume of case law has developed over entitlement to these in particular circumstances. This issue is dealt with on the basis of the terms of the employee's contract.

10.9 Further reading

Cabrelli, 'Liability and remedies for breach of the contract of employment at common law: some recent developments' (2016) 45(2) *Industrial Law Journal* 207.

Emmett, 'Dismissal procedures: making redundancies under the new regime' (2004) 55(Nov) *Employment Law Journal* 6.

Newman, 'The implications of the Woolworths redundancy decision' (2013) Jul/Aug *Employment Law Journal* 10.

Chapter 11

Discrimination

Chapter contents

11.1 Overview

This chapter provides an overview of discrimination law as it has developed in the United Kingdom. It deals with the forms of discrimination prohibited under the Equality Act 2010, together with the burden of proof. The different protected characteristics are dealt with in subsequent chapters.

Discrimination law (more accurately, anti-discrimination law) is a huge and expanding area, but entirely a product of statute. UK Discrimination Law developed piecemeal from the 1960s as a response to social and political change, the emergence of more liberal attitudes towards matters such as sexual orientation and gender identity, and a series of EU Directives.

This haphazard growth of anti-discrimination legislation produced a confused and inconsistent body of law, which the Labour government under Gordon Brown (Prime Minister 2007–2010) sought to rationalise by consolidating it into the Equality Act 2010. Some inconsistencies remain, and discrimination against part-time employees and employees on fixed-term contracts remains the subject of separate legislation (see Chapter 6).

11.2 Introduction and contextual background

At common law, the principle of freedom of contract applies to employment contracts as to any other. As such, at common law the employer can employ, or refuse to employ, anyone for whatever reason he wishes, including reasons based on the sex or race of that person, any disability he might have, or his religious beliefs. All this has now been overtaken by legislation.

The original impetus for legislation in this area came from international law, in the immediate aftermath of the Second World War. The United Nations Universal Declaration of Human Rights 1948 states that everyone is entitled to all rights and freedoms 'without distinction of any kind, such as race, colour, sex, language, religion, political or other opinion, national or social origin, property, birth or status'. As with other instruments of the same period, such as the European Convention on Human Rights of 1951, this represents the mood of a period which sought to ensure that the horrors of the Nazi period (1933–1945) and the Stalinist purges (1937–1940) could never happen again. Such statements were reiterated by the International Labour Organisation's Conventions of 1958 and 1980.

However, the most important single influence on UK law in this sphere has come from Britain's membership of the European Union, previously the European Community and originally the European Economic Community, from 1 January 1973 onwards, in a context of major social changes.

Britain has often been described as a nation of immigrants. During the late seventeenth and early eighteenth centuries, England became a haven for the Huguenots – French Protestants fleeing persecution during the long reign of Louis XIV (1643–1715) – particularly after the revocation of the Edict of Nantes in 1685 deprived them of the limited toleration they had previously enjoyed. As refugees from Catholicism during a time of intense hatred of Catholics, the Huguenots were welcomed in this country. The majority were prosperous small businessmen and skilled craftsmen and quickly assimilated. In particular, some of their descendants became prominent in banking and the Armed Forces.

One of the few liberal measures credited to Oliver Cromwell during the Commonwealth of 1649–1660 was the repeal of the prohibition imposed by Edward I in 1290 on Jews entering or living in England. This resulted in an influx of Jews, mainly of Spanish and Portuguese origins, in the same period and later. The most notable of these was the future Prime Minister, Benjamin Disraeli, whose grandfather settled in London in 1748. Though they maintained their religion, these Sephardic Jews too assimilated, and, like many Huguenots, some became prominent in the financial sphere.

The next large wave of immigration came in the 1840s and early 1850s from Ireland as a result of the Potato Famine. Unlike the Huguenots and Jews, they came largely from the working classes and settled mainly in the major ports, notably in Liverpool, 50 per cent of whose population was born in Ireland according to the 1851 census, and Glasgow. Irish immigration continued in smaller numbers for the rest of the century and beyond, with a further upsurge in the mid-twentieth century. At the end of the nineteenth century, there came a second and much larger wave of Jewish immigration, this time of *Ashkenazi* Jews escaping oppression in Tsarist Russia, which then controlled the eastern half of Poland, together with the Baltic States of Estonia, Latvia and Lithuania, all of which had large Jewish populations. These settled mainly in London and other large cities. Although some prospered, as with the Irish, many did not.

So far, we have been speaking of white immigrants, who to a greater or lesser extent became assimilated into the general population around them, though the Jews and Catholic Irish maintained their separate religious beliefs and practices. Before the Second World War, non-white immigrants were much fewer in number, and those who settled permanently did so mainly in the major ports. Others came to Britain as students, particularly from India – Mahatma Gandhi was called to the Bar at the Inner Temple in 1891 – but returned home after completing their studies.

There is evidence that black and Indian visitors to Britain before the Second World War were largely welcomed, if regarded with some curiosity by people who had never previously seen a non-white person. Ranjitsinhji, future Maharajah of Nawanagar, entered Cambridge University in 1889. Having failed to become a barrister, he concentrated on cricket, based himself in England and became the leading batsman of his day, with a considerable following among cricket aficionados. Learie Constantine, another celebrated cricketer, settled in Lancashire in 1928 because, he concluded, there were better opportunities there for black players and less racism than in his native Trinidad. Many British people were outraged at the high degree of racial segregation practised by the US forces stationed in Britain during the Second World War. Indeed, Constantine and his family were required to leave a London hotel in 1943 because the management feared complaints from Americans staying there.[1]

This pattern changed from the late 1940s onwards. For the first time, there was large-scale non-white immigration into Britain from various Commonwealth countries, particularly the Caribbean and the Indian sub-continent, but also West and East Africa. Some industries actively sought Asian immigrants, on the basis that they were prepared to work longer hours in worse conditions for lower pay than their British counterparts. In consequence, immigrants from India, Pakistan and what became Bangladesh[2] were particularly concentrated in the Lancashire cotton industry, the Yorkshire wool industry, in 'one-industry towns', such as Oldham, Rochdale, and Bradford. Large numbers of West Indians came to England to work in public transport and the National Health Service. Again, they tended to be concentrated in limited areas of the country, and very largely in urban conurbations. Meanwhile, students came in larger quantities as the number of universities expanded, and many remained after graduation.

In addition, refugees and other 'displaced persons' settled here in considerable numbers as a result of the Second World War and Communist rule in Eastern Europe. Poles were the most numerous single group, though there were also Ukrainians, Hungarians, Yugoslavs and Jews of many nationalities. Again, they tended to settle in specific areas – West Yorkshire and the East Midlands received considerable influxes.

All this produced tensions. There were serious riots in Notting Hill in August 1958. Further, in a period when Employment Law was, with few and specific exceptions, entirely based on

1 *Constantine v Imperial Hotels Ltd* [1944] KB 693. See also Nevil Shute's 1947 novel, *The Chequer Board*.

2 The modern Pakistan and Bangladesh were a single country, separated by the Indian territory of Kashmir, from independence in 1947 until 1971. During that period Bangladesh was known as East Pakistan.

freedom of contract, the system was ripe for exploitation of individual immigrants. Employers frequently refused to employ people of colour, and landlords refused to accept them as tenants (a particularly serious issue in a time of continued housing shortage in the aftermath of the Second World War). In 1963, after the Bristol Bus Company refused to employ West Indians, the local people in Bristol staged a four-month boycott of bus services which eventually led the company to climb down.

This was one of the triggers for the Race Relations Act 1965, which enabled a person to sue another person who refused to serve him, or served him with unreasonable delay, or overcharged him, on the grounds of colour, race, or national or ethnic origins. However, the Act specifically excluded shops and housing providers, as well as employment, so it achieved very little. The Race Relations Act 1968 extended the coverage to housing, employment and public services, but it remained of relatively little effect.

❖ THINKING POINT

Why was there a major increase in overt racism at the same time as the increase in the ethnic minority population?

In the same period when mass immigration began, and later, it was becoming more usual for women to continue working outside the home after marriage, particularly from the late 1960s, when the expansion of university education meant that many more women were taking up professional careers. At the same time, a feminist movement emerged, initially in the United States, then in Britain. Rather later, increasing house prices provided a further impetus, in that two incomes were frequently needed to service a mortgage.

Along with Britain's membership of the EEC from 1973, all this provided the context for the introduction of the Sex Discrimination Act 1975, and the first comprehensive Race Relations Act in 1976. At the same time, in 1975, the Equal Pay Act 1970 came into force.

There was then a hiatus in anti-discrimination legislation until 1995, when the Disability Discrimination Act was passed. The Disabled Persons (Employment) Act 1944, passed in anticipation of large numbers of servicemen returning disabled from the war and needing jobs, defined disability for the first time.[3] It created a registration system for disabled people, along with a quota system requiring employers to employ a minimum percentage of disabled people. The quotas were, however, largely ignored.

The 1995 Act again arose from a changing social context. It was recognised that the 1944 Act had been a failure, and that disability itself was a much broader concept than generally believed – many disabilities were 'hidden' from sight. Further, a disability rights movement had emerged, seeking the dismantling of barriers preventing disabled people from gaining equal access to education, employment and services. A philosophy, known as the social model of disability developed, believing that the problems disabled people faced were not caused by the disability itself, but by society's attitudes to them. This philosophy is most obvious in relation to HIV infection and AIDS.

3 1.-(i) In this Act the expression 'disabled person' means a person who, on account of injury, disease, or congenital deformity, is substantially handicapped in obtaining or keeping employment, or in undertaking work on his own account, of a kind which apart from that injury, disease or deformity would be suited to his age, experience and qualifications; and the expression 'disablement', in relation to any person, shall be construed accordingly.

The first years of the twenty-first century brought a further flurry of anti-discrimination legislation, in part dealing with gaps in the existing law. The Sex Discrimination Act dealt only with a person's physical sex, i.e. being a man or a woman (interestingly, that was not defined), along with marital status (being married; there was no protection for single people or cohabitees). It did not cover transgender individuals or matters relating to sexual orientation. There were a number of court cases where homosexual persons of either sex argued discrimination on grounds of sexual orientation, but each failed on the basis that the proper comparator required under SDA s. 5(3) for a homosexual person of one sex was not a heterosexual person of the other sex but a homosexual person of the other sex, the sexual orientation being a 'relevant circumstance' for this purpose. This issue was dealt with under the Employment Equality (Sexual Orientation) Regulations 2003, which made it unlawful to discriminate against a person on grounds of their sexual orientation.

Legislation was passed to enable women to take maternity leave, but initially this was only available where the employee had two years' continuous employment before the 14th week prior to the expected week of the birth. Until the House of Lords judgment in *Webb v EMO Air Cargo* ([1992] UKHL 13) the Sex Discrimination Act offered no protection to pregnant women who did not qualify for maternity leave.

The Race Relations Act did not cover a person's religion, though case law ruled Jews and Sikhs to be distinct racial groups for the purposes of the Act. Again, this loophole was closed in 2003, by the Employment Equality (Religion and Belief) Regulations, which also covered discrimination on the grounds of philosophical belief, though not political belief.

The Sex Discrimination (Gender Reassignment) Regulations 1999 made it unlawful to discriminate directly (see below) against a person on grounds of gender reassignment, though only in matters involving employment or vocational training.

The Employment Equality (Age) Regulations 2006 came into force on 1 October 2006.

11.3 The Equality Act 2010

As discrimination legislation was passed piecemeal and came into force at different times, it was inconsistent and sometimes contradictory. The Equality Act 2010, which came into force on 1 October 2010, was passed in order to rationalise the law and create a coherent code based on 'protected characteristics'. There was a general election and change of government between the Act receiving the royal assent and coming into force, and not all the provisions originally included were actually brought into force. There are currently no plans to bring them into force.

The protected characteristics are (s. 4):

- age;
- disability;
- gender reassignment;
- marriage and civil partnership;
- pregnancy and maternity;
- race;
- religion or belief;
- sex; and
- sexual orientation.

The Act then prohibits the following when based on a protected characteristic:

- direct discrimination;
- indirect discrimination;

- harassment; and
- victimisation.

There are also specific provisions relating to individual protected characteristics, particularly disability, and specific provisions related to equal pay. The latter largely reproduce the provisions of the Equal Pay Act 1970 (see Chapter 10).

It is important to note that the Act does not apply only in the employment sphere, but to self-employed individuals and in the supply of goods and services, including education.

The Act received the Royal Assent on 8 April 2010, just before Parliament was prorogued prior to the 2010 election. S. 216 provided that all but a small minority of its provisions were to be brought into effect by Order on a date appointed by a Minister of the Crown. Most of the provisions originally included were brought into force on 1 October 2010, but a decision was taken by the Coalition Government not to proceed with others in the foreseeable future, and at the time of writing they have yet to be brought into force.

The following chapters deal with specific protected characteristics, but first we must deal with the burden of proof, and with the prohibited conduct applicable to all the protected characteristics, which is defined in ss. 13, 19, and 26–27.

11.4 Burden of proof

As with civil matters generally, the standard of proof in discrimination cases is balance of probabilities. The issue of where the burden of proof lies – with claimant or defendant – is more complex.

In most civil matters the burden of proof is on the claimant. Initially, this was the position under the anti-discrimination legislation, so that the claimant in a direct discrimination case, for example, would have to show that there had been less favourable treatment, and that this was a consequence of race or sex. Establishing the less favourable treatment was not normally particularly difficult, but in practice the defendant was unlikely to admit to a racist or sexist motivation, so that it became difficult to establish the causal link with the claimant's race or sex.

❖ EXAMPLE

Patrick, a young black man, applied for a job. He was interviewed, but the job was offered to a white candidate. When he asked the reason he was not offered the job, he was told that the other candidate was better at interview.

Recognising this difficulty for claimants, courts and tribunals were prepared to reverse the burden of proof in individual cases, if they considered that the facts were such as to give rise to a presumption of discrimination. The burden would then be on the defendant to satisfy the tribunal that there was a non-discriminatory reason for the less favourable treatment.

In *Khanna v MOD* [1981] ICR 653 the court concluded that the fact that the claimant had been passed over for promotion 22 times, and on the most recent occasion the person promoted was less qualified and experienced than she was, created a presumption of direct racial discrimination. This precedent established the principle that the courts *could* infer that racial or sexual discrimination underlay the less favourable treatment, but not *when* or *whether* they should. In *King v Great Britain China Centre* [1991] IRLR 513, Neil LJ said that a difference in treatment and a difference in gender will often point to the possibility of discrimination. In such circumstances the tribunal will look to the employer for an explanation and if one is not forthcoming, or is inadequate, it is legitimate to infer that discrimination has occurred. In that case the Claimant, a native Mandarin speaker, applied for a post where a knowledge of Mandarin was described as essential, but the successful candidate did not speak any Chinese language.

In *Strathclyde Regional Council v Zafar* ([1997] UKHL 54) the House of Lords made it clear that a court or tribunal had discretion to adopt such an approach, but that it was not bound to.

The European Commission then concluded that 'too few' claimants were bringing successful claims of race or sex discrimination, and introduced two Directives requiring Member States to amend the burden of proof (EC Directive 97/80, dealing with sex discrimination claims and EC Directive 2000/43, on racial discrimination claims). These were given effect in the United Kingdom by, respectively, the Sex Discrimination Act (Indirect Discrimination and Burden of Proof) Regulations 2001, and Race Relations Act 1976 (Amendment) Regulations 2003. Both required the tribunal considering a complaint of direct discrimination to consider whether the claimant had established facts from which they *could* infer direct discrimination. If this threshold was passed, the burden then shifted to the defendant to demonstrate that there was in fact no discrimination.

A series of cases then followed, dealing with the approach to be taken by courts and tribunals applying the test. The issue was first considered by the EAT in *Barton v Investec Henderson Crosthwaite Securities Ltd* ([2003] IRLR 332, EAT), where Judge Ansell set out the approach tribunals should now take to the burden of proof in cases of alleged sex discrimination:

1) It is for the Claimant to prove on the balance of probabilities facts from which the Tribunal could conclude, in the absence of an adequate explanation, that the respondents have committed an act of unlawful discrimination.
2) If the Claimant cannot prove such facts he will fail.
3) It is important to bear in mind that it is unusual to find direct evidence of sex discrimination, i.e. evidence that sex discrimination was the motive for an act or omission.
4) In deciding whether the Claimant has proved such facts, it is important to remember that the outcome at this stage of the analysis will usually depend on what inferences it is proper to draw from the primary facts.
5) When the Claimant has proved facts from which inferences could be drawn that the respondents have treated him less favourably on grounds of sex, then the burden of proof moves to the respondent to disprove those inferences.
6) To discharge that burden it is necessary for the respondent to prove, on the balance of probabilities, that the treatment was in no sense whatever on the grounds of sex, since 'no discrimination whatsoever' is permitted under the Burden of Proof Directive.
7) The Tribunal is required to assess not merely whether the respondent has proved an explanation for the facts from which the inferences could be drawn, but also that it is adequate to discharge the burden of proof that *sex was no part of the reasons* for the treatment in question.[4]

The test was modified by the EAT in *Chamberlins Solicitors v Emokpae* [2004] UKEAT/0989/03/DM. The Claimant was employed as a legal assistant by a small firm of solicitors in London for some two months before she was dismissed after rumours (apparently baseless) spread about an affair between her and one of the solicitors, Mr Emezie. The Tribunal accepted the following as facts:

4 My emphasis.

1) there was a climate of gossip and rumour within the firm;
2) there was unwise familiarity from Mr Emezie towards the Claimant;
3) the Claimant had been summarily dismissed in a manner which was procedurally unfair.

The EAT approved the test in *Barton v Investec, mutatis mutandis*, and then applied it to the facts they were dealing with. However, the EAT accepted that *Barton* was too onerous, in that it required the employer to prove that there was no discrimination at all. Since *Nagarajan v London Regional Transport* ([1999] IRLR 572), less favourable treatment is unlawful if gender has a *significant* effect on the outcome. Therefore, if gender is only a small factor among a large number of predominant factors, it will not be the reason for the treatment.

Applying this adjustment to the facts of the present case, the EAT concluded that the decision would not differ. There were only two possible explanations for the Claimant's dismissal. Either the rumours about her relationship with Mr Emezie, based on her sex, were the reason for her dismissal, or they were not, and the Tribunal had found as a fact that they were.

The Equality Act now applies the same burden of proof to allegations of discrimination based on any protected characteristics. s. 136 provides as follows:

136 Burden of proof

(1) This section applies to any proceedings relating to a contravention of this Act.
(2) If there are facts from which the court could decide, in the absence of any other explanation, that a person (A) contravened the provision concerned, the court must hold that the contravention occurred.
(3) But subsection (2) does not apply if A shows that A did not contravene the provision.

Hewage v Grampian Health Board [2012] UKSC 37 is the most recent Supreme Court decision in this area, but takes us no further. It confirms that the burden of proof at the initial stage is on the claimant, and that the tribunal must hear the evidence of both sides at this stage. However, it does not establish what the claimant needs to prove, save that a mere difference of race or sex from an actual or hypothetical comparator is not sufficient to shift the burden of proof.

11.5 Prohibited conduct under the Equality Act 2010

11.5.1 Direct discrimination

S. 13 provides:

Direct discrimination

(1) A person (A) discriminates against another (B) if, because of a protected characteristic, A treats B less favourably than A treats or would treat others.

Direct discrimination is the simplest and most obvious form of discrimination, involving the treating of an individual less favourably than a comparable individual without that protected characteristic, because of the protected characteristic. A causal link must be shown between the treatment and the protected characteristic; it is not enough for there to be a difference of, say, race or sex, between the complainant and the comparator (*Strathclyde Regional Council v Zafar* [1997] UKHL 54).

'Less favourable' treatment does not mean simply treatment that is different, something which has caused issues in the past. However, once less favourable treatment and the causal link with the relevant prohibited characteristic has been established, there is generally no defence to direct discrimination.

11.5.1.1 'Less favourable treatment'

Case law shows that treatment may be different without being less favourable. This can be seen in relation to employers' dress codes.

It is not unusual for employers to require their employees to wear some form of uniform, or specify what may or may not be worn at work. Such dress codes may include provisions about hair styles or colour, the wearing of jewellery, visible tattoos, and body piercings. Royal Air Force Dress Regulations, for example, set detailed requirements which differ between men and women.

> **AP1358**
>
> **Growth of Hair and Beards – Male Personnel. (QR209 & 210).**
>
> **0149. Hair.** The hair of the head is to be well cut and trimmed. Sideburns are to be short and well-trimmed and are not to extend below a line running through the mid-point of the ear. Extreme styles of haircuts and colouring are not permitted. If the hair is dyed or highlighted, the colour chosen is to be natural and in a uniform shade appropriate to the individual. The commanding officer shall be the arbiter upon what is or not an acceptable style or length of cut.
>
> **a. Rastafarians**. Male Rastafarian hair is to follow the same general rules for other Service personnel in that it is to be neat and tidy and not of an exaggerated nature. Dreadlocks are to be no longer than the collar and able to be worn with all types of military headdress in such a way that is compatible with the image of the Royal Air Force.
>
> **0150. Beards.** Male personnel are to be clean-shaven when in uniform. Beards may only be permitted on religious grounds or when specially authorised by COs on medical grounds under the provisions of AP1269. The beard is to be a full one and, with the exception of Sikhs (see below), it is to be kept short and neatly trimmed.
>
> **a. Sikhs.** Sikhs may wear beards and their hair long in the Sikh tradition. The hair of the head is to be so arranged that it is placed under the turban.
>
> For occupational or operational reasons, where a hazard clearly exists, personnel authorised to wear beards on religious or medical grounds may be ordered to modify or remove facial hair to such an extent as to enable the correct wearing of respirator or breathing apparatus[. . .]
>
> **0151. Moustaches.** If a moustache is worn, the upper lip is to be unshaven and the moustache is not to extend below the edge of the mouth.
>
> **Hairdressing and Cosmetics – Female Personnel.**
>
> **0152.** Female personnel are to arrange their hair in a manner that permits Service Dress cap to be worn correctly; hair is not to show under the front or peak of the cap and the style is to be kept neat and no longer than the bottom edge of the collar at the back of the Service jacket. PMRAFNS personnel are to wear their hair off the collar when engaged in nursing duties. Extreme styles of haircuts and colouring are not permitted, if the hair is dyed or highlighted, the colour chosen is to be natural and in a uniform shade appropriate to the individual.

The commanding officer shall be the arbiter upon what is or not an acceptable style or length of cut. Narrow fabric-covered hair bands (scrunches) may be worn with working dress, but must be inconspicuous and either of a similar colour to the hair or black. Hair bands are not to be worn on parade. Combs, when worn, must be plain and of a similar colour to the wearer's hair. Exceptionally, when required on tasks or training which require them to wear respirators or other similar safety equipment, females with long hair may wear their hair in a ponytail if this facilitates safe fitting of such items. When the need to wear this equipment has passed, the hair must be put up.

a. Rastafarians. Female Rastafarian hair is to follow the same rules for other female personnel.

0153. In addition to the provisions of Para. 0150, female aircrew who are required to wear flying helmets or aircrew respirators for the performance of their aircrew duties are to wear their hair in a manner which:

a. Is sufficiently short that the fit and stability of their flying helmet or aircrew respirator is not compromised.

b. Allows the hair to fit completely and comfortably inside their flying helmet or aircrew respirator without the use of hairpins, clips or other hair-restraining device that might constitute an operational or flight safety hazard.

0154. Nail Varnish & Cosmetics. When in uniform female personnel are forbidden to use brightly coloured nail varnish and cosmetics of a conspicuous nature. Mixed nail colours and non-traditional colours such as blue, green, silver, black etc., are not permitted. The commanding officer shall be the arbiter upon what is or not an acceptable colour. Nursing staff are forbidden to use nail varnish of any kind when on ward duty. Female aircrew are forbidden to wear cosmetics of any kind when performing flying duties that require the use of oxygen masks or aircrew respirators.

Wearing of Trinkets & Jewellery.

0155. Males. In the case of male personnel, the wearing of watch-chains and trinkets in such a manner as to be seen is not permitted when wearing uniform. A wedding ring and/or one other plain signet or precious metal ring. A watch of inconspicuous style may also be worn. Thumb rings are not permitted. Earrings are not to be worn.

0156. Females. The prohibition in Para. 0152 is equally applied to female personnel who are similarly forbidden to wear jewellery when in uniform. They may, however wear a wedding and/or engagement ring plus one other plain metal ring. Thumb rings are not permitted. A watch of inconspicuous style may also be worn. Additionally, if ears are pierced, one small, unobtrusive plain yellow gold spherical stud earring may be worn in each ear lobe at all times except when on parade.

❖ THINKING POINT

Under these Regulations, are men less favourably treated than women in being forbidden to wear earrings? Are they less favourably treated in being required to have their hair short, while women may have long hair, provided it is worn in a bun?

Schmidt v Austicks Bookshops ([1977] IRLR 360, EAT) was the first case in this area and to some degree set a pattern for later cases. The Claimant's employers required her to wear a skirt at work, and an overall when serving the public. The only restriction on men was that they were forbidden to wear T-shirts. Phillips J considered the overall issue to be too trivial to amount to a detriment. As to skirts:

> The rules were plainly designed to assist in creating what to the employers was a satisfactory image and to assist in relations with the public. . . . The restriction applied only when she was working with and in sight of the public. . . . The evidence showed that although there was less scope for positive rules in the case of the men, in that the choice of wearing apparel was more limited, there were restrictions in their case too. For example, they were not allowed to wear T-shirts, and it is quite certain, on a reasonable examination of the evidence, that they would not have been allowed to wear, had they sought to, any out-of the-way-clothing. . . . There were in force rules restricting wearing apparel and governing appearance which applied to men and also applied to women, although, obviously, women and men being different, the rules in the two cases were not the same. We should be prepared to accept . . . an alternative contention . . . that in any event, insofar as comparison was possible, the employers treated both male and female staff alike in that both sexes were restricted in the choice of clothing for wear at work and were both informed that a certain garment should not be worn during working hours [. . .]
>
> It seems to us . . . that an approach of that sort is a better approach and more likely to lead to a sensible result, than an approach which examines the situation point by point and garment by garment . . .
>
> An employer is entitled to a large measure of discretion in controlling the image of his establishment, including the appearance of staff, and especially so when, as a result of their duties, they come into contact with the public.
>
> On this basis, the employer may impose an appearance code on his workforce, with the objective of presenting a suitable image and assisting relations with the public. Generally speaking, employers require their employees to maintain a conventional appearance at work; as what is considered conventional differs between men and women, specific requirements may be different provided the overall standard is the same.

This approach was followed by the EAT in *Smith v Safeway plc* [1995] 132, EAT, where a male delicatessen assistant was dismissed after refusing to get his hair cut when his pony tail grew too long to be contained under his hat. The relevant rule for male employees stated: 'Tidy hair not below shirt collar length. No unconventional hair styles or colouring'. The equivalent provision for women stated, 'Shoulder-length hair must be clipped back. No unconventional hair styles or colouring'. There was no suggestion that the rules were based on hygiene considerations. The tribunal applied *Schmidt* and considered that it was lawful to apply different rules to men and women provided they enforced a common standard of smartness. The EAT allowed the appeal by a majority.

> [The Claimant argued that hair length] could not be equated with dress. Dress can be changed on leaving work whereas hair is worn into public life. Hair length is not a function of any physiological difference between men and women. Differences are a question only of custom or fashion. Unlike differences in dress, there are no counterbalancing features; the rule discriminates against men [. . .]
>
> The lay members of this tribunal have no difficulty in holding that the treatment was less favourable and self-evidently so. The requirements . . . with respect to hair style are capable of being applied to both men and women in such a way as to take account of convention (and therefore to be compatible with *Schmidt*) without placing the restriction they do on hair length for men only [. . .]

> [According to the chairman] *Schmidt* [is] concerned with appearance. Employers are entitled to lay down reasonable requirements as to the way employees present themselves at work, if, for example, they come into contact with the public. Employers can have regard to current conventions and decline to accept what is 'out-of-the-way'. . . . What is conventional and what is out-of-the-way for men will often be different [from that] . . . for women. If the employer is entitled to require an appearance which is not out-of-the-way, it is difficult to distinguish between dress and other aspects of personal appearance, including hair style. Provided requirements for men and women can reasonably be related to current perceptions of what is a conventional appearance for men and for women, the requirements do not treat one sex less favourably than the other. The sexes are treated differently but equally by the standards of what is conventional.

On appeal, the Court of Appeal approved the Chairman's approach and ruled in favour of the employer (*Smith v Safeways plc* [1996] IRLR 456, CA).

Per Phillips LJ:

> In my judgment, a package approach to the effects of an appearance code necessarily follows once one accepts that the code is not required to make provisions which apply identically to men and women. . . . One has to consider the effect of any [one] item in the overall context of the code as a whole [. . .]
>
> Appearance depends in part on ephemera: clothes, rings and jewellery worn; but it also depends on more permanent characteristics: tattoos, hair style, hair colouring and hair length. The approach adopted in *Schmidt* can in my judgment properly be applied to both types of characteristic [. . .]
>
> I can accept that one of the objects of the prohibition of sex discrimination was to relieve the sexes of unequal treatment resulting from conventional attitudes, but I do not believe that this renders discriminatory an appearance code which applies what is conventional. On the contrary, I am inclined to think that such a code is likely to operate unfavourably with regard to one or other of the sexes unless it applies such a standard. . . . A code which applies conventional standards is one which, so far as the criterion of appearance is concerned, applies an even-handed approach between men and women, and not one which is discriminatory.

11.5.1.2 Less favourable treatment than whom? – The comparator

The decision on whether the claimant has been less favourably treated requires a comparison exercise, since 'less favourable' is a relative concept, not an absolute one. The legislation permits the claimant to rely on an actual or hypothetical comparator, whose relevant circumstances are the same or not materially different. Generally speaking, the comparator is a real or hypothetical individual employed by the same employer, or, where the claimant is a person seeking employment, another candidate, whose characteristics are the same as the claimant's except for the relevant protected characteristic.

SDA s. 5(3) provided, 'A comparison of the cases of persons of different sex or marital status under section 1(1) or 3(1) must be such that the relevant circumstances in the one case are the same, or not materially different, in the other'. This gave rise to case law on what constituted 'relevant circumstances', particularly in relation to pregnancy and sexual orientation. Neither of these was specifically dealt with by the Act, so the issue of the comparator became critical.

In the case of pregnancy, less favourable treatment – dismissal or refusal of promotion, for example – was usually based, not on the pregnancy itself, but on its consequences, most obviously a lengthy absence from work. But pregnancy is, by its nature, an exclusively female condition, so what are the 'relevant characteristics' of the comparator for the purpose of determining whether a pregnant woman has been 'less favourably' treated?

In *Turley v Allders Department Stores Ltd* ([1980] I.C.R. 66) a majority of the EAT held that dismissal of a woman on the pure ground of pregnancy could not constitute unlawful discrimination, as comparison with a man who was in a like position was impossible. Subsequently, the EAT followed the dissenting view in *Turley*, ruling that a valid comparison could be made with a man who was off work for medical reasons for the same length of time (*Hayes v Malleable Working Men's Club and Institute* [1985] I.C.R. 703). This produced a conclusion that there had been no 'less favourable' treatment, as such a man would be treated in the same manner as the claimant. There the position remained until the House of Lords decision in *Webb v EMO Air Cargo* (No. 2) ([1992] UKHL 13).

Mrs Webb was offered and accepted a post as an Import Operations Clerk, and began work on 1 July 1987. She was informed at her interview that the job was available because one of the four Import Operations Clerks, Valerie Stewart, was due to give birth in February 1988. The intention was that Mrs Stewart would train Mrs Webb to do the job before going on maternity leave at the end of 1988, Mrs Webb would replace her during her absence, but would continue to work after Mrs Stewart returned. In mid-July, Mrs Webb suspected she was pregnant, and was dismissed in the week that the pregnancy was confirmed, on the basis that she would be away during the period that she should have been replacing Mrs Stewart. At that time, a right to maternity leave only applied where the woman had completed two years' continuous employment by the end of the 14th week before the expected week of childbirth.

Following *Hayes*, the Court of Appeal ruled against Mrs Webb. On the issue of the comparator, Glidewell LJ said ([1992] 2 All E.R. 43, 52):

> To postulate a pregnant man is an absurdity, but I see no difficulty in comparing a pregnant woman with a man who has a medical condition which will require him to be absent for the same period of time and at the same time as does the woman's pregnancy.

Mrs Webb appealed to the House of Lords. In the initial hearing (*Webb v EMO Air Cargo* [1992] UKHL 13) Lord Keith of Kinkel distinguished her case from that where an employer used pregnancy itself as a criterion for dismissal or refusal to employ. Since pregnancy was an exclusively female condition, that employer was adopting a gender-based criterion, which represented unlawful direct discrimination. He drew a parallel with *James v Eastleigh Borough Council* ([1990] 2 AC 751), where the criterion applied by the Council was that the person must be receiving the state pension. Mr and Mrs James were both 62, but because of the differential pension ages then in force, only Mrs James met the criterion. 'But for' his sex, Mr James would also have been receiving the state pension at the same age.

The position in *Webb* was more subtle. Mrs Webb was not dismissed because she was pregnant, but because, as a result of pregnancy, she would be absent from work at the same time as Mrs Stewart. The issue for the House of Lords was whether, for the purposes of SDA s. 5(3), it was legitimate to take account of absence caused by pregnancy and expected childbirth, by using a man absent for the same length of time as a comparator.

Lord Keith continued, stating that he did not think the 'but for' test established in *James* was applicable here:

> The appellant was not dismissed simply because she was pregnant but because her pregnancy had the consequence that she would not be available for work at the critical period. It is true that but for her sex she would not have been pregnant, and but for her pregnancy she would not have been unavailable then. If the 'but for' test applies to that situation, it must equally apply where the reason for the woman's being unavailable at the critical time is that she is then due to have an operation of a peculiarly gynaecological nature, such as a hysterectomy. But a man may require to undergo an operation for some condition which is peculiar to males, such as an abnormal prostate. Is the 'but for his sex' test to be applied so as to produce a

> finding of unlawful discrimination where he is not engaged because the impending operation will make him unavailable when his services are particularly required?[. . .]
>
> The problem of postulating relevant circumstances for the purpose of making a comparison with the treatment accorded to hypothetical members of the opposite sex did not arise. The circumstances in the case of a woman due to have a hysterectomy are different from the circumstances in the case of a man due to have a prostate operation. The question is whether they are materially different, and the answer must be that they are not, because both sets of circumstances have the result that the person concerned is not going to be available at the critical time. Then it has to be considered whether there is something special about pregnancy which ought to lead to the conclusion that the case of a woman due to be unavailable for that reason is materially different from the case of a man due to be unavailable because of an expected prostate operation. In logic, there would not appear to be any valid reason for that conclusion. It is true that pregnancy may be said to be a normal condition, not an abnormal pathological condition such as to require a hysterectomy, but the consequences of both are the same, namely unavailability of the person when particularly needed. The argument for the appellant is that when comparison is made between a pregnant woman, who is going to be unavailable on account of her confinement at the critical time, and a man, then because a man could not be unavailable for the same reason dismissal of or failure to engage the pregnant woman constitutes discrimination. But the correct comparison is not with any man but with a hypothetical man who would also be unavailable at the critical time. The relevant circumstance for purposes of the comparison required by section 5(3) to be made is expected unavailability at the material time. The precise reason for the unavailability is not a relevant circumstance, and in particular it is not relevant that the reason is a condition which is capable of affecting only women, or for that matter only men.

On this basis, Lord Keith concluded that there had been no unlawful discrimination under the SDA. However, consideration of the relevant EU law produced a different and, arguably, distinctly artificial, result.

Article 2(1) of the Equal Treatment Directive (Directive 76/207) provides:

> For the purposes of the following provisions, the principle of equal treatment shall mean that there shall be no discrimination whatsoever on grounds of sex either directly or indirectly by reference in particular to marital or family status.

Lord Keith contrasted the conclusions of the ECJ in two cases where a claimant argued that national law breached the Equal Treatment Directive. The first was *Dekker v Stichting Vormingscentrum voor Jong Volwassenen (V.J.V. -Centrum) Plus* [1990] E.C.R. I-3941, where a Dutch woman was interviewed for a job when three months pregnant, and rejected because of the cost to the employer of paying her 100 per cent of salary while on maternity leave, while being unable to recover the cost of paying her salary from the relevant insurance scheme, as the fact of her pregnancy was known at the outset. In those circumstances, they could not afford to pay a replacement for Mrs Dekker, which would have led to staff shortages. The Dutch courts held that under the relevant national law Mrs Dekker had been discriminated against, but that the discrimination was justified. The Dutch Supreme Court referred a question of compatibility of the relevant Dutch law with the Directive to the ECJ, which held:

> 10. Consideration must be given to the question whether a refusal of employment in the circumstances to which the national court has referred may be regarded as direct discrimination on grounds of sex for the purposes of the Directive. The answer depends on whether the

> fundamental reason for the refusal of employment is one which applies without distinction to workers of either sex or, conversely, whether it applies exclusively to one sex.
>
> 11. The reason given by the employer for refusing to appoint Mrs. Dekker is basically that it could not have obtained reimbursement from the [insurance scheme] of the daily benefits which it would have had to pay her for the duration of her absence due to pregnancy, and yet at the same time it would have been obliged to employ a replacement. That situation arises because, on the one hand, the national scheme in question assimilates pregnancy to sickness and, on the other, the [Dutch legislation] contains no provision excluding pregnancy from the cases in which the [insurance scheme] is entitled to refuse reimbursement of the daily benefits.
>
> 12. In that regard it should be observed that only women can be refused employment on grounds of pregnancy and such a refusal therefore constitutes direct discrimination on grounds of sex. A refusal of employment on account of the financial consequences of absence due to pregnancy must be regarded as based, essentially, on the fact of pregnancy. Such discrimination cannot be justified on grounds relating to the financial loss which an employer who appointed a pregnant woman would suffer for the duration of her maternity leave.

The second case was the Danish case of *Handels-og Kontorfunktionaerernes Forbund i Danmark v Dansk Arbejdsgiverforening* [1990] E.C.R. I-3979, decided on the same day as *Dekker*. Mrs Hertz spent much of her pregnancy on sick leave, and then, having returned to work after maternity leave, took frequent periods of sick leave as a result of complications arising from the birth. After she had accumulated 100 days' sick leave in one year, her employer dismissed her. As in *Dekker*, the Danish courts ruled that there was no breach of domestic anti-discrimination legislation, but referred the issue of compatibility of that domestic law with the Directive to the ECJ, which ruled:

> It follows from the provisions of the Directive . . . that the dismissal of a female worker on account of pregnancy constitutes direct discrimination on grounds of sex, as is a refusal to appoint a pregnant woman. . . . On the other hand, the dismissal of a female worker on account of repeated periods of sick leave which are not attributable to pregnancy or confinement does not constitute direct discrimination on grounds of sex, inasmuch as such periods of sick leave would lead to the dismissal of a male worker in the same circumstances.
>
> The Directive does not envisage the case of an illness attributable to pregnancy or confinement. It does, however, admit of national provisions guaranteeing women specific rights on account of pregnancy and maternity, such as maternity leave. During the maternity leave accorded to her pursuant to national law, a woman is accordingly protected against dismissal due to absence. It is for every Member State to fix periods of maternity leave in such a way as to enable female workers to absent themselves during the period in which the disorders inherent in pregnancy and confinement occur.
>
> In the case of an illness manifesting itself after the maternity leave, there is no reason to distinguish an illness attributable to pregnancy or confinement from any other illness. Such a pathological condition is therefore covered by the general rules applicable in the event of illness.
>
> Male and female workers are equally exposed to illness. Although certain disorders are, it is true, specific to one or other sex, the only question is whether a woman is dismissed on account of absence due to illness in the same circumstances as a man; if that is the case, then there is no direct discrimination on grounds of sex.

Lord Keith concluded that the ECJ made a distinction between the 'normal incidents' of pregnancy and childbirth, and 'uncommon complications' arising from them. The former gave rise to specific legal protection which was solely applicable to women, and no comparison exercise was possible. The latter was treated by the Directive as comparable with sickness or injury of any other kind.

The claimant in *Dekker* was, ultimately, discriminated against because of the pregnancy itself and the consequent absence.

In the *Dekker* case the European Court held that the fundamental reason for the refusal of employment was pregnancy, a reason which did not apply to workers of either sex without distinction but which applied exclusively to the female sex, and that this constituted direct discrimination on grounds of sex. That the refusal of employment was not on grounds of pregnancy as such, but on account of the adverse financial consequences to the employer of absence of the worker due to pregnancy was regarded as not material because, in the Court's view, the refusal was essentially based on the fact of pregnancy.

Following the example of the Dutch and Danish Supreme Courts, the Lords sought a ruling from the ECJ on the compatibility of s. 5(3) with the Directive in relation to pregnancy. Unsurprisingly, the ECJ ruled that pregnancy and childbirth were matters unique to women and could not be compared with illness or injury, s. 5(3) must be interpreted in a manner which gave effect to the purpose of the Directive. Applying that ruling (*Webb v EMO Air Cargo* (No.2), the Lords concluded, somewhat artificially, that the proper comparator for a woman dismissed on grounds of a forthcoming absence due to pregnancy and childbirth was a man who was not absent from work at all. This would inevitably result in a finding of unlawful discrimination, since the pregnant woman would always have been less favourably treated than the comparator.

Subsequently, ERA 1996 ss. 70–75 created a right to maternity leave for pregnant women for a minimum of 28 weeks regardless of continuity of employment (later increased to one year).

The SDA did not contain specific provisions regarding sexual orientation either, a gap which remained until 2003. In a number of cases, homosexuals argued that their proper comparator was a heterosexual person of the same or opposite sex. However, the courts ruled consistently that homosexuality was a relevant characteristic, and so the proper comparator was a homosexual person of the opposite sex. Since in the same circumstances such a person would have been treated in the same fashion, there was no less favourable treatment on grounds of sex, and so no discrimination.

For example, in *Grant v South-West Trains* Case C-249/96 [1998] ECR I-3739, the Claimant, a woman employed by a railway company, argued that it was discriminatory not to extend travel concessions available to spouses or opposite-sex cohabitees to her female partner. The issue of compatibility with the Equal Treatment Directive was referred to the ECJ, which ruled that there was no breach:

> The refusal to allow Ms Grant the concessions is based on the fact that . . . she does not live with a 'spouse' or a person of the opposite sex with whom she has had a meaningful relationship for at least two years.
>
> That condition, the effect of which is that the worker must live in a stable relationship with a person of the opposite sex in order to benefit from the travel concessions, is . . . applied regardless of the sex of the worker concerned. Thus, travel concessions are refused to a male worker if he is living with a person of the same sex, just as they are to a female worker if she is living with a person of the same sex.
>
> Since the condition imposed by the undertaking's regulations applies in the same way to female and male workers, it cannot be regarded as constituting discrimination based on sex.

11.5.1.3 Cause and effect

Having established that there has been less favourable treatment, the next issue is whether it is 'because of' a protected characteristic. The question of burden of proof has already been considered, but what test do the courts apply in establishing the necessary connection between protected characteristic and treatment?

This issue was considered by the House of Lords in *James v Eastleigh Borough Council* [1990] 2 AC 751, and established the judicial interpretation of the phrase 'on the grounds of' his or her sex, used in the Sex Discrimination Act 1975 s. 1(1)(a). Mr and Mrs James were both aged 61. As was not unusual, Eastleigh Borough Council operated a policy of allowing free admission to swimming pools to persons of state pension age. Mrs James was entitled to free admission because she had attained the state pension age for women at 60. Mr James was not, as he had not reached the state pension age for men of 65. There was no intention to discriminate on the part of the council – it was simply giving concessions to pensioners and Mr James did not become a pensioner until he reached 65. The House of Lords affirmed that the test for discrimination is objective and motive or intention is irrelevant. If the complainant was receiving less favourable treatment for reasons of sex, there was discrimination. Further, to use a criterion which was itself discriminatory to create an advantage means that the action resulting from the use of that criterion must be discriminatory. The state retirement age was then discriminatory because it gave men less favourable treatment; therefore, to give a concession based on state pension ages was discriminatory.

Under *James v Eastleigh Borough Council*, the question for the Tribunal was whether the person has been treated less favourably than another person because of sex or race, that he would not have been treated in that way *but for* his sex or race. Since then, the 'reason why' test has supervened, but the practical difference between the two is difficult to detect. The 'reason why' test was originally defined in the victimisation case of *Nagarajan v London Regional Transport* ([2000] AC 501), and subsequently extended to direct discrimination in *Shamoon v Chief Constable of the Royal Ulster Constabulary* ([2003] UKHL 11). In *Nagarajan*, the Claimant, who was of Indian origin, applied for a job with LRT having brought several claims of racial discrimination against them in the past. Although he was interviewed, he was not offered the job, and brought an action for victimisation, claiming that he had been less favourably treated by reason of having brought claims previously. The Tribunal found in his favour on three grounds:

- All three members of the interviewing panel were aware of the earlier proceedings.
- The Claimant was given 1 out of 10 for 'articulacy' despite his having worked as a transport information assistant dealing with verbal inquiries for four months without complaint.
- One of the panel considered that the Claimant was 'very anti-management'.

From this the Tribunal concluded that the interviewers 'were consciously or subconsciously influenced by the fact that the Claimant had previously brought industrial tribunal proceedings against LRT'.

LRT appealed on the basis that an employer could only be liable if shown to be 'consciously motivated' by the bringing of proceedings, and, here, no conscious motivation could be made out.

Lord Nicholls:

S. 2 should be read in the context of s. 1. S. 1(1)(a) is concerned with direct discrimination. . . . This is the crucial question. Was it on grounds of race? Or was it for some other reason?

For the purposes of direct discrimination under s. 1(1)(a) . . . the reason why the alleged discriminator acted on racial grounds is irrelevant. Racial discrimination is not negatived by the discriminator's motive or intention or reason or purpose . . . in treating another person less favourably on racial grounds [. . .]

A variety of phrases, with different shades of meaning, have been used to explain how the legislation applies in such cases; discrimination requires that racial grounds were a cause, the activating cause, a substantial and effective cause, a substantial reason, an important factor. No one phrase is obviously preferable to all others, although, in the application of this legislation, legalistic phrases, as well as subtle distinctions, are better avoided so far as possible. If racial grounds or protected acts had a significant effect on the outcome, discrimination is made out.

This confirms that the conscious motivation of the defendant is irrelevant; the issue is simply whether the reason for the less favourable treatment was a protected characteristic of the claimant, either directly, or indirectly as in *James*, where a criterion based on gender was applied. The second point is that the discriminatory reason need not be the sole reason for the treatment.

There is no case law under the Equality Act to suggest any change.

11.5.1.4 Defences to direct discrimination

Once direct discrimination is established, the employer has no defence unless he can persuade the tribunal that a genuine occupational requirement (GOR) applies. In particular, the fact that the employer believes he is acting in the claimant's best interests is no defence to a finding of less favourable treatment.

In *Greig v Community Industries* ([1979] IRLR 158) the claimant was one of two teenage girls on a youth training scheme in which all the other participants were boys. The other girl left, and the organisers withdrew the claimant from the scheme on the basis that it would be too difficult for her to cope on her own in an exclusively male environment. Her claim of direct discrimination was upheld.

❖ THINKING POINT

The Times reported on 10 December 2015 that the owner of Port Vale football club had decided against offering the black former Dutch international Jimmy Floyd Hasselbaink the post of manager in 2013 because of 'the racial issue the club had'. Norman Smurthwaite was reported as telling the *Stoke Sentinel*:

> I didn't take him because of the racial issue the club had got. I did not think it was fair on him. Can you imagine the poor bloke getting abuse, along with the normal abuse, if results were going against him? He would have been right for the club . . . but I don't think the club would have been right for him. Ninety-nine per cent of our fans are excellent but a small minority leave us with policing and other issues.

If there was indeed concern about the behaviour of a minority of Port Vale fans, how could the club have dealt with it?

The SDA and RRA contained lists of specific GORs (originally Genuine Occupational Qualifications – GOQs), but the Equality Act takes a more general approach, though there are specific GORs for certain protected characteristics, in particular religion and belief.

SDA s. 7 provided:

Exception where sex is a genuine occupational qualification

(1) In relation to sex discrimination—
 (a) section 6(1)(a) or (c) does not apply to any employment where being a man is a genuine occupational qualification for the job, and
 (b) section 6(2)(a) does not apply to opportunities for promotion or transfer to, or training for, such employment.

(2) Being a man is a genuine occupational qualification for a job only where—

(a) the essential nature of the job calls for a man for reasons of physiology (excluding physical strength or stamina) or, in dramatic performances or other entertainment, for reasons of authenticity, so that the essential nature of the job would be materially different if carried out by a woman; or

(b) the job needs to be held by a man to preserve decency or privacy because—

(i) it is likely to involve physical contact with men in circumstances where they might reasonably object to its being carried out by a woman, or

(ii) the holder of the job is likely to do his work in circumstances where men might reasonably object to the presence of a woman because they are in a state of undress or are using sanitary facilities; or

(ba) the job is likely to involve the holder of the job doing his work, or living, in a private home and needs to be held by a man because objection might reasonably be taken to allowing to a woman–

(i) the degree of physical or social contact with a person living in the home, or

(ii) the knowledge of intimate details of such a person's life, which is likely, because of the nature or circumstances of the job or of the home, to be allowed to, or available to, the holder of the job; or

(c) the nature or location of the establishment makes it impracticable for the holder of the job to live elsewhere than in premises provided by the employer, and—

(i) the only such premises which are available for persons holding that kind of job are lived in, or normally lived in, by men and are not equipped with separate sleeping accommodation for women and sanitary facilities which could be used by women in privacy from men, and

(ii) it is not reasonable to expect the employer either to equip those premises with such accommodation and facilities or to provide other premises for women; or

(d) the nature of the establishment, or of the part of it within which the work is done, requires the job to be held by a man because—

(i) it is, or is part of, a hospital, prison or other establishment for persons requiring special care, supervision or attention, and

(ii) those persons are all men (disregarding any woman whose presence is exceptional), and

(iii) it is reasonable, having regard to the essential character of the establishment or that part, that the job should not be held by a woman; or

(e) the holder of the job provides individuals with personal services promoting their welfare or education, or similar personal services, and those services can most effectively be provided by a man, or

(f) [. . .]

(g) the job needs to be held by a man because it is likely to involve the performance of duties outside the United Kingdom in a country whose laws or customs are such that the duties could not, or could not effectively, be performed by a woman, or

(h) the job is one of two to be held

(i) by a married couple,

(ii) by a couple who are civil partners of each other, or

(iii) by a married couple or a couple who are civil partners of each other.

(3) Subsection (2) applies where some only of the duties of the job fall within paragraphs (a) to (g) as well as where all of them do.

(4) Paragraph (a), (b), (c), (d), (e). . . or (g) of subsection (2) does not apply in relation to the filling of a vacancy at a time when the employer already has male employees—

(a) who are capable of carrying out the duties falling within that paragraph, and

(b) whom it would be reasonable to employ on those duties, and
(c) whose numbers are sufficient to meet the employer's likely requirements in respect of those duties without undue inconvenience.

RRA s. 5 provided:

Exceptions for genuine occupational qualifications

(1) In relation to racial discrimination
   (a) section 4(1)(a) or (c) does not apply to any employment where being of a particular racial group is a genuine occupational qualification for the job; and
   (b) section 4(2)(b) does not apply to opportunities for promotion or transfer to, or training for, such employment.
(2) Being of a particular racial group is a genuine occupational qualification for a job only where—
   (a) the job involves participation in a dramatic performance or other entertainment in a capacity for which a person of that racial group is required for reasons of authenticity; or
   (b) the job involves participation as an artist's or photographic model in the production of a work of art, visual image or sequence of visual images for which a person of that racial group is required for reasons of authenticity; or
   (c) the job involves working in a place where food or drink is (for payment or not) provided to and consumed by members of the public or a section of the public in a particular setting for which, in that job, a person of that racial group is required for reasons of authenticity; or
   (d) the holder of the job provides persons of that racial group with personal services promoting their welfare, and those services can most effectively be provided by a person of that racial group.
(3) Subsection (2) applies where only some of the duties of the job fall within paragraph (a), (b), (c) or (d) as well as where all of them do.
(4) Paragraph (a), (b), (c) or (d) of subsection (2) does not apply in relation to the filling of a vacancy at a time when the employer already has employees of the racial group in question—
   (a) who are capable of carrying out the duties falling within that paragraph; and
   (b) whom it would be reasonable to employ on those duties; and
   (c) whose numbers are sufficient to meet the employer's likely requirements in respect of those duties without undue inconvenience.

Clearly there are overlaps between the two lists, most obviously in relation to 'authenticity'.

Case law shows that GORs were interpreted very narrowly, and tribunals made use of the exception to the GOR principle available where the employer already had employees available to perform the task at issue. In *Wylie v Dee & Co (Menswear) Ltd* [1978] IRLR 103 a woman was turned down for a job in a menswear shop. The employer argued that the nature of the job required the taking of inside leg measurements and therefore a GOR applied. The tribunal found, however, that the shop had separate changing cubicles and seven male assistants who could be called upon to measure inside legs if required, so that a GOR did not exist.

By contrast, in *Lasertop Ltd v Webster* [1997] ICR 828 the EAT concluded a GOR did apply where a man applied for a post as a salesman/trainee manager, selling memberships of a women's health club due to be opened by the Respondent company. He was rejected and told that the jobs were for 'ladies only'. The Respondents claimed a GOR on the ground that the job was required to be held by a woman to preserve the decency of the members. The Tribunal rejected this argument on the basis that duties in the changing room, sauna, sunbed room and lavatories would occupy a comparatively small part of the jobholder's time and the company would have sufficient female staff capable of carrying out those duties without undue inconvenience.

Allowing the Respondent's appeal, the EAT held that the law had to be applied to the circumstances prevailing when the *prima facie* discrimination took place, that is, at the time the Claimant was refused employment. At that time, the company had no employees, and therefore no female employees capable of carrying out those duties which a man could not do. The EAT admitted that this interpretation produced a gap in the law where a business was in the course of being set up.

❖ THINKING POINT

Was it actually necessary for prospective members to be *escorted* into the changing rooms, sauna, sunbed room and lavatories? Would the EAT have taken a more liberal approach, in accordance with the purpose of the legislation, had the sexes been reversed and a woman was seeking a job in an all-male establishment?

❖ THINKING POINT

Some years ago a woman engendered considerable media publicity when she brought an action for sex discrimination against St George's Chapel, Windsor, after she applied for a post as a baritone lay clerk (salaried adult chorister) in the chapel's world-renowned choir. She signed her application with her initials, and complained of discrimination in that the choirmaster sent a letter in reply beginning 'Dear Mr', and then informed her that she could not be considered for the post because no woman could sing baritone. Her action failed on the technical point that St George's Chapel is a 'royal peculiar' (a church under the direct authority of the Sovereign, who was not bound by the SDA), but could the choirmaster argue a GOR?

The Equality Act has substituted a single formulation, found in sch. 9 s. 1(1).

> 1(1) A person (A) does not contravene a provision mentioned in sub-paragraph (2) by applying in relation to work a requirement to have a particular protected characteristic, if A shows that, having regard to the nature or context of the work—
>
> (a) it is an occupational requirement,
> (b) the application of the requirement is a proportionate means of achieving a legitimate aim, and
> (c) the person to whom A applies the requirement does not meet it (or A has reasonable grounds for not being satisfied that the person meets it).

As yet there is little case law, most of it dealing with alleged age discrimination in relation to eligibility for redundancy packages. This will be examined in Chapter 15.

The Equality Act also provides specific GORs in connection with certain protected characteristics, particularly in relation to religion and belief. These will be examined in the relevant chapters.

11.5.2 Indirect discrimination

Indirect discrimination is a more subtle concept than direct discrimination, and may arise in practice without any discriminatory intent. It involves the situation, not where an employer treats a particular group or its individual members less favourably than another group, rather, the employer treats everyone concerned in the same way, but that treatment has detrimental effects towards those sharing a particular protected characteristic.

❖ EXAMPLE

An employer sets a minimum height requirement for job applicants of 5ft 8 inches, about the average height for men in the general British population. As the average height for women is much lower – about 5ft 4 inches – a smaller proportion of women than men will be able to meet that minimum height requirement and so be eligible for the job.

In contrast to direct discrimination, an employer may rely on a defence of justification in the face of a claim of indirect discrimination, expressed in the Equality Act in the terms that the criterion having the discriminatory effect is 'a proportionate means of achieving a legitimate aim'.

❖ EXAMPLE

The Royal Air Force sets very precise upper and lower limits on length of leg for prospective aircrew, because of the ejector seats used in fast jet aircraft. If a person's legs (particularly thighs) are too long, he will catch his knees on the edge of the windscreen while ejecting. If too short, he will not be able to sit correctly on the seat, and is at greater risk of being injured by the forces of ejection (ejector seats are rocket-powered in order to break through the aircraft's slipstream at high speed). The limits are rigorously enforced – the author is aware of one candidate who was rejected because her overall leg length was one centimetre too low. Clearly, the proportion of women candidates rejected because their legs are too short is higher than that of men, while the converse is true in relation to the upper limit. The issue has not been tested in court, but the Ministry of Defence relies on the safety argument, along with the high cost of modifying cockpits and ejector seats, in establishing that the limits are a proportionate means of achieving a legitimate aim.

The purpose of the legislation creating the concept of indirect discrimination was to induce employers, particularly at the recruitment stage, to change their practices in order to remove unnecessary criteria which limited opportunity for women and minority ethnic groups. The defence of justification recognises, however, that some criteria or practices may have a discriminatory effect but be necessary in order, for example, to maintain professional standards.

In *Hampson v Department of Education and Science* ([1991] 1 AC 171) the Claimant, an ethnic Chinese woman, completed a two-year English-medium teacher training course in Hong Kong, and a further one-year course enabling her to teach in the higher years of Hong Kong secondary schools. She then moved to this country, and applied for 'qualified teacher' status, in order to teach in secondary schools in England and Wales. Under the Teachers (Education) Regulations 1982, in order to be accorded such a status a person had to have completed a Postgraduate Certificate in Education, or a Bachelor of Education degree, or a Certificate in Education, awarded by a UK institution, or a course 'approved [by the Secretary of State for Education] as a course for the initial training of teachers in schools' (sch. 5 1(1)(a)). The Secretary of State did not approve the course taken by Mrs Hampson. It was accepted that the requirement was indirectly discriminatory against ethnic minority and other non-British teachers since they were more likely to have trained abroad, but the House of Lords held that the requirement was justified as a means of ensuring high standards in state education.

The Equality Act s. 19 provides:

(1) A person (A) discriminates against another (B) if A applies to B a provision, criterion or practice which is discriminatory in relation to a relevant protected characteristic of B's.
(2) For the purposes of subsection (1), a provision, criterion or practice is discriminatory in relation to a relevant protected characteristic of B's if—
  (a) A applies, or would apply, it to persons with whom B does not share the characteristic,
  (b) It puts, or would put, persons with whom B shares the characteristic at a particular disadvantage when compared with persons with whom B does not share it,
  (c) It puts, or would put, B at that disadvantage, and
  (d) A cannot show it to be a proportionate means of achieving a legitimate aim.

There must therefore be a provision, criterion or practice (PCP) which the employer applies to a person with a particular protected characteristic, and applies or would apply it to others with that protected characteristic. This PCP must put that claimant at a particular disadvantage, and put, or would put, others with the same protected characteristic at a particular disadvantage in comparison with those without that characteristic. If those requirements are satisfied, then the employer may escape a finding of unlawful discrimination by showing that, despite its discriminatory effect, the PCP is a proportionate means of achieving a legitimate aim.

❖ EXAMPLE

Andrea runs a small company which provides a translating service for engineering and science texts. She has been receiving an increasing number of requests for translations from Russian, and advertises for 'an experienced translator with fluency in Russian and knowledge of technical vocabulary and processes'. Chloe, who has a degree in Russian and experience of translating Russian literature, applies for the job and is rejected on grounds of insufficient technical vocabulary. The Employment Tribunal concludes that the requirement for technical vocabulary is indirectly discriminatory against women, since a smaller proportion of women than men are likely to work in technical spheres, but, given the nature of the job, a requirement for technical vocabulary and knowledge of technical processes is a proportionate means of achieving the legitimate aim of providing an efficient technical translation service.

A problem area in dealing with indirect discrimination is that there has as yet been little case law under the Equality Act definition, which differs considerably from that contained in earlier legislation.

11.5.2.1 Provision, criterion or practice (PCP)

This can be a formal requirement, or something quite informal. For example, in a decided case, a woman was interviewed for a job as a messenger on an RAF station. Given the distances involved, a bicycle was provided. The Claimant was turned down on the basis that, at 5ft 1 inch, she was too small to ride that particular bicycle. The EAT, unsurprisingly, rejected the employer's claim of justification, saying that the Claimant already had her own bicycle and the employer had given no valid reason why she could not use it at work.

Under the SDA as originally passed, there could be no indirect discrimination in relation to matters which were not regarded by the employer as absolute requirements. In practice, however, 'desirable' characteristics might well be treated by an employer as essential. For instance, a job advertisement for a law lecturer might well state that experience of teaching LLB students is essential and experience of teaching Employment Law or Company Law an advantage. The reality is that an applicant without experience of teaching Employment or Company Law is unlikely to progress even as far as an interview, unless there are very few candidates with such experience. The concept of 'provision, criterion or practice' now recognises this.

PCPs may be quite subtle, and may arise without any intention to discriminate, hence in many indirect discrimination cases the first task of the Tribunal is to determine whether a PCP exists, and what it is. In *Ministry of Defence v MacMillan* ([2004] EATS/0003/04) Mrs MacMillan was a Chief Petty Officer in the Royal Navy. Having joined the Women's Royal Naval Service (WRNS) before it was disbanded in 1990, she had been able to opt to serve in shore jobs only. She was married to a policeman and they had two young children. After a period in which her husband moved between various police forces in order to fit in with her postings, the two reached a decision to settle in Stirling, where Mrs MacMillan's parents lived, in order that they could help with childcare. Initially, Mrs MacMillan was posted to Faslane, 45 miles from Stirling, and permitted flexibility in her daily starting time. However, she was then posted to Prestwick, 60 miles from Stirling, and where she was required to start work at 8.00am, five days per week. It was accepted that married quarters were available at Prestwick, had she chosen to move there. Mrs MacMillan argued that being required to work full-time, and, specifically, to start work at 8.00am, was indirectly discriminatory against women. The Tribunal accepted that the requirement to start work at 8.00am was a PCP.

In practice, the majority of indirect discrimination cases involve sex, particularly in relation to requirements to work shifts, or to work full-time, though there are increasing numbers of cases being brought on grounds of religion, notably by members of minority Christian groups over requirements to work on Sundays.

11.5.2.2 The comparative group

Prior to the Equality Act, there was indirect discrimination where 'a considerably smaller proportion' of the group sharing the claimant's characteristic *could comply* with the PCP in comparison with the group without that characteristic (SDA and RRA as originally passed), or, under the two Acts as amended in 2003, a 'considerably larger proportion' of the claimant's group *could not comply*. In *MacMillan*, therefore, the Claimant had to show that a considerably larger proportion of women in the relevant population could not comply with the PCP of being able to start work at 8.00am, as compared with the men in that population. In practice, such a PCP created difficulties for all personnel living at a distance from Prestwick, in contrast to those living at the naval base. Individuals might choose to live at a distance for a variety of reasons, but, most commonly, would tend to be married personnel with children wishing to remain in a single location to ensure a consistent education for them. Clearly, this group would include both men and women, and it is far from clear whether women would be in the majority. Further, the proportions of women and men affected by the PCP might vary widely, depending on how the relevant population was defined.

The identification of the population therefore becomes important. On the facts of *Macmillan*, was the relevant population all naval personnel, all married personnel, all married personnel with children, all Chief Petty Officers, all married Chief Petty Officers, and so on? Each group would produce differing proportions of men and women unable to comply with the PCP, so that, on some populations, there could be a finding of indirect discrimination, on others not.

Jones v Chief Adjudication Officer [1990] IRLR 533 was not an employment case but concerned eligibility for social security benefits. Mustill LJ set out the steps which a tribunal should go through in dealing with an indirect sex discrimination claim under the original legislation, whether in the employment field or elsewhere. Mustill LJ assumed that the Claimant was a woman, and that she had to satisfy a single positive criterion in order to be selected:

- identify the criterion at issue;
- identify the relevant population, comprising all those who satisfy the other criteria for selection;
- divide the relevant population into groups representing those who satisfy the criterion at issue and those who do not;
- predict statistically what proportion of each group should consist of women;
- ascertain what the actual male/female balances in the two groups is;
- compare the actual and predicted balances;
- if women are found to be under-represented in the group which satisfy the criterion and over-represented in the group which do not, it is proved that the criterion is discriminatory.

❖ THINKING POINT

What actually constitutes under-representation? However it is defined, to what extent does any 'under-representation' actually result from discrimination, as distinct from choices made by individuals, or factors outside the employer's control? For example, the majority of plumbers are men, so an employer seeking an experienced plumber will have a preponderance of male candidates.

Following Lord Mustill's test in *Jones v Chief Adjudication Officer*, in *Taylor v Commissioners of the Inland Revenue* ([1999] EAT/498/98), the EAT concluded that, in circumstances where more than one PCP was applied, the relevant population was all those individuals who could fulfil those PCPs which the claimant could not.

Mrs Taylor, a trainee chartered surveyor, began employment as a Valuation Assistant in the Inland Revenue Valuation Office in 1988. In 1992 she was promoted to Valuation Executive. On 20 June 1993 she went on maternity leave. During September 1993, while she was on maternity leave, an appraisal was carried out in which on a scale of 1–5 she was graded 4 (not fitted for promotion because of lack of experience). The Claimant gained her RICS membership in November 1993, thus becoming a chartered surveyor, but instead of returning to work when her maternity leave ended on 26 December, she took a career break under the Inland Revenue's scheme. This allowed for a total absence of up to six years, during which time all terms and conditions of employment, including eligibility for promotion, continued to apply. The Claimant did not return to work until May 1996. In 1994–1995 the Inland Revenue instituted a re-grading scheme under which Valuation Executives who met the following criteria would be promoted to Senior Valuer:

- at least three years' service;
- obtaining of RICS membership before 31 December 1993;
- receiving a promotability grading of 2 or above in the individual's most recent appraisal.

Due to the Claimant's career break, her most recent appraisal was that in September 1993, which gave her 4 for promotability. She fulfilled the first two criteria, but not the third. She was not promoted on this occasion, whereas 12 of the 85 Valuation Executives were. Following the Claimant's return to work, her union sought promotion for her on the basis that she would, but for the career break, be on a par with her contemporaries who had joined in 1988, most of whom were now Senior Valuers. The Employer's reply was to the effect that the Claimant would be considered for promotion when she fulfilled the necessary criteria. In January 1997, seven months after returning to work, the Claimant was graded 1 for promotability. She sought retrospective regrading, which was rejected.

The Claimant alleged indirect sex discrimination, on the basis that, but for the career break, she would have satisfied the third criterion and been promoted on 1 October 1995, and that that criterion disproportionately affected women.

The majority of the Tribunal accepted the Inland Revenue's submission that the three criteria adopted in the 1995 promotion exercise were indivisible, and therefore that the relevant pool was all 85 Valuation Executives. The Chairman, dissenting, held that as a matter of ordinary language the Inland Revenue applied three conditions or requirements to the Valuation Executives. He concluded, following the *dicta* of Evans LJ in *Jones v University of Manchester*, that the pool is the persons who satisfy all criteria but the one at issue, that the correct pool was the 23 Valuation Executives who met the first two criteria.

The difference in the pool had a significant effect on the statistical exercise necessary to judge the question of disproportionate impact. Of the 85 Valuation Executives, 63 were men and 22 women. Twelve complied with all three criteria, of whom eight were men (12.7 per cent of men) and four were women (18.2 per cent of women). There was therefore no disproportionately detrimental impact on women, rather the reverse. However, of the 23 who met the first two criteria, 12 were men and 11 were women. Eight of the 12 men met all three conditions and were promoted (66 per cent), but only four of the 11 women (36 per cent). Thus, a disproportionate impact was made out.

The EAT upheld the chairman's approach. However, since then concern has been expressed in cases such as *Faulkner v Chief Constable of Hampshire* ([2007] UKEAT/0505/05/LA) that this approach can produce pools which are too small to be statistically reliable. This is seen in *Cheshire & Wirral Partnership NHS Trust v Abbott* [2006] EWCA (Civ) 523. This was an equal pay case brought on grounds of work of equal value, where the Claimants argued indirect discrimination in that a bonus was paid to porters, who were all male and had been employed by the NHS throughout, but not to domestic staff, a largely female group who had been transferred to an outside contractor under compulsory competitive tendering and then transferred back. The Employer argued that the relevant population included the caterers, a mixed group who had also remained employed by the NHS throughout and received the bonus.

The Court of Appeal ruled that in a claim for indirect sex discrimination it was for the claimant to identify a comparator group, but the employment tribunal provided a safeguard and was under an obligation to ensure that the comparator group was not artificial and limited. While it was for the claimant to identify the comparator group and the statistical evidence, the tribunal provided a safeguard and was under an obligation to ensure that the statistics were valid and not fortuitous, and to ensure that the claimant did not identify a comparator group that was artificial. It was important to identify a pool of comparators logically, and it was difficult to see why the EAT in this case found it appropriate to limit itself to the porters when others had also received the bonus. Comparisons had to be made between the disadvantaged group and the advantaged group, and the more reliable result would occur if as large a group as possible was considered. To limit the comparator group to the porters and to omit the caterers was arbitrary and bolstered the Claimants' case. However, it was clear on the facts of the case that the Claimants were almost exclusively female, whilst the porters and caterers were predominantly male and received the bonus. Accordingly, there was indirect sexual discrimination.

In *Faulkner v Chief Constable of Hampshire* Mrs Faulkner was a police officer, married to a police officer senior to her in rank, and argued that the force policy forbidding couples from serving together where one was senior to the other was indirectly discriminatory against women, who tended to be junior to their husbands. Initially, the comparison exercise was carried out only among married and cohabiting personnel, since they were the population affected by the policy. However, the EAT came down strongly in favour of broadly defined pools, and concluded that the relevant population was all personnel working for Hampshire Police, whether police officers or civilians, as the policy was applicable to all of them. In fact, the EAT concluded that the policy was indirectly discriminatory however the population was defined, but that it was justified. In any event, part of the detriment suffered by Mrs Faulkner resulted, not from the PCP, but decisions taken jointly with her husband, as was also the case with Mrs MacMillan (see further on).

Earlier case law, such as *Jones v University of Manchester* ([1993] IRLR 218, CA) established that arguments based on too narrow a comparative group were bound to fail. The university advertised for a graduate careers adviser aged 27–35. The age condition was imposed in order to have someone reasonably close in age and outlook to the students. The applicant, aged 46, claimed that the requirement was indirectly discriminatory against women who had obtained their degrees as mature students – she had graduated at 40 and female mature students tend to be older than males. The claim failed on the basis that the chosen population was too narrow; the university was not seeking a person who had obtained a degree as a mature student, but a person who had graduated at any age and was now aged 27–35.

> Evans LJ:
>
> If the numbers of women and of men, respectively, remaining after the requirement is applied are to be compared as 'proportions' of something other than the total number of those who can comply, then the question arises, as proportions of what? One possibility is, as proportions of 'all men' and 'all women', even of 'all humanity'. . . . The other possibility is what Mustill LJ called 'the relevant population', meaning all persons who satisfy the relevant criteria apart from the requirement or condition which is under consideration. . . . In my judgment, [this latter approach] is much to be preferred. . . . It is in effect the total number of those persons, men and women, who answer the description contained in the advertisement, apart from the age requirement. Here, that means all graduates with the relevant experience.

Though there is uncertainty over definition of the relevant population for the purposes of the comparison exercise, case law is clear that there must be a population, not a single individual. The authority for this is the rather curious case of *Coker and Osamor v Lord Chancellor and Lord Chancellor's Department*.

The 1969 Civil Service Order in Council allows for the appointment of paid Special Advisers to Cabinet Ministers as an exception to the normal rules on Civil Service appointments on the basis of fair and open competition. The Lord Chancellor, Lord Irvine, decided to appoint Garry Hart, a partner at Herbert Smith, as his Special Adviser, and sought the approval of the Prime Minister, which was given. The post was never advertised. Jane Coker, a solicitor, claimed that she had been directly and indirectly discriminated against on grounds of sex in relation to the arrangements made for the appointment of a Special Adviser to the Lord Chancellor. Martha Osamor, an adviser in a law centre, claimed there had been direct and indirect discrimination on grounds of both sex and race.

At first instance ([1999] IRLR 396, ET) the tribunal found that Miss Coker's claim was in part well-founded, but dismissed Miss Osamor's claim. The Lord Chancellor imposed a 'requirement or condition' that the successful candidate for the post of Special Adviser must be a person known to him. The assertion by the Lord Chancellor's Department that the relevant requirement was that the Lord Chancellor wished to appoint someone of whom he had long experience and in whom he had complete trust and confidence was not supported by evidence. On his own admission, in a written answer given to the tribunal, the Lord Chancellor was only concerned to appoint someone from a circle of people well-known to him.

The requirement clearly had a disproportionate impact as between men and women, taking as the pool for comparison those people who were eligible for the position in the light of the criteria set out by the Lord Chancellor in his letter to the Prime Minister seeking approval for the appointment of Garry Hart. The tribunal rejected the argument of the Lord Chancellor's Department that this pool was too small to show any statistically significant difference between the proportions of men and women able to satisfy the requirement, since only Mr Hart satisfied the requirement.

The tribunal's conclusion that a substantially smaller proportion of women could satisfy the requirement seems artificial. If there was only a pool of one, it cannot be assumed that a substantially smaller proportion of women could satisfy the test, since that one person might happen to be a woman. Equally, if the pool were larger, the tribunal did not consider the relative proportions of men and women in the Lord Chancellor's circle.

The tribunal's decision was considered by the EAT, which held that the tribunal erred in finding that a requirement that the successful candidate be personally known to the Lord Chancellor had a disproportionate effect as between men and women. There was no relevant pool because the Lord Chancellor had only ever intended to appoint a particular person – thus he could be said to have discriminated against every other person, irrespective of race or sex. The case was a very special one on its facts. The Claimants appealed.

The Court of Appeal ruled (*Coker and Osamor v Lord Chancellor* [2001] EWCA 1756, CA) that where a requirement excludes almost the entirety of a pool, it cannot constitute indirect sex discrimination. The test of indirect discrimination focuses on the effect of the requirement at issue on the pool of potential candidates. There can only be a discriminatory effect if a significant proportion of the pool is able to satisfy the requirement. Only in that situation will it be possible for the requirement to have differential effects as between different groups. Accordingly, making an appointment from within a circle of family, friends and acquaintances is seldom likely to represent indirect discrimination. Those known to the employer will represent a minute proportion of those qualified for the post.

This seems a distinctly anomalous decision, not least because the whole philosophy of anti-discrimination legislation is against recruitment from the 'old boy network'.

11.5.2.3 Differential effects

Prior to their amendment in 2003, the SDA and RRA required that a 'considerably smaller proportion' of the group within the relevant population (however delineated) to which the claimant belonged were able to comply with the PCP than the rest of the population. From 2003 the formula was that a *considerably larger* proportion of the claimant's group *could not* comply. It has since been argued that on the formulation now contained in the Equality Act there is no need for a comparison exercise at all – it is enough that the claimant is adversely affected by the requirement. This argument was advanced in *Ministry Defence v MacMillan*, where Mrs MacMillan argued that a comparison exercise was unnecessary where a PCP was 'intrinsically detrimental' to women, but was rejected by the EAT.

In the event, most of the case law dealing with the new formulation has come in relation to age discrimination. In *Homer v Chief Constable of West Yorkshire Police* ([2012] UKSC 15) Lady Hale said that there was no longer any need for detailed statistics to demonstrate the alleged discriminatory effect.

> Previous formulations relied upon disparate impact – so that if there was a significant disparity in the proportion of men affected by a requirement who could comply with it and the proportion of women who could do so, then that constituted indirect discrimination. But, as Mr Allen points out on behalf of Mr Homer, the new formulation was not intended to make it more difficult to establish indirect discrimination: quite the reverse. . . . It was intended to do away with the need for statistical comparisons where no statistics might exist. It was intended to do away with the complexities involved in identifying those who could comply and those who could not and how great the disparity had to be. Now all that is needed is a particular disadvantage when compared with other people who do not share the characteristic in question. It was not intended to lead us to ignore the fact that certain protected characteristics are more likely to be associated with particular disadvantages.

If some form of comparison exercise remains necessary, how much difference in the proportions of men and women disadvantaged is necessary to constitute indirect discrimination? Further, to what extent will the claimant be required to produce clear statistical evidence?

Early case law emphasised the importance of clear statistical evidence and the avoidance of making assumptions. In *Kidd v DRG (UK)* [1985] IRLR 190 the employer had a redundancy selection procedure which selected part-time employees first. Within the workplace the majority of women worked full-time but Mrs Kidd argued that on a national basis more women than men worked part-time and therefore the policy was discriminatory. She assumed that this contention was self-evident, but the EAT did not agree, holding that, in the absence of statistical evidence, it was no longer safe to assume that more women than men, or more married women than single women, did work part-time because of domestic responsibilities.

The danger of making assumptions can also be seen in *Barry v Midland Bank plc* ([1999] 2 All ER 974, HL), which involved a voluntary redundancy scheme under which redundancy pay was calculated on the basis of the employee's salary at the date of redundancy. The Claimant had worked full-time for 11 years, and part-time for a further two years. She argued that the scheme represented indirect discrimination against women, who were more likely than men to work part-time. One might assume that bank work provides an ideal environment for women wishing to work part-time, but the House of Lords accepted the employer's statistics that of their 45,420 employees, of whom 28,590 were women, only 58 worked part time, although 55 of these were women. The Lords rejected Mrs Barry's claim on the grounds of justification (see below), but noted that the scheme as constituted actually benefited women who returned to full-time work after a period as part-timers.

This approach was, however, challenged in *Meade-Hill v British Council* ([1996] 1 All ER 79), where the Claimant argued that a mobility clause in her contract was indirectly discriminatory against women, since they were more likely than men to be 'secondary earners' and so unable to relocate. This decision can be criticised on several grounds, not least that the Court of Appeal failed to identify a specific comparative group, but seems to have proceeded on the basis of assumptions relating to the population at large. For our purposes, here the issue of concern is that Stephen Brown LJ, giving the judgment of the court (but not experienced in employment cases) stated that he would take judicial notice of the fact that fewer women than men could comply with a condition which might require them to relocate, because it was common knowledge that women were more likely to be 'secondary earners' and there was therefore no need to call statistical evidence to this effect. This reliance on assumptions is seen again in the House of Lords reasoning in *London Underground v Edwards (No.2)* ([1998] IRLR 364).

If the claimant must show a differential effect between groups within the relevant population, how much difference is required? Once again, early case law stressed the importance of a clear difference in the proportions of men and women able to comply with the PCP, demonstrated by statistical evidence. *Staffordshire County Council v Black* ([1995] IRLR 234, EAT) involved a redundancy scheme which gave better terms to full-time teachers than part-time teachers. The Tribunal accepted that there was a requirement or condition that a teacher had to be employed full-time at the date of the redundancy in order to qualify for the maximum additional service credit. The proportion of women teachers over 50 who worked full-time was 89.5 per cent, which was held not to be considerably smaller than the 97 per cent of male teachers over 50 who worked full-time. The EAT upheld this finding. According to Morison J:

> What is or is not 'considerably smaller proportion' is a matter for the Industrial Tribunal. The figures speak for themselves. Overall there are more full-time women teachers than men. No doubt for historical reasons there are proportionately slightly less women (sic) than men in the over-50 age range, although again, in absolute terms there are more women than men doing full-time work in that bracket. A difference of 7.5 percentage points, in the context, is very small. . . . It is not unhelpful to keep in mind that the European Court refers to 'a much lower proportion' or a 'considerably lower proportion'.

The Northern Ireland Court of Appeal concluded in *McAusland v Dungannon District Council* ([1993] IRLR 583, NICA) that there was no hard-and-fast rule as to what constituted a 'considerably smaller proportion'. This case was brought under the Fair Employment (Northern Ireland) Act, 1989 dealing with discrimination on grounds of religious belief or political opinion, and alleged that a job requirement to be working in local government indirectly discriminated against Catholics. The comparison was between the proportions of Catholics and Protestants who were in local government. There was a 29 per cent difference between the two, and the applicant argued that a 'four-fifths rule', as found in US law, should be adopted (there is discrimination if the proportion of the claimant's group which is able to comply with the requirement is fewer than four-fifths of that of the other group). McDermott LJ said:

> [The words 'considerably smaller'] are words in daily usage and do not require definition. They were not defined by Parliament and we think no useful purpose would be served by any judicial definition or interpretation. . . . In our judgment, Parliament has chosen to leave these words undefined, relying on the good sense and experience of [the Tribunal] to produce a fair and relevant conclusion.
>
> The introduction of [the four-fifths] rule, if considered wise or helpful, should be by Parliament and not by judicial decision. We think it would be unwise to introduce such a test without a real knowledge of American law, a true understanding of the application of the rule in practice and the benefit of in-depth research on the impact of such a rule on industrial relations in the UK.

In *London Underground Ltd v Edwards (No.2)* the House of Lords ruled that a difference of less than 5 per cent produced a considerably smaller proportion of women able to comply. They relied on distinctly stereotypical assumptions in order to do so.

Miss Edwards, a single parent with a young child, was originally employed on rostering arrangements which allowed her to work 8.00am to 4.00pm on weekdays, plus alternate Sundays, with Saturdays as a rest day, although she did not receive the shift bonuses available for working unsocial hours. In 1991, as part of a cost-saving plan, the employers announced a new flexible shift system, under which duties would begin at 4.45am, and shifts would vary in length, with drivers receiving a standard salary for an average 38.5-hour week. It was possible for employees to swap shifts between themselves, but this was difficult in practice, since the trade-off was likely to be a longer shift for the same money. Mrs Edwards was not prepared to work the new system, and when negotiations between the employers and the union over special arrangements for single parents broke down, she resigned and claimed sex discrimination.

Her complaint was upheld by an industrial tribunal, which held that indirect discrimination was established since a considerably smaller proportion of female single parents than male single parents could comply with the new rosters. That discrimination was not justified, since the employers had themselves contemplated alternative arrangements for single parents, though they had abandoned them as a result of opposition from the union. The EAT allowed the employer's appeal on the basis that a pool consisting only of drivers who were single parents was too narrow, and the correct pool was all the drivers affected by the new arrangements. Despite the fact that only one woman among the 21 female train drivers could not comply with new flexible rostering arrangements, whereas all 2,023 male drivers could comply, the proportion of women who could comply (95.2 per cent) was 'considerably smaller' than the proportion of men (100 per cent).

The matter was remitted to a second industrial tribunal which held that 95.2 per cent was a considerably smaller proportion than 100 per cent. On appeal, the EAT held that a tribunal was entitled to have regard to the absolute numbers of people in the relevant populations, to consider whether the number of women was so small as to be statistically unreliable, and to have regard to the possibility that, where the percentage of women employees is very small indeed, there may be some generalised assumption that the work is 'men's work'. Further, in judging the proportionate impact on a very small number, the tribunal is entitled to look not only at the situation as it was at the date of the complaint, but as it might be had the percentage of women been larger.

The House of Lords then held that the tribunal had not erred in law in finding that 95.2 per cent was a considerably smaller proportion than 100 per cent. The need to show that a 'considerably smaller proportion' of women than men could comply with the requirement had a dual statutory purpose:

1) to set a threshold for intervention where there is a substantial rather than marginally disparate impact, so that a *prima facie* case of indirect discrimination can be shown to exist, sufficient to require the employer to justify the application of the condition or requirement at issue;
2) to ensure that a tribunal may be confident that the disparate impact of the condition is genuine and not simply the product of unreliable statistics or fortuitous circumstances.

It was not appropriate to lay down a rule of thumb in deciding what proportion amounts to 'considerably smaller'. A margin of flexibility is required in order to suit widely differing circumstances.

Here, the tribunal did not err in finding that the requirement bore disproportionately as between men and women even though only one woman was adversely affected by it. Given that the legislation is concerned essentially to contrast the impact of a given requirement as between men and women, it would be wrong to ignore the fact that not one man was disadvantaged by the requirement, despite the vast preponderance of men within the group – almost 20 to 1. The tribunal was also entitled to use its general knowledge and to take account of the fact that ten times as many women single parents as men have care of a child. It was further entitled to infer from the small number of women employed as train drivers that it was either difficult or unattractive for women to work in this role and that the figure of 95.2 per cent of women being able to comply with the requirement was likely to be a maximum rather than a minimum figure.

❖ THINKING POINT

1) Are we going back to stereotypical assumptions here?
2) There seems also to be an assumption that the very small number of women train drivers constituted evidence of discrimination – is this necessarily the case?
3) The Lords also seem to be saying that the other 20 women drivers were likely to be highly unrepresentative of the female workforce and much more likely than average to be able to comply with the new arrangements. Again, is this a stereotypical assumption?

Perhaps surprisingly, it seems to have been accepted without argument since *London Underground v Edwards* that small percentage differences are capable of giving rise to indirect sex discrimination against women even when there is not a huge preponderance of men in the relevant workforce.

Chief Constable of West Midlands Police v Blackburn ([2007] UKEAT/0007/07, EAT) is an equal pay case, but involves arguments of indirect discrimination and was eventually decided on the basis that the discrimination was justified. Police forces are required to provide 24/7 cover and generally require sergeants and constables to be available for shift work 24/7, customarily in three shifts, running from 0700–1500, 1400–2200 and 2200–0700. Individuals may be excused from this requirement on the basis of family commitments or for medical reasons. Under the Police Regulations 2003 individual police forces were given power to introduce 'special priority payments' (SPPs) to reward those working in 'the most demanding and difficult front line operational roles'. SPPs add an extra 2.5–3 per cent to the pay of those who qualify, about £800 for a constable at the time the facts of the case arose. West Midlands Police brought in SPPs for those who were available to work 24/7, with the aim of rewarding those who worked the full shift pattern and encouraging more people to make themselves available to do so. It was calculated that some 91.5 per cent of women were available to work 24/7 and qualified for SPPs, as against 96.6 per cent of men. The Chief Constable argued justification in relation to indirect discrimination and genuine material difference under the Equal Pay Act. The Claimants argued that because they were *prevented* from working 24/7 by a factor which mainly affected women – childcare commitments – they should be paid SPPs as if they were available 24/7. It was not disputed that those not available 24/7 for medical reasons were mainly men, though no percentage calculation was reported. Interestingly, although the male to female ratio in West Midlands Police was about 60:40, rather than close to 20:1, it seems to have been accepted without argument that 91.5 per cent was a considerably smaller proportion than 96.6 per cent.

11.5.2.4 Disadvantage to the claimant

The SDA and RRA originally provided that indirect discrimination could only be proved where the claimant suffered a detriment as a result of being unable to comply with the PCP. This test could be satisfied quite easily where, for example, the claimant was made redundant as a result of being unable to satisfy a requirement to work full-time. However, many situations were not as clear-cut. Could there be a detriment where a person unable to satisfy a PCP in a job advertisement was discouraged from applying for the job at all? Could there be indirect discrimination where a person was able to comply with the PCP but only with difficulty, for example, by making major changes to domestic arrangements in order to accommodate new shift patterns? Strictly speaking, in neither case would there be indirect discrimination, hence the Equality Act formula now only requires that the claimant be put at a particular disadvantage by the PCP. This clearly begs the question of what constitutes a disadvantage.

❖ **THINKING POINT**

In *Ministry of Defence v MacMillan* the EAT ultimately concluded that any detriment to Mrs MacMillan arose not from the PCP itself but from her decision to base herself and her family in Stirling rather than live in married quarters at the naval base. Under the 'disadvantage' test, it might be argued that no man would have been required to choose between work and family in that fashion. However, it is far from unusual for male military personnel to commute at weekends, possibly over very long distances, between their units and the family home, living in barracks accommodation during the week. Does that constitute 'disadvantage'? Further, Mr MacMillan had moved between police forces at least twice in order to accommodate his wife's career, and no man had the option to serve purely in shore jobs, as Mrs MacMillan had.

In *Faulkner v Hampshire Police* the reasoning on detriment to the claimant was similar to that in *MacMillan*. Mrs Faulkner argued that moving to a different police station to avoid serving directly under her husband represented a detriment. However, the EAT noted that where a couple were faced with this situation, Hampshire Police gave them a free choice as to whether the husband or wife should be the one to move. As in *MacMillan*, any detriment was caused by specific decisions made by her, acting with her husband. In any case, the policy was found to be justified (see below).

11.5.2.5 Justification

As stated earlier, in considering the defence of justification, we are faced with the difficulty that the defence is now framed in different terms, and there is a dearth of case law under the new definition.

Early case law under the Sex Discrimination Act required the tribunal to carry out a balancing act between the discriminatory effect of the PCP and the reasonable needs of the employer (*Cobb v Secretary of State for Employment and Manpower Services Commission* [1989] IRLR 464). In *Hampson v Department of Education and Science* ([1991] 1 AC 171) for example, the requirement that candidates for 'qualified teacher status' have obtained British teaching qualifications, or overseas qualifications recognised by the Department of Education and Science as equivalent, was indirectly discriminatory against non-British teachers. However, the DES had a responsibility to ensure high standards of teaching in state schools, and the House of Lords concluded that ensuring that all teachers were trained to a consistent standard acted as justification for the requirement.

Another case involving teachers establishes that justification can go beyond straightforward efficiency. *St Matthias Church of England School v Crizzle* ([1993] ICR 401) involved a voluntary aided school where there was a requirement for any applicant for the post of head to be a communicant in the Church of England. The Claimant was an Asian Christian who was not a communicant and claimed that the requirement was indirectly discriminatory under the Race Relations Act.[5] The tribunal decided that the requirement that the head of a Church of England be a communicant was not necessary for efficient education and therefore not justifiable. The EAT held, however, that the school was concerned with spiritual matters as well as efficient secular education. This was a legitimate objective, and, as a means of achieving it, the requirement that the head be a communicant was reasonable when weighed against its discriminatory effect.

5 His claims that he was not a communicant in the Church of England seems a little strange, as practice in the Church of England allows anyone who is a communicant in his own church to take communion.

The case of *Chief Constable of West Midlands Police v Blackburn* has already been mentioned. Following the conclusion that the PCP of being available for 24/7 shifts to receive the additional pay was indirectly discriminatory against women, the Chief Constable argued justification, and genuine material difference in relation to his failure to provide equal pay. The EAT's conclusions, upheld by the Court of Appeal, are robust and worth quoting at length. They found that the Chief Constable's aim of rewarding those who did work nights was a legitimate one and it was unrealistic to say that it could equally be achieved if those who were released from that obligation received SPPs as if they did work nights.

> The purpose of the scheme adopted by the Chief Constable is to single out and reward those working nights; we find it difficult to see how that objective is achieved if those who do not work nights are also paid the same amount. Those doing the work are not then being marked out for special treatment, which is the very purpose of the payment.
>
> More fundamentally, we consider that the approach of the Tribunal misunderstands the principle underlying indirect discrimination. The premise is that the predominantly male group is paid more than the predominantly female group for some reason other than sex. The question is whether it can be justified to make that payment.
>
> It can be justified if it is in pursuance of an objective which is legitimate and where the means chosen are proportionate to that objective. To say that the employer can afford to eliminate the difference in pay simply fails to engage with the defence at all. It is no answer to a defence of justification for a difference in pay to say that there is no need for the difference in the first place. If the employer had made these payments to the claimants, as the Tribunal suggested that they should, then the issue of justification would not have arisen at all because there would have been no pay differential to justify[. . .]
>
> Nothing in the Equal Pay Act requires an employer to deem that women have done what they have not done. The payment of money to compensate for the economic disadvantages suffered by those who have child care responsibilities is not what the Equal Pay Act requires. Nor is the assessment of the employer's ability to pay sums of this kind a task which Parliament could conceivably have expected Tribunals to do[. . .]
>
> The Tribunal was wrong to say that paying the claimants as if they had worked was simply a logical consequence of excusing the women from doing the work in the first place, and indeed Ms Gill did not seek to support the Tribunal's observations on this point. It is highly desirable that employers adopt flexible work practices which will enable women to work part time or at hours compatible with their child care, even if that involves incurring some cost in achieving that. But it does not follow at all that they should then pay the women on the basis of the work they would have done if they had not had the child care responsibilities.

A recent case in which justification was considered in detail was *Faulkner v Chief Constable of Hampshire*. The Chief Constable justified the policy of separating married couples where one was senior to the other on the following grounds:

> Such relationships may unintentionally impair operational efficiency or affect the integrity of service delivery, for example:
>
> - involvement with recruitment, selection, discipline, grievance
> - inflexibility re annual leave, duties, etc.
> - difficulties in team building, other staff may fear favouritism
> - can cause embarrassment to other staff
> - public or staff perception of fairness, impartiality or objectivity
> - evidence issues
> - emotional responses to other's work, e.g. on exposure to risk

> It is the duty of staff who are in a partnership to inform the Divisional Commander or Department Head of that fact.
>
> As a matter of policy, partners should not have roles which involve them being supervisor and subordinate to one another. The supervisor/subordinate relationship is a unique one where fairness and objectivity are essential for both the partners involved and the perception of colleagues. The situation could influence, or be seen by colleagues to influence, the supervisor on a daily basis on matters of deployment, discipline, etc. This policy is intended to both avoid such perceptions (whether real or imagined) and not put the partners in a potentially difficult situation.

The tribunal held the policy to be justified, not only on the basis of the rationale given above, but, where it was applied to individual couples, it was left to the couple themselves to decide which member should move to another station.

Barry v Midland Bank is an older case, but demonstrates that courts and tribunals are prepared to consider simplicity and certainty as part of justification. The House of Lords upheld a decision that there was no sex discrimination in calculating severance pay on the basis of part-time earnings, even though more women than men worked part-time. Administrative convenience and the aim of cushioning redundant employees against the effects of unemployment and job loss were objective reasons unconnected with sex to explain the difference in severance pay between the Claimant and her male comparators.

The Claimant was employed from July 1979 to April 1990 as a full-time clerk working 35 hours per week. Following maternity leave, she returned to work in October 1990, working alternate weeks and therefore a notional 171/2 hour week. In 1992 the bank invited volunteers for redundancy, with severance pay as provided for by a collective agreement, under which the amount payable was based mainly on completed years of service, whether in full-time or part-time employment and on the pay the employee was receiving at the date of termination. Having 13 years' service, the Claimant was entitled to 42 weeks' pay, and received severance pay of £5,806.08. She complained to an Industrial Tribunal on the basis that the calculation took insufficient account of the fact that 11 of the 13 years were full-time, and claimed that the scheme was sexually discriminatory since more women than men worked part-time.

In December 1992, the bank employed 45,420 people, of whom 28,590 were women. The overwhelming majority of both men and women worked full-time; only 58 people worked part time, 55 of them women. The Claimant named as comparators two male full-time clerks in the same department whose jobs had been rated as equivalent to hers, and claimed, *inter alia*, that the calculation of severance pay constituted a breach of her right under Art. 141 to equal pay for equal work and was not objectively justified. She argued that her severance pay should have been calculated on what would have been her full-time salary at the date of severance, with one year of part-time service being treated as six months' full-time service. This method of calculation would have produced an additional £2,274.72.

In the court's opinion, there could be no doubt that the primary objective of the scheme, to cushion the employee against the effect of unemployment, and the secondary objectives, to compensate the employee for the loss of a job and to reward previous loyalty, were legitimate and non-discriminatory. Further, it seemed plain that the form of the scheme was both appropriate and reasonably necessary. The scheme could not be redrafted so as to calculate the severance payment in the way suggested by the Claimant without detracting from the primary objective of the scheme.

The aims of the scheme, and its clarity and simplicity, were objective reasons independent of sex explaining the difference in severance pay between the Claimant and her comparators, under both EPA s. 1(3) and Art. 141. It was also noted that such a scheme was bound to have both winners and losers; a woman who had recently returned to full-time work after a long period of part-time work because of family commitments would benefit disproportionately.

As yet, there is little case law relating to the new formulation of justification – that the PCP is a proportionate means of achieving a legitimate aim – except in relation to age discrimination. Case law on redundancy schemes suggests that the prevention of 'double recovery' can justify limiting voluntary redundancy to, say, employees under 55, who will not also benefit from early access to pension benefits.

In *Loxley v BAE Systems* ([2008] UKEAT/0156/08/RN EAT) the Claimant appealed against a decision that the Employer had not unlawfully discriminated against him on grounds of age in refusing him payments under their voluntary redundancy scheme when he volunteered for redundancy aged 61. The scheme provided that benefits were only paid to those under the age of 60 at the date of redundancy. Those aged 60 or more were entitled to an immediate pension under the employer's pension scheme, without actuarial reduction, and would receive statutory redundancy payments only. Although the compulsory retirement age had been increased from 60 to 65 after the scheme had been introduced, and later there had been some modification to the operation of the pension scheme by agreement with relevant trade unions, no change had been made to the cut-off age for redundancy payments under the scheme. The employer argued that the prohibition on employees over 60 from receiving benefits under the voluntary redundancy scheme was necessary in order to prevent double recovery, i.e. a person benefitting from both the redundancy scheme and the pension scheme.

The EAT concluded that preventing a windfall could be a legitimate feature of the redundancy scheme. One of the purposes of a redundancy payments scheme such as this was to cushion workers from the effect of losing their income. That was not required to the same extent where pensions were paid. However, it was not inevitably and in all situations justified for individuals entitled to an immediate receipt of a pension to be excluded from a redundancy scheme. It would depend upon the nature of both schemes. The fact that an employee was entitled to immediate pension benefits would always be a highly relevant factor which an employer could properly consider when determining what redundancy rights, if any, an employee ought to receive. It might justify excluding the employee from the redundancy scheme altogether.

The tribunal had to ask whether the employer's treatment of the Claimant, namely his exclusion from the scheme, had achieved a legitimate objective and had been proportionate to any disadvantage suffered. His pension entitlement might be more valuable than any redundancy entitlement, but the tribunal had failed to analyse the available financial information about the benefits. The fact that an agreement had been made with the trade unions was also potentially a relevant consideration when determining whether treatment was proportionate, *Palacios de la Villa v Cortefiel Servicios SA* (C-411/05) (2008) All ER (EC) 249 ECJ (Grand Chamber) considered. The EAT concluded that the tribunal's decision was therefore flawed and it was appropriate for the matter to be heard again by a fresh tribunal.

11.5.3 Harassment

Harassment is a concept not included specifically in either the Sex Discrimination Act or the Race Relations Act, but was left to be handled under direct or indirect discrimination. Case law over the years demonstrated that there could at times be difficulty in establishing that actions considered to be harassment constituted direct or indirect discrimination for the purposes of one or other Act. In particular, if the behaviour complained of was directed equally at persons of both sexes it could not be actionable as direct discrimination.

Macdonald v Advocate General for Scotland; Pearce v Governing Body of Mayfield School [2003] UKHL 34 involved two conjoined appeals. Mr Macdonald was administratively discharged from the RAF after admitting to being homosexual, under a blanket policy applied by the Ministry of Defence at the relevant time. He argued both direct discrimination on grounds of sex, together with sexual harassment in the form of highly intrusive questioning at a security vetting interview. Ms Pearce, a teacher, had been subjected to a lengthy campaign of name-calling and similar harassment by pupils at her school after they discovered that she was a lesbian. The Lords held that in both cases the harassment had occurred because of their sexual orientation, not their physical sex, and so neither had been less favourably treated on grounds of sex than the proper comparator, who was a homosexual person of the other sex, not a heterosexual person of either sex.

Per Lord Hope of Craighead

> There is no escape, then, from the need to resort to a comparison. The words 'less favourable treatment' in section 1(1)(a) render this inevitable. It may be that the conduct complained of is so specific to the claimant's gender that there is no need to do more than to ask the question, to which the answer may well be, . . . *res ipsa loquitur*. . . . But that conclusion may be more easily drawn in cases of sexual harassment which do not involve any homophobic element than in cases such as those of Mr Macdonald and Ms Pearce where the context for the abuse is the abuser's belief that the victim is a homosexual. This is because those who abuse homosexuals tend to pick on them not because of their gender but because they are homosexual. The form which the abuse takes may well be specific to the gender of the person who is being abused, but this is because the terminology which is used to describe homosexuals and the acts which they can perform with each other tend to vary according to the gender of those who are involved in this relationship. That is not to exclude the possibility that an abuser may treat a woman who is a homosexual less favourably than he would treat a male homosexual. That may indeed happen, and an employment tribunal must always be alert to this possibility. But whether this is so will be a question of fact in each case.
>
> The facts as found by the employment tribunal in the cases of Mr Macdonald and Ms Pearce leave no room for doubt on this issue. In Mr Macdonald's case the finding is that the interview would have been no less intrusive if it had been a female homosexual officer who was being interviewed. In Ms Pearce's case the finding is that the pupils would not have treated a hypothetical homosexual male teacher more favourably. On these findings they were not discriminated against on the ground of their sex.

The Employment Equality (Sex Discrimination) Regulations 2005 amended the Sex Discrimination Act to make specific provision for both *sexual harassment*, i.e. conduct which is sexual in nature but not necessarily motivated by a person's sex, and *harassment on the ground of a person's sex*, which may not necessarily be sexual in nature (an example in the guidance is deliberately putting equipment on a shelf too high for most women to reach easily).

The definition in the 2005 Regulations provided that a person subjected a woman to harassment if:

- on the ground of her sex, he engaged in unwanted conduct that had the purpose or effect of violating her dignity, or of creating an intimidating, hostile, degrading, humiliating or offensive environment for her; or
- he engaged in any form of unwanted verbal, non-verbal or physical conduct of a sexual nature that had the purpose or effect of violating her dignity, or of creating an intimidating, hostile, degrading, humiliating, or offensive environment for her; or
- on the ground of her rejection of or submission to unwanted conduct of the kind mentioned above, he treated her less favourably than he would treat her had she not rejected, or submitted to, the conduct.

Analogous definitions were applied to harassment based on other protected characteristics.

On that basis, harassment might occur entirely inadvertently. The harasser may not intend to violate a woman's dignity, or to create an intimidating, hostile, degrading, humiliating or offensive environment for her, it will be enough if his actions or words have that effect – or the complainant claims they have. Further, if the harasser's *purpose* was to create an intimidating environment, his conduct is actionable even if it does not have this *effect*. Clearly, this creates a potential problem, as 'banter' between colleagues is a normal feature of the working environment, and individuals' sensitivities vary enormously.

Consider the following example involving the author's uncle:

❖ EXAMPLE

James works for a large firm which pays all its employees a Christmas bonus. He is very religious and considering becoming a clergyman in the Church of England. He is also very opinionated and has a tendency to 'lecture' his colleagues, though not on religious matters. The day the bonus is paid, a colleague remarks to him, 'Hey, James, what are you going to spend it on, a portable pulpit?'

Does this constitute harassment on grounds of religion and belief?[6]

The case of *English v Thomas Sanderson Blinds* ([2008] EWCA Civ 1421) complicates matters. There the Court of Appeal held that the Claimant, whom his tormentors accepted was a happily married heterosexual man with three teenage children, had nevertheless been subjected to unlawful homophobic abuse, triggered, apparently, by his having been brought up in Brighton and gone to boarding school. They reached this conclusion by construing the expression 'on the grounds of' sexual orientation in the 2003 Regulations (then in force) and by analogy with cases such as *Weathersfield v Sargent* [1999] IRLR 94. Sedley LJ then made the following policy points:

> This said, however, the single critical assumed fact was that the appellant was repeatedly taunted as gay. In my judgment it did not matter whether he was gay or not. The calculated insult to his dignity, which depended not at all on his actual sexuality, and the consequently intolerable working environment were sufficient to bring his case both within Regulation 5 and within the 1976 Directive. The incessant mockery ('banter' trivialises it) created a degrading and hostile working environment, and it did so on grounds of sexual orientation. That is the way I would prefer to put it. Alternatively, however, it can be properly said that the fact that the appellant is not gay, and that his tormentors know it, has just as much to do with sexual orientation – his own, as it happens – as if he were gay.
>
> If, as is common ground, tormenting a man who is believed to be gay but is not amounts to unlawful harassment, the distance from there to tormenting a man who is being treated as if he were gay when he is not is barely perceptible. In both cases the man's sexual orientation, in both cases imaginary, is the basis – that is to say, the ground – of the harassment. There is no Pandora's box here: simply a consistent application of the principle that, while you cannot legislate against prejudice, you can set out in specified circumstances to stop people's lives being made a misery by it.
>
> There are also policy reasons why the distinction should be regarded as one without a difference. Sexual orientation is not an either-or affair. Some people are bisexual; some are asexual; some, including heterosexuals, have unusual interests or proclivities. All of these may

6 In fact, the author's uncle thoroughly enjoyed the joke!

desire to keep their orientation to themselves but still be vulnerable to harassment by people who know or sense what their orientation is. It cannot possibly have been the intention, when legislation was introduced to stop sexual harassment in the workplace, that such a claimant must declare his or her true sexual orientation in order to establish that the abuse was 'on grounds of sexual orientation'. What is required that the claimant's (or someone else's) sexual orientation, whether real or supposed, should have been the basis of harassment directed at him or her. That is what was going on here, even on the limited facts which were assumed to be the only relevant ones. The case would have been exactly the same if Mr English had elected, for whatever reason, to remain silent about his actual sexual orientation – for example because he took the principled position that it was nothing to the point. And the same would be the case if he were actually gay or bisexual but preferred not to disclose it.

A further difficulty is that the legislation does not set a minimum level of behaviour which may constitute harassment, nor state whether the harasser must be aware that his conduct is unwanted. In *Reed v Stedman* ([1999] IRLR 299 the EAT ruled that if a victim made it clear to the perpetrator that she found particular conduct unwelcome, continuation of this conduct constituted harassment, even though some people might consider her unduly sensitive. However, certain types of conduct, unless expressly invited, would generally be considered unwelcome and no 'warning off' would be needed, although the EAT stopped short of defining these.

The Equality Act now provides:

s. 26 Harassment

(1) A person (A) harasses another (B) if—
   (a) A engages in unwanted conduct related to a relevant protected characteristic, and
   (b) the conduct has the purpose or effect of—
      (i) violating B's dignity, or
      (ii) creating an intimidating, hostile, degrading, humiliating or offensive environment for B.
(2) A also harasses B if—
   (a) A engages in unwanted conduct of a sexual nature, and
   (b) the conduct has the purpose or effect referred to in subsection (1)(b).
(3) A also harasses B if—
   (a) A or another person engages in unwanted conduct of a sexual nature or that is related to gender reassignment or sex,
   (b) the conduct has the purpose or effect referred to in subsection (1)(b), and
   (c) because of B's rejection of or submission to the conduct, A treats B less favourably than A would treat B if B had not rejected or submitted to the conduct.
(4) In deciding whether conduct has the effect referred to in subsection (1)(b), each of the following must be taken into account—
   (a) the perception of B;
   (b) the other circumstances of the case;
   (c) whether it is reasonable for the conduct to have that effect.
(5) The relevant protected characteristics are—
   - age;
   - disability;
   - gender reassignment;
   - race;
   - religion or belief;
   - sex;
   - sexual orientation.

This definition repeats that in the 2005 Regulations, albeit extending it to all protected characteristics. On this definition, the question of whether a particular form of conduct constitutes harassment is not solely based on the complainant's subjective reaction. There is an element of objectivity involved, since the tribunal must also consider 'the other circumstances of the case', and whether it is reasonable for the complainant to feel that the conduct has violated his or her dignity, or created an intimidating, hostile, degrading, humiliating or offensive environment for him or her. However, case law suggests that the conduct may be relatively minor – a joke which misfires can be enough.

The events at issue in *Richmond Pharmacology v Dhaliwal* [2009] UKEAT/0458/08/CEA occurred in 2007, and were dealt with under the Race Relations Act s. 3A, inserted into the 1976 Act by the Race Relations Act 1976 (Amendment) Regulations 2003. The Claimant, a British woman of Indian parentage, submitted her resignation as a project manager with a small research company. Her departure, with only one month's notice instead of the two months earlier agreed, was going to cause the employer some difficulty, and the Medical Director (also a woman) asked her to ensure that she worked her notice in a professional manner. The Medical Director then remarked that their field was a small one, adding 'We will probably bump into each other in future, unless you are married off in India'. There was a factual issue as to whether the Medical Director had said 'married *off* in India', or 'married *or* in India', which the Tribunal resolved in favour of the former. The Claimant alleged that she was very upset by the remark, and that her dignity had been violated. The Medical Director argued that there had been no intention to violate the Claimant's dignity, and that the remark had to be seen in the context of previous and entirely friendly discussions, where the Claimant had talked of visiting India, and that her parents were keen for her to marry.

Underhill J stated that a tribunal dealing with the issue of whether unlawful harassment had taken place should take the following approach.

> As a matter of formal analysis, it is not difficult to break down the necessary elements of liability under s.3A. They can be expressed as threefold:
>
> (1) *The unwanted conduct.* Did the respondent engage in unwanted conduct?
> (2) *The purpose or effect of that conduct.* Did the conduct in question either:
>   a) have the *purpose or*
>   b) have the *effect* of either:
>   (i) violating the claimant's dignity or (ii) creating an adverse environment for her? (We will refer to (i) and (ii) as 'the proscribed consequences').
> (3) *The grounds for the conduct.* Was that conduct on the grounds of the claimant's race (or ethnic or national origins)?
>
> But that formal breakdown conceals the fact that there are – or will at least in some cases be – substantial overlaps between the questions that arise in relation to each element. To take one obvious example, the question whether the conduct complained of was 'unwanted' will overlap with the question of whether it creates an adverse environment for the claimant. There is also evidently a considerable overlap between the two defined proscribed consequences, notwithstanding that they are expressed as alternatives: many or most acts which are found to create an adverse environment for an employee will also violate her dignity (though it may be less general for the reverse to apply). The tribunal's eventual decision may often depend on what are, in practice, undifferentiated factual issues which cover more than one element in the analysis [. . .]
>
> We would make four other points which we hope may be of assistance to tribunals seeking to apply s. 3A.
>
> First, such case-law as there was in relation to 'harassment' as a variety of discrimination prior to the implementation of the Directive is unlikely to be helpful. . . . Still less assistance is

likely to be gained from the entirely separate provisions of the Protection from Harassment Act 1997 and the associated case law [. . .]

Secondly, it is important to note the formal breakdown of 'element (2)' into two alternative bases of liability – 'purpose' and 'effect'. That means that a respondent may be held liable on the basis that the effect of his conduct has been to produce the proscribed consequences even if that was not his purpose; and, conversely, that he may be liable if he acted for the purposes of producing the proscribed consequences but did not in fact do so (or in any event has not been shown to have done so). It might be thought that successful claims of the latter kind will be rare, since in a case where the respondent has intended to bring about the proscribed consequences, and his conduct has had a sufficient impact on the claimant for her to bring proceedings, it would be *prima facie* surprising if the tribunal were not to find that those consequences had occurred. For that reason, we suspect that in most cases the primary focus will be on the effect of the unwanted conduct rather than on the respondent's purpose (though that does not necessarily exclude consideration of the respondent's mental processes because of 'element (3)' as discussed below).

Thirdly, although the proviso in s-s. (2) is rather clumsily expressed, its broad thrust seems to us to be clear. A respondent should not be held liable merely because his conduct has had the effect of producing a proscribed consequence: it should be *reasonable* that that consequence has occurred. That, as [Counsel] rightly submitted to us, creates an objective standard. However, he suggested that, that being so, the phrase 'having regard to . . . the perception of that other person' was liable to cause confusion and to lead tribunals to apply a 'subjective' test by the back door. We do not believe that there is a real difficulty here. The proscribed consequences are, of their nature, concerned with the feelings of the putative victim: that is, the victim must have felt, or perceived, her dignity to have been violated or an adverse environment to have been created. That can, if you like, be described as introducing a 'subjective' element; but overall the criterion is objective because what the tribunal is required to consider is whether, if the claimant has experienced those feelings or perceptions, it was reasonable for her to do so. Thus, if, for example, the tribunal believes that the claimant was unreasonably prone to take offence, then, even if she did genuinely feel her dignity to have been violated, there will have been no harassment within the meaning of the section. Whether it was reasonable for a claimant to have felt her dignity to have been violated is quintessentially a matter for the factual assessment of the tribunal. It will be important for it to have regard to all the relevant circumstances, including the context of the conduct in question. One question that may be material is whether it should reasonably have been apparent whether the conduct was, or was not, intended to cause offence (or, more precisely, to produce the proscribed consequences): the same remark may have a very different weight if it was evidently innocently intended than if it was evidently intended to hurt [. . .]

Fourthly, 'element (3)' involves an inquiry which will be very familiar to tribunals from other types of discrimination claim. There is ample case-law on the nature of the inquiry required by the (interchangeable) statutory phrases 'on the grounds of' or 'by reason that'. . . . [Counsel] made it clear that no issue arose on this point in the present appeal. But we should observe that the inquiry into the perpetrator's grounds for acting as he did – . . . 'the reason why' he acted – is logically distinct from any issue which may arise for the purpose of 'element (2)' about whether he intended to produce the proscribed consequences: a perpetrator may intend to violate a claimant's dignity for reasons other than her race (or indeed any of the other reasons proscribed by the discrimination legislation). It is also worth observing that, although establishing the reason why a respondent in a discrimination case acted in the way complained of typically involves an examination of the 'mental processes' . . . of the decision-taker, that is not always so. In some cases, the 'ground' of the action complained of is inherently racial. The best-known example in the case-law, though in fact relating to sex discrimination, is the

> decision of the House of Lords in *James v Eastleigh Borough Council* [1990] 2 AC 751 ([1990] ICR 554). In that case the criterion applied by the Council inherently discriminated between men and women, and no consideration of the thought processes of the decision-makers was necessary: the application of the inherently discriminatory criterion could without more be identified as 'the reason why' the plaintiff had suffered the detriment of which she complained. It is only because in most cases the detriment complained of does not consist in the application of an overtly discriminatory criterion of that sort that the 'reason' (or 'grounds') for the act has to be sought by considering the respondent's motivation (not motive). It seems to us particularly important to bear that point in mind in harassment cases. Where the nature of the conduct complained of consists, for example, of overtly racial abuse, the respondent can be found to be acting on racial grounds without troubling to consider his mental processes.

Underhill J then considered the Tribunal's reasoning and concluded that they had been entitled to find that the Medical Director's allusion to 'forced marriage' was capable of violating the Claimant's dignity, adding:

> We accept that not every racially slanted adverse comment or conduct may constitute the violation of a person's dignity. Dignity is not necessarily violated by things said or done which are trivial or transitory, particularly if it should have been clear that any offence was unintended. While it is very important that employers, and tribunals, are sensitive to the hurt that can be caused by racially offensive comments or conduct (or indeed comments or conduct on other grounds covered by the cognate legislation to which we have referred), it is also important not to encourage a culture of hypersensitivity or the imposition of legal liability in respect of every unfortunate phrase. We accept that the facts here may have been close to the borderline, as the Tribunal indeed indicated by the size of its award. But we are satisfied that the Tribunal, which clearly considered the case most conscientiously, was entitled to hold that what it found [the Medical Director] to have said did indeed fall on the wrong side of the line. We can see no error of law in its decision and this appeal must be dismissed.

Case law since *Richmond Pharmacology v Dhaliwal* has followed this approach. *GMB Union v Henderson* ([2015] UKEAT/0073/14/DM) involves an appeal from a Tribunal decision that the Claimant had been subjected to direct discrimination and harassment on grounds of his political beliefs, though he had not been unfairly dismissed. Mr Henderson worked as a Regional Organiser for the GMB, covering the London area, including GMB members working at the Houses of Parliament. The Employment Tribunal said:

> The Tribunal found that the Claimant is an advocate of left-wing democratic socialism and that this includes:
>
> (i) a belief in establishing 'socialism through democratic processes and [propagating] its ideals within the context of a democratic political system through a working-class industrial and political movement';
> (ii) a belief in workers' control, that is a term meaning 'participation in the management of factories and other commercial enterprises by the people who work there. Crossing workers' picket lines contradicts this aim because it undermines workers' ability to control their workplaces'.

Mr Henderson's duties included working with the Labour Party on the union's political activities. He was also, in his personal capacity, a member of the Labour Party. In November 2011 GMB members working at the House of Commons voted to take strike action, with a picket line at the House. The strike vote included a provision that Labour MPs should not cross the picket line.

The Claimant was tasked by the GMB with organising the picket line. He publicised the picket to the media, stating that Labour MPs were expected not to cross the picket line, and the issue was raised during Prime Minister's Questions on 30 November. The GMB General Secretary, Paul Kenny, took the view that Claimant had unwisely courted publicity and caused embarrassment to both the union and the Labour Party, and, according to the Tribunal's findings, telephoned the Claimant to shout at him. The Claimant contended that from then on there was a deliberate campaign by Paul Kenny and other senior union officials intended to force him to resign. This constituted a form of bullying and made him ill. Specifically, there were daily complaints about his work, and extra duties on top of an already excessive workload.

The Tribunal rejected these allegations, finding that the Claimant's superiors had little control over the flow of work to him, and that there were very few complaints about him. On the contrary, a major factor in his workload was that he was increasing his involvement with the Labour Party and seeking to become a county councillor in the Clacton area, where he lived. In this sphere, he came into conflict with his local Labour Party, culminating with his suspension in late July 2012. He was off work with stress throughout May and June, and then given a phased return to full-time work.

On 26 July, the Claimant contacted Paul Kenny for advice about his problems with the Labour Party. Subsequently, Paul Kenny passed relevant emails to the Claimant's immediate superior, Mr Hayes. The Tribunal found that Mr Hayes was annoyed that the Claimant had bypassed him by going direct to the General Secretary.

> Mr Hayes replied [to the Claimant] stating that because the role of County Councillor makes demands on time both during the day and evening there can be a conflict with the regional office's unspecified hours' requirements. He felt common sense and common courtesy suggested that the Claimant should have discussed his intention to stand as a candidate in advance; and refuted the fact that the Claimant had an onerous workload.

The Tribunal then found that on 31 July Mr Warr, another senior manager, wrote to Mr Hayes raising six concerns over the claimant's behaviour from 23 July onwards. The Claimant raised a grievance against Mr Warr and was then off sick from 17 August to 26 September. On 21 August, an investigation was convened into the Claimant's conduct, but the Claimant refused to attend an investigatory meeting until his grievance had been heard. Eventually, the investigation went ahead without him, and found seven matters on which there was a case to answer:

(1) consistently refusing to carry out reasonable management instructions;
(2) engaging in external political work while absent from his GMB position due to work-related stress and anxiety;
(3) challenging the authority of line management and the regional secretary;
(4) conduct that was likely to bring the respondent and its working relations into serious disrepute and undermining trust and confidence;
(5) making serious allegations of collusion between the GMB and the Labour Party in respect of his suspension from the Labour Party;
(6) failing to disclose his intention to stand for public office which might conflict with his unspecified hours and contractual obligations;
(7) failure to observe union procedures.

Meanwhile, the Claimant had issued a second grievance, replacing the first:

> He complained of bullying and victimisation including that he was being overworked deliberately; that he had been required to produce a sick-note unnecessarily; he had been verbally abused

> by Mr Warr; his request to work at Chelmsford had been unreasonably refused; and again he referred to being suspended from the Labour Party and that Mr Warr and Paul Kenny had failed to assist him in respect of the unfairness to him in being debarred from holding office while an internal Labour Party investigation was taking place.

The Claimant went on:

> The only conclusion I can come to is that extreme right-wing elements in both the GMB and the Labour Party have colluded to prevent a left-wing Unionist and a Labour Party activist from a working-class background making genuine progress in our movement.

The Tribunal specifically rejected the claim of collusion. The union considered the most serious allegations to be the making of unfounded allegations of collusion between the GMB and the Labour Party, and challenging the authority of the line management and the Regional Secretary; the Tribunal found that the Claimant admitted no wrongdoing and put forward no mitigation. The Tribunal then accepted that though the union considered alternatives to dismissal, they concluded that the relationship with the Claimant had broken down, and that he was guilty of gross misconduct. Subsequently, the union rejected his appeal against dismissal.

The Tribunal found the harassment claim to be proven:

> There was unwanted conduct in that Paul Kenny shouted at the Claimant describing him as too left-wing in the picketing incident; he was threatened with disciplinary action by Mr Warr if he failed to retract a statement to Alan Olive that he had an extremely onerous workload; and he was refused a two to three-week relocation to Chelmsford by Mr Hayes. This conduct was related to his protected belief and had the purpose of creating a hostile environment.

The union appealed against this finding. The EAT found that only in the first case was the 'unwanted conduct' related to the Claimant's protected characteristic – his political beliefs – and therefore only this incident constituted unlawful harassment.

According to Judge David Richardson in *Warby v Wunda Group Plc*:

> The legislation . . . does not prohibit all harassment, still less every argument or dispute in the workplace; it is concerned only with harassment which is related to a characteristic protected by equality law[. . .]
>
> In our judgement, when a Tribunal is considering whether facts have been proved from which it could conclude that harassment was on the grounds of sex or race, it is always relevant, at the first stage, to take into account the context of the conduct which is alleged to have been perpetrated on the grounds of sex or race. The context may, for example, point strongly towards or strongly against a conclusion that harassment was on the grounds of sex or race. The Tribunal should not leave the context out of account at the first stage and consider it only as part of the explanation at the second stage, after the burden of proof has passed.

The EAT then found the Tribunal had been in error in concluding that the union's purpose in the three incidents at issue was to creating an intimidating, hostile or humiliating environment for Mr Henderson. Quite simply, the incidents were too trivial.

> Although isolated acts may be regarded as harassment, they must reach a degree of seriousness before doing so. True it is that the Claimant was shouted at and that his letter was described as over the top and too left-wing, but this did not prevent him from answering back to Paul Kenny . . . and nor did it prevent him from contacting Paul Kenny subsequently, for support in

relation to his Labour Party difficulties. To conclude that the telephone conversation between Paul Kenny and the Claimant in November 2011 was an act of unlawful harassment is to trivialise the language of the statute.

11.5.4 Victimisation

s. 27 Victimisation

(1) A person (A) victimises another person (B) if A subjects B to a detriment because—
   (a) B does a protected act, or
   (b) A believes that B has done, or may do, a protected act.
(2) Each of the following is a protected act—
   (a) bringing proceedings under this Act;
   (b) giving evidence or information in connection with proceedings under this Act;
   (c) doing any other thing for the purposes of or in connection with this Act;
   (d) making an allegation (whether or not express) that A or another person has contravened this Act.
(3) Giving false evidence or information, or making a false allegation, is not a protected act if the evidence or information is given, or the allegation is made, in bad faith.
(4) This section applies only where the person subjected to a detriment is an individual.

Therefore, victimisation requires that the Claimant must have been involved in previous allegations of discrimination, not limited to acting as a claimant or as a witness, and whether or not legal proceedings have been instituted. These are known as 'protected acts'. There must be a causal link between the protected acts and the less favourable treatment. The test of less favourable treatment is the same as in direct discrimination. The burden of proof is also the same. Unlike direct discrimination, however, there is no need for a formal comparison exercise, although the according of different (more favourable) treatment to a person who has not done a protected act may act as evidence of victimisation (see *Chief Constable of Greater Manchester Police v Bailey* [2015] UKEAT/0166/15/DA).

In *Nagarajan v London Regional Transport* [1999] IRLR 572 it was made clear that the Tribunal must focus on the thought processes of the alleged discriminator when determining whether the less favourable treatment is due to a protected act. Further, the protected act need not be the sole or principal motivation for that treatment, provided it was a *significant* influence. It is also clear that, as in direct discrimination, the treatment at issue must be less favourable, not merely unreasonable, and the fact that a claimant is regarded by the employer as a troublemaker does not of itself mean that he has been victimised, as there must be a causal link with protected acts (cf. *Leeds Teaching Hospital NHS Trust v Blake* [2015] UKEAT/0430/14/BA).

11.6 Further reading

Arlow, '*Ganga v Chelmsford Diocesan Board of Finance and anor*: licence to officiate – revocation – qualifications body – section 54 Equality Act 2010 (Case Comment)' 2016, 18(2), *Ecclesiastical Law Journal* 252.

Burton, 'Neoliberalism and the Equality Act 2010: a missed opportunity for gender justice?' (2014) 43(2) *Industrial Law Journal* 122.

Cranmer, 'Whether discrimination on grounds of caste prohibited by s. 9(1) Equality Act 2010' (2015) 174 *Law & Justice* 129.

Talbot & Brownsell, 'Legislative Comment: 2010: changes to previous law' (2011) 2 *Private Client Business* 104.

Chapter 12

Disability discrimination

Chapter contents

12.1 Overview

This chapter deals with discrimination on the grounds of disability, a category created by the Disability Discrimination Act 1995 and now embodied in the Equality Act 2010. Not only does the legislation prohibit discrimination on grounds of disability, it also imposes a duty on employees to make 'reasonable adjustments' in order to enable a disabled person to work.

12.2 Introduction

Legislation dealing with disability in the workplace first emerged as a result of the Second World War. In addition to some 360,000 military dead, and 60,000 civilian dead, large numbers, particularly young men of working age, lost limbs, were paralysed, blinded or suffered after-effects from wounds or poison gas. They were added to those surviving from the First World War, a large proportion still of working age. The Disabled Persons (Employment) Act 1944 was passed in anticipation of large numbers of disabled servicemen returning from the war and needing jobs. This defined disability for the first time, going beyond war casualties to include congenital conditions and the consequences of injury or disease occurring in any circumstances:

> 1.-(i) In this Act the expression 'disabled person' means a person who, on account of injury, disease, or congenital deformity, is substantially handicapped in obtaining or keeping employment, or in undertaking work on his own account, of a kind which apart from that injury, disease or deformity would be suited to his age, experience and qualifications; and the expression 'disablement', in relation to any person, shall be construed accordingly.

Though not explicitly stated, the definition covers mental as well as physical disabilities.

Having defined disability, the 1944 Act created a registration system for disabled people, along with a quota system requiring employers to employ a minimum percentage of disabled people. The quotas were, however, largely ignored and so ineffective. A more successful initiative based on the Act was the creation of Remploy, an organisation which employed disabled people in specialised factories. At its peak, there were 83 factories, but, increasingly, public policy emphasised integrating disabled people into conventional employment rather than consigning them to sheltered workshops.

In addition to wartime casualties, an epidemic of polio, which lasted from 1946 until vaccination in infancy became routine in the late 1950s, produced disability in considerable numbers of young people. The disease mainly affects children and young adults, and causes paralysis, particularly of respiratory muscles, leaving patients unable to breathe unaided, a condition which may be temporary or permanent. In the same period, tuberculosis remained common, both the pulmonary form, spread by person-to-person contact, and the bovine form spread by contaminated milk. The latter affected the spine and resulted in lengthy periods of treatment. Again, bovine TB mainly affected children, particularly in rural areas, since they were the largest consumers of milk. It eventually disappeared as a result of pasteurisation.

A third large-scale source of disability in children and then young people was the drug thalidomide, used as a treatment for morning sickness in pregnancy between 1957 and 1961. Thalidomide produced deformities in children born to mothers who had taken it in early pregnancy, typically missing or deformed limbs. In the early 1970s, the parents of these children launched a compensation claim against the manufacturers, and acted as a pressure group seeking improved education and treatment for those disabled by the drug.

For much of the twentieth century, disabled children were usually taught at special schools specific to their disability. The former Labour Home Secretary, David Blunkett, blind from birth, has spoken movingly of being sent to a distant boarding school at the age of five. By the 1980s, public policy was moving towards integration of disabled children into mainstream schools.

The Disability Discrimination Act was passed in 1995, the parts relating to employment coming into force on 2 December 1996. Initially, it applied only to employers with 20 or more employees. Having defined disability in broad terms, to cover both physical and mental conditions, it then created a duty on employers to make 'reasonable adjustments' in order to enable disabled people to work. The philosophy underlying the Act was to encourage employers to make reasonable adjustments; the provisions creating the concept of disability discrimination for a reason relating to disability were secondary. At this stage the Act did not prohibit discrimination based on the disability itself, but based on the *consequences* of that disability. Most obviously, this meant absence from work or inability to carry out certain functions of the work – for instance, a blind person being unable to drive. Unlike sex and race discrimination legislation, there was no prohibition on indirect discrimination. Further, there was a defence of justification in relation to discrimination for a reason related to disability. This was controversial, but recognised that there were some types of work that were incompatible with some types of disability – again, the inability of a blind person to work as a driver is an obvious example.

Over the 14 years it was in force, the 1995 Act was amended several times, first to extend its scope to all employers, whatever the number of persons employed. In 1998 the threshold size of organisation was lowered to 15 employees, but this still exempted about 90 per cent of employers and 25 per cent of employees from the ambit of the Act. Further changes were brought into effect on 1 October 2004 in order to bring UK law on disability discrimination into line with EC Directive 2000/78, so that the following, *inter alia*, came within the scope of the Act:

- all employees and applicants for employment, irrespective of the size of the organisation;
- police, prison officers and firefighters;
- partners and prospective partners in businesses;
- persons undertaking or seeking work experience, as against the placement providers;
- barristers and pupil barristers, as against barrister's clerks and other barristers, but not solicitors or clients; and
- employees working wholly outside Great Britain, provided the employer has a place of business in Great Britain, the work is for the purposes of the business carried on at that establishment and the employee is ordinarily resident in Great Britain at the time he applies for, or is offered the job, or at any time during the course of the employment.

These categories are now covered by the Equality Act. Members of the Armed Forces continue to be outside the scope of the disability discrimination legislation.

The Act now covers the provision of goods and services, including education, but this book deals only with disability discrimination in relation to employment.

The second significant change was the introduction of a concept of direct discrimination – based on the disability itself. With some changes, the provisions of the Disability Discrimination Act were then incorporated into the Equality Act 2010. As with other protected characteristics, however, most of the relevant case law arose under the earlier legislation.

12.3 What is a disability?

The Equality Act definition of disability reproduces that in the Disability Discrimination Act. To be protected, an individual must have a disability (s. 6) or have had a disability (s. 6(4)). A disability is defined as a physical or mental impairment, which has a substantial and long term effect on the person's ability to carry out normal day-to-day activities (s. 6(1)). In other words, the physical or mental impairment must be the cause of the substantial and long term adverse effects.

'Substantial' is not defined, other than a threshold level of 'more than trivial' (Disability Discrimination Act Guidance para. A1). Whether the effect is substantial in any individual case is a matter for the tribunal's own judgment. Where the applicant claims to be suffering from the same degree of impairment at the time of the hearing, the tribunal may take account of the way he manages before them, though they should be in mind of the relatively strange and adversarial environment in which they are operating (*Goodwin v Patent Office* [1999] IRLR 4).

'Long term' means that the effect must have lasted 12 months, or be expected to last for 12 months or the rest of the person's life if this is likely to be less (sch. 1 para. 2(1)).

What if the substantial adverse effect has ceased by the time the cause of action arises? Sch. 1 para. 2(2) provides that an impairment will be treated as continuing to have such an effect if the effect is likely to recur.

Under *Swift v Chief Constable of Wiltshire Constabulary* [2004] IRLR 540, a tribunal applying para. 2(2) should follow the test below:

a) Was there at some stage an impairment that had a substantial adverse effect on the applicant's ability to carry out normal day-to-day activities?
b) Did the impairment cease to have such an effect? If so, when?
c) What was the substantial adverse effect?
d) Is *that* substantial adverse effect likely to recur?

The tribunal must be satisfied that the same effect is likely to recur – it is more probable than not that it will recur – and that it will again amount to a substantial adverse effect on the applicant's ability to carry out normal day-to-day activities, though it is not necessary that the recurrence be likely to last for at least 12 months. In *Swift* the EAT also stated that it was not necessary for the illness that caused the impairment to recur; it was possible for a change in surrounding circumstances to increase the effect of the impairment without the illness itself recurring. Here, the Claimant had to establish that an impairment which affected memory or ability to concentrate to the extent that it had a substantial effect on her ability to carry out normal day-to-day activities was likely to recur. An occasional panic attack or sleepless night would not be sufficient.

'Severe disfigurement', which is not defined, is specifically stated in sch. 1 para. 3(1) to be treated as having a substantial adverse effect on a person's ability to carry out normal day-to-day activities. Para. 6 provides that cancer, multiple sclerosis and HIV infection are also disabilities.

If the impairment is not specifically stated to be a disability in sch. 1, it must have long-term adverse effects on the person's ability to carry out normal day-to-day activities. Under the 1995 Act, sch. 1 para. 4 gave a list of normal day-to-day activities:

- mobility;
- manual dexterity;
- physical co-ordination;
- continence;
- ability to lift, carry or move everyday objects;
- speech;
- hearing or eyesight;
- memory or the ability to learn or understand;
- ability to concentrate;
- perception of risk of physical danger.

This list is not included in the Equality Act, but remains useful as a means of focusing attention on the consequences of disability.

The Guidance then contained examples in each of these categories as to what would and would not be considered to constitute substantial adverse effects. For example, under Manual Dexterity:

It would be reasonable to regard as having a substantial adverse effect:

- Loss of function in one or both hands, such that the person cannot use the hand or hands
- Inability to handle a knife and fork at the same time
- Ability to press the buttons on keyboards or keypads, but only much more slowly than is normal for most people

It would not be reasonable to regard as having a substantial adverse effect:

- Inability to undertake activities requiring delicate hand movements, such as threading a small needle
- Inability to reach typing speeds standardised for secretarial work
- Inability to pick up a single small item, such as a pin.

More generally, relevant factors which tribunals should take into consideration include:

- time taken to carry out an activity;
- the way in which an activity is carried out;
- cumulative effects of an impairment;
- whether reasonable coping strategies would prevent the disability having a substantial adverse effect;
- the effects of environment.

In the recent case of *Metroline Travel Ltd v Stoute* ([2015] UKEAT/0302/14/JOJ) the EAT concluded that Type 2 diabetes controlled by diet alone was not a disability, as abstaining from sugary drinks and similar was a reasonable coping strategy which prevented the substantial adverse effect of hypoglycaemic attacks.

The Equality Act sch. 1 s.1 states that regulations may be made stating that a specified condition is or is not an impairment.

Under the Disability Discrimination (Meaning of Disability) Regulations 1996 the following were specifically excluded from being disabilities:

- severe disfigurement consisting of tattoos or body piercings;
- addiction or dependency on alcohol, nicotine or any other substance, except where the addiction was originally the result of administering prescribed drugs or other medicines;
- a tendency to start fires;
- a tendency to steal;
- a tendency to physical or sexual abuse of other persons;
- exhibitionism;
- voyeurism;
- hayfever.

This list is clearly based on public policy considerations. It remains in force and raises difficulties when, for example, a person with depression is also an alcoholic.

Case law suggests that the Tribunal should ignore the excluded condition and make its decision on whether the claimant is disabled on the basis of the non-excluded condition. In *Power v Panasonic UK Ltd* [2003] IRLR 151 the EAT held that the Tribunal had erred by asking whether the applicant's alcoholism was the cause of her depression. The proper approach was to ask whether the depression itself had a substantial adverse effect on her ability to carry out normal day-to-day activities. In *Murray v Newham Citizens Advice Bureau* [2003] IRLR 340 the EAT ruled that in order to fall within the exclusions in the 1996 Regulations, excluded conditions must be free-standing, rather than arising as a consequence of a recognised disability. Therefore, the Claimant's tendency to violence arising from paranoid schizophrenia fell outside the exclusions.

Edmund Nuttall Ltd v Butterfield EAT [2005] UKEAT/0028/05 is worth considering in some detail. The Claimant was arrested by the police after he twice exposed himself to different groups of women. After he was released from custody on bail, he attended a work meeting where he broke down and was admitted to hospital. He was diagnosed as suffering from a moderately severe depressive illness. The Claimant instructed solicitors in connection with the criminal proceedings, who advised him that he was not legally required to inform the employer of those proceedings unless they were relevant to his job. He told the employer that he had been disqualified from driving but did not mention the offences of indecent exposure. At this stage, the employer was happy for him to remain in employment. Subsequently the Claimant pleaded guilty to indecent exposure and was put on probation. His probation officer informed him that he had to disclose the offences of indecent exposure. The Claimant informed the employer and the directors decided that he had to be dismissed as he had misled them, and because his conduct could potentially bring the company into disrepute and might be repeated in the future.

The Claimant applied to an Employment Tribunal who found that he was disabled under the Disability Discrimination Act 1995 s. 1 and that the employer had treated him less favourably because of that condition, as, had he not been suffering from the mental illness, he would not have committed the offences. The Tribunal also found that he was not guilty of contributory conduct. The employer submitted that by virtue of the 1996 Regulations it was entitled to treat someone less favourably if they tended to exhibitionism, even if they were regarded as disabled.

The EAT held:

(1) It was clear that the sole reason for the Claimant's dismissal related to his exhibitionism, a condition that did not amount to an impairment under Reg. 4. The dismissal did not relate to his depressive illness, which was a 'legitimate' impairment. Where a legitimate medical impairment underlay an excluded condition that was the reason for less favourable treatment, disability was not a reason for the less favourable treatment. The Claimant had also misled the employer as to the true position and therefore the tribunal's finding of discrimination had to be set aside.

(2) The Tribunal appeared to have found that the reason for dismissal related to the Claimant's conduct. The Tribunal had been right to conclude that dismissal for that reason was procedurally unfair, in that the employer had pre-judged the matter and its outcome prior to the initial disciplinary hearing. It was also correct to conclude that the dismissal was substantively unfair, in that it fell outside the range of reasonable responses, due to the employer's failure to investigate the possibility of the Claimant re-offending.

(3) The Tribunal's finding that the Claimant was not guilty of culpable or blameworthy conduct was perverse. Committing offences and concealing the truth from his employer was plainly culpable conduct. Therefore, the case was remitted to a fresh tribunal.

This case demonstrates that a dismissal may not be contrary to disability discrimination legislation, but still be unfair under the ordinary law of unfair dismissal.

The statutory definition of disability has been the subject of much criticism. In particular, it has been argued that it does not go far enough. Some 'disability activists' argue that disability is not a physical reality so much as a social construct – the problem is not the limitations resulting from a medical condition but the assumptions made by a society composed largely of able-bodied people of 'normal' intelligence. This argument is perhaps made particularly forcefully in relation to people infected by HIV but who may not show any physical effects from the virus for many years.

12.3.1 Progressive conditions

DDA s. 8(1) dealt with progressive conditions, specifically including cancer, multiple sclerosis, muscular dystrophy and HIV infection. Originally it provided that where the person had an impairment as a result of such a condition, but the effect of that impairment was not yet substantial, the effect was to be taken as substantial if it was likely to become substantial. This would seem to have covered the position of a person in the early stages of, say, multiple sclerosis or cancer, with a small degree of adverse effect, but not a person infected with HIV who had yet to show any symptoms. This changed with effect from 5 December 2005 to cover such conditions from the date of diagnosis, irrespective of whether the person was showing symptoms. This provision is now included in Equality Act 2010 sch. 1 para. 6.

12.3.2 Effects of medical treatment

Clearly, the effects of many conditions can be significantly reduced, or for practical purposes eliminated altogether, by medication, such as insulin in the case of diabetics and anticonvulsants for epileptics. There is also the disgraced South African athlete, Oscar Pistorius, who had both legs amputated below the knee as an infant, and ran in the 2012 Olympics on 'blades', having earlier run 10.91 seconds for the 100m (Usain Bolt's world record is 9.58 seconds).

The Equality Act sch. 1 para. 5 deals with the effects of medical treatment and use of artificial aids, providing as follows:

> (1) An impairment which would be likely to have a substantial adverse effect on the ability of the person concerned to carry out normal day-to-day activities, but for the fact that measures are being taken to treat or correct it, is to be treated as having that effect.

This means that the ability of, say, a person with one leg to carry out normal day-to-day activities must be evaluated on the basis that he does not use an artificial leg.

It should be noted that the making of reasonable adjustments is not equivalent to medical treatment and its effects (*Wolfe v North Middlesex Hospitals NHS Trust* [2015] UKEAT/0065/14/MC). In that case, the Claimant, a nurse, developed an anxiety disorder as a result of being bullied while working on a particular ward. On medical advice, she was temporarily redeployed to an outpatient clinic, where her symptoms ceased. The EAT accepted the analogy of a person allergic to sunlight; living permanently in a darkened room would avoid the effects of the allergy, but the allergy would re-emerge on leaving the darkened room. Here, the Tribunal accepted that the anxiety disorder would show itself once more if the Claimant was required to return to the original ward, or, indeed, work on any other ward.

❖ THINKING POINT

Last year, Mary was diagnosed with early stage cervical cancer following routine screening. The affected area was removed, and Mary has just been given the all-clear after a course of chemotherapy. Is she a disabled person, and, in the absence of a recurrence of the cancer, or after-effects from treatment, how long should she continue to be regarded as disabled?

12.3.3 Case law on disability

Inevitably, there has been a great deal of case law on the issue of whether a person is within the scope of the Act, much of it dealing with conditions which might well not be considered 'disabilities' in the ordinary sense of the word, and/or are wholly or partly controlled by medication. In practice, decisions seem very much to be taken on the facts of individual cases, though some general guidance has been given.

Goodwin v Patent Office ([1999] ICR 302, EAT) sets out the approach to be taken by tribunals. The Claimant had been diagnosed as having paranoid schizophrenia, and was dismissed because of bizarre behaviour consistent with that illness. It was not disputed that he suffered from auditory hallucinations which affected his concentration. The Tribunal concluded that the effect on his ability to carry out normal day-to-day activities was not 'substantial' as he was able to hold down a job demanding high intellectual abilities and to carry out domestic tasks without assistance. The EAT held that the Tribunal had misdirected themselves in concentrating on what the Applicant could do, rather than on what he could not do, or could only do with difficulty.

Per Morison J:

> Section 1(1) defines the circumstances in which a person has a disability within the meaning of the Act. The words of the section require a Tribunal to look at the evidence by reference to four different conditions [. . .]
>
> [1] Does the applicant have an impairment which is either mental or physical?[. . .]
> [2] Does the impairment affect the applicant's ability to carry out normal day-to-day activities in one of the respects set out in [sch. 1 para. 4(1)], and does it have an adverse effect?
> [3] Is the adverse [effect] substantial?
> [4] Is the adverse [effect] long-term?
>
> Frequently, there will be a complete overlap between conditions [3] and [4], but it will be as well to bear all four of them in mind. Tribunals may find it helpful to address each of the questions but at the same time be aware of the risk that disaggregation should not take one's eye off the whole picture.

Morison J went on to say that the question of whether a condition had an adverse effect on a person's ability to carry out day-to-day activities may be very difficult to judge, given the adjustments that disabled people often made to their lives.

> Thus a person whose capacity to communicate through normal speech was obviously impaired might well choose . . . to live on their own. If one asked such a person whether they managed to carry on their daily lives without undue problems, the answer might well be 'yes', yet their ability to lead a 'normal' life had obviously been impaired. Such a person would be unable to communicate through speech and the ability to communicate through speech is obviously a capacity which is needed for carrying out normal day-to-day activities, whether at work or at home. If asked whether they could use the telephone, or ask for directions or which bus to take, the answer would be 'no'. Those might be regarded as day-to-day activities contemplated by the legislation, and that person's ability to carry them out would clearly be regarded as adversely affected. Furthermore, disabled persons are likely, habitually, to 'play down' the effect that their disabilities have on their daily lives.

In *Vicary v British Telecommunications plc* ([1999] IRLR 680) the EAT considered the meaning of normal day-to day activities. The Claimant, a clerical assistant, appealed against a tribunal decision that she was not disabled. She had a weakness in her arms which meant that she was unable to prepare vegetables, cut meat or potatoes, carry full saucepans or baskets of washing, open jars, read without resting the book on the arm of the chair, do heavy shopping or DIY, file her nails, curl her hair with tongs, shake quilts, groom animals, iron, polish furniture, knit, sew, or cut with scissors. The Tribunal were of the view that a loss of strength could not be equated with loss of function, that she could reasonably be expected to modify her behaviour in opening jars, reading, etc., to compensate for the loss of strength, and that DIY, nail filing, hair-curling, ironing, quilt-shaking, etc., could not be regarded as normal day-to-day activities as set out in the Guidance, since they were not carried out by most people 'on a daily or frequent and fairly regular basis'.

The EAT found the conclusion that the Claimant was not disabled surprising.

Per Morison J:

> The Employment Tribunal has not considered the interpretation of the word 'substantial'. It seems to us clear that they must have approached the case on the basis that 'substantial' means more than what the word means in this context. . . . Paragraph 6 of Annex 1 of the Code of Practice. . . . 'A substantial adverse effect is something which is more than a minor or trivial effect. The requirement that an effect must be substantial reflects the more general understanding of disability as a limitation going beyond the normal differences in ability which might exist among people [. . .]
>
> In this case there was in fact no need for the Employment Tribunal to refer to the Guidance once they had properly understood the meaning of the word 'substantial'. Having concluded that the ability of the Applicant to do the activities specified [above] was impaired, the Tribunal inevitably should have concluded that the Applicant was a person suffering from a disability within the meaning of the Act. Instead, the Employment Tribunal appears to have used the Guidance in a somewhat literal fashion so as to arrive at the surprising conclusion that the Applicant was not substantially impaired in her ability to carry out normal day-to-day activities [. . .]
>
> It is clear that an ability to prepare vegetables, cut up meat and carry a meal on a tray would all be regarded as examples of normal day-to-day activities. An inability to carry out those functions would, in our view, obviously be regarded as a substantial impairment of an ability to carry out normal day-to-day activities.
>
> Furthermore, the Tribunal's conclusion . . . that DIY tasks, filing nails, tonging hair, ironing, shaking quilts, grooming animals, polishing furniture, knitting and sewing and cutting with scissors were not normal day-to-day activities 'as set out in the Guidance' misunderstands the nature of the guidance given. Paragraph C9 of the Guidance makes it clear that the lists of examples which follow 'are not exhaustive; they are only meant to be illustrative'. It seems to us obvious that making beds, doing housework. . ., sewing and cutting with scissors would be regarded as normal day-to-day activities, as would minor DIY tasks, filing nails, curling hair and ironing. These are all activities which most people do on a frequent or fairly regular basis [. . .]
>
> The fact that a person is able to mitigate the effects of their disability does not mean that they are not disabled within the meaning of the Act. It seems to us obvious that it would be a substantial impairment on normal day-to-day activity if the Applicant could not use a hand-held bag or carry washing, other than in small quantities, or unload her shopping trolley, other than in small quantities.

Morison J went on to state that it was for the Tribunal, not any medical expert called, to determine what was a normal day-to-day activity and whether any impairment was 'substantial'.

In *Ekpe v Commissioner of Police for the Metropolis* ([2001] IRLR 605) the EAT thought that 'normal day-to-day activities' should be defined as anything not abnormal or unusual. What was normal did not depend on whether the majority of people could do them, and could not exclude activities carried out mainly by people of one sex.

According to the EAT in *Cruickshank v Motorcast Ltd* ([2002] IRLR 24) the Tribunal is not prevented from assessing the ability to carry out normal day-to-day activities according to the Claimant's condition in the working environment. There, the working environment had both caused and exacerbated the Claimant's asthma. Where the effect of an impairment varies according to a person's general pattern of life, the Tribunal must first identify the particular circumstances in, and the background against which, his ability to carry out normal day-to-day activities should be judged. Here, the Claimant had been dismissed because he was incapable of working, there was no reason to exclude evidence of his abilities while at work. The Tribunal had therefore erred in law in considering only his abilities when not at work and holding on that basis that he was not disabled. Relevant factors in such a situation would include:

- how long the adverse effect continued;
- how long it took for the condition to improve when the Claimant left the working environment; and
- what the Claimant was capable of doing in terms of normal day-to-day activities both at work and in the evenings, at work and during longer absences.

It has been suggested that this decision means that whether a particular person is disabled or not may depend on the type of employment. However, this is explicable in terms of public policy. An employer should not be able to dismiss an employee on the basis that his condition would improve if he gave up work – or that particular work. Instead, the legislation seeks to encourage the employer to make 'reasonable adjustments' in order to enable the disabled employee to continue working.

In *Hewett v Motorola Ltd* ([2004] IRLR 455) the EAT found that the 'ability to learn or understand' is not limited to the ability to learn or understand *information*, so that a person with Asperger's Syndrome was held to be disabled on the basis of his limited ability to understand social interactions.

The Equality Act does not include the list of 'normal day-to-day activities' contained in the 1995 Act. There is also no requirement, as there was in the 1995 Act as originally passed, for a mental impairment to be 'clinically well-recognised', which led to somewhat sterile debates on where a claimant's mental health issue could be fitted into the World Health Organisation's *International Statistical Classification of Diseases and Related Health Problems*. On this basis, establishing whether an individual is to be considered as disabled for the purpose of the Equality Act involves a commonsense application of the test – does he have a physical or mental impairment which has a substantial and long-term effect on his ability to carry out normal day-to-day activities?

This does leave the issue of whether a person is to be regarded as disabled when only his ability to carry out highly specialised tasks is affected. For example, is a professional footballer who can no longer play in the Premier League because of a knee injury disabled? Or a leading violinist unable to take part in lengthy rehearsals and performances because of repetitive strain injury? In *Banaszczyk v Booker* ([2016] UKEAT/0132/15/RN) the EAT concluded that 'normal day-to-day activities' included work of a kind done by significant numbers of people. The Claimant was a warehouse operative whose work included lifting boxes weighing up to 25kg on and off pallets. As a result of back problems, he was unable to carry out the work at the same speed as his colleagues. The EAT rejected the employer's argument that the weight involved, or the requirement to achieve a minimum hourly 'pick rate' – the number of boxes moved – took the activity outside the normal day-to-day category and into a highly specialist zone. If this line of reasoning is followed, then the tribunal should approach the issue on a common-sense basis, though this leaves open the issue of the point at which an activity becomes too uncommon or specialised for the inability to carry it out to qualify as a disability.

12.3.4 Employer's Knowledge

What is the position when the employee is a disabled person within the meaning of the Equality Act, but the employer is not aware of it? This is an issue which, until recently, was unique to disability discrimination, since a person's race and sex are normally clearly evident. In many cases, the fact of the employee's disability will be obvious to those around him. In other cases, the disability will be 'hidden' – diabetes makes a good example. In still others, the employee may take steps to conceal the condition and/or its effects.

The language of DDA s. 5(1) was *for a reason which relates to the disabled person's disability*. This was broad enough to encompass matters going beyond the direct effects of the disability, but, logically, it would seem unjust to find an employer liable when he did not know of the disability and quite possibly could not know. How does case law deal with this issue?

O'Neill v Symm & Co Ltd ([1998] ICR 481) was the first case on this issue to reach the EAT. In August 1996, the Claimant was interviewed for the post of accounts clerk and stated that she had had two months off work in April and May because of viral pneumonia. The employers understood her to mean that she was now fully recovered and fit for work. She started work on 3 September 1996 and by 3 December had taken 14 or 15 days off work. She had supplied no sick note, which was required under her contract, and on 3 December the employer wrote to her terminating her employment.

The Claimant claimed at the tribunal that she had submitted a sick note specifying 'ME/chronic fatigue syndrome' which the employer should have received on 2 September, before she started work, and that they had dismissed her contrary to the DDA. The tribunal was satisfied that the dismissal resulted solely from the absences and non-production of a doctor's certificate, and that at all material times the employer was unaware that the Claimant was suffering from ME. It was held that she did suffer from a disability within the meaning of the Act, but that she was not dismissed or discriminated against by reason of disability.

It was held that the issue for the EAT was what was connoted by the word 'reason'. It seemed to the EAT that it must involve knowledge of matters which were material. What was material to discrimination on the grounds of disability was knowledge of the disability, just as what was material in relation to the pregnancy provisions was knowledge of the pregnancy. It followed that the tribunal had not erred in law in regarding as relevant the employer's lack of knowledge that the Claimant suffered from ME and was therefore a disabled person for the purposes of s. 5(1).

The Claimant also submitted that the tribunal had erred in its application of s. 5(2)(a), under which an employer also discriminates if he fails to comply with the duty imposed by s. 6 to make reasonable adjustments. Again, the tribunal had concluded that the duty to make reasonable adjustments did not apply where the employer was unaware of the disability.

It seems material that the employer not only *did not know* that the Claimant had a disability at the time of the events giving rise to the dismissal, *but could not have known*, since the medical certificate allegedly sent around the end of August (before the applicant actually started work) had never been received and there was nothing in the pattern of absence to suggest disability.

By contrast, in *Heinz Co. Ltd. v Kenrick* ([2000] IRLR 144) the EAT held that the Claimant had been discriminated against at a time when the Claimant's condition had yet to be diagnosed. He was dismissed after a year's absence with an illness which was the subject of much investigation, but not given a diagnosis of ME until after the dismissal. It could thus be argued that not only did the employer not know that the Claimant was disabled, the Claimant did not know either.

On appeal, the EAT concluded that the reason for the less favourable treatment had to be judged objectively, rather than according to the employer's knowledge. However, knowledge could become relevant if the employer raised justifiability as a defence.

Per Lindsay J:

> *O'Neill* . . . appears to conclude that there cannot be some less favourable treatment of a person by an employer within s. 5(1)(a) . . . unless the employer has knowledge of the disability 'or at least the material features of it as set out in sch. 1' [. . .]
>
> We would hesitate before adopting this view. . . . Its adoption, if [Counsel's] argument on behalf of Heinz in this case is a guide, would, we fear, lead in many cases to hair-splitting medical evidence. We were addressed on whether CFS [Chronic Fatigue Syndrome] was a physical or mental condition, or some combination of the two, was it psychosomatic, was it clinically well-recognised, was it long-term? One can readily imagine cases in which, if detailed knowledge were to be relevant as *O'Neill* was argued to require, there would need to be medical evidence as to the labels which could be attached to this or that symptom or aggregation of symptoms as a person's condition deteriorated or improved. We cannot think such an approach was within the legislation's broad intendment [. . .]
>
> There is no language in s. 5(1) that requires that the relationship between the disability and the treatment should be judged subjectively, through the eyes of the employer, so that the applicable test should be the objective one of whether the relationship exists, not whether the employer knew of it. Indeed, unless the test is objective there will be difficulties with credible and honest but obtuse employers who fail to recognise or acknowledge the obvious [. . .]
>
> The phrase 'which relates to' . . . widens the description of the reasons which may be relevant beyond what the case would have been had the Act said 'by reason of . . . the disability'. As we see it, the expression may include a reason deriving from how the disability manifests itself even where there is no knowledge of the disability as such. This, we think, opens no floodgates but it does require employers to pause to consider whether the reason for some dismissal that they have in mind might relate to disability and, if it might, to reflect on the Act and Code before dismissing. There is . . . no need to imply into the statute a requirement not expressly present, namely that the employer should know of the disability as such or as to whether its material features fall within or without sch. 1. . . . This is not to say, though, that such knowledge or its absence may not be highly material to justifiability.

On this basis, the decisions in *O'Neill* and *Kenrick*, apparently conflicting, are easily reconciled. In *O'Neill*, the Claimant had a series of short-term absences over the first three months of her employment, a pattern suggestive of persistent absenteeism rather than disability. By contrast, Mr Kenrick had a single lengthy period of absence during which his condition was under investigation by the medical profession. This should have put his employers on notice of potential disability, and so they could be said to be under constructive notice. Further, ME/CFS was at that time something of a 'dustbin diagnosis', applied when a person had experienced a particular set of symptoms for a set period without any more concrete diagnosis.

Lewisham LBC v Malcolm [2008] UKHL 43 was not an employment case, but concerns a local authority seeking possession of a council flat, after the tenant had breached the terms of his tenancy by sub-letting it. It was, however, a rare case involving the Disability Discrimination Act which was taken to the House of Lords. The Lords' reasoning seems to require that the person responsible for the less favourable treatment must be aware of the disability. Here the Lords were satisfied that the council had sought possession because the tenant had illegally sub-let the property, and that they did not know at that time that he was schizophrenic. They concluded that the council could not be liable for disability-related discrimination as the disability was not 'at the forefront of their minds'.

Further, in deciding whether the treatment of a disabled person was 'less favourable' than that of a non-disabled person, the proper comparator was a non-disabled person whose circumstances were otherwise the same. Here the reason for the Claimant's treatment was his sub-letting of the flat, and the Lords were satisfied that a non-disabled tenant would have been treated in the same fashion.

If this reasoning is followed, an employer cannot be liable for disability-related discrimination unless he knows – or possibly *ought reasonably to have known* – of the disability. Many cases may fall between the two factual extremes of *O'Neill* and *Kenrick*. Should an employer faced with an employee who has a lot of brief absences for similar reasons consider that there may be an underlying medical cause which may, in turn, amount to a disability? There is a difference between liability for discrimination arising from disability and the duty to make reasonable adjustments, which is applicable only where the employer is aware of the disability and the disadvantage suffering by the disabled employee in the working environment (see below).

More recent case law emphasises that employers cannot simply rely on the advice of their medical advisers and must make their own decisions, bearing in mind the possibility that the employee concerned may prove to be disabled. In *Gallop v Newport City Council* ([2013] EWCA(CIV) 1583) a case decided under the DDA as the facts arose when it was still in force, the Claimant worked for the Council from 1997 as a grounds technician. On 13 May 2004, he emailed the Council to say that he was suffering from stress, setting out various symptoms. The Council referred him to their Occupational Health Department. On 25 May, Occupational Health informed the Council that he had some stress-related symptoms which were likely to be work-related but that he was not suffering from clinical depression. Some adjustments were made to his workload, and he remained at work until 1 August 2005. Again, Occupational Health stated that he was suffering from a work-related illness, but not depression. He began a phased return to work on 1 November 2005, and spent January–July 2006 on secondment to the cemeteries department. He went off sick again on 15 August 2006, remaining away until 19 February 2007. On 11 April 2007, he was signed off sick again. During this absence two doctors from Occupational Health wrote to the Council stating that Mr Gallop was not disabled for the purposes of the DDA.

The Claimant returned to work on 25 February 2008, and was promptly suspended on the basis of allegations of bullying going back to 2005. He was dismissed on 23 May by reason of these allegations. The Council argued that although the Claimant had a mental impairment it was not substantial or long-lasting, and he was therefore not disabled for the purposes of the DDA. If *Heinz v Kenrick* were followed then it could be argued that the Council, faced with three lengthy absences for the same reason in fewer than three years (three months, six months and ten months), had constructive knowledge of potential disability.

The Court of Appeal held that the employer could not simply rely on the opinion of his medical advisers in deciding whether a person was or was not disabled. On the facts of this case, the Occupational Health doctors had not specifically considered each of the three elements of the test of disability in DDA s. 1, and therefore their view that Mr Gallop was not a disabled person was simply a general statement of opinion.

Per Rimer LJ:

> The problem with certain types of disability, or claimed disability, is that it is only when eventually the ET rules on the question that it is known whether the claimant was in fact a disabled person. In the meantime, however, the responsible employer has to make his own judgment as to whether the employee is or is not disabled. In making that judgment, the employer will rightly want assistance and guidance from occupational health or other medical advisers.
>
> That assistance and guidance may be to the effect that the employee is a disabled person; and, unless the employer has good reason to disagree with the basis of such advice, he will ordinarily respect it in his dealings with the employee. In other cases, the guidance may be that the opinion of the adviser is that the employee is not a disabled person. In such cases, the employer must not forget that it is still he, the employer, who has to make the factual judgment

> as to whether the employee is or is not disabled: he cannot simply rubber stamp the adviser's opinion that he is not.
>
> I add that this case illustrates the need for the employer, when seeking outside advice from clinicians, not simply to ask in general terms whether the employee is a disabled person within the meaning of the legislation but to pose specific *practical* questions directed to the particular circumstances of the putative disability. The answers to such questions will then provide real assistance to the employer in forming his judgment as to whether the criteria for disability are satisfied.

The Claimant in *Morgan v Armadillo Managed Services Ltd* ([2013] UKEAT/0567/12/RN, EAT) worked for a small IT company. During a visit to Gibraltar on behalf of the company, Mr Morgan was attacked in the street on the night of 14–15 April 2011 and badly injured. On 11 May, the chief executive, Mark Newns, received a medical certificate which stated that the Claimant was suffering from double vision resulting from the assault. On 12 May Mr Newns wrote to the Claimant stating that he would be writing to invite him to a disciplinary meeting over allegations that he had been drunk in front of a client on the evening before the assault, and that he would receive only statutory sick pay until he returned to work. At no time did the employer seek to deny that the assault had taken place or that it was unconnected with work. In August, Mr Newns wrote to the Claimant stating that he would not be paid commission for the period since 15 April, on the basis that he had not been at work. Following his resignation, the Claimant, who had insufficient continuity of employment to claim unfair dismissal, claimed disability discrimination in respect of the failure to pay sick pay and commission. The EAT concluded, on the basis of *Gallop*, that actual or constructive knowledge of the fact of disability was required for both direct discrimination and disability-related discrimination. They went on to hold that the reason the Claimant was not paid commission was not his disability, but the assault. The first point seems fair, but surely the latter is splitting hairs?

Equality Act s. 15(2) resolves the issue (one hopes!) by providing that an employer will not be liable for discrimination arising from a disability if he does not know, and cannot reasonably know, that the employee is disabled. That does leave open the question of whether knowledge is essential for liability for indirect discrimination.

12.4 Duty to make reasonable adjustments

The duty to make reasonable adjustments is contained in s. 20 of the Equality Act and applies when the employer knows or ought to know that a disabled person is put at a 'substantial disadvantage' in the working environment in comparison with persons who are not disabled, by one or more of the following:

- a provision, criterion or practice (PCP);
- a physical feature;
- absence of an 'auxiliary aid'.

The duty is to take such steps as are reasonable to have to take to avoid the disadvantage, or to provide the auxiliary aid necessary. The concept of reasonable adjustments is expressed in general, indeed vague terms, and it is useful to refer to the non-exhaustive list of reasonable adjustments contained in s. 18B(2) (formerly s. 6(3)):

- making adjustments to premises;
- allocating some of the disabled employee's duties to another;
- transferring him to another vacancy;

- altering his working hours;
- assigning him to a different place of work;
- allowing time off for rehabilitation, assessment or treatment;
- arranging training;
- acquiring or modifying equipment;
- modifying instructions or reference manuals;
- modifying procedures for testing or assessment;
- providing a reader or interpreter;
- providing supervision.

Frequently in practice, a package of adjustments will be necessary. For example, a person injured in an accident may need alterations to premises such as the addition of a ramp, a phased return to work, including part-time hours and the temporary transfer of some of his responsibilities to a colleague. He may need time off for physiotherapy, or retraining, or, if unable to return to his previous role, a move to a different post together with specific training for it.

12.4.1 When does the duty arise?

Case law on reasonable adjustments turns on the issue of whether the duty has been observed, and when, chronologically speaking, the duty comes into effect. It is often argued by claimants that they were unable to return to work because the employer did not put any reasonable adjustments in place. The employer will then argue that no duty arose because at the material time there was no sign of the claimant returning to work. Clearly, such cases involve a lack of communication between the parties, but how is this issue dealt with by tribunals?

This question arose most recently in the Scottish case of *Doran v Department of Work and Pensions* ([2014] UKEATS/0017/14/SM). This is a case decided under the DDA, but there are no substantive differences from the relevant Equality Act provisions. Lady Stacey, sitting alone, held that no duty to make reasonable adjustments arose when the claimant was certified as unfit for any work and had given no indication of when she might be able to return to work.

Miss Doran began working for the DWP on 5 May 2009 on a fixed-term contract, initially until 4 May 2010, but subsequently extended to 4 November 2010. On 11 January 2010, she went off sick, initially with dental problems, though she then sent in a succession of one- and two-week sick notes referring to stress-related illness. The employer referred Miss Doran to Occupational Health, who interviewed her by telephone on 12 February and concluded that although she was not at that time to be regarded as disabled, she was unfit to return to work. They advised a phased return to work over four weeks. Her GP advised that she was not fit to return to her normal work, which involved answering telephone inquiries all day. The employer arranged a review meeting, but after this the Claimant was signed off work for another four weeks. Another review meeting was scheduled for 22 March, which the claimant did not attend. From then on the claimant sent in medical certificates stating that she was unfit for work, with no suggestion that she could return with appropriate adjustments, although the employer had already offered a phased return to work, and a demotion which meant she would not be required to spend long periods on the telephone.

The Claimant was dismissed by letter dated 26 May, at a time when she was still certified as being unfit for work and her GP had written to the employer to say that expecting her to attend meetings at work was counter-productive. She said at the appeal hearing on 22 July that she thought that the only option she had been given were returning to full-time work over four weeks, and being demoted, and that she was being punished for being ill. She was not certified as fit for work until 20 September, and was unfit again from January to June 2011. From September 2011, she took a full-time college course, and the Tribunal considered that she had effectively ruled herself out of the labour market. The employer stated in evidence that it was its normal practice to consider dismissal after three months' absence, but an employee would be allowed to return to work provided the total absence was fewer than six months. The Tribunal accepted evidence that at the time of the dismissal the Claimant had been absent for four and a half months and was not fit for work for a further four months.

The Claimant contended at the Employment Tribunal that the following adjustments should have been made:

- redeployment within the business;
- temporary reduction in the number of days which the claimant was required to work;
- structured rehabilitation plan prepared by occupational health to assist the Claimant in her return to work;
- flexible working;
- reduced hours per day;
- light duties.

The Tribunal directed themselves on the case of *Environment Agency v Rowan* [2008] IRLR 20 which states that an employment tribunal considering a claim for discrimination by failing to make reasonable adjustments must identify:

a) the provision criterion or practice (PCP) applied by or on behalf of the employer, or;
b) the physical feature of premises occupied by the employer
c) the identity of non-disabled comparators (where appropriate); and
d) the nature and extent of the substantial disadvantage suffered by the claimant.

The Tribunal then applied these requirements to the facts before them. They found that the evidence before them did not show that the claimant was being required either to return to her previous role without adjustment or to return with a fixed four-week phased return. That had just been floated for discussion with her; she had said the period was too short but that was not evidence of any insistence on a period of that length and no other. They thought the PCP actually applied was the application of the respondent's attendance procedure, in particular, consideration of whether the claimant was capable of achieving satisfactory attendance levels within a reasonable period.

The Employment Tribunal then found that the evidence suggested that the disadvantage the Claimant was put under by the policy was her dismissal following an inability to return within what the respondent considered a reasonable period of time. The proper comparators were non-disabled employees who were able to attend work and carry out the tasks required of them. They found that the Claimant was at a disadvantage in comparison with them, and therefore the duty to make reasonable adjustments could arise, subject to a timing issue.

Central to argument over the timing issue was the case of *NCH Scotland v McHugh* UKEATS/0010/06, where the EAT had held from the case of *Home Office v Collins* [2005] EWCA 598 that it was reasonable for the employer not to pursue the possibility of a phased return to part-time work until the employee could indicate a definite date for her return. The EAT decided that a managed programme of rehabilitation depends on all the circumstances of the case, plainly including a return to work date. While the claimant was unable or unwilling to give a return to work indication any adjustments would be futile.

The Employment Tribunal accepted Ms Shaw's submission that since the claimant had not indicated to the respondent a start date, or given any other sign that she would be returning to work at a particular time, the duty was not triggered. They concluded that the respondent did not discriminate against the claimant by failing to comply with the duty to make reasonable adjustments, since on binding authority the duty had not yet been triggered. The adjustments contended for could only be regarded as reasonable when the claimant was back at work, or had at least indicated a start date when she would return.

The EAT upheld the Tribunal's decision. On that basis, the duty to make reasonable adjustments does not arise until there are clear indications that the disabled employee will be able to work at a particular date provided adjustments are in place. To argue that the duty to make reasonable adjustments only arises once the disabled employee is back at work is unrealistic, as in many situations it will not be possible for him to return to work unless adjustments have already been made – the obvious example is where physical changes to the workplace are needed to enable access by a person in a wheelchair. It is submitted that, in practice, the duty to make reasonable adjustments should arise at the time when the employee is able to return to work subject to adjustments. This requires regular communication between the parties; the employer should then discuss and agree the necessary adjustments with the employee, the employee's medical advisers, and the employers' occupational health department.

12.4.2 What are reasonable adjustments?

The glib answer to the question of what constitutes reasonable adjustments is that it all depends on the facts of the individual case. It is also a truism that issues of what are reasonable adjustments only reach the tribunals when there is a dispute, often in circumstances where, as in *Doran*, the employee has been dismissed and argues that this would have been avoided had the employer made reasonable adjustments. In particular, it is frequently argued where an employee is dismissed under the employer's absence policy (as in *Doran*) that a reasonable adjustment would have been to disregard all absences arising from disability. A similar argument is made in relation to selection for redundancy, where absence is often used as one among several criteria.

❖ EXAMPLE

The employer has 20 employees and decides to make four redundant. A selection matrix is adopted which gives employees a score by applying the following criteria:

- length of employment;
- qualifications;
- experience; and
- 'Bradford Score' over the past two years.

The Bradford Score is a method of monitoring absence which emphasises frequent short-term absence, using the formula:

Number of absences × Number of absences × Total days of absence

Neil is diabetic. The resultant problems in maintaining stable blood glucose levels cause periodic hypoglycaemic attacks, and also affect his immune system, making him susceptible to infections. In consequence, he has had 20 absences over the last two years, all of one to three days, totalling 49 days. His Bradford Score is therefore:

$20 \times 20 \times 49 = 19{,}600$

Although Neil scores well on length of employment, qualifications and experience, his Bradford Score makes him the worst performer in the selection exercise by some distance, and he is therefore selected for redundancy. He argues that if all his diabetes-related absences were disregarded, he would be left only with one absence of two days caused by a badly sprained ankle, which would give him a Bradford Score of 2 (1 × 1 × 2), and he would not have been selected for redundancy.

Case law in this area turns on the purpose behind the duty to make reasonable adjustments. In *O'Hanlon v HM Revenue & Customs Commissioners* ([2007] EWCA Civ 283, CA), decided under the DDA, the Claimant suffered from depression and had intermittent long periods of absence. She argued that the employer's normal policy of paying full sick pay for a maximum period of six months, and half-pay for a further six months, placed her at a substantial disadvantage in comparison with non-disabled employees and that a reasonable adjustment would be to pay her full sick pay for all periods of absence of whatever length.

The Court of Appeal's response was robust. They asked what the purpose was underlying the duty to make reasonable adjustments. It was, they concluded, to enable the disabled person to work. Payment of sick pay did not assist the individual to return to work; indeed, generous sick pay schemes might have the opposite effect, by encouraging employees to remain off work even after they had recovered. Therefore, extending an already generous sick pay scheme to the benefit of the Claimant was not a reasonable adjustment.

Since *O'Hanlon* was decided, the Equality Act has extended the scope of indirect discrimination to disability, but it seems possible that the employer can argue justification, on the basis that extended periods of sick pay will act as a disincentive to returning to work.

The first case on the issue under the Equality Act is *Griffiths v Secretary of State for Work and Pensions* ([2014] UKEAT/0372/13/JOJ), where the Claimant did not argue indirect discrimination, but only a failure to make reasonable adjustments when the employer issued an attendance warning after she was absent for 62 consecutive days as a result of fibromyalgia and post-viral fatigue. It was not disputed that the Claimant was a disabled person. The absence policy provided that a warning could be issued once an employee had reached a 'consideration point' of eight days' absence in any one-year period. The Tribunal first considered whether the duty to make reasonable adjustments had been triggered – had the Claimant been placed at a substantial disadvantage by the employer's absence policy in comparison with a non-disabled person? The majority had decided that she had not, given that the absence policy gave the employer discretion to disregard a disabled employee's disability-related absences and to adjust 'consideration points'. The minority disagreed, on the basis that a disabled person was more likely to have sufficient absences and so reach any 'consideration point'.

On appeal, Counsel for the Claimant argued that being given a warning as a first stage towards possible dismissal constituted a substantial disadvantage, which was more likely to affect a disabled person, because he was more likely to be absent from work. This disadvantage could only be avoided by the employer using the discretionary provisions in the policy, which had not been done in the Claimant's case. The EAT, however, concluded that the Tribunal's decision had been correct on the basis of the applicable law.

This conclusion dealt with the issue in the appeal, but the EAT went on to consider the conclusion reached by the Tribunal that a retrospective adjustment of the 'consideration point' to ignore the previous 62-day absence, and to ignore disability-related absences in future, was not a reasonable adjustment. Again, they upheld the Tribunal's decision, in part on the basis that the adjustment sought was outside the purpose of the duty to make reasonable adjustments. In any case, it went beyond the boundary of what was reasonable.

It could be argued that a certain amount of hair-splitting was involved in this decision. On the natural and ordinary meaning of the words used, 'consideration points' based on absence will put individuals with some types of disability at a disadvantage, since they are more likely to have periods of absence. If an absence policy includes discretion to ignore disability-related absences, the disadvantage can only be rectified if the discretion is used.

The duty is to make 'reasonable adjustments', not all adjustments demanded by the claimant. Cases such as *Griffiths* demonstrate that there is a point beyond which the employer cannot be expected to go. A good example is *Hay v Surrey CC* [2007] EWCA Civ 93, CA (Civ Div). The Claimant was employed by the local authority as a mobile library manager, which involved her driving a van and stacking and lifting books from low shelves. Medical reports indicated that a degenerative knee condition prevented her from properly carrying out her role; in particular, she could not drive the van, nor crouch down to move books from the shelves. The employer offered her an alternative post in a static library, which she refused, arguing that she should remain in the mobile library, and be provided with an assistant to drive the van and move books. After she was dismissed, the Claimant alleged unfair dismissal on the grounds of disability discrimination, on the basis that the local authority should have made sufficient use of the reasonable adjustments that she had suggested so that she could have continued acting as mobile library manager despite her admitted disability. The Court of Appeal concluded that redeployment to a static library was a reasonable adjustment, so that the local authority had satisfied the duty, and made it clear that 'reasonable adjustments' did not mean changing the job out of all recognition.

Other protected characteristics, with the exception of pregnancy and maternity, 'work both ways', so that treating a person more favourably than another by reason of, say, sex or race, involves direct discrimination against that other by treating them less favourably. Thus, subject to limited exceptions, giving a job to a black person because he is black is direct discrimination against a white applicant. However, disability discrimination legislation specifically provides that an employer may treat a disabled person more favourably than a non-disabled person without liability towards the non-disabled person (now Equality Act s. 13(3)). This provision was part of the reasoning in *Archibald v Fife Council* [2004] UKHL 32, HL, which was the first case on reasonable adjustments to reach the House of Lords.

Mrs Archibald worked for the Council for two years as a road sweeper, but in 1999 she became unable to walk as the result of complications of an operation. Clearly, she was incapable of continuing to work as a road sweeper. Mindful of their responsibilities under the DDA, the Council retrained her for office work and encouraged her to apply for office jobs within the organisation as they became available. They considered that they could not simply move her into a vacancy because, as a road sweeper, Mrs Archibald was at the bottom of the national pay scale for local authority manual workers. All office jobs were therefore higher in pay and status, and the Council considered that, without a competitive appointment process, they were limited to moving the Claimant to a post at the same level or lower. Specifically, under the Local Government and Housing Act 1989 s. 7 all staff employed by a local authority are required to be appointed 'on merit'. Mrs Archibald applied for over 100 admin jobs and was rejected for all of them, which she considered was caused by prejudice against her as a former road sweeper. Eventually, as she was still physically incapable of working as a road sweeper, and the Council's redeployment procedures had been exhausted, she was dismissed.

Mrs Archibald's argument was that she should not have been required to go through competitive interviews for an administrative post if she could show that she was qualified and suitable for that post. The EAT dismissed her appeal on the basis that here was nothing in the arrangements for selection which placed her at a substantial disadvantage compared with a non-disabled person because the requirement for competitive interviews applied to everybody, and therefore that the duty to make reasonable adjustments was not triggered.

Baroness Hale gave the lead judgment in the House of Lords. Again, her approach and conclusions deserve consideration in detail.

> It is common ground that the Act entails a measure of positive discrimination, in the sense that employers are required to take steps to help disabled people which they are not required to take for others. It is also common ground that employers are only required to take those steps which in all the circumstances it is reasonable for them to take. . . . The debate is about what triggers the duty. The Council argue that its purpose is to enable the disabled person to overcome the obstacles which her disability puts in the way of her doing the job *for which she has applied or is already employed*. . . . Once these obstacles have been cleared out of the way,

> there is a 'level playing field' and the disabled person is free to compete on her merits with anyone else. . . . This duty cannot arise where the disability means that she cannot do the job at all and there is no adjustment to the arrangements for that job which can make any difference.
>
> The Disability Rights Commission [interveners in the case] argue that in such a case the duty is indeed triggered. The control mechanism lies in the fact that the employer is only required to take such steps as it is reasonable for them to have to take. They are not expected to do the impossible. But among the possible steps is . . . transfer to fill an existing vacancy, which must include an existing vacancy for a different job. Inability to do the present job cannot mean that there is no duty at all. The Act was clearly intended to apply to existing employees who become disabled as well as the Code of Practice . . ., which says this under the heading 'transferring the person to fill an existing vacancy [. . .]
>
> Underlying the debate there may be . . . a fundamental philosophical difference about the permissible limits of the positive discrimination which the duty to make reasonable adjustments inevitably entails. The Act predates the Council Directive 2000/78/EC establishing a general framework for equal treatment in employment and occupation ('the framework Directive'). That Directive cannot constitute grounds for reducing the level of protection against discrimination already afforded by Member States (Art. 8.2). Nevertheless, both sides seek to rely on its principles. The Council point to the opening words of Recital 1 – 'This Directive does not require the recruitment, promotion, maintenance in employment or training of an individual who is not competent, capable and available to perform the essential functions of the post concerned or to undergo the relevant training', while the Commission point to its concluding words – 'without prejudice to the obligation to provide reasonable accommodation for people with disabilities'. The Council argue that it is a framework for equal, not preferential treatment. Article 1 provides its purpose:
>
>> The purpose of this Directive is to lay down a general framework for combating discrimination on the grounds of religion or belief, disability, age or sexual orientation as regards employment and occupation, with a view to putting into effect in the Member States the principle of equal treatment.

Lady Hale accepted that the Directive required positive action by employers in favour of disabled people in some circumstances, but went on to say that the role of the court in the case before her was essentially one of statutory construction. She considered 'arrangements' to be a broad concept.

> [DDA] s. 6(1) applies to 'any arrangements' made by or on behalf of an employer. These arrangements have to relate either to the arrangements for determining to whom employment will be offered, or to 'any term, condition or arrangements on which employment, promotion, a transfer, training or any other benefit is offered or afforded' (s. 6(2)). Subject to that, the term 'arrangements' is undefined. It could clearly relate to the Council's redeployment policy, but in this case that did not put Mrs Archibald at a substantial disadvantage compared with anyone else. It could equally apply to the terms on which Mrs Archibald held her road sweeping job. An employer's arrangements for dividing up the work he needs to have done into different jobs are just as capable of being 'arrangements' as are an employer's arrangements for deciding who gets what job or how much each is paid. Some employers might combine cooking and bottle-washing in one job while others might treat them quite differently. The job descriptions for all their posts are 'arrangements' which they make in relation to the terms, conditions and arrangements on which they offer employment. Also included in those arrangements is the liability of anyone who becomes incapable of fulfilling the job description to be dismissed.
>
> The next question, therefore, is whether those arrangements placed her 'at a substantial disadvantage in comparison with persons who are not disabled'. The answer to that was clear.

The job description required her to walk and sweep and she could not for the foreseeable future do that. Hence she was eventually dismissed for incapacity. Any steps which the Council might have to take under s. 6(1) must be 'in order to prevent the arrangements . . . having that effect'. 'That effect' clearly refers to her being placed at a substantial disadvantage in comparison with non-disabled persons[. . .]

The duty is to take such steps as it is reasonable in the circumstances of the case for the employer to have to take. Could this ever include transferring her to fill an existing vacancy at a slightly higher grade without competitive interview? It is noteworthy that the Council did do a great deal to help Mrs Archibald. They arranged retraining for her. They kept her on the books for a great deal longer than they normally would have done while she retrained and then looked for alternative posts. They automatically short-listed her for the posts for which she applied. They went rather beyond their normal policies in cases of redundancy or ill-health. They were behaving as if they did have a duty towards her under s. 6(1) even if they did not think that they did. They would have been prepared to transfer her without competitive interview to another job at the same or a lower grade, even though there might be others better qualified to do it. But as she was at the bottom of the manual grade and all office jobs were nominally at a higher grade, there was no equal or lower grade job to which she could be transferred.

S. 6(3)(c) merely refers to 'an existing vacancy'. It does not qualify this by any words such as 'at the same or a lower grade'. It does refer to 'transferring' rather than 'promoting' her, but as a matter of language a transfer can be upwards as well as sideways or downwards. Furthermore, transferring her 'to fill' an existing vacancy is clearly more than allowing her to apply, short-listing or considering her for an existing vacancy. If that were all it meant, it would add nothing to the existing non-discrimination requirements: the employer is already required by s. 4(2)(b) not to discriminate against a disabled employee in the opportunities afforded for promotion, transfer, training or any other benefit.

On the face of it, therefore, transferring Mrs Archibald to a sedentary position which she was qualified to fill was among the steps which it might have been reasonable in all the circumstances for the Council to have to take once she could no longer walk and sweep. Is there any reason to hold to the contrary?

The Employment Tribunal thought that there was. They relied on that part of s. 6(7) which provides that 'nothing in this Part is to be taken to require an employer to treat a disabled person more favourably than he treat or would treat others'. But this is prefaced by the words, 'Subject to the provisions of this Section. . .', so that, to the extent that the duty to make reasonable adjustments requires it, the employer is not only permitted but obliged to treat a disabled person more favourably than others.

There is another possible reason to the contrary in the case of a local authority employer such as this. s. 7 of the Local Government and Housing Act 1989 requires all staff engaged by a local authority to be appointed 'on merit'. This is an extremely important principle. Regrettably local government does offer opportunities for corrupt appointment practices which have on occasions resulted in people being appointed who were not even competent, let alone the best person available, to do the job. Advertisement and competitive interview is one way of securing that appointments are made on merit. But this is not the only way of doing so. Furthermore, this obligation has always been subject to the requirements of the law relating to disabled persons. When the 1989 Act was passed, it was subject to the quota requirement in the Disabled Persons (Employment) Act 1944. This meant that a person who did not qualify 'on merit' might have to be appointed to fill the quota. Now that the 1944 Act has been replaced by the 1995 Act, the duty in s.7 (1) of the 1989 Act is (in s. 7(2)(f)) made subject to ss. 5–6 of the 1995 Act. Thus, local government appointments must always be on merit, subject to the duty to make reasonable adjustments. Usually, those will be reasonable adjustments to the post which is being offered so as to make it accessible to a disabled applicant. But s. 7(2)(f) refers generally to ss. 5–6,

> so that it is capable of including the step of transferring a disabled person from a post she can no longer do to a post which she can do, provided that this is a reasonable step for the employer to have to take.
>
> This will depend on all the circumstances of the case, having regard in particular to the factors laid down in s. 6(4). An important component in the circumstances must be the Council's redeployment policy. This currently distinguishes between transfer to a post at the same or a lower grade and transfer to a post at a higher grade. Generally, it must be reasonable for a Council to maintain this distinction. But it might be reasonable to expect a small modification either in general or in the particular case to meet the needs of a well-qualified and well-motivated employee who has become disabled. Manual grades are often technically lower than non-manual grades even if the difference in pay is minimal. . . . We are not talking here of high grade positions where it is not only possible but important to make fine judgements about who will be best for the job. We are talking of positions which a great many people could fill and for which no one candidate may obviously be 'the best'. There is no law against discriminating against people with a background in manual work, but it might be reasonable for an employer to have to take that difficulty into account when considering the transfer of a disabled worker who could no longer do that type of work. I only say 'might' because it depends upon all the circumstances of the case. While the 1995 Act clearly lays great emphasis on the circumstances of the individual case, the general policy of achieving fairness and transparency in local government appointments is also extremely important. The real question may be whether this should have been seen as a sideways rather than an upwards move.

Ultimately, the Lords concluded unanimously that on the facts of this case it was a reasonable adjustment for the Council to move Mrs Archibald into an office job for which she was qualified without a competitive selection process.

Case law shows that individual circumstances are central in deciding whether an employer has fulfilled the duty to make reasonable adjustments. For example, it is clear from *Hay v Surrey County Council* that there is no duty to change a job out of all recognition, and, generally speaking, there is no duty to create a job specifically to accommodate a disabled person. However, in *Southampton City College v Randall* ([2005] UKEAT/0372/05/DM) the EAT concluded that creating a specific job and awarding it to the Claimant was capable of being a reasonable adjustment at a time when the employer was carrying out a major reorganisation. Mr Randall, a lecturer in engineering, developed a throat problem which affected his voice and made it difficult for him to teach large groups of students. After a period of sick leave, he sought to return to work. By this time, a restructuring process was in train. As part of the restructuring, the college created the role of co-ordinating lecturer, which was similar to Mr Randall's existing role, but with less teaching. He applied for the new role, but another employee was appointed. He was then offered the opportunity to apply for ill-health retirement or redundancy but he resigned and claimed constructive dismissal and disability discrimination.

The tribunal held that Mr Randall was subjected to less favourable treatment compared with other employees for a reason related to his disability, that the college had a duty to devise a job that would take account of the effects of his disability and had unjustifiably failed to comply with its duty to make reasonable adjustments. The tribunal also held that the dismissal was automatically unfair. The college appealed.

The EAT held that the creation of a new post in substitution of an existing post was not precluded by s. 6(3) from being a reasonable adjustment. Whether an employer was obliged to create a new post depended on the facts of the case. Here, Mr Randall's line manager had a blank sheet of paper so far as the job specification was concerned. Accordingly, it was possible to devise a job that would take account of the effects of Mr Randall's disability. On the factual evidence, he could have remained employed by the college. However, the college had not considered the question of reasonable adjustments at all. The duty under s. 6(1) could not be complied with unless an employer made a proper assessment of what needed to be done to eliminate a disabled person's disadvantage. As the Tribunal held, in the absence of such an assessment, it would often be impossible for an employer to know what adjustments might be reasonable.

This case demonstrates in addition that the first essential of the duty to make reasonable adjustments is to make an assessment of what needs to be done to eliminate the disadvantage caused to the disabled person by the 'arrangements' at work. That in turn requires identification of the disadvantage. It is also made explicit in the legislation that the duty to make reasonable adjustments only arises where the employer has actual or constructive notice of the disability (sch. 8, s. 20).

Once this initial assessment is complete, the nature of reasonable adjustments depends very much on the facts of the individual case. In *Croft Vets Ltd v Butcher* ([2013] UKEAT/0430/12/LA) the EAT upheld a decision of the Tribunal that it was a reasonable adjustment for the employer to pay for the employee to have private medical treatment for depression, even though this would not guarantee her return to work, although they emphasised that the point was not of general application but specific to the facts of the case. Mrs Butcher had worked for the employers as an office manager since 1996. She went off sick with depression on 4 May 2010 and never returned to work. A psychiatrist engaged by the employer to prepare a medical report saw the Claimant in August, and made recommendations in a report dated 19 August. These recommendations included funding for private psychological sessions. Meanwhile, the employers were prepared to make substantial reductions to the Claimant's workload when she returned to work.

Matters drifted until 23 November, when the Claimant resigned. Subsequently, she claimed disability discrimination and constructive dismissal. The Tribunal held that paying for psychological treatment was a reasonable adjustment on these facts, and their decision was upheld by the EAT, who noted, in particular, that there had been no discussion with the Claimant after the psychiatrist's report. Indeed, there was no direct communication with her after July (as with many other cases, this demonstrates the importance of regular communication from the employer to the absent employee).

12.5 Direct discrimination on grounds of disability

Though direct discrimination is fairly frequently argued, it is rarely found by the Tribunal. Most appeals in which direct discrimination is discussed prove to involve situations where the first-instance Tribunal has confused direct discrimination with discrimination arising from disability. Alternative, the Tribunal may have failed to identify the appropriate comparator.

The definition of direct discrimination is now found in Equality Act s. 13(1) and is that applied to all the protected characteristics. There can be no liability where the employer is unaware of the disability, contrary to the position in discrimination arising from disability. The burden of proof process is the same as that applicable to direct discrimination on the basis of other protected characteristics.

From the very limited case law, it would seem that the paucity of successful claims for direct discrimination on grounds of disability is because of the difficulty in establishing that the claimant has been treated less favourably than a non-disabled comparator who was, for example, absent for the same period. For example, in *Matinpour v Rotherham MBC* ([2011] UKEAT/0406/11), the Claimant, who had been off work for 14 months because of his disability, failed to persuade the tribunal that a person who had been off work for 14 months because of, for example, a broken leg, would not have been dismissed. In *Wilcox v Birmingham CAB Services* ([2011] UKEAT/0293/10/DM) the Claimant resigned and claimed constructive dismissal and disability discrimination after an 18-month absence. The tribunal found no evidence that she had been treated less favourably than a real or hypothetical non-disabled comparator who was off work for the same length of time. The EAT, in turn, found no reason to disturb that conclusion.

The situation in *JP Morgan Europe Ltd v Chwiedan* ([2010] UKEAT/0286/09) is rather more complex, since the EAT remitted the issue of direct discrimination to a fresh tribunal on the basis that the original tribunal had become confused between the tests for direct discrimination and disability-related discrimination. The Claimant was a merchant banker who became disabled in 2007 as the result of a skiing accident, and argued that he had been discriminated against by being made redundant and, separately, by being paid a lower bonus than in previous years, before he was disabled. The EAT concluded that the tribunal had found facts from which they could infer direct discrimination in the absence of a non-discriminatory explanation from the employer. However, the EAT added a note of caution, given that the reason for both the reduced bonus and the redundancy was that the Claimant did some 60 per cent of his work for a single client, and was unable, because of the disability, to work longer hours and seek more clients.

> At this point in time it is important to note that the Employment Tribunal (a) has not constructed a comparator so far as direct discrimination is concerned; (b) the Employment Tribunal has not explained what the discrimination was. If the direct discrimination was simply that the Respondent believed that it was uneconomic to make reasonable adjustments, or that it was unable to make greater profits from clients because of the Claimant's disability, that discrimination would appear to be disability-related rather than direct. *Only if there was some prejudice against people in a back brace and using crutches might it be said to be direct discrimination and this would need to be explained.*[1]

In *Stockton upon Tees Borough Council v Aylott* ([2008] UKEAT/0401/08/CEA) the Claimant was bipolar and was eventually dismissed. He worked for the Council from 2003 and, on 2 January 2005, following difficulties with colleagues, submitted 17 grievances. It was agreed that he should go on paid leave until these were resolved. In February, the Council decided to deal with the matter under its Dignity At Work policy. After long delays, adjustments were agreed – that he would have weekly meetings with his line manager and not have any responsibility for managing others – and the Claimant returned to work on 6 February 2006. However, he went off sick on 22 February with stress-related chest pains. On 13 April (Maundy Thursday) he attempted to return at 1500. There was then an altercation with a superior, and reports of strange behaviour. It was subsequently noted that this was the day he was due to be reduced to half-pay, having exhausted his entitlement to full pay while sick. On 18 April, the next working day, a decision was taken to suspend the Claimant, but, meanwhile, he had been admitted to a psychiatric hospital. Thereafter, he was treated as being off sick, and a decision was taken that there should be no investigation until he was fit to return to work. On 23 August, the Claimant was invited to a meeting to take place on 1 September, but it transpired that he had been back in hospital for most of August. On 6 September, with no sign of his returning to work, a decision was taken to dismiss him with effect from 6 November.

As regards direct discrimination the Tribunal concluded:

> The Tribunal is satisfied that the claimant has established facts from which a Tribunal could conclude, in the absence of an adequate explanation, amounted to direct discrimination on grounds of the claimant's disability. The appropriate comparator is someone who has been off for a similar number of days but did not have the claimant's particular disability. The Tribunal is satisfied that the claimant has shown that the respondents (sic) treatment of him upon his

1 My emphasis.

> return from sickness, by imposing deadlines and referring to his performance, and strict monitoring followed by the response to his return to work in April 2006 and his dismissal were sufficient to shift the burden of proof. A comparator who had a similar sickness record in respect of, for example, a complicated broken bone or other surgical problem, would not have been subjected to the same treatment.

In respect of the decision to suspend Mr Aylott and to conduct a disciplinary investigation after he failed to return to work after 13 April 2006, the Tribunal held:

> [On 13 April] Paul Diggins ignored Sue Daniels' instructions to have a welfare/return to work meeting with the claimant and send him home. Instead he gave the Claimant tasks and deadlines which provoked the heated meeting. The subsequent decision to carry out a disciplinary investigation and to suspend the Claimant was extremely harsh when an informal approach would have been appropriate. Once again, the Tribunal finds that this was direct discrimination based on the stereotypical view of mental illness [. . .]
>
> The Tribunal finds that the dismissal was discriminatory. It was on grounds of the claimant's disability. There was a fear of the claimant's return based on a stereotypical view of mental illness.

The Council appealed.

The EAT first considered the issue of the proper comparator, and concluded:

> For the purposes of ascertaining whether there has been discrimination on grounds of disability, a hypothetical comparator does not have to be a clone of the complainant. However [DDA] Section 3A(5) requires the comparison to be with a non- disabled person
>
> > '. . . whose relevant circumstances, including his abilities, are the same as, or not materially different from, those of the disabled person'.
>
> In our judgment, for a meaningful comparison to be made, the hypothetical comparator should have all the attributes or features which materially affected the employer's decision to carry out the act which is said to be discriminatory.
>
> 78. Even if, contrary to our findings above, the Tribunal had been entitled to consider claims that the Council had discriminated against Mr Aylott by monitoring his performance and setting deadlines after his return to work in February 2006, in our judgment the Tribunal erred in law in failing to select a hypothetical comparator who, in addition a similar sickness absence record to that of the complainant, had the other characteristics relevant to the acts of which complaint was made. An appropriate hypothetical comparator for the purpose of considering whether Mr Aylott had been discriminated against in monitoring his performance and setting deadlines, in addition to having a similar sickness absence record, would have been a person who had recently been moved to a different post and whose past behaviour and performance had caused concern.

As regards the dismissal, the Tribunal committed an error of law in failing to identify an appropriate comparator.

Although the Tribunal was entitled to conclude that the burden of proof had passed to the Council, the Tribunal failed to give adequate reasons for its conclusion that the Claimant had been directly discriminated against:

> In our judgment the findings of '. . . direct discrimination based on the stereotypical view of mental illness' are too vague to support a conclusion that disability discrimination is made out.

> What does 'a stereotypical view of mental illness' mean? Did the Tribunal consider that Mr Aylott would be violent, be offensive, fail to perform his duties, have further long periods of absence? In our judgment this phrase falls far short of a finding as to the reason for conduct of the Council of which complaint is made and which is necessary for the identification of the characteristics of an appropriate comparator.

As in other cases, the Tribunal's decision was quashed and the matter referred to a fresh tribunal.

12.6 Unfavourable treatment on grounds related to disability

Equality Act s. 15 defines discrimination arising from disability as follows:

(1) A person (A) discriminates against a disabled person (B) if—
   (a) A treats B unfavourably because of something arising in consequence of B's disability, and
   (b) A cannot show that the treatment is a proportionate means of achieving a legitimate aim.
(2) Subsection (1) does not apply if A shows that A did not know, and could not reasonably have been expected to know, that B had the disability.

No comparator is required; it must simply be shown that the disabled person is treated 'unfavourably'.

❖ THINKING POINT

What constitutes 'unfavourable' treatment? For example, is being able to retire early on an enhanced pension actually unfavourable treatment?

This is a major difference from the DDA, which referred to 'less favourable' treatment, and therefore required a non-disabled comparator and a comparison exercise. The original requirement for a comparator was removed from the Equality Act at the draft stage as a result of the House of Lords decision in *Malcolm*. The Tribunal must now consider whether the disabled person was treated 'unfavourably' and whether that unfavourable treatment was for a reason related to the disability. Little appellate case law is available as yet, and we can consider whether some of the existing cases would have been decided differently under the new test.

In *London Clubs Management Ltd v Hood* ([2001] IRLR 719, EAT) a disabled employee was not discriminated against for a reason which related to his disability when he was denied sick pay, when the entire workforce was subject to a ban on sick pay. There was no 'less favourable' treatment. This case might well be decided differently on the basis of indirect discrimination (see below), which has now been extended to disability, but would this be seen as unfavourable treatment in any event?

Child Support Agency (Dudley) v Truman ([2008] UKEAT/0293/08/CEA) was decided on the basis that the proper comparator for a disabled person who could only work from home due to disability was a person who could only work from home for other reasons. Since such a person would not have been treated any differently when the employer ceased to permit any employee to work from home there was no discrimination for a reason related to disability. It was common ground that Mrs Truman was a disabled person by reason of back problems – she had had three prolapsed discs removed. These prevented her from working on the employer's premises when her office moved, because of difficulties with access. However, the Employment Tribunal's conclusion that there was a failure to make reasonable adjustments was not appealed and so stood.

Again, this case might well be decided differently on the basis of indirect discrimination.

The issue of what constitutes unfavourable treatment was considered for the first time in the disability context in *Trustees of Swansea University Pension & Assurance Scheme v Williams* [2015] UKEAT/0415/14/DM. The Claimant worked for Swansea University as a laboratory technician, and was working half-time at the time he was granted ill-health retirement at the age of 38, on the basis that he was permanently unfit for work. He was entitled to a pension based on his continuing to work until his retirement age (under the pension scheme) of 67, and his salary as at the date of retirement. However, he argued that basing the pension on salary as at the date of retirement, rather than full-time salary, was unfavourable treatment arising from disability, since many disabled people would be unable to work full-time. This issue was considered on appeal by Langstaff J.

> One of the difficulties in dealing with cases of discrimination on the grounds of disability is that although every person who is treated as disabled by the Equality Act 2010 is defined as such by application of a common definition, the disabilities of each can be very different and may share few common features. An individual may be disabled physically, or mentally, from working or at work. Different faculties or functions may be affected, and to differing degrees. In the present case, the effect of the disabilities of some of those entitled to take ill-health retirement might permit retirement from work a very short time after first manifesting their disability; others with different disabilities might soldier on for some considerable period. The position of a person suffering from a stroke might differ significantly from that of a person with multiple sclerosis, and both of those from that of a person with a cancer: but all would undoubtedly be classed as 'disabled' for the purposes of the Equality Act [. . .]
>
> Accordingly, anyone who is permanently incapacitated so that they cannot work in the foreseeable future is disabled, whether or not the disability is brought about as a result of a slow and progressive process, by recognition of a continuing state of affairs which renders continued work untenable, or by reason of some sudden cataclysmic physical, neurological or mental event.
>
> It follows that those who are so significantly disabled as to be eligible for ill-health retirement under the terms of the scheme would be entitled to its benefits; and, conversely, no one would be entitled to the benefits of the scheme unless sufficiently seriously disabled. By comparison with any non-disabled person, a former employee having taken ill-health retirement would be treated favourably. To hold the opposite would be perverse. The scheme rules provided for this. In short, the scheme rules (taken overall) favoured those who were disabled. It could not be otherwise. It was obviously the intention in making them that they should do so [. . .]
>
> As to the reasoning by reference to other possible discrimination claims, the meaning of the word 'unfavourably' cannot, in my view, be equated with the concept of 'detriment' used elsewhere in the Equality Act 2010. The word 'unfavourably' is deliberately chosen. So, too, the choice not to use the word 'detriment' must be assumed to be deliberate: the draftsman would have been well aware of the use of the word 'detriment' elsewhere within the Equality Act, and avoided it. Nor, as the parties were agreed, does the word 'unfavourably' require a comparison with an identifiable comparator, whether actual or hypothetical, as would the description 'less favourable'. 'Less' invites evidence to be provided in proof of 'less than whom?'; 'un. . .' is by

contrast to be measured against an objective sense of that which is adverse as compared with that which is beneficial.

Section 15 as such was introduced into the Equality Act 2010 for the first time. The word 'unfavourably' is used elsewhere in the Act in respect of provisions which have a longer pedigree. Thus, in Section 18, a person is held to discriminate against a woman if in a protected period in relation to a pregnancy of hers that person treats her unfavourably because of the pregnancy or because of illness suffered by her as a result of it (section 18(2): see also sections 18(3) and (4)). In this use, it has the sense of placing a hurdle in front of, or creating a particular difficulty for, or disadvantaging a person because of something which arises in consequence of their disability. Since the word 'unfavourable' is the same word in section 15 as it is in section 18, in the same part of the same Act, it is likely that the draftsman had in mind that it would mean much the same in both.

I accept [Counsel for the Claimant's] submission that it is for a Tribunal to recognise when an individual has been treated unfavourably. It is impossible to be prescriptive of every circumstance in which that might occur. But it is, I think, not only possible but necessary to identify sufficiently those features which will be relevant in the assessment which this recognition necessarily involves. In my judgment, treatment which is advantageous cannot be said to be 'unfavourable' merely because it is thought it could have been more advantageous, or, put the other way around, because it is insufficiently advantageous. The determination of that which is unfavourable involves an assessment in which a broad view is to be taken and which is to be judged by broad experience of life. Persons may be said to have been treated unfavourably if they are not in as good a position as others generally would be. Sometimes this may be obvious: as for example, where a person may suffer a life event which would generally be regarded as adverse – taking the *Malcolm* case as an example, eviction; or being surcharged; being required to work harder, longer, or for less. . . . This approach is both consistent with and reflective of the sense in which 'unfavourably' is applied in a case coming within section 18.

Langstaff J concluded that the Tribunal had misconstrued the word 'unfavourable'. By definition, ill-health retirement under the pension scheme was only available to disabled persons. It was true that persons whose disability came on suddenly and who went straight from full-time work and full-time salary to retirement received a larger pension, and so were treated more favourably than those whose condition gradually worsened and had a period of part-time work and so part-time salary. That the latter group were treated less favourably than the former did not make their treatment 'unfavourable' for the purposes of s. 15. In any event, Langstaff J noted, the Claimant had gone part-time at his own request, as a reasonable adjustment to enable him to continue working. A reasonable adjustment could not at the same time be unfavourable treatment, and there was no duty to pay a person who worked part-time as a reasonable adjustment as if he was working full-time.

In *T-Systems Ltd v Lewis* [2015] UKEAT/0042/15/JOJ, Richardson J said that 'unfavourable treatment' was something said or done; it was not the mental process followed by the employer in making a decision. Here, therefore, the unfavourable treatment was the decision to dismiss the employee, not the factors taken into account in making the decision. Here, the Claimant was diabetic and the employer, which was implementing a new shift system, required a medical report that the Claimant was fit to work the new shift pattern. For a combination of reasons, the report did not arrive until after all the other employees affected were ready to work the new shifts. The Claimant refused to make a decision on whether to accept the new shifts or accept voluntary redundancy without the report. The employer lost patience and dismissed the Claimant. Although the Tribunal had been mistaken in their approach, the EAT upheld their conclusion that the

Claimant had been subjected to unfavourable treatment (dismissal) for a reason arising from the disability.

Warner v Armfield Retail & Leisure Ltd ([2013] UKEAT/0376/12/SM) was an unusual case in that the Tribunal accepted the employer's argument that the Claimant's contract had been frustrated by a long-term absence due to disability, and the EAT upheld that conclusion. Frustration (see Chapter 4) is a doctrine of ordinary contract law, applicable where something happens wholly outside the control of the parties to the contract, which renders performance of the contract either impossible or substantially different from that envisaged. A classic example in the employment sphere is found in *Morgan v Manser* [1948] 1 KB 184, where the parties concluded a contract specifying a ten-year fixed-term of employment, scant months before the Second World War broke out and the employee was called up into the army, in which he remained until 1946. In employment, frustration is, however, most frequently argued where the employee has been away from work for a lengthy period through illness.

In *Warner* the Claimant had a serious stroke on 12 February 2010. On 27 January 2011, almost a year later, the employer sent him a P45 and a letter stating that his employment was at an end. The Claimant argued, *inter alia*, disability-related discrimination and failure to make reasonable adjustments. It is important to note the nature of the employment; this was a small company with only four employees, two of whom, including the Claimant, were site managers, whose job involved long hours and frequent travel across a large part of Great Britain. An occupational health assessment in October 2011 found that his mobility, manual dexterity, memory and concentration were all substantially affected. Given the way in which the dismissal was handled, there seems to have been no consideration of reasonable adjustments, but, on the facts of the case, there were no possible reasonable adjustments which would have enabled the Claimant to continue working in that organisation. In turn, this meant that the Claimant's dismissal (as the termination of his employment was treated for the purpose of the Equality Act) was justified. As to frustration, the EAT concluded:

> In the case of a disabled person, before the doctrine of frustration can apply there is an additional factor which the Tribunal must consider over and above the factors already identified in the authorities – namely whether the employer is in breach of a duty to make reasonable adjustments. While there is something which . . . it is reasonable to expect the employer to have to do in order to keep the employee in employment, the doctrine of frustration can have no application. But where, as the Tribunal found in this case, there was no breach of the duty to make reasonable adjustments, the Tribunal was entitled to find that the contract was frustrated.

12.6.1 Causal link between disability and treatment

In *Summer Bridge Doors Ltd v Pickering* ([2003] EAT 1088/02) the EAT followed the approach used in the sex discrimination case of *O'Neill v Governors of St Thomas More RC School* [1996] (IRLR 372) (where the claimant was dismissed after becoming pregnant by the school's Catholic chaplain) in holding that a disability-related reason need not be the only reason for the less favourable treatment, provided it is an *effective* reason. Here the reason for the employer's refusal to allow the Applicant to return to work was that she had fallen down the stairs as the result of an unstable knee.

In *Murphy v Slough Borough Council* ([2004] EAT 1157/02) the link between the disability and the treatment was more subtle. The Claimant had a congenital heart condition which made pregnancy and giving birth highly dangerous. She and her husband therefore obtained a child by using a surrogate mother. It was held that the employer's refusal to allow her maternity leave, rather than the then shorter adoption leave, was because she had not borne the child herself, which was a reason related to her disability.

12.6.2 Justification of unfavourable treatment

A defence of justification is available to employers who have treated a disabled employee unfavourably for a reason arising from the disability (s. 15(1)(b)). This was originally contained in the DDA and is included in the Equality Act, although, arguably, the threshold is now higher, as the unfavourable treatment must be a proportionate means of achieving a legitimate aim. The inclusion of such a defence has been heavily criticised, but it can be argued that the provision was included in order to reflect practical realities, that a person's physical or mental condition may be incompatible with certain types of employment.

Prior to the Equality Act, case law showed that the issue of justification of less favourable treatment under the DDA was intimately related to the duty to make reasonable adjustments. Courts and tribunals took a narrow view of the defence of justification, and it would seem that only if there were no 'reasonable adjustments' which could be made to negate the effect of the disability, or if such adjustments had been tried or at least considered without success, would the defence be accepted. Whether this approach will continue under the Equality Act is unclear, but early signs suggest that this is the case.

Under the DDA, if there were no reasonable adjustments which could have been made and which would have prevented the less favourable treatment, then that treatment was justified. In *Kenny* for example, it was held not to be a reasonable adjustment to expect the employer to provide a carer, but the employer had not taken sufficient steps to establish whether the services of a carer could have been obtained from another source. Therefore, the defence was made out. In *Hay*, by contrast, the employer had offered reasonable adjustments – by agreeing to move the claimant to a static library where her disability would not affect her performance of her duties. When the claimant refused this solution, her dismissal was justified.

❖ THINKING POINT

What is the threshold of justification – at what level of expense, inconvenience, etc., to the employer, and burden to the disabled employee's colleagues, does unfavourable treatment become justified or the making of adjustments cease to be reasonable?

Warner v Armfield Retail & Leisure Ltd suggests that under the new law the Tribunal will continue to consider whether reasonable adjustments could have been made which would have prevented the unfavourable treatment.

Dominique v Toll Global Forwarding Ltd ([2014] UKEAT/0308/13/LA) is another recent case. The employee had worked for the employer and its predecessor companies in the charging department (dealing with incoming and outgoing bills) since 1979. In 2007 he had a stroke. It was common ground that he had residual physical disabilities, and the Tribunal accepted his evidence that there were also cognitive effects. In 2010 he was selected for redundancy on the basis that he had the lowest score in his department against a series of criteria which included accuracy, and willingness to help colleagues (something the employee was unable to do because of his physical disabilities). In particular, he made frequent mistakes and was unable to cope with a new computer system. He argued that a failure to exclude or modify these criteria represented a failure to make reasonable adjustments and disability-related discrimination. However, given the nature of the employer's business (a fairly small family-run company), and the employee's role, the Tribunal held that the selection system was justified, including the two criteria at issue. In any event, the EAT considered that modifying the criteria would not have prevented the employee's selection for redundancy.

More recently still, in *O'Brien v Bolton St Catherine's Academy* ([2017] EWCA Civ 145), the Court of Appeal ruled that the test of justification in respect of a disability-related dismissal is the same as that of reasonableness in unfair dismissal (see Chapter 9).

12.7 Indirect discrimination and disability

Once more, there is very little case law in this area; the great majority of disability discrimination cases involve failure to make reasonable adjustments and/or unfavourable treatment for a reason related to disability. It may be argued that the great majority of cases where indirect discrimination might be argued can be dealt with under disability-related discrimination, though there are exceptions. The obvious exception is where an employer has a policy of not paying sick pay to any employee, or as in *Truman*, a policy forbidding any employee from working from home. However, although case law under the DDA found that the treatment accorded to disabled claimants in such circumstances was not 'less favourable' under the *Malcolm* test, it is now highly likely to be held 'unfavourable'. Further, the employer may well be able to justify the absence of sick pay on the basis that it does not facilitate a return to work.

❖ THINKING POINT

Are there circumstances in which the employer could argue justification in respect of a refusal to allow employees to work from home?

12.8 Further reading

Busby, 'Case Comment: A small step or a giant leap? *Archibald v Fife Council*' (2005) 9(1) *Edinburgh Law Review* 133.

Johnstone, 'Duty to make adjustments where disability manifests itself in behaviour' (2010) 203 *Equal Opportunities Review* 31.

Lewis, 'Obesity and disability' (2015) Mar *Charity Finance* 14.

Maroto & Pettinicchio, 'The limitations of disability antidiscrimination legislation: policymaking and the economic well-being of people with disabilities' (2014) 36(4) *Law & Policy* 370.

Phillips, 'The Equality Act 2010: impact on mental health-related disability claims' (2012) 109(Jun) *Employment Law Bulletin* 2.

Chapter 13

Discrimination on the grounds of pregnancy and maternity

Chapter contents

13.1 Overview

This chapter looks at entitlement to maternity leave as the result of the birth of a child, to leave following adoption, and to paternity leave. It also considers the circumstances in which an employer will be held to discriminate against an employee on the grounds of pregnancy or the taking of such leave.

13.2 Introduction

'Pregnancy and maternity' are protected characteristics under the Equality Act 2010, but most of the legal protection in this area comes from other legislation, the Employment Rights Act 1996 and the Maternity and Parental Leave Regulations 1999, as amended.

Though pregnancy and giving birth are uniquely female conditions, the Sex Discrimination Act 1975 did not make specific provision for them. A woman claiming to have been discriminated on the grounds of pregnancy, giving birth, or having recently given birth, had therefore to rely on the ordinary law relating to direct or indirect discrimination, or victimisation (there was at that time no specific legislation covering harassment). An employee who had accumulated the required period of continuous employment could also argue unfair dismissal if dismissed because of absence caused by pregnancy or childbirth, but no successful actions appear to have been reported.

The EEC Equal Treatment Directive 1976 (Council Directive 76/207/EEC) required EEC member states to give effect to the principle of equal treatment between men and women in employment, and came into effect in August 1978. From this date, under the ordinary principles of enforcement of EU law in the English courts, its provisions became enforceable by employees of 'state bodies', though not by employees in the private sector. However, no statutory provision was made in the United Kingdom for maternity leave until as late as 1993. In the interim, a number of cases established that a woman dismissed because of pregnancy was most unlikely to succeed in an action under the Sex Discrimination Act.

In *Turley v Allders Department Stores Ltd* ([1980] ICR 66) the EAT rejected the Claimant's argument of direct discrimination on the very straightforward basis that no comparison was possible between the treatment of a pregnant woman and any man. In *Hayes v Malleable Working Men's Club and Institute* ([1985] IRLR 367) the EAT altered their approach by finding that the proper comparator for a pregnant woman should be a man absent from work for the same period through illness, which, in practical terms, opened the possibility to a successful claim. However, it then became necessary for a Claimant to persuade a tribunal that such a man would not have been dismissed or subjected to other less favourable treatment, which would be unusual. This approach was criticised in many quarters for the following reasons:[1]

a) Pregnancy is not an illness, but 'a normal, natural and necessary event which should be celebrated'. To treat it as an illness is demeaning to women.
b) The amount of time off resulting from a typical pregnancy, both before and after the birth, is far longer than the majority of periods of sickness, and raises the possibility, even the likelihood, that a man absent for such a period would also be dismissed.
c) This approach meant that pregnant women must not be treated worse than sick men. If a sick man with the same length of service would also be dismissed, there was no discrimination. Alternatively, if an employer did not pay women while absent because of pregnancy, there would be no discrimination if he did not pay sick pay to men.

---

1 See e.g. Connelly, *Townshend-Smith on Discrimination Law: Text, Cases and Materials*, 2nd edn 2004, p. 197.

d) In workplaces with few male employees, or an absence of formal personnel policies, it might be impossible in practice to rebut an employer's argument that the hypothetical sick man would have been treated in exactly the same way.

These criticisms can themselves be criticised, not least because pregnancy and childbearing, unlike most illness or injury, are ultimately a matter of choice rather than circumstances forced on the employee.

❖ THINKING POINT

Is it fair to treat a person who is absent from work for a lengthy period for reasons of her own choosing, which are not available to members of the other sex, better than a person absent as the result of, say, a broken leg? Could it be argued that there are public policy reasons in operation? If so, what are they?

It was not until 1991 that the position began to change, as the result of the ECJ case of *Dekker v Stichting Vormingscentrum voor Jonge Volwassen Plus* (Case C-177/88 [1991] IRLR 27). A Dutch woman applied for a job while pregnant, and was refused employment on the grounds that the employer could not afford to pay her while absent and at the same time pay her replacement. This was because their insurance policy would not cover the cost of her pay as her absence would be due to 'foreseeable incapacity'. The ECJ held that refusal of employment on grounds of pregnancy is direct discrimination on grounds of sex.

> As employment can only be refused on grounds of pregnancy to women, such a refusal is direct discrimination on grounds of sex. A refusal to employ because of the financial consequences of absence connected with pregnancy must be deemed to be based primarily on the fact of pregnancy. Such discrimination cannot be justified by the financial detriment in the case of recruitment of a pregnant woman suffered by the employer during her maternity leave [. . .]
>
> An employer is acting in direct contravention of the principle of equal treatment . . . if he refuses to enter into a contract of employment with a female applicant found suitable by him for the post in question, where such refusal is on the ground of the possible adverse consequences . . . arising from employing a woman who is pregnant at the time of the application, because of a government regulation . . . which treats inability to work because of pregnancy and confinement in the same way as inability to work because of illness [. . .]
>
> The answer to the question of whether the refusal to recruit a woman constitutes direct or indirect discrimination depends on the motive for such a refusal. If this motive resides in the fact that the person concerned is pregnant, this decision is directly related to the applicant's sex. . . . It is of no importance that there were no male applicants [. . .]
>
> The Directive does not make the liability of the discriminator in any way dependent on the evidence of fault or the absence of any grounds of legal justification. . . . A contravention of the prohibition of discrimination in itself should be sufficient in order for full liability of the discriminator to arise. No grounds for justification existing in national law can be accepted.

❖ THINKING POINT

Does this not place an unrealistic burden on employers, given that they may be required to take on an individual who, within a short time of starting work, may be away for a year? Would an employer be expected to take on any other person who intends almost immediately to be away for a lengthy period?

Following *Dekker* and the House of Lords decision in *Webb v EMO Air Cargo* ([1992] UKHL 13), the Employment Rights Act 1996 s. 99(1) gave the Secretary of State the right to make regulations on entitlement to maternity leave, and provided protection against dismissal on grounds of pregnancy, childbirth or taking maternity leave. Such dismissal is an 'automatic' unfair dismissal, with no requirement for a prior period of continuous employment. All the claimant must demonstrate is the causal link between the dismissal and the pregnancy, childbirth or maternity leave. Initially, maternity leave was only available to those who had two years' continuous employment, but since then has been gradually extended. The current provisions are found in the Maternity and Parental Leave Regulations 1999 (SI 1999/3312) as amended.[2]

S. 99 Leave for family reasons.

(1) An employee who is dismissed shall be regarded for the purposes of this Part as unfairly dismissed if—
   (a) the reason or principal reason for the dismissal is of a prescribed kind, or
   (b) the dismissal takes place in prescribed circumstances.

(2) In this section 'prescribed' means prescribed by regulations made by the Secretary of State.

(3) A reason or set of circumstances prescribed under this section must relate to—
   (a) pregnancy, childbirth or maternity,
   (b) ordinary, compulsory or additional maternity leave.

(4) A reason or set of circumstances prescribed under subsection (1) satisfies subsection (3)(c) or (d) if it relates to action which an employee—
   (a) takes,
   (b) agrees to take, or
   (c) refuses to take,
   under or in respect of a collective or workforce agreement which deals with parental leave.

The main issue in this area is establishing the causal link between the pregnancy or childbirth and the dismissal, given that the employer is not precluded from dismissing a pregnant employee for some other reason. The most obvious alternative reason is redundancy, but misconduct or incapability may also be argued from time to time. Case law establishes that the dismissal will be automatically unfair if the pregnancy is a significant factor in the decision to dismiss.

In *O'Neill v Governors of St Thomas More School and Bedfordshire CC* ([1996] IRLR 372, EAT), the claimant was a teacher of religious education at a Catholic school, and expected to provide a moral example

2 By the Maternity and Parental Leave (Amendment) Regulations 2002 (SI 2002/2789) and the Maternity and Paternity and Adoption Leave (Amendment) Regulations 2006 (SI 2006/2041).

to her pupils. She became pregnant in the course of an affair with a Catholic priest. The Tribunal concluded that the primary reason for the dismissal was not the pregnancy but the immorality, but their decision was reversed by the EAT. According to Mummery LJ:

> [Following *Webb (No.2)*] the Appellant's claim is not . . . to be determined by a comparison of her treatment with the treatment of a hypothetical male comparator proposed by the governors as a male teacher of RE [Religious Education] who had fathered a child by a Roman Catholic nun and where there had been press publicity about this relationship. Such a comparison is not legally appropriate under the interpretation of the 1975 Act in the light of the ruling of the ECJ [in *Webb*]. Pregnant women in employment occupy a special position which attracts special protection[. . .]
>
> The basic question is what, out of a whole complex of facts before the Tribunal, is the 'effective and predominant' cause or the 'real and efficient' cause of the act complained of? . . . The event or factor alleged to be causative of the matter complained of need not be the only or even the main cause of the result complained of (though it must be more than just the occasion for the result complained of)[. . .]
>
> In our view, the distinction made by the Tribunal between pregnancy *per se* and pregnancy in the circumstances of this case is legally erroneous. . . . The concept of 'pregnancy *per se*' is misleading, because it suggests pregnancy as the sole ground of dismissal. Pregnancy always has surrounding circumstances, some arising prior to the state of pregnancy, some accompanying it, some consequential on it. The critical question is whether, on an objective consideration of all the surrounding circumstances, the dismissal or other treatment complained of . . . is on the ground of pregnancy. It need not be only on that ground. It need not even be mainly on that ground. Thus, the fact that the employer's ground for dismissal is that the pregnant woman will become unavailable for work because of her pregnancy does not make it any the less a dismissal on the ground of pregnancy . . . In the present case, the other factors in the circumstances surrounding the pregnancy . . . are all causally related to the fact that the applicant was pregnant – the paternity of the child, the publicity of that fact and the consequent untenability of the applicant's position. . . . Her pregnancy precipitated and permeated the decision to dismiss her.

❖ THINKING POINT

Is Mummery LJ being over-simplistic? Would this dismissal have occurred if either:

- Ms O'Neill had been a married woman and pregnant by her husband?
- If the fact of the affair with a priest had become known, without the pregnancy?

In 2005, s. 3A was inserted into the Sex Discrimination Act specifically to cover direct discrimination on grounds of pregnancy, and pregnancy and the taking of maternity leave are now specifically included in the Equality Act as protected characteristics.

Importantly, there can be no discrimination on grounds of pregnancy if the employer is unaware of the pregnancy, as established in *Ramdoolar v Bycity Ltd* [2005] ICR 368, where the dismissal of a pregnant woman for poor performance at work was held not to be automatically unfair because the employer did not know of the pregnancy.

Equality Act s. 18 provides that a woman may not be treated *unfavourably* because of pregnancy or because of illness resulting from pregnancy, during a 'protected period' which begins at the outset of the pregnancy and ends at the end of additional maternity leave or, if the woman returns to work at an earlier date, when she returns to work.

The employer's responsibility towards a pregnant employee begins when he is informed of the pregnancy, although the definition of the protected period creates a potential retrospective liability for unfavourable treatment (there is as yet no case law dealing with this). By ERA s. 55 a pregnant woman is entitled not to be unreasonably refused time off for ante-natal appointments, and is entitled to be paid for that time off. This begs two questions. First, what constitutes an unreasonable refusal – for example, is the employer entitled to expect a woman who works part-time to arrange her ante-natal appointments for times when she will not be working in any event? Second, what is the scope of 'ante-natal appointments'? Do they, for example, include relaxation classes?

In some types of employment, the employer may be required to suspend a pregnant employee from work. ERA s. 66 is applicable where, because of pregnancy, a woman cannot safely continue with her existing job, most obviously where the job involves exposure to ionising radiation such as x-rays. If allowing the woman to continue to work would involve contravention of either:

- any statutory requirement; or
- any recommendation contained in a Code of Practice issued under the Health & Safety at Work Act 1974,

and there is no suitable alternative work (s. 67) available the employer should suspend the employee from work.

During such a suspension, the employee is entitled to be paid.

The employer is also required to carry out a risk assessment in relation to a pregnant employee (which may be individual or generic), and the conclusions must be communicated to the employee concerned (see e.g. *Stevenson v JM Skinner & Co* [2008] UKEAT/0584/07/DA0). It may be noted that in that case the employer had acted within s. 66 in suspending a pregnant employee after she injured herself falling down the stairs during a dizzy spell, and the layout of the building made it impossible for her to continue working safely.

13.3 Entitlement to maternity leave

The right to maternity leave only applies to employees, though pregnant women who are not employees (including workers and the self-employed) are protected from discrimination by Equality Act 2010 s. 18. Only a woman who bears a child is entitled to maternity leave, though a person (male or female) who legally adopts a child is entitled to adoption leave of the same duration (see below). There is now no qualifying period of continuous employment, although the woman must meet the notice requirements set out in reg. 4(1).

An employee who gives birth to a child is entitled to a total of one year's maternity leave, without any requirement for a qualifying period of continuous employment. This entitlement falls into three parts:

- compulsory maternity leave;
- ordinary maternity leave;
- additional maternity leave.

As maternity leave is only available to women who give birth, and adoption leave to those with whom a child is 'placed for adoption' there is currently a gap in provision where children are produced via surrogacy arrangements. The Human Fertilisation and Embryology Act 1990, as amended, provides that the woman who bears the child is the legal parent, along with any partner she has, but enables the 'commissioning parents' to obtain a parental order transferring legal parenthood to themselves within the first six months after the child's birth, provided one of them is genetically related to the child, i.e. provided the egg or sperm. If the commissioning parents and the child are not genetically related, then an adoption order is required. An adoption order is only available if a registered adoption agency (such as a local authority) is used. In the case of births since 5 April 2015 commissioning parents who intend to seek a parental order, or who obtain an adoption order in respect of a child obtained through surrogacy are entitled to adoption leave and pay, but there is a clear gap in the law where neither applies. Note that both types of order require the consent of the 'host mother' and any other person who has parental responsibility for the child.

Although the purpose of maternity leave is to enable the mother to spend time with the child, she remains entitled to full maternity leave if the child dies during the maternity leave period, and even if the child is stillborn, as 'childbirth' is defined as the birth of a living child or the birth of a child whether living or dead at any time after 24 weeks of pregnancy (ERA s. 235(1)). Nor is there any requirement for the mother actually to bring up the child herself.

13.3.1 Compulsory maternity leave

This is dealt with by ERA s. 72, and begins at the child's birth. An employer is required to prohibit a woman from returning to work for a period of two weeks beginning with the day of childbirth. Breach of this requirement is a criminal offence, punishable by a fine not exceeding £500, though the mother commits no offence. Compulsory maternity leave normally forms part of ordinary maternity leave.

The requirement for compulsory maternity leave has been criticised in some quarters, where it is argued that it should be for the mother herself to decide how soon to return to work after giving birth.

13.3.2 Ordinary maternity leave

S. 71 as amended.

This lasts for 26 weeks and may begin not earlier than the beginning of the 11th week before the estimated week of childbirth (unless the baby is born earlier) and not later than the actual birth of the child.

In order to take ordinary maternity leave, the woman must notify the employer of the following, not later than the end of the 15th week before the expected week of childbirth, or as soon as reasonably practicable:

- her pregnancy;
- the estimated week of childbirth; and
- the date on which she intends to start maternity leave (in writing if the employer so requests).

If the employer so requests, she must provide him with a certificate from a registered medical practitioner or midwife stating the estimated week of childbirth.

Case law shows that it will not be reasonably practicable to give notice by the end of the 15th week before the expected week of childbirth if the mother does not realise she is pregnant until after that time, but the test is likely to be difficult to satisfy in other circumstances.

The employee need not give notice of her intention to take additional maternity leave at this stage.

Having given the necessary notice, the woman is then free to begin her maternity leave at any time from the 11th week before the estimated week of childbirth up to the birth itself. However, under reg. 6(1), if she is absent from work wholly or partly because of pregnancy in the four weeks before the estimated week of childbirth she must start her maternity leave at that point. In that case, she must notify the employer as soon as reasonably practicable (reg. 4(3)). Similarly, the birth of the child before the estimated week of childbirth automatically triggers the start of maternity leave, and again the woman must notify the employer of the position as soon as reasonably practicable (reg. 4(4)).

Within 28 days of receiving the employee's notice of when ordinary maternity leave will start or has started, the employer must inform her of when her additional maternity leave will end (i.e. when her total entitlement to maternity leave runs out).

❖ EXAMPLE

Christine became pregnant last summer and gave the employer notice on 2 October that the expected week of childbirth was the week beginning 28 January, and that she intended to go on maternity leave as from 2 January. However, a surfeit of Christmas shopping and parties brought on premature labour, and the baby was born on Christmas Eve (24 December). Christine informed the employer as soon as the office reopened on 2 January, and later in January the employer wrote to her stating that her additional maternity leave would end on 23 December.

During ordinary maternity leave:

- the employment contract continues to subsist and the employee's continuous employment continues to accrue;
- the employee is bound by any obligations arising out of her employment, other than those inconsistent with being on maternity leave, such as the duty to be available for work. Thus, for example, she is bound by any duty of confidence;
- the employee is entitled to receive all contractual and non-contractual benefits except remuneration (defined in reg. 9 as 'sums payable to the employee by way of wages or salary'), so that she retains any benefits in kind such as private medical insurance, but is not entitled to be paid unless the employer's maternity leave scheme provides otherwise;
- statutory and contractual leave accrues during this period.

The effect of the provisions about remuneration can be seen in *Hoyland v Asda Stores* [2006] IRLR 468, where the employer operated a bonus scheme for employees. In practice, an annual bonus was, according to a set formula, to all employees with 12 months' continuous employment who were employed on the specified date. Where an employee was absent for more than eight weeks in one year, the bonus was paid on a pro rata basis. The employee was absent on maternity leave for six months and her bonus was reduced accordingly. The EAT held that the bonus fell within reg. 9 and so was not required to be paid, and also within a similar provision in SDA s. 6(6). The Scottish Court of Session upheld the decision but said that claims of this nature might be brought on the basis of the equality clause implied into all employment contracts by Equal Pay Act 1970 s. 1(2)(e), by virtue of which a bonus may be apportioned to take account of maternity leave other than compulsory maternity leave. The point was not argued, and on the facts, the bonus had been apportioned, so there was no breach of s. 1(2)(e), though on different facts there might be scope for disputing the apportionment.

Entitlement to non-cash benefits while on maternity leave was recently considered in *Peninsula Business Services Ltd v Donaldson* ([2016] UKEAT/0249/15/DM). The employer provided only statutory maternity pay to employees on maternity leave, but gave employees the opportunity to receive childcare vouchers under a salary sacrifice scheme. Such schemes involve the provision of a benefit in kind in return for a reduction in basic salary, and are beneficial to employees because they are not liable for tax or national insurance on the cash value of the benefit. They are also beneficial to the employer, who does not have to pay employers' national insurance contributions on the value of the benefit. The employer had a policy of suspending entitlement to the vouchers during maternity leave, and refused the Claimant's application to join the scheme when she was pregnant with her second child, as she would not agree that the provision of vouchers would be suspended during her forthcoming maternity leave. The issue for the EAT was whether the vouchers came within the meaning of 'remuneration'; if so, the employer was entitled not to provide them during maternity leave, though the Claimant could still argue that she was being directly discriminated against on grounds of pregnancy under Equality Act 2010 s. 18, and/or the employer was failing to give effect to the equality clause implied into all employment contracts by Equality Act s. 66.

The EAT faced a complex array of statutory provisions, and ruled first that the Equality Act contained two distinct strands of provisions covering sex discrimination. Discrimination in relation to terms and conditions of employment, not limited to pay, was initially dealt with by the Equal Pay Act, other forms of discrimination – 'detrimental acts' – by the Sex Discrimination Act 1975 s. 6. In respect of the latter, the Equality Act specifically excludes the possibility of a claim for indirect discrimination based on pregnancy (s. 19(3)). S. 70 also excludes the possibility of an indirect discrimination claim based on pregnancy in relation to terms and conditions. The EAT doubted whether direct discrimination under the 2010 Act was applicable, but proceeded on the basis that it was, along with the provisions of ERA s. 71 and the 1999 Regulations reg. 9.

Reg. 9 provides:

9. — (1) An employee who takes ordinary maternity leave—

(a) is entitled, during the period of leave, to the benefit of all of the terms and conditions of employment which would have applied if she had not been absent, and

(b) is bound, during that period, by any obligations arising under those terms and conditions, subject only to the exception in section 71(4)(b) of the 1996 Act.

(2) In paragraph (1)(a), 'terms and conditions' has the meaning given by section 71(5) of the 1996 Act, and accordingly does not include terms and conditions about remuneration.

(3) For the purposes of section 71 of the 1996 Act, only sums payable to an employee by way of wages or salary are to be treated as remuneration.

The EAT concluded that vouchers provided via a salary sacrifice scheme were 'remuneration' and so were within the scope of reg. 9(2)(3). The employer was therefore not acting unlawfully in refusing to provide them during maternity leave, although if he had been providing vouchers in addition to salary, he would have been required under reg. 9(1) to continue to do so. In the opinion of the EAT, there were strong public policy reasons for adopting this interpretation.

> Though the phrase [salary sacrifice] is in common use, and is referred to by that colloquial description in the legislation . . . it is something of a misnomer. It is in reality not a sacrifice but a diversion of salary, which the employee has earned but which is redirected prior to it being placed within the employee's pay packet, in order to purchase vouchers to the value of the salary utilised.
>
> This view is critical. It means that we accept that the voucher is properly to be regarded as part of remuneration. The fact that it is deemed to be a 'non-cash benefit' by the taxing

statutes for the purposes of personal taxation does not deprive it of this character. The question is factual, and not to be determined by labels adopted for other purposes. The sum by which the voucher is purchased is that which is payable to the employee: for the purpose of the purchase it is diverted. If the consequence were not beneficial tax treatment, the position would be obvious: if an employee invited an employer to make a direct payment on her behalf, and to deduct the sum paid from his monthly salary, no one would suggest that the payment was anything other than part of her remuneration. If it were used to purchase goods, it would not be regarded as arranging for a payment in kind (i.e. those goods) to be made by her employer to her.

The consequence of holding otherwise produces consequences which we do not think could have been contemplated in the legislature. The law takes steps to permit the payment of lower sums by way of salary to those on maternity leave. It is not discrimination, nor contrary to the 1999 Regulations, to do so. The employee receiving a salary without entering a sacrifice scheme is not entitled by law to receive any more than legislation requires as a minimum. If that employee previously paid for childcare out of that salary, she would have no more money than if she did not. Where, instead, the same money (overall) is used by arrangement with the employee to pay for childcare without the cost of it forming part of her pay packet, it is difficult to see why in principle she should be entitled not only to the minimum for which statute provides but also for the amount spent on childcare in addition. The tax benefit disappears: but this is a benefit which only applies as a consequence of being in receipt of the higher salary to which the Claimant is no longer entitled.

The Lay Members point out that to require the continued provision of vouchers during maternity leave both produces a windfall benefit for a Claimant who is in such a scheme but also – more importantly – imposes a cost upon the employer. The policy behind the provision of childcare vouchers through a salary sacrifice recognised in the taxing statutes as entitling the maker of it to favourable tax treatment is to enable more women with young children to remain in or return to the workplace. This is a real benefit economically to the employer, who then has a wider range of skilled and valuable workers from which to choose, as well as a real benefit to employees by alleviating to some extent the costs of remaining in work. It incentivises women to remain at work; and therefore is overall of economic benefit to the country. But the scheme is entirely voluntary on the employer's part. If entering such a scheme had the consequence that once employees became pregnant the employer would face a cost beyond that it would already face by provision of statutory maternity pay, it would have the effect of discouraging employers from offering such a scheme. This is particularly acute where small and medium enterprises are concerned. Both Lay Members, from their different perspectives, regard such a consequence as very damaging to a valuable policy. We do not think that Parliament can have intended this consequence.

A woman who takes ordinary maternity leave is entitled to return to the job in which she was employed before her absence with all seniority and pension rights as they would have been had she not been absent.

Until 1 April 2007 an employee automatically brought her maternity leave to an end if she returned to work before it expired. However, reg. 12A now allows the employer and employee to agree that she should work for a maximum of ten days during the total period of maternity leave without bringing that leave to an end. 'Work' for this purposes includes training and any other activity undertaken in order to enable the employee to keep in touch with the workplace (often referred to as 'keeping in touch days'). Any such work may be undertaken solely by agreement and those ten days do not extend the maternity leave period.

13.3.3 Additional maternity leave

S. 73 as amended.

Unless the employee chooses to return to work at the end of her ordinary maternity leave, additional maternity leave begins automatically, without any need for notice, and continues for up to 26 weeks. Until 2008 a woman's entitlements during additional maternity leave were much more limited than during ordinary maternity leave, but that is now no longer the case, and there is in practice no difference between the two.

13.3.4 Returning to work after maternity leave

The employee does not need to give any notice if she simply intends to return at the end of her additional maternity leave. However, if she chooses to return earlier – for example, at the end of her ordinary maternity leave, or part way through either ordinary or additional maternity leave – she must give the employer eight weeks' notice of the date on which she intends to return. If she gives less than this minimum, the employer is entitled to postpone her return to a date which ensures he gains eight weeks' notice. This provision was included in the legislation in order to make it easier for employers to plan for her absence.

The employee's statutory entitlement is to return to the job in which she was employed before her absence, or, if this is not reasonably practicable for a reason other than redundancy, to a suitable and appropriate job:

- on no less favourable terms and conditions as to remuneration than those applicable had she not been absent; and
- with seniority, pension and similar rights preserved as they would have been had the period of employment prior to additional maternity leave been continuous.

'Job' is defined as the nature of the work which the employee is employed to do in accordance with her contract and the capacity and place in which she is employed (MPLR 1999 reg. 2(1)).

The exact nature of this entitlement was considered in *Blundell v Governing Body of St Andrew's Catholic Primary School* (UKEAT/0529/06). The Claimant was a primary school teacher and, in common with most teachers at the school and other primary schools, class teacher for a particular class. She claimed that requiring her to be class teacher for a different class on her return was in breach of her right to return to the same 'job'. The EAT found against her, ruling that she was entitled to return to the job of class teacher, but not necessarily in the same class, and were influenced by the fact that the school had an established practice of moving teachers between classes at the start of a school year.

If, for a reason other than redundancy, it is impracticable for the employee to return to the same job as previously (for example, there has been a business reorganisation during her absence), the terms and conditions of the new job must not be less favourable than the old. The DTI Guidance states that an employee who refuses an offer of a suitable job under this head will have 'effectively resigned'. However, she may argue unfair dismissal and/or sex discrimination on the basis that the offer is not suitable. There is a great deal of case law both in this area and in relation to redundancy.

At present, there is no specific right to return under different terms and conditions – for example, choosing to work part-time. However, the employee has the right to request flexible working patterns (see below), and she may be able to argue that a failure to allow her to work part-time constitutes indirect sex discrimination.

13.3.5 Failure to return to work at the end of additional maternity leave

Failure to return does not of itself terminate the employment contract. Whether it does so is dependent on the *employee's* intention. Case law establishes that the employer should take steps to establish the reason for the failure to return and whether the employee intends to return (*Rashid v Asian Community Care Services Ltd* (EAT 480/99). Failure to treat the employee in the same way as any other person returning late from leave or sickness could potentially give rise to an indirect discrimination claim, or unfair dismissal.

If, however, the employee fails to return due to sickness, the DTI Guidance states that she should be treated in the same way as any other sick employee. This is in accordance with ECJ case law, which does not provide special protection in relation to illness resulting from childbirth or maternity leave.

Note that the employee continues to accrue statutory and contractual leave while on maternity leave, and there is nothing to prevent her from taking some or all of it at the end of her maternity leave and before returning to work.

❖ THINKING POINT

Rose gave birth to her first child, John, on 12 September, and went on maternity leave from that date. Having been erroneously informed that she could not get pregnant while breast feeding, Rose and her husband dispensed with contraception. Their second son, James, was born on 10 September the following year, just before Rose's maternity leave was due to end. Is Rose entitled to take a second period of maternity leave without returning to work in between? If so, what procedural requirements must be observed?

Would your answer be any different if Rose had, in fact, begun her maternity leave a month before John's birth and returned to work briefly before James's arrival?

13.3.6 Redundancy during maternity leave

MPLA reg. 10 and reg. 20.

If, by reason of redundancy, it is not practicable for the employer to continue to employ the employee under her existing contract on her return from maternity leave, she must be offered a suitable alternative vacancy before the contract ends, provided such a vacancy exists. The new contract must be such that:

- the kind of work to be done is suitable for the employee and appropriate for her to do in the circumstances; and
- the provisions as to the capacity and place the woman is employed, and other terms and conditions of employment, are not substantially less favourable than the previous terms and conditions of her employment.

Reg. 10(2) provides:

> (2) Where there is a suitable available vacancy, the employee is entitled to be offered (before the end of her employment under her existing contract) alternative employment with her employer or his successor, or an associated employer, under a new contract of employment

which (. . . takes effect immediately on the ending of her employment under the previous contract).

If this provision is not complied with, the dismissal will be automatically unfair (MPLR 1999 reg. 20).

Reg. 10(2) raises the issue of when the duty to offer the vacancy takes effect. Is it applicable when the individual's job has been identified as redundant and redeployment is being considered, or only when she has actually been put under notice of redundancy? This was the issue in *Sefton Borough Council v Wainwright* [2014] UKEAT/0168/14/LA. In February 2011 the employer began a restructuring process in order to make financial savings. In June 2012, they concluded that Mrs Wainwright's post was redundant, along with a similar post held by a Mr Pierce, shortly before she went on her third period of maternity leave. On 26 July, both Mrs Wainwright, by then on maternity leave, and Mr Pierce, were informed that they were at risk of redundancy. A new post was created, for which both were considered suitable. The employer stated that, had Mrs Wainwright been the only candidate, she would have been offered the new post. As there were two well-qualified candidates, the employer felt it necessary to carry out a competitive process, including interviews, which concluded that Mr Pierce was the better-fitted to the job. When Mrs Wainwright brought a claim on the basis of reg. 10, the employer argued that the duty had only arisen *after* the post created in the restructuring had been offered to Mr Pierce, and Mrs Wainwright had been given notice of her redundancy. The EAT upheld the Tribunal's conclusion that to accept the employer's approach weakened the protection accorded by reg. 10, as employers could state that there was only a redundancy after others had been 'redeployed' into what might otherwise have been suitable available vacancies.

If the woman is redundant and no suitable alternative vacancy exists, she is entitled to a redundancy payment in the normal way.

13.3.7 Detriment short of dismissal

S. 47C, MPLR 1999, reg. 19.

An employee is entitled not to be subjected to any detriment by her employer because she:

- is pregnant;
- has given birth to a child and is on maternity leave;
- is on maternity suspension. i.e. forbidden to work;
- took or availed herself of the benefits of ordinary maternity leave;
- took or sought to take additional maternity leave;
- failed to return after additional maternity leave, in circumstances where either:
  - o the employer did not give her notice of the date on which the additional maternity leave would end and she reasonably believed that it had not ended; or
  - o the employer gave fewer than 28 days' notice of the end of her additional maternity leave and it was not reasonably practicable for her to return on the date given;
- undertook, considered undertaking or refused to undertake work during maternity leave in accordance with reg. 12A (the 'keeping in touch' provisions).

13.3.8 Automatic unfair dismissal

S. 99 as amended.

A dismissal is automatically unfair if the reason, or principal reason, is connected with the fact that the employee:

- is pregnant;
- has given birth to a child and is on maternity leave;
- is on maternity suspension;
- took or availed herself of the benefits of ordinary maternity leave;
- took or sought to take additional maternity leave;
- failed to return after additional maternity leave, in circumstances where either:
  - the employer did not give her notice of the date on which the additional maternity leave would end and she reasonably believed that it had not ended; or
  - the employer gave fewer than 28 days' notice of the end of her additional maternity leave and it was not reasonably practicable for her to return on the date given;
- undertook, considered undertaking or refused to undertake work during maternity leave in accordance with reg.12A (the 'keeping in touch' provisions).

Ramdoolar v Bycity Ltd (EAT/0236/04) makes it clear that the employer must know or believe that the employee is pregnant before he can be liable for automatic unfair dismissal on grounds of pregnancy. This cancels the suggestion made *obiter* in the Disability Discrimination Act case of *Heinz (HJ) Co v Kenrick* [2000] IRLR 144, that it was enough that the reason for dismissal was objectively connected with the fact of pregnancy, i.e. if the employee was sacked for repeatedly fainting at work, where the fainting was caused by the pregnancy.

Protection from dismissal for taking maternity leave only applies during the maternity leave. The point has yet to be tested, but presumably a woman who is dismissed for a failure to return at the end of maternity leave for a non-childbirth-related reason will not be automatically unfairly dismissed, though she may still argue unfair dismissal under the general law.

In *Visa International Service Organisation v Paul* [2004] IRLR 42 the EAT concluded that the employer's failure to keep the claimant informed of opportunities in her department while she was on maternity leave constituted a breach of the duty of trust and confidence, so that when she resigned during the maternity leave it was a constructive dismissal, and automatically unfair since it was for a reason connected with maternity leave.

Under ERA s. 92(4) a woman dismissed during pregnancy or maternity leave is entitled to written reasons for dismissal without the need to request them. This does not apply to other employees.

13.4 Maternity pay

The ECJ ruled in *Gillespie v Northern Health & Social Services Board* [1996] IRLR 214 that nothing in EU equal pay law requires an employer to pay an employee her normal pay while on maternity leave. All that is necessary is that she receive an amount which is adequate and not so low as to jeopardise the general purpose of maternity leave. On this basis, the employer is required only to pay Statutory Maternity Pay unless the employee's contract provides otherwise.

DWP v Sutcliffe [2007] UK/EAT/0319/07/ZT establishes that a person is not entitled to Statutory Sick Pay while on maternity leave.

An employee who has been continuously employed for 26 weeks before the expected week of childbirth and earning not less than the lower earnings limit for national insurance contributions is entitled to Statutory Maternity Pay.

Statutory Maternity Pay is paid for a maximum of 39 weeks at the following rates:

- 90 per cent of salary for the first six weeks;
- £145.18 (2018–2019 figure) for the remaining 33 weeks (or 90 per cent of the employee's average earnings if less).

A woman who does not qualify for Statutory Maternity Pay may qualify for Maternity Allowance, which is paid by the Department of Work and Pensions at a rate of £145.18 per week or 90 per cent of weekly earnings if lower. This is available provided the woman has worked on an employed or self-employed basis at any time in the 15 months before the expected week of childbirth.

13.5 Adoption leave and adoption pay

This is dealt with in the Paternity and Adoption Leave Regulations 2002, as amended. Rights to adoption leave and adoption pay are broadly similar to maternity rights though not identical. In particular:

- there is a qualifying period of continuous employment before a person becomes entitled to adoption leave;
- while maternity leave is only available to mothers, i.e. the persons who physically bear children, adoption leave is available to adoptive fathers, though where the child is adopted jointly by a couple, only one may take adoption leave. Note that at present those women who acquire children via surrogacy arrangements are not entitled to maternity leave as such. They, or their husband or other partner are entitled to adoption leave if they have obtained, or intend to obtain, a parental order (if one or other is genetically related to the child) or an adoption order (if neither is genetically related to the child). An adoption order can only be sought through a registered adoption agency (usually a local authority).

13.5.1 Adoption leave

13.5.1.1 Ordinary adoption leave

An employee who is the 'adopter' of a child is entitled to take up to 26 weeks' ordinary adoption leave provided the following conditions are satisfied:

- an 'adopter' is defined in reg. 2(1) as a person who has been matched with a child for adoption, or, where two people have been matched with the child, the person who elects to be the adopter for adoption leave purposes. Reg. 2(4) provides that an employee is matched with a child for adoption when an adoption agency (usually a local authority) decides that the person would be a suitable adoptive parent for *that* child (whether individually or jointly);
- the adopter must have 26 weeks' continuous employment;
- the adopter must have notified the agency that he agrees to adopt the child and has agreed the date of placement;
- the adopter must have complied with the notice provisions in reg. 17.

Reg. 17(1) provides that the adopter must inform his employer of the following no later than seven days after he is informed that he has been matched for adoption, in writing if the employer requests:

- the date the child is expected to be placed;
- the date the adopter intends to begin adoption leave;
- if requested, evidence from the adoption agency of entitlement to adoption leave.

An employee may vary the date he intends to begin ordinary adoption leave in the same way that a pregnant employee can vary the date she intends to begin ordinary maternity leave. However, given that a child cannot be matched for adoption until it has been born, nor, in the case of surrogacy, can a parental order be made until after the birth, it follows that adoption leave, unlike maternity leave, cannot begin before the child's birth.

Having received the necessary notice from the adopter, the employer must inform him of the date his additional adoption leave will end.

The terms and conditions of employment applicable during ordinary adoption leave are identical with those of ordinary maternity leave (reg. 19).

13.5.1.2 Additional adoption leave

Regs 20 and 21A.

This begins on the expiry of ordinary adoption leave. The terms and conditions of employment which apply during additional adoption leave are identical with those of additional maternity leave, including 'keeping in touch' days.

13.5.1.3 Returning to work after adoption leave

Regs 23, 25–26.

The adopter's rights to return, and the position as regards redundancy are exactly the same as in maternity leave.

13.5.1.4 Detrimental treatment and automatic unfair dismissal

Regs 28–29.

Again, the position is exactly the same as in maternity leave.

13.5.2 Statutory Adoption Pay

As with Statutory Maternity Pay, Statutory Adoption Pay is payable where the adopter meets the minimum national insurance contribution requirements. It is payable for 39 weeks at the same rate as Statutory Maternity Pay.

13.6 Paternity leave

This is now something of a misnomer, as a person taking paternity leave need not be the father of the child, nor even a man. A partner of the mother of a child (whether or not the father of the child) is entitled to 14 days' paternity leave following the birth or adoption of a child.

To qualify for paternity leave following the birth of a child the person must:

- be an employee;
- be taking the leave to look after the child or to support the child's mother;
- have 26 weeks' continuous employment by the start of the 14th week before the expected week of childbirth;
- be the child's father or the husband or partner of the mother;
- have or expect to have responsibility for the child's upbringing.

To qualify for paternity leave following adoption of a child, a person must:

- be an employee;
- be either an adopter of the child in the case of joint adoptions, or the partner of the adopter;
- have or expect to have responsibility for the child's upbringing, along with the adopter;
- have 26 weeks' continuous employment;

- continue to work for the employer from the week in which the adopter is notified of being matched with the child up to the date of the placement;
- be taking the leave in order to support the adopter, to look after the child, or both.

'Partner' is defined as 'anyone who lives with the mother in an enduring family relationship and is not a relative'. It can therefore include a same-sex partner but not, for example, the mother's mother or sister.

Statutory Paternity Pay is payable at the same rate and under the same conditions as Statutory Maternity Pay.

13.6.1 Notice

In the case of paternity leave following the birth of a child, the employee must give notice of his intention to take paternity leave in or before the 15th week before the expected week of childbirth, or as soon as reasonably practicable, in writing if the employer so requests, stating:

- the expected week of childbirth;
- the length of absence; and
- the date the leave is intended to start.

In the case of paternity leave after adoption, this information (*mutatis mutandis*) must be given no more than seven days after the day that the adopter is notified of the matching with the child, or as soon as reasonably practicable.

In either case, if the employer so requests, the employee must sign a declaration stating that:

- the purpose of the leave is to look after the child or support the mother or adopter;
- he is the father of the child, or husband or partner of the mother or adopter;
- he expects to have responsibility for the child's upbringing.

Under the current legislation the employee may choose whether to take one week or two consecutive weeks' paternity leave. He cannot take odd days. He may start his leave either:

- from the actual date of the child's birth or adoption;
- from a chosen number of days or weeks after the actual date of the birth or adoption; or
- from a chosen date after the first day of the expected week of childbirth or adoption.

The leave must be completed:

- within 56 days after the actual date of birth or adoption; or
- if the child is born or adopted earlier than the expected week, within the period from the actual date of birth or adoption up to 56 days after the expected week of birth.

Only one period of paternity leave is available for each pregnancy or adoption, regardless of the number of children born or adopted at one time.

❖ **EXAMPLE**

Andrew's wife Helen was due to give birth on 1 April. He gave the necessary notice on 10 January, some 16 weeks before the expected week of the birth. In fact, Helen gave birth to twins on 2 March. Her mother came to stay in the household for the next three weeks. Andrew found things much more peaceful at work, and decided to take his paternity leave after she left, beginning on 25 March.

There is no statutory provision about changing the date the paternity leave is due to start. This is perhaps a little surprising, given that very few infants arrive on the due date! In practice, a father will either start his paternity leave when the child is actually born, or agree a date after that with his employer. The original notice is essentially a warning of his intention to go on paternity leave, and, as with maternity leave, gives the employer the opportunity to plan for the employee's absence.

13.6.2 Terms and conditions of employment during paternity leave

These are the same as those applicable to a woman on ordinary maternity leave.

13.6.3 Right to return to work after paternity leave

The position differs according to whether the employee takes paternity leave alone, or takes other 'family' leave – such as parental leave (see below) – before or after.

- If the employee takes paternity leave alone, he is entitled to return to the job in which he was employed before paternity leave.
- If the employee takes paternity leave directly before or after a period of parental leave of not fewer than four weeks, the position is the same as for a woman taking additional maternity leave, i.e. he is entitled to return to either:
  - the same job; or
  - if this is not reasonably practicable, for a reason other than redundancy, to another job which is suitable and appropriate.

On his return, his terms and conditions of employment must be not less favourable than those applying at the time of his departure.

The position as to detrimental treatment and automatically unfair dismissal is identical with that pertaining to maternity leave and adoption leave.

In practice, since paternity leave is so much shorter than maternity leave, dismissal or detrimental treatment are less likely to occur.

13.7 Shared parental leave

This is a very recent development, so there is no case law as yet. The legislation now permits a mother to share her period of maternity leave with her husband or other partner, but no additional leave is made available. The current legislation is the Shared Parental Leave Regulations 2014, which is applicable where the expected week of childbirth is after 5 April 2015. The provisions are complex, particularly in relation to the notice requirements. Failure to comply with the notice requirements disentitles the individual to share in the leave, and therefore a large volume of case law may be anticipated.

From 6 April 2011, in the case of births where the expected week of childbirth was on or after that date, the mother could transfer a single block of up to 26 weeks' maternity leave to a partner entitled to paternity leave, from not earlier than the 20th week after the birth, provided the mother returned to work at that point.

The current entitlement is much more flexible. It enables the mother and her partner (who may not necessarily be the child's father, or a man) to divide up to 50 weeks of the mother's maternity leave between them as they think fit. Provided the necessary procedural requirements are satisfied, both can be on leave at the same time. Statutory parental leave is also available in the case of adoptions.

To be entitled to shared parental leave, the individual must share responsibility for the child with:

- their husband, wife, civil partner or joint adopter;
- the child's other parent; or
- their partner (the definition requires the two to be living under the same roof).

In the absence of case law, there is no definition of what is meant by 'share responsibility'. However, the definition of partner excludes blood relations,[3] so that the mother cannot, for example, share leave with her mother or sister. In addition, the eligible person must have 26 weeks' continuous employment by the 15th week before the expected week of childbirth *and* continue to be employed by that employer at the date they take shared parental leave. Notice of the intention to share leave must be given *by the mother* to her employer not fewer than eight weeks before the partner's portion of the leave begins. If notice is given before the birth, and the child is subsequently born eight weeks or more early, then the requirement for eight weeks' notice is waived.

❖ THINKING POINT

Stella shares a flat with her father's former girlfriend, Miriam (her father moved abroad years ago and is no longer in contact with either of them). Both work for the same employer. Recently, Stella became pregnant as the result of a brief fling with Neil, who has also moved elsewhere. Ten weeks before the expected date of childbirth, Stella gave notice that Miriam would be sharing parental leave with her, and would be away for the first three months of the child's life.

Is Miriam entitled to share parental leave with Stella?

3 Reg. 3(1). The mother's child, parent, grandchild, grandparent, sibling, aunt, uncle, niece or nephew. Step-relations or relations by marriage are not mentioned, which, in the absence of case law to the contrary, leaves open the possibility of a mother sharing her leave with, for example, her stepmother.

Having received the notice, the mother's employer may request that she provide:

- a copy of the child's birth certificate (once the child has been born, if the child has yet to be born); and
- the name and address of the partner's employer.

The mother then has 14 days to provide this information.

Having given notice of intention to share the leave, the mother may then give up to three notices specifying when the leave is to be taken.

Therefore, there are three forms of notice involved:

(1) notice by the mother of her own intention to take maternity leave (not later than the end of the 15th week before the expected week of childbirth);
(2) notice by the mother of her intention to share the leave with her partner (not later than eight weeks before the partner begins his share of the leave);
(3) notice of specific dates of the beginning and end of shares in the leave. Up to three may be given, the last not later than eight weeks before the partner begins his share of the leave.

Potentially, all three notices may be given together, two together, or all three separately. The more liberal regime in relation to dates of sharing probably reflects a recognition that plans may change after the child is born.

Unlike the old additional paternity leave, it is not necessary for the mother to return to work for the partner to be able to take shared parental leave, provided the minimum eight weeks' notice is given. However, the mother must take compulsory maternity leave of two weeks in all cases. The parents, whether separately or together, may choose to take up to 50 weeks of the leave in up to three separate blocks, provided all leave is completed before the child's first birthday. A total of 50 weeks' leave is available to be shared between the two parents, so that if, for example, the mother chose to take 26 weeks off, the father would have 24 weeks available, which he could take either at the same time as the mother, or after she returns to work, or a combination of both. If the parents choose to take the leave in separate blocks, each block must be a minimum of two weeks, unless the employer agrees to shorter periods, for example, by allowing the partner to work one week on, one week off.

Note that the partner's entitlement is in addition to his entitlement to paternity leave, but the Regulations require that paternity leave is used *before* the partner begins his element of shared parental leave.

❖ EXAMPLE

Peter and Mary's first child was due to be born on 1 April 2017. In December 2016, Mary gave notice to her own employer of her intention to take maternity leave with effect from 3 March, together with notice to Peter's employer that he intended to share in her leave. The notice stipulated that Mary would take 26 weeks' leave, and Peter would take the remaining 24 weeks, in addition to his two weeks' paternity leave. Peter would take his paternity leave in the first two weeks after the birth, then four weeks of the shared parental leave immediately after. When Mary returned to work, Peter would then take the remaining 20 weeks and stay at home with the baby.

As events turned out, their son Philip was born three weeks early, a week after Mary began her maternity leave. Peter's employer agreed that he could go on paternity leave at once, followed by four weeks' shared parental leave. He then returned to work. Mary stayed at home until Philip was 25 weeks old, when Peter took over for the remaining 21 weeks of the leave. Each received Statutory Parental Pay during their periods of leave.

13.7.1 Payment during shared parental leave

As yet the only case law in this area is the first-instance decision in Snell v Network Rail ETS/4100178/2016, which establishes that it is unlawful as direct discrimination against men and contrary to the principle of equal pay to pay a man taking shared parental leave only Statutory Paternity Pay while the mother received her contractual salary. However, it was not unlawful to alter the mother's pay so that she received only Statutory Maternity Pay.

13.8 Further reading

Ewing, 'Surrogacy: beyond equality? (Case Comment)' (2014) 120(Apr) *Employment Law Bulletin* 6.
Fox, 'Protection in contemplation of pregnancy?' (2008) 85(Jun) *Employment Law Bulletin* 3.
James, 'Family-friendly employment laws (re)assessed: the potential of care ethics' (2016) 45(4) *Industrial Law Journal* 477.
Newman, 'Postnatal depression after maternity leave ended' (2014) 247 *Equal Opportunities Review* 27.

Chapter 14

Discrimination on the grounds of sexual orientation and gender reassignment

Chapter contents

14.1 Overview

These two areas are among the most controversial in Discrimination Law, whether within the employment sphere or elsewhere. The concepts of sex and racial discrimination were introduced to deal with discrimination on grounds of what people were – male or female, or members of a particular national or racial group. Disability discrimination also deals primarily with characteristics which are outside the individual's control, and, often, visible to those around him. Sexual orientation is, however, not simply a matter of what a person is, but what he or she *does* – whether and how he or she chooses to express his or her sexual orientation. Gender reassignment also involves a departure from what sex a person was born to how they appear physically to be.

14.2 Introduction

There is considerable dispute about the numbers of homosexual, bisexual and transgender people in the British population. Official estimates of the proportion of homosexuals and bisexuals vary between 1.5 per cent and 7 per cent, and the number of transgender people as between 300,000 and 500,000.

Male homosexual behaviour has been condemned by the Christian churches for many centuries, but female homosexual behaviour (lesbianism) attracted little official attention until very recently. Prior to the Reformation, sexual acts between men were treated as offences under ecclesiastical law. The Buggery Act 1533 was the first parliamentary legislation in this area, prescribing death by hanging for acts of anal intercourse (sodomy) between men, and sexual activity with animals (bestiality). The Offences Against the Person Act 1861 s. 61 abolished the death penalty for sodomy, but retained lesser penalties, and the Criminal Law Amendment Act 1885 extended the scope of the legislation to include *any* sexual activity between males.

This prohibition became increasingly controversial during the 1950s. Following the conviction and imprisonment of the 3rd Baron Montagu of Beaulieu and two others in 1953, the Conservative government set up a committee under Sir John Wolfenden, previously a public-school headmaster and the then Vice-Chancellor of the University of Reading, to report on the law relating to homosexual offences. The Wolfenden Committee reported in 1957 with a near-unanimous recommendation for the decriminalization of homosexual acts between consenting adults (aged over 21 – then the age of majority) in private. This was eventually brought into effect by the Sexual Offences Act 1967 in England and Wales, but not until 1980 in Scotland and 1982 in Northern Ireland. However, the relaxation of the law was limited in its scope, since homosexual acts involving members of either sex remained contrary to military law until 2000 (generally speaking, members of the Armed Forces found to be active homosexuals were administratively discharged rather than court martialled), and the phrase 'in private' was interpreted by the courts to mean in a person's own home (not, for example, in a hotel room) and without the presence of a third person.

The Gay Liberation movement emerged and became increasingly vocal from the 1970s onwards, but something of a backlash occurred in the 1980s, not least because of the emergence of HIV infection, which occurred disproportionately among male homosexuals, and revelations of the promiscuous lives led by some of them. During the Conservative government of 1987–1992 Parliament passed Section 28 of the Local Government Act 1988, prohibiting 'the intentional promotion of homosexuality' by any local authority and 'the teaching in any maintained school of the acceptability of homosexuality as a pretended family relationship'. Though Section 28 was extremely controversial right up to its repeal in 2002, no cases actually reached the higher courts.

By the Sexual Offences (Amendment) Act 2000 the age of consent for homosexual acts was reduced to 16, in line with that for heterosexual acts, although the Parliament Acts were used to overcome opposition in the House of Lords. In 2003 a further Sexual Offences Act rendered the definition of sexual offences neutral as between men and women, so that, for example, male-on-male rape had the same status as male-on-female rape (though, as rape requires penetration by the penis, it remains impossible in law for a woman to rape a man or another woman).

Further changes came in the sphere of family law. By the Civil Partnerships Act 2004, same sex couples were able to register civil partnerships, though they remained unable to marry until 2014 (Marriage (Same Sex Couples) Act 2013). The official rationale was to enable same sex couples the opportunity to enjoy the same financial and property rights as married couples, in particular the ability for one party to pass their entire estate to the other free from Inheritance Tax, but in practice the creation of civil partnerships represented public acceptance of homosexual unions.[1]

The Adoption and Children Act 2002, in permitting unmarried couples to adopt children, enabled same sex couples to adopt. The Human Fertilisation and Embryology Act 2008 came into force in 2009 and enables lesbians and their partners to access IVF without restriction, and applies the same presumptions on acquisition of parental responsibility as are applicable to married couples. In consequence, both partners can be legal parents of a child born to one of them by IVF. In the same year, by an amendment to the Registration of Births and Deaths Regulations 1987, both female partners could be registered as parents on the child's birth certificate. From 2010, male couples entering into surrogacy arrangements could gain parental orders making both legal parents of the child concerned. The best-known example in this country is probably that of Elton John and David Furnish, who have two children via an American surrogate.

Transsexualism and transgenderism as a social and legal issue emerged in roughly the same period, although there are a number of instances from the eighteenth century of women serving in the army under male identities. As in folk songs such as *Sweet Polly Oliver*, their motive was nearly always to find husbands or boyfriends who had unwisely enlisted. Hannah Snell, born in 1723, claimed in later life to have enlisted in the 6th Foot in 1746 under the name of her brother-in-law, James Gray, in order to find her husband, who had deserted her and their child. More certainly, she joined the Royal Marines in 1747, and saw action in India, where she was wounded. On returning from India, she revealed her true identity, and petitioned the Duke of Cumberland, then Commander-in-Chief of the army, for a pension. Phoebe Hessel, born Phoebe Smith in 1713, enlisted in the 5th Northumberland Foot along with her future husband, Samuel Golding, and served in Gibraltar, the West Indies, and on the continent during the War of the Austrian Succession. The two married after leaving the army, and settled in Plymouth, where they had nine children. After Golding's death, Phoebe married Thomas Hessel, and moved to Brighton, where she died in 1821, aged 108. Her grave may still be seen there.

A more prominent example of a woman living as a man is Dr James Barry, born Margaret Ann Bulkeley at some time in the 1790s. Barry studied medicine at the University of Edinburgh from 1809–1813 (the uncertainly about his date of birth is because he may well have claimed to be younger than he was in order to account for an unbroken voice, delicate features and lack of facial hair). He then joined the British Army Medical Department and rose to become an Inspector-General of Military Hospitals, equivalent to a Major-General. Though professionally highly competent – he carried out one of the earliest caesareans in which both mother and child survived[2] – Barry was

1 The Civil Partnerships Act removed one injustice by allowing same-sex couples, who under the law of the time could not marry, to enjoy the same financial advances as married couples. However, there remains the injustice that other pairings who share lives and property – for example, two sisters or a mother and adult child who live under the same roof and may own property together – cannot enter into civil partnerships, since the 2004 Act applies the same 'prohibited degrees' as does the law regulating marriage.

2 Before the development of anaesthetics and antiseptic surgery in the mid-nineteenth century, caesareans were carried out as a desperate measure to save the child when childbirth had gone badly wrong and the deaths of both mother and child were otherwise certain.

a difficult and quarrelsome individual, who fought two duels with pistols and incurred the lasting enmity of Florence Nightingale when they encountered one another during the Crimean War. Barry's masquerade as a man was so successful that it was only revealed after his death in 1865, when the charwoman laying out the body discovered that it was that of a woman, moreover, a woman with stretch marks showing that she had borne a child.

Lillias Irma Valerie Barker, born on Jersey in 1895, gained some notoriety in the 1920s under the name of Colonel Sir Victor Barker. Having previously married as a woman and had two children, Barker then married as a man in 1923, but was subsequently exposed and served a prison sentence for perjury in making a false statement to enable the marriage ceremony to take place. Subsequently, Barker ran a restaurant for a brief period before being made bankrupt in 1928, and received further criminal convictions, one in relation to the bankruptcy, the second for theft.

Interestingly, given the media prominence today of male-to female transsexuals as against female-to-male transsexuals, there is little information on men passing themselves off as women in past centuries. The first male-to-female transsexual to come to public notice was April Ashley, born as George Jamieson in 1935. After working as a female impersonator in the late 1950s, and a gender reassignment operation in Casablanca in 1960, Ashley became a model, and was 'outed' as a transsexual by the *Sunday People* in 1961. In 1963 Ashley married Arthur Corbett, later 3rd Baron Rowallan, but the marriage broke down within a fortnight. After Ashley claimed maintenance payments, Corbett petitioned to have the marriage annulled on the basis that it was void *ab initio* since the parties were not respectively male and female. The annulment was finally granted in 1970, and established that transsexuals could not as a matter of law change their physical sex (*Corbett v Corbett* [1970] 2 All Er 33), though the court noted that the Ministry of Pensions and National Insurance had already been prepared to treat Ashley as a woman for their own purposes. This approach was followed by the Court of Appeal on similar facts in *Bellinger v Bellinger* ([2001] EWCA Civ 1140).

The first gender reassignment operations were carried out in Britain in 1949–1951. Medical evidence accepted by the court in *Corbett* suggested that there were about 190 post-operative male-to-female transsexuals in Britain at this time, together with unknown numbers who had had hormone treatment without surgery or were simply living as the opposite gender. There is no mention in the report of female-to-male transsexuals.

The Sex Discrimination (Gender Reassignment) Regulations 1999 prohibited direct discrimination against transsexuals, including discrimination on grounds of undergoing gender reassignment treatment, but not indirect discrimination, so that the effects were relatively limited.

The legal position arising from *Corbett* remained unchanged until 2005, when the Gender Recognition Act 2004 came into force, allowing transgender people to change their legal sex for all purposes, including marriage, and be granted a new birth certificate (rather in the way that an adopted child is given a new birth certificate showing the adoptive parents as parents). The procedure requires the individual to live in the new gender for at least two years, and apply to a Gender Recognition Panel for the issue of a Gender Recognition Certificate on the basis of evidence that transition has taken place. Importantly, gender reassignment surgery is not required, but is treated merely as evidence of transgenderism, so that, in theory at least, a person may receive a Gender Recognition Certificate as a woman while remaining physically a man.

The Gender Recognition Act followed the decision of the European Court of Human rights in *Goodwin v United Kingdom* ([2002] ECHR 588), where a male-to-female transsexual who had had gender reassignment surgery argued that the current state of the law, under which a transsexual remained for legal purposes a member of his original physical sex, constituted a breach of the Article 8 right to respect for private life, home and correspondence. It was argued in particular that the fact that a post-operative transsexual could not obtain a new birth certificate made it impossible to keep his original sex confidential.

The Sex Discrimination Act dealt only with a person's physical sex, i.e. being a man or a woman (interestingly, that was not defined), along with marital status (being married; there was no protection for single people or cohabitees). It did not cover transgender individuals or matters relating to sexual orientation. There were a number of court cases where homosexual persons of either sex argued discrimination on grounds of sexual orientation, but each failed on the basis that the proper comparator required under SDA s. 5(3) for a homosexual person of one sex was not a heterosexual person of the same or the other sex but a homosexual person of the other sex, the sexual orientation being a 'relevant circumstance' for this purpose. This issue was dealt with under the Employment Equality (Sexual Orientation) Regulations 2003, which made it unlawful to discriminate against a person on grounds of their sexual orientation.

14.3 Legislation and case law

Under the Equality Act 2010 both sexual orientation and transgenderism are protected characteristics, defined in the following terms:

> **7 Gender reassignment**
>
> (1) A person has the protected characteristic of gender reassignment if the person is proposing to undergo, is undergoing or has undergone a process (or part of a process) for the purpose of reassigning the person's sex by changing physiological or other attributes of sex.
>
> (2) A reference to a transsexual person is a reference to a person who has the protected characteristic of gender reassignment.
>
> **12 Sexual orientation**
>
> (1) Sexual orientation means a person's sexual orientation towards—
> (a) persons of the same sex,
> (b) persons of the opposite sex, or
> (c) persons of either sex.

Given the controversy attendant on both issues, it is perhaps surprising that there is very little case law under these provisions in the employment sphere. The bulk of such case law as there is involves the interplay between the protected characteristics of sexual orientation and religion and belief. According to the Employment Appeal Tribunal website, at the time of writing only nine cases dealing solely with sexual orientation have reached them since November 2008, one of which was entirely on quantum, and none at all on transsexualism. This suggests that difficulties are very largely resolved by negotiation at local level before reaching the Employment Tribunal.

The Equality Act Sch. 9 contains certain exemptions from its requirements 'for the purposes of an organized religion'. Para. 2 sets out exemptions for religious requirements relating to sex, marriage or civil partnership and sexual orientation in respect of:

- s. 39(1)(a) or (c) or (2)(b) or (c) (employee selection arrangements, terms of employment, refusal to appoint and dismissal);
- s. 49(3)(a) or (c) or (6)(b) or (c) (selection arrangements, terms of appointment, refusal to appoint and dismissal in relation to personal offices);
- s. 50(3)(a) or (c) or (6)(b) or (c) (selection arrangements, terms of appointment, refusal to appoint and dismissal in relation to public offices);
- s. 51(1) (recommendations for appointments to public offices).

Clearly, these exceptions allow the Roman Catholic Church to maintain a celibate male priesthood, but were recently considered in the case of *Pemberton v Inwood* ([2016] UKEAT/0072/16/BA).

Canon Pemberton, a Church of England clergyman, divorced his wife in 2007 and subsequently cohabited with a male partner, whom he married after the Marriage (Same Sex Couples) Act 2013. The Respondent, then the Bishop of Southwell, revoked Canon Pemberton's Permission to Officiate (PTO), thus preventing him from working in a parish, and refused him an Extra-Parochial Ministry Licence (EPML), which also prevented him from taking up a post as an NHS chaplain which he had been offered. He subsequently claimed direct discrimination on grounds of sexual orientation and/or marital status, together with harassment on grounds of sexual orientation. The Bishop argued that his actions fell within sch. 9 para. 2, since homosexual marriage was contrary to the doctrines of the church.

Canon Pemberton argued that the Bishop of Southwell was a 'qualifications body' for the purposes of Equality Act s. 53, and so under a duty not to discriminate against a person on grounds of a protected characteristic by refusing to grant a qualification or withdrawing a qualification previously granted. The Bishop denied that he was a qualifications body, and in the alternative argued that if the PTO or EPML were 'relevant qualifications' for the purpose of s. 54(2), they were granted for the purposes of employment in an organized religion and so the exemptions in sch. 9 para. 2 applied.

The Employment Tribunal ruled in favour of the Bishop in relation to the EPML and the allegations of harassment. The EPML was a relevant qualification and so the exemption under para. 2 was available. Although Canon Pemberton had suffered humiliation and distress by reason of the Bishop's actions, the Bishop had acted in this fashion because he had defied church doctrine rather than because of his sexual orientation. In any case, the Bishop had not acted unlawfully in refusing the EPML, and a lawful act could not constitute harassment. However, the PTO was not a relevant qualification on the facts of this case, since it was not required for the role of NHS chaplain, so that para. 2 did not apply.

On appeal by Canon Pemberton and a cross-appeal by the Bishop, the EAT upheld the original decision. As the NHS required a chaplain to hold an EPML from the bishop of the relevant diocese, an EPML was a relevant qualification for the purpose of employment in an organized religion. The exemption thus applied, although another reasonable bishop might not have refused an EPML in these circumstances. The Tribunal had also been entitled to find that entering into a same-sex marriage was contrary to the doctrines of the Church of England; it was noted that the General Synod had opposed the passing of the 2013 Act, and, specifically, the churches were not required to carry out same-sex marriage ceremonies. The Bishop's refusal to grant Canon Pemberton an EPML was not based on his sexual orientation, or his same sex marriage, but on the fact that he was no longer 'in good standing' with the church.

Case law under the 2003 Regulations confined the scope of these exceptions to employment in the church itself, and not, for example, to employment in church schools and religious charities.

Other case law which has reached the EAT has tended to involve subtleties of situation, and, perhaps inevitably, workplace banter.

In *Lisboa v Realpubs Ltd* ([2010] UKEAT/0224/10/RN) the employer took over a pub which had been well-known locally and even nationally as a 'gay pub', and relaunched it as a gastropub under a new name with the intention of developing a broader clientele. Both the Tribunal and the EAT accepted that this policy was entirely lawful. The Claimant, who was openly homosexual, argued that this involved less favourable treatment of existing customers on grounds of their sexual orientation. As the EAT put it, 'We would characterise the critical issue in this way: a policy of embracing diversity and welcoming inclusiveness is laudable; discriminating against gay customers and staff on grounds of their sexual orientation is not; it is unlawful'.

Mr Lisboa's employment began on 1 December 2008, and ended with his resignation with effect from 11 January 2009, which, he argued, constituted constructive dismissal and wrongful dismissal. His allegations were directed in the main towards actions by Mr Heap, a director of the company, who, he claimed, took active steps to discourage the previous clientele from returning to the pub, by, for example, asking one of the staff to put up a notice saying, 'This is not a gay pub'. Overall, the Claimant's allegations fell into two categories:

- comments by Mr Heap directed at his sexual orientation;
- a course of conduct by the employer under which he was put under pressure to make the pub less welcoming to homosexual customers than to other customers.

The Tribunal found direct discrimination against the Claimant in respect of three of Mr Heap's comments, but rejected his claims on the second ground. Their reasoning ran as follows:

> The law does not legislate against prejudice: it offers a remedy only where adverse *treatment* on a proscribed ground is made out. We find that nothing was done to make the pub unwelcoming to gay customers or less welcoming to gay customers than other patrons. Nor was any instruction given to that effect. Realpubs are a hard-headed commercial enterprise. The last thing in the minds of its directors was to alienate their established customers. Their objective was to broaden the appeal of the pub, increase the numbers coming in and widen its clientele. If that aim had been achieved (as apparently, it has not), the inevitable consequence would have been a 'watering down' of the gay element within the client base. But a reduction in the percentage of gay customers would not have amounted to an exclusion of gay people or less favourable treatment of them, even if some established customers might have disapproved. Rather it would have been the natural fulfilment of the unobjectionable 're-positioning' strategy. And once it is accepted that the strategy was lawful, it seems to us that measures such as redressing the gender imbalance among bar staff (whether or not that entailed sex discrimination) and 'showcasing' families or mixed-sex groups by seating them prominently in the pub are not properly seen as instances of discrimination against gay customers but rather as manifestations of the legitimate policy of seeking to 'sell' the pub to a wider public (of course, matters would have been different had there even evidence of, for example, an instruction to reserve the more comfortable or attractive tables or seating areas for non-gay customers or to enforce any form of segregation by reference to sexual orientation. But that is not what happened).
>
> There certainly was evidence of a policy to exclude *some* gay customers. Mr Heap made it clear in his evidence that Realpubs would not tolerate offensive behaviour and would take steps to ensure that miscreants did not return. But that was a policy aimed at managing misconduct, not disadvantaging individuals because of their sexuality. We are quite satisfied that the reference in Mr Heap's email of 8 December 2008 to barring 'over the top' old customers alluded to those who, by illegal, outrageous or otherwise unacceptable behaviour, had contributed to the 'fallen' image of the pub. We reject Mr Cooper's suggestion that 'over the top' merely meant 'camp'.
>
> The instruction by Mr Heap to the Claimant to warn the amorous gay couple would have constituted an instruction to discriminate had we found that a corresponding instruction would not have been given in the case of a heterosexual couple but we are unable to make such a finding. Indeed, we are confident that, in such circumstances, Mr Heap's reaction would have been the same. In this context, we have noted the unchallenged testimony of Ms Christian that Realpubs operate an 'anti-petting policy' across their entire chain of pubs.
>
> The Claimant's argument in relation to the second ground was based on *Weathersfield v Sargent* ([1999] IRLR 94, CA), where a white employee successfully argued constructive dismissal and racial discrimination after being instructed not to hire vans to black or Asian clients. The EAT admitted that the situation they were dealing with was a good deal more subtle than that in *Weathersfield v Sargent*.

As the ET observed . . . a strategy aimed at re-positioning the pub as one that appealed to all sections of the public rather than being known as an essentially 'gay pub' is, without more, unexceptionable. The question on this part of the case, as the ET recognised, is whether the Respondents, particularly through Mr Heap, went too far in embracing a policy of putting pressure on gay customers and/or in taking negative steps which made the venue less welcoming to gay customers.

In order to answer that question, [Counsel for the Claimant] submits, it is necessary to look at the picture presented by the overall factual matrix as found. Here, he argues, the ET applied a wrong approach. Instead of looking at the overall effect of the Respondents' implementation of their re-positioning policy on the customers and as a result on the Claimant, as a gay employee, the ET at para. 48 limited themselves to the commercial aim of Realpubs, to broaden the appeal of the Pembroke Arms to a wider clientele than that which frequented the old Coleherne Arms, which they considered to be lawful and having accepted that that strategy was lawful, then characterised matters such as gender imbalance among bar staff (which they thought may have led to possible sex discrimination against the male members of staff who left between 5 December and 5 January), and 'showcasing' families or mixed-sex groups by seating them prominently in the pub were not as instances of discrimination against gay customers but simply manifestations of selling the pub to a wider public.

[Counsel] submits that the correct question for the ET is to ask itself whether gay customers would or might reasonably take the view that, as a result of the measures adopted, they were disadvantaged compared with straight customers. Putting his case at its highest [Counsel] poses the question in this way; what would have been the cumulative effect for an established gay customer if all the measures proposed, particularly by Mr Heap, had been implemented? Such a customer would be aware of an aggressive marketing campaign on the streets making sure everyone knows that it is not exclusively a gay pub; confirmed by a sign saying 'this is not a gay pub'; with windows crammed with overtly straight customers, leaving him to find a table at the back; with the bar staff culled of those male employees known to attract the established clientele and with a director making homophobic remarks to the manager (and his assistant, the Claimant, a gay man) about customers and staff within the pub. The answer, proffers [Counsel] is that the customer would plainly feel less welcome than straight customers [. . .]

The ET was required to make a judgment as to whether the factual matrix as a whole, as they found it to be, showed that Realpubs and in particular their director, Mr Heap, in advancing a legitimate policy of widening the appeal of the pub following its re-launch, implemented it in such a way that the old gay clientele was less favourably treated than the desired straight/family customer base on grounds of their sexual orientation. . . . The ET failed to ask itself that critical question at para. 48 of their Reasons. Their error lay in stopping their enquiry at the point where they found that the re-positioning strategy was lawful.

❖ THINKING POINT

One of the factors influencing the EAT's decision was that Mr Heap visited the pub with his family shortly after the reopening, and sat near a window where they could be seen by passers-by. Taken in isolation, does such behaviour suggest a hostility towards homosexuals?

14.4 Further reading

Anon, 'Gender identity in the workplace' (2016) 1047 *IDS Employment Law Brief* 10.
Connolly, 'Preddy v Bull (Case Comment)' (2013) 114(Apr) *Employment Law Bulletin* 7.
Dunne, 'Ten years of gender recognition in the United Kingdom: still a "model for reform"?' (2015) Oct *Public Law* 530.
Johnson & Vanderbeck, 'Sexual orientation equality and religious exceptionalism in the law of the United Kingdom: the role of the Church of England' (2017) 6(3) *Oxford Journal of Law and Religion* 498.
McIlroy, 'Legislation in a context of moral disagreement: the case of the sexual orientation regulations' (2007) 159 *Law & Justice Christian Law Review* 114.

Chapter 15

Discrimination on the grounds of age

Chapter contents

15.1 Overview

Age was the last of the current protected characteristics to be created, by the Employment Equality (Age) Regulations 2006, which came into force on 1 October 2006. This chapter examines the legislation, and considers the way it operates in case law.

15.2 Introduction

The Equality Act 2010 s. 5 now provides:

5 Age

(1) In relation to the protected characteristic of age—
  (a) a reference to a person who has a particular protected characteristic is a reference to a person of a particular age group;
  (b) a reference to persons who share a protected characteristic is a reference to persons of the same age group.

(2) A reference to an age group is a reference to a group of persons defined by reference to age, whether by reference to a particular age or to a range of ages.

Age is both an absolute and a relative concept, so a person may argue discrimination on grounds of being a particular age, or of being older, younger, or the same age as those around him.

As is usual under the Equality Act, direct discrimination, indirect discrimination, harassment and victimisation on grounds of age are prohibited. Unusually, there is a defence of justification in respect of direct discrimination as well as indirect discrimination.

Under the original 2006 Regulations, the employer was permitted to apply a default retirement age of 65 years or higher, provided he followed a statutory procedure which enabled the employee to request to be allowed to continue working after that default age, either indefinitely or for a set period. This provision was repealed with effect from 1 October 2011. The law now enables an employer to require employees to retire at a particular age only if he can show this to be a proportionate means of achieving a legitimate aim. Perhaps unsurprisingly, much of the existing case law deals with compulsory retirement. Redundancy schemes also give rise to both direct and indirect discrimination issues, as employers seek to minimise costs by excluding certain age groups, often to prevent a person from benefitting from both voluntary redundancy and an immediate pension. Given that the main issue in both groups of cases is the operation of the defence, it is convenient to consider them together, although, according to Lady Hale in *Seldon v Clarkson Wright and Jakes* (see below), the defence to direct discrimination is couched in much narrower terms.

15.3 Retirement ages

The leading case on compulsory retirement is *Seldon v Clarkson Wright and Jakes* ([2012] UKSC 16), where a partner in a City legal firm argued direct discrimination in being required to retire from the partnership at 65 under the provisions of the partnership deed. The partnership argued objective justification on the basis that the requirement was justified on the basis of the following aims:

29.1 ensuring that associates are given the opportunity of partnership after a reasonable period as an associate, thereby ensuring that associates do not leave the firm;

> 29.2 ensuring that there is a turnover of partners such that any partner can expect to become Senior Partner in due course;
>
> 29.3 facilitating the planning of the partnership and workforce across individual departments by having a realistic long term expectation as to when vacancies will arise;
>
> 29.4 limiting the need to expel partners by way of performance management, thus contributing to a congenial and supportive culture in the Respondent firm;
>
> 29.5 enabling and encouraging employees and partners to make adequate financial provision for retirement;
>
> 29.6 protecting the partnership model of the Respondent. If equity partners could not be forced to retire at 65, but employees (including salaried partners) could be, it would be preferable to keep lawyers at the Respondent as employees or salaried partners rather than equity partners.

At the time the facts of the case arose, the 2006 Regulations were still in force, including the default retirement age of 65, although this did not apply to partners, as distinct from employees. As the Regulations had been made in order to implement an EU Directive (Council Directive 2000/78/EC) the Supreme Court concluded that they had to be interpreted in accordance with the purpose of that Directive, and that the issue of what constituted legitimate aims must be determined in that light. Article 2(2)(i) of the Directive sets out the 'ordinary' test of justification in indirect discrimination cases (that the provision, criterion or practice is a proportionate means of achieving a legitimate aim). Article 6(1) deals specifically with age discrimination, and provides as follows:

> Notwithstanding article 2(2), Member States may provide that differences of treatment on grounds of age shall not constitute discrimination, if, within the context of national law, they are objectively and reasonably justified by a legitimate aim, including legitimate employment policy, labour market and vocational training objectives, and if the means of achieving that aim are appropriate and necessary.
>
> Such differences of treatment may include, among others:
>
> (a) the setting of special conditions on access to employment and vocational training, employment and occupation, including dismissal and remuneration conditions, for young people, older workers and persons with caring responsibilities in order to promote their vocational integration or ensure their protection;
> (b) the fixing of minimum conditions of age, professional experience or seniority in service for access to employment or to certain advantages linked to employment;
> (c) the fixing of a maximum age for recruitment which is based on the training requirements of the post in question or the need for a reasonable period of employment before retirement.

Lady Hale, speaking for the majority in the Supreme Court, then considered the ECJ case law on Article 6(1):

> The distinction drawn in the evolving case law of the European Court of Justice . . . ('Luxembourg') is between aims relating to 'employment policy, the labour market or vocational training', which are legitimate, and 'purely individual reasons particular to the employer's situation, such as cost reduction or improving competitiveness', which in general are not.

The Supreme Court considered a number of ECJ cases from outside the United Kingdom, dealing not only with retirement ages, but other restrictions based on age. Emerging from this was the important point that, where a restriction had more than one aim, the two could not be inconsistent with one another, and that, whatever the aim or number of aims, the means adopted to achieve the aim could not be inconsistent with it. For example, in the German case of *David Hütter v Technische Universität Graz*, Case C-88/08 [2009] All ER (EC) 1129, the law governing public service pay stipulated that service before the age of 18 was not to be taken into account in determining an employee's pay grade. The effect of this was to discriminate against those who chose to take apprenticeships in the public sector rather than staying in general education until age 18 or later. The ECJ accepted that the aims of not discouraging people from remaining in secondary education, not making apprenticeships unduly costly for the public sector and of promoting the integration of apprentices into the labour market, were social policy aims which could constitute justification. However, these aims were contradictory – most obviously the first and last, and the law was not, in the ECJ's view, 'appropriate' to achieve them.

Lady Hale said, in relation to Art. 6(1):

> What messages, then, can we take from the European case law?
>
> (1) All the references to the European Court discussed above have concerned national laws or provisions in collective agreements authorised by national laws. They have not concerned provisions in individual contracts of employment or partnership, as this case does. However, the *Bartsch* case, mentioned at [2] above, did concern the rules of a particular employer's pension fund; and the *Prigge* case, [49] above, concerned a collective agreement governing the employees of a single employer, *Deutsche Lufthansa*.
>
> (2) If it is sought to justify direct age discrimination under article 6(1), the aims of the measure must be social policy objectives, such as those related to employment policy, the labour market or vocational training. These are of a public interest nature, which is 'distinguishable from purely individual reasons particular to the employer's situation, such as cost reduction or improving competitiveness' (*Age Concern*, *Fuchs*).
>
> (3) It would appear from that, as Advocate General Bot pointed out in *Kücükdeveci*, that flexibility for employers is not in itself a legitimate aim; but a certain degree of flexibility may be permitted to employers in the pursuit of legitimate social policy objectives.
>
> (4) A number of legitimate aims, some of which overlap, have been recognised in the context of direct age discrimination claims:
>
> (i) promoting access to employment for younger people (*Palacios de la Villa*, *Hütter*, *Kücükdeveci*);
>
> (ii) the efficient planning of the departure and recruitment of staff (*Fuchs*);
>
> (iii) sharing out employment opportunities fairly between the generations (*Petersen*, *Rosenbladt*, *Fuchs*);
>
> (iv) ensuring a mix of generations of staff so as to promote the exchange of experience and new ideas (*Georgiev*, *Fuchs*);
>
> (v) rewarding experience (*Hütter*, *Hennigs*);
>
> (vi) cushioning the blow for long serving employees who may find it hard to find new employment if dismissed (*Ingeniørforeningen i Danmark*);
>
> (vii) facilitating the participation of older workers in the workforce (*Fuchs*, see also. *Mangold v Helm*, Case C-144/04 [2006] 1 CMLR 43);
>
> (viii) avoiding the need to dismiss employees on the ground that they are no longer capable of doing the job which may be humiliating for the employee concerned (*Rosenbladt*); or
>
> (ix) avoiding disputes about the employee's fitness for work over a certain age (*Fuchs*).
>
> (5) However, the measure in question must be both appropriate to achieve its legitimate aim or aims and necessary in order to do so. Measures based on age may not be appropriate to the aims of rewarding experience or protecting long service (*Hütter*, *Kücükdeveci*, *Ingeniørforeningen i Danmark*).

(6) The gravity of the effect upon the employees discriminated against must be weighed against the importance of the legitimate aims in assessing the necessity of the particular measure chosen (*Fuchs*).

(7) The scope of the tests for justifying indirect discrimination under article 2(2)(b) and for justifying any age discrimination under article 6(1) is not identical. It is for the member states, rather than the individual employer, to establish the legitimacy of the aim pursued (*Age Concern*).

Lady Hale went on:

> It seems, therefore, that the United Kingdom has chosen to give employers and partnerships the flexibility to choose which objectives to pursue, provided always that (i) these objectives can count as legitimate objectives of a public interest nature within the meaning of the Directive and (ii) are consistent with the social policy aims of the state and (iii) the means used are proportionate, that is both appropriate to the aim and (reasonably) necessary to achieve it.
>
> Two different kinds of legitimate objective have been identified by the Luxembourg court. The first kind may be summed up as *inter-generational fairness*. This is comparatively uncontroversial. It can mean a variety of things, depending upon the particular circumstances of the employment concerned: for example, it can mean facilitating access to employment by young people; it can mean enabling older people to remain in the workforce; it can mean sharing limited opportunities to work in a particular profession fairly between the generations; it can mean promoting diversity and the interchange of ideas between younger and older workers.
>
> The second kind may be summed up as *dignity*. This has been variously put as avoiding the need to dismiss older workers on the grounds of incapacity or underperformance, thus preserving their dignity and avoiding humiliation, and as avoiding the need for costly and divisive disputes about capacity or underperformance. Either way, it is much more controversial. As Age UK argue, the philosophy underlying all the anti-discrimination laws is the dignity of each individual, the right to be treated equally irrespective of either irrational prejudice or stereotypical assumptions which may be true of some but not of others. The assumptions underlying these objectives look suspiciously like stereotyping[. . .]
>
> I confess to some sympathy with the position taken by Age UK. The fact that most women are less physically strong than most men does not justify refusing a job requiring strength to a woman candidate just because she is a woman. The fact that this particular woman is not strong enough for the job would justify refusing it to her. It would be consistent with this principle to hold that the fact that most people over a certain age have slower reactions than most people under that age does not justify sacking everyone who reaches that age irrespective of whether or not they still do have the necessary speed of reaction. But we know that the Luxembourg court [ECJ] has held that the avoidance of unseemly debates about capacity is capable of being a legitimate aim. The focus must therefore turn to whether this is a legitimate aim in the particular circumstances of the case.
>
> The fact that a particular aim is capable of being a legitimate aim under the Directive (and therefore the domestic legislation) is only the beginning of the story. . . . Once an aim has been identified, it has still to be asked whether it is legitimate in the particular circumstances of the employment concerned. For example, improving the recruitment of young people, in order to achieve a balanced and diverse workforce, is in principle a legitimate aim. But if there is in fact no problem in recruiting the young and the problem is in retaining the older and more experienced workers then it may not be a legitimate aim for the business concerned. Avoiding the need for performance management may be a legitimate aim, but if in fact the business

already has sophisticated performance management measures in place, it may not be legitimate to avoid them for only one section of the workforce.

Finally, of course, the means chosen have to be both appropriate and necessary. It is one thing to say that the aim is to achieve a balanced and diverse workforce. It is another thing to say that a mandatory retirement age of 65 is both appropriate and necessary to achieving this end. It is one thing to say that the aim is to avoid the need for performance management procedures. It is another to say that a mandatory retirement age of 65 is appropriate and necessary to achieving this end. The means must be carefully scrutinised in the context of the particular business concerned in order to see whether they do meet the objective and there are no other, less discriminatory, measures which would do so.

This leads to the final issue, which is whether the measure must be justified, not only in general but also in its application to the particular individual. After all, the regulation applies to a particular act of direct discrimination, where 'on grounds of B's age, A treats B less favourably than he treats or would treat other persons' and 'A cannot show the treatment . . . to be a proportionate means of achieving a legitimate aim'. The argument on behalf of Mr Seldon, therefore, is that the partnership, A, had to show that its particular less favourable treatment of him, B, was justified. This could be another distinction between direct and indirect discrimination, because for indirect discrimination the regulation only requires A to show that the 'provision, criterion or practice' is a proportionate means of achieving a legitimate aim. Hence, it is argued, the partnership should have to show, not only that the mandatory retirement rule was a proportionate means of achieving a legitimate aim, but also that applying it to Mr Seldon could be justified at the time.

The answer given in the EAT, at [58], with which the Court of Appeal agreed, at [36], was that:

'Typically, legitimate aims can only be achieved by the application of general rules or policies. The adoption of a general rule, as opposed to a series of responses to particular individual circumstances, is itself an important element in the justification. It is what gives predictability and consistency, itself an important virtue'.

Thus, the EAT would not rule out the possibility that there may be cases where the particular application of the rule must be justified, but they suspected that these would be extremely rare.

I would accept that where it is justified to have a general rule, then the existence of that rule will usually justify the treatment which results from it. In the particular context of inter-generational fairness, it must be relevant that at an earlier stage in his life, a partner or employee may well have benefited from a rule which obliged his seniors to retire at a particular age. Nor can it be entirely irrelevant that the rule in question was re-negotiated comparatively recently between the partners. It is true that they did not then appreciate that the forthcoming Age Regulations would apply to them. But it is some indication that at the time they thought that it was fair to have such a rule. Luxembourg has drawn a distinction between laws and regulations which are unilaterally imposed and collective agreements which are the product of bargaining between the social partners on a presumably more equal basis (*Rosenbladt, Hennigs*).

There is therefore a distinction between justifying the application of the rule to a particular individual, which in many cases would negate the purpose of having a rule, and justifying the rule in the particular circumstances of the business.[1] All businesses will now have to give careful consideration to what, if any, mandatory retirement rules can be justified.

---

1 My emphasis.

> In common with both the EAT and the Court of Appeal, I would pay tribute to the careful judgment of the ET. Their conclusions are particularly impressive given that they were deciding the case in November 2007, before any of the European jurisprudence discussed earlier had emerged. They did approach the justification of direct discrimination in the same way as they would have approached the justification of indirect discrimination, whereas we now know that there is a difference between the two. However, they identified three aims for the compulsory retirement age, which the Court of Appeal summed up as 'dead men's shoes' and 'collegiality'. Mr Seldon, with the support of Age UK, has argued that these were individual aims of the business rather than the sort of social policy aims contemplated by the Directive. I do not think that that is fair. The first two identified aims were staff retention and workforce planning, both of which are directly related to the legitimate social policy aim of sharing out professional employment opportunities fairly between the generations (and were recognised as legitimate in *Fuchs*). The third was limiting the need to expel partners by way of performance management, which is directly related to the 'dignity' aims accepted in *Rosenbladt* and *Fuchs*. . . . I would therefore accept that the identified aims were legitimate.
>
> As to whether the means chosen were proportionate, in the article 6(1) sense of being both appropriate and (reasonably) necessary to achieving those aims, the case is already to go back to the ET on the basis that it had not been shown that the choice of 65 was an appropriate means of achieving the third aim. The question, therefore, was whether the ET would have regarded the first two aims as sufficient by themselves. In answering that question, I would not rule out their considering whether the choice of a mandatory age of 65 was a proportionate means of achieving the first two aims. There is a difference between justifying *a* retirement age and justifying *this* retirement age. Taken to extremes, their first two aims might be thought to justify almost any retirement age. The ET did not unpick the question of the age chosen and discuss it in relation to each of the objectives. It would be unduly constraining to deny them the opportunity of doing so now. I would emphasise, however, that they are considering the circumstances as they were in 2006, when there was a designated retirement age of 65 for employees, and not as they are now.

On this basis, the Supreme Court referred the question of justification of the specific retirement age of 65 back to the original Tribunal.

Harrod v Chief Constable of West Midlands Police ([2017] EWCA Civ 191) was a case brought by a number of police officers who argued that their being required to retire 'in the interests of efficiency' after completing 30 years' service constituted indirect discrimination on grounds of age.

Police Pensions Regulations 1987 Regulation A19 then provided:

> Compulsory retirement on grounds of efficiency of the force
>
> A19.- (1) This Regulation shall apply to a regular policeman, other than a chief officer of police, deputy chief constable or assistant chief constable, who if required to retire would be entitled to receive a pension of an amount not fewer than two thirds of his average pensionable pay[. . .]
>
> (2) If a Police Authority determine that the retention in the force of a regular policeman to whom this Regulation applies would not be in the general interests of efficiency, he may be required to retire on such date as the police authority determine.

Various police forces had adopted a practice of requiring police officers to retire under Reg. A19 once they completed 30 years' service and so were entitled to a full pension, as a cost-saving measure. The Tribunal accepted evidence that the police pension system was unusually generous and the majority of those retired on this basis did not contest the requirement to retire. In a previous case, in *Police Superintendents' Association of England & Wales and Ors v Chief Constable of Bedfordshire Police and Secretary of State for the Home Department* ([2013] EWHC 2173 (Admin)), the court held that Reg. A19 was applicable to collective retirements as well as individual.

The judge held that pure budget saving would not be sufficient to permit the use of A19: there must be some efficiency gain. But that did not limit consideration to the effectiveness of the individual officer concerned. King J held that the phrase 'general interests of efficiency' must in principle be capable of extending to the question of how to accommodate the need for a police force to live within its means.

Following the 2010 Election, a Comprehensive Spending Review required each police force to cut 20 per cent from its spending. Seven forces used Reg. A19 to require almost all officers who reached 30 years' service to retire. The Tribunal found that there was no serious attempt to ask them to take career breaks or go part-time, or to encourage those with fewer than 30 years' service to retire early. There was a clear discriminatory effect on those aged between 48 (the minimum possible age for achieving 30 years' service) and 65, the formal police retirement age. It was accepted that this discriminatory effect was inherent in Reg. A19 itself.

Bean LJ, giving the leading judgment, concluded that although the exercise of the power under Reg. A19 was discretionary, its terms made it impossible to require any other officers to retire early, as only those with 30 years' service were eligible. Further, police terms of service made it impossible to make them redundant, but the situation was analogous to redundancy, where the courts and tribunals would not question the employer's decision that redundancies were necessary.

> Police officers have a high degree of security of tenure, although, since they are not employees, they cannot bring claims for unfair dismissal. But it is instructive to consider how the decision of the Forces would have been analysed if the officers had been employees to whom the unfair dismissal and redundancy provisions of the Employment Rights Act 1996 applied. Suppose that a particular Force had 100 officers in post with 30 years' service, of whom between 80 and 95 might be expected to retire, but the employers, faced with significant budget cuts, decided to require all 100 to do so.
>
> In such a case the reasons for the dismissals would be redundancy. The employers' decision to reduce headcount by 100 could not in practice be successfully challenged. It has been established law at the level of this court and below at least since *James W Cook and Co (Withenhoe) Ltd v Tipper* [1990] ICR 716 that it is not open to an employment tribunal to investigate the commercial or economic reasons which prompt the closure of a business or a reduction in the workforce. *In the absence of a statutory provision such as Regulation A19, any decision to limit the selection pool for the 100 posts to employees with 30 years' service or more would be vulnerable to challenge on the grounds of age discrimination (and possibly also unfair dismissal or sex discrimination). But if a statutory provision such as A19 made it unlawful to include anyone with fewer than 30 years' service in the pool, the selection method would be inevitable and a claim whether for unfair dismissal or age discrimination would fail.*
>
> This case, in my view, is no different. The decision to reduce officer headcount to the fullest extent available was taken in the interests of achieving certainty of costs reduction and it was not for the Tribunal to devise an alternative scheme involving the loss of fewer posts. The second element of the decision, to confine dismissals to officers with more than 30 years' service, cannot be impugned either, because no other method of selection was lawful. The only possible conclusion from these two propositions, in my view, is that the Respondents' actions were justified and that the Appellants had no valid claim for age discrimination.
>
> [Counsel] emphasised in his submissions to us that the Tribunal are the statutory fact-finders and that, as many cases of high authority have held, discrimination cases are particularly fact sensitive. But the legal approach – determining the questions to be answered – is not fact sensitive; it is the answers which are fact sensitive. The Tribunal, after a painstaking analysis

of the facts, took the view that the Respondents could have managed with fewer compulsory retirements than they did. But that, with respect, was an answer to the wrong question. The Respondents had to justify the selection, which they did by reliance on A19. They did not have to justify the numbers.

Elias LJ added:

The PCP which needs to be justified within the meaning of section 19 of the Equality Act is the PCP adopted by A which puts B, and those with whom he shares the relevant characteristic, at a particular disadvantage when compared with persons who do not share that characteristic. What renders the act discriminatory is not subjecting persons to a disadvantage; it is the fact that the disadvantage is suffered by some and not others and that the selection of those to be disadvantaged is based on the adoption of a PCP which is not a proportionate means of achieving a legitimate aim. In this case the disadvantage which the claimants suffer is the act of dismissal. The act of dismissal is not itself an act of discrimination. What potentially renders it discriminatory is the way in which those to be subject to dismissal are chosen. It is the selection process which creates the risk of discrimination, not the decision to dismiss.

In this case the selection process undoubtedly gives rise to prima facie discrimination on grounds of age. That is the effect of applying the criteria in Regulation A19. It is not disputed, however, that in the circumstances the adoption of those criteria is a proportionate way of achieving a legitimate aim. The dismissals are on grounds of efficiency – that has not been challenged and it is a legitimate aim; and adopting the selection criteria required by Parliament is a proportionate means of achieving it.

The ET considered that the relevant practice was that the Forces would, subject to certain exceptions, 'require all officers to retire at ?APP'. Then, in the course of its judgment the ET said this (para.72):

'When looking at the appropriateness and necessity of the application it has to be appreciated the prima facie discrimination has been made out and that such discrimination should be avoided if reasonably possible'.

On this basis the tribunal engaged with the question whether dismissals could be reasonably avoided and concluded that the Chief Constables did not need to dismiss as many staff as they did, or at least they did not satisfy the tribunal that they needed to do so. Accordingly, the Appellants suffered the disadvantage of dismissal when they need not have done.

I have considerable difficulty with that analysis. Assuming that to be true, why does that render the dismissals discriminatory? The logic is that a claimant will have no discrimination claim if the tribunal is satisfied that an authority has dismissed no more staff than in the tribunal's view it was reasonably necessary to dismiss, but will have a claim if the number is greater than that. But how does it become discrimination on age or any other grounds because more officers are dismissed than the exigencies of the business require? In my judgment this is eliding the disadvantage with the discrimination and wrongly requiring the Chief Constables to justify both the dismissals and the process of selection. It is telling them that they should have adopted a different scheme and made their cuts in some other way.

There is another fundamental problem with the tribunal's analysis. The assumption underlying this argument is that the employer should be obliged to minimise dismissals and should take any reasonable steps to avoid them. But . . . there is no general legal obligation to that effect. It is not the job of tribunals to question management decisions in that way, and they are not equipped to do so. Tribunals do of course have extensive jurisdiction relating to dismissals. For example, in unfair dismissal claims they can properly seek to ensure that dismissals are for a good reason; they can enforce obligations to consult before redundancies are effected; and they can require an employer to show that a dismissal ostensibly for

> redundancy is genuinely for that reason. But that is a far cry from reviewing the decision of management as to the number of staff required to run their business. That will often involve difficult decisions about how resources should be prioritised. In my judgment discrimination law does not, and was not intended to, open up questions of this kind to scrutiny by tribunals.

Taken together, these two cases provide authority for the following:

- if statute prevents any other method of selection from being used, any discriminatory effect will be justified, on the basis that this was the intention of Parliament;
- if this is not the case, then cost-saving in isolation cannot be justification; it must be linked to some form of social policy objective.

15.4 Redundancy/early retirement

HM Land Registry v Benson ([2011] UKEAT/0197/11/RN) involved five employees aged 50–54, who were refused a place on an early retirement scheme because it would be disproportionately expensive to grant them an unreduced pension at their relatively early age, although the terms of the relevant pension scheme permitted them to retire. As part of a scheme to reduce employee numbers and costs it was decided to merge three sets of offices which were close to one another, in Birkenhead, South Wales and Lytham St Anne's. One class of employee (Registration Executives) were offered early retirement if over 50 and given the opportunity to volunteer for redundancy if under 50. Both schemes were generous. In particular, the early retirement scheme included an unreduced pension payable up to ten years early (Civil Service pensions were then payable at 60). It was made clear that not all volunteers would necessarily be selected; depending on numbers, a selection could be required. As things turned out, both the redundancy and early retirement schemes were over-subscribed and a selection was made on the basis of the cost of providing the early pension. In practice, 75 per cent of applicants aged 55–59 were selected for early retirement, and 69 per cent of those aged 44–49 for redundancy (the redundancy scheme was based on a maximum of six years' pay, so much cheaper for the employer than the early retirement scheme). It was accepted that the cost criterion was indirectly discriminatory in its effect; the issue was whether a defence of justification applied. The Tribunal concluded that cost-saving was a legitimate aim, but that its application was not proportionate, as the Land Registry could have given early retirement to all those who applied, although this would have added £19 million to the cost of the scheme, for which only £12 million had been allocated.

The Appellants were among 142 applicants from the two Lytham St Anne's offices, of whom 117 were ultimately selected for early retirement or redundancy, as applicable. The selectors worked on the basis of selecting the maximum number of people who could be paid off for £12 million across the three pairs of offices. Across the six offices, 238 were selected from 404 applicants. The Tribunal found that the Civil Service unions had been strongly opposed to any selection criteria which involved assessment of performance or value to the organization, and this was the main reason the cost criterion was applied to the virtual exclusion of any other. The Tribunal's reasoning on justification was based on a surmise that it was not essential for the cost of the scheme to be limited to £12 million, since the employer had not shown the additional £19.7 million required to enable all the applicants to depart was 'unaffordable'.

The EAT concluded as follows:

> The essence of the Tribunal's reasoning was that the Appellant had not demonstrated a 'real need' to limit its spending on the Scheme to £12m. . . . It held that it had not done so because it had not shown that payment of the additional £19.7m was 'unaffordable'. By that it evidently

meant that the Appellant had not shown that the funds were absolutely unavailable, in the sense that they could not be paid without insolvency: it pointed out that the Appellant's reserves far exceeded that amount (albeit that Treasury approval was needed to spend them) . . . In our view, to apply a test of unaffordability in that sense is to fall into the error of treating the language of 'real need', or 'reasonable needs'. . . as connoting a requirement of absolute necessity. It is well established that that is not the case: see the judgments of the Court of Appeal in *Barry* ([1999] ICR 319, at p. 336 A–B) and in *Cadman v Health and Safety Executive* [2005] ICR 1546, and of Elias P in this Tribunal in *Blackburn* (above), at paras 17–21 (pp. 509–510).

The effect of that principle, applied to a case like the present, seems to us to be that an employer's decision about how to allocate his resources, and specifically his financial resources, should constitute a 'real need' – or, to revert to the language of aim and means, a 'legitimate aim' – even if it is shown that he could have afforded to make a different allocation with a lesser impact on the class of employee in question. To say that an employer can only establish justification if he shows that he could not make the payment in question without insolvency is to adopt a test of absolute necessity. *The task of the employment tribunal is to accept the employer's legitimate decision as to the allocation of his resources as representing a genuine 'need' but to balance it against the impact complained of.*[2] This is of course essentially the same point, adjusted to the different formulation of the test, as we make at para. 34 above. If the Tribunal had carried out that exercise it would, we believe, inevitably have come to the same conclusion as we have reached, on our approach[. . .]

38. We have not in reaching this conclusion lost sight of the fact that the cheapness criterion was indeed disproportionately unfavourable to employees in the Claimants' age group, and we can well understand their disappointment at their non-selection. But it is fundamental that not all measures with a discriminatory impact are unlawful. Sometimes they have to be put up with. And we are bound to say, though this is not central to our reasoning, that in the present case the impact is not as severe as in many cases. Those affected did not lose their jobs or lose any other benefit which they had a positive expectation of receiving: rather, they lost out on the chance to take advantage of a benefit – admittedly a very substantial benefit – on which they had no right to count and which could indeed be described as a windfall. It is also important to emphasise that a central element in our conclusion is the Tribunal's finding that the Appellant had no real alternative, if it was to select at all, to using the cheapness criterion. We are not sure that that was an inevitable conclusion, and in other similar cases the evidence might well produce a different result. It does not, accordingly, follow from this decision that the use of a similarly discriminatory criterion will necessarily be justified in other cases.

Lockwood v Department of Work and Pensions ([2013] EWCA Civ 1195) involved a 26-year-old civil servant made compulsorily redundant after just under eight years' service. The established civil service redundancy scheme provided for a payment calculated as follows, subject to an overall maximum of three years' pay:

(a) one month's pay for each year of service, plus
(b) the lesser of:
    (i) one month's pay for each year of service given after five years' service and
    (ii) one month's pay for each year of service given after the employee's 30th birthday, plus
(c) one month's pay for each year of service after the employee's 35th birthday.

2 My emphasis.

She was entitled to a payment of £10,849, but, had she been over 35 with the same length of service, she would have received an additional £17,690. She argued that this amounted to direct discrimination on grounds of age. As with *Benson*, there was no question of the discriminatory effect on younger employees, particularly those under 30; the sole issue was the operation of the justification defence.

Evidence provided by the civil service which was accepted by the Tribunal made it clear that the reason for the more generous provision for employees aged over 35 was that, statistically, they were likely to have more difficulty than younger employees to obtain alternative employment and to have acquired long-term responsibilities such as marriage, children and mortgagees. It was important to treat all employees in the same category in the same way, and not to apply an element of means testing to individual cases. Further, to provide compensation to younger employees on the same basis as older employees would greatly increase the cost of the scheme and the consequent burden on the public purse.

The EAT concluded that the Employee's circumstances were materially different from those of the chosen comparators, and thus there was no direct discrimination. In any event, they accepted that any discriminatory effect was objectively justified on the basis of the legitimate aim of providing an adequate financial cushion where it was most likely to be needed, and that it was proportionate when balanced against the disparate effect.

The Court of Appeal concluded that the employee's relevant circumstances were not materially different from those of employees aged over 35; in both cases the relevant circumstance was their age, though the age itself was different. There was no difference between a comparison between black and white employees in a race discrimination case, and comparing persons of different ages in an age discrimination case. It followed from this that the employee had been treated less favourably than the comparators; the issue was whether this was objectively justified. The Court of Appeal concluded that the Tribunal had carried out a proper balancing act, applying relevant factors, and that there was no reason to disturb their conclusion on justification, though a different Tribunal might have come to a different conclusion.

Case law in this area shows that the Court of Appeal and EAT will play close attention to the employer's purpose in devising and applying the details of the scheme, and whether that purpose is legitimate. In practice, once satisfied that the purpose is legitimate, they are more likely than not to accept that the means are proportionate, despite the discriminatory effect on some individuals and/or groups.

MacCulloch v ICI [2008] was a case which was not dissimilar to *Lockwood* on its facts. The employer operated a scheme for redundancy compensation which was based on annual salary and years of employment, and was relatively complex, giving maximum entitlement (up to 175 per cent of salary) to employees made redundant between the ages of 50 and 57, on the basis that this group would find it most difficult to obtain alternative employment, *and* were still some years away from receiving their occupational pensions. After 57, the redundancy payments reduced relatively rapidly, such that a person aged 61 years and four months at his redundancy would receive only 50 per cent of salary, the same as a person in his early 30s. The employee was aged just under 37 at her redundancy, and had been employed for seven years and eight months. Her redundancy payment was based on 55 per cent of salary, whereas a person aged 50–57 with ten years' service would have received 175 per cent of salary. She argued that the scheme was directly discriminatory because of the age criterion, and indirectly discriminatory on grounds of age because it rewarded longer service, albeit to a maximum of ten years.

The Tribunal reached this conclusion on legitimate aims:

> 13. The Tribunal directed itself that in order to determine the issue of justification it had to determine whether the scheme could be treated as a proportionate means to achieve a legitimate aim. As a bare statement of the test for justification, that is consistent with the principles we have outlined.

> 14. The employers identified a number of aims of the scheme. First, it was alleged that one of its purposes, reflected in the ten-year service criterion, was to encourage and reward loyalty. The Tribunal accepted that this was a legitimate aim, and indeed was one of the aims underlying the statutory redundancy payments scheme in its present format. We note that it is also one of the potential justifications expressly referred to in regulation 32.
>
> 15. A second aim relied upon by the employers, also accepted by the Tribunal, was that it was legitimate to give a larger financial payment to older workers because they were more vulnerable in the job market and it gave them some protection from the stress which losing employment would otherwise create. The Tribunal concluded that it did not require evidence from any express research study to support that conclusion. The Tribunal observed that it had ample evidence, from its own knowledge, that older workers out of a job had real difficulty in obtaining new employment. That may not be how matters ought to be, given the protection against age discrimination, but that is still the practical reality.
>
> 16. Finally, the Tribunal also accepted the third reason relied upon by the employers, namely that it was extremely popular being a generous scheme which applied to all members of staff, regardless of where they worked or whether they were manual or white collar. The respondents submitted that having these generous payments for older workers encouraged people to leave who might not otherwise have done so, thereby making available space for more junior employees. It also avoided compulsory redundancies and made it easier to manage change.
>
> 17. The Tribunal was not, however, persuaded that it was a legitimate objective that the company should honour contractual promises it had made to the work force. As the Tribunal noted, if the scheme were unlawful because of discrimination on grounds of age then the scheme would have to be amended to make it legally compliant whatever expectations the parties might have.

The Court of Appeal concluded that the Tribunal had considered whether the aims of the scheme were legitimate in a proper fashion, but had then failed to consider whether the means were proportionate, and remitted the matter to the same Tribunal, adding as follows:

> The treatment of the claimant was the result of the application of fixed rules. She fell into a particular category, depending on age and length of service, and was treated accordingly. We accept, as [Counsel] submits, that the extent to which she (and others similarly placed) are disadvantaged by the rules of the scheme, when compared with her comparators, is highly relevant to the proportionality issue (assuming that legitimate aims have been established). But the reason for the claimant's treatment is the adoption and application of the scheme, and it is the aims of the scheme which must justify (or not) her particular treatment.
>
> 35. The question then arises whether the means to achieve those aims, having regard to the detrimental effect on the individual, are justified. Even in that context however, we do not think that the position of the individual can be regarded without any consideration for the scheme as a whole. It seems to us that in carrying out the proportionality exercise it will still be necessary to bear in mind that any change in the differential between the claimant's payment and the sum paid to her comparator will necessarily have an impact on the structure of the scheme as a whole. So, whilst the proportionality test must focus on the extent of the disadvantage, the balancing exercise will have to have regard to the impact which a different scheme would have on the whole range of employees.
>
> 36. The fact that the rules are fixed and do not vary with individual circumstances is a feature of the scheme which itself needs justifying – although we surmise that in practice that will not be difficult in a scheme of this nature since transparency and equality of treatment are important principles in their own right. However, we do not accept that in assessing justification

for a scheme of this kind it is necessary or appropriate to focus on the matters specifically referable to the individual but not shared by others of the same age or length of service. The employer has never sought to treat the claimant less favourably as an individual, but only in so far as she falls into a particular category defined by age and length of service. No doubt where a scheme envisages the exercise of discretions depending on individual circumstance, different considerations may arise. But that is not this case.

15.5 Other discriminatory acts

Homer v Chief Constable of West Yorkshire Police ([2012] UKSC 15) involved alleged indirect discrimination in relation to qualifications. The Claimant retired from the police as a Detective Inspector in October 1995 at the age of 51, and went to work as a legal adviser for the Police National Legal Database. At the time, a law degree was not required for this work, and all legal advisers received the same salary. In 2006, in order to improve recruitment by offering career progression, the PNLD adopted a new salary structure based on three thresholds, the last of which required the individual to hold a law degree. By the time the Claimant's final appeal against a refusal to regrade him was heard in November 2006, the 2006 Regulations were in force and he was aged 62. It was the expectation of both sides that he would retire in the summer of 2009, when he reached 65. A part-time law degree would take a minimum of four years, which would take him beyond his expected retirement age.

The Tribunal accepted that persons aged 60–65 were put at a particular disadvantage by the requirement, as they would not have time to obtain a law degree before their normal retirement age. The EAT and Court of Appeal, however, held that the reason for the disadvantage was not age of itself, but the proximity of leaving work, and the proper group for comparison purposes was those giving up work for other reasons.

The Supreme Court rejected this approach. Again, Lady Hale gave the leading judgment:

> This argument involves taking the particular disadvantage which is suffered by a particular age group for a reason which is related to their age and equating it with a similar disadvantage which is suffered by others but for a completely different reason unrelated to their age. If it were translated into other contexts it would have alarming consequences for the law of discrimination generally. Take, for example, a requirement that employees in a particular job must have a beard. This puts women at a particular disadvantage because very few of them are able to grow a beard. But the argument leaves sex out of account and says that it is the inability to grow a beard which puts women at a particular disadvantage and so they must be compared with other people who for whatever reason, whether it be illness or immaturity, are unable to grow a beard.
>
> Ironically, it is perhaps easier to make the argument under the current formulation of the concept of indirect discrimination, which is now also to be found in the Equality Act 2010. Previous formulations relied upon disparate impact – so that if there was a significant disparity in the proportion of men affected by a requirement who could comply with it and the proportion of women who could do so, then that constituted indirect discrimination. But, as Mr Allen points out on behalf of Mr Homer, the new formulation was not intended to make it more difficult to establish indirect discrimination: quite the reverse. . . . It was intended to do away with the need for statistical comparisons where no statistics might exist. It was intended to do away with the complexities involved in identifying those who could comply and those who could not and how great the disparity had to be. Now all that is needed is a particular disadvantage when compared with other people who do not share the characteristic in question. It was not intended to lead

us to ignore the fact that certain protected characteristics are more likely to be associated with particular disadvantages.

In any event, it cannot be right to equate leaving work because of impending retirement with other reasons for doing so. They are materially different. A person who leaves work for family reasons or takes early retirement generally has some choice in the matter. Indeed, she may factor into her decision whether it would be advisable to obtain the law degree and with it the higher grading before doing so. A person who is coming up against the mandatory retirement age does not have the same choice. Any extension depends upon the decision of the employer which cannot be depended upon at the relevant time. At the relevant time for this case, regulation 30 of the Age Regulations provided that the decision to retire an employee at the age of 65 did not need to be justified. Hence, as Mr Allen puts it, this is a case of running up against the buffers of a mandatory retirement age rather than a matter of choice.

Nor is this a question of asking for more favourable treatment for people of their age. It obviously should be possible to cure the discrimination in a non-discriminatory way. In *London Underground Ltd v Edwards (No 2)* [1999] ICR 494, for example, the new rosters for underground train drivers were held to be indirectly discriminatory because all the men could comply with them but not all the women could do so: it was a 'striking fact' that not a single man was disadvantaged despite the overwhelming preponderance of men in the pool of train drivers affected. The reason, of course, was that the new rosters had a greater impact upon single parents and single parents are predominantly (though not exclusively) female. But the problem could be solved, not by making an exception for the women, but by making arrangements for single parents of whatever sex. This problem could have been solved by making arrangements for people appointed before the new criterion was introduced.

Ingenious though the argument put forward by Mr Lewis is, therefore, to my mind it is too ingenious. The law of indirect discrimination is an attempt to level the playing field by subjecting to scrutiny requirements which look neutral on their face but in reality work to the comparative disadvantage of people with a particular protected characteristic. A requirement which works to the comparative disadvantage of a person approaching compulsory retirement age is indirectly discriminatory on grounds of age. There is, as Lord Justice Maurice Kay acknowledged, 'unreality in differentiating between age and retirement' [34]. Put simply, the reason for the disadvantage was that people in this age group did not have time to acquire a law degree. And the reason why they did not have time to acquire a law degree was that they were soon to reach the age of retirement. The resulting scrutiny may ultimately lead to the conclusion that the requirement can be justified. But if it cannot, then it can be modified so as to remove the disadvantage.

Having allowed the Claimant's appeal on that issue, and so established that indirect discrimination had occurred, the Supreme Court moved on to consider whether the requirement for a law degree was justified.

As Mummery LJ explained in *R (Elias) v Secretary of State for Defence* [2006] EWCA Civ 1293,

[T]he objective of the measure in question must correspond to a real need and the means used must be appropriate with a view to achieving the objective and be necessary to that end. So, it is necessary to weigh the need against the seriousness of the detriment to the disadvantaged group.

He went on, at [165], to commend the three-stage test for determining proportionality derived from *de Freitas v Permanent Secretary of Ministry of Agriculture, Fisheries, Lands and Housing* [1999] 1 AC 69, 80:

First, is the objective sufficiently important to justify limiting a fundamental right? Secondly, is the measure rationally connected to the objective? Thirdly, are the means chosen no more than is necessary to accomplish the objective?

As the Court of Appeal held in *Hardy & Hansons plc v Lax* [2005] EWCA Civ 846, [2005] ICR 1565 [31, 32], it is not enough that a reasonable employer might think the criterion justified. The tribunal itself has to weigh the real needs of the undertaking, against the discriminatory effects of the requirement.

The ET found that the aim of requiring a law degree was to facilitate the recruitment and retention of staff of appropriate calibre within the PNLD. It is not disputed that this was a legitimate aim. When it comes to considering proportionality, however, it is necessary to distinguish the aim of recruitment from the aim of retention. It is also necessary to distinguish the aim of retaining newly or recently recruited staff, who stand to benefit from the opportunity of career progression, and the aim of retaining existing staff, who were recruited under a different system, and who may or may not be motivated to stay by such an incentive. It was clearly important to the developing organisation to retain the skills and expertise of its existing highly valued staff, including Mr Homer. This means, as the EAT pointed out, that it was necessary to distinguish between the justification of the criteria for recruitment and the justification of the criteria for the thresholds above that, and in particular the third threshold.

The ET (perhaps in reliance on the IDS handbook on age discrimination) regarded the terms 'appropriate', 'necessary' and 'proportionate' as 'equally interchangeable' [29, 31]. It is clear from the European and domestic jurisprudence cited above that this is not correct. Although the regulation refers only to a 'proportionate means of achieving a legitimate aim', this has to be read in the light of the Directive which it implements. To be proportionate, a measure has to be *both* an appropriate means of achieving the legitimate aim *and* (reasonably) necessary in order to do so. Some measures may simply be inappropriate to the aim in question: thus, for example, the aim of rewarding experience is not achieved by age related pay scales which apply irrespective of experience (*Hennigs v Eisenbahn-Bundesamt*; *Land Berlin v Mai*, Joined Cases C-297/10 and C-298/10 [2012] 1 CMLR 18); the aim of making it easier to recruit young people is not achieved by a measure which applies long after the employees have ceased to be young (*Kücükdeveci v Swedex GmbH & Co KG*, Case C-555/07, [2011] 2 CMLR 33). So, it has to be asked whether requiring existing employees to have a law degree before they can achieve the highest grade is appropriate to the aims of recruiting and retaining new staff or retaining existing staff within the organisation. The EAT expressed some scepticism about this [45, 46].

A measure may be appropriate to achieving the aim but go further than is (reasonably) necessary in order to do so and thus be disproportionate. The EAT suggested that 'what has to be justified is the discriminatory effect of the unacceptable criterion' [44]. Mr Lewis points out that this is incorrect: both the Directive and the Regulations require that the criterion itself be justified rather than that its discriminatory effect be justified (there may well be a difference here between justification under the anti-discrimination law derived from the European Union and the justification of discrimination in the enjoyment of convention rights under the European Convention of Human Rights).

Part of the assessment of whether the criterion can be justified entails a comparison of the impact of that criterion upon the affected group as against the importance of the aim to the employer. That comparison was lacking, both in the ET and in the EAT. Mr Homer (and anyone else in his position, had there been someone) was not being sacked or downgraded for not having a law degree. He was merely being denied the additional benefits associated with being at the highest grade. The most important benefit in practice is likely to have been the impact upon his final salary and thus upon the retirement pension to which he became entitled. So, it has to be asked whether it was reasonably necessary in order to achieve the legitimate aims of the scheme to deny those benefits to people in his position? The ET did not ask itself that question.

> To some extent the answer depends upon whether there were non-discriminatory alternatives available. It is not clear whether the ET were suggesting that an exception should have been made for Mr Homer (who was on any view an exceptional case) or whether they were suggesting that the criterion should have been modified to include qualifications other than law degrees. As the EAT said, an ad hominem exception may be the right answer in personnel management terms but it is not the answer to a discrimination claim. Any exception has to be made for everyone who is adversely affected by the rule. 'Grandfather clauses' preserving the existing status and seniority, with attendant benefits, of existing employees are not at all uncommon when salary structures are revised. So, it is relevant to ask whether such a clause could have represented a more proportionate means of achieving the legitimate aims of the organisation. On the other hand, what is in issue here is not preserving existing benefits but affording entry to a newly created higher grade.

As in *Seldon*, the issue of justification on the facts of that case was remitted to the original Tribunal for a decision, but the case is a useful one in establishing what may constitute a legitimate aim.

15.6 Further reading

Blackham, 'Falling on their feet: young workers, employment and age discrimination (Case Comment)' (2015) 44(2) *Industrial Law Journal* 246.

Connolly, 'Objectively justifying compulsory retirement (Case Comment)' (2012) 109(Jun) *Employment Law Bulletin* 6.

Monaghan, 'Justifying direct age discrimination: when will a mandatory retirement age not amount to direct age discrimination? *Seldon v Clarkson Wright and Jakes* (Case Comment)' (2012) 6 *Journal of Business Law* 479.

Rodgers, 'Labour law and the "public interest": discrimination and beyond' (2011) 2(4) *European Labour Law Journal* 302.

Chapter 16

Leave for family and dependants

Chapter contents

16.1 Overview

This chapter covers the employee's statutory entitlement to unpaid leave in two circumstances:

- to deal with emergencies at short notice;
- to look after his children at times which are foreseeable in advance, such as school holidays.

It also deals with the employee's right to request flexible working.

16.2 Introduction

As with many areas of Employment Law, employees' entitlements to time off for domestic reasons have grown up piecemeal and there are various inconsistencies. All entitlements derive from statute and underlying them is recognition that in most families with dependent children both parents are likely to be working. The leave available is unpaid, unless the employment contract provides otherwise. Parental leave (not to be confused with Statutory Parental Leave) is available to cover planned absences for parents to care for their own children (for example, during school holidays), while time off for dependants is designed to enable individuals to take leave at short notice (or no notice at all) to deal with emergencies involving their dependants (a broader category than their children). Significantly, it is only intended to enable the employee to deal with the immediate emergency, and should not last more than two to three days at a time.

Overall, there is the difficulty, for both employers and employees, that entitlements have developed piecemeal, with overlaps between them (and also with Shared Parental Leave in particular), and differing procedural requirements.

16.3 Parental leave

Under MPLR 1999 as amended an employee may take up to 18 weeks' unpaid leave in the first 18 years of his child's life, at a maximum of four weeks per year, provided:

- he is a parent of the child;
- he has responsibility for the child; and
- the leave is taken to look after the child.

Note that the entitlement is 18 weeks *per child* for each parent, so that a parent with three children is entitled to 54 weeks in total. This is applicable even in the case of twins and other multiple births. Since the leave is available to each parent – and may be taken separately or together – a couple have a total of 36 weeks per child, which may be utilised as they think fit, with the limitation that it may only be taken in periods of one week or multiples thereof.

The concept behind parental leave is that it can be taken when the parent needs time off to look after the child for reasons which are predictable well in advance – school holidays in the case of a child who is at school, when a childminder is on holiday, or perhaps when the child is or has been in hospital for a planned operation. It therefore differs from time off for dependants, which is intended to cover emergencies.

In *South Coast Trains Ltd v Rodway* ([2004] IRLR 777, EAT) it was ruled that parental leave could only be taken in blocks of one week. Therefore, an employer who refused to allow the employee one day's parental leave was entitled to do so.

16.3.1 Evidential and notice requirements

MPLR 1999 sch. 2 applies in default of a collective agreement to the contrary.

a) The employer may request evidence of:
   - The employee's responsibility or expected responsibility for the child.
   - The date of the child's birth or placement for adoption.

b) The employee must give:
   - At least 21 days' notice of the date his leave will start, together with the date the leave will end.
   - Where an expectant father wishes to take parental leave from the date of the child's birth, he must give at least 21 days' notice of the expected week of childbirth, together with the length of leave he intends to take. Bear in mind that he can now take paternity leave, either immediately after the birth or later, provided that it is completed within 56 days of the birth.
   - In the case of adoption, the parent must give at least 21 days' notice of the week the child is expected to be placed, and the length of the leave he intends to take.

c) Parental leave may only be taken in blocks of one week, and a maximum of four weeks for any one child per year. However, where the employee has more than one child, he is entitled to the relevant multiple of four weeks, and, he may, of course, look after more than one of his children at a time.

d) The employer has limited powers to postpone the taking of parental leave:
   - He cannot postpone the taking of leave at the time of birth or adoption where the employee has given the proper notice.
   - He may postpone parental leave where he considers that the operation of the business would be unduly disrupted if the employee took leave during the period requested. The employer must notify the employee in writing within seven days of the employee's notice, that he is postponing the leave, and he must allow the employee to take the leave within six months.
   - The DTI Guidance gives the following examples of good reasons for postponing parental leave:
     - Where the work is at a seasonal peak
     - Where a significant proportion of the workforce applies for parental leave at the same time (school holidays!)
     - Where the employee's role is such that his absence at a particular time would unduly harm the business.

❖ EXAMPLE

Simon and Jane both work for the same small firm and have a four-year-old daughter who started school in September. On 20 January, they both put in applications for a week's parental leave to cover the half-term week (10–14 February). On 22 January, the manager replied, saying that because several other employees wanted the same week off (either as parental leave or taken out of their ordinary leave), he could not allow them both to take parental leave at the same time. He suggested that Simon and Jane decide between them who should take parental leave at half-term, and the other could take it during the Easter school holidays. This is what happened.

❖ THINKING POINT

Miranda has a seven-year-old daughter at primary school. She applied for and was granted one week's parental leave to cover the May half-term period. On Sunday, the day before she was due to return to work, her employer discovered from her Facebook page that she spent Monday to Friday of that week cycling from London to Paris in aid of a breast cancer charity, after leaving her daughter with her parents.

What should the employer do?

16.3.2 Remedies for refusal or unreasonable postponement of parental leave

The employee must make application to an Employment Tribunal within three months of the date of refusal. The Tribunal has powers to make a declaration and to award such compensation as it considers just and equitable, having regard to the employer's behaviour and any loss sustained by the employee.

16.3.3 Terms and conditions during parental leave

These are the same as those applicable to a woman during additional maternity leave.

16.3.4 Returning to work after parental leave

The position is the same as is applicable to a woman returning from ordinary maternity leave.

However, for redundancy purposes an employee on parental leave should be treated as though he is not absent from work.

16.3.5 Detriment and automatic unfair dismissal

The position is identical to that applicable to maternity leave.

16.4 Flexible working

A right to *request* flexible working has been available to parents of children under six since April 2003. Eligibility was then gradually extended, and the right now applies to *all* employees, after 26 weeks' continuous employment. The current provisions are set out in ERA 1996 s. 80F as amended.

S.80F enables an employee who qualifies to request a change in the terms and conditions of his employment relating to:

- hours of work;
- time of work; and
- place of work.

The philosophy is that a qualifying employee should be able to propose a change in his work which suits him, for example:

- going part-time;
- working from home one day a week;
- compressing five working days into four; or
- starting and finishing work earlier or later.

❖ EXAMPLE

Pat has an elderly mother who recently had a stroke and lives some 50 miles from her. The family are keen that she should stay in her own home as long as possible, but a certain amount of looking after is needed, along with shopping and dealing with household tasks. Pat applies to work her 35-hour week in four 'long' days rather than five days, so giving her a free day during the week to spend time with her mother, in rotation with other relations.

❖ EXAMPLE

Chris is a member of the British youth triathlon squad, which involves him in regular competitions and training camps at weekends, often at considerable distances from home. In order to make it easier to combine this with his work, he applies to finish work at 3.00pm on Fridays and start again at 11.00am on Mondays, increasing the length of his working days for the rest of the week to compensate.

16.4.1 Application

S. 80F(2) provides that an application for flexible working may be made only once in any 12-month period and must be in writing and dated. It must state:

- whether and when any previous application has been made;
- the change to the working pattern which is requested;
- the date for the change to come into effect; and
- the effect the change may have on the employer, and how this can be dealt with.

In practice, a letter which covers these points will suffice unless the employer has a specific form.

16.4.2 Grounds for refusal of request

The legislation applies a presumption that any request for flexible working should be granted. S. 80G(1)(b) provides that a request may only be refused on one or more of the following grounds, and places the burden of proof on the employer:

- additional costs;
- detrimental effect on ability to meet customer demand;
- inability to reorganise work among existing staff;
- inability to recruit existing staff;
- detrimental effect on quality;

- detrimental effect on performance;
- insufficient work available during the periods the employee wants to work;
- planned structural changes.

16.4.3 Procedure following receipt of application

- Within 28 days the employer must arrange a meeting with the employee to discuss the application. The employee is entitled to be accompanied by a colleague;
- within 14 days after the meeting the employer must write to the employee giving formal written notice of the decision.
  - If the request is accepted, the notice should be dated and should state the working pattern agreed and the date it takes effect;
  - if the request is refused, the employer must set out the s. 80G(1)(b) reason for the refusal and inform the employee of the appeal process.

16.4.4 Appeal process

- Within 14 days of the notice of refusal the employee must set out the grounds of appeal in writing;
- within 14 days of the appeal notice the employer must hold a meeting to discuss the matter (or he may uphold the appeal before the meeting and inform the employee of this in writing);
- within 14 days of the appeal meeting the employer must write to the employee either upholding the appeal (and stating the new working pattern and the date it will take effect), or dismissing the appeal, stating the s. 80G(1)(b) grounds and the reasons they apply.

Following the dismissal of his appeal to the employer, the employee may bring a claim to an Employment Tribunal, on one of the following grounds only (s. 80H):

- the employer has not followed the procedure set out in the Regulations;
- the employer's ground for rejecting the application was not within those listed in s. 80G(1)(b);
- the employer's decision was based on incorrect facts.

Essentially, the tribunal's role is to ensure that the employer followed the proper procedure and considered the request seriously.

The application to the tribunal must be made within three months of the date the employee was notified of the employer's decision on his appeal or the date a breach of the Regulations occurred. The tribunal may extend this time limit if satisfied that it was not reasonably practicable for the employee to bring the application within this time.

So far, there has been very little case law in relation to flexible working, which suggests that few applications are refused.

In the unreported first-instance case of *Clarke v Telewest Communications* the employee requested that on returning from maternity leave her hours should change from Monday to Friday 10.00–18.30, plus some weekends, to Monday to Friday 09.30–17.00 only. The employer offered various alternative patterns, but all included some combination of evenings and weekends. The Tribunal found that:

- the employer failed to reply promptly to the original request and to hold a meeting within 28 days of the original request;
- the decision to refuse the request was in reality made before the meeting and without proper consideration;

- there was no adequate explanation of the refusal; and
- the written reasons for the refusal did not set out the s. 80g(1)(b) and so the employee was denied a proper opportunity to appeal.

Note that the Tribunal's decision was entirely based on procedural matters and nothing was said about the merits of the employer's decision.

Armstrong v DB Regio Tyne and Wear Ltd ET/2500602/11 is another first-instance decision, where the Tribunal made it clear that a man's application for flexible working should not be taken less seriously than a woman's. The case is worth examining in detail.

Mr Armstrong's young daughter suffered from a rare genetic disorder. His wife was doing an Open University course. They had a childminder on Mondays and Tuesdays, but had no family in the immediate area to help out with childcare responsibilities. In 2009 Mr Armstrong was put on the 'support' roster, rather than the main roster, which allowed him to work the same shifts every week, rather than having to work varied shift patterns on the main roster. The support roster allowed Mr Armstrong to work stable hours every Sunday, Monday, Tuesday and Friday. There was also a 'family-friendly' roster.

After DB took over the running of the Metro system on a TUPE-transfer, they reviewed the rosters to make more efficient use of drivers. Mr Louis-Fernand, a manager, met all the drivers on the support roster. In July 2010, Mr Louis-Fernand had an 'informal' meeting with Mr Armstrong, who was asked if his wife might be able to be more flexible in her working arrangements and if the couple could explore the possibility of using a different childminder if the current one could not accommodate changes. Mr Louis-Fernand reported that Mr Armstrong had a 'very poor excuse' for being on the support roster and that he should be removed from it. Mr Armstrong was informed that he would be taken off the support roster from December 2010.

Mr Armstrong appealed, reiterating that he needed every Wednesday and Thursday off to look after his daughter and every Monday and Tuesday morning free to take his children to the childminder. He argued that, if he was put on the main roster, although he would be able to swap shifts, he would have to do so up to four times every week. His appeal was unsuccessful.

The overall result of Mr Louis-Fernand's review was that the total number of drivers on the 'support' roster and 'family-friendly' roster was reduced from 13 to seven. Of those seven who remained, three were men and four were women. No women were taken off either roster, although some had to compromise by adjusting their working hours. A new 'red' roster replaced the old system. Three more men and one woman applied to be placed for the first time on the red roster. The female driver was successful, but the three male drivers' applications were rejected.

There was an initial period in December 2010 when Mr Armstrong was allowed to change shifts by his supervisor, but this stopped after another supervisor complained. Mr Armstrong tried shift swapping after that, but soon went off sick with ulcerative colitis, said by his doctor to have been brought on by stress. He claimed sex discrimination in the Employment Tribunal. His comparators were:

- Employee E – a woman who was allowed to stay on the roster because she has custody of her autistic grandson, albeit working one more day than she wanted to;
- Employee F – a woman with a son with attention deficit and hyperactivity disorder and autism who was able to stay on the roster, on the condition that she slightly alter her working hours;
- Employee C – a single mother, who successfully applied to be put on the roster for the first time after the review.

The Tribunal accepted that Employees E and F were appropriate comparators. Like Mr Armstrong, Employee E had a reason related to her child's medical condition for needing to be on the roster and had a partner who worked. Although she could not use any childcare assistance because the child could become violent, the Tribunal did not consider Mr Armstrong's childcare problems to be materially different.

The tribunal found Employee F's position to be even more similar to that of Mr Armstrong. Employee F also shared caring responsibility with a partner for a child with a serious medical condition. She had to take her son to school and he was much more attached to her than the father, making it important that she have flexibility.

However, the Tribunal found that Employee C was not an appropriate comparator. She had sole responsibility for a child and did not have a supportive partner to share the burden. The Tribunal accepted that the employer was right to draw a distinction between her and Mr Armstrong.

Next, the Employment Tribunal concluded that Mr Armstrong had demonstrated that there was evidence that he had suffered less favourable treatment on the ground of sex. On the review, only men were removed from the roster and, after the review, the only new applicant who succeeded in being put on it was female – Employee C, who had argued that she was the only female driver left on the main, non-flexible roster after the review. According to the Tribunal, there was an 'obvious lack of proportionality between the genders' on the new red roster.

On the burden of proof shifting, the Tribunal found that the employer had not shown that the less favourable treatment was for a reason other than Mr Armstrong's sex. Mr Louis-Fernand had used language to suggest that he was dismissive of Mr Armstrong's case, including saying that he had a 'very poor excuse' for wanting to work flexibly. No such language was used in relation to any of the female staff.

It seemed to the Tribunal that men had to fight harder to stay on the roster. It gave the examples of:

- a male employee who was expected to make an application to the Family Court to vary his access to his child, armed with evidence of the new roster;
- employee F, who was allowed without question to stay on the roster, even though her husband assisted with the care of their autistic son; and
- employee E, for whom there was no suggestion that her husband might be approached to change his shifts to care for their autistic grandson.

The Tribunal detected 'undercurrents too of some stereotypical views of women in employment'. The application to stay on the support roster by one male employee whose wife worked part time in a pub was turned down because, in the words of the Tribunal, the employer thought that 'her job was less important than his', presumably because she earned less.

The employment tribunal upheld Mr Armstrong's claim of sex discrimination and, although he had not suffered any financial loss, awarded him £5,000 for injury to feelings.

16.4.5 Remedies

S. 80I

The Tribunal may make an order for reconsideration of the application, and may award compensation of up to eight weeks' pay (statutory maximum for a week's pay applies), based on what it considers just and equitable. If discrimination on the grounds of a protected characteristic is found, as in *Armstrong*, the Tribunal may make an award for injury to feelings.

16.4.6 Detriment and automatic unfair dismissal

Once again, employees who work flexibly, or make application to work flexibly are protected against dismissal or detriment in the same way as those who take or seek to take maternity leave.

In addition, provided the employee has one year's continuity of employment, he can bring a claim for 'ordinary' unfair dismissal on the basis of constructive dismissal if an application for flexible working is refused or handled perversely or unreasonably (*Clarke v Telewest Communications*).

There is some overlap with sex discrimination legislation in that:

- a woman returning from maternity leave may argue that a refusal of flexible working constitutes indirect sex discrimination, on the basis that a requirement to work a 'traditional' working pattern creates a detriment for a considerably larger proportion of women than men;
- a man could bring a claim for direct sex discrimination if he can show that his application was treated less favourably than that of a woman in the same circumstances. This situation is seen in *Armstrong*.

16.5 Time off for dependants

ERA 1996 s. 57A(1) provides that an employee is entitled to be permitted to take 'reasonable' unpaid time off in order to take action necessary:

- to assist a dependant who is ill, injured, has given birth or been assaulted;
- to arrange care for an ill or injured dependant;
- as the result of the death of a dependant;
- due to the disruption or ending of care arrangements; or
- to deal with an incident at the child's school.

'Dependant' is defined (s. 57A(3)(4)(5)) as:

- the employee's spouse, partner, child, parent or a person who lives in the same household, but not a tenant, boarder or lodger;
- a person who reasonably relies upon the employee for help, when that person is ill, injured or assaulted, or to make arrangements for that person's care only.

❖ THINKING POINT

At 9.00am on Monday morning Peter rings from the Casualty Department of Derriford Hospital to say that an hour ago, just before he was due to set out for work, he found his next-door neighbour, old Mr Miller, in a heap at the bottom of the stairs. He explains that he has Mr Miller's spare key and generally keeps an eye on him. He decided to check on him this morning as he hadn't seen him all day Sunday, which is unusual. He is not sure whether Mr Miller is going to be kept in hospital, and wants to hang on there to make sure he isn't on his own until his daughter, Alice, who lives in Birmingham, can get here. Peter says that, realistically, he may not make it in today, certainly not until after lunch, but will keep the office informed.

Later in the day, Peter arrives at work and says that Mr Miller has broken his hip and is being kept in hospital. In due course, he would like to help out when Mr Miller is fit enough to come home. Can he discuss that when the situation is clearer?

Will Alice Miller also be able to get time off from her job in Birmingham to deal with the crisis involving her father? If so, how long?

Unlike parental leave, the intention behind the legislation is that the employee should be able to have time off at no notice or very short notice in order to take immediate action to deal with emergencies. However, this point was stretched somewhat in the case of *Royal Bank of Scotland plc v Harrison* ([2008] UKEAT/0093/08). The employee discovered on 8 December that her childminder would not be available on 22 December and subsequently argued that her taking that day off to look after the child fell within s. 57A. The employer argued that s. 57A only applied to emergencies and circumstances that arose suddenly. The EAT, however, ruled that 'unexpected' was to be judged at the time the situation arose, so that, although Mrs Harrison had a fortnight to make alternative arrangements, the need to take time off work could still be 'unexpected'.

By s. 57A(2) the employee must inform the employer as soon as practicable of:

- the reason for his absence; and
- how long he expects to be absent.

There is no statutory requirement for this information to be given in writing, so a telephone call or text will suffice, although there is nothing to prevent the employer from imposing more specific requirements. The issue of notification was considered by the EAT in *Ellis v Ratcliff Palfinger Ltd* ([2014] UKEAT/0438/13/BA). The employer's terms and conditions of employment included provision for two weeks' paternity leave on full pay, provided the employee gave 15 weeks' notice in line with the statutory requirements. Although Mr Ellis's wife was pregnant, he gave no notice before the birth of his intention to take paternity leave. The terms and conditions then provided as follows in relation to absence:

- If employees were absent from work due to an illness or injury, which incapacitated them from doing work they are employed to do, they must notify their line manager by telephone no later than 30 minutes after they were due to begin work.
- Thereafter the employee should keep in contact at intervals appropriate to the illness or condition preventing them from working.
- In any event, there should be contact, at the very least, once a week.
- In the first instance, absent employees were to contact their line manager and, if they were not immediately available, a message was to be left on the Respondent's absence line.

Note that these provisions referred specifically to absence by reason of illness or injury. Mr Ellis had worked for the employer since 2009, but on 25 November 2011 he was given a final written warning for repeated absences. Mrs Ellis was due to give birth on or about 6 February 2012. On that day, a Monday, the two went several times to the hospital, but each time Mrs Ellis was sent home. Mr Ellis did not contact the employer direct, though his father rang the employer that afternoon to say that he was at the hospital with his wife, who was about to give birth. Despite staying off work again on the Tuesday, Mr Ellis did not make contact until Wednesday, after the manager's son, a friend of his, had texted to tell him to contact work urgently. Later, Mr Ellis spoke to the manager, who criticised him for neither coming to work nor keeping in contact. That evening, 8 February, Mr Ellis left a voicemail to say he would not be in the next day. The Tribunal rejected his claims that he told the employer he would not be back until Monday 13 February. By that time the child had been born.

At the disciplinary hearing on 15 February, Mr Ellis claimed that he did not contact the employer on 7 February because his mobile battery had run out. He was dismissed with one month's notice on the basis of his failure to contact the employer, which, in their view, amounted to failure to obey a reasonable instruction.

At the Tribunal, Mr Ellis argued automatic unfair dismissal under ERA s. 99, on the basis that he had been dismissed for taking time off for dependants within s. 57A. However, the Tribunal rejected this argument. The Employment Judge said, robustly:

> 6.7 The view I have come to is that the claimant is not entitled to rely on s. 99 and s. 57(A) because the claimant did not tell his employer the reason for his absence as soon as reasonably practicable.
>
> 6.8 In this day and age of mobile phones even if the claimant's mobile phone had run out of battery early on the Monday or the Tuesday, there would have been no difficulty in him recharging his mobile phone and making appropriate phone calls early in the morning to his employers. I particularly take the point that once his wife had gone into childbirth there was every opportunity for him to go into the hospital corridor and make a quick telephone call to his employers which he failed to do. Even if for some reason his mobile phone was not working there would have been no difficulty, in my view, from him borrowing a mobile phone from somebody else to make the necessary phone calls. Even if that was not possible from the claimant's own evidence, he used the pay phone in the hospital to phone his father to make a telephone call on the Monday, and I can see no reason whatsoever why he could not have gone to the pay phone and made these phone calls from the pay phone on Tuesday and Wednesday.
>
> 6.9 So, in those circumstances I do not consider that s. 99 applies. In those circumstances I am satisfied that at the end of the day that the principal reason for the claimant's dismissal was his misconduct and that the respondent was satisfied, in their own mind, that the claimant had been guilty of all the matters that they alleged against him and they carried out a fair procedure in coming to that conclusion.

The EAT upheld that decision.

❖ THINKING POINT

Would the Tribunal have come to the same decision if the employee had not already been under a final warning for absence?

Qua v John Ford Morrison Solicitors ([2003] IRLR 184) is the leading case at present on the meaning of 'reasonable' time off. The employee was absent from work on eight separate occasions, for a total of 17 days, in order to look after her asthmatic son. The EAT stated that when determining what is reasonable time off work, the tribunal should work from the *employee's* perspective and ignore the disruption to the employer. An employee is entitled to take reasonable time off to look after a sick child, but the purpose of s. 57A leave is intended to enable the employee to deal with the unforeseen. Once a parent knows that his child is suffering from a medical condition which involves relapses, the situation does not fall within s. 57A. The employee is entitled to reasonable time off to make arrangements for the longer term, but not to take three weeks off work to look after the child herself. The EAT set out the following general principles:

- In determining how much time off is reasonable, an employer should always take account of the employee's individual circumstances. It may be that, in the vast majority of cases, not more than a few hours or, at most, one or two days would be regarded as reasonable to deal with the particular problem which has arisen. That said, there is no limit to the number of times an employee can be absent from work when unforeseen circumstances arise.
- The right to time off work when a dependant is suddenly or unexpectedly taken ill (or is injured or assaulted) is a right, in the first instance, to provide any necessary assistance; and, in the second, to make longer-term (or to restore disrupted) arrangements for care. Employees

do not have the right to take time off work in order to provide care for a sick or injured dependant themselves.

- Employees wishing to take more than a reasonable amount of time off (i.e. beyond the time needed to provide immediate assistance and make arrangements for longer-term care) may apply to their employers to take that extra time as part of their annual holiday entitlement, negotiate leave of absence without pay, or (in a situation involving a child) exercise their qualified legal right to take a period of unpaid parental leave.
- An employer's operational needs cannot be relevant to a consideration of the amount of time an employee reasonably needs to deal with an emergency involving a dependant. Indeed, an employee might well have to leave their desk or workstation at a moment's notice to attend to a dependant who is suddenly taken ill (or is injured or assaulted) at a time which the employer could show caused acute, or even insurmountable, operational problems. But taking into account the employer's needs as relevant to the overall reasonableness of the amount of time taken would frustrate the clear purpose of the legislation, which is to ensure that employees are permitted time off to deal with such an event, whenever it occurs, without fear of reprisals – so long as they inform their employers of the reasons for their absence and tell their employers how long they expect to be away.
- Unless unable to do so until after they have returned to work, employees are duty bound to inform their employers, as soon as is reasonably practicable, of the reasons for their absence (or continued absence) from work and must inform their employers about the expected duration of absence. A failure to comply with either of these requirements negates an employee's entitlement to take time off under s. 57A. However, absent employees are not obliged to telephone their employers every day to keep them informed of developments, although many would want to do so.
- Employers have no statutory right to demand that employees taking time off under s. 57A justify their absences by producing documentary evidence (e.g. medical notes, or death certificates). However, there is nothing to prevent employees suspected of abusing their statutory rights volunteering to produce such evidence to avoid disciplinary action or dismissal.

The last point is perhaps surprising, given that there is scope for abuse.

In the first-instance decision of *Naisbett v Npower Ltd* (ET/2502795/12) the Tribunal held that five absences totalling seven days in a period of a year by the mother of a three-year-old to deal with her daughter's minor illnesses did not go beyond what was reasonable. It may have been relevant to the decision that the employee's husband worked away from home and her parents also had full-time jobs and so could provide only limited assistance.

Forster v Cartwright Black Solicitors ([2004] UKEAT/0179/04/DM) dealt with the issue of how much time off is reasonable following the death of a close family member, and the purpose for which time off is permitted. Mrs Forster began working for the employer on 5 August 2002. In October she had three days off ill. Her father died in January 2003, and she was given 12 days paid bereavement leave. She had two days off sick in May, and then her mother died. She had a further five days' bereavement leave, and was then immediately given a sick note for two weeks on grounds of 'bereavement reaction', followed by a second. After the second sick note was sent to the employer, she was called in to a meeting on 12 June, and dismissed on grounds of her latest absence and absence record generally. As she did not have sufficient continuity of employment to claim unfair dismissal, the only way she could contest the dismissal was to claim automatic unfair dismissal on the basis of s. 99.

The basis of the decision was the interpretation of s. 57A(1)(c), permitting time off 'in consequence of the death of a dependant'. Mrs Forster submitted that this included absence to protect her health following the deaths of both parents in four months. The Tribunal, whose decision was upheld by the EAT, took the approach that the purpose of permitting time off following the death of a dependant went beyond enabling the employee to attend the funeral, but only as far as dealing with practical matters arising from the death, arranging the funeral, registering the death, and dealing with the estate. On that basis, Mrs Forster's two periods of sick leave did not fall within s. 57A, and therefore her dismissal was not automatically unfair.

McCulloch & Wallis Ltd v Moore [2003] is another unreported EAT case, and again emphasises the importance of the employee keeping the employer informed of the situation. Miss Moore, who did not have sufficient continuity to claim unfair dismissal, flew to Ireland at short notice after her father was injured in a road accident.

After three or four days without news, her employers (who suspected that she was taking more time off than was strictly necessary, given that she had brothers and sisters in Ireland) wrote to her instructing her to return to work on a specified date or face dismissal. The employee ignored her employer's instructions and remained at her father's bedside until he died on the day after the expected return date.

As there was no evidence to suggest that she needed to spend more time off work after having made arrangements for her father's admission to hospital (given that there were other members of the family close by) and she had not informed her employers that her father's condition had deteriorated and that he was not expected to survive, the EAT held that she had forfeited her rights under s. 57A by taking more than a reasonable amount of time off and by neglecting to inform her employers of the reasons for her continued absence from work and for how long she expected to be absent.

Nevertheless, the EAT was critical of her employer's decision to dismiss, and considered that she would have succeeded in an ordinary unfair dismissal case, had she had the necessary length of service.

Overall, the case law suggests that tribunals will apply a common-sense approach, and make their decisions very much on the facts of individual cases.

16.5.1 Detriment and automatic unfair dismissal

Yet again, an employee taking or seeking to take time off for dependants is protected in the same way as a woman taking maternity leave. However, the case law is clear that protection can be forfeited by a failure to inform the employer not only of the reason for taking time off at the outset, but if more time is needed – beyond one to two days – and why.

16.5.2 Remedies

An employee refused time off under this provision may make application to a tribunal within three months of the refusal. The tribunal make a declaration, and award such compensation as is just and equitable, having regard to the employer's behaviour and any loss to the employee. As yet there is no case law on the quantum of compensation.

16.6 Further reading

Busby, 'Carers and the Equality Act 2010: protected characteristics and identity' (2011) 11(2) *Contemporary Issues in Law* 71.

Golynker, 'Family-friendly reform of employment in the UK: an overstretched flexibility' (2015) 37(3) *Journal of Social Welfare & Family Law* 378.

Lewis, 'Balancing "time to work" and 'time to care": policy issues and the implications for mothers, fathers and children' (2009) 21(4) *Child and Family Law Quarterly* 443.

Mair, 'An ideal balance?' (2013) 117(Oct) *Employment Law Bulletin* 2.

Chapter 17

Equal pay

Chapter contents

17.1 Overview

Equal pay law is an element of anti-discrimination law. It is entirely based on statute and is a relatively recent development, the Equal Pay Act having only been passed in 1970. Unusually, it was not brought into force until 1975, as the Government wished to give employers the opportunity to equalise pay between men and women voluntarily.

The concept of equal pay is limited in scope. It is not concerned with 'fair' pay, but only that pay is the same between men and women. The circumstances in which a person of one sex may claim equal pay with a person of the other sex are also relatively narrowly defined. In particular, the claimant (usually but by no means invariably a woman) must identify a specific individual working for the same employer with whom her work and pay package may be compared. In many low-paid and low-skilled areas of work traditionally done by women, such as care assistants in residential homes, there may simply be no men with whom the necessary comparison exercise can be made. This is perhaps the most significant element in the continuance of a gender pay gap after 40 years of equal pay legislation.

The provisions of the Equal Pay Act have in the main been consolidated into the Equality Act 2010. The changes introduced in the 2010 Act will be considered later in this chapter.

17.2 Historical context

Before the Equal Pay Act 1970 came into force in 1975 there was nothing whatever in law to preclude an employer from paying women employees less than their male counterparts for doing the same work. Indeed, differential pay levels were so much the accepted norm that in *Roberts v Hopwood* [1925] AC 578 the House of Lords found Poplar Borough Council to be in breach of its fiduciary duty to its ratepayers by setting a minimum wage for its workforce at a figure well above that then prevailing for unskilled labourers (£4), and by paying this minimum to women as well as men. This case was brought by the District Auditor and decided on judicial review principles. The Lords deemed the Council's desire to be a model employer and to promote sex equality irrelevant factors in comparison with its duty to make proper use of public money.

Why should this have been the case? Despite the emergence of implied duties intended to protect the employee from the consequences of imbalances in bargaining power, the common law places a considerable value on freedom to negotiate the terms of the employment contract. From 1924, there was machinery to compel employers to pay set minimum wages to agricultural workers, as defined,[1] but employers were otherwise left to set their own pay rates, with or without trade union agreement. If women were prepared to do the same work for lower pay, that was of no concern to the courts.

Second, and more significantly, unequal pay was very much a reflection of the way society organised itself. To generalise to a degree, during the nineteenth and early twentieth centuries, social organisation was geared to households rather than individuals. At a time when the absence of effective contraception meant that marriage was followed sooner rather than later by children born at intervals of one to two years, a married man was the head of a household consisting, at a minimum, of himself, his wife and a number of dependent children. This unit might well be joined by his own or his wife's parents, particularly if widowed; unmarried or widowed siblings; and any orphaned children of relations. As head of a household, the married man was expected to provide for that household from his income. The wages of other adults in his household were secondary

1 Agricultural Wages (Regulation) Act 1924 and Agricultural Wages Act 1948. The latter was largely repealed by the Enterprise and Regulatory Reform Act 2013.

income. If the household could manage on the income of the head of the household alone, it would seek to do so; the only other earners in the household would be the young adult sons who were future heads of households. On this model, females only worked for pay from financial necessity, and their incomes were of secondary importance to those of their husbands or fathers. In a similar fashion, it was regularly argued before 1918 that there was no need for universal suffrage, as the Representation of the People Acts of 1867 and 1883 had created a 'household franchise', under which most male householders had the vote and exercised it on behalf of their households. This model of society does, of course, ignore the large numbers of widows in the population, often with dependent children, as well as those who remained unmarried and did not live under the same roof as their fathers or brothers. Many men and women worked in domestic service, and lived in, receiving food and board and a small wage.

From the early twentieth century, increasing numbers of middle class women moved into the workforce, in particular into teaching and administrative and clerical work. The invention of the typewriter greatly increased opportunities for women. Women also attended university, though Oxford and Cambridge did not at this time award them degrees. The Sex Disqualification Removal Act 1919 opened the professions to women, who thereafter qualified in some numbers as doctors, barristers, solicitors and accountants. One pioneer entrant into a male preserve was Miss Victoria Drummond, born into a distinguished Scottish family in 1894 with Queen Victoria among her godmothers. She became a Merchant Navy engineer officer via the traditional route of an apprenticeship ashore. Miss Drummond spent some 40 years at sea and was awarded the MBE for her gallant service at sea during the Second World War.[2] However, in this period there was no political pressure for equal pay. The leading feminists of the period, such as Eleanor Rathbone, instead campaigned for family allowances, so that married women could provide for their children independently of their husbands.

Pressure for equal pay came only from the late 1950s onwards. The Treaty of Rome, establishing the then European Economic Community, included a principle of equal pay for equal work as Article 119 (now Article 141). The Labour Party manifesto for the 1959 General Election included a commitment to equal pay for men and women. However, although a Labour government came to power in the autumn of 1964 and the TUC Conference of 1965 endorsed a principle of equal pay, no progress was made until the final months before the 1970 election. A major trigger seems to have been the strike among women sewing machinists making car seats at the Ford works at Dagenham in 1968, in protest against being paid 15 per cent less than men doing work graded by the company as equivalent in skill. An Equal Pay Bill was introduced into the Commons early in 1970 by Harold Wilson's government, and received the Royal Assent just before Parliament was prorogued at the end of May. A major element of the plans of the incoming Conservative government under Edward Heath was entry into the EEC; the Equal Pay Act gave effect to the requirements of Article 141, and was permitted to come into force without amendment (unlike the Equality Act 2010, where some provisions were repealed under the Coalition after the 2010 election, before they had come into force).

---

2 See Drummond, 1994. Though Victoria Drummond struggled from time to time against the prejudice of traditionalists of both sexes (a Board of Trade examiner privately admitted that she had been failed 31 times for a Chief Engineer's Certificate solely because she was a woman), she was highly regarded by most of her male counterparts. One described her as follows: 'She is about the most courageous woman I ever saw. She seems to be without fear or nerves, is very good at her job and has an uncanny power over engines, for which I once thanked God'. In the fashion of the day, Miss Drummond never married, despite at least one proposal, and lived between voyages with her two unmarried sisters. Happily, the Institute of Marine Engineering, Science and Technology, as the Institute of Marine Engineers has now become, takes considerable pride in its first lady member, and has a Victoria Drummond Room in its headquarters.

The Equal Pay Act as originally passed included only two routes to claiming equal pay with a male comparator:

- 'like work', that is, work which is the same or broadly similar;
- 'work rated equivalent', that is, work rated as equivalent in a job evaluation scheme (JES) previously carried out by the employer.

The first category dealt with the issue of women being paid less than men for doing the same or very similar work, often under different job titles, and was very largely successful; claims based on like work quickly became uncommon. However, this category did not address the issue of gender segregation in employment, where men and women tend to be concentrated in different types of work, even when working for the same employers, and 'women's work' tends to pay less than 'men's work'. The category of 'work rated equivalent' was intended to deal with this, but was limited in its effect because an employer could not be compelled to carry out a JES, and without a previous JES there was no possibility of a claim under this head.

In the case of *Commission for the European Communities v United Kingdom* [1982] IRLR 333, the European Court of Justice ruled that the Equal Pay Act did not give full effect to the principle of equal pay contained in Article 119, as it was not possible for a woman who was not doing like work with a man to claim equal pay unless the employer had carried out a JES. This gap in the Act's coverage was remedied by the introduction of the Equal Pay Act (Amendment) Regulations 1983, which created the route of 'work of equal value'. This mirrors work rated equivalent, with the important difference that the claimant first submits a claim for equal pay on the basis of work of equal value, and the Employment Tribunal commissions an independent expert to carry out an evaluation of the work done by the claimant and her chosen comparator.

The Equality Act 2010, which consolidates all pre-existing anti-discrimination legislation into a single statute, largely reproduces the Equal Pay Act as amended by the 1983 Regulations. The most important change is in the defence available to the employer. As little case law under the 2010 Act has reached appellate level at the time of writing, it is necessary to look in detail at the provisions of the 1970 Act and case law under it.

17.3 What is equal pay?

In ordinary colloquial English, 'equal' is usually taken to mean 'the same'. 'Equal pay' should therefore mean 'the same pay'. As with many things, it is rather more complicated than that, principally because a person's remuneration package may well contain several elements, not only the basic salary, but provision of a company car, employer's pension contribution and perhaps private medical insurance. Another employee might receive a standard hourly rate for his normal working hours, and be paid at overtime rates for hours outside the norm. Some employees may receive bonuses. For example, a group of claimants, mainly care assistants and canteen staff, in *Redcar & Cleveland Council v Bainbridge* ([2008] EWCA Civ 885), sought equal pay with a mainly male group of gardeners whose hourly pay rate was lower than theirs, but who received an attendance bonus which increased their basic pay by about 40 per cent.

Article 141 of the Treaty of Rome provides a comprehensive definition of 'pay' for the purposes of equal pay:

> Pay means the ordinary, basic or minimum wage or salary and any other consideration, whether in cash or in kind, which the worker receives, directly or indirectly, in respect of his employment from his employer.

The Equal Pay Act 1970 s. 1(1) (now Equality Act s. 66) inserted an 'equality clause' into all employment contracts, requiring men and women to receive the same contractual terms and conditions, including pay. Perhaps surprisingly, this has been consistently interpreted by the courts as meaning not simply that the value of the overall pay package must be the same, but that each individual element of the women's' pay package must be the same or better than each element of the men's'.

This was made clear by the House of Lords in *Hayward v Cammell Laird Shipbuilders* [1988] AC 894. The claimant established that her work as a canteen cook in a shipyard was of equal value with more highly paid male employees – electricians, plasterers and insulation fitters. Although her basic pay was lower than theirs, she had more favourable sick pay arrangements and also received free meals in the canteen. The employer argued that her overall pay package was the same or better than that of the comparators, but the Lords concluded that under the Act she was entitled to the same basic rate of pay, and the more favourable terms of her contract were unaffected. These terms were not automatically incorporated into the men's contracts – if the men wished to benefit from such terms they would ultimately have to pursue an equal pay claim using Miss Hayward's contract as the comparison.

In *Brownbill v St Helens & Knowsley Hospitals NHS Trust* [2011] EWCA Civ 903 the claimants made a comparison with comparators who were paid at higher rates for unsocial hours than they were, although their own package was already more favourable overall, due to higher hourly pay rates. Granting them the higher unsocial hours payment would place the men in a still worse position. The Court of Appeal held that the legislation required the comparison to be made on a term-by-term basis, irrespective of the overall package. The Court of Appeal did, however, note that pay packages for the different groups (here the women were healthcare assistants and a receptionist, the men car park attendants, drivers and a theatre porter) had, as is often the case, developed over the years in haphazard fashion. *Brownbill* was a case under the Equal Pay Act, but it would seem that the issue remains under the Equality Act.

It should be noted that the requirement for equal pay may be satisfied by equalising the pay of the comparators *downwards*, rather than raising the pay of the claimants.

17.4 The Equal Pay Act 1970 as amended

S.1 of the Act provided as follows:

> (1) The provisions of this section shall have effect with a view to securing that employers give equal treatment as regards terms and conditions of employment to men and to women, that is to say that (subject to the provisions of this section and of section 6 below)
>
> (a) for men and women employed on like work the terms and conditions of one sex are not in any respect less favourable than those of the other; and
>
> (b) for men and women employed on work rated as equivalent (within the meaning of subsection (5) below) the terms and conditions of one sex are not less favourable than those of the other in any respect in which the terms and conditions of both are determined by the rating of their work.

The following provisions of this section and section 2 below are framed with reference to women and their treatment relative to men, but are to be read as applying equally in a converse case to men and their treatment relative to women.

> (2) It shall be a term of the contract under which a woman is employed at an establishment in Great Britain that she shall be given equal treatment with men in the same employment,

that is to say men employed by her employer or any associated employer at the same establishment or at establishments in Great Britain which include that one and at which common terms and conditions of employment are observed either generally or for employees of the relevant class.

(3) Where a woman is employed at an establishment in Great Britain otherwise than under a contract which includes (directly or by reference to a collective agreement or otherwise) a term satisfying subsection (2) above, the terms and conditions of her employment shall include an implied term giving effect to that subsection.

(4) A woman is to be regarded as employed on like work with men if, but only if, her work and theirs is of the same or a broadly similar nature, and the differences (if any) between the things she does and the things they do are not of practical importance in relation to terms and conditions of employment; and accordingly in comparing her work with theirs regard shall be had to the frequency or otherwise with which any such differences occur in practice as well as to the nature and extent of the differences.

(5) A woman is to be regarded as employed on work rated as equivalent with that of any men if, but only if, her job and their job have been given an equal value, in terms of the demand made on a worker under various headings (for instance effort, skill, decision), on a study undertaken with a view to evaluating in those terms the jobs to be done by all or any of the employees in an undertaking or group of undertakings, or would have been given an equal value but for the evaluation being made on a system setting different values for men and women on the same demand under any heading.

(6) Subject to the following subsections, for purposes of this section–

(a) 'employed' means employed under a contract of service or of apprenticeship or a contract personally to execute any work or labour, and related expressions shall be construed accordingly;

(b) a person is to be regarded as employed at an establishment if he is employed to work in the establishment or, in the case of a person employed to work otherwise than in an establishment, if his employment is carried out from the establishment;

(c) two employers are to be treated as associated if one is a company of which the other (directly or indirectly) has control or if both are companies of which a third person (directly or indirectly) has control.

Therefore, a woman, or group of women, could claim equal pay with a man, or group of men, provided they were:

- employees of the same employer or 'associated employers', as defined;
- working at the same establishment or at different establishments under 'common terms and conditions'; or
- doing 'like work', 'work rated equivalent', or 'work of equal value'.

Each of these requirements must be considered in turn.

17.4.1 The same employer or associated employers

This issue gave rise to some case law but perhaps not as much as might be anticipated. 'Associated employers' was defined to include two common situations:

- one company was a subsidiary of another – both were associated employees;
- two or more companies were within a group under the ultimate control of another (an example would be the department store conglomerate House of Fraser) – all were associated employees.

One problem area in this sphere was within the public sector. Teachers in maintained schools within the state education system are employed by local education authorities. Although these are technically separate bodies, the terms and conditions of employment and pay scales for those teachers are set by a series of collective agreements at national level. Could one LEA be an associated employer of another? The decision reached by the courts in *South Ayrshire Council v Morton* [2002] IRLR 257 was perhaps not in accordance with the strict letter of s. 1(6)(c), since a local council is not a 'company', but certainly gave effect to its purpose.

Mrs Morton was the head teacher of a primary school and received a salary on the requisite point on the scale for primary school heads. However, in Scotland the pay scales for primary school heads (75 per cent women) were lower than those for secondary school heads (75 per cent men). Both scales were set by the Scottish Joint Negotiating Committee (SJNC), a quasi-autonomous body set up under the Education (Scotland) Act 1980, and prior to devolution under the general control of the Secretary of State for Scotland. The 32 local education authorities in Scotland were required to give effect to the salary scales but had discretion on how to do it. Mrs Morton, a primary school head employed by South Ayrshire Council, sought to use as comparator a male secondary school head employed by Highland Council. The Court of Session concluded that s. 1(6) had to be interpreted into conformity with Art. 141, following the ECJ case of *Defrenne v SABENA* Case 149/77 [1978] ECR 1365. Gill LJC said:

> The present case is a good example of what Article 141 is about. The Respondent contends that there is an objective and meaningful comparison to be made between her work and that of her comparator. . . . We consider that an SJNC settlement conducted under statutory authority and overall governmental control constitutes a national collective agreement of the kind contemplated in *Defrenne*. . . . In our view, it is logical and reasonable to suggest that in a uniform statutory regime governing pay and conditions in the public sector of education, comparisons may be made across the boundaries of the authorities that are statutorily obligation to give effect to it [. . .]
>
> The material considerations are that the claimant and her comparators are in the same branch of public service and are subject to a uniform system of national pay and conditions set by a statutory body whose decision is binding on their employers. It seems reasonable to us to refer to them as being engaged in the same service [. . .]
>
> This case involves teachers directly employed by local education authorities. What about those working in voluntary-aided schools, mainly 'faith schools', which are also part of the state system, but are controlled by their governing bodies, who work in cooperation with the LEAs? The LEAs are represented on the governing bodies. It is arguable that as teachers in such schools are paid according to national pay scales, although employed by the governing bodies, they come within the principle in *South Ayrshire Council v Morton,* but what is the position of ancillary workers in voluntary-aided schools who seek to make comparisons with workers employed by local authorities?

This was considered in *Dolphin v Hartlepool BC, South Tyneside MBC v Middleton* [2006] EAT 10/7/2006, where an issue arose in conjoined appeals as to whether female employees could rely upon their chosen male comparators for the purpose of bringing equal pay claims. In the first case, the female employees were employed by the governing body of voluntary aided schools as support staff. They brought equal pay claims comparing themselves with male manual workers who did not work in schools but were employed by the local authority. The support staff submitted that the tribunal had erred in finding that they and their comparators were not employed in the same service, since in practice the schools' governing body applied the same grade and remuneration to support staff posts as the local authority.

The EAT held that the support staff had been assigned to work in schools but their chosen comparators had not worked in schools. Further, the support staff could not show that a single body, either the local authority or the schools' governing body, was responsible for ensuring equal treatment, contrary to the position in *South Ayrshire Council v Morton*. In the circumstances, they and their chosen comparators were not in the same service for the purpose of equal pay claims under Art. 141, and were therefore not entitled to compare themselves with their chosen comparators. Given the decision in *North v Dumfries and Galloway Council* [2013] UKSC 45, a different basis might be reached today, on the basis that it would not be material that the chosen comparators had not worked in schools.

Increasing numbers of state schools, whether maintained or voluntary-aided, are now becoming academies, which are, under the Academies Act 2010, independent of local authority control and may set their own salaries for staff. The conversion of a state school into an academy will involve a TUPE transfer (see Chapter 8), but the duration of protection of pay and other contractual terms and conditions remains unclear.

Case law also shows that the *Morton* principle is likely to be narrowly interpreted. *Lawrence v Regent Office Care Ltd* Case C-320/00 [2002] IRLR 822, ECJ, involved the contracting out of school cleaning and catering services in some areas of North Yorkshire to Regent. This would now be a TUPE transfer, but was not under the TUPE Regulations then in force. In the areas where Regent took over, the employees concerned were made redundant and re-employed by Regent at lower pay rates (one of the abuses which the TUPE Regulations are intended to prevent). Women workers now employed by Regent brought an equal pay claim using men who continued to be employed by the Council as comparators. The ECJ ruled:

> Where, as in the main proceedings here, the differences identified in the pay conditions of workers performing equal work or work of equal value cannot be attributed to a single source, there is no body which is responsible for the inequality and which could restore equal treatment. Such a situation does not come within the scope of Article 141.

So, according to *Lawrence*, the test of whether the claimant and comparator come within the concept of being employed by the same employer or by associated employers is whether there is a 'single source' for their pay and conditions. This was held not to be the case in the Civil Service after pay began to be determined department by department rather than across the service as a whole (*Robertson v Department for Environment, Food and Rural Affairs* [2005] EWCA Civ 138).

17.4.2 Working at the same establishment or at different establishments under 'common terms and conditions'

Interestingly, there is no case law on what constitutes 'the same establishment', other than that the test is a geographical one. As to 'common terms and conditions', it is very important to note that this has nothing to do with the type of the work that the claimant and comparator are doing. 'Common terms and conditions' refers to contractual terms and conditions other than the job description. It is also not simply a matter of the terms and conditions under which the particular claimant and her comparator work, but instead that there are common terms and conditions under which both male and female workers operate. However, 'common' does not mean 'the same' or, necessarily, similar, since the threshold of commonality is set very low.

In *Leverton v Clwyd County Council* [1988] IRLR 239 a nursery nurse sought to compare herself with higher paid clerical workers employed by the council at a different site. The Court of Appeal held that the clerical workers were not valid male comparators, as the claimant worked 32 hours per week and had 70 days' annual holiday; the comparators worked a 37-hour week with 20 days' holiday. The court held that although common terms and conditions did not mean identical terms, there had to be a sufficient degree of commonality to enable a proper comparison to be made. Here, two fundamental terms – hours of work and holidays – were radically different, and as such the clerical workers were not valid comparators within s. 1(6). The House of Lords, by contrast, took the view that there were common terms and conditions, since the terms and conditions of both classes of employee arose from a common collective agreement.

More recently, the Supreme Court has made it clear that the purpose of the requirement for common terms and conditions is simply to enable a realistic comparison to be drawn between claimant and comparator. In *North v Dumfries and Galloway Council* [2013] UKSC 45, 251 female classroom assistants and nursery nurses working in the Council's schools, sought comparison with certain manual workers employed by the same local authority. These men were employed under a different collective agreement from the classroom assistants, unlike the claimant and comparators in *Leverton v Clwyd*, and operated across a range of premises, not just schools. Under their terms and conditions the women worked 35 hours per week in school terms only. The men worked full-time throughout the year. Critically, as far as the women were concerned, the men were entitled to various bonuses which substantially increased their pay. The Supreme Court stated that the test was that the claimants must 'satisfy the Tribunal that if their comparators were employed at their establishment, they would be employed under broadly similar terms to those that they are employed under at present'. It was also not enough for the employer to say that the comparators would never be employed at the same establishment; the purpose of the legislation was to allow comparisons to be made between workers who did not and never would work in the same workplace, provided they worked for the same or associated employers. It was immaterial that male janitors were employed at the schools, i.e. the same establishments, and at other schools on the same terms and conditions as the claimants, who did not wish to use them as comparators as they were already receiving the same pay. *North* also confirmed the single source test of 'the same employer'.

17.4.3 Choice of comparator

Case law also establishes that the choice of comparator is a matter for the claimant, although the Tribunal has a role in determining the validity of the chosen comparator (*Ainsworth v Glass Tubes and Components* [1977] IRLR 74). There is no requirement that the comparator be fairly representative of a group of workers (*Thomas v National Coal Board* [1987] IRLR 451). However, under the equal pay provisions the claimant must select a specific man or group of men; she cannot rely on a hypothetical man. *Pickstone v Freemans plc* [1988] 2 All ER 803 dealt with the position where a woman is doing the same work as a man and is paid the same as him, but wishes to bring an equal value claim using as a comparator a man doing a different job and paid more. The Court of Appeal concluded that this was lawful, as otherwise unscrupulous employers could defeat equal pay claims by installing a 'token man' into 'woman's work'.

The claimant may choose a man employed in her post prior to her. According to *Diocese of Hallam v Connaughton* [1996] IRLR 505, she could also choose a successor. However, while the Equal Pay Act was still in force, the EAT overruled that decision (*Walton Centre for Neurology and Neuro Surgery NHS Trust v Bewdley* [2008] UKEAT/0564/07/MAA), on the basis that a successor was effectively a hypothetical comparator. The Equality Act s. 64(2) states specifically that there is no requirement that the work of the claimant and comparator be done contemporaneously, which presumably is intended to allow claims for equal pay with a successor once more, but there is as yet no case law to confirm this.

17.4.4 Bringing a claim

Having found a comparator, the claimant then needs to submit a claim using the Court Service's online system. Form ET1 needs to be received by the Court Service not more than six months after the employment has terminated (Equality Act s. 129). As the majority of equal pay claims are brought while employment is continuing, this is not normally an issue, although it may be if the claim involves equal pay with a successor. In *Birmingham City Council v Abdulla* [2012] UKSC 47 the Supreme Court ruled that since an equal pay claim involved breach of contract and payment of moneys due, it could be brought in the High Court for up to six years after the termination of employment. That the time limit for bringing the claim in the Employment Tribunal had expired was irrelevant. Further, s. 140 of the Equality Act allows equal pay claims to be transferred between court and tribunal in either direction as appropriate. Not infrequently, the inequality in pay has been perpetuated over a long period, so how far can a claim be backdated? The limit is normally six years, but under Equality Act s. 132(4) this can be extended if the employer has previously concealed information necessary for the bringing of a claim.

Having found a comparator and satisfied the Tribunal that the comparison is a valid one, the claimant must then demonstrate that she and he are doing like work, work rated equivalent or work of equal value.

17.4.5 Like work

The concept of like work is relatively straightforward. The work of the claimant and comparator must be the same or broadly similar in nature, and any differences must not be of practical importance. In 1970 it was commonplace for men and women to do similar work but with different job titles – the men might be called clerks and the women secretaries – and s. 1(4) is worded in terms which allow for this. Case law, all from the early period after the 1970 Act came into force, centres on what constitutes differences 'of practical importance'.

In *Capper Pass v Lawton* [1977] ICR 83 the EAT explained how s. 1(4) should be applied. The claimant was employed in the director's dining room, alone, cooking ten–20 meals per day, and sought equal pay with assistant chefs in the staff canteen who cooked 350 meals per day and were supervised. She worked 40 hours per week, the assistant chefs worked 45 hours. The EAT upheld her claim to equal pay. Phillips J said that in applying s. 1(4) the job should not be dissected minutely. First, the tribunal should consider whether the work is the same or broadly similar by looking at the duties and responsibilities. Second, they should look to see what in practice is done, whether there are differences and whether these are of practical importance. On this basis, what is done and when it is done is important, and a job can be split into three basic areas:

- duties;
- responsibilities;
- hours.

In *E. Coomes (Holdings) v Shields* [1978] IRLR 263 CA, the claimant and comparator were cashiers working in a betting shop. The employer argued that they could not be doing like work, as male cashiers, who received a higher hourly rate of pay, had the additional duties of transporting cash between different shops and ejecting unruly customers.

According to Lord Denning MR:

> Instances of [work of] the 'same nature' are men and women bank cashiers at the same counter, or men and woman serving meals in the same restaurant. Instances of a 'broadly similar nature' are men and women shop assistants in different sections of the same department store [. . .]
>
> Second, there must be an inquiry into:
>
> (i) The differences 'between the things that the woman does and the things that the men do'; and

(ii) A comparison of them so as to see 'the nature and extent of the differences' and the 'frequency or otherwise with which such differences occur in practice'; and

(iii) A decision as to whether those differences are, or are not, of practical importance in regard to the terms and conditions of employment.

This inquiry involves consideration of what happens in practice rather than what is stated in the contract. Here, the Court of Appeal held that the 'difference' in duties was not of practical importance because there had never in fact been any disturbances, and the men were seldom required to take cash between branches.

Lord Denning went on to say that 'equal pay' meant the same hourly rate of pay, and that employees should not receive a higher hourly rate merely for working a greater number of hours, although this might be appropriate in the case of overtime, night shifts, and other unsocial hours. If one of these applied, then the parties would not be doing like work.

Case law shows that close attention is paid to realities, rather than contractual provisions, and decisions very much turn on these realities. In *Electrolux v Hutchinson* [1977] ICR 252 there was an obligation in the men's contracts to work overtime at weekends or at night if so required. In other respects, the work was broadly similar. In practice the men were rarely required to work overtime and the court held that the women concerned were entitled to equal pay. By contrast, in *Thomas v National Coal Board* [1987] IRLR 451, the fact that the male comparator worked permanent nights unsupervised was a difference of practical importance and the claimant, therefore, was not entitled to equal pay. In *Kerr v Lister* [1977] IRLR 259 men and women working on the night shift were paid the same rate, which was higher than that paid to the women who worked on the day shift. It was held that the differences in the rates of pay had nothing to do with sex. The higher rate was paid to attract employees of either sex to the night shift, and there was a material difference between the day shift and the night shift.

Similar reasoning was used in the much more recent case of *Chief Constable of West Midlands Police v Blackburn* [2007] UKEAT/0007/07, EAT. Under the Police Regulations 2003 individual police forces were given power to introduce 'special priority payments' (SPPs) to reward those working in 'the most demanding and difficult front line operational roles'. The Chief Constable of West Midlands chose to use this provision to pay SPPs to Sergeants and Constables who were prepared to work 24/7 shifts, but not to those (mainly women) who had opted out of being available for night shifts for domestic reasons. The EAT accepted that having to work night shifts placed extra demands on individuals, and that the Chief Constable's purpose in granting SPPs was to encourage more individuals to make themselves available for night shifts. This reasoning was upheld by the Court of Appeal.

Perhaps unsurprisingly, equal pay claims based on like work, not uncommon in the 1970s, have now almost disappeared.

17.4.6 Work rated equivalent

The concept of work rated equivalent operates when the employer has carried out a job evaluation scheme, *and* that scheme has rated the jobs done by the claimant and her comparator equivalent in terms of the demands on the job holder. Essentially, the law requires the employer to give effect to the findings of the JES. The converse also applies, so that if the JES has found the two jobs not to be equivalent, the aspiring claimant cannot bring an equal value claim as an alternative unless she can prove that the JES was carried out in a sexually discriminatory fashion (Equality Act s. 64(4)–(5); *Green v Broxtowe DC* [1977] IRLR 34; *Neil v Ford Motor Co* [1984] IRLR 339).

The Equality Act s. 65(4), couched in the same terms as s. 1(5) of the Equal Pay Act, provides:

(4) A's work is rated as equivalent to B's work if a job evaluation study—
  (a) gives an equal value to A's job and B's job in terms of the demands made on a worker, or
  (b) would give an equal value to A's job and B's job in those terms were the evaluation not made on a sex-specific system.

The Equality Act s. 80(5) then states that a job evaluation study is a study undertaken with a view to evaluating, in terms of the demands made on a person by reference to factors such as effort, skill and decision-making, the jobs to be done

(a) by some or all of the workers in an undertaking or group of undertakings, or
(b) in the case of the armed forces, by some or all of the members of the armed forces.

What is a JES in practical terms? Generally speaking, an employer will carry out a JES when seeking to reorganise its pay structure, and quite possibly its terms and conditions of employment generally. For example, over many years, the terms and conditions of employment for local authority employees were governed by a series of collective agreements which divided the employees in to three distinct groups, each with a different set of terms and conditions contained in a particular 'Book':

- manual workers – 'White Book';
- administrative, professional, technical and clerical workers – 'Purple Book';
- skilled manual workers – 'Red Book'.

In 1997 there was a 'Single Status' collective agreement at national level to merge the White Book and Purple Book into a single set of terms and conditions known as the Green Book, and to move all employees previously on the White and Purple Book terms onto the new Green Book. For this purpose, individual local authorities were required to carry out a JES among their workforces (see *Redcar & Cleveland Borough Council v Bainbridge* [2008] EWCA Civ 885). One of the purposes of the Single Status agreement was to remove the inequalities of pay which had developed in local authority employment, by, for example, the introduction of attendance or productivity bonuses for some types of worker but not others, and to pave the way for equal pay between the sexes.

It is important to note that there is nothing in law to compel an employer to carry out a JES, and he may be reluctant to do so, on grounds of expense and potential divisions among the workforce.

How then should a JES be carried out? This has been the subject of a good deal of case law, mostly brought by equal pay claimants arguing that the JES which found a lack of equivalence in job demands was not carried out in a valid fashion, or employers arguing that a claimant could not use an equal value claim to bypass an unfavourable JES. Case law developed under the Equal Pay Act then shows that the employer cannot simply make 'whole job comparisons' (*Bromley v Quick* [1988] IRLR 249). Instead, the employer must set out the requirements needed to carry out the jobs ('factors'), assess them according to a numerical scale, and add those figures together to produce an overall result. *Hayward v Cammell Laird*, though an equal value case, provides a useful example of a set of factors:

- physical demands;
- environmental considerations;
- skill and knowledge;
- planning and decision making;
- responsibility.

It has been argued that a JES should not give 'undue weight' to criteria favouring men, such as a need for physical strength, or working in a poor physical environment, such as a building site, but this begs the question of what constitutes undue weight, quite apart from the possibility that excluding that as a criterion may go against the essential nature of a job entirely.

Once a JES has been completed, both employer and employee are bound by its results, unless it can be proved that it has been carried out in a discriminatory fashion. In *O'Brien v Sim-Chem Ltd* [1980] IRLR 373 a JES was carried out by the company but before the claimant was paid her increased salary the government announced a voluntary incomes policy and so the implementation of the scheme was postponed. The House of Lords ruled that once the scheme had been completed the comparison of the respective terms in the man's and woman's contracts could be made, thus the equality clause was effective at that point.

17.4.7 Work of equal value

The critical difference between work rated equivalent and work of equal value is that in the first case the employer has carried out a JES and the claimant is seeking to enforce its results. In the second case, there has been no JES (or the claimant argues that a JES was carried out in a discriminatory fashion), and, following the application, the Tribunal commissions a study of the jobs performed by the claimant and comparator equivalent to a JES.

The equal value route to claiming equal pay was introduced by the Equal Pay (Amendment) Regulations 1983, following the ruling of the European Court of Justice in *Commission of the European Communities v United Kingdom* [1982] IRLR 333, that the Equal Pay Act did not give effect to the principle of equal pay contained in the Equal Pay Directive (Directive 75/117/EEC). This is unsurprising, as the Act pre-dated the Directive.

Case law establishes that a woman is free to bring a claim based on equal value with men doing different work from her, even when there are men doing like work with her. This was the position in *Pickstone v Freemans plc* [1988] 2 All ER 803, where the claimant was a warehouse operative doing like-work with a group of male warehouse operatives. All received the same pay. She was permitted to bring an equal value claim using a male checker warehouse operative who received higher pay as a comparator, on the basis that for the court to rule otherwise would allow unscrupulous employers to keep women's pay down by introducing a 'token man' into 'women's work'.

The procedure for equal value claims is now as follows:

a) Where a JES has been carried out and concluded that the two jobs are not equivalent, the tribunal *must* dismiss the equal value claim unless it has reasonable grounds for concluding that the JES was discriminatory or otherwise unreliable.
b) The tribunal may:
   - choose to determine the question of equal value itself; or
   - appoint an independent expert from the ACAS panel to prepare a report.
c) The tribunal should then make orders setting a timetable for the next stages of the case.
d) If an independent expert is appointed, a second stage hearing takes place to resolve facts in dispute and simplify the expert's task.
e) Once the expert's report is available, there is a final hearing at which the tribunal decides whether the jobs are of equal value and to consider any defence put forward by the employer. It is for the tribunal to decide whether the jobs are of equal value (though they will not usually depart from the expert's view).

17.4.8 Employer's defences

This is the main area of substantive change resulting from the Equality Act 2010, but as yet there is little case law to demonstrate the effects of the new defence.

Before going any further, it must be made clear that defences are of no relevance where the claimant fails to establish any breach of the principle of equal pay. This was the ruling in the high-profile case of *Villalba v Merrill Lynch* [2006] EAT. The Claimant appealed against a decision dismissing her claims for sex discrimination and unequal pay, but upholding certain complaints of discrimination on grounds of victimisation and finding V's dismissal to be unfair. She had been employed by Merrill Lynch several years and had held various responsible posts. When promoted to a different role she experienced difficulties with that role and with her immediate superior. In respect of equal pay, the Claimant admitted that the tribunal had been entitled to find, on the facts, that there was no sex discrimination. However, she argued, the ECJ case of *Brunnhofer v Bank der Osterreichischen Postsparkasse AG* [2001] IRLR 571 established that in order to rebut an equal pay claim, the employer was also obliged to demonstrate that there was objective justification for the difference in pay between the employee and her chosen comparators. The tribunal had failed to require Merrill Lynch to do that. The Claimant argued that once a woman was held to be working on work of equal value with a male comparator, the employer must show that there was an objective justification for the difference in pay, or else the claim must succeed. She submitted that it was not enough simply to demonstrate that there was no discrimination on grounds of sex.

The EAT held that the Equal Pay Act 1970, the Equal Pay Directive 75/117 and Article 141 were all concerned with eradicating discrimination between men and women. If the Claimant were correct in her argument, and objective justification needed to be established in every case where a woman could raise a presumption of equal pay because she was employed on work of equal value with her chosen comparator, then the effect was to convert a law that was designed to eliminate discrimination on grounds of sex into fair wages legislation. There was something fundamentally inconsistent with the idea that laws which were designed to eliminate sex discrimination should be construed so as to give relief even where there was no hint of any kind of discrimination on grounds of sex at all. In *Brunnhofer* the court was not intending to break fresh ground and did not perceive itself as so doing. *Brunnhofer* did not establish that the elimination of discrimination on grounds of sex required objective justification for differences in pay in circumstances where an employer had successfully rebutted a presumption of direct sex discrimination and there was no independent evidence of any kind to show that sex had any influence on the difference in pay.

The Equal Pay Act s. 1(3) provided as follows:

> An equality clause shall not operate in relation to a variation between the woman's contract and the man's contract if the employer proves that the variation is genuinely due to a material factor which is not the difference of sex, and that factor –
>
> (a) In the case of an equality clause falling within subsection (2)(a) or (b) above [like work or work rated equivalent], *must* be a material difference between the woman's case and the man's; and
>
> (b) In the case of an equality clause falling within subsection (2)(c) above [equal value] *may* be such a difference.[3]

Dissected, this means that the burden of proving the defence is higher in cases based on like work or work rated equivalent than in equal value cases. Case law then shows what factors may operate

3 My emphasis.

as defences to equal pay claims. Early judgments were clear that only differences other than sex in the 'personal equation' between the claimant and comparator could qualify. The most obvious examples are qualifications and experience. In *Fletcher v Clay Cross Quarry Services Ltd* [1979] 1 All ER 474 Lord Denning MR rejected the employer's argument that the comparator had to be paid more than the claimant because he would not have accepted the job if he had been paid less than in his previous post. Lord Denning stated that paying a man more than a woman merely because he asked for it the Equal Pay Act would be 'a dead letter'.

Later cases broadened the ambit of the defence quite considerably, though the issue of whether the employer could use 'market forces' to pay a man more than a woman (or the reverse) remained a grey area.

When a person is moved to a less demanding job for medical reasons, or his original job becoming redundant and he is moved to another post in the organisation, he is often paid his former salary for a specified period. This practice is sometimes known as 'red-circling'. In *Methven v Cow Industrial Polymers Ltd* [1980] IRLR 289 red-circling was held capable of being a genuine material difference accounting for a difference in pay between men and women doing like work, but only where the Tribunal was satisfied that the man's pay had not been red-circled solely on grounds of sex, and that the job he had previously done was open to women as well as men. *NAAFI v Varley* [1976] IRLR 408 established that a difference in place of work could qualify as a genuine material difference, where the Tribunal is satisfied that there is a clear difference in the cost of living at the locations where the claimant and comparator work.

Jenkins v Kingsgate Clothing Productions Ltd [1981] IRLR 388 involved an employer who paid a higher hourly rate to full-time employees than part-timers. Most of the latter, including the claimant, were women, and it was argued that this practice constituted indirect discrimination against women. The employer argued that the higher rate was paid to full-time workers because the machinery lay idle for part of the week when operated by part-timers, and that there was also a higher rate of absenteeism among part-timers. The employer therefore wished to encourage full-time working by offering higher pay. After a reference to the ECJ, the EAT held that economic necessity was capable of being a genuine material difference provided there was evidence that this was indeed the reason for the difference in pay, the reason actually existed and there was no intention to discriminate.

No judgment in a decided case followed this decision and therefore the reasoning in *Jenkins* was assumed to be confined to its own facts until the case of *Chief Constable of West Midlands Police v Blackburn* [2007] UKEAT/0007/07, EAT, some 25 years later.

The case of *Rainey v Greater Glasgow Health Board* [1987] 1 AC 224 HL is worth examining in detail. Mrs Rainey was a prosthetist (a fitter of artificial limbs). The Health Board established a new limb-fitting service, and recruited qualified prosthetists from two areas; those already working in the NHS elsewhere in Scotland, and those working for private sector providers in Glasgow. As those from the private sector had been paid significantly more than the NHS prosthetists, they were put on a separate and more favourable pay scale in order to encourage them to apply for the posts available. No provision was made for phasing out this pay scale over time. Mrs Rainey and other women prosthetists had been recruited from within the NHS and remained on the relevant NHS pay scale. They made claims based on like work with male prosthetists on the private sector scale. It was accepted that the two groups were indeed doing like work, and the burden was then on the Health Board to satisfy the court that there was a genuine material difference, not related to sex, which underlay the pay differential. Note that there were male and female prosthetists on both pay scales.

Per Lord Keith of Kinkel:

> The difference must be 'material', which I would construe as meaning 'significant and relevant', and it must be between 'her case and his'. Consideration of a person's case must necessarily

involve consideration of all the circumstances of that case. These may well go beyond . . . the personal qualities by way of skill, experience or training which the individual brings to the job. Some circumstances may on examination prove to be not significant or not relevant, but others may do so, though not relating to the personal qualities of the employee. In particular, where there is no question of intentional sex discrimination whether direct or indirect (and there is none here) a difference which is connected with economic factors affecting the efficient carrying on of the employer's business or other activity may well be relevant [. . .]

In *Bilka-Kaufhaus GmbH v Weber von Hartz* [1986] ECR 1607 (ECJ) the European Court . . . made it clear that it was not sufficient for the employer merely to show absence of any intention to discriminate, saying. . .:

It is for the national court, which has sole jurisdiction to make findings of fact, to determine whether and to what extent the grounds put forward by the employer to explain the adoption of a pay practice which applies independently of a worker's sex but in fact affects more women than men may be regarded as objectively justified on economic grounds. If the national court finds that the measures chosen by Bilka correspond to a real need on the part of the undertaking, are appropriate with a view to achieving the objectives pursued, and are necessary to that end, the fact that the measures affect a far greater number of women than men is not sufficient to show that they constitute an infringement of Article [141] [. . .]

I consider that read as a whole the ruling of the European Court would not exclude objectively justified grounds which are other than economic, such as administrative efficiency in a concern not engaged in commerce or business [. . .]

The position in 1980 [when the facts of the case arose] was that all National Health Service employees were paid on the Whitley Council scale, and that the Whitley Council negotiating machinery applied to them. The prosthetic service [operated by the Board] was intended to be a branch of the [NHS]. It is therefore easy to see that from an administrative point of view it would have been highly anomalous and inconvenient if prosthetists alone, over the whole tract of future time for which the prosthetic service would endure, were to have been subject to a different salary scale and different negotiation machinery. . . . Accordingly, there were sound objectively justified administrative reasons, in my view, for placing prosthetists in general, men and women alike, on the Whitley Council scale and subjecting them to its negotiation machinery. There is no suggestion that it was unreasonable to place them at the particular point on the Whitley Council scale which was in fact selected, ascertained by reference to the position of medical physics technicians and entirely regardless of sex. It is in any event the fact that the general scale of remuneration for prosthetists was laid down accordingly by the Secretary of State. It was not a case of the appellant being paid less than the norm, but of [the comparator] being paid more. He was paid more because of the necessity to attract him and other privately employed prosthetists into forming the nucleus of the new service [. . .]

Counsel for the appellant put forward an argument based on SDA s. 1(1)(b) . . . This provision has the effect of prohibiting indirect discrimination between women and men. In my opinion it does not, for present purposes, add anything to [EPA s. 1(3)], since, upon the view which I have taken as to the proper construction of the latter, a difference which demonstrated unjustified direct discrimination would not discharge the onus placed on the employer [to prove that the factor relied on is independent of sex]. Further, there would not appear to be any material distinction in principle between the need to demonstrate objectively justified grounds of difference for the purpose of s. 1(3) and the need to justify a requirement or condition under [SDA s. 1(1)(b)(i).

To summarise *Rainey*, although the appellant lost on the facts, because administrative efficiency in a non-profit-making organisation (in particular the need to maintain the integrity of the Whitley

Council pay scales for professions ancillary to medicine), Lord Keith's *dicta* are authority for the following points:

- indirect sex discrimination in relation to pay is contrary to the Equal Pay Act;
- ECJ jurisprudence on Article 141 must be included in the interpretation of the defence against providing equal pay in s. 1(3). This includes ECJ decisions post-*Bilka*.

Perhaps surprisingly, the House of Lords in *Rainey* did not consider the indirect discrimination issue, given that all the prosthetists recruited from the private sector and thus on the higher pay scale were men, and those on the NHS pay scale included all the women prosthetists. Further, there was no limit on the duration of the higher pay scale, so that it could not be said that the two would be reconciled within a defined period. On that basis, there is a strong argument that indirect discrimination did indeed arise, and that the employer should have been expected to demonstrate objective justification. However, the issue of indirect discrimination was first considered in detail by the ECJ in *Enderby v Frenchay Health Authority* [1993] ECR I-5535.

Again, the case involved a woman working in a profession ancillary to medicine, with pay scales governed by the Whitley Council, this time speech therapy, a job which is, in practice, done almost exclusively by women. Mrs Enderby brought an equal value claim using clinical psychologists and pharmacists as comparators, and the defence was raised by the employers that the differences in pay were the result of different bargaining structures and that the separate pay scales for the different groups were each internally non-discriminatory. The Court of Appeal referred the following questions to the ECJ:

- whether the employer's reliance on separate bargaining structures was justifiable under Article 141;
- whether 'if the employer could establish that serious shortages in one of the comparator professions explained, part, but not all, of the difference in pay, the whole or only part of that difference could be regarded as justified'.

> Judgment:
>
> It is normally for the person alleging facts in support of a claim to adduce proof of such facts. Thus, in principle, the burden of proving the existence of sex discrimination as to pay lies with the worker who, believing himself to be the victim of such discrimination, begins legal proceedings against his employer with the aim of removing that discrimination.
>
> However, it is clear from the case law of the [ECJ] that the onus may shift when it is necessary to avoid depriving workers who appear to be the victims of discrimination of any effective means of enforcing the principle of equal pay. Accordingly, when a measure distinguishing between employees on the basis of their hours of work has in practice an adverse impact on substantially more members of one or other sex, that measure must be regarded as contrary to the objective pursued by Article [141] unless the employer shows that it is based on objectively justified factors unrelated to any discrimination on grounds of sex. . . . [Note that *Jenkins* was decided before *Bilka* and *Rainey*]. Similarly, where an undertaking applies a system of pay which is wholly lacking in transparency, it is for the employer to prove that his practice in the matter of wages is not discriminatory, if a female worker establishes, in relation to a relatively large number of employees, that the average pay for women is less than that for men [. . .]
>
> If the pay of speech therapists is significantly lower than that of pharmacists and if the former are *almost exclusively* women while the latter are *predominantly* men,[4] there is a *prima*

4 My emphasis.

facie case of sex discrimination, at least where the two jobs in question are of equal value and the statistics describing that situation are valid [. . .]

The fact that the rates of pay at issue are decided by collective bargaining processes conducted separately for each of the two professional groups concerned, without any discriminatory effect within each group, does not preclude a finding of *prima facie* discrimination where the results of these processes show that two groups with the same employer and the same trade union are treated differently. If the employer could rely on the absence of discrimination within each of the collective bargaining processes as sufficient justification for the difference in pay, he could . . . easily circumvent the principle of equal pay by using separate bargaining processes [. . .]

If . . . the national court has been able to determine *precisely* what proportion of the increase in pay is attributable to market forces, it must necessarily accept that the pay differential is objectively justified to the extent of that proportion. When national authorities have to apply Community law, they must apply the principle of proportionality. If that is not the case, it is for the national court to assess whether the role of market forces in determining the rate of pay was sufficiently significant to provide objective justification for all or part of the difference.

Enderby provides authority for the following:

- A *prima facie* case of indirect discrimination arises where men and women are doing work of equal value and those in work done *almost exclusively* by women are paid less than those in jobs done *predominantly* by men.
- Nevertheless, the employer will have a defence if he can show objectively justified grounds for imposing the condition or requirement which gives rise to the discrimination.
- Market forces (not defined) are capable of acting as justification for all or part of a difference in pay involving a *prima facie* case of indirect discrimination.

Presumably, the same principle would apply to equal pay claims based on like work and work rated equivalent, although that issue did not arise in *Enderby*. This proved to be the case in relation to subsequent decisions. The ECJ in *Enderby* spoke of situations where one job was done *almost exclusively* by women and the other *predominantly* by men. 'Almost exclusively', on the ordinary meaning of the expression, suggests around 95 per cent female or more, while 'predominantly' involves a majority of men but a considerably less extreme imbalance of the sexes – perhaps a two-thirds to one-third male majority – not a group 95 per cent or more male, and one which may have a significant minority of women. Later case law seems to accept that the *Enderby* principle may apply in situations where the discrepancy in the proportions of men and women employed is much less.

The claimants in *British Road Services Ltd v Loughran* [1997] IRLR 92 were employed as clerical officers at the employers' Mallusk depot in Northern Ireland, there being nine women and seven men employed as clerical staff there. In the overall group in Northern Ireland and Scotland, 75 per cent of clerical staff were women. The claimants sought to claim like work with warehouse operatives at Mallusk, an all-male group. The pay scales for the two groups were determined by separate collective agreements. The employers sought to argue that the existence of these separate agreements constituted a genuine material factor, and that the principle in *Enderby* applied only where the group including the applicant was exclusively or almost exclusively female.

The Northern Ireland Court of Appeal rejected this approach. On the facts, in a situation where the applicant's group was 75 per cent female and the comparative group was exclusively male, the tribunal was entitled to conclude that the proportions of males and females in each group were sufficiently representative to provide a reliable indication of the existence of unequal treatment, that the differing percentages were not purely fortuitous or the result of short-term phenomena, and that the existence of separate collective agreements was not an objectively justified genuine material factor.

Tyne & Wear Passenger Transport Executive v Best EAT (21/12/2006) establishes, however, that the *Enderby* principle cannot apply where both the advantaged and the disadvantaged groups are largely male. Here, Metro train drivers working on one route were also required to collect fares and were paid at a higher rate than the 'pure' drivers working on the other route, who included the claimant, but of whom 92 per cent were men.

The claimants in *Ratcliffe v North Yorkshire County Council* [1995] ICR 833 (HL) were school dinner ladies, whose jobs had been rated equivalent to those done by various groups of mainly male employees. Required by legislation to offer various services, including school meals, out to the private sector via competitive tendering, the Council formed a number of Direct Services Organisations (DSOs) to compete for the relevant contracts. In order that the school meals DSO could compete successfully with the outside providers to offer the lowest tender, the Council reduced the dinner ladies' pay by 25 per cent. They subsequently argued that the need to secure the school meals contract was a genuine material difference, not based on sex, between the cases of the dinner ladies and the comparators, for whom there had not been the commercial necessity for a pay cut. The Tribunal found in favour of the claimants, and their decision was ultimately restored by the House of Lords after the EAT allowed the employer's appeal. Both noted that the external organisation competing for the contract employed only women, and, in practice, those women were prepared to work for very low pay in return for working hours which fitted around their domestic commitments. According to Lord Slynn, who gave the lead judgment, the external competitor discriminated directly against their women employers in terms of pay, and by reducing their own employees' pay to match those levels, the Council also discriminated directly, since they were paying women less than men on work rated equivalent.

The women could not have found other suitable work and were obliged to take the wages offered if they wished to continue with this work. The fact that two men were employed on the same work at the same rate of pay does not detract from the conclusion that there was discrimination between the women involved and their male comparators. It means no more than that the two men were underpaid compared with other men doing jobs rated as equivalent.

The factor relied on by the employer – the need to reduce pay in order to undercut the competitor for the tender – acted to the disadvantage of women, and, according to the Lords, was directly discriminatory. That being so, there was no possible justification for it in law, and therefore it could not constitute a defence. On the basis of ECJ case law, such as *Bilka*, a factor which is indirectly discriminatory is capable of being justified. This begs the question of when a factor is directly discriminatory, and it is arguable that Lord Slynn was in fact mistaken in concluding that the need in *Ratcliffe* to win the tender was directly rather than indirectly discriminatory. The central question here is whether the women were less favourably treated than the comparators *because they were women*, or because they worked in the school meals service.

According to other case law arising from the 1970 Act defences, there was no requirement for the employer to show that a factor relied on as a defence was justified if he could establish that it was neither directly nor indirectly discriminatory (cf. *Strathclyde Regional Council v Wallace* [1998] ICR 205, HL). However, to take one example, what if the factor relied on is experience, as is by no means uncommon? *Cadman v Health & Safety Executive* [2004] IRLR 971, CA is not an equal pay case but establishes that experience and length of service as criteria are capable of being indirectly discriminatory against women (who tend to spend periods working part-time or out of the workplace altogether), and also on grounds of age (specifically against younger employees). Such discrimination can only be justified if the employer can establish that experience makes the employee better at carrying out his role. Further, granting pay increments on the basis of length of service can only be justified for a limited period – no more than five years – as performance will eventually plateau.

Chief Constable of West Midlands Police v Blackburn [2007] UKEAT/0007/07, EAT, shows that the courts and tribunals were prepared to take a robust approach to the purpose of the Equal Pay Act. Police forces are required to provide 24/7 cover and generally require sergeants and constables to be available for shift work 24/7, customarily in three shifts, running from 0700–1500, 1400–2200 and 2200–0700. Individuals may be excused from this requirement on the basis of family commitments or for medical reasons. Under the Police Regulations 2003 individual police forces were given power to introduce 'special priority payments' (SPPs) to reward those working in 'the most demanding and difficult front line operational roles'. SPPs add an extra 2.5–3 per cent to the pay of those who qualify. West Midlands Police brought in SPPs for those who were available to work 24/7, with the aim of rewarding those who worked the full shift pattern and encouraging more people to make themselves available to do so. It was calculated that some 91.5 per cent of women were available to work 24/7 and qualified for SPPs, as against 96.6 per cent of men. It was not disputed (perhaps surprisingly, but see *London Underground v Edwards (No.2)* [1997] IRLR 157, AC) that this represented indirect discrimination, but the Chief Constable argued justification and genuine material difference. The Claimants argued that because they were *prevented* from working 24/7 by a factor which mainly affected women – childcare commitments – that they should be paid SPPs as if they were available 24/7. It was not disputed that those not available 24/7 for medical reasons were mainly men, though no percentage calculation was done. It was also not disputed that the Claimants were doing like work with their comparator.

The EAT reversed the Tribunal decision that a GMD did not apply. The aim of rewarding those who did work nights was a legitimate one and it was unrealistic to say that it could equally be achieved if those who were released from that obligation received SPPs as if they did work nights.

> The purpose of the scheme adopted by the Chief Constable is to single out and reward those working nights; we find it difficult to see how that objective is achieved if those who do not work nights are also paid the same amount. Those doing the work are not then being marked out for special treatment, which is the very purpose of the payment.
>
> More fundamentally, we consider that the approach of the Tribunal misunderstands the principle underlying indirect discrimination. The premise is that the predominantly male group is paid more than the predominantly female group for some reason other than sex. The question is whether it can be justified to make that payment.
>
> It can be justified if it is in pursuance of an objective which is legitimate and where the means chosen are proportionate to that objective. To say that the employer can afford to eliminate the difference in pay simply fails to engage with the defence at all. It is no answer to a defence of justification for a difference in pay to say that there is no need for the difference in the first place. If the employer had made these payments to the claimants, as the Tribunal suggested that they should, then the issue of justification would not have arisen at all because there would have been no pay differential to justify.
>
> 43. The error is akin to that pointed out by the EAT in *Redcar and Cleveland Borough Council v Bainbridge* [2007] IRLR 91, para. 62. The assumption appears to be that the employers should do their utmost to ensure that women and men on equal work are paid the same. That is not what the law requires. As the EAT observed:

> 'The right is to equal pay unless there is a genuine material factor explaining the difference; it is not a right to the same pay even where the genuine material factor continues to explain and justify the difference'.

The Tribunal's conclusion is that the employer cannot justify because they can secure equalisation by deeming the women to have done what they have, in fact, not done. This is in truth a conclusion of staggering consequence. Taken logically, it would mean that in all cases of indirect discrimination the employer would have to satisfy the Tribunal that notwithstanding that he has a legitimate objective in differentiating between the pay given to the predominantly male and female groups, he is acting reasonably in not paying the women on the basis that they can be taken to have done the same work as the men[. . .]

If the argument is right then logically there would be no reason in principle why a woman who is working part time, and whose employer has specifically accommodated her to be able to do that, could not say that she should be paid the same as the full timer, the employer paying her for the hours she was not able to work because of her domestic responsibilities. Tribunals would be making judgments as to whether an employer could really be expected to bear the cost of indirectly discriminatory treatment. That is not their function. Paradoxically, it would also mean that the more severe the indirect discrimination, the greater the cost to the employer of eradicating it, and the greater the likelihood of his being able in those circumstances to satisfy the Tribunal that the cost would be disproportionate.

Nothing in the Equal Pay Act requires an employer to deem that women have done what they have not done. The payment of money to compensate for the economic disadvantages suffered by those who have child care responsibilities is not what the Equal Pay Act requires. Nor is the assessment of the employer's ability to pay sums of this kind a task which Parliament could conceivably have expected Tribunals to do[. . .]

The Tribunal was wrong to say that paying the claimants as if they had worked was simply a logical consequence of excusing the women from doing the work in the first place. . . . It is highly desirable that employers adopt flexible work practices which will enable women to work part time or at hours compatible with their child care, even if that involves incurring some cost in achieving that. But it does not follow at all that they should then pay the women on the basis of the work they would have done if they had not had the child care responsibilities.

17.4.9 The employer's defence under the Equality Act 2010

69 Defence of material factor

(1) The sex equality clause in A's terms has no effect in relation to a difference between A's terms and B's terms if the responsible person shows that the difference is because of a material factor reliance on which—

  (a) does not involve treating A less favourably because of A's sex than the responsible person treats B, and

  (b) if the factor is within subsection (2), is a proportionate means of achieving a legitimate aim.

(2) A factor is within this subsection if A shows that, as a result of the factor, A and persons of the same sex doing work equal to A's are put at a particular disadvantage when compared with persons of the opposite sex doing work equal to A's.

(3) For the purposes of subsection (1), the long-term objective of reducing inequality between men's and women's terms of work is always to be regarded as a legitimate aim.

(4) A sex equality rule has no effect in relation to a difference between A and B in the effect of a relevant matter if the trustees or managers of the scheme in question show that the difference is because of a material factor which is not the difference of sex.
(5) 'Relevant matter' has the meaning given in section 67.
(6) For the purposes of this section, a factor is not material unless it is a material difference between A's case and B's.

The new defence requires that the factor relied on by the employer:

- is not based on sex;
- if it gives rise to indirect discrimination, the factor must be a proportionate means of achieving a legitimate aim.

On this basis, a decision such as that in *Strathclyde Regional Council v Wallace* remains good law, on the basis that there was no indirect discrimination. *Chief Constable of West Midlands v Blackburn* was decided on the basis that although there was indirect discrimination in requiring Sergeants and Constables to be available 24/7 in order to receive SPPs, this requirement was a proportionate means of achieving the legitimate aim of rewarding those who accepted the additional burden of working night shifts, and encouraging a greater proportion to do so.

As yet there is no specific case law on the new defence beyond first instance. However, analogous case law from other areas of discrimination law (mainly age discrimination) suggests that financial savings alone can never be a legitimate aim.

In *Loxley v BAE Systems* [2008] EAT 29/7/2008 the employee appealed against a Tribunal decision that the employer had not unjustifiably discriminated against him on the grounds of his age. The employer's voluntary redundancy scheme provided that benefits were only paid to those under the age of 60 at the date of redundancy. Those aged 60 or more were entitled to an immediate pension. Although the compulsory retirement age had been increased from 60 to 65 after the scheme had been introduced, and later there had been some modification to the operation of the pension scheme by agreement with relevant trade unions, no change had been made to the cut-off age for redundancy payments under the scheme. On this basis, a person could not benefit from both a redundancy payment and an immediate pension.

The EAT concluded that preventing a windfall could be a legitimate feature of a redundancy scheme. One of the purposes of a scheme such as this was to cushion workers from the effect of losing their income. That was not required to the same extent where pensions were paid. However, exclusion of individuals entitled to an immediate receipt of a pension from a redundancy scheme was not automatically justified. Whether it was justified would depend upon the nature of both schemes. The fact that an employee was entitled to immediate pension benefits would always be a highly relevant factor which an employer could properly consider when determining what redundancy rights, if any, an employee ought to receive. It might justify excluding the employee from the redundancy scheme altogether.

The tribunal had to ask whether the employer's treatment of the employee, namely his exclusion from the scheme, had achieved a legitimate objective and had been proportional to any disadvantage he suffered. His pension entitlement might be more valuable than any redundancy entitlement, but neither tribunal was in a position to assess that. The tribunal had failed to analyse the available financial information about the benefits. That an agreement had been made with the trade unions was also potentially a relevant consideration when determining whether treatment was proportionate, *Palacios de la Villa v Cortefiel Servicios SA* (C-411/05) [2008] All ER (EC) 249 ECJ (Grand Chamber) considered. The decision was therefore flawed and it was appropriate for the matter to be heard again by a fresh tribunal.

17.5 Further reading

Connolly, 'The gender pay gap, hypothetical comparators and the Equality Act 2010' (2011) 101(Feb) *Employment Law Bulletin* 6.

Drummond, The Remarkable Life of Victoria Drummond – Marine Engineer, *London: Institute of Marine Engineers*, 1994.

Gow & Middlemiss, 'Equal pay legislation and its impact on the gender pay gap' (2011) 11(4) *International Journal of Discrimination and the Law* 164.

Johnson, 'Wilson v Health and Safety Executive: employment law – equal pay (Case Comment)' (2010) 15(1) *Coventry Law Journal* 42.

Malone, 'Reforming equal pay law in Britain: some proposals' (2015) 256 *Equal Opportunities Review* 10.

Robison, 'Equal pay in local government: what has been achieved?' (2017) 138 *Employment Law Bulletin* 2.

Chapter 18

Internal trade union law

Chapter contents

18.1 Overview

This chapter is concerned with judicial and statutory regulation of trade union internal affairs.

- The definition of a trade union is applied by the Certification Officer in order for the union to be entered on the 'list' of trade unions, necessary in order for the union to apply for a certificate of independence.
- Once certified as independent a trade union is entitled to protection from anti-union discrimination and to apply for recognition for collective bargaining purposes.
- Under ss. 10(1) and 12(1) of the Trade Union and Labour Relations (Consolidation) Act 1992 a trade union has the legal status as an unincorporated association of workers with specific attributes usually associated with corporations, such as the right to make contracts, to be subject to the criminal law, to sue and be sued in their own name.
- Until 1979 the legal regulation of union internal affairs was almost exclusively dependent on the common law through enforcement of the union rule book, a contract between each member and the union. Since 1979 numerous legislative developments have meant that individual members have specific statutory rights enforceable in the courts.
- A trade union cannot hold property in its own name, but through trustees. If funds are not administered in accordance with the trust, individual members are entitled to take action to remove the trustees under the common law and statute.
- Union financial matters are subject to extensive statutory regulation, including, *inter alia*, the requirement to keep appropriate accounting records, to make an annual financial return, to co-operate with appointed union auditors, and to permit union members to inspect union accounts. There are civil and criminal sanctions should a trade union violate these requirements.
- Historically, the control over union decisions on admission, discipline and expulsion was based solely on the common law through the enforcement of the terms of the rule book or by reliance on judicially developed principles of public policy. A member of a union alleging wrongful discipline or expulsion due to a failure of the union to abide by the rules can bring an action to enforce the rules. Additionally, there are provisions contained in the Trade Union and Labour Relations (Consolidation) Act 1992 that permit the individual union member to complain of 'unjustified discipline' when a disciplinary act, as defined in the statute, has been taken against the applicant. Legislation also gives union members the right not to be expelled from a union and to join a trade union of their choice.
- Until 1984 there was no statutory requirement for trade unions to hold internal elections. If the union rule book contained provisions on elections, control could be via enforcement of the terms of the rule book. Statute has now introduced compulsory elections and election procedures which displaces any relevant rules of the union and is enforceable by application to the Certification Officer or the High Court for a declaration and an enforcement order.
- Historically, the use of trade union funds for political purposes was illegal as outside the powers of a trade union as outlined in the Trade Union Act 1871. The Trade Union Act 1913 permitted a trade union to create a 'political fund' to be used for political purposes financed by a political levy on individual members. More recent statutory amendments now require a ballot of the membership every ten years to validate the political fund and detailed rules have been introduced that govern the operation of the fund.

18.2 The definition of a trade union

The Trade Union and Labour Relations (Consolidation) Act (TULR(C)A) 1992 s. 1(a), defines a trade union as an organisation which consists of 'workers of one or more descriptions and whose principal purposes include the regulation of relations between workers of that description or those descriptions and employers or employers' associations'. This statutory definition of what constitutes a trade union is applied by the Certification Officer in determining whether the organisation can be entered on the list of trade unions. Listing is voluntary, but it does have some advantages as entry on the list is the gateway to tax advantages for the union such as tax relief on provident or friendly funds. More importantly, without listing, the union would be unable to apply for a certificate of independence which is a prerequisite for the union to be eligible for certain additional rights that support a trade union's collective bargaining function.

This definition was considered by the Court of Appeal in *British Association of Advisers and Lecturers in Physical Education (BAALPE) v NUT*.[1] BAALPE had terminated an affiliation agreement with the NUT, and as a consequence, the NUT moved to exclude BAALPE from the Soulbury panel – the negotiating body for certain employees in the education field. On the issuing of a writ against the NUT alleging breach of contract, the preliminary issue to be decided was whether BAALPE was a competent body to initiate proceedings. The NUT argued that as a small and ineffective organisation, BAALPE did not satisfy the definition of a trade union and so was incapable of suing in its own name. The Court of Appeal stressed, however, that so long as BAALPE's principal purpose was to regulate relations between its members and the employer via collective bargaining, how effective it is at doing so, was not a relevant consideration. By participating in the Soulbury committee, BAALPE had satisfied this principal purpose test and so qualified as a trade union.[2]

One consequence of the BAALPE decision is that any organisation, which satisfies the definition in TULR(C)A s. 1(a), no matter how small or ineffective, may be regarded as a trade union. In *Midland Cold Storage v Turner*,[3] the court was willing to apply the definition to a temporary joint shop stewards' committee comprising of only seven members.[4] This has significance when courts are determining whether, and against whom, an injunction should be granted to restrain unlawful industrial action (see later Chapter 20).

18.3 Listing and the test for independence

Where an organisation wishes to be entered on the list of trade unions in order to apply for state support, s. 3 TULR(C)A 1992 outlines the procedure for an application to the Certification Officer. Once the Certification Officer is satisfied that the organisation complies with the definition in s. 1(a) and so qualifies as a trade union, the name of the trade union is included on the list. The union's appearance on the list is good evidence of status as a trade union and a certificate is issued to this effect.[5] Should an organisation wish to appeal from the decision of the Certification Officer not to enter its name on the list or to remove their name from the list, then an appeal lies to the Employment Appeal Tribunal (EAT) on law.[6]

Only listed unions can apply for a certificate of independence. Once in possession of a certificate of independence trade unions are the recipients of a degree of state support to enhance

---

1 [1986] IRLR 497.

2 Note that professional bodies that have the function of administering the profession rather than representing members in negotiations with employers are not trade unions as they are not 'an organisation of workers', nor exclusively 'regulate relations between workers and employers'. See *Carter v Law Society* [1973] IRLR 497 and s. 296(1) TULR(C)A 1992 on the definition of 'worker'.

3 [1972] ICR 230. See also *Express & Star Ltd v NGA* [1985] IRLR 455 and *NGN Ltd v SOGAT 82* [1986] IRLR 337.

4 See also the application of the test in *Akinosun v Certification Officer* [2013] IRLR 937.

5 Section 2(4).

6 Section 9.

the effectiveness of their activities. The most important benefits granted are the right of individual members to be protected against anti-union action so enabling them to join the union and engage in union activities without fear of victimisation or discrimination[7] and the right of the trade union to apply for recognition.[8]

Once an independent union has been recognised by the relevant employer, various other rights that facilitate collective bargaining are provided, such as, the right to information for collective bargaining purposes,[9] right of consultation on redundancies,[10] right of consultation on a proposed transfer of an undertaking[11] and the right to time off for trade union officials and members to engage in trade union activities and duties[12] (see Chapter 19). The aim of this system of listing and certifying independence is not to enhance employer or state control over union affairs, but rather to identify which organisations are genuine trade unions and thus deserving of support for their legitimate trade union activities.

In determining independence, the question the Certification Officer must consider is whether the applicant organisation is:

a) not under the domination or control of an employer or group of employers or of one or more employers' associations, and
b) is not liable to interference by an employer or any such group or association (arising out of the provision of financial or material support or by any other means whatsoever) tending towards such control.[13]

Disputes over the use of the Certification Officer's discretion were particularly prevalent in the 1970s as a consequence of the large growth in 'white collar' staff associations in the banking, insurance and chemical industries. There were some allegations that many of these organisations were management inspired 'sweet heart' staff associations or 'house unions' easily influenced by employers. The purpose behind the test for independence is to exclude such weak and dependent staff associations from obtaining the statutory benefits available to *bona fide* trade unions.

In determining whether the applicant union is independent the Certification Officer will take into account information provided under the following headings[14]:

1) *Finance*: Who provides the finance for the union? If the employer does so, then that is strong evidence that the union is 'under the domination or control of the employer'. If the financial base of the union is weak and the union receives some limited financial assistance from an employer, this implies the union is 'vulnerable to interference' by the employer.
2) *Other support*: Does the employer provide any other support such as premises and office facilities? If they are provided for free or at low cost, this is evidence of dependence on the employer.
3) *History*: Was the union originally created by the employer and controlled by the employer? If so, has it now grown from being a 'creature of management into something more independent'.

7 Sections 146 and 152.
8 Sections 70A and Schedule A1.
9 Section 181.
10 Section 188.
11 TUPE Regulations (SI 1981 No 1794).
12 Sections 168 and 170.
13 Section 5.
14 Criteria approved by the Court of Appeal in *Blue Circle Staff Association v C.O.* [1977] IRLR 20 and *Squibb UK Staff Association v C.O.* [1979] 2 All ER 452.

4) *Membership base*: Does the union only recruit from one employer or is it a more broadly based union? If it recruits solely from one employer, then it is more likely to be 'vulnerable to interference' from that employer.
5) *Organisation and structure*: Are the rules settled by the employer so that the employer can control or interfere with the union? The rules should also allow the members of the union to play a full part in the decision-making process and exclude the employer or senior members of the management from any involvement in union affairs.
6) *Negotiating record*: What is the union's general attitude to negotiations with the employer?

The Certification Officer will consider the full circumstances and nature of the case in deciding whether, overall, the union is under the domination or control of the employer or, if not, whether the union is liable to interference by the employer. In *Blue Circle Staff Association v Certification Officer*[15] the EAT approved the refusal of a certificate as the staff association had been created and then dominated by the employer for some years. Although there was evidence of some progress towards independence the staff association had still not satisfied the heavy burden of showing that it had divested itself of this control by the employer as 'the process of asserting genuine and effective independence after some years of such domination by management as has occurred in this case is likely to be protracted'.[16]

In *Squibb UK Staff Association v Certification Officer*,[17] the provision of financial support and other assistance from the employer combined with the record of ineffective bargaining and the small membership base meant that this staff association was 'exposed to the risk of' interference which would tend towards control by the employer. Even though there was little likelihood of the employer bringing pressure to bear by withdrawing this material support; if it were to be withdrawn, the association would be sufficiently weakened to be unable to resist employer interference and continue independently.

The *Squibb* interpretation of the test was applied by the Certification Officer in *GCHQ v Certification Officer*.[18] After the rights of association in trade unions had been withdrawn by the Conservative administration in 1984 from members of staff at GCHQ, the question arose as to whether the new GCHQ staff federation which replaced representation by national trade unions was entitled to a certificate of independence. As the staff association's ability to negotiate on behalf of its members, its freedom of action and indeed its very existence depended on the approval of the management, the staff association was clearly 'exposed or vulnerable or at the risk of interference' and failed to satisfy s. 5(b).

Once granted, a certificate of independence is conclusive evidence of independence.[19] But likewise, a withdrawal or cancellation of the certificate of independence under s. 7 is conclusive evidence that the trade union is not independent. An appeal on law against a refusal, withdrawal or cancellation of a certificate proceeds to the Employment Appeal Tribunal.[20]

---

15 [1977] ICR 224.
16 Cumming Bruce J, p. 234.
17 [1979] 2 All ER 452.
18 [1993] IRLR 260.
19 Section 8.
20 Section 9. A union opposed to the granting of a certificate of independence to a rival organisation cannot themselves appeal against this decision – *General Municipal Workers Union v C.O. & Imperial Group Staff Association* [1977] ICR 183.

18.4 Trade union legal status

The legal status of a trade union is of some importance, since it is this status that determines the legal capacity of the organisation. For example, whether legal action can be taken by and against a trade union in its own name, the way property is held, the liability of officers of the union, are all matters determined by the particular legal status imputed to a union. The question that arises is whether a union has the legal status of an individual, of a partnership between individuals, of a statutory or private corporation, or has an exclusive category of status reserved to itself.

Although trade unions had become lawful organisations with the passage of the Trade Union Act 1871, this statute did not deal directly with the issue of legal status. Those unions that had registered under the Trade Union Acts of 1871 and 1876 had conferred on them by the courts a degree of legal personality equivalent to quasi-corporate status.

The leading case of this era was *Taff Vale Railway Co v Amalgamated Society of Railway Servants*[21]. The majority in the House of Lords concluded that the existence of specific provisions in the Trade Union Acts of 1871 and 1876 (establishing a system of union registration, legalising trade union contracts, authorising the ownership of property through trustees and imposing duties of account on officers) meant that Parliament must have intended to treat a registered trade union as if it was a legal entity subject to the same duties and liabilities as an individual or corporation. This majority decision was subsequently unanimously re-affirmed by the House of Lords in *Osborne v Amalgamated Society of Railway Workers*.[22]

This analysis of trade union status was followed in subsequent cases. In *Gillian v National Union of General and Municipal Workers Union*,[23] the Court of Appeal, relying heavily on *Taff Vale*, went so far as to propound the view that as a registered trade union was a distinct legal person separate from the individuals comprising it, a trade union possessed sufficient characteristics of a company so as to have an independent legal personality capable of being defamed.[24]

While these cases show that unions were treated by the courts for many purposes as invested with the characteristics of corporate bodies, it remained unclear what the true extent of trade union quasi-legal status was. In 1968 the Donovan Commission reported that any uncertainty should be ended by statute formally providing for the incorporation of trade unions.[25] Consequently, the Industrial Relations Act 1971, provided for the formal incorporation of trade unions, although this full incorporated status was only available to those unions that registered under the Act.

In 1974 the new Labour government repealed the majority of the provisions of the Industrial Relations Act and replaced it with the Trade Union and Labour Relations Act 1974. The aim of s. 2(1) of the 1974 Act was to put on a statutory footing the status of a trade union as an unincorporated association of workers with specific attributes usually associated with corporations. This section first asserted that a 'trade union shall not be, or treated as if it were, a body corporate' and specified that any attempted incorporation under the Companies Acts would be void. It continued by providing specific authority for unions to enter into contracts, for property to be held in trust for the benefit of the trade union as an entity, for unions to be subject to the criminal law, for unions to sue and be sued in their own name and for civil judgments to be enforced as if the union was a company.[26]

---

21 [1901] AC 426.

22 [1910] AC 87.

23 [1946] KB 81.

24 See also *Bonsor v Musicians Union* [1956] AC 104 where the House of Lords held that a trade union as a quasi-corporate body had the capacity to make contracts and therefore could be sued by a member for wrongful expulsion in breach of the rule book.

25 Royal Commission on Trades Unions and Employers' Associations, Cmnd 3623, 1968, para. 782.

26 Provisions now repeated in sections 10(1)(2), 12(1) (2) TULR(C)A 1992.

The question arose in *EETPU v Times Newspapers Ltd*[27] whether the provisions of this section furnished unions with the same level of status as had been bestowed by the courts from 1901–1971 so as to permit the union to sue in defamation. Individuals as natural legal persons can, of course, be libelled, as can corporations who, since they possess full artificial legal personality, can sue to protect their trading reputation. For the EETPU to sustain the action it was necessary that sufficient legal personality be attributed to the union in the same way that it is attributed to companies.

Prior to s. 2(1), the Court of Appeal in *Gillian* had, as we saw earlier, established that unions registered under the 1871 Act possessed this degree of separate personality and consequently had a reputation to protect. O'Connor J in *EETPU* held that this was not now the case. Despite the fact that section 2(1) conferred on unions most of the elements of corporate status, the words of the section – 'shall not be treated as a corporate body' – limited union legal status to something less than had previously been the case. As a union was specifically not a corporate body it clearly did not possess the reputation of a corporate body. For the union to take action for defamation depended on whether the list of powers and liabilities contained in statute specifically conferred such a power on a union. As the list did not do so the EETPU could not maintain an action in their own name in relation to their reputation.

18.5 Trade union governance: judicial and statutory control

Historically, internal legal regulation was almost exclusively the preserve of the common law through the enforcement of the provisions of the rule book – which operates as the union's constitution, setting out the procedures of how the union is to be governed and administered. The rule book also acts as a contract of association between the union and each individual member. Where there is a breach of the provisions of the constitution or of other specific rights and obligations outlined in the rule book, any member is entitled to take legal action against their union on the basis that there has been a breach of contract.[28] Where a member and the union are in dispute over union action which is allegedly contrary to provisions in the rule book, the court can intervene to interpret the relevant provision of the rules to establish whether a breach of contract has occurred and to provide an appropriate remedy. In addition, the courts have often examined rule books to ascertain the objects or powers of a trade union. Where a union has acted in breach of the objects of the union derived from the rule book, the courts will declare such action as *ultra vires*, that is, beyond the powers of the union.

For most of the twentieth century the subject matter and content of the rules has primarily been a matter for the union itself. While there has been some statutory interference with the contents of the rule book since 1871,[29] the extent of interference has developed substantially in more recent years. Few areas of the union rule book have been left untouched by the passage of legislation since 1979. For example, ss. 28–45 TULR(C)A 1992 regulates, in some detail, trade union financial affairs, ss. 46–61 TULR(C)A 1992 completely replaces any existing provisions contained in union rules on elections to its executive committee. Where rights on admission are

---

27 [1980] QB 585.

28 This is subject to the rule in *Foss v Harbottle* [1843] 2 Hare 461 which is discussed on p. 352.

29 The Trade Union Act 1871 limited the requirements in the rules to the appointment of trustees and financial scrutiny of union finances. The Trade Union Labour Relations Act 1974 required unions to have rules on only two particular subjects – to allow a member to terminate his or her membership on reasonable notice and on the appointment and removal of auditors, retained in TULR(C)A 1992 as s. 69 and ss. 33–35 respectively.

concerned, ss. 174–177 TULR(C)A 1992 provide all individuals with a right to join a union of their choice. Discipline and expulsion is another area now heavily regulated by statute. Sections 64–67 TULR(C)A 1992 give every member the right not to be unjustifiably disciplined. In all these examples the provisions of the rule book, determined by the representatives of the membership as a whole, are over-ridden, with statute either nullifying the rules or displacing them. The remainder of this chapter considers the residual role of actions on the rule book and examines the development and extent of statutory regulation in these areas.

❖ THINKING POINT

Why do you think the statutory regulation of trade union activity has increased so dramatically since 1979?

18.6 Financial regulation: trustees and union funds

As a trade union is not a distinct legal person it cannot hold property in its own name; as an unincorporated association (albeit with special powers) a trade union must hold property vested in trustees. The assets of the union are not held by the trustees on trust for the members individually but rather for the members collectively.[30]

The union rule book is the document that sets out the terms of the trust, the powers and duties of the trustees and the procedure for the appointment and removal of trustees. It may provide for the holders of certain offices of the union to be trustees, or for the trustees to be elected by the annual conference. There is no requirement for trustees to be members of the national executive and often they are not. However, typically it is the executive committee that has the real power to make financial decisions as the trustees are normally required to act in accordance with the lawful directions of the national executive committee.

As the trust should be administered in accordance with the terms of the trust deed, any disposition of property outside the terms of the trust contained in the rule book is unlawful and trustees are then liable to the union for breach of trust. Although only the union has the authority to take action under the trust as the terms of the trust are contractual terms contained in the rule book, an action to enforce the rule book would in theory allow individual members a right to sue the trustees for breach of trust.[31]

In these circumstances the individual member must overcome the rule in *Foss v Harbottle*.[32] This rule provides that an individual member has no right to complain of a breach of the rule book in circumstances where the wrong has been committed against the union itself – as the proper claimant is the union, not the individual member, or if the breach is an internal irregularity that could be condoned by a simple majority of the membership. Thus, it would seem where *Foss v Harbottle* applies, the member's only option is to publicise the breach and to request the union to take action. However, the rule does not apply in certain circumstances, such as where the action

30 See section 12(1) TULR(C)A 1992 which specifies that 'all property belonging to the trade union shall be vested in trustees in trust for the union'.

31 See *Oddy v TSSA* [1973] ICR 524.

32 [1843] 2 Hare 461.

of the trustees is *ultra vires*. The doctrine of *ultra vires* will apply if funds are used for purposes that are not permitted by the rules.[33] In such a situation the member does have standing to take an action on the basis of the breach of trust arising from the rule book.

An opportunity for individual union members to enforce this form of common law right was provided during the miners' strike of 1984–1985. During the strike, fines were imposed on the NUM for contempt of court for refusing to adhere to a series of court orders. The NUM executive declined to pay and as a precaution ordered the trustees of the union to send union funds abroad out of the jurisdiction of the UK courts. As a consequence of the continuing contempt a sequestrator was appointed to recover the amount due. The trustees refused to authorise payment of the appropriate sums to the court appointed sequestrator and took action to frustrate the efforts of the sequestrator in tracking down union funds.

In *Clarke v Heathfield (No2)*[34] an NUM member successfully took action to have the union trustees removed from office for this breach of trust with the official receiver appointed in their place to administer the union's assets. Although the trustees were complying with their duties as trustees under the rule book by obeying the instructions of the national executive committee, these instructions were not in themselves lawful. By complying with unlawful instructions, the trustees were consequently in breach of the terms of the trust and acting *ultra vires*. Mervyn Davies J concluded that as the trustees were aware that their actions would very likely result in further substantial fines against the union and a reduction in the size of the funds available for lawful purposes they were not 'fit and proper persons' to administer the property of the union.[35]

Additional control of union financial matters can be enforced through the general law of trusts. This enables the union to challenge the way the assets are being used if there has been a breach of a fiduciary duty by the trustees. Individual union members cannot sue directly for breach of fiduciary duty as the duty is owed to the union. However, where a breach of fiduciary duty is alleged there will usually also have been a breach of the trust deed derived from the rule book and so, subject to the rule in *Foss v Harbottle*, an action would proceed based on breach of contract.[36]

After the litigation during the miners' strike of 1984–1985, over the use of trade union funds for furthering the dispute, the Conservative government believed the common law remedies available to union members were inadequate in controlling the abuse of these funds as trustees were too often willing to follow unlawful orders given by the NUM national executive.[37] The Green Paper *Trade Unions and Their Members* outlined the need to improve safeguards on the use of union assets in the interests of members who contribute to union funds. The Green Paper noted that the safeguard of union funds by trustees 'comes under strain where the union finds itself in conflict with the law' and that 'persons bearing the title of trustees may properly be required to prevent the unlawful use of the assets they are supposed to be protecting'.[38] The authors of the Green Paper

---

33 In practice the rule book of a union gives the national executive the power to give directions to trustees regarding the disposition of property. The main role of the trustees is thus to obey the lawful instructions of the executive. If these instructions are themselves unlawful and a trustee follows such an instruction an actionable breach of trust has been committed. For example, in *Bennett v National Amalgamated Society of Operative House and Ship Painters and Decorators* [1916] 85 LJ Ch 298, union trustees were instructed to buy shares in a commercial concern where there was no power to do so in the rules. As this was an *ultra vires* payment the individual member had standing to take an action based on the breach of trust derived from the rule book. See also *Carter v United Society of Boilermakers* [1916] 85 LJ Ch 289.

34 [1985] ICR 606.

35 See also *Taylor v NUM (Derbyshire Area) (No 3)* [1985] IRLR 99, where trustees following an unlawful instruction from the national executive misapplied union funds by providing strike pay to miners engaged in an unlawful strike.

36 As an example, see *Cowan v Scargill* [1984] IRLR 260.

37 For example, during the miners' strike trustees permitted union funds to be used to pay picket line fines (see *Thomas v NUM (South Wales Area)* [1985] 2 All ER 1). Section 15 of TULR(C)A 1992 now prohibits the use of union funds to indemnify unlawful conduct.

38 Cmnd 95. 1987, paras 3.1 and 3.14.

came to the conclusion that if trustees do not obey the general law any member should have the right to take action quickly and efficiently to remove the offending trustee.

This right was subsequently provided by the Employment Act 1988 which is now contained in s. 16 TULR(C)A 1992. This section states that where trustees carry out or propose to carry out their functions unlawfully, such as by breaking the union rules, refusing to carry out a court order or by breaking their general fiduciary duties, any member can take action in the High Court which has the power to make a variety of orders. The court may require the trustees to protect or recover property, by, for example, carrying out a particular investment policy or by paying a fine so as to recover property from a receiver.

The court has discretion to remove trustees and can appoint a receiver to administer the remaining union property.[39] Where trustees have not been removed, but a court order has been granted, if the trustees propose to apply or do apply any union funds in contravention of that court order, then the court must remove all the trustees of the union, unless one or more can satisfy the court that there is good cause why they should not be removed. Importantly, interlocutory relief is available where the court 'considers it appropriate'. This allows the court to remove the trustee on an emergency motion. Removal of trustees at the interlocutory stage would normally take place right at the beginning of an industrial dispute and so would cut off funding during the crucial early period of the dispute.

The right to ensure trustee compliance with the law exists side by side with the existing common law right to sue for breach of trust.[40] In the future it is far more likely that a member will initiate action on the basis of the statute than under the common law. Although during the miners' strike, the common-law action did eventually result in trustees being removed and union property moved out of the reach of union officials, the new statutory right is a quicker, more effective and flexible remedy, giving clear express rights to union members and particular powers to the court.

Moreover, the statutory remedy specifically provides for the appointment of a receiver and so resolves the previous uncertainty that existed about whether the court had power under their inherent jurisdiction to provide such a remedy.[41]

18.7 Financial regulation: union accounts

As trade unions are funded directly through members' subscriptions, and as they control substantial funds to enable them to provide a variety of services to their membership, it is indisputable that there should be a degree of democratic accountability and fiscal regulation to ensure their financial integrity. Due to the serious consequences of improper financial control, unions have never been left to devise their own financial systems without any interference, although the degree of regulation has increased dramatically in the years after the miners' strike of 1984–1985.

Basic controls over union financial affairs and the disposition of union property was provided by the Trade Union Act 1871, mirroring the type of regulation provided by the Companies Acts of 1844–1862. Trade unions were under an obligation to produce properly audited accounts and

39 Section 16(3).

40 Section 16(6).

41 Section 4 of the Trade Union Act 1871 had prevented a receiver being appointed as the section excluded the courts from interfering in any agreement relating to the application of funds of the union (See *Sansom v London and Provincial Union of Licensed Vehicle Workers* [1920] 36 TLR 666). The High Court took advantage of the repeal of the Trade Union Act by the Industrial Relations Act 1971 and by the absence of such a section in the Trade Union and Labour Relations Act 1974 to appoint receivers in some of the miners' cases. Up until the events of the miners' strike there had been no recorded cases where this had occurred.

to deposit an annual financial return with the Chief Registrar. This limited statutory regulation of trade unions was increased dramatically with the passage of the Industrial Relations Act 1971 which introduced a full regulatory framework for all trade union activities including financial administration.

On repeal of the Industrial Relations Act 1971, it was accepted that the financial regulation of trade unions should not revert back to the limited control under the Trade Union Act 1871. The Donovan Commission in 1968 had examined the issue of financial administration and had found that the lack of regulation had not resulted in any large scale financial corruption or fraud. However, it also found that inefficiency or waste was not easily identified where inexperienced or untrained staff were involved in preparing union accounts and other financial documents. The reasoning behind the regime introduced by the Trade Union and Labour Relations Act 1974 was to cure the problems created by reliance on amateur staff to discharge accounting and other financial tasks. This was achieved by the introduction of a legally enforceable framework of professional support. The substance of these requirements previously contained in the Trade Union Labour Relations Act 1974 ss. 10–12 and Schedule 2 Part 1 have been retained and consolidated into TULR(C)A ss. 28–45.

Under s. 28 trade unions must have a proper system of financial control. Appropriate accounting records must be kept, either at branch or national level, so as to satisfactorily provide a 'true and fair view of the state of the affairs of the trade union . . . and to explain its transactions'. Section 32 makes it compulsory for a union to submit an annual financial return to the Certification Officer. The return must include the audited accounts (balance sheet and revenue accounts), a copy of union rules, the auditor's report and a note on any change of union officers.[42] The annual return is available for public inspection and a copy of the annual return must be supplied to members and others on request.[43]

The role of union auditors, their specific duties and the content of their report is guided by ss. 33–37. These sections establish the principle that independent professionally qualified auditors must be appointed to report on the accounts that are submitted with the annual return.[44] In particular the auditors must report on i) whether the union has kept proper financial records under s. 28; ii) whether the union has maintained a satisfactory system of checking accounts and finances under s. 28; and iii) whether the accounts in the annual return correspond to the union's accounting records. Under s. 37 auditors have extensive rights of access to all financial documents, the right to demand information from union officers and to attend and speak at union general meetings. Where the union refuses or wilfully neglects to perform these duties, criminal liability is imposed under s. 45(1). Furthermore, under s. 45(2), liability also accrues to an officer whose duty it was, unless s/he reasonably believed some other competent person had been authorised to carry out the duty and had done so.[45] It is also an offence for any person in the course of performing the above duties to wilfully alter or cause to be altered any financial document with intent to falsify, so as to enable a trade union to evade any of their financial duties.[46]

The experience of the miners' strike of 1984–1985 resulted in further regulation. As the strike was called in contravention of the rule book, litigation was initiated by members to challenge the way union finances were applied to prosecute the strike. Furthermore, as the union refused to obey the orders of the court and found itself in contempt, action was also taken by members to safeguard unions assets against sequestration. In the Green Paper *Trade Unions and Their Members*[47] it was noted

42 Section 32(3).
43 Section 32(5)(6).
44 Sections 33–35.
45 Sections 45(3).
46 Section 45(4).
47 Cmnd 95, 1987, para. 3.25.

that these actions were hampered by the lack of information available to individual members and by the obstructive attitude of the NUM.

Reforms were introduced by the Employment Act 1988, building on the common law decisions during this period, with the aim of making it easier for union members to ascertain wrongdoing by establishing their right to demand access to financial information. The reasoning behind these provisions is that without an unfettered right to obtain such information a member would not be able to make an informed decision about whether to initiate an action against the union. These obligations have now been consolidated into TULR(C)A 1992 as ss. 29–31. Under s. 29 unions must have all their accounting records available for possible inspection by any member for a period of six years.[48] Section 30 permits a member to inspect the past and current accounts of the national union or of any branch or section of the union accompanied, if necessary, by an accountant.[49] The member who wishes to inspect union accounts is entitled to take copies as required, subject to reasonable administrative charges.

The union must comply with this request within 28 days. Should access not be forthcoming or if some or all of the requirements outlined in s. 30 are denied, a court order can be obtained under s. 31 enforcing the right to inspect. Should the order be ignored, the union or union officials will be held in contempt and heavy fines or possible sequestration of funds may be the consequence. Alternatively, an application can be made to the Certification Officer for an order enforceable in the same way as a court order.

Although the Trade Union and Labour Relations Act 1974 and the Employment Act 1988 imposed a comprehensive regime of financial regulation and a package of rights for members to enforce, the Green Paper *Industrial Relations in the 1990s*,[50] published in July 1991 presaged further reforms. The Green Paper referred to the miners' strike when noting that existing rights were insufficient to control financial wrongdoing. As a consequence of allegations in the press that NUM funds had been misapplied during the strike, the NUM had appointed Gavin Lightman QC to conduct an inquiry. As a consequence of his report the Certification Officer initiated a prosecution of members of the NUM national executive which failed partly due to the inadmissibility of much of the evidence collected for the report.

The response of the Government to the failure of this prosecution was the conclusion in the Green Paper that the relevant law required strengthening, particularly in the area of the investigation of financial irregularities, the offences that may be committed and the provision of financial information to members. The Green Paper suggested that additional powers should be given to the Certification Officer to find and prosecute irregularities and that those convicted of offences should be barred from holding national office. In addition, it was argued that there should be automatic and extensive disclosure of financial information to enable members to assess whether offences have been committed and to enhance the evidence gathering process for prosecutions.

Despite opposition from unions, the substance of the Green Paper was enacted in the Trade Union Reform and Employment Rights Act 1993 amending the TULR(C)A 1992. Section 32A of the TULR(C)A requires a union that has been in existence for more than 12 months to provide an annual financial statement[51] to its members no later than eight weeks after the annual report has

---

48 Note that this right permits any member to obtain information of all national or branch accounts and so deals with the issue that arose in *Hughes v TGWU* [1985] IRLR 382, where a union member was unable to examine the accounts of branches other than his own as the rules did not permit it.

49 Section 30 provides statutory support to the decision by Vinelott J in *Taylor v NUM (Derbyshire Area) (No 2)* [1985] IRLR 65, who had held that where the rule book gives the member the right to inspect the union accounting records, an implied right exists to have an accountant present for the purposes of interpreting the data.

50 Cm 1602, 1991.

51 The financial statement is a summary of the union's annual return containing the auditor's report on the union accounts and details of all income and expenditure of the union.

been sent to the Certification Officer. Either a copy of the statement can be sent to members or it can publish via the union's normal channel of communication, that is, publication in the union newspaper or journal. The annual statement must also be sent to the Certification Officer as soon as is reasonably practicable and a copy provided free to any member who requests it.

The Certification Officer's functions were also extended by the 1993 Act. The Certification Officer has additional powers to investigate union financial matters at national or branch level and to prosecute irregularities. Section 37A allows the Certification Officer, where there is 'good reason', to direct a trade union to produce 'relevant documents', defined as accounting documents or other documents dealing with financial affairs.

The Certification Officer also possesses the power to appoint inspectors to investigate the financial affairs of a trade union. This power of investigation is only activated if it appears that the union has failed to comply with any rule of the union, or duty relating to its financial affairs imposed by the statute, or a person concerned with the management of the union has been convicted of an offence regarding the management of union funds.

If an investigation is undertaken all relevant financial documents in the possession of officials or agents of the union must be produced. Such persons must co-operate with the investigation by attending any meeting with an inspector and by giving any other assistance they are reasonably able to give as required. The same duties are imposed on any other person who appears to the inspector to be in possession of relevant information. A person who is required to explain any documents or to assist an investigation may not refuse to comply on the grounds that it may incriminate them. They will be protected from prosecution unless the financial explanations they give are inconsistent with a statement or explanation made previously.[52]

Where an investigation is taking place, the inspector appointed must keep the Certification Officer informed and provide the Certification Officer with any information requested.[53] Additionally, the inspector may make a written interim report as directed by the Certification Officer and on the conclusion of the investigation a final report must be made. Most importantly, in the light of the failure of the Lightman prosecution, a certified copy of the report is admissible in any legal proceedings.

Offences for breach of the duties or requirements concerning inspection and investigation in TULR(C)A ss. 37A and 37B are dealt with by s. 45(5) of the TULR(C)A. It is an offence for an official or agent of a trade union to intentionally conceal the financial affairs of the union. However, where proceedings are brought for failing to produce documents, it is a defence for the accused to prove they were not in their possession and it was not reasonably practicable for them to comply with the requirement.[54] Where a person purports to comply with ss. 37A or 37B and knowingly or recklessly provides a false explanation or statement, an offence is committed as a breach of s. 45(9).

In addition, two other offences are specifically created. It is an offence to intentionally defeat the law by destroying, mutilating or falsifying a financial document or by making a false entry in a financial document[55] and to fraudulently part with, alter or delete anything in a financial document.[56]

Penalties for all offences relating to the financial administration of trade unions are contained in s. 45A. All of the offences are tried summarily in the Magistrates Court and may result, on

52 Sections 37A(7) and 37B(7). However, refusal to disclose information on the grounds of legal professional privilege is expressly retained by s. 37E(3).

53 Section 37C.

54 Section 45(6).

55 Section 45(7).

56 Section 45(8).

conviction, in either a fine of up to £5,000 for the offences under s. 45(1)–(5) or imprisonment for up to six months and/or a fine of up to £5,000 for those under s. 45(4) and (7)–(9).

Section 45B provides for a penalty of disqualification for persons convicted of any of the offences in s. 45. A trade union is under a duty to ensure that any member of the executive, the president and general secretary is disqualified from a position in the union for five years if convicted of an offence of maladministration under s. 45(1)–(5). Where such a person is convicted of the offences of corruption detailed in s. 45(4)(7)(8) or (9) the period of disqualification is ten years. An exception to disqualification arises where the president or general secretary is not a voting member of the executive or holds the position under the rules for only 12 months and has not held the position before.

A member of a trade union who believes the union has failed to comply with s. 45B by not disqualifying offenders may apply to the Certification Officer or the court for a declaration.[57] A declaration by the court or Certification Officer may be enforced by an order requiring the union to take steps to remedy the failure specified in the declaration. This order, once made, is enforceable by any member of the trade union.

❖ THINKING POINT

Why do you think trade union finances are more heavily regulated than the financial affairs of a company?

18.8 Admission, discipline and expulsion: common law control

Until 1980, control of union decision making in the area of admission, discipline and expulsion was solely based on common law, either through the enforcement of the terms of the contract of association or by reliance on judicially developed common law principles founded on public policy. The common law has now been supplemented by an extensive statutory regime to control internal union decisions. Although recourse to the enforcement of common law rights is thus far less frequent, the common law (in the form of the enforcement of the union rule book) still retains a residual supervisory role.

However, the enforcement of contractual rights has not always been a wholly effective way of regulating union decisions to expel or refuse admission. For example, where contractual requirements are fully observed – such as where the rule clearly allows for the expulsion of the member and full consideration is given to the application of correct procedure – the courts' capacity to intervene on the basis of a breach of contract is severely restricted. Alternatively, where a decision is made to refuse an application for membership, common law control based on a wrongful application of the rule book is clearly inadequate as there is no contractual relationship between the applicant and the union.

Historically, the solution for the courts was to broaden their jurisdiction, supplementing control via the rule book by the generation of additional common law doctrines justified on

57 Section 45C.

grounds of public policy. Many of these legal principles were developed to restrain the operation of the 'closed shop', either where a member was expelled, resulting in a loss of their job, or where an application for membership was denied, denying the applicant the opportunity of working in that trade or occupation.

In the forefront of these developments – in moulding the common law by way of public policy, to fit the requirements of 'justice' – was Lord Denning. He justified this use of public policy in *Enderby Town Football Club v Football Association Ltd*[58] where, after describing cases of judicial intervention in contractual disputes between members and their associations, he said:

> All these are cases where the judges have decided, avowedly or not, according to what is best for the public good. I know that over 300 years ago Hobart C.J. said 'Public policy is an unruly horse'. It has often been repeated since. So unruly is the horse, it is said that no judge should ever try to mount it, lest it run away with him. I disagree. With a good man in the saddle, the unruly horse can be kept in control. It can jump over obstacles. It can leap the fences put up by fictions and come down on the side of justice.[59]

In a series of cases in the 1960s and 1970s Lord Denning was at the forefront of controlling trade union decision making over admission and expulsion by the application of these doctrines. For example, in *Nagle v Fielden*[60] the 'right to work' as a legal principle was introduced to control the decisions of the Jockey Club which had excluded[61] the plaintiff merely on the grounds of her gender. Lord Denning distinguished the legal position of the ordinary social club that had a right to deny membership to any applicant, with that of powerful associations that do not have this unfettered right as the common law

> has for centuries recognised that a man has a right to work at his trade or profession without being unjustly excluded from it. He is not to be shut out from it at the whim of those having the governance of it. If they make a rule which enables them to reject his application arbitrarily or capriciously, not reasonably, that rule is bad. It is against public policy.[62]

Subsequently, Denning applied this principle in a number of trade union cases. For example, in *Edwards v Society of Graphical and Allied Trades*[63] the plaintiff, who was a temporary member, had failed to pay his union fees for six weeks and was excluded from membership under the rules of the union. His applications for readmission were rejected and he was subsequently dismissed by his employer who operated a closed shop. Building on the principles derived from *Nagle*, Lord Denning held that an arbitrary refusal to re-admit was invalid as being contrary to the 'right to work' principle outlined in *Nagle v Fielden*.

Other doctrines developed in this era included the 'by-law theory'. In a series of judgments in trade union cases spanning a period of 30 years until his retirement in 1983, Lord Denning often referred to the contract of association between union and member as a 'legal fiction'.[64] The essence of Denning's view was that union rules were not mutually agreed contractual obligations but were

58 [1971] 1 All ER 215.
59 Ibid. p. 219.
60 [1966] 2 QB 633.
61 For a review of the early cases, see Rideout, 1966.
62 Ibid. p. 644.
63 [1971] Ch 354. For comment, see Elias, 1971.
64 For example, see *Abbot v Sullivan* [1952] 1 All ER 226; *Bonsor v Musicians Union* [1956)]3 All ER 518; *Lee v Showmen's Guild of Great Britain* [1952] 1 All ER 1175; and *Boulting v ACTAT* [1963] 1 All ER 716.

imposed on a new member who had no choice but to accept the rule book unaltered. Therefore, as union rules were more in the nature of a legislative code or set of regulations laid down by a governing body, they could be treated as analogous to statutory by-laws. Union rules could thus be regulated in the same way that statutory by-laws are regulated – where a trade union applies an irrational and unfair interpretation of the rule it can be struck down as unreasonable and *ultra vires*.[65]

These principles, derived from case law of the 1960s and 1970s and the particular industrial circumstances pertaining to that era, are really of only historical interest – all decided in the context of the closed shop, which is now unenforceable by statutory changes. Indeed, on many occasions these decisions were overturned on appeal with the House of Lords less convinced of Lord Denning's legal analysis.[66]

A more conventional use of the common law is for the courts to analyse the content of the union rule book (the contract of association) to ascertain whether the union has complied with the procedural and substantive requirements of the contract when disciplining or expelling a member.

❖ THINKING POINT

What do you think these common-law concepts tell you about judicial attitudes at the time to trade union rules on admission and exclusion from membership?

18.8.1 Enforcement of the rule book

The law of contract, through a member's individual contract of association, regulates the relationship between the member and the union. As the rule book outlines the terms of the contract between the member and the union, a member alleging wrongful discipline or expulsion due to a failure of the union to abide by the rules may bring an action to enforce the rules.

As judicial control is exercised through the application of the contract of association between member and union, it follows that any failure to comply strictly with the requirements of the rules will render the decision to discipline or to expel unlawful. Consequently, courts will scrutinise the operation of disciplinary rules very carefully to ensure that the rule which is applied by the union clearly does provide the union with the power to act, to impose the particular sanction and that all procedural requirements outlined in the rules have been followed. Moreover, if the power to expel or discipline a member or the power to impose a particular sanction is not explicit, but is vague or unclear, then, as it fails to provide the authority for the action taken by the union, the court will declare it unenforceable. Where the power to act does not arise at all under the contract then the courts will not usually imply a power to discipline or expel a member.[67] The Certification Officer now has concurrent authority with the High Court to deliberate on a breach of the rules in a number of areas, such as union elections and discipline and expulsion.

65 See *Edwards v SOGAT* [1971] Ch 354; *Faramus v FAA* [1963] 1 All ER 636.

66 For example, see Lord Diplock's judgment in *Faramus v FAA* [1964] AC 925 and in *Cheall v APEX* [1983] IRLR 215.

67 See *Spring v National Amalgamated Stevedores' and Dockers' Society* [1956] 2 All ER 221, cf. *McVitae v Unison* [1996] IRLR 33.

18.8.2 Substantive and procedural compliance

Any divergence from the powers outlined in the rules will be unlawful. In *Blackall v National Union of Foundary Workers*,[68] Blackall was expelled for being 19 weeks in arrears with his subscriptions. The relevant rule allowed for an expulsion where a member was 20 weeks in arrears. As there had not been strict adherence to the rule the expulsion was unlawful. A similar situation arose in *Bonsor v Musicians Union*.[69] The relevant rule specified that if a member was more than six weeks in arrears then the branch could resolve to expel the member. Bonsor had failed to pay his subscriptions for a year. The branch secretary decided personally to inform the plaintiff he was expelled. As the power of expelling a member was vested in the branch committee and could not be delegated, the expulsion was contrary to the rules and therefore void.

In addition to complying with the substantive rules on discipline or expulsion, the union must comply with any additional procedural requirements stipulated in the rules. Thus, the domestic tribunal must be properly constituted and duly convened as required under the rules.[70] Any rules providing for a specific period of notice to be given before the convening of the disciplinary tribunal, or for a right to attend the hearing, must be adhered to[71] and the procedures for investigating a charge outlined in the rules must be followed.[72]

If there is a failure to comply with the appeal procedures enshrined in the rules, the original decision of the tribunal is of course void. That failure may also, in appropriate circumstances, invalidate any subsequent charges. In *Silvester v National Union of Printing, Bookbinding and Paper Workers*[73] the plaintiff was charged with acting to the detriment of the union for refusing to obey an instruction of the union. The plaintiff continued to defy the union and so further charges were brought against him. His right to appeal under the rules for the first charge was refused as an investigation of the other charges had not yet been completed. The court held that the wrongful denial of the appeal on the first charge invalidated the proceedings and vitiated the decision on all the charges.[74]

18.8.3 Construction of the rules

The domestic disciplinary tribunal is ordinarily regarded as having exclusive jurisdiction over any findings of fact. Yet where questions of law arise, the findings of a domestic tribunal can be disturbed by the courts as in matters of law the courts claim ultimate jurisdiction. It is a question of law whether there is sufficient evidence reasonably capable of supporting the findings of fact by the domestic tribunal. In effect the court is entitled to take it upon itself to assess the weight of evidence presented to the tribunal.[75]

Even where the facts are clearly supported by the evidence, the decision is reviewable by the courts where the tribunal has incorrectly interpreted the offence cited in the rules. For example, in *Radford v NATSOPA*,[76] Radford was charged with taking 'wilful action against the union' for consulting a solicitor during a previous dispute with the union. Plowman J justified intervention on the

68 [1923] 39 TLR 431.
69 [1956] AC 1.
70 *Leary v National Union of Vehicle Builders* [1971] Ch 34.
71 *Lawlor v Union of Post Office Workers* [1965] Ch 712.
72 *Santer v National Graphical Society* [1973] ICR 60.
73 [1966] 1 KIR 679.
74 See also *Braithwaite v EETU* [1969] 2 All ER 859.
75 For example, Denning in *Breen v AEU* [1971] 2 QB 175, emphasised that where a tribunal has taken into account irrelevant evidence, the court is wholly justified in declaring the decision of the tribunal null and void.
76 [1972] ICR 484.

grounds that the courts are 'peculiarly appropriate' bodies to consider the true construction of the rules and to examine the sufficiency of evidence to support findings of fact. On these facts, he unsurprisingly held that consulting a solicitor could not be reasonably construed as satisfying the test of 'wilful action against the union'.[77]

A further safeguard for the disciplined member is that the courts insist that the rule book is construed in such a way so that any ambiguity in the rules is resolved in favour of the individual. This is achieved by the courts interpreting the rules 'so as to give a reasonable interpretation which accords with what in our opinion must have been intended'.[78] This allows the courts some discretion over how the rule book should be construed. The court adopts, what is to the court, the most reasonable interpretation in the circumstances.[79]

18.8.4 Ousting the jurisdiction of the court

Denning LJ in *Lee v Showmen's Guild*[80] underlined the exclusivity of the court's jurisdiction when he said that 'the true construction of the contract is to be decided by the courts and by no one else'.[81] This is clear authority that an internal tribunal cannot ordinarily usurp the authority of the court in matters of law. Indeed, any formal attempt to oust the jurisdiction of the court by the provision of a clause in the rule book purporting to exclude the power of the court to intervene will be struck down as void and unenforceable.[82]

However, the courts have an inherent discretion to stay proceedings until domestic procedures have been exhausted.[83] This discretion, however, cannot be enforced by a formal mandatory provision in the rule book delaying access to the courts until there has been recourse to domestic proceedings. Such a rule would act to fetter the courts lawful discretion and is *prima facie* contrary to public policy, yet it may be valid in appropriate circumstances. Goff J dealt with this issue in *Leigh v NUR*[84] when he said

> where there is an express provision in the rules that the plaintiff must first exhaust his domestic remedies, the court is not absolutely bound by that because its jurisdiction cannot be ousted, but the plaintiff will have to show just cause why it should interfere with the contractual position.[85]

'Just cause' may be satisfied where there is clear evidence of bias in the domestic tribunal, capricious or arbitrary behaviour by the union, excessive delay,[86] or possibly where the factual issues are not in dispute and so only an issue of law is to be considered.[87] In these limited circumstances, the courts, at common law, may well be willing to recognise and give effect to a partial ouster of their jurisdiction and so use their discretion to stay legal proceedings pending the outcome of the domestic tribunal.[88]

---

77 See also *Esterman v NALGO* [1974] ICR 625.
78 Viscount Dilhorne in *Goring v British Actors' Equity* [1978] ICR 791 at p. 795.
79 See *MacLelland v NUJ* [1975] ICR 116.
80 [1952] 2 QB 329.
81 Ibid. p. 344.
82 *Scott v Avery* [1856] 5 HL Cas 811.
83 *Lawlor v UPW* [1965] Ch 712 and *White v Kuzych* [1951]1All ER 353.
84 [1970] Ch 326.
85 Ibid. p. 334.
86 *Leigh v NUR* [1970] Ch 326.
87 *Radford v NATSOPA* [1972] ICR 484.
88 This is of course on the assumption that the domestic procedures are effective and will preserve the status quo pending the decision of the tribunal. *Hiles v Associated Society of Woodworkers* [1968] Ch 440.

The common law position on the legality of delaying access to the courts has now been supplemented by a statutory provision, s. 63 of TULR(C)A 1992, which now provides a right for members to have access to the courts to pursue a grievance against their union, notwithstanding any contrary rule in the rule book. This right not to be denied access to the courts is limited to the situation where the member has already made an application under the rules of the union and six months have elapsed from the date of the application without a determination by the union, unless the reason for the delay was because of the unreasonable conduct of the member. If the member enforces their statutory right, the court is bound to adjudicate without regard to any rule limiting its jurisdiction, even if the matter would have been more quickly, efficiently and conveniently disposed of under domestic procedures.

Section 63(6) states that this right is provided without prejudice to any principle of common law. Thus, it is still possible that if 'just cause' is demonstrated, the member may still ignore any rule requiring the exhaustion of domestic remedies, before the six-month period has elapsed.

If disciplinary procedures are incorporated into the rule book the courts will act to enforce this procedure and declare any disciplinary action contrary to the procedure unlawful. Where the procedural safeguards in the rule book are inadequate or incomplete, the courts will still require that certain minimum procedural requirements are met. These are broadly known as the rules of natural justice. There is a need for union tribunals to observe the principles of natural justice owing to the existence of implied obligations of law to that effect in the contract of association. As implied terms of law they cannot be excluded by any contrary provision in the rule book on the basis that such an agreement would be void as contrary to public policy.[89]

There are broadly two constituents of natural justice:

1) The disciplinary decision must have been reached without bias on the part of the panel hearing the charges.[90]
2) There must be a fair hearing. This means the accused is entitled to appropriate notice of the charges, the right to be heard in answer to these charges, the right to attend and to put his or her case to the tribunal.[91]

❖ THINKING POINT

Why do you think actions on the rule book have declined so much in recent years?

18.9 Admission, discipline and expulsion: statutory control

Until the passage of the Industrial Relations Act 1971, there was little statutory regulation limiting a union's power to admit, discipline or expel a member. The Trade Union Act 1913 enforced a

89 See *Lee v Showmen's Guild* [1952] 2 QB 329; *Radford v NATSOPA* [1972] ICR 484; *Breen v AEU* [1971] 2 QB 175; cf. *Lawlor v UPW* [1965] Ch 712.

90 See *White v Kuzych* [1951] AC 585; *Taylor v National Union of Seamen* [1967] 1 All ER 767; *Roebuck v NUM (Yorkshire Area)(No2)* [1978] ICR 678.

91 See *Santer v NGA* [1973] ICR 60; *Annamunthodo v Oil Workers' Union* [1961] AC 945; *Leary v National Union of Vehicle Builders'* [1971] 1 All ER 767; *Ecclestone v NUJ* [1999] IRLR 166.

requirement that a union could not refuse to admit or discipline an individual solely on the grounds that they refused to contribute to the political fund. Other than this, very limited provision, control was based solely on judicial construction of the rule book and on doctrines of public policy considered earlier.

In 1968 the Donovan Commission[92] recommended the establishment of an independent committee to investigate and provide redress for the limited number of cases where unreasonable exclusion was alleged.[93] The Conservative government elected in 1970 responded to this recommendation by including in the Industrial Relations Act 1971, a provision providing for full statutory control over disciplinary matters. This section was broader than had been thought strictly necessary by the Donovan Commission as it was not exclusively concerned with admissions or expulsions where a closed shop operated but provided members with a general right of complaint against disciplinary action by trade unions.

Section 5 was abolished in 1976. As a consequence of the furore created by this abolition, the Trades Union Congress set up an Independent Review Committee to investigate and deliberate on admission and expulsion cases where a closed shop existed. The Committee played an important role in controlling over-zealous disciplinary action by trade unions. However, after 1980 the role of the Independent Review Committee diminished. Section 4 of the Employment Act 1980 created a new statutory right to complain to an industrial tribunal of unreasonable exclusion from a trade union where a closed shop operated. Other legislative interventions made it more difficult for trade unions to establish new closed shops and to enforce existing ones. The Independent Review Committee, now effectively redundant, was formally disbanded in 1989.

The crucial component of the right in s. 4 of the 1980 Act was the 'reasonableness' of the exclusion or expulsion.[94] The application of the test of reasonableness was tightly circumscribed by a Code of Practice on Closed Shop Agreements and Arrangements published by the Department of Employment in 1980 and revised in 1983. The contents of the Code were admissible in evidence and both tribunals and courts were directed to take notice of the Code in determining 'reasonableness'.[95]

The Code contained both substantive and procedural elements. Procedurally, the Code stated that rules on exclusion must be clear and well known, with sufficient appeal procedures and that the principles of natural justice should be observed when taking the decision to exclude the applicant. By far the most controversial element of the Code was the recommendation that no member should be excluded or other disciplinary action taken if a member refuses to take industrial action[96] or crosses a picket line.[97]

The 1988 Employment Act expanded the protection for union members from the limited protection in s. 4 against exclusion from a union where a closed shop existed, to include situations where disciplinary sanctions were taken against them, short of exclusion and without regard as to whether a closed shop existed at their place of employment. In the Green Paper *Trade Unions and Their Members*,[98] which preceded the publication of the Employment Bill, the government particularly focused its criticisms on trade unions that impose sanctions on members who refuse to take industrial action. The government took the view that the freedom of choice of the individual to

92 Cmnd 3623, para. 610.
93 Paras 612 and 658–669.
94 For a more detailed explanation of the background to this statutory development, see Elias, 1980.
95 Section 3(8).
96 Para. 61.
97 Para. 62.
98 Cmnd 95, 1987, paras 210–213.

work rather than take industrial action must be unaffected by the threat of discipline and that the common law provided inadequate protection for union members who were in conflict with their union over their right to choose to go to work.[99] This, it was suggested, was supported by the evidence of disciplinary action being unjustly taken during several high profile disputes, such as during the Rail dispute in 1982 and most importantly the experience of the miners' strike of 1984–1985 and the Wapping dispute in 1986.[100]

Consequently, a new statutory right 'not to be unjustifiably disciplined' was introduced by the Employment Act 1988. The provisions of the Employment Act 1988, which established this right, have now been incorporated into TULR(C)A 1992 as ss. 64–68. Essentially, a union member has the right to complain of 'unjustifiable discipline' where a disciplinary act, as defined in the statute, has been taken against the applicant.

18.9.1 The right not to be unjustifiably disciplined[101]

An individual is 'disciplined' by a union if action is taken that falls within section 64(2). This includes matters such as expulsion from the union, the imposition of a fine or enforcing the payment of other monetary sum, such as by confiscating subscriptions. It also embraces more general action such as where the member is deprived of 'access to, any benefits, services or facilities . . . of the union'[102] or where a member is subjected to 'some other detriment'.

The EAT has taken a broad view of the meaning of the term 'some other detriment'. In *Transport & General Workers Union v Webber*,[103] the EAT held that refusal to allow the applicant to attend a union meeting was capable of amounting to 'some other detriment'. In *NALGO v Killorn*,[104] the EAT defined 'other detriment' as 'some disadvantage of whatever nature'. Therefore, the action of the union in advertising the names of members in a union newsletter who had not taken strike action, so causing them embarrassment, was 'other detriment' for the purposes of the Act.

The disciplining of the member is 'unjustifiable' if it is for one or more of several reasons outlined in s. 65. These include:

1) failing to take part in or support a strike or other industrial action,[105] or for opposing such action;
2) failing to contravene a contract of employment (such as by obeying an instruction by a manager to cover for strikers), or for encouraging others to comply with their contract of employment (such as by urging others not to take strike action);
3) asserting that there has been a breach of the rule book or of a statutory requirement;
4) failing to agree or withdrawing agreement for the 'check off' system of deduction of union subscriptions from source;
5) resigning or proposing to resign from the union or becoming or proposing to become a member of another union;

---

99 The importance the Government attributed to this right to work is clear from the introductory statement to para. 210 – 'The right of the individual to go to work despite a call to take industrial action is an essential freedom'.

100 See para. 213.

101 For an overview of the cases decided in the first three years refer to Kidner, 1991.

102 As access to benefits, services or facilities derive from the use of membership any suspension of membership, whether temporary or not, is a deprivation under the Act – see *NALGO v Killorn* [1990] IRLR 464.

103 [1990] IRLR 462.

104 [1990] IRLR 464.

105 The Court of Appeal in *Fire Brigades Union v Knowles* [1996] IRLR 617 affirmed the decision of the EAT that a union ban on full-time fire personnel taking on additional duties was not 'other industrial action' as it was imposed for safety reasons.

6) working with or proposing to work with non-union labour or members of another union, working for or proposing to work for an employer who employs non-union or members of another union;
7) requiring the union to comply with its statutory duties or for consulting or seeking the advice and assistance of the Certification Officer.

❖ THINKING POINT

Will a trade union member attract the protection of the statutory provision where the applicant is disciplined for committing several offences – of which only one is 'unjustifiable' under the legislation?

18.9.1.1 Remedies and procedure

Section 66(2) provides that the applicant must apply to an employment tribunal with the complaint within three months of the determination to impose the penalty which infringes the right. This time limit can be extended if 'it was not reasonably practicable for the complaint to be presented before the end of that period' or 'any delay is . . . attributable to a reasonable attempt to appeal against the determination or have it reconsidered or reviewed, within such further period as the tribunal considers reasonable'.[106] This allows members to apply for an internal appeal without any prejudice to their right to complain to an employment tribunal of a breach of this statutory right.

The tribunal then has the power to grant a declaration that the application is well founded.[107] Once a declaration has been made, further remedies of restitution of any financial penalty or compensation are available under section 67 in a further application to an employment tribunal. An application for compensation or for reimbursement of a payment or fine by the member should be made within six months, but not before four weeks from the time of the declaration. This is to allow the union to reflect on the decision of the tribunal and to voluntarily make amends.

Compensation awarded is dependent on what is considered to be 'just and equitable in the circumstances'.[108] However, the section provides for the duty of the applicant to mitigate loss[109] and that contributory fault by the applicant may justify a reduction in compensation.[110] The amount of compensation awarded should not exceed the maximum basic and compensatory award for unfair dismissal.[111] However, if the infringement of the applicant's rights has not been revoked a minimum award must be made.[112]

The operation of these compensatory provisions was considered by the EAT in *Bradley & Others v NALGO*[113] where an award for distress or injury to feelings was permissible, although the EAT held that any award should be of a modest nature.

106 Section 66(2)(b).
107 Section 66(3).
108 Section 67(5).
109 Section 67(6).
110 Section 67(7).
111 Section 67(8).
112 Section 67(8A).
113 [1991] IRLR 159.

18.9.2 The right to membership

The Trade Union Reform and Employment Rights Act 1993 repealed the provisions on unreasonable exclusion and expulsion where a closed shop operated and introduced a new s. 174 of TULR(C)A 1992 guaranteeing the right of every person to join a trade union of their choice and the right not to be expelled from a trade union unless the exclusion[114] or expulsion is expressly permitted by the statute. Section 174(2) outlines the permissible reasons:

a) If an applicant or member is excluded because they do not satisfy an 'enforceable membership requirement' contained in the rule book, then the exclusion is permitted. The statute continues by stating that a membership requirement in the rule book is only 'enforceable' in three circumstances – if it limits membership by virtue of requiring specified qualifications or experience, or membership is limited to members of a specified trade or profession, or to particular grades or categories of jobs.[115]
b) Where the union only recruits in a certain geographical area, or from only one employer, then the rejection of an application from outside that area or from someone who works for another employer, is justified.
c) The exclusion or expulsion is permitted if it is wholly because of the conduct of the individual. What constitutes sufficient misconduct for the purposes of the section is clearly open to interpretation. However, certain types of conduct can never be a valid reason for exclusion or expulsion. It would be unlawful to exclude or expel a person for having been or presently being a member of another trade union,[116] or for having been or presently being employed by a particular employer. Additionally, conduct which would constitute 'unjustifiable discipline' under s. 65 is not a sufficient reason for exclusion or expulsion under this section.[117]

Until repealed by the Employment Act 2008 it was also an automatic breach of the provisions to exclude or expel an individual for being, or having been, a member of a political party. In *ASLEF v UK*[118] the union expelled a member (Lee) of the British National Party as its racist views were in direct contravention of union policy on equality. Lee successfully argued that this expulsion was contrary to his rights under s. 174 – with the result that ASLEF had to re-admit him to the union. In response ASLEF brought proceedings before the European Court of Human Rights on the basis that the UK legislative provision (s. 174) was contrary to the right under Article 11 of the European Convention for unions, in certain circumstances, to exclude individuals from membership. In earlier cases the Strasbourg Court had indicated that the provision in Article 11 – the right to form and join trade unions – included the right of trade unions to a degree of autonomy from the state so as to administer their affairs without undue interference and to determine their own rule book provisions in this area, subject to the need to protect individuals who were excluded arbitrarily or suffered personal hardship by the exclusion.[119]

Building on these previous decisions the Strasbourg Court in *ASLEF v UK*[120] held that s. 174 failed to strike the appropriate balance between the rights of the individual and the rights of the

114 In *NACODS v Gluchowski* [1996] IRLR 252, the EAT concluded that 'exclusion' for the purposes of liability under s. 174 must be construed strictly. A temporary suspension of membership did not amount to exclusion from the union.
115 Section 174(3).
116 Section 174(4). This thus provides that a refusal of an application because it would result in a breach of the Bridlington Principles on inter-union membership disputes would be unlawful.
117 Section 174(4).
118 [2007] IRLR 361.
119 *Cheall v UK* [1986] EHRR 74; *Johansson v Sweden* [1990] 65 DLR 202.
120 n 118.

trade union. This provision, that introduced a blanket ban on exclusion, was a disproportionate and unjustified interference with ASLEF's right to refuse entry to an individual, taking account of the fact that Lee had not suffered any detriment by his loss of union membership.[121]

Consequently, the Employment Act 2008 has introduced a new s. 174 (2)(D) and (4A)–(4H) into the TULR(C)A 1992. These provisions now state that an individual is not protected from exclusion or expulsion if membership of a particular political party is contrary to the rules or objectives of the union. However, the action of the union can still be unlawful if exclusion or expulsion is taken not in accordance with the union rules, or contrary to rules of natural justice (such as a failure to give advance notice of the exclusion or expulsion and to allow representations prior to the decision to expel or exclude), or if, as a consequence of exclusion or expulsion, the individual would lose his or her livelihood or suffer some other exceptional hardship.

18.9.2.1 Remedies

An application for a declaration is first made to an employment tribunal, within six months of the date of exclusion or expulsion. Once obtaining a declaration that he or she was excluded or expelled contrary to the statute, the applicant may claim compensation after a waiting period of four weeks (to give the union the opportunity to rescind its decision). The tribunal calculates compensation based on what is considered to be 'just and equitable', subject to the maximum of the basic award and compensatory award available for unfair dismissal. However, where the union does not readmit or admit, then similarly with an award for 'unjustifiable discipline', there is a minimum that must be awarded – the current minimum (at the time of writing) is £9,118. If the tribunal finds the applicant was at fault in any way the rules of contributory fault apply.[122]

18.10 Union elections

18.10.1 Common law control

Until the advent of extensive statutory intervention (with the passage of legislation from the Employment Act 1980 to the Trade Union Reform and Employment Rights Act 1993), there was no statutory requirement to hold elections for union positions. Yet, as a matter of general law, if specific provisions on elections and election procedure existed in the union rules then a member could force the union to abide by these provisions by the contractual enforcement of the terms of the rule book. In *Leigh v NUR* [1970],[123] the rule book of the NUR stipulated that the union general secretary had the authority to vet nominations for election to the post of president of the union. Where approval was improperly denied to a potential candidate the court granted an injunction to restrain the holding of the election.[124] An action on the rule book was also successful in *Wise v USDAW*[125] where the executive council of the union acted outside of the rules when altering nomination procedure.

---

121 Note that numerous commentators have suggested that a full challenge to the statutory provisions on admission, expulsion and discipline (ss. 60–65 and s. 174) as a breach of Article 11 of the European Convention could be successfully mounted as a consequence of the more robust approach of the Strasbourg Court to union rights demonstrated by the decision in *ASLEF* and cases such as, *inter alia*, *Wilson & Palmer v UK* [2002] 35 EHRR 20; *Demir v Turkey* [2009] IRLR 456. The EAT in *Unison v Kelly* [2012] IRLR 442, however, rejected the argument that s. 65 violated Article 11 of the Convention. Protecting the rights of union members to hold the union to account when there is a breach of the rule book was 'necessary in a democratic society' and therefore justified under Article 11(2). See Ewing, 2007, 2009 and Barrow, 2013.

122 Section 176(5).

123 [1970] Ch 326.

124 For a fuller examination of actions on the rule book, see Kidner, 1973.

There are of course limitations to this system of control. As members' rights are based solely on the enforcement of the rule book, members cannot object to the lack of elections or demand adherence to a preferred procedure if such matters are not contained in the rules. Furthermore, existing rules, even by an interventionist court, can only be construed so far. *Hughes v TGWU*[126] illustrates this point. Hughes applied to the High Court for an order requiring the union to release full information about the result of the election in each branch and for the right to full access to union records to ascertain the accuracy of this information. As the rules did not provide for the release of such detailed information this request was denied by the court.

Even where there has been an irregularity in the conduct of an election and a breach of the rule book there have been occasions where the courts have refused to arbitrate in a dispute between member and union. For example, the *Foss v Harbottle* principle was applied in *Goodfellow v London & Provincial Union of Vehicle Workers*[127] to justify non-intervention in the circumstances of an irregularity in election procedure. Non-interference in election disputes has also been justified on more pragmatic grounds. Walton J held in *Brown v AUEW*,[128] that so long as an irregularity in election procedure was only of a minor nature causing no substantial injustice, an election result was still valid. In *Douglas v GMPU*[129] the union executive council ordered a fresh election to the post of general president of the union because of allegations that the plaintiff, who had been elected, had acted in breach of the rules by making unauthorised comments to the press prior to the election. Morison J, in reinstating the result of the original election, adopted the reasoning in *Brown v AUEW*.[130] As the alleged minor breach of the rules would not have truly affected the result of the election the executive council's decision to rerun the election was unreasonable and perverse.

18.10.2 Statutory control

The Conservative government elected in 1979 believed intervention in the internal democratic process of trade unions was justified for several reasons. Most importantly, not all trade unions maintained the system of direct elections to senior trade union positions favoured by the new administration.[131] There was also at this time heavy media and government criticism of the militant leadership of many unions. Legislation, it was believed, was necessary in order to give effective control of the union back to its membership and to establish a minimum standard of democracy.

The legislative strategy described below – the imposition of direct balloted elections and compulsory election procedure – was criticised for ignoring the existence of an already well developed system of democracy appropriate to the needs of trade unions. Unions have always had rules governing elections and election procedure at all strata of the union, not just for the national executive. Although unions did not always utilise a system of direct elections to senior positions

125 [1996] IRLR 609.
126 [1985] IRLR 382.
127 (1919) *The Times*, 8 September.
128 [1976] ICR 147.
129 [1995] IRLR 426.
130 n 128.
131 For criticisms of union arrangements prior to the statutory changes, see the Green Paper, *Democracy in Trade Unions* Cmnd 8778, 1983, para. 39.

the various methods employed reflected the historical development and organisational complexity of trade unions.[132]

The diversity of democratic methods utilised within the decentralised structure of a trade union enabled the views of the membership to be communicated to the union hierarchy at a number of levels. It has also been suggested that representative democracy, designed for a system of 'government' and 'opposition' is unsuited to trade unions as it encourages the existence of oppositionist factions or groupings.[133] This potentially damages the necessary cohesion which a trade union requires to effectively represent the interests of its membership in negotiation with employers. If representative democracy disrupts, rather than strengthens collective action, then union ability to exercise this essential function is weakened.[134]

The first stage of the 'democratising' of trade unions in order to enhance democratic control was based on a strategy of encouraging rather than compelling trade unions to hold balloted internal elections. Section 1 of the Employment Act 1980 made state funds available for those unions willing to hold secret ballots on a number of matters,[135] including national and certain local internal elections. The scheme was administered by the Certification Officer and funds were provided to defray the costs of the printing of the ballot paper, other stationery and postal costs. However, in practice the operation of the provisions failed to sufficiently encourage trade unions to change their methods of democracy. Thus, the next stage of reform was to introduce more directive legislation enforcing mandatory union elections under a specified procedure.

The Green Paper *Democracy in Trade Unions*[136] put forward the government's case for the introduction of a prescriptive regime. The Green Paper alleged that there was evidence that the national executive of certain unions were not properly representative and accountable to the membership as a whole,[137] that union rules were too easily manipulated by the leadership of unions,[138] and that allegations of corruption of the election process were too numerous to ignore.[139]

As a consequence of these criticisms, fundamental reforms on compulsory elections and election procedure were introduced by Part 1 of the Trade Union Act 1984.[140] Important amendments extending statutory control have since been made by the Employment Act 1988 and the Trade Union Reform and Employment Rights Act 1993. All these provisions have now been consolidated into TULR(C)A 1992 Chapter IV ss. 46–56. This extensive regime for elections, where necessary, displaces any relevant rules of the union.

18.10.2.1 Duty to hold elections

The original provision in the Trade Union Act 1984 only required voting members of a union's executive committee to be directly elected. The Employment Act 1988 extended this to all members of the executive committee who are entitled to attend and speak or hold national office, whether

---

132 Methods used differed between unions. Where amalgamations have occurred at different phases of a union's history special arrangements for election to the national executive may have been in place to meet the needs of special occupational groups or sections. Alternatively, in some unions indirect elections (such as appointment via a special delegate conference) may have been used to determine membership of all or part of a union's national executive.

133 The danger of hostile groupings in what is essentially a 'fighting organisation' is cogently examined by Kahn-Freund, 1983.

134 These and other points are discussed in more detail by Davies & Freedland, 1984, pp. 670–685 and by Kahn-Freund, 1983, pp. 270–290. See also Fredman, 1992.

135 Finance was also provided to hold ballots on other matters such as to amend union rules, on amalgamations and on industrial action. Thus, funds for union elections were part of a wider strategy to encourage member participation in union decision making.

136 Cmnd 8778, 1984.

137 Paras 1 and 7.

138 Para. 10.

139 Para. 12.

140 The background to the passage of the 1984 Act and the perceived justifications are fully examined by R. Martin in Fosh & Littler, 1986, Chapter 5.

they have a vote or not,[141] and enforced a requirement that elections to the national executive must be fully postal.[142] Section 46 of the TULR(C)A 1992 now provides for mandatory direct elections by secret postal ballot every five years of any member of the union principal executive committee and those who hold the offices of president and general secretary or their nearest equivalents. However, due to amendments introduced by the Employment Relations Act 2004, a president of the union does not need to be elected separately if they had been previously elected to the union executive.[143]

18.10.2.2 Exclusion of a candidate for election

It is a basic right that each individual union member is entitled not to be unreasonably excluded from standing as a candidate, nor may a candidate be required to be a member of a political party.[144] Many unions have special eligibility rules (such as a bar on candidates with criminal convictions or a minimum age requirement). A policy of requiring particular qualifications or a number of nominations by other members or branches before a member could stand as a candidate is not unlawful so long the nomination process is well advertised by the union. However, the exclusion from candidature must be objectively justified. In *Paul v NALGO*,[145] the rules of the union stated that candidates for Vice President had to be nominated by the executive or by district councils of the union. Paul argued this was contrary to s. 47(1) as an ordinary member would need to personally persuade members of the executive or district council to nominate him or her. Refusal would mean an ordinary member was excluded from standing as a candidate. The Certification Officer upheld this complaint as this was an unreasonably exclusive nomination system that could not be objectively justified. Although the procedure did not actually preclude members from standing, in practical terms it made it very difficult for them to exercise their right.[146]

The right not to be unreasonably excluded from standing as a candidate is qualified by s. 47(3) which permits the rules of a union to exclude a whole class of members. In order to disqualify a class it must be possible to establish in advance who is within that class. A 'class of members' can be defined as a number of individuals possessing some common attribute identifiable by description, such as all new members or retired members, but not determined by reference to a subjective test, such as 'those persons approved by the national executive'.[147]

18.10.2.3 The scrutineer and independent counting officer

The scrutineer's role is to oversee the election and ensure it is run fairly. The scrutineer is charged with a duty to supervise the production and distribution of ballot papers and on request from a union member or a candidate, or where it is appropriate to do so, to check the union register of members[148] (which acts as the electoral roll) for accuracy.[149] All ballot papers must be returned direct to the scrutineer who retains custody of them for at least a year to assist any member who wishes to complain of irregularities in the election.

---

141 This became known as the 'Scargill clause' as the NUM general secretary had previously given up his vote on the executive committee to avoid adherence to the 1984 Act.

142 The 1984 Act had originally provided that secret postal ballots were the preferred method of election, but that workplace secret ballots were acceptable in certain circumstances. Even though there were criticisms in the Green Paper (at para. 5.8) of the organisation of workplace ballots for elections in the TGWU and the CPSA it was surprising that they were forbidden by the 1988 Act as workplace ballots guarantee a far higher level of turnout and thus are inherently more 'democratic'.

143 Section 46(4A)(5A).

144 Section 47(1) (2). Prior to s. 47(2), discrimination on political grounds had been lawful – *Leigh v NUR* [1970] Ch 326.

145 [1987] IRLR 43.

146 See also *UNISON v Staunton* [2009] IRLR 418.

147 *Ecclestone v NUJ* [1999] IRLR 166.

148 A union is required under s. 24 to maintain this register.

149 Section 49(3).

The scrutineer is under a duty to make a report on the election, detailing the results of the election and commenting on its fairness and whether there has been full union compliance with the statute.[150] A copy of the report must be sent to all members or alternatively the report may be published in the union journal. This report must contain certain specific information, such as the number of ballot papers distributed, number returned, number of valid votes for each candidate, a record of whether the register of members was inspected and the performance of any independent counting officers, if appointed.[151]

The scrutineer is supposed to be competent, impartial and independent of the union. The union is under a duty not to interfere in the scrutineer's work and to co-operate at all times.[152] The Scrutineer Regulations (SI 1993/1909), details who is qualified to act as a scrutineer. A union may appoint a firm of solicitors or accountants that satisfy certain additional conditions or appoint one of three specialist named organisations; the Electoral Reform Society, the Industrial Society or Unity Balloting Services.

In addition to the appointment of a scrutineer, a union must appoint a counting officer to store, distribute and count the voting papers once they are returned.[153] The section does provide that the scrutineer may take on these functions. In practice this has often been the case. Otherwise the criteria for appointment is similar to that for the scrutineer; of paramount importance is the independence and impartiality of the appointee.

18.10.2.4 The electorate and method of voting

The union is under a duty, as far as is reasonably practicable, to compile and maintain a register of names and addresses of their members which acts as the union's electoral roll. A failure to maintain this register's accuracy is a breach of the statute.[154] A member has the right to inspect this register and the scrutineer has a duty to inspect where he or she is requested to do so by a member.

To ensure no members are unreasonably excluded from voting, the electorate who are entitled to vote are clearly defined by the legislation. All members are so entitled unless they belong to a specified class excluded by the rules. The classes that may be lawfully excluded are those members who are unemployed, in arrears with their subscriptions, apprentices, trainees, students, new members or those on holiday.[155] Additionally, where a member of the executive represents a particular union constituency, based on a trade group, a geographical area or a section of the union, then it is permissible for the union to limit participation in the election of that representative to the appropriate group of members.[156]

All members must be allowed to vote without interference or any constraint imposed by the union, its officials or employees or other members.[157] Conduct that puts members in fear of voting freely, so preventing them from exercising their right to vote for a candidate of their choice is in breach of this provision. Thus, the mere direct endorsement by the union of one candidate over another is not an interference or constraint prohibited under the Act.[158]

---

150 Section 52.

151 Section 52(1)(2A)(2B) and section 52(2B). The scrutineer's report is important evidence when complaints by members or candidates are received and investigated by the Certification Officer.

152 Section 49(6)(7).

153 Section 51A.

154 Section 24(1). Clearly the register will not be absolutely up to date as changes in membership are inevitable in those unions with a rapid turnover of membership. Thus, where minor errors arise this will not be a breach of the section, see *Paul v NALGO* [1987] IRLR 43.

155 Section 50(2).

156 Section 50(3).

157 Section 51(3).

158 See *Paul v NALGO* [1987] IRLR 43 and *Re USDAW* D/1/94 13 January 1994.

Section 51 permits a union to choose the method of direct election; this may be the 'first past the post' method or the single transferable vote system.[159] Whatever system is chosen, the election must be a fully postal ballot with each vote given equal weighting.[160] The section further requires that votes given are fairly and accurately counted although an inaccuracy that occurs accidentally which doesn't affect the result of the election can be disregarded.

18.10.2.5 Remedies and procedure

Should a candidate be elected improperly, that does not invalidate his or her actions as a member of the executive, or as general secretary or president.[161] Rather, where there has been a failure to comply with these detailed requirements, any candidate and any person who was a member of the union at the time of the election has the option of making a complaint within a year of the default to the Certification Officer[162] or the High Court[163] for a declaration.

Unless the complaint to the Certification Officer is frivolous or vexatious the Certification Officer will investigate the circumstances and must give the trade union and the applicant the opportunity to present their case before making or refusing the declaration requested.

Both the court and the Certification Officer have the power to make an enforcement order (and the court may also grant interlocutory relief).[164] An enforcement order may require the union to hold the election again in accordance with the provisions of the Act, or to take other steps to remedy the failure specified in the declaration or to abstain from such acts in the future. A failure to adhere to an enforcement order is a contempt of court by the trade union – the ultimate sanction is a fine and sequestration of assets.

A complainant has a choice whether to make a single application or consecutive applications to both the Certification Officer and the court, but not concurrent applications. Furthermore, where union omissions result in a *prima facie* breach of a union rule and a statutory requirement, a member has the option to choose which cause of action to pursue.[165]

18.11 Trade unions and political activities[166]

Trade unions were formed in the late eighteenth and early nineteenth century to represent and protect their members' interests at the workplace. As a system of collective bargaining was gradually established many tangible benefits for many trade union members was achieved by union-employer negotiation. Yet collective bargaining could only deliver a partial and uneven level of protection as it depended on the willingness of employers to engage in bargaining in good faith, or on the power of the union to draw the employer to the negotiating table.

Towards the end of the nineteenth century trade unions increasingly turned to the political system as an alternative means of improving the welfare of their members and in order to secure the repeal of the remnants of the anti-trade union legislation from the early period of the nineteenth century. Consequently, in the late nineteenth and early twentieth century the union movement

159 Any form of indirect election (such as elections to an electoral college which appoints or votes for members of the executive), is unlawful – see *Paul v NALGO* [1987] IRLR 43 and *Whiteman v AUEW* D/1/87 3 February 1987.

160 However, a system weighted to prevent the over representation of the membership in any one geographical area is permissible – *R v C.O. ex p EPEA* [1990] IRLR 398.

161 Section 61(2).

162 Section 55.

163 Section 56.

164 Sections 55(5A) and 56(4)(7).

165 *Venness & Chalkey v NUPE* [1991] IRLR 76.

166 For general background, see Ewing, 1982.

sought political influence to win industrial, social and economic advantages for their mass membership and to secure the repeal of anti-union legislation and judicial decisions.[167]

Early union strategy had entailed working within the existing political framework as a pressure group to achieve limited objectives. When the mainstream parties failed to respond to union concerns the union movement turned to fostering direct Parliamentary representation as the means to win benefits for their mass membership and their working-class constituency. Trade union influence was predominant in the formation of the Labour Representation Committee in 1900 which in 1906 changed its name to the Labour Party.

Union support for the Labour Party was temporarily halted by the House of Lords judgment in *Osborne v ASRS*.[168] Osborne challenged the rule which provided for a compulsory levy for the payment of funds to the Labour Party to support their candidates for election. The majority in the House of Lords applied the '*ultra vires*' doctrine in a hitherto novel manner. Rather than apply the doctrine by reference to the objects set out in the rule book, the House of Lords examined the definition of a trade union contained in the Trade Union Acts of 1871 and 1876 and concluded that the powers of a trade union were limited to matters that fell within this definition. As there was nothing in the statutory provisions that indicated that parliamentary representation was a permissible object of a trade union the funding of political activities was *ultra vires*, that is, outside the powers of the trade union.

As a consequence of this decision, not only was political expenditure illegal (serious as that was), but the use of funds for any purposes such as for educational or insurance purposes, whether allowed under the rule book or not, was illegal if these purposes did not fall within the statutory definition. The decision was thus viewed with some concern by trade unions that had for many years engaged in a variety of activities that were authorised under their constitution but were now illegal as '*ultra vires* the statute'.

After the election of 1912, the Liberal government, under pressure from the Labour Party and wishing to retain some influence with the union movement, piloted through a Bill to reverse the Osborne judgment – this became the Trade Union Act 1913. The Act essentially restored the *ultra vires* doctrine to the form which had applied prior to the *Osborne* case. It provided that a union could apply its funds for any object or purpose so long as they were authorised by the rules of the union.

However, in the specific area of political expenditure the trade unions had to accept some limitations on their freedom to spend their funds. Expenditure for political purposes had to be from a specific 'political fund' administered separately from the union general fund, established by a ballot of the membership and financed by a 'political levy' on individual members. The Act also defined and limited the political activities that could be supported by expenditure from the political fund. Furthermore, provisions were incorporated into the Act to ensure that no union member would be forced to contribute to the political fund if it was anathema to their personal convictions or conscience, and to safeguard them from discrimination within the union.

It is this framework, reformed in crucial respects during the 1980s, that still regulates trade union political expenditure today. The regulations concerning the procedure for establishing a political fund and the uses and limitations of such a fund, altered by the Trade Union Act 1984, the Employment Act 1988, the Trade Union Reform and Employment Rights Act 1993 and the Trade Union Act 2016, have now been incorporated into the TULR(C)A 1992 Chapter VI ss. 71–96.

---

167 For a more detailed analysis of union campaigns in this period, see Webb & Webb, 1926, pp. 284–290 and Pelling, 1993, Chapter 4.

168 [1910] AC 87

18.11.1 Adopting political fund rules

A specified procedure for the adoption of political objects was imposed on trade unions by the Trade Union Act 1913. The lawful application of funds 'in the furtherance of political objects' was dependent on the union adopting special rules in compliance with the provisions of the Act and approved by the Chief Registrar.[169] Adoption was only effective if a resolution, incorporating these rules into the rule book, was passed in a 'once and for all' ballot of members. The resolution established the special political fund from which all the political expenditure must come; ensured that any payments to further political objects were made out of the political fund; listed the political objects as defined in the Act; contained provisions permitting any member to contract out of contributing to the political fund and proscribed discrimination against such a non-contributor.

In the Green Paper *Democracy in Trade Unions*,[170] the government expressed the view that there was a need for this procedure to be tightened up. In particular, the requirement that unions only needed to ballot once was criticised as anachronistic. A ballot held up to 70 years ago could not legitimately represent the wishes of the contemporary membership of a trade union.[171] A regular ballot, every ten years, was recommended to take into account the wishes of new members and those members whose views had changed. Consequently, the previous 'once and for all' ballot that authorised expenditure on the political objects has now been superseded by the requirement (originally contained in the Trade Union Act 1984) that a postal ballot is necessary every ten years to affirm this authorisation.[172]

The statutory procedure for adopting political fund rules, although in many areas similar to the original provisions contained in the Trade Union Act 1913, differ in some crucial respects. The arrangements for the ballot (or re-ballot) are overseen by the Certification Officer who has a general duty of supervision of the procedure. The Certification Officer has to approve the organisation of the ballot[173] and the political fund rules that are to be incorporated into the rule book as a consequence of the ballot.[174] Although these rules need to be submitted to the Certification Officer for approval, 'model' political fund rules can be provided by the Certification Officer if required. The model rules follow the detailed statutory requirements outlined in s. 82(1) regarding the conduct of the ballot, the political objects and the government of the political fund. The rules on the government of the political fund provide for the separation of the fund from other union funds, allow for the contracting out from the fund and proscribe discrimination for non-contributors, although permitting the exclusion of non-contributors from the control and management of the fund.

The statutory requirements on ballot supervision are very similar to those in force for leadership elections. The difference being that these obligations are enshrined in the union rules, so technically any complaint relates to a breach of the rule book rather than the statute. The rules must provide for the appointment of an independent scrutineer (and independent counting officer) to oversee the ballot and submit a report on the operation of the ballot.[175] The rules will also establish the right of all members to an entitlement to vote and to be given a reasonable opportunity to vote without interference.[176]

---

169 The modern day equivalent of the Chief Registrar is the Certification Officer.

170 Cmnd 8778, 1983.

171 Paras 84–86.

172 Section 73(3). A simple majority is required to adopt or re-adopt the political objects resolution.

173 Section 74(1).

174 Section 74(3).

175 Sections 75 and 78, s. 77A.

176 Sections 76 and 77.

18.11.2 The political objects

The original provisions contained in the Trade Union Act 1913 limited the political activities that could be financially supported by the political fund to clearly defined 'political objects'. Lawful expenditure was limited to matters such as:

- the payment of expenses incurred either directly or indirectly by a candidate or prospective candidate for election to Parliament or to any public office;
- the holding of a political meeting or the distribution of any literature or documents in support of such a candidate or prospective candidate;
- the maintenance of any person who is a Member of Parliament or who holds a public office;
- payment in connection with the registration of electors or the selection of a candidate for Parliament or any public office; and
- the holding of political meetings or the distribution of political literature or political documents.

Whether loans to political parties can be regarded as political expenditure for the purposes of the Act was considered in *Richards v NUM*.[177] Richards alleged that using money from the union general fund to finance the purchase of the Labour Party headquarters was a breach of the rules. The Certification Officer regarded the contribution, whether a straightforward commercial investment or not, as 'expenditure' within the meaning of the rule. Therefore, since the principal function of the building was to hold gatherings of a political nature, this was expenditure 'on the holding of political meetings' and so infringed the political fund rules.[178]

A further matter raised in *Richards* concerned payments by the NUM for a lobby of Parliament by union members. The Certification Officer held that a lobby of Parliament to further industrial matters that implicitly supported the Labour Party's political position was improperly funded from the general fund as it was also expenditure on a 'political meeting'.

An issue of some concern to trade unions is whether contributions to campaigns or causes that are not 'party political', although of an ideological nature, ought to be funded solely from the political fund. In *Coleman v POEU*[179] Coleman's union branch contributed an affiliation fee of £8 from its general fund to the local Trade Councils 'Campaign against the Cuts', which had as its object a campaign against government public spending cuts and economic policies. The fee contributed to the financing of public meetings and the publication of campaign literature. The Certification Officer rejected the argument that this fee should have been paid out of the political fund. 'Political' for the purposes of the Act, meant 'party political'. This literature was merely expressing a general point of view and since it was not expressly in support of a particular political party, the contributions were not infringing the rules.

Government concern over some of these decisions was demonstrated by critical comment on trade union political activity in the Green Paper *Democracy in Trade Unions*.[180] As a consequence, the Trade Union Act 1984 substantially amended the definition of political objects and broadened the scope of 'political' activities that may only be funded by the political fund.[181] In addition to the activities originally contained in the Trade Union Act 1913, s. 71 of the Trade Union and Labour Relations (Consolidation) Act now includes:

---

177 [1981] IRLR 247.
178 See also *ASTMS v Parkin* [1983] IRLR 448.
179 [1981] IRLR 427.
180 Cmnd 8778, 1983, paras 103–104.
181 Generally on these changes, see Ewing, 1984.

a) the provision of any service or property for use by or on behalf of a political party[182];
b) the production, publication or distribution of any literature, document, film, sound recording or advertisement the main purpose of which is to persuade people to vote for a political party or candidate or to persuade them not to vote for a political party or candidate.[183]

In addition to these changes, other elements of the original political objects have been amended. The definition of 'political office' has been expanded to include Members of the European Parliament and any position within a political party.[184] Expenditure on holding conferences or meetings, the main purpose of which includes the transaction of business connected with a political party is also now explicitly subject to the rules on the political fund.[185]

The High Court was called upon to interpret the scope of the reforms in *Paul v NALGO*.[186] The union did not have a political fund but had initiated a publicity campaign at election time entitled 'Make People Matter' using the general fund. The campaign was aimed at publicising criticisms of public expenditure cuts in the public services. Paul argued this was a political campaign contrary to the new definition as it intended to persuade the electorate not to vote Conservative at the General Election.

Browne-Wilkinson V-C thought the crucial issue was determining the purpose of the union in disseminating the information in their campaign. The main purpose could be surmised by an examination of the content of the literature in the light of all the surrounding circumstances. An important circumstance was the impending election. According to Browne-Wilkinson, the high level of criticism of the Conservative government and the request to readers to consider their voting intentions with the material in mind was evidence that this was a political campaign to persuade people to vote against the Conservative party.

18.11.3 The political fund levy and the non-contributor

The 1913 Act established the principle that a member cannot be compelled to contribute to the political fund. Members of a union automatically contribute to a union's political fund unless they specifically object. If a member gives notice of his or her objections, then the political fund rules in the rule book must provide for exemption from the obligation to contribute.

The procedure for opting out of the political levy is detailed in s. 84 TULR(C)A 1992. Once political objects are adopted the union must issue an 'exemption notice' notifying its members in writing of their right to opt out of the obligation to contribute.[187] The notice must make it clear that paying into the political fund is not a condition of membership and indicate how subscription relief will be provided for those who contract out.[188]

The principle of contracting out was challenged in the 1984 Green Paper *Democracy in Trade Unions*.[189] The Green Paper noted the high level of trade union members who pay the political contribution and expressed doubt that the vast majority had positively taken a decision not to

---

182 This gives statutory support to the Certification Officer's decision in *Richards v NUM* [1981] IRLR 247 and *Parkin v ASTMS* [1983] IRLR 448.
183 This alteration has the effect of overturning the Certification Officer's decision in *Coleman v POEU* [1981] IRLR 427.
184 Thus, union expenditure on internal Labour Party elections (local or national) is now regulated.
185 This includes expenditure incurred by delegates or participants in connection with their attendance.
186 [1987] IRLR 413.
187 Section 84(2).
188 Section 85.
189 Cmnd 8778, 1983.

exercise their right to opt out.[190] It was suggested that inertia and the lack of awareness of this right was the more likely explanation for this failure to contract out.[191] The TUC successfully forestalled legislative intervention by consulting with government representatives and agreeing to issue a 'Statement of Guidelines' to affiliated unions to encourage greater openness on financial matters in general and on the political fund in particular.

However, this issue was revisited by the Conservative administration elected in 2015. Provisions have been introduced via the Trade Union Act 2016 to enforce a process of 'opting in' to the political fund. Section 11 Trade Union Act 2016 amends s. 84 TULR(C)A 1992 by requiring that all new members of a trade union (those who join after the commencement of the provision and after a transition period, decided by regulations) must be given a choice to contribute or not to the fund. Where a trade union sets up a new political fund then all members must be given that choice. A new s. 84A requires unions to send annual information to all new members setting out their right to withdraw from the political fund once they have 'opted in'. Furthermore, section 12 of the 2016 Act inserts a new s. 32ZB into TULR(C)A 1992, which requires trade unions to provide detailed information about their political expenditure in their annual return to the Certification Officer.

18.11.4 Discrimination and the non-contributor

The political fund rules must contain provisions ensuring that a member who is exempt from the obligation to contribute is not excluded from any benefits of the union or is placed indirectly or directly at any disadvantage compared with other members of the union.[192] However, there is a statutory exception – discrimination is permissible in relation to the control or management of the political fund. The right to discriminate is, however, not automatic. It is necessary to have a rule allowing for the exclusion of non-contributors. Within the ambit of the expression 'control and management' are included matters of policy on how to distribute the political fund. Therefore, an exempt member can be excluded from voting on a motion dealing with the reselection of a union sponsored MP.[193]

In *Birch v NUR*,[194] the plaintiff, a non-contributor, was an elected chair of his union branch. As chair Birch had a multiplicity of union functions to perform, one of which was the management of the political fund. He was subsequently declared ineligible to hold this position and removed from office. Birch applied to the High Court for a declaration on the grounds that he was put at a disadvantage by his exclusion from holding union office. Danckwerts J decided that even though the Registrar had approved the union rules, they still offended against the condition of non-discrimination in the Act. Birch was not just denied the opportunity to manage the political fund, but also excluded from involvement in union affairs as a whole.

18.11.5 The non-contributor and the 'check off'

The 'check off' is the deduction of union subscriptions direct from salary by an employer who forwards it on to the union. Often it is administratively convenient for an employer to deduct the

190 Para. 89.

191 Paras 92–94. For an alternative interpretation, see Ewing & Rees, 1983.

192 See the interpretation of this in *Richards v NUM* [1981] IRLR 247 – a non-contributor who was excluded from inspecting the political fund accounting records had not been discriminated against as he could not possibly have any interest in such records. Now cf. s. 30 TULR(C)A 1992 on the statutory right of access to union accounts.

193 *ASTMS v Parkin* [1983] 448.

194 [1950] Ch 602.

total contribution from each member without adjusting the amount to reflect the reduced subscription rate paid by those who are exempt from contributing to the political fund. Where this is the procedure the union reimburses a lump sum to the non-contributors.

The Green Paper, *Democracy in Trade Unions*[195] criticised the reimbursement of a lump sum as an affront to individual rights. Consequently now s. 86 of the TULR(C)A 1992 provides that once an employee certifies in writing to their employer or their union that they are a non-contributor to the political fund, the employer is under a duty to ensure that the check off of union dues reflects this.[196] A potential problem for trade unions is that where it is administratively awkward to apply a system accurately, employers may be tempted to suspend check off arrangements altogether or simply check off the lower rate for every union member leaving the union to collect the political levy separately. It has been argued that this reform was motivated more to limit the political funds available to trade unions rather than because of a concern for the individual rights of non-contributors.

Where the complaint is of a breach of the political fund rules the Certification Officer and High Court have joint jurisdiction. In a hearing before the Certification Officer both parties are given the opportunity to make representations. The Certification Officer has the discretion to make an order requiring the union to remedy the breach. This is enforceable in the County Court.[197] There is a right of appeal to the EAT from the Certification Officer's decision.

Where the complaint is that the rules for holding the ballot have been infringed, the High Court has concurrent jurisdiction with the Certification Officer to grant a declaration and enforcement order.[198] Where there has been a breach of the statute (such as where the trade union has no political fund rules and yet has made a political donation), the Certification Officer has authority to hear the complaint.

❖ THINKING POINT

Taking account of the principle of freedom of association, is the existing statutory regulation of trade union internal affairs overly intrusive?

18.12 Further reading

Barrow, 'Trade Union Rights in the United Kingdom and Article 11 of the European Convention: Past Failures and Future Possibilities' (2013) 1 *European Human Rights Law Review* 56.

Davies & Freedland, *Labour Law: Text and Materials*, London: Butterworths Law,1984.

Elias, 'Closing in on the closed shop' (1980) 9 *Industrial Law Journal* 201.

Elias & Ewing, *Trade Union Democracy: Members' Rights and the Law*, London: Mansell Publishing, 1987.

195 Cmnd 8778, 1983.

196 This right is enforceable in the employment tribunal via a declaration and a compensation order for an amount equal to two weeks' pay (s. 87(4)). Alternatively, once a declaration has been made, s. 88 provides that the inaccurate check off can be treated as an unauthorised deduction under the Employment Rights Act 1996.

197 Section 82(4A)(4B).

198 Section 79(2).

Ewing, *Trade Unions, The Labour Party and the Law*, Edinburgh: Edinburgh University Press, 1983.
Ewing, 'Trade union political funds: The 1913 Act revisited' (1984) 13 *Industrial Law Journal* 227.
Ewing, 'The strike, the courts and the rule book' (1985) 14 *Industrial Law Journal* 160.
Ewing, 'The implications of the ASLEF case' (2007) 36 *Industrial Law Journal* 425.
Ewing, 'Implementing the ASLEF decision' (2009) 38 *Industrial Law Journal* 50.
Ewing & Rees, 'Democracy in trade unions: the political levy' (1983) 133 *New Law Journal* 100.
Fosh & Littler (eds), *Industrial Relations and the Law in the 1980s*, London: Avebury, 1985, Chapter 5.
Freedman, 'The new rights: labour law and ideology in the Thatcher years' (1992) 12 *Oxford Journal of Legal Studies* 24.
Hendy & Ewing, 'Trade unions, human rights and the BNP' (2005) 34 *Industrial Law Journal* 197.
Kahn-Freund, *Labour and the Law*, London: Stevens & Sons Ltd, 1983.
Kahn-Freund, 'Trade unions, law and society' (1984) 33 *Modern Law Review* 241.
Kidner, 'The right to be a candidate for union office' (1973) 2 *Industrial Law Journal* 65.
Kidner, 'Unjustified discipline by a trade union' (1991) 20 *Industrial Law Journal* 284.
Pelling, *A History of British Trade Unionism*, Basingstoke: Palgrave Macmillan,1993.
Rideout, 'Upon training an unruly horse' (1966) 29 *Modern Law Review* 424.
Webb & Webb, The History of Trade Unionism, London: Longmans, Green and Co., 1926.

Chapter 19

Freedom of association and collective bargaining

Chapter contents

19.1 Overview

This chapter analyses the extent of legal support for freedom of association and collective bargaining. In summary:

- The rights to paid and unpaid time off supports freedom of association and collective bargaining by reinforcing union strength and facilitates the trade union bargaining function.
- A reasonable level of paid time off is available to officials of a trade union for collective bargaining purposes or for industrial relations training so long as the activity is closely connected to the bargaining negotiations or the training is relevant to trade union duties.
- Unpaid time off is available to members and officials of trade unions to enable them to participate in trade union activities such as attending union meetings.
- Section 152 Trade Union Labour Relations (Consolidation) Act 1992 provides protection for employees who are dismissed on the grounds of union membership or participation in trade union activities. The union activities must be at an appropriate time (outside of working hours or with the employer's permission). Protection may be available even where the dismissal occurs because of the employee's record of engaging in union activities in a previous employment.
- A worker also has the right not to be subjected to a detriment on grounds of union membership or due to participation in trade union activities. Examples of detriment include; demoting an employee, cutting his or her wages, transferring an employee into an inferior job. The detriment must be focused on the individual and so must not only occur incidentally as a consequence of an employer's attack on a trade union. The purpose of the employer's actions must be to prevent, deter or penalise the worker. Where an employer encourages employees to leave a trade union by providing an incentive to employees to do so, this is specifically actionable under section 145A Trade Union Labour Relations (Consolidation) Act 1992.
- An individual seeking employment also has the right not to be discriminated against in recruitment and there are specific regulations providing a remedy should an individual be 'blacklisted' (where trade unionists are denied employment, dismissed or otherwise discriminated because they are on a list of individuals supplied to an employer).
- Trade unions have certain collective rights – to information for collective bargaining purposes, to consultation on redundancies, on a transfer of an undertaking, on health and safety procedure and to set up a European and domestic works council.
- Information must be disclosed to trade unions if the information is relevant to collective bargaining and it would be 'good industrial relations' to disclose it. There are exceptions to the right, such as where disclosure would cause 'substantial injury to the undertaking'.
- Employers must consult with a recognised trade where at least 20 employees are to be made redundant. An employer must provide certain information in advance of the redundancy and consult on ways of avoiding the dismissals, mitigating the effects and reducing the numbers to be made redundant. Similarly, where an employee is affected by transferred ownership of the undertaking they work for, both employers involved in the transfer must consult with recognised trade unions and inform the union of the proposed arrangements in some detail.
- The European Works Council Directive (introduced into UK law by the Transnational Information and Consultation of Employees Regulations 1999) establishes a consistent system of worker participation in all transnational European enterprises so as to ensure that workers are kept informed of developments across all the European subsidiaries. Works councils should be set up where the undertaking has 1000 employees in the European Union and a minimum of 150 in at least two member states.
- The Information and Consultation Directive (introduced into UK law by the Information and Consultation of Employees Regulations 2004) provides for consultation on employment issues

with recognised trade unions or other elected employee representatives at a national level where the undertaking has at least 50 employees.

- Many of the rights trade unions enjoy depend on a union being recognised for collective bargaining purposes by an employer. Until 1999 recognition was a totally voluntary decision for an employer (although an experimental compulsory recognition procedure operated from 1977–1979). The Employment Relations Act 1999 has introduced a statutory (and complex) recognition procedure where trade unions apply for recognition by an application to the Central Arbitration Committee. Should a majority of workers (and at least 40 per cent of them) vote in a ballot for recognition then a declaration of recognition should be made. The method of collective bargaining is a matter of negotiation between trade union and employer, but a compulsory method can be imposed if the parties fail to agree.

19.2 Introduction

The right of workers to join and participate in trade union affairs and a union's freedom to engage in collective bargaining are the cornerstones of the British industrial relations system. These bedrock principles are inextricably linked as, manifestly, without unhindered free association of workers in trade unions, collective bargaining, by its very nature, cannot function. Even with free association, collective bargaining is undermined where unions are unable to organise effectively – such as where trade union members and officials are discouraged or formally penalised for participating in trade union affairs. Furthermore, a prerequisite for collective negotiation is formal recognition of a trade union and the provision of information by an employer to a union in order to facilitate collective bargaining.

The right to associate in trade unions *per se*, without hindrance from the state, was secured by the repeal of the criminal conspiracy laws in the nineteenth century. This right, however, is of little value where an employer's hostility to trade unions is manifested by discrimination against trade union members at the workplace. Consequently, an important facet of freedom of association in trade unions is the liberty to join trade unions and participate in union activities without retribution from employers. One strategy for securing effective freedom of association is to rely solely on trade union strength. An alternative approach is to develop a system of legal rights to augment trade union efforts. The Labour government from 1974–1979, following the recommendations of the Donovan Commission,[1] set up to examine industrial relations in the United Kingdom, legislated extensively in this area. The Trade Union and Labour Relations Act 1974 provided collective trade union rights to information and union recognition, and the Employment Protection Act 1975 provided associated individual rights to union members and officials to encourage and underpin collective bargaining.

These individual rights (for example, to paid and unpaid time off, protection against dismissal or victimisation for trade union membership or activities, protection against anti-union hiring policies) have an additional collective dimension – according to Lord Wedderburn, the 1975 statute was 'building a collective "right to associate" out of the bricks of certain individual employment rights'.[2] The provision of rights to individual union members and officials builds union strength by reinforcing the internal organisation of trade unions. It is in this way that the protection of individual rights assists unions in their collective bargaining function. The original provisions were,

---

1 Royal Commission on Trade Unions and Employers Associations, Cmnd 3623, 1968.

2 Wedderburn, 1976.

of course, created in an era of strong support for collective bargaining and freedom of association. Government policy from 1979–1997 was opposed to this way of conducting industrial relations. However, although legislative restrictions in this era weakened their effectiveness, the overall structure of the individual rights regime was retained and the more recent Labour administrations (from 1997–2009) have added additional individual rights (such as the right for all individual employees to be accompanied by a union official or other person of the employee's choice at grievance or disciplinary proceedings).

The Conservative administration elected in 2015 have made some changes to trade union 'facility time' (time off for trade union duties and activities) in the public sector. Specifically, in order to 'promote transparency and public scrutiny of facility time' ministers may require public sector bodies to publish details of time allocated to trade union representatives[3] and have reserve powers to modify statutory or contractual rights in this area.[4] Although there has been no use of these powers to date there is now the possibility that the regime described below may be reformed in the near future.

19.3 Individual rights for union members and officials – paid and unpaid time off

These rights were originally contained in the Employment Protection Act 1975 as part of the 'Social Contract' agreement between the Labour government and the Trades Union Congress (TUC). They were consolidated into ss. 27 and 28 of the Employment Protection (Consolidation) Act 1978, amended by the Employment Act 1989 and then reconsolidated as ss. 168–173 of the Trade Union and Labour Relations (Consolidation) Act (TULR(C)A) 1992. Arguably, trade union officials are more likely to carry out their duties effectively if they possess skills and knowledge relevant to their duties. Therefore, the rationale behind the original provision of these rights was that collective bargaining would be more effectively discharged if workplace representatives had the opportunity to acquire the skills of negotiation and the time to perform their negotiating functions. The efficient performance of collective bargaining is logically in the interests of employers, as well as trade unions. The Conservatives unease at the provision of these rights was voiced in the White Paper, *Building Businesses – Not Barriers*.[5] Disquiet was expressed at the wide-ranging nature of the industrial relations duties for which trade union officials have a statutory right to paid time off and the financial implications for employers.

The consequence of these and other criticisms were amendments to the time off provisions contained in the Employment Act 1989 which narrowly circumscribed the application of the rights. The reforms, however, did not totally dismantle this form of assistance for collective bargaining. They have ensured that, where an employer has voluntarily recognised a union, time off for the purposes of negotiation and training is provided so long as it is restricted solely to those collective bargaining matters the union is specifically recognised for. ACAS is under a duty to provide practical guidance on the application of these rights. Consequently, a revised ACAS Code of Practice (No 3) on *Time off for Trade Union Duties and Activities* (2010) sets out advice on the application of the law.

3 Section 13 Trade Union Act 2016, inserting a new s. 172A into TULR(C)A 1992.
4 Section 14 Trade Union Act 2016, inserting a new s. 172B into TULR(C)A 1992.
5 Cmnd 9794, 1986, Chapter 7.

❖ THINKING POINT

Why do you think these individual rights for trade unionists were not repealed in their entirety by subsequent Conservative administrations from 1979–1997?

19.3.1 Paid time off

Section 168(1) provides that

> an employee who is an official,[6] of an independent trade union recognised by the employer is permitted to take time off during working hours for the purpose of carrying out any duties of his, as such an official, concerned with—
>
> (a) negotiations with the employer related to or connected with matters falling within s. 178(2) (collective bargaining) for which the trade union is recognised by the employer, or
>
> (b) the performance on behalf of employees of the employer of functions related to or connected within that provision which the employer has agreed may be so performed by the trade union.

The matters of collective bargaining referred to above are further defined by reference to s. 178(2) and listed as: terms and conditions of employment; health and safety; recruitment, dismissal and redundancy; job allocation and demarcation disputes; discipline; membership or non-membership of a union; facilities for officials of trade unions; and recognition procedures and other machinery for negotiation or consultation on the above matters. Thus, even if the matter is an issue of collective bargaining as defined in the Act by s. 178(2) and by the Code of Practice, it will not be the subject of paid leave if the employer does not recognise the union for bargaining purposes on that specific subject matter.

As noted above the duties undertaken by the official must be '*concerned with* negotiations . . . related to . . . collective bargaining'. Clearly, time off to engage in the actual process of negotiation is covered by this phrase. The question, however, arises whether it is limited to the mere conduct of negotiations or whether a far broader interpretation may be applied which includes planning and preparatory work prior to the negotiations. The Court of Appeal in *Adlington v British Bakeries (Northern) Ltd*[7] interpreted this phrase by holding that attendance at a meeting to discuss strategy for future negotiation must be 'sufficiently proximate' to the actual negotiations. If attendance at a preparatory meeting was too remote in time to actual negotiations or too remote in its purposes from those negotiations, then in practical terms, the attendance will not be *concerned with* the industrial relations issue.[8]

In *London Ambulance Service v Charlton*[9] the Employment Appeals Tribunal (EAT) specifically followed the *Adlington* 'proximity' formulation. The EAT explained that there is no need for actual negotiations to take place between the two sides: a union official is carrying out a duty which 'concerns' these negotiations so long as the genuine purpose of attendance at the meeting was to enable the official

6 Defined in s. 119 TULR(C)A 1992 as elected or appointed union officers and workplace representatives.
7 [1989] IRLR 218.
8 See also *Ashley v Ministry of Defence* [1984] IRLR 57.
9 [1992] IRLR 510.

to actively prepare for the forthcoming negotiations. Paragraph 14 of the Code of Practice provides some guidance on the required degree of proximity. It states that the trade union duties 'must be connected with or related to the negotiations or the performance of functions both in time and subject matter'. The Code of Practice thus suggests that the preparatory meeting must be close in time to the actual negotiations and that the preparations must specifically relate to the subject matter of the negotiations that are to take place.

Section 168(2) of TULR(C)A 1992 also provides that an employer:

> shall also permit such an employee to take time off during his working hours for the purpose of undergoing training in aspects of industrial relations—
> (a) relevant to the carrying out of such duties as are mentioned in sub-s (1); and
> (b) approved by the Trades Union Congress or by the independent trade union of which he is an official.

It is a question of fact and degree whether there is a sufficient link between the training and the specific duties to be discharged for it to be 'relevant' for the purposes of this section. The Code of Practice provides some guidance on this issue. Paragraph 26 suggests that training is relevant if it is appropriate to the actual role and duties of the union official. This is dependent upon the structure of the union, the level of bargaining arrangements and the scope of the recognition agreement. The Code advises that time off should be considered where the official has special responsibilities, or where the official has only recently been elected and has little experience, or if existing collective agreements have to be reconsidered because of legislative changes or because of structural changes in the forum for negotiations.[10]

The Employment Act 2002 has also introduced a right for an employee who is a 'union learning representative' to take reasonable paid time off to undertake relevant learning and training duties.[11] These duties include advising on training issues and arranging appropriate learning and training needs. The ACAS Code provides guidance on the extent of the learning representative's duties and the procedure to apply for time off. Furthermore, from April 2011 a new legal right has been created for employees to request unpaid time off for the purposes of training.[12]

19.3.1.1 Reasonableness

Even though the applicant trade union official may have established that the purposes for which time off is required falls within the section, it does not mean the official is now necessarily entitled to the time off. Section 168(3) makes clear that the amount of time off to be taken, the purposes for which it is taken, the occasions on which it is taken and the conditions to which it is subject depend on a test of reasonableness. Guidelines on the circumstances an employer should appraise in determining what is 'reasonable' are found in the Code of Practice.

Paragraph 42 outlines some general considerations to be taken into account that apply to both paid and unpaid time off. The paragraph notes that 'trade unions should be aware of the wide variety of difficulties and operational requirements to be taken into account by employers when seeking or agreeing arrangements for time off'. These 'difficulties and operational requirements' include the size of the enterprise and of the workforce, the inconvenience to the employer because of the effect on the production process of the absent employee, the need to secure safety and security at the workplace and 'the need to maintain a service to the public'. Thus, in *Thomas Scott*

10 For a judicial analysis of this guidance, see See *Young v Carr Fasteners* [1979] ICR 844; *Ministry of Defence v Crook* [1982] IRLR 488.
11 Section 168A TULR(C)A 1992.
12 Sections 63D–63K Employment Rights Act 1996 (inserted by s. 40 Apprenticeship, Skills, Children and Learning Act 2009).

(Bakers) Ltd v Allen,[13] the Court of Appeal refused to interfere with the tribunal's view that the request by 11 shop stewards for all to take paid time off to attend a negotiation strategy meeting was properly denied as it would have disrupted the employer's business to an unacceptable level. Paragraph 55 recognises that although each application should be considered on its own merits, past time off may be a factor in determining the reasonableness of a request.[14]

19.3.1.2 Payment

Once the relevant employee has received permission from the employer for time off, s. 169 details the requirements on payment. Where the employee's pay is calculated by reference to a fixed salary, he or she is entitled to be paid for the work he would ordinarily have been doing during the period of absence. Where pay varies with the amount of work done (such as piecework), pay is calculated by reference to the average hourly earnings of the employee concerned. Where the union has negotiated a separate agreement on time off, this may be incorporated into their member's employment contract. This contractual provision exists as a supplement to the statutory right, which is a minimum entitlement, a so-called floor that the contractual arrangements can improve on, but cannot reduce or exclude.

Both paragraph 19 of the Code on payment for time off for trade union duties and paragraph 35 on payment for time off for training, state that there is 'no statutory requirement to pay for time off where the duty is carried out at a time when the official would not otherwise be at work'. In *Hairsine v Hull CC*,[15] an employee who was an evening shift worker attended with his employer's permission, an industrial relations training course during normal daytime business hours on one day a week for 12 weeks. He requested payment as if he had worked normally. The EAT held that, on construction of section 168 and with guidance from the Code of Practice, the employer's refusal to pay was justified. Payment only needed to be made where, if he had not been on the course, he would have normally been at work.[16]

When an official requests paid time off to attend a meeting or a training course where only a proportion of the business transacted is covered by the statutory definition, then the official is still entitled to time off but may find that the assessment of pay is reduced. In *RHP Bearings v Brookes*,[17] the EAT concluded that, where an official was requesting time off for mixed purposes, on the failure of the employer and union to agree to share the reimbursement costs, the tribunal should assess how much of the meeting was devoted to a statutory purpose and award an appropriate level of pay.[18]

19.3.2 Unpaid time off for trade union activities

Under s. 170(1), an ordinary member of a recognised independent trade union is entitled to take time off work to engage in 'any activities of the union'. In contrast to the position in relation to paid time off for trade union duties, this right is not limited within the statute by the need for the

---

13 [1983] IRLR 329.

14 See as examples of this approach, *Wignall v British Gas* [1984] ICR 716; *Borders Regional Council v Maule* [1993] IRLR 199.

15 [1992] IRLR 211.

16 It should be noted that the ECJ has held in *Arbeiterwohl Fahrt der Stadt Berlin v Botel* [1992] IRLR 423 that it is a breach of the Equal Pay directive (75/117/EC) for a part-time female worker to be paid less than a male full-timer for time spent on the same trade union duties out of working hours. This was followed by the EAT in *Davies v Neath Borough Council* [1999] IRLR 769. The rights of part-timers to paid time off are re-inforced by the Part Time Workers (Prevention of less Favourable Treatment) Regulations 2000 (SI 2000/1551).

17 [1979] IRLR 452.

18 See also *Beal v Beecham Ltd* [1983] IRLR 192.

activities to be directly connected to matters of collective bargaining or any recognition agreement. However, although activities of the union could thus have a very broad application, the EAT in *Luce v London Borough of Bexley*,[19] has substantially narrowed the application of the phrase.

A number of members of the National Union of Teachers were refused unpaid leave to attend a lobby of Parliament against the Education Reform Bill. Although the proposed legislation was of vital concern to the members of the union, the EAT held, on the evidence, that the lobby of Parliament was intended to convey a political or ideological message and so was not an appropriate trade union activity for the purposes of the statute – the activity should be one which is in some way linked to the employment relationship, that is, between that employer, that employee and the trade union. The Code of Practice does not provide a full explanation of what constitutes 'activities of a trade union'. It merely gives examples of trade union activities in paragraph 37 and does not link the trade union activity with any requirement that it has to be related to the employment relationship.

❖ THINKING POINT

Should the right to unpaid time for trade union activities only apply to matters strictly related to the employment relationship or should the definition of trade union activities be given a broader interpretation?

Section 170(1)(b) also provides members who are representatives of the union the right to unpaid time off to take part in union activities relevant to their position. Thus, shop stewards who act as a channel of communication between the membership and the employer are entitled to time off for workplace negotiations with employers. Paragraph 38 of the Code of Practice also expands the statutory provision by recommending that a member who is also a workplace representative of the union should be provided with unpaid time off to discuss union business at branch, area or regional meetings or to attend the union annual conference or national executive committee.[20]

19.3.2.1 Procedure and remedies

The Code of Practice notes that there are positive advantages in employers and unions coming to formal agreements on the issue of paid and unpaid time off. A formal agreement, which may have to be relatively flexible in smaller organisations, should provide clear guidelines on when time off should be granted, for how long, and whether it should be paid. An individual application can be judged against this agreement thereby ensuring fair and equal treatment and avoiding any misunderstandings that may otherwise arise from an application of the statutory right. The Code stresses that should an agreement be made, this does not of itself supersede the statutory entitlement. The implication is that any agreement cannot provide a worse entitlement than the statutory minimum.

19 [1990] IRLR 422.

20 Section 170(3) repeats the test of reasonableness contained in s. 168(3) on paid time off. As is the case with paid time off, once it is has been determined that the activity qualifies under the section, the amount of time off has to be reasonable in all the circumstances.

There is no specific procedure outlined in the Act for requesting paid or unpaid time off. The Code of Practice does, however, state that were paid time off is requested, as much notice as possible of the application should be provided with full details of the purpose of the time off, the proposed duration and timing and location where it will be used. Similar requirements for paid time off to attend a training course are outlined in paragraph 30. Should informal or formal negotiation at the workplace be unsuccessful, then the Code reiterates the right of an official or union member to complain under ss. 168(4) or 170(4) to an employment tribunal within three months that their rights to time off have been infringed as the 'employer has failed to permit him to take time off as required by this section'. Should the complaint be successful, the tribunal will issue a declaration that it is well founded. Compensation payable will be what the tribunal considers to be 'just and equitable' in the circumstances which may include compensation for injury to feelings and other non-pecuniary loss.[21] Protection against dismissal for bringing proceedings to enforce the statutory right to time off or for alleging the employer has infringed this right is provided by s. 104(4)(c) of the Employment Rights Act 1996.

19.4 Protection against dismissal and detriment

Unlike rights to time off, protection against dismissal on grounds of union membership or union activities were originally found in the Industrial Relations Act 1971. Amended by the Employment Protection Act 1975, these provisions were later incorporated into s. 58(1)(a), (b) of the Employment Protection (Consolidation) Act 1978, now contained in s. 152(1)(a), (b), (ba), (c) of TULR(C)A 1992. A dismissal on the grounds of union membership or activity is automatically unfair without the need for any qualifying term of employment or for the employee to show that the dismissal was unreasonable in any way.

19.4.1 Dismissal for union membership

Section 152(1)(a) of the TULR(C)A 1992 states that:

> the dismissal of an employee shall be regarded as unfair if the reason for it . . . was that that the employee—
> (a) was, or proposed to become, a member of an independent trade union.

This sub-section protects those individuals who are dismissed solely because they possess membership of, or wish to join, a trade union.[22] It thus deals with the more extreme anti-union prejudices of employers. It may be thought that where an employee is actively enjoying the benefits of membership, this is more logically protected by sub-s. (1)(b) which protects a union member against dismissal for union activities. However, in *Discount Tobacco v Armitage*[23] where the employee was dismissed for taking advantage of their union membership, the claim was framed solely by reference to s. 152(1)(a). The claimant had asked for a written statement of terms and conditions of employment. When it was not forthcoming, she asked a union official to write to her employer on her behalf. She subsequently received the statement of terms, but also received her dismissal notice. The EAT concluded that making use of union membership in this way was a necessarily

---

21 See *Corner v Buckinghamshire CC* [1978] IRLR 320; *Skiggs v South West Trains Ltd* [2005] IRLR 459.
22 Section 152(1)(c) also provides protection for dismissal for refusing to join a trade union.
23 [1990] IRLR 15.

incidental act to union membership. Knox J noted that to construe the section in a narrow way would emasculate the protection as

> the scope [of the provision] would be reduced almost to vanishing point, since it would only be just the fact that a person was a member of a union, without regard to the consequences of that membership, that would be the subject matter of that statutory provision.[24]

The construction Knox J put on s. 152(1)(a) was explicitly endorsed in the Court of Appeal by Dillon LJ in *Wilson v Associated Newspapers* and *Palmer v Associated British Ports*[25] a case on the parallel provision in s. 146(1)(a). This view, however, that the concept of membership also includes active use of membership, was doubted by the House of Lords judgment in this case.[26] This issue has now been resolved by an amendment to this provision introduced by the Employment Relations Act 2004. TULR(C)A 1992 s. 152(1)(ba) now states that it is unlawful to dismiss where the union member has made use, or proposed to make use, of trade union services at an appropriate time.[27]

19.4.2 Dismissal for participation in trade union activities

Section 152(1)(b) protects individual union members where they have been dismissed for having:

> taken part, or proposed to take part, in the activities of an independent trade union at an appropriate time.

The statute provides guidance as to when it is an 'appropriate time' to engage in trade union activities. Section 152(2) states that 'appropriate time' means:

(a) a time outside the employee's working hours, or
(b) a time within his working hours at which, in accordance with arrangements agreed with or consent given by his employer, it is permissible for him to take part in the activities of a trade union . . . or make use of trade union services.

'Working hours' is further defined under this section as 'any time when, in accordance with his contract of employment, he is required to be at work'. Only at the times above does a worker have the protection of an automatic unfair dismissal claim should he or she be dismissed for trade union activities. This is because an unfettered right to engage in trade union activities at other times could, arguably, interfere with the smooth running of an employer's business.

In *Zucker v Astrid Jewels Ltd*,[28] two specific issues fell for adjudication: the interpretation of the term 'working hours' and the nature of implied consent. The applicant was a vigorous proponent of trade union membership and discussed trade union matters with her colleagues during her tea and lunch breaks and whilst engaging in her duties at work as a machinist. The EAT held that the discussion of union affairs on her employer's premises at a designated break time was not during 'working hours' and so was undertaken at a protected time. Secondly, although conversation at the machines was during the course of work, the employer had always permitted general conversation

---

24 Ibid p. 16.
25 [1993] IRLR 336.
26 [1995] ICR 406.
27 This same amendment was made to the analogous provisions under s. 146 TULR(C)A 1992.
28 [1978] IRLR 385.

and had not attempted to control their content. Consequently, the applicant's union recruitment activities while at work was 'in accordance with arrangements (impliedly) agreed with or consented to by the employer'.

However, the Court of Appeal, in *Marley Tile Co v Shaw*,[29] responded with caution to the possibility of inferring consent by silence. The Court of Appeal found that although the applicant, in calling a meeting of members at the workplace, was engaged in trade union activities, the employer's failure to ban the meeting or to comment at all to the employee on his course of action could not be regarded as tantamount to implied consent or permission for the employee's action. This does not, however, imply that silence from an employer can never constitute consent. Arguably, if an employee is an accredited shop steward and had called meetings before without dissent from an employer, the employer's previous behaviour is evidence of an established customary arrangement amounting to permission for meetings of that type to be held at that time.[30]

An issue of some importance is whether the section provides protection where the applicant is dismissed due to trade union activities undertaken before he or she joined the present employer. In *Birmingham DC v Beyer*,[31] the plaintiff gave a false name and bogus reference to obscure his past record as a previously active trade unionist which he knew would count against him in obtaining employment. When this became known to the employer, he was dismissed. The EAT was unequivocal in declaring that engaging in deceit cannot be a trade union activity, whatever the circumstances and that, as the legislation is limited to protecting trade union activity at an 'appropriate time', activities outside and before employment began are excluded.

The same issue was considered by the Court of Appeal some years later in *Fitzpatrick v BRB*.[32] The Court of Appeal first confirmed the decision in *Beyer* that where a dismissal was genuinely for the deceit in failing to inform the employer about past trade union activities, then an applicant would lose the protection of this provision as this would not be a dismissal for 'trade union activities'. However, the Court of Appeal then went on to note that the section makes it unlawful to dismiss an employee not just for taking part in union activities, but also for 'proposing to take part' in union activities. Therefore, an employee may gain the protection of the section where the reason for a dismissal is clearly initiated by a belief that the employee is proposing to repeat such activities in his or her current employment.

19.4.2.1 Appropriate activities

Although there is no statutory definition of 'activities of an independent trade union', the matters listed in the ACAS Code on *Time Off for Trade Union Duties and Activities* have been construed, for the purposes of this section, as relevant 'activities'. These comprise; attendance at branch meetings, voting in elections and attendance at emergency meetings on industrial action. So long as they are activities undertaken with permission or outside work times, such as at lunchtime, then participation is protected. Local officials (such as shop stewards) will also be protected where they engage in union activities commensurate to their post, such as taking up individual grievances with management or calling a meeting with members.[33] These examples are not exhaustive and certainly other matters can fall within the scope of appropriate activities.[34]

---

29 [1980] ICR 72.

30 See also *Robb v Leon Motor Services Ltd* [1978] IRLR 26.

31 [1977] IRLR 211.

32 [1991] IRLR 376.

33 See *British Airways Ltd v Francis* [1981] IRLR 1.

34 Note the contrasting decisions of *Dixon v West Ella Developments Ltd* [1978] ICR 856 and *Chant v Acqua Boats* [1978] ICR 643 on the construction of the phrase 'activities of an independent trade union'.

19.4.2.2 Trade union organising activity and industrial action

Where a union is not recognised at a workplace, the recruitment of members may conflict with the anti-union policies of the employer. Can this organising process be protected by an application of the individual right not to be dismissed for union membership or activities? In *Carrington v Therm-a-Star Ltd*,[35] the Court of Appeal subscribed to a cautious approach of the construction of the section. After a recruitment drive by the Transport and General Workers Union, over 90 per cent of the workforce of a new factory had joined or had applied to join the union. The union district official then approached the employer for the purposes of obtaining recognition. In a response to this enquiry, the employer immediately made 20 employees redundant, most of whom were union members or those who had intended to join. It was found on the facts that the reason for the dismissals was not redundancy, but rather a response to the union's attempt to obtain recognition – as a retaliation against the union. Donaldson MR in the Court of Appeal accepted that the union and the employees had a justifiable grievance, and that the section was clearly aimed at a mischief very similar to that which befell the employees. But, on a true construction of the statute, the section operated only to protect individuals where they have been dismissed for their personal trade union activity. The employer's reaction was a blanket response to a general trade union activity.[36]

Where a trade union is already recognised, there is no doubt that, subject to consent, recruitment activity *per se* is protected. It seems trade union officers may go about this function in a robust manner. In *Bass Taverns Ltd v Burgess*[37] the Court of Appeal noted that, in order to sell the services of the union, some implicit or explicit criticism of an employer is made. So long as any criticism is not expressed in bad faith, union officers are still engaging in appropriate trade union activities as there is no obligation on them to perform union functions in a manner approved by an employer.[38]

It has not always been clear whether industrial action is an 'appropriate' trade union activity for the purposes of this section. The EAT, in *Drew v St Edmundsbury BC*,[39] denied protection to trade unionists who engaged in industrial action as industrial action was an inappropriate trade union activity. However, even if industrial action is regarded as appropriate union activity, any claim for dismissal under s. 152 would be unlikely to succeed. First, industrial action would have to take place at an 'appropriate time', which as we have seen is outside working hours or with the employer's agreement. The very nature of industrial action is that it rarely takes place after work.[40] In any event, s. 238A of the TULR(C)A 1992 (introduced by the Employment Relations Act 1999) now provides a new category of automatically unfair dismissal where an employee takes 'protected' industrial action.

19.4.2.3 Remedies

There are special compensation provisions for an unfair dismissal on union grounds. A basic award is calculated according to the rules pertaining to ordinary unfair dismissal cases. However, where dismissal was for trade union membership or activities, a minimum figure of £5,970 must be awarded (at the time of writing). The compensatory award is also calculated according to ordinary unfair dismissal rules. This will usually include a sum for future loss. Where an individual has been

35 [1984] ICR 208.

36 Note there is a degree of protection for those officals engaged in union activities prior to a recognition ballot under the statutory recognition procedure, see pp. 420–429.

37 [1995] IRLR 596.

38 See also *Mihaj v Sodexho* [2015] UKEAT/0139.

39 [1980] ICR 513.

40 See *Britool v Roberts* [1993] IRLR 481, where participating in the planning and organisation of industrial action outside of working hours could be a protected activity as it takes place at an 'appropriate time'.

dismissed for union reasons, it may well be that his opportunity to work in that industry is seriously limited and the figure under this head of loss could be substantial.

Like claims for unfair dismissal on other grounds, an order for reinstatement or re-engagement is possible, but unlikely. An employer can resist a re-employment order if it can be shown that it is 'not practicable' to re-employ the dismissed worker. One factor the tribunal considers is the effect of the re-employment order on the employer's business arrangements.[41] However, further compensation provisions exist if an order is made and the employer fails to comply. Section 33(2) of the Employment Relations Act 1999 amends the relevant compensation provisions in the Employment Rights Act 1996 by providing for an 'additional' award – an employee is entitled to up to 52 week's pay on a refusal to re-employ. Furthermore, under s. 161 Employment Rights Act 1996, an interim remedy is available for an applicant who alleges dismissal on the grounds of union membership or union activities. This is in the form of an order for temporary reinstatement or re-engagement. Interim relief thus has the effect of ensuring that the applicant is paid until the hearing of the case.

19.4.3 Protection against detriment short of dismissal

The right to claim unfair dismissal for trade union membership and for engaging in trade union activities is supplemented by additional protection where an employer disciplines or victimises an employee for these reasons. The provisions formerly contained in the Employment Protection Act 1975 and then s. 23(1)(a), (b) of the Employment Protection (Consolidation)Act 1978 were reproduced (after amendments introduced by the Employment Relations Act 1999 and 2004) in s. 146(1)(a), (b), (ba), (c) of the TULR(C)A 1992 as:

> (1) A worker has the right not to be subjected to any detriment as an individual by his employer, whether by an act or a deliberate failure to act, for the sole or main purpose of—
>
> (a) preventing or deterring him from being or seeking to become a member of an independent trade union, or penalising him for doing so;
>
> (b) preventing or deterring him from taking part in the activities of an independent trade union at an appropriate time, or penalising him for doing so;
>
> (ba) preventing or deterring him from making use of trade union services at an appropriate time, or penalising him for doing so;
>
> (c) compelling him to become a member of a trade union.

The terms 'appropriate activities' and 'appropriate time' were considered earlier when examining protection under s. 152. Consequently, the cases on the interpretation of these terms previously considered also apply for the purposes of this section.

19.4.3.1 Actions and omissions

Positive acts, such as demoting an employee, cutting his or her wages, transferring or actively harassing an employee clearly constitutes detrimental action taken by an employer for the purpose of the section. In appropriate circumstances, threatening to take action which would constitute a detriment has also satisfied the statutory requirement.[42] Guidance as to whether an omission to act, by for example, withholding a benefit, is regarded as detrimental 'action' for the purposes of the

---

41 See *London Port Authority v Payne* [1994] IRLR 9.

42 See *Brassington v Cauldron Wholesalers Ltd* [1978] ICR 405.

section was provided by s. 298 of the TULR(C)A 1992 which stated 'In this Act, unless the context otherwise requires – "act" and "action" . . . includes omission, and references to doing an act or taking action shall be construed accordingly'. Consequently, the courts have consistently interpreted an employer's failure to provide a benefit to an employee as 'taking action' against that employee.[43]

However, the House of Lords in *Wilson v Associated Newspapers; Palmer v Associated British Ports*,[44] by a majority, held that the failure of the employers to pay wage increases to those employees who declined to agree to the termination of union representation on wages and conditions was not 'action' within the meaning of s. 146. As it was an omission it was not capable of amounting to a contravention of the section. The Labour government elected in 1997 identified this outcome as a 'loophole' in the protection offered to trade unionists and, subsequently, amended s. 146(1) by sch. 2 to the Employment Relations Act 1999 – protection now exists where the detriment is 'by an act or a deliberate failure to act'.

The action taken by the employer must be directed against the employee as an individual. Action taken against the union that has indirectly negative consequences for employees, is not 'action short of dismissal' for the purposes of the section. This issue arose in *National Coal Board v Ridgway*.[45] After the defeat of the National Union of Mineworkers (NUM) in the miners' strike, the Union of Democratic Mineworkers (UDM) was formed, consisting of many miners who had opposed the strike. The National Coal Board recognised the UDM for bargaining purposes and negotiated a pay rise with this union. At pits where neither the NUM nor the UDM were in a majority, the NCB decided to grant the pay rise to members of the UDM only. Ridgway and other members of the NUM who were denied the pay rise complained that the failure to increase their pay was action taken against them as individuals which penalised them for membership of the NUM.

The majority of the Court of Appeal in *Ridgway*, with May LJ dissenting, held that the action of withholding a pay award was action against an individual. As individuals, they were penalised by the loss of money, which was a direct loss to them as individuals. This was not merely an attack on the union with indirect consequences for their members.[46]

19.4.3.2 The 'purpose' of the action

The existence of a mere detriment or disadvantage that prevents, deters or penalises an individual is not enough to satisfy the section. It is also necessary to show the employer's purpose in doing this was to stop the employee from joining or staying in a union or from engaging in union activities. An issue of significance is whether members of a union have the protection of the section where the employer is motivated by hostility to trade unions at the workplace but the employer argues that the action is taken to alter the contractual relationship with the employees and the negative impact on those who are union members is an unavoidable by-product. Whether action of this kind is contrary to this section was considered fully in *Associated Newspapers v Wilson; Associated British Ports v Palmer*[47] (*Wilson* and *Palmer*) in the House of Lords.

In the first case, the employers had derecognised the union, terminated collective bargaining arrangements and awarded pay rises only to those who agreed to new contracts of employment. In the second, the employers offered a pay rise to staff who entered into a 'personal' contract of employment, with the proviso that they gave up their right to union representation for collective

---

43 See *Carlson v The Post Office* [1981] ICR 343 – refusing a union member a car parking permit; *Department of Transport v Gallacher* [1993] ICR 654 – failing to promote a union member.

44 [1995] ICR 406.

45 [1987] IRLR 80.

46 See also *FW Farnworth v McCoid* [1999] IRLR 626.

47 [1995] ICR 406.

bargaining purposes. Those employees who refused the offer still had their terms and conditions agreed through the collective bargaining system, but were denied the pay rise. In both cases, the common issue to determine was the employer's purpose. Was it to penalise the applicants for their union membership, to deter them from continuing as union members, or merely to further a change in the employment relationship between the employer and their individual employees, from collective bargaining to individual bargaining?

The House of Lords held that that the ultimate purpose of the discrimination was to further a legitimate industrial relations objective, to amend bargaining structures at the place of work – the action did not have as its purpose an intention to penalise or deter *per se*. The real intention behind the employers' actions was to enhance business efficiency by reforming the system of contractual negotiations with employees – thus it was not an actionable detriment for an employer to offer differential payments to employees if the object is to encourage them to relinquish their union membership and their right to trade union representation in order to achieve a change in bargaining relationships.

The decisions in *Wilson* and *Palmer* (and subsequent Conservative statutory amendments to the law enshrining the decision in statute) were heavily criticised by trade unionists at the time as they clearly provided employers with the opportunity to lawfully discriminate against union members as individuals and so further limit trade union influence at the workplace. Subsequently, the Labour Government's White Paper, *Fairness at Work*,[48] identified this form of discrimination as 'contrary to its commitment to ensuring individuals are free to choose whether to join a trade union'.[49] The White Paper, however, did not explicitly propose to repeal the Conservative amendment or to deal with the *Wilson* and *Palmer* judgments. Rather than introducing substantive amendments, the government instead reserved the right to deal with these issues in the future by the passage of secondary legislation. To complicate matters still further, the government accepted (during the passage of the legislation in the House of Lords) a Conservative amendment that provided that an employee must not be formally victimised for being a union member *per se*, but that it is still legitimate to offer individualised contracts that have the practical impact of undermining collective bargaining.[50]

As the Employment Relations Act 1999 failed to resolve this issue to the satisfaction of trade unionists, the unions lodged a claim with the European Court of Human Rights in Strasbourg that UK law that permitted this level of victimisation or discrimination against an individual who wishes their union to represent their interests is in violation of Article 11 of the European Convention of Human Rights. Article 11 provides, *inter alia*, that everyone has the right to form and join trade unions 'for the protection of their interests' and that any restrictions on this right must be 'necessary in a democratic society . . . for the protection of the rights and freedoms of others'. Building on commentary in the earlier decisions in *National Union of Belgium Police v Belgium*[51] and *Swedish Engine Drivers Union v Sweden*,[52] the European Court of Human Rights held that an individual is entitled not just to join a trade union but also that it was an inherent right within Article 11 for members of a trade union to be represented at the workplace by their trade union, as otherwise the right was virtually worthless. United Kingdom law (common law as identified in the House of Lords judgment in *Wilson* and *Palmer* and the statutory provisions) that permitted employers to discriminate against employees who were not prepared to renounce this right was thus in violation of Article 11.[53]

---

48 Cmnd 3968, 1998.

49 Para. 4.25.

50 For further analysis of the House of Lords decision and the implications of the case, see Simpson, 1995 and Ewing, 2000.

51 [1975] 1 EHRR 578

52 [1976] 1 EHRR 617

53 *Wilson and the NUJ, Palmer and RMT v United Kingdom* [2002] IRLR 568. For further analysis of the ECHR decision, see Ewing, 2003.

Furthermore, the Strasbourg court noted that the Article 11 right had a collective element – the employer's actions were frustrating a trade union's ability to protect its members' interests, itself guaranteed by Article 11.

As a consequence of this decision the law was amended by the Employment Relations Act 2004 which introduced ss. 145A–145F into the TULR(C)A 1992 that now outlaws inducements designed to deter union membership and activities. Section 145A provides that a worker has the right not to be offered financial inducements intended to deter membership or non-membership, or engage in union activities or to make use of union services. Section 145B further extends this to inducements made to encourage employees to opt out of collective bargaining. A specific remedy, limited to this provision, is provided in s. 145E. Where the tribunal finds the complaint well founded a fixed payment of £3,907 is awarded (as at the time of writing).

19.4.3.3 Remedies

The procedure for determining a complaint is contained in s. 147. The complaint must be made to an employment tribunal within three months of the action occurring, unless it was not reasonably practicable for the complaint to be presented within the three-month period. Should the tribunal find the complaint justified, a declaration must be made to that effect. A compensation order may then be made. Compensation is assessed according to what the tribunal thinks is 'just and equitable in all the circumstances having regard to the infringement of the complainant's rights . . . by the employer's act complained of and to any loss sustained by the complainant which is attributable to that action'.[54]

The basis of the discretionary monetary award is purely one of compensation for the employee. Any actual financial loss is clearly recoverable, such as loss of pay through attendance at the tribunal. Compensation for non-pecuniary loss would be appropriate in certain circumstances, such as where the application has caused stress and anxiety or where the employee has been deprived of union benefits.[55]

19.4.4 The right not to be discriminated against in recruitment

This right was introduced by the Employment Act 1990, now enacted in ss. 137–143 of the TULR(C)A 1992. These provisions provide some protection against anti-union hiring policies and should be considered in conjunction with both the Court of Appeal's judgment in *Fitzpatrick v BRB*[56] which, in some circumstances, protects those who are dismissed for union activities prior to their employment and with the new 'blacklisting' provisions considered below.

Any individual 'seeking employment' has the right not to be refused employment because he or she is a member of a trade union or specified trade union. Refusal in s. 137(5) is defined in some detail, beyond merely refusing an application or enquiry. It also includes causing the withdrawal of an application, refusing to make an offer after an interview or making an offer, but on unreasonable terms or conditions or withdrawing an offer after it has been made. Under s. 138, it is unlawful for an employment agency to refuse its services to any person on grounds of union membership.

Complaints of discrimination in recruitment are heard by an employment tribunal. One problem for those denied employment in these circumstances is that the burden of proof is on the applicant. Where it is impossible to obtain direct evidence of the unlawful reason, the tribunal may

---

54 Section 149(2).

55 See *Cleveland Ambulance NHS Trust v Blane* [1997] IRLR 332.

56 [1991] IRLR 376.

accept inferences of anti-union bias from all the surrounding circumstances. If a complaint is upheld, a declaration to that effect will be made. The tribunal also has the authority to make a declaration that the employer takes action to eliminate or reduce the effects of the unlawful conduct on the individual. A compensation order may be made up to the limit of the compensatory award for unfair dismissal which can include an award for injury to feelings. A question of some importance is whether the union member who is denied access to employment because of his or her known reputation as a union activist will be able to rely on this right. Such an individual would not be able to mount a challenge under this legislation as protection is arguably limited to refusal on grounds of union membership per se.[57] This issue is now resolved through the provision of new blacklisting regulations introduced in 2010.

19.4.5 The right not to be 'blacklisted'

The blacklisting of trade union members and activists (where trade unionists are denied employment or discriminated at the workplace) has caused trade unions some concern over a number of years. Blacklisting in certain industries – such as construction and finance – was arguably rife throughout the post-war period and was the subject of a complaint by the Trades Union Congress (TUC) to the International Labour Organisation (ILO) in 1991, and was subsequently condemned by the supervisory institutions of the ILO as acts of anti-union discrimination in violation of Article 1 of ILO Convention No. 98 on the right to organise in trade unions.[58]

The Labour government, in the White Paper *Fairness at Work*, gave a commitment to prohibit the formation and use of such lists.[59] The provisions, however, contained in s. 3 of the 1999 Act, did not actually proscribe blacklisting. They provided the Secretary of State with authority to introduce regulations to prohibit the use, sale or supply of such lists. Although draft regulations were issued in 2003, a decision was made by the Department of Trade and Industry not to introduce them for parliamentary approval at that time so as to limit the risk of the over regulation of businesses.[60] Ministers revisited this issue as a consequence of the substantial evidence of widespread blacklisting in the construction industry uncovered after an investigation by the Information Commissioner under the Data Protection Act 1998. The Government responded to the Information Commissioner's investigation by announcing an intention to legislate on the issue of blacklisting after due consultation. The Regulations, to prohibit the blacklisting of trade unionists, were published and laid before Parliament in February 2010 for approval in accordance with section 42 of the Employment Relations Act 1999, subsequently approved by a resolution of each House of Parliament, and came into force on 2 March 2010.[61]

Regulation 3(1) contains the general prohibition that 'no person shall compile, use, sell or supply a prohibited list'. A 'prohibited list' (i.e. a trade union blacklist) is defined in Regulation 3(2) and contains two elements. First, it is a list which 'contains details of persons who are or have been members of trade unions or persons who are taking part or have taken part in the activities of trade unions'.[62] The second requirement is that the list must have been 'compiled' for a discriminatory purpose 'with a view to being used by employers or employment agencies for the purposes of discrimination in relation to recruitment or in relation to the treatment of workers'.[63]

---

57 For a contrary view of the legislation, see *Harrison v Kent County Council* [1995] ICR 434.

58 297th Report Case No 1618, para. 22.

59 Para. 4.52.

60 DTI Regulatory Impact Assessment, para. 2.

61 Employment Relations Act 1999 (Blacklists) Regulations 2010 (SI 2010/493). For a detailed analysis, see Barrow, 2010.

62 Regulation 3(2)(a).

63 Regulation 3(2)(b).

A discriminatory purpose is defined in the same way as in other areas of discrimination – the employer treats the claimant less favourably than another individual when recruiting or in employment generally due to their membership of a union or union activity.

Regulation 4 creates five exceptions to this general prohibition in Regulation 3 relating to the compilation, sale, supply or use of 'prohibited lists'. Regulation 4(2) provides that where an individual or organisation unknowingly supplies a prohibited list or could not be reasonably be expected to know they are supplying a prohibited list there is no contravention of Regulation 3.[64] Another exception relates to investigative journalism. Where a person compiles, uses or supplies a prohibited list and the main purpose for doing so is to demonstrate a contravention of the Regulations, no violation occurs so long it is justified in the public interest and the consent of the individuals on the list has been obtained. The third exception relates to situations where information about an individual's involvement in trade union issues is an important factor in a job selection process, such as for certain academic jobs or personnel roles.[65] The final exception introduced by Regulation 4 provides that individuals or organisations are not in breach of the Regulations if the compilation, sale, supply or use, of the prohibited lists, are in order to comply with a statutory or other legal requirement, connected with legal proceedings or to obtain or provide legal advice about compliance with the Regulations. This latter exception enables lawyers to access evidence about blacklists when advising clients about their compliance with the Regulations, but it does not permit the operation of a blacklist on behalf of a client.

Where there is a contravention of the regulations, a claimant who has suffered loss may take action in the county court or the employment tribunal. Regulation 13 provides that an action lies by a person affected (who has suffered loss or potential loss) to the county court for breach of statutory duty. This widens the scope of those who are entitled to take action and gain legal redress beyond those who work under a contract of employment. Unions themselves can take action in the county court if they have suffered loss or may suffer a loss, as a consequence of a breach of the general prohibition in the Regulations. Where the court upholds the complaint, it may award unlimited damages which may include compensation for injury to feelings.[66] The court may also make an order to restrain or prevent the defendant from breaching the general prohibition.[67] For example, an order may require the defendant to cease using a prohibited list.

The Regulations also provide for complaints to be made to an employment tribunal where an employer refuses employment to the claimant or where an employment agency refuses its services for a reason related to a prohibited list, and make it unlawful for an employer to dismiss an employee or to subject a worker to any other detriment for a reason related to a prohibited list. Regulation 12 amends the Employment Rights Act 1996 by inserting a new section 104F into the 1996 Act, introducing a new category of automatic unfair dismissal where an employee is dismissed for a reason relating to a 'prohibited list'. A number of consequential amendments to the Employment Rights Act 1996 and other primary legislation have been made to reflect that. Regulation 9 makes it unlawful for an employer to impose any detriment on a worker as a consequence of using a prohibited list. A detriment may include, for example, a failure to promote or shortlist for a post, reducing pay, but not specifically the fact of a claimant appearing on a blacklist as there is a need for the claimant to suffer some practical consequences of their listing.

The remedies available under an application to an employment tribunal for a breach of the Regulations follow the model provided under existing trade union law where individuals are

64 This exception allows the Royal Mail or other postal services to deliver a prohibited list without fear of committing an offence.

65 Regulation 4(4)(a).

66 Regulation 13(3)(b).

67 Regulation 13(3)(a).

discriminated against on the grounds of their trade union membership and activities, with some minor amendments. Where the tribunal finds a complaint under Regulation 5 or 6 is well founded a declaration to that effect is made and compensation may be awarded to the claimant.[68] The tribunal also has the power to make a recommendation that the employer or employment agency take action to eliminate or reduce the adverse impact of their unlawful act in refusing employment or employment agency services, but does not have the jurisdiction to grant an order to stop blacklisting by, for example, impounding the wrongful material.[69] An unreasonable failure to comply with a recommendation may result in an increase in compensation. When determining the level of compensation, the calculation is on the same basis as damages for breach of statutory duty – by reference to the amount of loss suffered as a result of the contravention of the general prohibition. It may include damages for injury to feelings and a minimum award applies (without regard to reductions, such as, for a failure to mitigate loss).[70] The maximum level of damages available is set at the same maximum amount that is available for unfair dismissal claims.[71]

19.4.6 The individual right to be accompanied in grievance or disciplinary hearings

The Employment Relations Act 1999, ss. 10–15, created a right for workers[72] to be accompanied in disciplinary or grievance hearings by a trade union official or a fellow worker. These provisions will allow a trade union official to enter an employer's premises to represent a union member, if the member so requests, even where a trade union (or that particular union) is not recognised.

19.4.6.1 Definition of disciplinary and grievance proceedings

Section 13(4) of the 1999 Act defines a disciplinary hearing as any hearing that could result in:

(a) the administration of a formal warning to a worker by his employer;
(b) the taking of some other action in respect of a worker by his employer (such as demotion, suspension or dismissal);
(c) the confirmation of a warning issued or some other action taken (as in an appeal by the worker concerned).

The right to be accompanied only applies to hearings that may result in formal disciplinary action taken against the worker or where a worker is challenging disciplinary action at an appeal. This view of the scope of disciplinary hearings is confirmed in paragraph 53 by the ACAS *Code of Practice on Disciplinary and Grievance Procedures* (2000) which contains detailed guidance on the operation of the law and is taken into account by tribunals when deliberating on a violation of the right.

The right to be accompanied at a grievance hearing applies only where the grievance issue 'concerns the performance of a duty by an employer in relation to a worker'.[73] This has been further

68 Regulation 8(1)(a).
69 Regulation 8(1)(b).
70 Regulation 8(2)(3).
71 A challenge to blacklisting – that the practice was contrary to Articles 8 and 11 of the European Convention – was made in *Smith v United Kingdom* [2017] IRLR 771 on the basis that agency workers were in practice excluded from protection from blacklisting as they were not employees of the end user of the blacklist. The application was declared inadmissible as the applicant was unable to establish he had suffered 'significant disadvantage' as required under Article 35(3)(b).
72 Defined in s. 230(3) TULR(C)A 1992.
73 Section 13(5).

defined in the Code of Practice to mean a legal duty arising from statute (such as an allegation concerning equal pay or health and safety) or common law (such as an allegation that the employer has broken a term of the employment contract). The intention is to ensure that the right is not available where an employee has a grievance that is trivial or irrelevant (to the employment relationship). The Code of Practice also specifically notes that a grievance regarding the future improvement of pay or other terms of the contract of employment is excluded, as it is not a complaint about existing terms. Hence, it is not possible for individuals to declare a grievance on issues that are properly a matter for collective trade union representation.

19.4.6.2 The scope of the right

The statutory right applies where a worker:

(a) is required or invited by his employer to attend a disciplinary or grievance hearing; and
(b) reasonably requests to be accompanied at the hearing.[74]

The section makes clear that the worker must ask to be accompanied. Additionally, the right only applies where the worker 'reasonably requests' to be accompanied. Once the worker makes the request, s. 10(2) states that the employer must allow the worker to be accompanied at the subsequent hearing by a single companion chosen by the worker, who is either another of the employer's workers or a designated trade union official. The companion is to be permitted to address the hearing (but not to answer questions on behalf of the worker) and to confer with the applicant during the hearing. The Code of Practice recommends that where a particular trade union is recognised in a workplace it is appropriate for an official from that union to be selected to accompany the worker at the hearing.[75]

The right to accompaniment does not place a statutory duty on the union automatically to provide a companion, although union members may have a contractual right to representation derived from their union rule book. The companion who accompanies the worker is entitled to reasonable time off with full pay during working hours to prepare for, and attend, the grievance or disciplinary hearing, enforceable by a complaint to an employment tribunal.[76] The Act also states that the accompaniment task is to be treated as a trade union duty or activity for the purposes of the protection contained in ss. 168–169 and ss. 171–173 of the TULR(C)A 1992.[77]

19.4.6.3 Remedies

Section 11 of the Act provides a remedy against an employer who has 'failed or threatened to fail' to allow the right of accompaniment under s. 10(2) or who has postponed proceedings under s. 10(4). A tribunal claim could thus be taken where the employer has threatened to deny a worker the right and the disciplinary matter or grievance is later withdrawn without a hearing. If an employment tribunal finds a complaint well founded, it can make an award of compensation to the worker not exceeding two weeks' pay.[78] This will be subject to the maximum week's pay limits within s. 227(1) Employment Rights Act 1996.

Section 12 of the Act also provides protection where a worker has suffered a detriment for exercising the right to be accompanied or to postpone the hearing or where the worker is the chosen companion and has been victimised for seeking to accompany the individual exercising

74 Section 10(1).
75 Para. 58.
76 Para. 59.
77 Section 10(7).
78 Section 11(3).

the right. Dismissal for exercising these rights is automatically unfair.[79] Claimants who have been subject to dismissal may also claim interim relief. If interim relief is granted, employment is continued (on full pay and benefits) pending the outcome of the full tribunal hearing.

19.5 Collective rights for trade unions: information

19.5.1 The right to information

The right to information was originally contained in ss. 17–21 of the Employment Protection Act 1975,[80] now found in ss. 181–185 of the TULR(C)A 1992. The object of the legislation at the outset was to encourage the flow of relevant information to trade unions so as to enhance and promote the conduct of ordered collective bargaining. This measure was retained during the Conservative period of office from 1979–1997 because it was thought that disclosure served an important economic function in limiting union claims as where a trade union has knowledge of a business's financial position, it would scale down any unrealistic demands and strike realistic bargaining positions.

Information for collective bargaining purposes is only available to recognised unions. This is a major weakness of the right as employers have the option of lawfully restricting the release of information by refusing to recognise trade unions or by withdrawing recognition.[81] In the vast majority of cases where a trade union is recognised and included in negotiations an employer will release information as a matter of course. It is precisely those employers who refuse to recognise and negotiate who deny trade unions information.

Recognition for collective bargaining purposes means recognition for the purposes of negotiations on the matters listed in s. 178(2).[82] Consequently, the extent of the recognition controls the extent of disclosure. This is demonstrated by the decision in *R v CAC, ex p Tioxide*.[83] Here the employer introduced a job evaluation scheme for the reassessment of salary scales. The union was given the opportunity to make representations on behalf of individuals during the process of job evaluation, but not to negotiate on the terms of the scheme. Forbes J held that the employer could lawfully withhold this information on the scheme. Although salary determination via a job evaluation scheme was a matter related to terms and conditions of employment for which the union was ordinarily recognised, the union was not specifically recognised for negotiating purposes on the application of the scheme.

19.5.1.1 The type of information to be disclosed

A general duty is imposed on an employer who recognises an independent trade union for collective bargaining negotiations to release information for this purpose. There are, however, checks on the flow of information.[84] Whether the information should be disclosed is dependent on the application of a dual test. It must be information 'without which the trade union representatives would be to

79 Section 12(4).

80 For the background to the passage of this measure, see Gospel, 1976.

81 Note that the Employment Relations Act 1999 provides a procedure for unions to gain automatic recognition where a majority of union members vote in a ballot. For details, see p. 421.

82 See p. 385.

83 [1981] ICR 843.

84 An employer is not required to produce original documents for inspection or for copying, information requested may be conveyed in an edited document. Nor is an employer required to compile or assemble information 'where it would involve work or expenditure out of all reasonable proportion to the value of the information in the conduct of collective bargaining'. See on this *Hoover Ltd and GMWU* (CAC Award 79/507).

a material extent impeded in carrying on collective bargaining . . . and which it would be in accordance with good industrial relations practice to disclose'.[85] For a trade union to be impeded to a 'material extent' in carrying on collective bargaining the information denied by an employer must be both of a relevant and significant nature – of some importance to the bargaining process.[86]

Section 181(4) of the TULR(C)A 1992 establishes that in determining what is in accordance with good industrial relations practice regard should be had to the ACAS Code of Practice on *Disclosure of Information to Trade Unions for Collective Bargaining Purposes*. The Code encourages the parties to conclude a voluntary agreement on what items will be disclosed, when and to whom.[87] If no separate agreement is made between employer and union, then, the substantive content of the Code is evidence of 'good industrial relations practice'. The Code outlines in paragraph 11 examples of material that might be the subject of disclosure. This list includes information on such matters as pay and benefits, recruitment policies and redundancy, promotion and other staffing plans, investment and financial information.

19.5.1.2 Exceptions to the right

Even where this dual test has been exercised a union is not entitled to demand information where one of five exceptions applies.[88] An employer is not obliged to give the applicant union the information requested if disclosure of the information is:

- against the interests of national security[89];
- would result in the contravention of a statute[90];
- is related specifically to an individual and consent has not been obtained for its release[91];
- is obtained by the employer for the purpose of legal proceedings;
- has been communicated in confidence or obtained in confidence[92];
- would cause substantial injury to the undertaking.[93]

19.5.1.3 Procedure for disclosure and remedies for non-disclosure

Section 183(1) of the TULR(C)A 1992 provides that a complaint of failure to disclose information must be presented to the Central Arbitration Committee (CAC) who, initially, will refer the complaint to ACAS to settle the matter by conciliation. If the complaint is not referred because the CAC believes it is not reasonably likely to be settled by conciliation or it is referred and the conciliation fails, the CAC will hear the complaint from the trade union. Where the CAC finds the complaint wholly or partly well founded a declaration is made to this effect. The declaration specifies a timescale by which the employer should comply with the disclosure of the information.[94]

---

85 Section 181(2)(a)(b).

86 See *Civil Service Union v CAC* [1980] IRLR 274.

87 Para. 22.

88 Section 182(1).

89 Section 183(6) specifies that a certificate signed by or on behalf of a Minister of the Crown to the effect that the disclosure of the information is against the interests of national security is conclusive evidence of that fact.

90 For example, refusal of disclosure was justified in *Joint Credit Card Co and NUBE* (CAC Award 78/212) because the release of information would otherwise be a breach of the Copyright Act.

91 Refusal was justified in *Chloride Legg Ltd and ACTSS* (CAC Award 84/15) because the union had requested personal information on salaries of staff who were not the subject of the pay claim by the union.

92 See *Civil Service Union v CAC* [1980] IRLR 274, where the High Court upheld the CAC's decision that given the commercial sensitivity surrounding the competitive tendering process, information on cleaning bids by private companies may be withheld on grounds of confidentiality.

93 The Code suggests at paras 14 and 15 that substantial injury to an undertaking occurs where the release of information would cause the loss of customers to a competitor or difficulty would be experienced with suppliers of goods or services or the ability to raise finance would be seriously impaired if the information was released.

94 Section 183(5).

Should the employer fail to comply with the declaration, s. 184 provides for a further complaint to the CAC. The union, on or after presenting the further complaint to the CAC, may apply to the CAC under s. 185 for a formal award of enhanced terms and conditions for the employees who are the subject of the claim. This award may reflect the terms and conditions specified in the claim, or it may reflect what would have been achieved by collective bargaining if the information had been released by the employer.

The new terms and conditions incorporated into the employment contracts of employees cannot be superseded or varied by a later collective agreement or by any subsequent implied or express agreement unless the agreement is more favourable than the CAC award.[95] This is to prevent employers from pressurising employees to revert to their previous terms and conditions.

It has been argued that the remedy for a refusal to disclose is inadequate as the union is not entitled to enforce release of the information to which it is entitled.[96] When the provisions were originally adopted the intention was to avoid overt legalism – to produce a system where the law facilitated the release of information rather than enforced disclosure. It was hoped that in practice complaints would be resolved through conciliation rather than by formal proceedings.[97]

19.6 Rights to consultation

Employers are under a statutory obligation to consult with recognised trade unions in the areas of: redundancy, on the transfer of an undertaking, on matters relating to health and safety at work, the administration of pension schemes and on issues of training.

19.6.1 Redundancy

The law on consultation in the event of redundancy developed as a response to European Community obligations contained in the European Directive on Approximation of Laws Relating to Redundancies. The provisions of this directive were enacted into domestic law during the period of the Social Contract as ss. 99–107 of the Employment Protection Act 1975; now found in ss. 188–192 of the TULR(C)A 1992 as amended by the Trade Union Reform and Employment Rights Act 1993, and by the Collective Redundancies and Transfer of Undertakings (Protection of Employment) (Amendment) Regulations 1995,[98] 1999,[99] and 2014.[100]

Throughout the 1980s there was persistent criticism that the UK had not correctly implemented the Directive. As a consequence, the European Commission in 1992 initiated infringement proceedings against the UK on the grounds that the domestic law defined redundancy dismissals too narrowly; failed to ensure that effective sanctions were in place to deter breach of the consultation provisions; did not require employers to consult 'with a view to reaching agreement' and supply the degree of information as prescribed in the Directive and omitted to lay down appropriate consultation provisions where there was no recognised union at the place of work.

---

95 Section 185(5).

96 See *Holokrome Ltd and ASTMS* (CAC Award 79/451).

97 It seems that to a great extent this has been the experience of the CAC. Very few cases proceed to an enforced award against an employer; disputes are settled by conciliation (referred to ACAS) or information is provided voluntarily once a formal claim is made. See Gospel & Lockwood, 1999.

98 SI 1995/2587.

99 SI 1999/1925.

100 SI 2014/16.

The last complaint was of particular importance.[101] Employers could effectively avoid community obligations by refusing to recognise, or by derecognising trade unions prior to the announcement of dismissals. This was clearly contrary to the Directive which imposed an absolute obligation on employers to consult with 'worker representatives'.

In response to the action by the European Commission and, in anticipation of an adverse judgment by the European Court of Justice (ECJ), amendments were made by the Trade Union Reform and Employment Rights Act 1993 on three of the four areas cited by the European Commission. Although the revised legislation on consultation now complied more closely with the requirements of the Directive there was still one glaring omission – the failure to extend the right of consultation to employee representatives where a trade union was not recognised.

In 1994 the ECJ held that on all of the four grounds above, the UK was in breach of the Directive.[102] The ECJ decision thus confirmed that the UK government was obliged to ensure that all workers had the opportunity to be consulted on redundancies whether or not their union was recognised. Consequently, in late 1995, the government introduced, by way of a statutory instrument, additional changes to the consultation provisions and transfer of undertaking regulations to conform to the ECJ decision. Following the passage of the 1995 Collective Redundancies and Transfer of Undertakings (Protection of Employment) (Amendment) Regulations, the duty imposed on an employer was to consult with 'appropriate representatives' of employees who may be dismissed, i.e. representatives of a recognised independent trade union or elected representatives of those employees.[103] The employee representatives may be elected specifically for the purpose of redundancy consultation or they may be already elected for a different purpose (such as for health and safety consultation).[104]

The most controversial aspect of the Regulations was that they gave no preference to consultation with recognised trade unions. Under the Regulations an employer could choose to consult with an ad hoc group elected for this purpose rather than with officials of a recognised union – thereby bypassing established employee representatives, sidelining union objections to a particular course of action and effectively frustrating the whole basis of the consultation provisions. The Regulations also allowed the employer to have a free hand in organising the election. The Regulations did not lay down any detailed rules on how the election should be administered nor provide any safeguards to ensure the independence of the elected representative from the employer.[105]

After the election of the Labour government in 1997 new Regulations[106] were introduced that now provide that where a trade union is recognised, union representatives of that union must be automatically consulted (even where some of the affected workers are not trade union members).[107] Where a recognised union is not present at the workplace explicit detailed regulation of the process of electing employee representatives has been introduced with the onus on the employer to ensure the election is fair. Employee representatives must be elected in accordance with prescribed procedures in a secret ballot; no affected employee may be unreasonably excluded from voting or

---

101 This was also a criticism of the Transfer of Undertakings Regulations implementing the Acquired Rights Directive.

102 *Commission of the European Community v UK* [1994] IRLR 392 (Case 383/92).

103 Regulation 3 which substituted a new s. 188(1)(2) of the TULR(C)A 1992.

104 Section 196(1).

105 A challenge to the way the directive was transposed was made in *R v Secretary of State for Trade and Industry, ex p Unison and others* [1996] IRLR 438. Otton LJ held that the lack of detailed safeguards against abuse of the election process did not amount to a defective implementation of the directive although a subjective determination of employee representatives 'at the whim of an employer' would be manifestly contrary to the Regulations.

106 SI 1999/1925.

107 Section 188(1B)(a).

for standing as a representative,[108] or be unfairly dismissed or suffer a detriment for taking part in an election of employee representatives.[109]

19.6.1.1 The proposal to dismiss

The duty to consult with appropriate representatives of employees who may be affected by the dismissals or affected by measures taken in connection with the dismissals[110] arises as soon as the employer is 'proposing to dismiss' 20 or more employees in one establishment[111] on grounds of redundancy. In *Hough v Leyland Daff Ltd*,[112] Knox J construed the expression 'proposing to dismiss' to mean that consultation only needs to begin when the actual decision has been made to make the employees redundant, i.e. when

> matters . . . have reached a stage where a specific proposal has been formulated and that is a later stage than the diagnosis of a problem and the appreciation that at least one way of dealing with it would be by declaring redundancies.[113]

In *Scotch Premier Meat Ltd v Burns*,[114] the EAT held that once an employer had decided on a plan of action which had two alternative scenarios, one of which included potential dismissals, then the employer was 'proposing to dismiss' within the meaning of s. 188.[115]

19.6.1.2 The nature and degree of consultation

The object of the statutory duty on employers is to give the representatives of the affected employees the opportunity to influence the decision by making constructive proposals to avoid or limit the effects of the redundancies. During the consultation process the union may suggest alternative methods of achieving the employer's objectives or ways of limiting the number of redundancies.

To facilitate and enhance the consultation process the appropriate representatives have the right to receive certain information on the employer's proposals for redundancy.[116] The employer must disclose, in writing, the reasons for the redundancies, the number of employees of a particular description to be made redundant, the total numbers of employees of that description, the proposed selection procedure, the proposed method of carrying out the dismissals and how any extra statutory redundancy payments are to be calculated.[117] An amended s. 188(2) of TULR(C)A 1992 provides guidance on the extent of consultation. The employer is required to engage in discussion 'about ways of a) avoiding the dismissals, b) reducing the numbers of employees to be dismissed, and c) mitigating the consequences of the dismissals'. The section further states that this consultation must 'be undertaken by the employer with a view to reaching agreement with the appropriate representatives'. The employer who refuses to consider union ideas or who does not make reasonable

---

108 Section 188(1B)(b).

109 Where affected employees fail to elect representatives, having had a genuine opportunity to do so, the employer may discharge the duty under the Act by providing appropriate information to the employees directly.

110 Section 188(1).

111 For the definition of 'establishment', see *Woolworths Ltd v USADAW* [2013] ICR 1300.

112 [1991] IRLR 194.

113 Ibid. p. 198.

114 [2000] IRLR 639

115 The Directive states that consultation should start once an employer is 'contemplating' redundancies. It has been argued that this is at an earlier stage than 'proposing to dismiss'. See the judgment of Glidewell LJ in *R v British Coal Corporation ex p Vardy* [1993] IRLR 104. Also on the interpretation of this expression, see *UK Coal Mining Ltd v NUM (Northumberland Area)* [2008] IRLR 4; *USA v Nolan* [2016] IRLR 34.

116 Section 188(4) as amended.

117 The statutory consultation period does not run until this information has been provided – *MSF v GEC Ferranti Ltd (No 2)* [1994] IRLR 113.

efforts to reach agreement will clearly fall foul of the law.[118] The provisions will also be broken where the consultation takes place, but it is a sham as the dismissal notices have already been issued,[119] or where little time has been allocated for the consultation exercise.[120]

The consultation must take place 'in good time'[121] but only where at least 20 employees are dismissed.[122] This is subject to a certain statutory minimum period which must elapse before the start of the first of the redundancies. Where 20 or more employees are to be dismissed consultation must start at least 30 days before the first dismissals take effect. Where 100 or more employees are to be dismissed consultation must take place at least 45 days before the first dismissals.[123]

19.6.1.3 The defence of special circumstances

If, because of special circumstances, 'it is not reasonably practicable' for the employer to comply with the requirement of consultation within the timeframes above or to disclose the necessary information or to engage in the consultation required by s. 188(2) then the employer only under a duty to take such 'steps . . . as are reasonably practicable in those circumstances'.[124]

The courts have interpreted this provision relatively strictly, and have not generally been willing to accept business difficulties as a special circumstance justifying a failure to provide information and to consult. The Court of Appeal in *Clarks of Hove Ltd v Bakers' Union*[125] held that a special circumstance was something 'out of the ordinary, something uncommon'. Here a decision to cease trading after a period of business difficulty, with the gradual running down of the business to eventual insolvency, was not sufficient to amount to a special circumstance.[126]

However, a sudden financial or physical disaster that results in the immediate closure of the business may well be a special circumstance if it was caused by something out of the control of the employer. In *USDAW v Leancut Bacon Ltd*,[127] there was a failure by the prospective purchaser to carry through the purchase of the business. Almost immediately the bank withdrew credit facilities and a receiver was appointed within days. This sudden development was held to be sufficiently grave to amount to a special circumstance.

There is an additional statutory provision, introduced by the Trade Union Reform and Employment Rights Act 1993, to put into effect the EC amendment Directive on Collective Redundancies.[128] It is not a special circumstance for an employer to argue that the requisite information was not provided because the decision leading to the redundancy was taken by a controlling company that refused to release the information required. It has also been held that it is not a special circumstance for the employer to argue they had misunderstood the effect of the relevant law.[129]

---

118 The 1993 Act deleted the previous requirement on employers to outline reasons for rejecting any suggestions put forward during the consultation exercise. For discussion of the requirements of 'fair consultation' (albeit in a different context), see *R v British Coal Corporation, ex p Price* [1994] IRLR 72 at p. 75.

119 *NUT v Avon County Council* [1978] IRLR 58.

120 *E Green & Son v ASTMS* [1984] IRLR 135.

121 Section 188(1A), replacing the previous requirement that consultation had to be 'at the earliest opportunity'.

122 Previously, before the 1993 amendments, an employer was under an obligation to consult where any number of employees were to be made redundant. On revising the legislation in 1993 the government took the opportunity to introduce these more restrictive provisions permitted by the directive.

123 The ECJ in *Junk v Kuhnal* [2005] IRLR 310, has held that dismissal notices should not be given until the appropriate consultation period has ended in order to ensure the consultation is meaningful.

124 Section 188(7). The burden of proof is on the employer to prove special circumstances existed and that all reasonably practicable steps were taken to comply with the duty to consult.

125 [1978] IRLR 366.

126 See also on insolvency, *AEEU v Clydesdale Group plc* [1995] IRLR 527.

127 [1981] IRLR 295.

128 EC Directive 92/56.

129 *E Ivor Hughes Educational Foundation v Morris* [2015] IRLR 704.

19.6.1.4 Remedies

Should an employer fail to comply with the duties to inform and consult, s. 189 outlines the procedure to be followed on the presentation of a complaint. The first stage is for the union or elected employee representative to make an application to an employment tribunal, either before the dismissals take place or within three months of them taking place.

If the complaint is well-founded then the tribunal will grant a declaration to this effect and may make what is termed a 'protective award' for the benefit of the affected employees. This award is calculated by reference to a 'protected period'. The employer is ordered to pay a sum of money equivalent to a week's pay for every week in the protected period. This period runs from the date the dismissals take effect or of the award, whichever is the earlier,[130] and 'is of such length as the tribunal determines to be just and equitable in all the circumstances having regard to the seriousness of the employer's default'.[131]

When assessing compensation for breach of these provisions, the tribunals will often consider what is 'just and equitable' by reference to what the employees would have lost in wages if the proper period of consultation under the statute had taken place. However, the severity of the employer's default may also be a factor to be taken into account in determining compensation. In circumstances where an employer has not been consulted, but it is clear that everything has been done to avoid the redundancies, then a nominal award may be appropriate. Conversely, where there is a severe and deliberate breach of the statute, a higher award may well be justified.[132] However, the protected period is subject to a maximum that a tribunal can award – 90 days' pay in all cases.[133]

Should an employee be fairly dismissed or unreasonably terminate their own contract during the protected period, then s. 191 provides that entitlement to payment for the reminder of the protective period lapses. An employee is also not entitled to payment if the employee is made an offer by the employer, before the protected period, to renew the contract on similar terms and conditions of employment, or an alternative offer of suitable employment is made and it is unreasonably refused. Section 191(4) provides that the employee is entitled to a trial period of four weeks. If the employee terminates the new contract within this period, the benefit of the protective award is not lost unless the employee acted unreasonably in doing so.

19.6.1.5 Conclusions

The changes to the statutory provisions have not altered the essentially procedural nature of the consultation requirements. Even though consultation is 'with a view to reaching agreement' on specified matters, employers are not obliged to take account of union views and so move towards the union position in order to strike a compromise agreement. Nor is it necessary for employers to justify their rejection of union suggestions.

Moreover, the efficacy of redundancy consultation has been weakened by what was described by the Conservative government at the time as a 'deregulation measure' to help small businesses. An employer must propose to dismiss at least 20 employees before there is a need to consult with unions or employee representatives. In practical terms, as the bulk of redundancies are small scale, unions have lost the opportunity to influence employer's plans in a large number of cases. It is also arguable that, even after the 1999 amendments, sanctions for breach of the consultation requirements

---

130 See *TGWU v Ledbury Preserves Ltd* [1986] IRLR 492.

131 Section 189(4)(b).

132 See *Spillers-French (Holdings) Ltd v USDAW* [1980] ICR 31; *Sovereign Distribution Services Ltd v TGWU* [1989] IRLR 334; *Susie RadinLtd v GMB* [2004] IRLR 400; *AMICUS v GBS Tooling Ltd* [2005] IRLR 683.

133 Section 189(4) as amended.

are still not a credible deterrent to the determined employer who can buy out the duty to consult and that the protective award may not satisfy the European Union requirement that sanctions for breach of European law must be 'effective, dissuasive and proportionate'.[134]

19.6.2 On a transfer of the undertaking

Rights of consultation on the transfer of an undertaking originally derive from the EC Directive on Acquired Rights.[135] The main objective of this directive is to protect the employment rights of employees where the ownership of an undertaking changes. The directive was enshrined into domestic law in 1981 by the passage of the Transfer of Undertakings (Protection of Employment) Regulations.[136] New consolidating Regulations (incorporating minor amendments necessary after a re-negotiated acquired rights directive was agreed) were introduced in 2006.[137] On a 'relevant transfer' the terms and conditions of affected employees are transferred to the new undertaking, thus protecting their continuity of employment.[138] Also transferred are the contents of any existing collective agreement[139] and any union recognition agreement.[140] A duty is also imposed on both parties to inform and consult with employee representatives on measures to be taken in connection with the transfer that affect employees.[141] Additionally, subject to an exception, it is automatically unfair to dismiss an employee for a reason connected with the transfer.[142]

In a similar vein to the criticisms levelled at the collective redundancies legislation it had been argued by the European Commission that the original 1981 Regulations did not faithfully incorporate the requirements of the directive as they had excluded the transfer of non-commercial ventures[143]; failed to specify that consultation must take place 'with a view to seeking agreement'; did not provide adequate sanctions that conformed to European Community standards and failed to identify appropriate employee representatives in the absence of trade union recognition. In response to infringement proceedings initiated by the Commission, changes were made to the Regulations by the Trade Union Reform and Employment Rights Act 1993. However, as was the case with the Collective Redundancies Directive, the government failed to ensure that proper consultation provisions were in place where a trade union was not recognised. The infringement proceedings thus culminated in the decision of the ECJ in *Commission of the European Community v UK*[144] that the UK remained in breach of the Directive on this ground. As we saw earlier, the UK government attempted to comply with this judgment by providing for employee representatives to be elected at the workplace for the purposes of consultation prior to the transfer.[145] Likewise the 1999

---

134 A stronger and possibly more appropriate sanction would be to permit the courts to grant injunctive relief prohibiting the redundancies until proper consultation had taken place. Despite the problem of enforcement the court in *R v British Coal Corporation, ex p Vardy* [1993] IRLR 104 granted a declaration that no redundancies should take effect until the statutory review procedure (under the Coal Industry Nationalisation Act 1946) had been followed.

135 77/187/EEC.

136 SI 1981/1794. See Hepple, 1982

137 Transfer of Undertakings (Protection of Employment) Regulations 2006 SI 2006/246.

138 Regulation 5.

139 Regulation 6.

140 Regulation 9.

141 Regulation 10.

142 Regulation 8.

143 The ECJ had consistently held that the exclusion of non-commercial organisations from the Regulations was contrary to the requirements of the Directive – see for example, *Dr Sophie Redmond Stichting v Bartol* [1992] IRLR 366 applied by the Court of Appeal in *Kenny v South Manchester College* [1993] IRLR 265.

144 [1994] IRLR 412.

145 The Collective Redundancies and Transfer of Undertakings (Protection of Employment) (Amendment) Regulations 1995 SI 1995/2587.

amendment Regulations[146] specifying the procedure to be followed for the election of representatives and for the primacy of trade union representation also applies for the purposes of TUPE consultation. However, the 2014 Regulations permit businesses that employ fewer than ten employees to consult directly with individuals without the need to organise elections for the purpose of consultation.[147]

19.6.2.1 The consultation and information provisions

Where there is 'a relevant transfer' (see Chapter 5) and where employees may be affected (such as by redundancy or a change in working conditions) Regulation 13 provides that both undertakings involved in the transfer must inform the relevant employee representatives of the proposed arrangements in some detail.

The requisite information must cover: when the relevant transfer is to take place, the reasons for the transfer, the 'legal, social and economic implications' for the affected employees of the transfer and the measures that each employer envisages will be taken that will affect their employees.[148] The information must be provided 'long enough before a relevant transfer to enable consultations to take place'.[149] The consultation must take place 'with a view to seeking agreement' on the measures put forward. During this process, representations may be made by the appropriate employee representatives. The employer must consider these representations and, if rejected, state the reasons for doing so.[150] There is no minimum period by which time consultation has to commence or last – the more complex the issues that arise on a transfer, the longer the period an employer should allow for consultations. Similarly to the compulsory consultation provisions on redundancy, a failure to inform and consult on a transfer of undertakings is not actionable where there are special circumstances, making it not reasonably practicable for the employer to perform the duty.[151] An employer is only obligated to take whatever steps of consultation are practicable in the circumstances. It may be assumed that the redundancy case law on this defence will also apply here.

19.6.2.2 Remedies

On a failure to consult or inform recognised trade unions in advance of the transfer, Regulation 15 states that a complaint may be presented by the relevant trade union or employee representative to an employment tribunal.[152] If the complaint is well-founded, the tribunal will make a declaration to that effect and award compensation to the relevant employees as the tribunal considers 'just and equitable having regard to the seriousness of the employer's default'.

Until amendments contained in the 1993 Act, the maximum award could not exceed two weeks' pay and employers were also able to set off this compensation against a redundancy protective award. As a consequence of criticism by the European Commission that this was not a credible and effective sanction, the compensation levels were increased in 1993 to a sum not exceeding four weeks' pay and the requirement of set off was abolished.[153] Due to criticisms that

---

146 The Collective Redundancies and Transfer of Undertakings (Protection of Employment)(Amendment) Regulations 1999 SI 1999/1925.

147 Regulation 13A.

148 Regulation 13(2).

149 See *IPCS v Secretary of State for Defence* [1987] IRLR 373.

150 Regulation 13(6) as amended.

151 Regulation 13(9).

152 The complaint must be made within 3 months of the date the transfer is completed unless 'not reasonably practicable'. There is no need to wait for the transfer to take place before presenting the complaint – see *South Durham Health Authority v UNISON* [1995] ICR 495. It even appears that the complaint may proceed even if the transfer does not in fact take place – see *BIFU v Barclays Bank plc* [1987] ICR 495.

153 Note the ECJ decision in *Marshall (No 2)* [1993] ICR 893 that compensation limits *per se* undermine the effectiveness of sanctions.

this was still not an appropriate deterrent, the 1999 Regulations[154] have raised the limit of compensation payable to a maximum of 13 weeks' pay.[155]

19.6.3 Health and safety and pensions

By virtue of the powers provided under the Health and Safety at Work Act 1974, the Safety Representatives and Safety Committees Regulations[156] which came into force in 1978, introduced the right of recognised trade unions to appoint safety representatives. Section 2(6) of the Health and Safety at Work Act 1974 places a duty on employers:

> to consult safety representatives with a view to the making and maintenance of arrangements which will enable (the employer) and his employees to co-operate effectively in promoting and developing measures to ensure the health and safety at work of employees and in checking the effectiveness of such measures.

Where requested in writing, by two or more safety representatives, the employer must set up a safety committee within three months of the request. The employer should consult with safety representatives and any relevant union as to how it should function. The powers of the committee and terms of reference are determined by reference to guidance notes provided by a Code of Practice under the Safety Representatives Regulations.

Should an employer refuse to consult with a recognised union about the setting-up of a safety committee after a request by the safety representatives, the union may complain to an inspector from the Health and Safety Commission. An improvement notice may then be issued requiring the committee to be established. It is possible for a recalcitrant employer to be prosecuted under the Act for failing in this duty.

In addition, the Management of Health and Safety at Work Regulations 1992 (amended by the 1999 Regulations[157]), enforcing the European 'Framework Directive' on Health and Safety,[158] contains further requirements on health and safety matters generally and consultation in particular. Regulation 4(a) extends the rights of consultation to ensure that every employer will consult 'in good time' on:

(a) the introduction of any measure that may substantially affect health and safety;
(b) arrangements for the appointment of employees to assist with health and safety and with the implementation of procedures where there is serious and imminent risk;
(c) the type of health and safety information provided to employees;
(d) the planning and organisation of health and safety training; and
(e) the health and safety implications of the introduction of new technology.

The Framework Directive requires (similarly to the Collective Redundancies and Acquired Rights Directives), that consultation must be with 'designated workers' representatives'. Regulations have therefore been introduced to ensure compliance with European law and the ECJ decision in

154 SI 1999/1925.
155 On the calculation of compensation, see *Sweetin v Coral Racing* [2006] IRLR 252.
156 SI 1977/500.
157 SI 1999/3242.
158 89/391/EC.

European Commission v UK.[159] The Health and Safety (Consultation with Employees) Regulations 1996 have extended rights of consultation to workers in non-unionised workplaces.[160]

Where an employer wishes to opt out of the State pension scheme by operating an occupational company pension for employees, the employer must obtain a contracting out certificate from the Occupational Pensions Board. Before doing so, any relevant trade union must be consulted. Once an occupational pension scheme is in operation s. 113 of the Pensions Schemes Act 1993 and the Occupational Pension Schemes Regulations 1996 and 2013[161] provide that certain information must be released to members of the scheme and their union representatives recognised for the purposes of collective bargaining.

19.6.4 Training

Where an independent trade union is recognised in accordance with the statutory recognition procedure and a method of collective bargaining has been specified by the CAC, that trade union is entitled to be consulted on training issues within the relevant bargaining unit.[162] The employer is under a duty to call a meeting with trade union representatives within six months to consult on the employer's training policy *per se*, and on arrangements for training in the following six-month period. Follow up meetings should take place within six months of the previous meeting.[163] Two weeks prior to the meeting the employer must provide the union with certain relevant information – that without which the union would be impeded to a material extent in participating in the meeting and which it would be in accordance with good industrial relations to disclose.[164] This repeats the formula applied to the right to information for collective bargaining purposes discussed earlier in the chapter and the same restrictions on disclosure apply. The employer must also 'take account' of written representations from the union stemming from matters raised at a consultative meeting.[165]

Where an employer has failed to comply with this duty to consult on training matters, the union concerned may complain to an employment tribunal for a declaration to this effect and for an award of compensation equivalent to two weeks' pay for each individual member of the relevant bargaining unit, enforceable by the individual, rather than the union complainant.[166]

19.6.5 Information and consultation – the European dimension

The principle of employee information, consultation and participation as an aspect of European social policy has been supported by European Community institutions since 1974. The early initiatives in this area were the Acquired Rights Directive and the Collective Redundancies Directive discussed earlier. These two Directives arose out of the 1974–1976 Action Programme on Social Policy undertaken by the Commission to harmonise the laws of Member States on employment matters. Although worker participation was a theme of the Action Programme, the Commission failed to develop initiatives on this issue as a consequence of the opposition of a number of Member States to the harmonisation of labour standards in this area.

159 [1994] IRLR 412.
160 1996/1513.
161 SI 1996/1172; SI 2013/2734.
162 S. 70B(1)(2) TULR(C)A 1992.
163 S. 70B (3).
164 S. 70B(4).
165 S. 70B(6).
166 S. 70C.

The first attempt by the European Commission to secure a degree of worker information and consultation was the 'Vredling' Draft Directive.[167] This was developed to provide rights of information and consultation to employees of undertakings with complex structures. Where there was a parent undertaking with one or more subsidiaries, the original Directive required the disclosure of wide ranging and explicit financial, economic and strategic information every six months by the dominant undertaking to the representatives of employees of its subsidiaries. Additional financial information concerning the relevant subsidiary had also to be disclosed.

As a consequence of widespread alarm in the European business community, amendments to the original draft Directive were made in 1983. Despite these amendments the draft Directive was not implemented and it has now been dropped by the Commission. However, many of the Vredling requirements have resurfaced in a different guise via the European company statute and the European Works Council Directive.

In 1989 the Community Charter of Fundamental Social Rights of Workers (the Social Charter) was adopted by the Council of Ministers in conjunction with an Action Programme to develop new legislative measures.[168] This was the social policy complement to the completion of the single internal market approved by all members of the community except the UK.[169]

The Social Charter Action Programme (1989) spawned the Draft Directive on Information and Consultation of Workers within European Scale Undertakings.[170] As this was a measure harmonising labour standards, the implementation of this draft Directive required a unanimous vote of all States under Article 100. With the UK vetoing this Directive the remaining 11 States turned to implementation procedures under the Maastricht Social Protocol. In 1992, as an addition to the Treaty of European Union (Maastricht Treaty), all members of the European Union except for the UK reaffirmed their commitment to minimum labour standards and the harmonisation of labour law across the European Union. As the UK opposed the extension of community competence in this area, an Intergovernmental Protocol on Social Policy, annexed to the Maastricht treaty, was agreed by the remaining members to enable implementation of the Social Charter Action Programme.[171] The European Works Council Directive[172] was finally passed under the Social Policy Protocol procedure and adopted by the Council of Ministers on 22 September 1994, with an implementation deadline of two years from that date. As a consequence of the 'Brexit' process there is a degree of uncertainty as to the future of European initiatives in this area for the United Kingdom. However, leaving the EU does not necessarily impact on the relevance of existing EU derived provisions, as most have been implemented into domestic law.

❖ THINKING POINT

Why was the Conservative Government at the time so opposed to the Social Charter and the European Action Programme?

167 OJ C297/80/EC.

168 The Community Charter of Social Rights had no specific legal status but was a solemn declaration of agreed principles in the area of social and employment policy. To implement these principles the Council adopted the Action Programme.

169 For an extensive analysis of the Social Charter and background to the Action Programme, see Bercusson, 1990; Hepple, 1990.

170 This was the original draft European Works Council Directive (OJ C39 1991).

171 This is otherwise known as the 'Social Policy Agreement'. See Fitzpatrick, 1992.

172 94/45/EC.

19.6.5.1 The European Works Council Directive

The aim of the Works Council Directive is to establish a consistent system of worker participation in all transnational European enterprises so as to ensure that workers are informed and consulted about decisions taken in other Member States. Works councils (committees of workers' representatives), must be set up in all undertakings which have at least 1,000 employees in the European Union and have a minimum of 150 employees in at least two other member states.

Where these conditions are met and where at least 100 employees or their representatives so request,[173] the directive calls for the 'central management' of the undertaking to organise the setting-up of a 'special negotiating body' between employee representatives and management to negotiate and agree in writing the composition, nature, functions, competences and operating rules of a works council. If negotiations within three years fail to agree to the structure and powers of a works council, the directive imposes a default model of minimum standards.

The default model lays down that the works council should consist of between three and 30 employees (at least one from each relevant member state) appointed by all employees or by employee representatives as determined by 'national law or practice'. The works council should meet with management at least once a year to be informed and consulted on the economic and financial situation of the undertaking, on investment proposals and any other company developments of relevance to employees, such as organisational change or the introduction of new working methods. A works council can insist on additional meetings where business decisions are to be made on matters (for instance on closures) likely to have a serious effect on the interests of employees.

As a consequence of the reversal of the UK's decision to opt out of the Social Policy Protocol agreed by the new Labour Government at the Amsterdam Conference of June 1997, a new Directive[174] was promulgated to extend the terms of the 1994 Directive to the UK. The Transnational Information and the Consultation of Employees Regulations 1999[175] have now been introduced (under the authority of the European Communities Act 1972) to implement the Directive. The Regulations as a whole reflect the requirements outlined in the Directive with additional detail provided on the issues of enforcement and employee representation.[176] In the absence of a valid voluntary agreement (or in response to a written request from at least 100 employees or their representatives in at least two member states) the negotiation procedure is triggered. Members of a 'special negotiation body' are to be elected by supervised ballot of the workforce unless an elected committee already exists – in which case members may be nominated from that group.[177] Members of the works council itself may be elected by employee representatives where they represent all UK employees or by a supervised ballot of all employees. Management will be able to withhold sensitive information to the works council where release might 'seriously harm the functioning of the undertaking concerned or would be prejudicial to it'.[178] The failure to release information on this ground can be challenged by an appeal to the CAC who can release the information if appropriate. To assuage employers' commercial concerns, the improper disclosure of confidential information has been made a breach of statutory duty enforceable in the courts.[179]

173 The ECJ has held in the *Bofrost* case [2001] IRLR 403 that employees or their representatives have the right to request information from their employer in order to ascertain whether a European undertaking exists for the purposes of the Directive. In the UK context Regulations enacting the Directive into domestic law do provide for this level of rights to information at this early stage.

174 97/74/EC.

175 SI 1999/3323.

176 See, Carley & Hall, 2000.

177 Regulations 11–15.

178 Regulation 24.

179 Regulation 23.

The CAC has the responsibility to adjudicate on disputes regarding compliance with the procedures leading up to the establishment of a special negotiating body or a works council and on whether information is being unreasonably withheld from legitimate employee representatives. Non-compliance with an order of the CAC is enforceable via contempt proceedings. Where a complaint refers to a refusal to co-operate in the setting up of a special negotiating body or a works council, the EAT has jurisdiction with the power to levy a civil fine on a transgressing employer of up to £75,000.[180]

For those UK companies that are not pan-European this is a major change in the minimum rights employees can expect under domestic law. The requirement on such employers to inform and consult with the workforce is on a far broader range of topics than previously required under British law and is not dependent on union recognition. Moreover, even though under the Directive and the Regulations trade unions do not have the exclusive sole right to representation on a works council, the employee representation structures are based predominantly on the trade union model. The so called 'twin track'[181] pattern of workplace representation that caused some alarm in trade union circles in the 1980s and 1990s (where an employer could opt to inform and consult elected non-union employee representatives rather than elected union representatives) has not been revived by the 1999 Regulations, although some disquiet has been caused by the diversity of employee representational structures permitted under the Regulations.

19.6.5.2 The information and consultation of employees' regulations 2004

The Works Council Directive is one of the few examples of a recent Commission proposal coming to fruition under the Social Policy Protocol in the labour law area. However, the European Commission has also been successful in promoting a new Information and Consultation Directive to be applied at the national level. The progress of the directive was given fresh impetus by the highly public failure of the car manufacturer Renault Vilevoorde to inform and consult workers before a decision was taken to shut down a major car plant in Belgium. In the wake of the Renault closure, and later Rover closures in the UK, concerns were raised concerning the effectiveness of the obligations imposed by the Collective Redundancies and European Works Council Directives.[182] In 1998, the Commission proposed a new framework of minimum standards of information and consultation at the national level in all undertakings with 50 or more employees, on issues concerning contractual and workplace change, threats to employment and the development of employment and economic policy.[183]

The UK government was initially opposed to the Directive, but assented in principle after transposition amendments were agreed at the June 2001 EU Council of Ministers conference.[184] The Information and Consultation Directive promulgated in 2002,[185] and introduced into United Kingdom law by the Information and Consultation of Employees Regulations 2004,[186] widens the level of consultation with employees at the national level and applies to all undertakings with more than 50 employees.

180 Regulations 20–22.

181 For further details, see Hall, 1996.

182 For background to the Rover controversy, see Villiers, 2000.

183 For background, see Bercusson, 2002.

184 The UK government negotiated a phased introduction of the Directive with it applying originally to undertakings with over 150 employees, reducing to 50 or more after 2008.

185 EC 2002/14.

186 SI 2004/3426.

For the consultation and information provisions to be activated, at least 10 per cent of employees must initiate a written request to their employer or the CAC.[187] Within three months of the request the employer must make arrangements for the election and appointment of employee representatives and initiate negotiations for an agreement for consultation on workplace issues. Any negotiated settlement must be approved by the workforce – by formal approval in writing of all the negotiating representatives or by a majority of the negotiating representatives in addition to the consent of a majority of the undertaking's employees determined by a ballot or otherwise in writing.

An employer does not need to agree to an employee request to negotiate an information and consultation system if a previous legitimate agreement, as defined under the regulations, exists. Such an agreement must be in writing, describe the structure for consultation, cover all the employees in the undertaking and have been previously approved by the employees (such as a union negotiated collective bargaining system).[188] However, where 10 per cent of the employees in the undertaking request an information and consultation agreement an employer must initiate negotiations; although an employer may deny the request if a ballot is held and the request has not been endorsed by at least 40 per cent of the employees in the undertaking and the majority of those voting.[189]

If there is no pre-existing consultation agreement or if a negotiation on a consultation agreement fails, then the default information and consultation procedure applies, the details of which are determined by the regulations, supplemented by extensive guidance notes.

The default provisions provide that the employer must ensure that employee representatives are elected by secret ballot by the relevant workforce.[190] Once elected, regulation 20(1) provides that the representatives are entitled to:

- receive information on the undertaking's[191] present and future activities and financial situation;
- be informed and consulted on employment developments within the undertaking and on any measures envisaged, in particular where there is a threat to employment within the undertaking;
- be informed and consulted with a view to reaching agreement on decisions relating to substantial changes in work organisation or in contractual relations.

These default requirements arguably extend consultation in areas such as multiple redundancies beyond the specific procedural requirements contained in the earlier collective redundancies regulations, and impacts on an employer's prerogative to unilaterally alter non-contractual works rules and to amend the contractual terms of its employees.

A complaint by an employee that the employer has violated the terms of a negotiated agreement or the default provisions proceeds to the CAC.[192] If the complaint is substantiated, a declaration is made to that effect and the CAC may order the employer to comply with the declaration. If the employer fails to comply the complainant can apply to the EAT for a penalty notice which can result in a fine of up to £75,000.[193] Should an employee or an ICE representative break their duty

187 Regulations 7(1)–(6).

188 Regulation 8(1).

189 For an analysis of how these regulations apply to trade union recognition agreements, see *Stewart v Moray Council* [2006] IRLR 592.

190 Regulation 19(3) states that one representative must be elected per 50 employees.

191 On the definition of an undertaking, see *PCSU v ACAS* [2017] IRLR 680.

192 Regulation 22.

193 For an example of the operation of the enforcement procedure see, *AMICUS v Macmillan Publishers Ltd* [2007] IRLR 885.

not to misuse confidential information provided during the process, then an action for breach of statutory duty may be initiated by the employer.[194]

❖ THINKING POINT

The European information and consultation initiatives support a form of industrial democracy which highlights consultation, dialogue and co-operative decision making. Are these employee participation strategies (which may not be based solely on a model of trade union representation) a suitable and effective substitute for the resolution of industrial issues by collective bargaining between employer and trade union?

19.7 Collective rights for trade unions: recognition

The collective rights for trade unions – such as the right to information and consultation on redundancy, on the transfer of an undertaking, health and safety and pensions – indirectly reinforce freedom of association and collective bargaining by promoting trade union influence at the workplace. However, a major drawback for trade unions is that most of these rights are dependent upon the trade union being recognised by an employer. Furthermore, there is little incentive for workers to join a union which is unable to negotiate on behalf of its members for enhanced terms and conditions of employment through collective bargaining. Without recognition, a union is marginalised at the workplace and cannot function in any meaningful or effective way.

The decision whether to recognise a trade union has historically been solely a matter for the employer and trade unions have often been ambivalent towards the concept of direct state support for recognition. This has been partly due to a concern that legal interference in voluntary arrangements between employer and union would damage the tradition of 'legal abstentionism' in industrial relations and partly because of a genuine belief held by many trade unionists that there was no need for legal measures to enforce recognition.

For much of the twentieth century recognition was assured in the public sector for both manual and white collar unions as the state, since the Whitley Reports of 1917, had pursued a positive policy of recognition and cooperation with public sector unions.[195] To an extent, recognition and bargaining rights were guaranteed in much of the private sector by trade union strength. This was particularly true in the traditional heavy industries which had a record of very high union membership and a history and culture of solidarity and collective action. Certainly, in evidence to the Donovan Commission, the TUC thought there was no need for legal support as 'trade unions in Britain have succeeded through their own efforts in strengthening their organisation and in obtaining recognition without relying on the assistance of government through legislation'.[196]

The Donovan Commission regarded this as a somewhat complacent view. In the less unionised industries recognition issues were still a major source of conflict between employers and unions.

194 Regulation 25.

195 In the state-run industries provisions for union recognition were included in the nationalisation statutes. For example, s. 46(1) of the Coal Industry Nationalisation Act 1946, s. 39 of the Iron and Steel Act 1949, s. 53 of the Electricity Act 1947 and s. 57 of the Gas Act 1948.

196 The Royal Commission on Trade Unions and Employers' Associations Cmnd 3623, 1968.

The Commission also identified a weakness in the developing white collar unions in the private sector. Without a history of solidarity and collective action few white-collar unions were able to achieve recognition in the face of employer opposition.

As the Donovan Commission proceeded on the basis that orderly industrial relations were best served by an extension of collective bargaining, this inconsistency of recognition across and between industries was unsatisfactory. To secure collective bargaining in all sectors of the economy an effective means of dealing with the problems of recognition was required. The Commission recommended the establishment of an independent tribunal to which recognition disputes could be referred. This tribunal would investigate all the circumstances of the dispute and would have the power to make recognition recommendations.[197]

In response to these proposals, the Labour government in 1968 set up by Royal Warrant the Commission on Industrial Relations. One of the roles of this Commission was to facilitate recognition by providing conciliation services where there was a recognition dispute. It could also inquire into the circumstances of a dispute and make recognition recommendations. A serious weakness, however, was the Commission's lack of enforcement powers. Before the success of this tribunal could be evaluated, the Labour government lost the 1970 election. The Conservatives in the Industrial Relations Act 1971 put the Commission on Industrial Relations onto a statutory footing and provided registered trade unions full rights of recognition. However, union hostility to the Act meant that these provisions never operated effectively. For the returning Labour government in 1974 the broadening of collective bargaining throughout industry was a central theme of their industrial and economic policy. An essential element of this policy was the extension of recognition. For the first time this was to be achieved through an enforcement procedure contained in ss. 11–16 of the Employment Protection Act 1975.

19.7.1 The statutory recognition procedure 1976–1980[198]

The statutory recognition procedure relied heavily on persuading employers to recognise trade unions by conciliation and mediation. It was only after an exhaustive process intended to encourage employers to voluntarily recognise and negotiate with unions that enforcement procedures were applied. Where an employer refused to voluntarily recognise a union for collective bargaining purposes, the union had the option of referring this refusal to the Advisory, Conciliation and Arbitration Service (ACAS) under s. 11 of the Act. If initial conciliation between the parties was unsuccessful, ACAS was then required to comply with a protracted procedure outlined in the statute before a recommendation of recognition could be made. This procedure provided for a process of consultation and inquiry with the employer, the union and all relevant employees. Where the employer refused to comply with a recommendation of recognition, ACAS was empowered to make a second attempt to settle the matter by conciliation.

If this was unsuccessful the statute then provided for the union to apply to the Central Arbitration Committee (CAC) for an arbitration award. The practice of the CAC was to make an award which enhanced terms and conditions of employment, equivalent to the bargain, which recognition, had it been granted, would have provided. The CAC did not regard it as within its role to penalise reluctant employers by imposing punitive awards. The only remedy for employers dissatisfied by an ACAS decision was to seek a judicial review of that decision by way of a declaration that ACAS was in breach of its statutory duty. This depended upon ACAS wrongly exercising its power to recommend recognition by failing to comply with the procedure outlined in ss. 11–16.

197 Paras 253–256.

198 For a full description of the procedure, see Dickens, 1978.

Although the scope for judicial intervention was relatively narrow, this did not stop the courts from vigorously examining the basis of ACAS decision making.

The statutory recognition procedure was not an unqualified success. Arguably, the sanction of an award of improved terms and conditions of employment was not a suitable disincentive to the employer who wished to retain a workplace free of union influence. Judicial interference sapped the power of ACAS to energetically pursue its duties under the Act.[199] Once it became clear that ACAS could be obstructed and that the sanctions imposed by the CAC were limited, employer non-co-operation increased accordingly. The Conservative government, elected in 1979, abolished the procedure in the Employment Act 1980.

Tighter procedure and stronger enforcement powers might have improved the rates of forced recognition. Yet the principle of voluntary collective bargaining which had informed labour relations for many years militated against the introduction of such a coercive system. This experience of legislative intervention in recognition disputes had implications for the structure of the recognition law introduced by the Employment Relations Act 1999 (considered below).

19.7.2 Recognition policy 1979–1997

Repeal of the statutory recognition procedure was the first stage in a Conservative legal strategy (allied with industrial and economic policy) to undermine existing recognition agreements and limit the incidence of new agreements so as to forestall the expansion of collective bargaining. In many nationalised industries, it was standard practice for the recognition of unions to be guaranteed by placing management under a duty to consult and recognise relevant unions. Conservative industrial policy was to privatise the nationalised industries and public utilities, abolishing the obligation to consult and negotiate with appropriate trade unions. Furthermore, recognition agreements in local and central government were undermined by the compulsory competitive tendering process, market testing and subsequent contracting out of public services. In other areas of the public sector the right to recognition was attacked directly through legislation.[200] The extent and nature of recognition during the 1980s and 1990s was also shaped and directed by economic forces, with some employers, in response to the new economic conditions created by free market and monetarist policies, reassessing their relationship with trade unions by embarking on policies of de-recognition and non-recognition (especially in the new high tech and white collar industries).

Where unions are faced with a reluctant employer who refuses recognition, or who withdraws recognition, the traditional response is to challenge such developments by resorting to collective action to force concessions from the employer. The capacity of trade unions to rely on such a strategy were seriously handicapped by legislative changes. New limits originally introduced by the Employment Act 1982 do not make recognition disputes themselves unlawful but weakened unions' ability to put pressure on employers to expand union recognition requirements across industries. For example, section 225 of the TULR(C)A 1992 provides that the immunity for industrial action is withdrawn where action is taken or threatened, against an employer, to induce

---

199 For examples of the judicial decisions in this period, see *Powley v ACAS* [1978] ICR 123; *Grunwick Ltd v ACAS* [1978] ICR 231; *UKAPE v ACAS* [1979] ICR 303.

200 The Burnham Committee as a forum for negotiation with teachers' unions was abolished in 1987 by the Teachers' Pay and Conditions Act. This development resulted in the ILO twice condemning the UK for a breach of Article 4 of Convention No 98 on the Right to Organise and to Collective Bargaining (1949). See the 275th Report of the Freedom of Association Committee (Case No 1518).

the incorporation into a commercial contract of a term or condition which requires that services are only performed, or goods only supplied, by a contractor that recognises trade unions or a particular trade union. The immunity is also withdrawn where action is taken to disrupt the supply of goods and services from a supplier who does not recognise trade unions. This exposes trade unions to actions in tort for the losses caused by the industrial action or for an injunction to stop the action, enforceable via contempt of court proceedings. It is also now unlawful for organisations – such as local or public authorities sympathetic to trade unions – to attempt to enforce recognition via their contractual arrangements with suppliers.[201] Section 186 of the TULR(C)A 1992 states that a term or condition of a contract for the supply of goods or services is void where it purports to require the party to the contract to recognise, consult or negotiate with one or more trade unions. This is strengthened by s. 187 of the TULR(C)A 1992 which provides that 'a person shall not refuse to deal with a supplier or prospective supplier' on the grounds that the supplier or prospective supplier does not, or is not likely to recognise, negotiate or consult with one or more trade unions.[202]

Conservative policies encouraging de-recognition and the dismantling of collective bargaining forced the union movement to reassess strategies to acquire recognition and rekindled interest in legal solutions to the recognition problem. Against this background of the decline in union recognition broad support for some form of legal machinery to secure, protect and maintain recognition had been growing in the union movement, and in the Labour Party, since the end of the 1980s.[203]

The Labour Party elected in May 1997 was committed to a legal right to recognition for the purposes of collective bargaining.[204] The new government outlined the substance of the new right in the Employment White Paper *Fairness at Work*,[205] published in May 1998. After extensive consultation with both sides of industry and some amendment to the original proposals, the Employment Relations Bill containing the recognition provisions was introduced in January 1999 and received the Royal Assent in July of that year. The provisions of the Act on recognition in sch. 1 (inserted into the Trade Union and Labour Relations (Consolidation) Act 1992 as sch. A1 and enforceable since 6 June 2000) amount to over 40 pages and 172 paragraphs. The schedule was drafted in such great detail and length precisely in order to avoid the pitfalls of the previous experiment on compulsory recognition contained in the 1975 Employment Protection Act. The government's view was that the major shortcoming of the 1975 Act was its lack of detailed criteria and procedures for making decisions and its failure to provide ACAS with appropriate guidance as to how it should exercise its discretion. Consequently, the 1999 version of a statutory right to recognition is far more comprehensive in its application. In 2003 the operation of the recognition provisions was reviewed (as part of the assessment of the Employment Relations Act 1999) and minor amendments were made to the procedure by the Employment Relations Act 2004.

---

201 Sections 144 and 145 apply the same approach to arrangements attempting to secure the recognition of a single union via closed shop arrangements.

202 A 'refusal to deal' with another is defined in s. 187(2) as excluding another person from tendering for a contract, or by excluding them from a list of approved suppliers of goods or services or otherwise refusing to enter into a contract with them. The imposition of a recognition term in a contract or a refusal to deal is also a tortious breach of statutory duty. It is actionable by the contracting party against whom it is aimed or 'any other person who may be adversely affected' by it.

203 During this period the debate was informed by a burgeoning academic literature on the issue. For example, see Townley, 1987; Ewing, 1990; Simpson, 1991.

204 See the Labour Party documents *Looking to the Future* (1990), *Building Prosperity – Flexibility, Efficiency and Fairness at Work* (1995), *New Labour, New Life for Britain* (1996), *Equiping Britain for the Future* (1997).

205 Cmnd 3968.

19.7.3 Recognition procedure

19.7.3.1 The application to the Central Arbitration Committee[206]

The process of applying for recognition under the statutory scheme is initiated by the union writing formally to the employer requesting recognition. The union must ensure the letter identifies the union and the proposed bargaining unit (defined as the 'group of workers' in respect of whom the union seeks to conduct collective bargaining) over which recognition is sought and states that it is made under Sch. A1 of the 1992 Act.[207] The request will automatically fail if the employer employs fewer than 21 employees or because the union making the request does not hold a certificate of independence.

If the employer recognises the union and the bargaining unit is agreed, then no further steps need be taken under the statutory procedure. If the employer does not accept the request for recognition but informs the union that it is willing to enter into negotiations, then the parties then have a period of 20 days, or an agreed longer period (with the assistance of ACAS if necessary), in which to agree the bargaining unit and the question of recognition. Once the parties reach agreement on both issues then the union claim under the statutory procedure is terminated.[208] If no agreement has been reached, or the employer has rejected the request or failed to respond to it,[209] the union may then apply to the CAC for a declaration of recognition.[210] The role of the CAC is then to decide whether the bargaining unit proposed by the union is appropriate, and if not, whether some other unit is appropriate; and whether the union has the support of a majority of workers within the bargaining unit for the purposes of automatic recognition.[211]

19.7.3.2 Determination of the bargaining unit

Once the CAC has accepted an application and the parties have not agreed a bargaining unit, the CAC must then decide the appropriate bargaining unit. In order to ensure that pre-existing bargaining arrangements are not disrupted, a recognition application will also not be admissible if the CAC is satisfied that any workers within the relevant bargaining unit (as proposed by the union or agreed with the employer) are already covered by a collective agreement between the employer and any other recognised union.[212] The exceptions are where an existing union with a limited collective agreement makes an application to obtain negotiating rights (that it previously did not have) on pay, holidays and hours or if the pre-existing agreement was made by the employer with a non-independent union in order to forestall a statutory application by another independent union.[213]

In deciding the appropriate unit, a number of matters may be taken into account by the CAC including:

- the views of the employer and of the union or unions;
- existing national and local bargaining arrangements;
- the desirability of avoiding small fragmented bargaining units;

206 The CAC is the body with the primary responsibility to adminster the new procedures. For further explantion of the CAC's role, see Chapter 1.

207 Para. 8.

208 Para. 10(4).

209 Para. 10(1)–(3).

210 Paras 11(1)(a)(b) and 12(1)(a)(b).

211 Paras 11(2) and 12(2).

212 Para. 35(1). On the application of this provision, see *TGWU v Asda* [2004] IRLR 836; *R (NUJ) v CAC* [2005] ICR 493; *R v CAC and MGN Ltd* [2006] IRLR 53; *Pharmacists' Defence Association v Boots Management Services Ltd* [2017] IRLR 355.

213 Para. 35(2)(4).

- the characteristics of the workers falling within the proposed unit and the location of the workers.[214]

However, the overriding criterion the CAC must consider is the need for the unit 'to be compatible with effective management'.[215] The employer's view of the make-up of the appropriate bargaining unit is a relevant, but not the sole determining factor.[216] This is an important issue as the determination of the bargaining unit may be decisive to the outcome of the application for recognition (particularly if a union is well organised amongst a particular group of workers or at a particular site, but is much weaker across the whole organisation). If the appropriate bargaining unit in that instance is widened to the workforce as a whole, then this clearly has implications for the outcome of the ballot.

Once the bargaining unit has been agreed by the parties, or the unit is determined by the CAC, then the next issue for the CAC to determine is whether the union has sufficient support within the bargaining unit in order to initiate the balloting process or to justify an automatic recognition declaration.

19.7.3.3 Automatic recognition

If agreement has been reached on the question of the bargaining unit, but not on the question of recognition itself, then the CAC has the task of determining whether the majority of workers within the bargaining unit support the union before ordering recognition. Unless the union has a majority of members at the bargaining unit (see below) the CAC must decide whether the union has *reasonable support* within the unit. Paragraph 36 defines this as meaning that at least 10 per cent of the proposed unit must be members of the relevant union, and also that a majority of the workers in the unit 'would be likely to favour recognition of the union'.[217] Once it is established that this level of support exists, the next stage is for the CAC to organise a ballot of all workers in the bargaining unit.

However, if there is already 50 per cent membership in the bargaining unit the automatic recognition provisions apply and the CAC will normally make a declaration (without the need for a ballot) that the union is to be recognised as entitled to conduct collective bargaining on behalf of the relevant workers.[218] However, paragraph 22 (4) states that the CAC must arrange for a ballot to be held if one of three qualifying conditions are found to exist, namely:

- the CAC is satisfied that a ballot should be held in the interests of good industrial relations[219];
- a significant number of the union members within the unit inform the CAC that they do not want the union to conduct collective bargaining on their behalf[220];

---

214 Para. 19B(3).

215 Para. 19B(2).

216 On the CAC's decision making, see *R v CAC ex p Kwik-Fit (GB) Ltd* [2003] IRLR 395; *R (Cable & Wireless Sevices Ltd) v CAC* [2008] IRLR 425; *Lidl v CAC* [2017] IRLR 646.

217 The legislation does not make it explicit how the CAC should arrive at its decision. However, the White Paper, *Fairness at Work*, expected that survey or other evidence such as a 'petition signed by a sufficient number of employees' would be sufficient and in practice the CAC has followed the suggestions of the White Paper. For example, in *New Millenium Experience Co. Ltd and British Actors Equity* (2000) TUR 1/6/00 a 'straw poll' conducted by the union was regarded as sufficient evidence of support for recognition, whilst in *TGWU and Stadium Electrical Components Ltd* (2000) TUR1/10/0 a petition of the requisite number of employees satisfied the CAC on this point.

218 Para. 22(1)(2).

219 See as examples *GPMU and Red Letter Bradford Ltd* TUR1/12/00; *TGWU and Economic Ships Ltd* TUR 1/121/01.

220 What would be a 'significant number' of union members depends on the size of the bargaining unit, and a number that is large enough to affect the outcome of the ballot. Where workers have been pressurised by an employer to write to the CAC this evidence will be disregarded – *R (ex p Gatwick Express) v CAC* [2006] EWHC 2035.

- there is evidence of membership produced which leads the CAC to conclude that there are doubts as to whether a significant number of the union members within the unit want the union to conduct collective bargaining.

19.7.3.4 The balloting process

The ballot must be conducted by a qualified independent person (QIP), appointed by the CAC, and must take place within a period of 20 days (or such longer period as the CAC may specify) starting with the day after the QIP was appointed.[221] Once the CAC has decided to arrange the ballot, it must 'as soon as reasonably practicable' inform the employer and the union of that decision, the name of the QIP, the period within which the ballot must be conducted, whether the ballot is postal and – if the ballot is not postal – details of the workplace or places where the ballot is to be conducted.[222] In deciding whether to choose workplace or postal ballots, the CAC must have regard to the likelihood of the ballot being affected by unfairness or malpractice if it were conducted at a workplace, costs and practicality and any other matters it considers appropriate.[223]

19.7.3.4.1 The employer's duties in the balloting process

The legislation states that the employer has three main duties in relation to the conduct of the ballot:

- the employer must co-operate generally in connection with the ballot, with the union and the QIP[224];
- the employer must give the union 'such access to the workers constituting the bargaining unit as is reasonable to enable the union to inform the workers of the object of the ballot and to seek their support and their opinions on the issues involved'[225];
- the employer must give the CAC the names and home addresses of the relevant workers and, 'as soon as reasonably practicable', the employer must inform the CAC of the name of any worker who subsequently joins or leaves the bargaining unit.[226]

If the employer fails to comply with any of the above statutory duties, the CAC may order the employer to remedy the failure. If the employer then fails to comply with that order, the CAC may make a declaration of recognition and dispense with the need to conduct a ballot. Additionally, employers must comply with the DTI (now BIS) Code of Practice *Access to Workers During Recognition and De-recognition Ballots* first published in May 2000 and now re-published as *Access and Unfair Practices during Recognition and De-recognition Ballots*, 2005 after amendments introduced by the Employment Relations Act 2004.[227]

The Code suggests that the parties should begin preparations as soon as the CAC notifies its intention to conduct a ballot and in particular encourages parties to establish an access agreement covering the union's programme for where and when it will contact the workers, and a mechanism for resolving any disputes that may arise during the operation of the agreement. Subject to any agreement the Code continues by laying down guidelines on matters such as: who is to be granted access, where and when access is to take place, the frequency and duration of union activities, written communications and atypical workers.

---

221 Para. 25(3).
222 Para. 25(9).
223 Para. 25(5).
224 Para. 26(2).
225 Para. 26(3).
226 Para. 26(4)
227 Section 5 Employment Relations Act 2004 inserting paragraph 19C–19F into sch. AI, TULR(C)A 1992.

Breach of the Code will not result in any legal sanction as such, but by virtue of s. 207 TULR(C)A 1992, its provisions are admissible in evidence and may be taken into account in any proceedings before any tribunal, court or the CAC. In considering whether to make orders and/or award of recognition the CAC will therefore have regard to the compliance by employers and unions with the provisions of the Code. The CAC has the power to order the employer to make good any failure to comply with its duties to allow reasonable access and in the event of further failure (after the issuing of an order by the CAC) to grant a declaration of recognition. The Code recommends that in the event of minor disputes the parties should attempt to resolve the differences themselves – utilising the conciliation facilities of ACAS if necessary or the good offices of the QIP, before referring the issue to the CAC.

The Employment Relations Act 2004 also introduced an additional regulation of the balloting process by exhorting the parties to refrain from using any 'unfair practice'.[228] An unfair practice is an offer, by either side, to influence the ballot by paying money to an individual to vote in a particular way, or to abstain from voting, or to coerce a worker to vote in a particular way, or to dismiss or threaten to dismiss a worker or take disciplinary action, or to subject a worker to any detriment or undue influence. If a complaint to the CAC of unfair practice is substantiated the CAC may issue a remedial order requiring the party concerned to take action to reverse the effect of the unfair practice. On failure to comply with a remedial order a declaration may be made that the union is recognised or not recognised.

19.7.3.5 The declaration of recognition

As soon as is 'reasonably practicable' after the result of the ballot is determined by the QIP, the CAC must inform the union and the employer of the result.[229] If a majority of those voting, and at least 40 per cent of the workers constituting the bargaining unit vote in favour of recognition, a declaration of recognition will be made.[230] However, gaining recognition is the first hurdle for the union. The next is actually to establish a viable procedure for conducting collective bargaining. The parties must agree (with or without the help of ACAS) a method by which they will conduct collective bargaining or the CAC will specify one. The parties will be expected to conduct negotiations – within what is known as the 'negotiation period' – with a view to agreeing the method by which they will conduct collective bargaining within a 30-day period.[231]

If no agreement on the method to conduct collective bargaining is made during the negotiation period, either party may apply to the CAC for assistance. The CAC then has 20 days to help the parties agree a method for conducting collective bargaining. If, at the end of this period, the parties have still not agreed the method by which they will conduct collective bargaining, the CAC then has the authority to specify the relevant method to the parties.[232] The specified procedure is deemed to have effect as though it were contained in a legally enforceable contract made by the parties.[233] The parties may agree that either the whole or parts of the method specified by the CAC should not have legally binding effect – or they may vary or replace the method specified by the CAC.[234]

---

228 Employment Relations Act 2004 section 10 inserting paragraph 27A into sch. AI, TULR(C)A 1992.
229 Para. 29(1).
230 Para. 29(2).
231 Para. 30(4).
232 Para. 31(3).
233 Para. 31(4).
234 Para. 31(5).

19.7.3.6 The model method for collective bargaining

The Trade Union Recognition (Method of Collective Bargaining) Order[235] was laid before Parliament on 12 May 2000 and came into force on 6 June 2000. This model makes provision for the establishment of a Joint Negotiating Body (JNB), whose members are to comprise equal numbers of union and employer representatives (with at least three on each side). The employer's representatives must have authority to negotiate and agree terms relating to pay, hours of work and holidays. The bargaining process starts with the submission by the union side of its claim, followed by a meeting of the JNB to consider the claim and the employer's response.

Any agreements on pay, hours and holidays are to be set in writing as a legally enforceable collective agreement (by way of an order for specific performance). Information must be disclosed by the employer in accordance with the ACAS Code of Practice on disclosure of information for collective bargaining purposes. Union representatives who are employees of the employer are to be given paid time off to prepare the claim and attend meetings, and to hold meetings with the bargaining unit to discuss the claim. The employer must also make certain facilities available to the union side of the JNB.[236]

19.7.3.7 Enforcement of recognition

The notion of collective agreements being legally enforceable is a new departure for British law, which has always traditionally regarded such agreements as being binding in honour only between the parties (see Chapter 2). The reason why agreements stemming from the statutory recognition procedure are contractually binding is in order to create an enforcement framework in the event that one of the parties fails to observe the method stipulated.[237] The enforcement mechanism specified for a failure to observe the terms of a method imposed by the CAC is an application to a court for an order for specific performance.[238] Failure to comply with an order for specific performance will be a contempt of court punishable by a fine and, in rare cases, imprisonment. This procedural remedy is not accompanied by a substantive sanction, such as in the form of a claim for improved terms and conditions as was the case under the Employment Protection Act 1975. It has been argued that this reliance on a procedural model for enforcement may well allow a recalcitrant employer to delay and prevaricate – accepting the form of recognition but denying the substance.

19.7.3.8 Changes to the bargaining unit after a declaration of recognition has been issued

Where either party believes that there have been material changes to the bargaining unit they may apply to the CAC for a determination as to whether the original unit is still viable and/or for a declaration of a new bargaining unit.[239] The CAC will only accept such an application where it is satisfied that there is *prima facie* evidence that the original unit is no longer appropriate because there is a change in the organisation or structure of the business carried on by the employer, a change in the business activities pursued by the employer or a substantial change in the number of workers employed in the original unit.[240]

---

235 SI 2000/1300.

236 Once the CAC has ordered recognition or refused the application another application in respect to the same bargaining unit cannot be made within 3 years (para. 39).

237 It should be noted that any agreement reached by the parties during the negotiation periods (not the CAC imposed method) will not be legally binding unless it states clearly they are intended to have legal effect.

238 Para. 31(6).

239 There is also a specific procedure that employers can activate where the bargaining unit has 'ceased to exist'.

240 Para. 67(2).

If the CAC accepts the application for decision, the parties then have an initial ten-day period – or such longer period as they might agree – in which to agree a new bargaining unit or units that differs from the original bargaining unit.[241] If the parties manage to agree a new unit or units the CAC must then issue a new declaration of recognition that replaces the original declaration, with modifications as to the method of collective bargaining if required.[242]

If the parties cannot agree on a new unit or units, the CAC must then decide whether the original unit or another unit (or units) is appropriate.[243] If the CAC decides that the original unit is no longer appropriate, and that another unit is (or units are) appropriate (by reference to the same process when determining the original bargaining unit) and there is no overlap with other units, then, depending on the level of support within the new unit, a new declaration of recognition will be made. If the CAC decides that the level of support does need to be assessed, then the inquiry process concerning the level of support for recognition that was carried out in relation to the original unit must be repeated as regards every new unit, up to and including a new ballot if necessary.

19.7.3.9 Joint applications

One of the difficulties with the 1975 Act concerned demarcation disputes and competing claims by different unions over the same groups of workers. These provisions attempt to remove any likelihood of a repetition of these problems by effectively stating that if more than one union wishes to make an application for recognition over the same group of workers, they must do so together and co-operatively. Where a number of unions make a joint application that application will not be admissible unless the unions show that they will co-operate with each other in a manner likely to secure and maintain stable and effective collective bargaining arrangements, and if the employer wishes, they will enter into 'single table' bargaining arrangements.[244] Furthermore, where the CAC has accepted an application from a union in relation to a bargaining unit (with the application pending), an application by another union in relation to another bargaining unit would not be admissible if there is any overlap of employees between the two.[245] If the CAC has received an application but not yet accepted it, and another application is then made, which satisfies the 10 per cent 'reasonable support' rule, then the CAC must proceed with that application only.[246]

19.7.4 De-recognition[247]

The statutory procedure allows for de-recognition applications to be made after a three-year period has elapsed since the declaration of recognition where:

- the employer contends that the size of its workforce has fallen below 21 workers[248];
- where the employer or workers believe that there is less than majority support for the collective bargaining arrangements;[249]

---

241 Para. 69(1)(4).
242 Para. 69(1)(3).
243 Para. 70(4)(5).
244 Para. 37(2).
245 Para. 38(1)(2).
246 Different rules apply where there are multiple competing applications – see para. 14.
247 The de-recognition procedure only applies to statutory recognition. Employers who are party to voluntary recognition agreements can still end them by simply giving the appropriate notice under the collective agreement.
248 Paras 99–103.
249 Paras 104–121.

- where the original declaration of recognition was made automatically on the basis of majority union membership and the employer believes that membership within the bargaining unit is now less than 50 per cent;[250]
- where a group of workers want to end voluntary recognition of a non-independent union.[251]

Where the employer believes that there is no longer majority support for recognition in the bargaining unit the de-recognition process effectively mirrors that which is followed once a recognition request has been served by a union on an employer under Part I of Sch. A1. Once a written request to end the bargaining arrangements is served on the union the parties then have time in which to conduct negotiations with a view to ending the bargaining arrangements.[252] If the union does not accept the request but is willing to negotiate (with the assistance of ACAS if requested), the parties have a period of 20 days or a longer period as agreed in which to conduct negotiations.[253] If no agreement is reached then the employer can then apply to the CAC for a secret ballot to be held on whether the bargaining arrangements should end.[254]

The CAC will not proceed with the de-recognition application unless it is satisfied that at least 10 per cent of the relevant workers want an end to the bargaining arrangements and there is *prima facie* evidence that a majority of those workers would support a de-recognition proposal.[255] If the CAC decides that the formal admissibility requirements are satisfied, it must proceed to conduct a secret ballot on the de-recognition question.[256] The balloting process (set out in paras 117–121), is the same as that undertaken when a union makes an application for recognition under Part I. The employer is under the same three statutory duties and the same 40 per cent threshold applies. If the result of the ballot is that a majority of workers voting and at least 40 per cent of workers in the bargaining unit favour derecognition, then the CAC will declare that the bargaining arrangements are to end on a specified date.[257]

A simplified de-recognition procedure will apply in cases where recognition has been automatic (i.e. without a ballot) by virtue of the levels of union membership.[258] Where the employer's application alleges that the number of union members has now dropped below 50 per cent, the employer and union have ten days in which to conduct negotiations with a view to ending the bargaining arrangements.[259] Where there is no agreement the employer may apply to the CAC for the holding of a secret ballot on the de-recognition question. If the CAC is satisfied that less than half of the workers in the bargaining unit are union members, then it will proceed to conduct a secret ballot on de-recognition.[260]

The final type of de-recognition application enables a union to eliminate employer bargaining arrangements with house staff associations so as to allow the union itself to formally apply for recognition. Thus, where an employer has a voluntary recognition agreement with a non-independent union, a worker or workers within the bargaining unit covered by the agreement may

---

250 Paras 122–133.

251 Paras 134–148.

252 Para. 105(1)(6).

253 Para. 105(2)(7).

254 Paras 106 and 107.

255 Just as is the case with unions seeking to gain recognition, employers desiring de-recognition will need to canvass the relevant workers in order to satisfy these requirements. A worker or workers disaffected with the recognised union may also seek to press for a de-recognition ballot.

256 Paras 111(5) and 117(1)(3).

257 Para. 121(3).

258 Para. 122.

259 Para. 128(1)(3).

260 A worker or workers disaffected with the recognised union may also apply to the CAC for a de-recognition ballot.

apply to the CAC for a de-recognition ballot. The request by the workers to the employer must comply with the usual admissibility requirements,[261] including the requirement that at least 10 per cent of the workers in the bargaining unit desire an end to the bargaining arrangements and a majority of the unit would similarly favour a cessation of the present arrangements.[262] If the application is admissible the balloting provisions discussed previously apply.

Note that if a union that has a statutory declaration of recognition or an agreement for recognition with an employer loses its certificate of independence, then the statutory bargaining arrangements cease to have effect and the parties will be deemed to be in a relationship of voluntary recognition.[263]

19.7.5 Protection against detriment and dismissal

Part VIII of Sch. A1 confers special protection against detriment, dismissal and selection for redundancy for workers involved with the statutory recognition and de-recognition process. Workers have the right not to be subjected to any detriment by their employer by an act or a deliberate failure to act on any one of eight grounds, enforceable by an application to an employment tribunal within three months of the act taking place.[264] The eight grounds are that the worker:

(1) acted with a view to obtaining or preventing recognition of a union by the employer under Sch. A1;
(2) indicated that s/he supported or did not support recognition of a union by the employer under Sch. A1;
(3) acted with a view to securing or preventing the ending of bargaining arrangements under Sch. A1;
(4) indicated that s/he supported or did not support the ending of bargaining arrangements under Sch. A1;
(5) influenced or sought to influence the way in which votes were to be cast by other workers in a ballot arranged under Sch. A1;
(6) influenced or sought to influence other workers to vote or abstain from voting in such a ballot;
(7) voted in such a ballot; or
(8) proposed to do, failed to do, or proposed to decline to do, any of the matters referred to above.

A worker will not be protected if the detriment or dismissal took place because the worker's act constituted an 'unreasonable act or omission' by him or her.[265]

Compensation is to be awarded on a just and equitable basis, having regard to the infringement complained of and any loss sustained by the complainant that is attributable to the act complained of. The loss will include any expenses reasonably incurred as a consequence of the act or failure in question, together with the loss of any benefit that the worker might otherwise have expected to receive. Compensation can be reduced on a 'just and equitable' basis where the worker contributed to the loss and workers must take reasonable steps to mitigate their loss. Where the detriment amounts to a dismissal, 'employees' are protected by specific provisions prohibiting unfair dismissal. The same cap on compensation that applies to employees making claims for ordinary unfair

261 The application would, of course, not be admissible if the union faced with de-recognition could demonstrate it possessed a certificate of independence.
262 Paras 137 and 139.
263 Para. 152.
264 Para. 156(1)(2).
265 Para. 156(3).

dismissal under the Employment Rights Act 1996 will apply.[266] Employees can also make applications for interim relief provided that any such application is lodged within seven days of the effective date of termination.[267]

19.7.6 Conclusions

The question of outright employer opposition to the idea of compulsory trade union recognition remains one of the most problematic areas for legislation in this field. Many employers will have never had any experience of collective bargaining and others will have become accustomed to excluding unions from the workplace. Coupled with creative legal advice and legislation that is extremely complex, there was thus initial concern that opposition to attempts to secure recognition could well find a fruitful outlet in litigation. The operation of the 1975 scheme suffered from a hostile judiciary unhappy with the idea of employers being forced to negotiate with trade unions, viewing it as a draconian incursion on the right of an individual to regulate his or her own working life, or for that matter, the right of an employer to run their business as they see fit. Accordingly, they adopted a policy of construing the provisions in a narrow, legalistic manner. However, this current procedure was drafted in great detail precisely in order to circumvent court challenges and the evidence of almost 20 years of the operation of the procedure is that this recognition procedure has not been undermined by judicial review applications. This more dynamic process combined with tighter legislative drafting has neutralised the threat of legal action and undue judicial interference.

One of the major problems ACAS found when implementing the 1975 version of recognition was the protracted consultation and inquiry procedure that ACAS was obliged to carry out. The procedure took too long – references took a year, on average, to reach the final report stage, and more than a fifth took 18 months. In the 1999 Act the government was careful to prescribe time limits for every stage of the process, with scope for extension where necessary. The legislative timetable allows for a maximum period of up to 80 working days – excluding extensions by agreement or as set by the CAC – from the initial trade union request for recognition to the holding of a ballot on the issue.

One arguably legitimate criticism of the present procedure is the narrow scope of the recognition award. Where the CAC makes an award of recognition to a trade union for the purpose of conducting collective bargaining, this only applies to negotiations on 'pay, hours and holidays', although the parties may voluntarily broaden the coverage of an agreement for recognition. The definition of 'pay, hours and holidays' has been subject to a narrow interpretation. In *BALPA v Jet2.com*[268] the court refused to accept that operational issues such as the rostering of pilot hours fell within the scope of collective bargaining for the purposes of the statutory procedure. Even though this decision was reversed on appeal,[269] it is still the case that unions need to establish that the issue under consideration falls within the narrow sphere of 'pay, hours and holidays'. In addition, questions concerning the effectiveness of the CAC imposed model method have been raised. This only enforces (by an order for specific performance) a procedural remedy culminating in the parties meeting for negotiations, it does not enforce actual negotiations on the substantive issues.[270]

---

266 Para. 160.

267 Similar protection exists where an employee is selected for redundancy on the eight grounds noted above.

268 [2015] IRLR 543.

269 *BALPA v Jet2.com* [2017] IRLR 233.

270 For a further critical review of the procedure see Dukes, 2008.

However, like the indirect impact of the 1975 recognition law, there is evidence that the introduction of the new recognition procedure has encouraged employers to agree voluntary recognition without the need for unions to formally apply to the CAC.[271]

19.8 Voluntary recognition

The statutory recognition procedure does not affect the rights and responsibilities of the parties who have negotiated a voluntary recognition agreement. Where the union is not formally recognised, the informal relationship between the employer and the union takes on an added significance. The courts may determine that at a point in the relationship between union and employer there exists implied recognition in law due to a course of dealing between the parties. What is required is for the employer in practice to negotiate with the union on one or more of the matters contained in s. 178(2). These are listed as terms and conditions of employment, working conditions, discipline, termination and suspension of employment, facilities for trade union officials, membership or non-membership of a trade union and machinery for negotiation and consultation relating to these matters or to trade union recognition. A union must have the agreement of the employer to negotiate on issues concerning one or more of these topics to qualify for the collective bargaining rights.[272]

Strict criteria are rigidly employed to determine whether there has been implied recognition. The approach of the courts is epitomised by Lord Denning's comment in *NUGSAT v Albury Brothers Ltd*[273] that 'a recognition issue is a most important matter for industry; and therefore an employer is not to be held to have recognised a trade union unless the evidence is clear'. This evidence may be clear from a previous course of dealing. In *NUTGW v Charles Ingram & Co Ltd*[274] actual negotiations on a variety of matters took place over an extensive period of time. The bald statement from the employers that the union was not recognised was insufficient as it was contradicted by the practical evidence of co-operation.[275]

In *NUGSAT v Albury Brothers*,[276] the mere entering into discussions by the employer over the payment of trade association rates for members was not sufficient evidence of implied recognition. Although a beginning had been made on negotiations, the consultation between the parties was too limited and inconclusive. There was no real evidence of an agreement to bargain or to strike a deal.[277]

A union may be recognised for limited bargaining purposes. What is required is a sustained course of conduct between the parties indicating that there is an agreement to negotiate on at least

271 In the first 5 years of the procedure 39,000 workers achieved recognition through the statutory procedure. In the same period 800,000 workers were the benficiaries of voluntary recognition agreements. For details, see Gall, 2005. By 2010 it has been noted that 56,000 workers were now the beneficiaries of the recognition procedure with an estimated 750,000 covered by new voluntary agreements. For details, see Gall, 2010.

272 S. 178(3). See *USDAW v Sketchley* [1981] ICR 644, where the EAT held that a limited express agreement for union representation of employees' grievances did not confer on the union general collective bargaining rights. See also *TGWU v Coutenham Products Ltd* [1977] IRLR 8.

273 [1979] ICR 84 at p. 89.

274 [1977] IRLR 147.

275 Thus whether there has been recognition is judged objectively on the facts rather than on the subjective view of either of the parties. See also *J Wilson & Sons Ltd v USDAW* [1978] ICR 614.

276 [1978] ICR 62.

277 Note *Cleveland CC v Springett* [1985] IRLR 131 where the Secretary of State had appointed an unrecognised union to the Burnham negotiating committee which determined national terms and conditions of employment. Recognition was not inferred from this act as (at 135) 'there is no place in any satisfactory system of employment law for the concept of enforced or automatic recognition thrust upon an employer by a third party'.

one of the listed matters of collective bargaining in s. 178(2). For example, on the facts in *Sketchley v USDAW*,[278] there existed an implied recognition agreement on redundancy issues. When it had become known to the union that the employer wished to dismiss workers for reason of redundancy, the union threatened strike action. As a consequence, the employer met with the union and it was agreed that certain advance information would be provided should redundancies occur. Although there was not sufficient evidence here for there to be implied recognition of the union for general bargaining purposes it was arguable that rights of consultation on redundancy had been granted to the union in consideration for their withdrawal of the threat of industrial action.

The union in *Cleveland County Council v Springett*[279] also argued that the employer had recognised the union for limited purposes. The Association of Polytechnic Teachers (APT) was not formally recognised by the employers, but was in practice permitted to appoint health and safety representatives to safety committees and to represent members in grievance proceedings. The EAT rejected the submission that the appointment of safety representatives (which was a statutory benefit for recognised unions under the Safety Representatives Regulations) had inferred recognition on matters of health and safety. The statutory provision provided rights to already recognised unions and did not of itself grant rights of recognition *per se*.

19.9 Further reading

Barrow, 'The Employment Relations Act 1999 (Blacklists) Regulations 2010' (2010) 39 *Industrial Law Journal* 300.

Bercusson, 'The European Community's Charter of Fundamental Social Rights' (1990) 53 *Modern Law Review* 643.

Bercusson, 'The European social model comes to Britain' (2002) 31 *Industrial Law Journal* 209.

Bogg, 'Politics, community, democracy: appraising CAC decision making in the first five years' (2006) 35 *Industrial Law Journal* 245.

Bogg, 'The mouse that never roared: unfair practices and union recognition' (2009) 38 *Industrial Law Journal* 390.

Carley & Hall, 'The implementation of the European Works Council Directive' (2000) 29 *Industrial Law Journal* 103.

Dickens, 'ACAS and union recognition procedure' (1978) 7 *Industrial Law Journal* 160.

Dukes, 'The Statutory Recognition Procedure 1999: no bias in favour of recognition' (2008) 37 *Industrial Law Journal* 236.

Ewing, 'Trade union recognition – a framework for discussion' (1990) 19 *Industrial Law Journal* 209.

Ewing, 'Dancing with daffodils' (2000) 50 *Federation News* 1.

Ewing, 'The implications of Wilson and Palmer' (2003) 32 *Industrial Law Journal* 1.

Fitzpatrick, 'Community social law after Maastricht' (1992) 21 *Industrial Law Journal* 199.

Gall, 'The first five years of Britain's statutory recognition procedure' (2005) 34 *Industrial Law Journal* 345.

Gall, 'The first 10 years of the statutory recognition procedure in Britain' (2010) 39 *Industrial Law Journal* 444.

Gall, 'Union recognition in Britain: the end of legally induced voluntarism?' (2012) 41(4) *Industrial Law Journal* 407.

Gospel, 'Disclosure of information to trade unions (1976) 5 *Industrial Law Journal* 223.

Gospel & Lockwood, 'Disclosure of information for collective bargaining: the CAC approach revisited' (1999) 28 *Industrial Law Journal* 233.

Hall, 'Beyond recognition? Employee representation and EU law' (1996) 25 *Industrial Law Journal* 15.

Hall, 'Accessing the ICE Regulations' (2005) 34 *Industrial Law Journal* 103.

278 [1981] ICR 644.

279 [1985] IRLR 131.

Hepple, 'The implementation of the Community Charter of Fundamental Social Rights' (1990) 53 *Modern Law Review* 643.
Simpson, *Trade Union Recognition and the Law*, Liverpool: Institute of Employment Rights, 1991.
Simpson, 'Freedom of Association and the right to organise: the failure of an individual rights strategy' (1995) 24 *Industrial Law Journal* 235.
Townley, 'A comparative analysis of recognition legal procedure' (1987) 25 *British Journal of Industrial Relations* 177.
Villiers, 'The Rover case - the role of the Works Council' (2000) 29 *Industrial Law Journal* 386.
Wedderburn, 'The Employment Protection Act 1975: collective aspects' (1976) 39 *Modern Law Review* 169.
Wedderburn, 'Consultation and collective bargaining in Europe: success or ideology? (1997) 26 *Industrial Law Journal* 1.

Chapter 20

Industrial action

Chapter contents

20.1 Overview

This chapter examines the legal regulation of industrial action.

- Where industrial action is taken by trade unions it is almost inevitable that one or more of the economic torts will be committed. Since the Trades Disputes Act 1906 trade unions have had a form of immunity from these torts so long as the dispute is a 'trade dispute'. There are circumstances where these immunities will be withdrawn leaving unions open to legal action.
- The main torts trade unions will be liable for on industrial action are inducing breach of contract and causing loss by unlawful means.
- Inducing breach of contract occurs where a union instructs workers to go on strike. By inducing the breach of employment contracts the employer suffers economic loss – such as loss of profits.
- Causing loss by unlawful means is a broad 'genus' tort which encompasses a number of sub torts such as loss caused by indirect inducement of breach of a commercial contract – where the union induces breach of an employment contract which itself causes breach of a commercial contract between the employer and supplier or customer.
- Other examples of causing loss by unlawful means include intimidation – where a threat is made by the union against a third party which causes that third party to act in a way to the detriment of the employer's economic interests.
- Trade unions have an immunity against actions that constitute these economic torts so long they act 'in contemplation or furtherance of a trade dispute'.
- In order to 'outflank' these immunities the courts historically have introduced new potential illegalities trade unions may commit such as inducing breach of statute and economic duress.
- The Conservative administrations from 1979 to 1993 and in 2016 introduced a number of restrictions on trade union strike action. Trade unions must comply with certain conditions for industrial action to be lawful. If these conditions are violated, the immunities from legal action are lifted.
- A trade union will lose their immunity if the industrial action is called without a valid ballot, or consists of prohibited secondary action, results in unlawful picketing, is taken to enforce a 'closed shop' or union recognition or to impose the use of union-only labour or is taken to enforce the re-instatement of dismissed strikers' where the industrial action was unofficial.

20.2 Introduction

A trade union, in seeking to achieve its objectives, must occasionally force an employer to the bargaining table by the tactical use of industrial action. Employees who respond to the call for industrial action will be in breach of their employment contracts. Strike action will also often cause breaches of commercial contracts between the employer (against whom the industrial action is directed) and other persons with whom the employer is doing business. Moreover, additional commercial contracts may be broken where employees in other enterprises take supportive secondary action to cut off supplies or the distribution of goods to the employer in the primary dispute.

In the circumstances described above, it is almost inevitable that one or more of the 'economic torts' will have been committed. Clearly an unfettered application of these torts – with employers, suppliers or other parties taking legal action for damages or for an injunction to stop the action – would seriously hinder trade union industrial activities and render them powerless to protect their members' interests. Consequently, since the Trade Disputes Act 1906, unions have been provided with certain 'immunities' to these torts, so long as the action taken is 'in contemplation and furtherance of a trade dispute'. Since 1979, the scope of these immunities have been gradually reduced, making it easier for employers and others to challenge industrial action in the courts.

An approach that has much to commend it is to examine trade union liability in three phases. This is the framework employed by Brightman J in *Marina Shipping v Laughton*,[1] subsequently approved by Lord Diplock in *Merkur Island Shipping Co v Laughton*.[2]

1) Has, *prima facie*, one or more of the economic torts been committed?
2) If so, do any of the immunities now found in the Trade Union and Labour Relations (Consolidation) Act (TULR(C)A) 1992, s. 219 apply?
3) Has the immunity been withdrawn by the legislation since 1980?

20.3 The economic torts

Historically, the relevant economic torts that a trade union may be liable for on taking industrial action were categorised as; inducing breach of contract, interference with trade or business, conspiracy and intimidation. In *OBG Ltd v Allan*[3] (OBG Ltd) the House of Lords went some way towards re-classifying these torts and modifying some of the requirements for liability. The Law Lords determined that there were two specific economic torts – inducing breach of contract and causing economic loss by unlawful means.[4] The latter tort incorporates what were previously the separate torts of interference with trade or business and intimidation.

20.3.1 Inducing breach of contract

This tort has its roots in the Statute of Labourers 1381,[5] although the action in its modern form dates from *Lumley v Gye*.[6] Here, the defendant persuaded an opera singer, who was under a contract to sing at the claimant's theatre, to break her contract with the claimant so as to perform at the defendant's theatre. These principles were subsequently applied to trade union strike action – extending the scope of the tort to include the inducement of breach of commercial supply contracts and contracts for the hire of goods and services.[7]

Inducing breach of contract is committed where the instigator of industrial action induces or procures without justification, knowingly and intentionally a breach of an employment or commercial contract. For example, direct inducement of breach of employment contracts occurs where union official A instructs union members to take strike action against company B. *Prima facie*, company B can sue A, the organiser of the action, in damages or for injunctive relief. Direct inducement to break a commercial contract arises where union official A persuades company B not to honour a supply contract to company C. Company C is then in a position to sue A.

Where A instructs union members to take strike action against company B, in order to stop the delivery of goods to company C, liability is for directly inducing a breach of employment contract and, where this causes a breach of a commercial contract of supply, the tort of causing loss by unlawful means is committed.

---

1 [1982] QB 1127.

2 [1983] IRLR 218.

3 [2008] 1 AC 1. For an analysis of the labour law implications of this case, see Simpson, 2007.

4 Lord Nicholls preferred the description 'interference with the claimant's business by unlawful means'.

5 Under this statute (which owed its origins to the system of serfdom), the law recognised the tort of 'enticement' of a servant from a master.

6 [1853] 2 E and B 216.

7 *Bowen v Hall* [1881] 6 QBD 333; *Temperton v Russell* [1893] 1 QB 715; *DC Thomson & Co v Deakin* [1952] Ch 646.

20.3.1.1 Intention to cause loss

An intention to cause loss by inducing a breach of contract must not be confused with motive. It is not necessary for the claimant to show that the defendant acted out of spite or ill will,[8] or that the defendant's aim was solely to damage the claimant. Liability for this tort requires an intention to procure a breach of contract but not necessarily an intention to cause the claimant harm. The act of the defendant may simply be a means of achieving the aim of protecting the defendant's own interests. Previously the Court of Appeal in *Millar v Bassey*[9] had attempted to link intention with foreseeability – if the defendant could foresee that the consequences of his or her actions could be a breach of contract, the defendant intends its breach. Lord Hoffman in *OBG Ltd*[10] (who gave the leading speech followed by the majority in the House of Lords) rejected this view. The fact that the claimant is a foreseeable victim of the defendant's conduct (with the defendant's act causing a breach of contract) is, on its own, not enough to demonstrate sufficient intention. A defendant intends to cause the breach where he or she takes deliberate steps knowing that breach will be a consequence of his or her actions – in practice the defendant will have directed or 'targeted' the action against the specific claimant. In the more straightforward cases of inducing breach of an employment contract, a union defendant is clearly aware that employees who follow a strike call will invariably break their contracts of employment.

Where commercial contracts are concerned, it is not always the case that the defendant knows that his or her actions will precipitate a breach of contract (due to the defendant's ignorance of the terms of such contracts). The Court of Appeal in *Emerald Construction v Lowthian*[11] refused to accept the assertion that, in these circumstances, a defendant does not possess the necessary intent to cause breach. Mere knowledge (actual or constructive) that a contract exists will suffice. Lord Hoffman considered this authority in *OBG Ltd*[12] and concurred with the view that, where the defendant possessed knowledge of the contract, the defendant has the necessary intention to cause its breach even where he or she does not act deliberately, but is reckless to whether a breach occurs or not.[13] Thus, the requirement for intention is satisfied not only where the defendant acts with the specific intention to cause a breach of the contract, as in actually foreseeing that a breach would occur and desiring these consequences, but is reckless as to the consequences of their actions to a particular claimant.[14]

20.3.1.2 Inducement to break the contract

The requirement that the defendant should induce the breach of contract provides the link of causation between the intention to commit the unlawful act and the loss suffered by the claimant. The clearest example of inducement is where union members are instructed to take industrial action, or threatened or coerced into doing so, resulting in a breach of an employment contract. A threat against a commercial company that strike action will be taken unless they break a commercial contract with a business with whom the union is in dispute also constitutes inducement.

---

8 Lord MacNaghten in *Quinn v Leathem* [1901] AC 495, p. 510.

9 [1994] EMLR 44.

10 n 3.

11 [1966] 1 WLR 691.

12 n 3.

13 Denning MR in *Emerald Construction v Lowthian* [1966] 1 WLR 691, p. 701 opined: 'if the officers deliberately sought to get this contract terminated, heedless of its terms, regardless whether it was terminated by breach or not, they would do wrong. For it is unlawful for a third party to procure a breach of contract knowingly, or recklessly, indifferent to whether it is a breach or not'.

14 Note that Lord Hoffman in *OBG Ltd* regarded the analysis of intent of the defendant to be based on a subjective test. Therefore, a defendant may not have the necessary intent to cause a breach where there is an honest belief that the action will not cause a breach of contract – *MBC of Solihull v NUT* [1985] IRLR 211.

However, there are a variety of ways of intervening in contractual relations short of this active inducement of breach. The Donovan Commission[15] identified a clear boundary between the giving of mere advice or information to an individual and actively encouraging, persuading or instructing a person to break a contract:

> a trade union official who advises a customer of an employer in dispute that he should consider his business relations with that employer in the light of the dispute, commits no tort even if in consequence of such advice the customer breaks his contract . . . [nor] will it . . . constitute an inducement to break a contract even if he calls attention to the possible dangers for the customer of continuing to deal with the employer in dispute.

In *Square Grip Reinforcement Co Ltd v MacDonald*,[16] Lord Milligan believed that statements or advice had to be construed in the context of the circumstances. Hence, an inducement had occurred where union officials provided workers with certain information concerning a recognition dispute elsewhere, knowing that on hearing this information the workers were highly likely to take industrial action. The Court of Appeal also reverted to the much wider construction of the term in *Union Traffic v TGWU*.[17] The court ruled that even where pickets are not actively persuading employees to break their employment contracts, their mere presence at the entrance to a workplace may be sufficient to amount to an inducement.

The modern position is therefore to construe the requirement of inducement quite widely. If the gist of the words used or the act committed, in the prevailing circumstances, causes a breach of the contract, then the element of inducement of breach has been satisfied. This was certainly the approach undertaken by the High Court in *Govia Thameslink Railway Ltd v ASLEF*[18] where it was held that a text message informing members of a break-down in negotiations and intention to ballot for industrial action could constitute an inducement to take action for the purposes of the tort.

❖ THINKING POINT

In *DC Thomson Ltd v Deakin*,[19] Jenkins LJ suggested that general exhortations issued in the course of a trade dispute such as 'Stop supplies to X', 'Refuse to handle X's goods', were not necessarily unlawful inducements. Do you think this approach to inducement would be followed to-day?

20.3.1.3 The defence of justification

Where all the ingredients of the tort are present it may still be possible for the defendant to escape liability if it can be shown in the particular circumstances of the case there was 'justification' in law for the inducement of breach. However, trade union action in inducing breach of contract for the purposes of achieving benefits for their membership is not sufficient justification, even where the defendant trade unionist was acting in good faith and with an absence of malice.

15 Royal Commission on Trade Unions and Employers' Associations, Cmnd 3623, 1968.
16 [1968] SLT 65.
17 [1989] IRLR 127.
18 [2016] IRLR 686.
19 [1952] Ch 646.

This was the essence of the judgment of Romer LJ in the Court of Appeal in *South Wales Miners' Federation v Glamorgan Coal Co.*[20] Miners were paid on a sliding scale dependent on the selling price of coal. The scarcer coal was, the higher the price of coal and the higher the miners' wages. To increase their members' wages, the trade union persuaded its members to turn up for work intermittently, so as to limit the supply of coal. Although the union had no dispute with the employer and took action genuinely believing that it was in the best interests of their members and of the employer, Romer LJ refused to apply the defence as:

> a defendant sued for knowingly procuring such a breach is not justified of necessity merely by showing that he had no personal animus against the employer or that it was to the advantage or interest of both the defendant and the workman that the contract should be broken.[21]

The defence has only been successfully invoked in cases where the defendant has acted in furtherance of a moral duty or in the public interest. For example, in *Brimelow v Casson*,[22] the defendant justifiably induced chorus girls to leave the claimant's employment because there was evidence that they were paid such low wages that they resorted to prostitution. Simonds J in *Camden Nominees v Foray*[23] doubted the decision in *Brimelow* and attempted to narrow the defence with the argument that the defence should be restricted to cases where persons act in pursuance of a legal, rather than moral duty – for example, a doctor who is in a legal relationship with his patient may instruct an employee to give up work for health reasons without attracting liability for inducing breach of the patient's contract of employment.[24]

20.4 Causing economic loss by unlawful means

This tort incorporates a number of unlawful activities that were previously classified as separate torts, including indirectly inducing a breach of contract, interference with trade or business, intimidation and conspiracy. They are all variants or sub-divisions of the broad overall, genus tort of causing loss by unlawful means. In *OBG Ltd*,[25] the House of Lords defined the unlawful means tort as where the defendant intentionally causes loss to the claimant by interfering directly with the freedom of a third party to deal with the claimant with the unlawful means being independently actionable by that third party.

20.4.1 Indirectly inducing breach of contract

Where a contract of employment is broken due to a direct inducement by trade union officials there may well be further contractual implications for the claimant employer. In this situation, commercial contracts of supply may be broken. In such a case the union may be liable for the tort of causing loss by unlawful means – previously identified as indirectly inducing a breach of the commercial contract. The unlawful means is the direct inducement causing the breach of employment contracts. The question as to whether there was an intention to cause the breach and loss to the claimant can be more complex because of the factual circumstances.

20 [1903] 2 KB 545.
21 Ibid. p. 574. See also, Slade J in *Grieg v Insole* [1978] I WLR 302, pp. 340–342.
22 [1924] 1 Ch 302.
23 [1940] Ch 352.
24 See also *Timeplan Education Group Ltd v National Union of Teachers* [1997] IRLR 457, p. 460.
25 n 3.

In some circumstances, loss may occur as an inevitable, but accidental, consequence of the industrial action. An intention to cause loss is inextricably linked to the level of knowledge the defendant has of the contract. As noted earlier, ordinarily, an instigator of industrial action is fully aware that employees work under a contract of employment and for employees to stop work is a breach of that contract. This is not always the case with commercial contracts of supply. However, where the contract that has been broken is one regularly employed in the defendant's trade or industry, a form of constructive knowledge of its terms can be ascribed to the defendant. We can see the application of this principle in *Merkur Island Shipping Co v Laughton*,[26] where a union instruction calling for strike action resulted in a breach of a complex 'merchant charter party' contract of hire concerning the sub-leasing of several ships. The House of Lords accepted the contention that even though the union official was not privy to the complex terms of the contract (and so did not know for certain exactly who the other parties were or that the action would cause a breach of the contract of hire), it could be assumed that such an official was well informed about these types of contracts common in the shipping industry.

The use of the device of 'deemed knowledge' was reaffirmed by the Court of Appeal in *Middlebrook Mushrooms Ltd v TGWU*[27] and by the House of Lords in *OBG Ltd*.[28] Lord Hoffman confirmed Lord Denning's view in *Emerald Construction Co Ltd v Lowthian*,[29] that it was not necessary for the union organisers of industrial action to have knowledge of the precise terms of a contract so long as they had 'the means of knowledge – which they deliberately disregarded. . . . Like the man who turns a blind eye'.[30]

Whether there is an actual breach of a commercial contract depends on an examination of the terms of that contract. Moreover, Jenkins LJ, in *DC Thomson Ltd v Deakin*,[31] considered that where the claimant is alleging breach of a commercial contract of supply it must be shown that, because of the withdrawal of the services of the employees concerned, the contract breaker was in practice unable to perform the contract. So, for example, where a commercial contract of supply is broken (due to strike action by lorry driver employees), but the goods or services could be provided by some other alternative means (such as by hiring alternative transport), it is arguable liability will not ensue as there has not been a breach of the contract of supply as a 'necessary consequence' of the defendant's act.

20.4.2 Interference with trade or business

As a consequence of an expansionist and innovative approach to trade union liability in order to outflank the immunities, there have been historical attempts by the judiciary to supplement the tort of inducing breach of contract by developing liability by way of interference with contract, trade or business, short of breach. The House of Lords have made it clear in OBG Ltd that liability can only be founded on unlawful behaviour that is independently actionable by the affected third party. Thus, earlier authorities (in particular *Torquay Hotel Ltd v Cousins*[32] and *Merkur Island v Laughton*[33])

26 [1983] IRLR 218.

27 [1993] ICR 612, *per* Neil LJ: 'in many cases a third party (to a contract) may be deemed to know of the almost certain existence of a contract and indeed of some of its likely terms'.

28 n 3.

29 [1966] 1 WLR 691, p. 700.

30 Ibid. p. 701.

31 [1952] Ch 646.

32 [1969] 2 Ch 106.

33 n 26.

establishing trade union liability based on bare interference without clear use of unlawful means have been disapproved.

In *Torquay Hotel v Cousins*[34] the claimant hotel owner had criticised the defendant's actions in a dispute the union had with other hotel owners in the region. In response, the union telephoned the oil company Esso, advising them directly that oil supplies to the hotel should cease and that any supplies delivered would be met by a picket line. The contract for the supply of oil between the hotel and Esso included a *force majeure* exemption clause which limited Esso's liability in circumstances where a failure to supply oil was due to an industrial dispute. Lord Denning argued that, although there had not been a breach of contract, interference short of breach was in itself actionable, as '[t]he time has come when the principle (of inducing breach of contract) should be extended to cover deliberate and direct interference with the execution of a contract'.[35] This doctrine was later re-affirmed in *Merkur Island v Laughton*.[36]

The House of Lords in *OBG Ltd*[37] criticised the judgments in *Torquay Hotel* and *Merkur Island*, making it clear that any interference short of breach must be accompanied by unlawful means – thus, where there is some independent unlawful means, interference short of breach can be actionable. This is demonstrated by *Hadmor Productions Ltd v Hamilton*.[38] The claimant was an independent TV production company which was engaged in contractual negotiations with Thames TV concerning the transmission of certain of their programmes. During the dispute, the defendants threatened to instruct their members at Thames TV to refuse to transmit any programmes produced by the claimant – a threat to induce a breach of employment contract. This was an actionable interference with the claimant's trade and business – as the threat to induce the breach of contract of employment constituted the tort of intimidation which is the unlawful means for purposes of liability.

20.4.3 Intimidation

A threat directed at a third party which causes them to act to the detriment of the claimant causing them economic damage is actionable as a variant of the tort of causing loss by unlawful means. This tort (known at the time as intimidation) can be traced back to eighteenth century cases, such as *Tarleton v McGawley*.[39] Here, the master of a trading ship A, off the coast of Africa, fired a warning shot at a canoe, the third party, which was about to trade with another ship, B, a commercial rival of ship A. As a result, the canoe turned back and the rival trading ship B lost business and subsequent profits. It was this threat of violence against the third party resulting in loss to ship B which was actionable as tortious intimidation.

In the industrial field, unions can secure their aims by the threat of industrial action and ordinarily do not need to resort to violent tactics.[40] Consequently, until the landmark case of *Rookes v Barnard*,[41] this tort was rarely committed by trade unionists threatening strike action. The House of Lords revolutionised the law on intimidation by holding that a threat to break an employment contract (that is, a threat to go on strike) was an unlawful threat for the purposes of the tort of intimidation. Lord Devlin commented that the threat to break or to induce others to break a contract

34 n 32.
35 Ibid. p. 138.
36 n 26.
37 n 3.
38 [1981] ICR 690.
39 (1793) 1 Peake 270.
40 For examples of actionable intimidation caused by threats of violence, see *NGN Ltd v SOGAT 82* [1986] IRLR 337.
41 [1964] AC 1129.

of employment was as much an illegal threat for the purposes of the tort as a threat to commit violence to person or property, as

> all that matters to the plaintiff is that, metaphorically speaking, a club has been used. It does not matter to the plaintiff what the club is made of – whether it is a physical club or an economic club, a tortious club or an otherwise illegal club.[42]

This decision of the House of Lords caused understandable alarm in the union movement. Kahn-Freund described the decision as a 'frontal attack upon the right to strike'. Lord Wedderburn observed that it was 'one strange result [of] the common law' that a mere threat to strike was unlawful when actual strike action itself was not.[43] The development of this tort was a highly effective method of 'outflanking' the existing immunities, until the Trade Disputes Act 1965, a year later, closed off liability by explicitly bestowing an immunity on strike organisers and union members for threatening to induce a breach of an employment contract or threatening to break an employment contract.

20.4.4 Conspiracy

Two forms of the tort of conspiracy may be distinguished: general conspiracy to injure, often known as simple conspiracy or lawful means conspiracy, and the more specific conspiracy to commit an unlawful act or unlawful means conspiracy. It is thought that the requirements for these torts have not been affected by the decision in *OBG Ltd.*[44]

Conspiracy to injure occurs where two or more persons combine for the intended purpose of injuring another without justification. It may well be that the activity in itself is lawful if undertaken by an individual but not when done in combination with another.[45] Thus *prima facie*, economic loss caused to an employer by interference with workers' contracts is actionable as a conspiracy to injure unless it could be said the union's actions were justified in some way.

In the commercial case of *Mogul Steamship Co v McGregor, Gow & Co*,[46] the Court of Appeal held that an association of ship-owners who had driven a rival ship-owner out of business by lowering their charges had not committed an actionable conspiracy as they had acted merely to protect their legitimate trade and their profits which was a justifiable aim of their competitive pricing policy. The real purpose of the combination was to advance the commercial interests of the association, not to cause the loss to the claimant.

In *Quinn v Leathem*,[47] trade union interests were barely recognised by the House of Lords. The defendants, wishing to enforce a closed shop, prevailed upon an important customer not to trade with the claimant after he had refused to dismiss non-union staff. The House of Lords justified a finding of actionable conspiracy on the grounds that the combination of workers had intentionally caused loss to the plaintiff and their main purpose in doing so was not to further their own legitimate interests in setting up a closed shop, but to injure the claimant for reasons of revenge.

This decision was a serious blow to trade union attempts to obtain benefits for their membership via industrial action and was one of the catalysts for the passage of the Trade Disputes Act 1906 which provided an immunity for this and other torts. However, the immunity for conspiracy is

42 Ibid. p. 1209.
43 *The Worker and the Law*, 3rd edn., 1986, p. 42.
44 n 33.
45 Bowen LJ in *Mogul* (1889) 23 QBD 598, p. 616.
46 (1889) 23 QB 598.
47 [1901] AC 495.

now rarely required as, in a change of judicial attitudes after the First World War, trade union objects were legitimised by a number of judgments.[48] The House of Lords' decision in *Crofter Handwoven Harris Tweed Co v Veitch*[49] confirmed that no liability will attach to a trade union engaged in a genuine trade dispute with a claimant, such as on an issue concerning terms and conditions of employment. Once the *bona fide* trade union purpose is established, whether or not the defendants knew damage to the claimant was a consequence of their actions is not relevant[50]; nor is the fact that the conspirators behave in 'a selfish, tyrannous and irresponsible' manner.[51]

Where there are mixed motives for the union's action, such as where the main purpose is to protect or enhance a legitimate interest, but another reason for the action is because of a degree of ill will towards the claimant, the legitimate interest must be 'predominant'.[52] For instance, in *Huntley v Thornton*,[53] members of a strike committee pressurised the employer to take action against a non-striking member of the union. This was an actionable conspiracy as the defendants were not furthering a trade dispute but a grudge or personal matter.

The second form of conspiracy occurs where a combination intentionally inflicts damage on another by the use of unlawful means. The conspirators have committed a separate unlawful act and this, committed in combination, is the additional tort of conspiracy. In the industrial context, there may be liability for conspiracy to commit the tort of inducing breach of contract. Pickets during a dispute may, by their actions, individually commit the tort of nuisance. They may together be additionally liable for the tort of conspiracy to commit a nuisance.

As these acts above are unlawful in themselves, there may be little need to frame an action in conspiracy because each of the individual conspirators will be liable for the wrong they have committed. Very occasionally, such an action in conspiracy may be used to sue an individual who has not committed any wrong but who was involved in the dispute. This occurred in *Rookes v Barnard*.[54] The full-time union official could not have been sued for the tort of intimidation in threatening to break a contract of employment because he was not employed by the third-party employer and so did not have a contract to break. But, in organising the threats to break the contracts of employment, he was sued for conspiring to commit the tort of intimidation.

The ambit of the tort was substantially narrowed by the judgment of the House of Lords in *Lonhro Ltd v Shell Petroleum Ltd*.[55] It was held by Lord Diplock that, for liability to arise, the conspirator's predominant purpose must be to injure the claimant rather than to further or preserve their own legitimate interests. Otherwise, he said, the tort would be extended beyond its natural parameters. However, more recent House of Lords authority has cast doubt on Diplock's judgment. In *Lonhro Ltd v Fayed*[56] the House of Lords refused to accept Diplock's reasoning in *Shell* and concluded that, as there must be a distinction between the two forms of conspiracy, an intention to injure the plaintiff was an issue relevant only to simple conspiracy. Consequently, if the conspiracy was unlawful – in that the parties were actively engaged in some illegal activity, such as breach of contract, tort or crime – then the predominant purpose of the combiners was irrelevant, whether or not the purpose was to further or protect a legitimate interest of their own.

48 See *White v Riley* [1921] 1 Ch 1; *Reynolds v Shipping Federation* [1924] 1 Ch 28; *Sorrell v Smith* [1925] AC 700.

49 [1942] AC 435.

50 Viscount Simon, p. 445.

51 *Stratford v Lindley* [1965] AC 269, p. 300, *per* Salmon LJ.

52 On the judicially defined legitimate objectives of trade unions and their members, see also *Scala Ballroom (Wolverhampton) Ltd v Ratcliffe* [1958] 1 WLR 1057; *Stratford v Lindley* [1965] AC 269.

53 [1957] 1 WLR 321.

54 [1964] AC 1129.

55 [1982] AC 173.

56 [1991] 3 All ER 303.

❖ THINKING POINT

Taking into account the clarification of the economic torts in *OBG Ltd*, do you think trade unions are more, or less likely, to violate these torts when engaging in industrial action?

20.5 The expansion of 'unlawful means' and other liabilities

The definition of unlawful means is a crucial issue in determining the liability of trade unions. The common form of unlawful means in industrial action is the tort of direct inducement to break a contract of employment. However, inducing breach of contract (as well as acts that were previously defined as the torts of intimidation and conspiracy) are not 'unlawful means' for the purposes of liability where the statutory immunities apply. This is because the statutory immunities provide that so long as the acts are 'in contemplation or furtherance of a trade dispute' such illegalities 'are not actionable', which has been interpreted to mean that they are not 'unlawful means'. Therefore, over the years since the Trades Disputes Act 1906, the courts have occasionally resorted to looking for new forms of illegalities, outside the protection of the immunities, to act as unlawful means for the purposes of tort liability.[57]

For example, the House of Lords in *Rookes v Barnard*[58] debated whether an employee's breach of employment contract committed during strike action could be unlawful means for the purposes of tort liability. To ensure that no future expansionist court resurrected the issue, the Labour government piloted through a provision in the Trade Union and Labour Relations Act 1974 which stated that 'for the avoidance of doubt' a bare breach of contract was not unlawful means for the purposes of establishing liability in tort. However, on the repeal of this provision by the Employment Act 1980, the law was returned to a state of some uncertainty.

Consequently, in *Barretts & Baird v IPCS*,[59] Henry J held that it was arguable that a breach of an employment contract *per se* can be unlawful means for the purposes of an action by a third party for breach of commercial contracts caused by the strike action so long as there was an intent to injure the third-party claimant. As this case was not appealed to a higher court, it must remain an open question whether the reasoning in the case is correct. Should this be followed in future cases it would have dramatic consequences. It would mean that those on strike would be liable in tort for inducing breach of commercial contracts whilst the organisers of the strike would continue to enjoy the protection of the immunities.

The courts have also generated further illegalities which provide employers with new causes of action in civil law unconstrained by the immunities, the most important being inducing breach of a statutory duty, economic duress and breach of an equitable obligation. These new liabilities

57 The conventional approach to this issue is to look for an act that is actionable in tort (such as nuisance or trespass: *MGN Ltd v NGA* [1984] IRLR 397). Some of the older examples of possible unlawful means are thus of very doubtful authority. See *Daily Mirror Newspaper Ltd v Gardner* [1968] 2 QB 762 (operating an agreement contrary to restrictive practices legislation); *Camellia Tanker v ITWF* [1976] ICR 274 (alleged breach of local bylaws); *Acrow (Automation) Ltd v Rex Chainbelt Inc* [1971] 1 WLR 1676 (contempt of court); *Associated Newspapers v Wade* [1979] IRLR 201 (interference with the freedom of the press contrary to Art. 10 of the European Convention on Human Rights).

58 [1964] AC 1129.

59 [1987] IRLR 3.

may be directly actionable in their own right as a tort or can be used as a form of unlawful means for the purposes of establishing the tort of causing loss by unlawful means.

20.5.1 Inducing breach of a statutory duty

Industrial action may result in the contravention of a statutory duty imposed on employees or on employers. In certain limited circumstances, employers or third party suppliers may have a remedy for this illegality. A clear example is provided in *Cunard Co v Stacey*[60] where the Court of Appeal construed the Merchant Shipping Act 1894 in such a way as to permit the employers to sue the union organisers of industrial action in tort who had induced their members to break provisions of the Act that criminalised strike action.

However, not every breach of a criminal statute is necessarily unlawful at civil law, as not every crime is a tort. In *Gouriet v UPW*,[61] Post Office workers, by delaying mail to South Africa, had *prima facie* committed criminal offences under the Post Office Act 1953. The High Court decision to refuse to permit an action in tort against the defendant on the grounds that there was no power within the statute for the claimant to sue for breach of statutory duty was subsequently supported by the House of Lords. This judgment was further endorsed by the House of Lords in *Lonhro Ltd v Shell Petroleum*.[62] Their Lordships made it clear that a breach of statutory duty (which may have criminal or civil ramifications) does not by itself give rise to a civil action by a particular plaintiff unless it can be shown, on the construction of the statute, that a duty is explicitly owed to the claimant as a member of an identifiable class.

Lord Denning MR attempted to develop a wider general rule in *Meade v Haringey BC*,[63] which does not depend upon the scope and language of the statute. Here, the parents of children who were unable to go to school because of strike action by ancillary staff issued writs to enforce the local authority to perform their statutory duty to provide full-time education under the Education Act 1944. According to Lord Denning the trade unions were the dominating influence in requiring the schools to be closed, this was therefore a call on the local authority to break its statutory duty to provide full-time education, which was arguably unlawful means for the purposes of an action in tort by those injured by the action.[64]

Considering the extent of public services regulated by statute, Denning's approach, if correct, would be of some significance, and of some concern, to public sector unions. However, Denning's broad formulation,[65] which gives third parties automatic rights of action on breach of statute, has been disavowed in subsequent cases which have reemphasised the strict 'construction' test for establishing an actionable breach of statutory duty.[66]

In *Associated British Ports v TGWU*,[67] the trade unions objected to proposals to abolish the statutory scheme regulating the supply of dock labour. After negotiations with employers failed, the unions threatened to take strike action. The House of Lords held that the clause solely imposed a contractual rather than a statutory requirement to work, therefore, the issue of breach of statutory duty and unlawful means did not arise. Lord Hoffman in *OBG Ltd*[68] has reiterated the principle that unlawful

60 [1955] 2 LR 247.

61 [1978] AC 435.

62 [1982] AC 173.

63 [1979] 2 All ER 1016.

64 Ibid. p. 1026.

65 Also strongly argued by Lord Denning in *ex p Island Records* [1978] Ch 122, p. 136.

66 See *Lonhro Ltd v Shell Petroleum Ltd* [1982] AC 173, p. 187; *RCA v Pollard* [1983] Ch 135, noted by Lord Wedderburn (1983) MLR 224; *CBS Songs Ltd v Amstrad Electronics* [1988] Ch 61; *Lonhro v Fayed* [1990] 2 QB 479, p. 489; *X (A Minor) v Bedfordshire CC* [1995] 3 All ER 353; *O'Rourke v Camden London BC* [1998] AC 188; *Michaels v Taylor Woodrow Developments Ltd* [2000] 4 All ER 645.

67 [1989] IRLR 399.

means requires the third party to be able to independently take action against the defendant. This, therefore, excludes breaches of statute where there is no civil cause of action by the relevant third party.[69]

20.5.2 Economic duress

Economic duress is a contractual doctrine, whereby a contract is declared void if it is entered into on the basis of duress. Usually, the doctrine operates where one party is in such a strong bargaining position that the will of the other party is coerced by the other's actions. In these circumstances, the coerced party may claim restitution of monies paid under the contract.

The use of the doctrine in the context of industrial disputes was first discussed in *Universe Tankships Inc of Monrovia v ITWF*.[70] A ship owned by the claimant was boycotted by members of the union on its arrival at the port of Milford Haven. In order to lift the boycott, the claimant agreed to pay a sum to the union's welfare fund. The claimant made a claim for restitution of this sum on the grounds that consent for entry into this special agreement was vitiated by the industrial pressure imposed by the union.

Although the majority of the House of Lords agreed that the use of economic duress to induce another person to part with money or property is not a tort *per se*, it was decided that the contractual doctrine was *prima facie* applicable in these circumstances.[71] Lords Diplock and Scarman continued, however, by stating that if the duress was applied 'in contemplation or furtherance of a trade dispute' then for reasons of 'public policy' the action for economic duress must fail. These issues were partially reconsidered by the House of Lords in *Dimskal Shipping v ITWF*.[72] The facts were very similar, in that a ship owned by the claimant was boycotted by the defendant, held in port and not released until the owners complied with the defendant's demands. These demands were, *inter alia*, that all crew received ITF employment contracts, backdated pay and the payment of sums to the ITF welfare fund. Following and affirming the previous House of Lords decision in *Universe Tankships*, it was held that this use of illegitimate economic pressure was a form of actionable duress. Consequently, as the payments were induced by duress the contracts were voidable at the instance of the claimant.

20.5.3 Inducing breach of an equitable obligation

In *Prudential Assurance Co v Lorenz*,[73] during an industrial dispute, union officials representing insurance agents working for the claimant company induced the agents not to submit their collected premiums to the company. Plowman J believed there was sufficient authority for the proposition that the defendants were interfering, not just with a contractual obligation under the agent's contract with the claimant, but with a general equitable duty 'to account' implied by the general law relating to fiduciary duties.

As there is no immunity for causes of action based on breach of equitable obligations, if this head of liability was expanded by a creative and innovative judiciary into a general liability for inducing breach of trust, unions would be open to substantial legal action. However, in *Metall und*

68 n 3.

69 As Lord Hoffman stated in *OBG Ltd* ibid. at para. 32B–32G 'it is not for the courts to create a cause of action out of a regulatory or criminal statute which Parliament did not intend to be actionable in private law'.

70 [1982] IRLR 200.

71 The majority also noted that the form the duress takes may provide evidence of the tort of intimidation.

72 [1992] IRLR 78.

73 [1971] 11 KIR 78.

Rohstoff AG v Donaldson Inc,[74] the Court of Appeal refused to extend liability to other equitable liabilities by specifically stating that there was no such tort of inducing breach of trust, so limiting the common-law action to the facts of *Prudential*.[75]

20.5.4 The right to secure the provision of goods or services

In the Green Paper, *Industrial Relations in the 1990s*,[76] it was argued that the 'distinctive feature of strikes and other forms of industrial action in the public services is that they are often targeted on the life of the community'.[77] It was thus proposed that those members of the public who were seriously inconvenienced by unlawful industrial action (such as commuters stranded by a transport strike) should be given the right to enforce the provision of these services by legal action.

In the Green Paper, this right was exclusively linked to the non-performance of public services. In the draft legislation, it was extended to services provided by all sectors of the economy. Despite the combined efforts of the CBI[78] and the TUC all representations for amendments to the draft legislation were rejected and the provisions were enacted in the Trade Union Reform and Employment Rights Act 1993, incorporated as ss. 235A–C of the TULR(C)A 1992.

The right operates where a trade union[79] or other person induces another to take part in unlawful industrial action[80] and the effect or likely effect of the industrial action is or will be to 'prevent or delay the supply of goods or services or reduce their quality'.[81] In these circumstances, an individual member of the public (whether or not legally entitled to the supply of the goods or services) can apply to the High Court for an injunction to prohibit the action. There is no requirement on the individual taking action to show they have been actually inconvenienced or suffered loss.

The provision at the time was criticised for providing third parties who are not involved in the dispute an opportunity to interfere in union-employer relations whatever their individual motivation. It was noted that an employer who is directly involved may have good reasons for not wishing to take action in the courts. The 'concerned citizen' is thus able to override the employer's wishes despite (or because of) the possibility of settlement. Although very few applications under this section have been made, it still remains in force.

20.6 Trade union immunities – the 'golden formula'

Where, as a consequence of the actions of trade union members or officials, one or more of the common law torts have been committed, the second stage of determining trade union liability is to ascertain whether any of the statutory immunities are applicable to the tortious act at issue.

---

74 [1989] 3 All ER 14.

75 Approved by Hoffman LJ in *Law Debenture Trust Corp v Ural Caspian Oil Corp Ltd* [1993] 1 WLR 138, p. 151.

76 Cm 1602, 1991, Chapter 4.

77 Para. 4.5.

78 The CBI was critical of the proposal because an employer may be legitimately hesitant in enforcing the law so as not to disturb the chances of a negotiated settlement. Where members of the public are entitled to do so, the results may be catastrophic for industrial relations.

79 By s. 235A(6), an act of inducement by a trade union is assumed if it has authorised or endorsed the act of another.

80 Industrial action is unlawful if it is actionable in tort *per se* by an employer. The Act also provides that it is unlawful if a valid ballot has not been held and the applicant is a union member with the right of complaint under TULR(C)A 1992, s. 62. This provides a right of action to the citizen should the industrial action not be in breach of contract (a necessary component of the tort of inducing breach of contract).

81 Section 235A(1).

As we have already observed, amendments to the Trade Disputes Act 1906 were necessary in the 1960s and 1970s as a consequence of judicial decisions which circumvented the immunities by expanding the scope of the established torts and by developing new forms of tort liability. The amended immunities were consolidated into the Trade Union and Labour Relations Act 1974. In contrast to previous legislative policy, statutory (rather than judicial) changes, initiated during the 1980s, have narrowed the circumstances when the immunities apply and enlarged the number of exceptions to them. The core immunities and all relevant amendments are now found by reference to the Trade Union and Labour Relations (Consolidation) Act (TULR(C)A) 1992.[82]

Protection for inducing breach of contract in the direct or indirect form (causing loss by unlawful means) or for the use of the tort as 'unlawful means' for other liability is provided by s. 219(1)(a). Immunity for the tort of intimidation (that is, threatening to induce a breach of contract) is found in s. 219(1)(b) and for the tort of conspiracy to injure in s. 219(2).[83]

These immunities only apply where the act that generates common law liability has been committed 'in contemplation or furtherance of a trade dispute'. This has become known as the 'golden formula'.[84] If the industrial action falls outside this formula, then the immunities will be suspended and an interlocutory injunction may be granted to halt the action and damages will be awarded against the organisers and the union. If the industrial action falls within this formula, then the immunities will apply unless they are withdrawn because the industrial action offends against one or more of the exceptions examined later in this chapter.

20.6.1 Contemplation (of a trade dispute)

The classic meaning of these words is contained in the speech of Lord Loreburn in *Conway v Wade*.[85] His Lordship said that, for the industrial action to be 'in contemplation . . . of a trade dispute', it is necessary for the dispute to be imminent and the act to be done 'in expectation of and with a view to it'.[86] Thus, where a union makes a genuine claim on an employer to improve the conditions or pay of its members and the employers reject the claim, a trade dispute is in contemplation even though no active dispute has yet arisen.

In *Cory Lighterage v TGWU*,[87] the Court of Appeal had held that, where a dispute does not arise because the employer has unexpectedly acceded to union demands, any pre-emptive union action is not 'in contemplation of a dispute'. This interpretation of the formula was reversed by the Trade Union and Labour Relations Act 1974 – now enacted as s. 244(4) of the TULR(C)A 1992. This establishes that an act, which if resisted would have led to a trade dispute, is to be treated as being in contemplation of a trade dispute, even though no dispute has in fact arisen because the other party has submitted to the demand.

20.6.2 Furtherance (of a trade dispute)

In order to 'further' a dispute, it must already be in existence. Acts taken in the course of the dispute must be discharged so as to support or aid and assist in the dispute.

---

82 As amended by the Trade Union Reform and Employment Rights Act 1993, the Employment Relations Acts 1999 and 2004 and the Trade Union Act 2016.

83 This is not extended to conspiracy to commit an unlawful act, e.g. conspiracy to commit a trespass or a statutory tort.

84 This expression was first coined by Wedderburn KW (now Lord) in *The Worker and the Law*, 1st edn., 1965, p. 222.

85 [1909] AC 506.

86 Ibid. p. 512.

87 [1973] IRLR 152.

In a trio of cases – *Express Newspapers Ltd v McShane*,[88] *NWL Ltd v Woods*[89] and *Duport Steel v Sirs*,[90] the Court of Appeal held that whether a particular act was 'furthering' a trade dispute should be interpreted objectively and must not be so remote that it has no real effect on the trade dispute. This meant that purely sympathetic secondary action, which did not in practical terms apply any pressure on the employer in the primary dispute, was unlawful. The House of Lords, however, in *Express Newspapers v McShane*[91] disagreed with this analysis. Their Lordships asserted that 'furtherance . . . of a trade dispute' should be examined in the context of what the union subjectively believed. Did the defendants honestly and genuinely believe the action they were taking would further union objectives in that dispute? If so, then they were acting in furtherance of the dispute.

❖ THINKING POINT

Does evidence of a bad motive – such as the union acting out of spite – cast light on the honesty of the intention?

The overruling of the Court of Appeal[92] on this issue meant that purely sympathetic secondary action remained lawful. In response, one of the first acts by the new Conservative government elected in 1979 (which had welcomed the Court of Appeal's decisions) was to legislate to withdraw the immunities in these circumstances. However, secondary action which was likely to achieve its objective continued to be protected, that is, action which disrupted a contract to supply goods or services to the primary employer or where secondary action was taken against an associated company because the primary employer had switched production to that associated company. These 'gateways' to legality were removed by the Employment Act 1990. Consequently, all secondary action is now unlawful and will result in a withdrawal of the immunities.

20.6.3 Trade dispute

A dispute has been defined as a 'fairly definite' difference of opinion.[93] Whether a dispute has arisen is not determined by the subjective view of the parties, but is to be reasonably inferred from the facts of the situation. For example, in *Bents Brewery Co Ltd v Hogan*,[94] a trade union official sent out a questionnaire to members of the union, who were employed as managers of public houses, requesting information on takings, wage bills, etc., in order to have this data available for a future wage claim. The disclosure of this information was in breach of the managers' contract of employment. On an action against the union for inducing breach of contract, the court accepted the argument that, as the questionnaire had simply been used to collect information for future collective bargaining purposes, there was no current dispute – no 'difference of opinion' in being

88 [1979] ICR 210.
89 [1979] IRLR 321.
90 [1980] IRLR 112.
91 [1980] ICR 42.
92 See also the House of Lords judgments in *NWL Ltd v Woods* [1979] IRLR 478 and *Duport Steel Ltd v Sirs* [1980] IRLR 116.
93 Lord Loreburn in *Conway v Wade* [1909] AC 506, p. 520.
94 [1945] 2 All ER 570.

or 'imminent'. A dispute would only arise if, after the results of the questionnaire had been considered, a claim was submitted and rejected.[95]

Whether the same objective test can be applied to determining when a dispute ends is open to doubt. In the majority of circumstances, a dispute ends in an agreement between the parties or where one side has abandoned the dispute. In *Stratford & Sons Ltd v Lindley*,[96] the House of Lords took account of objective evidence in deciding that the union had withdrawn from the recognition dispute. Contrary to this authority, the Court of Appeal, in *Newham BC v NALGO*,[97] introduced a subjective element to the test by suggesting that a dispute may continue for so long as one side genuinely believes that it has not been settled.

Once it is established that there is an actual or imminent dispute, the next issue to resolve is whether the dispute is a 'trade' dispute. Arguably the proper role of trade unions is to engage in collective bargaining on behalf of their members for improved terms and conditions of employment and to represent their members on all issues and disputes that arise at the workplace. Accordingly, it is not legitimate for a trade union to go beyond this narrow industrial role by seeking to influence government policy or to restrict an employer's freedom of action on other matters. The concept of the 'trade dispute' in the statute is, for that reason, drafted so as to distinguish genuine industrial disputes (where trade unions can legitimately expect to be protected from legal action) from political or personal grievances.

The definition of a trade dispute is contained in s. 244 of the TULR(C)A 1992.

> (1) In this Part a 'trade dispute' means a dispute between workers and their employer which relates wholly or mainly to one or more of the following:
>
> (a) terms and conditions of employment,[98] or the physical conditions in which any workers are required to work;
> (b) engagement or non-engagement, or termination or suspension of employment or the duties of employment, of one or more workers;
> (c) allocation of work or the duties of employment between workers or groups of workers;
> (d) matters of discipline;
> (e) a worker's membership or non-membership of a trade union;
> (f) facilities for officials of trade unions; and
> (g) machinery for negotiation or consultation, and other procedures, relating to any of the above matters, including the recognition of a union by an employer or employers' association.

In *BBC v Hearn*,[99] the union attempted to overcome the distinction between industrial and political or ideological disputes by contending that the dispute was about the failure of the employer to agree to the inclusion of a contractual term permitting their members to engage in an activity excluded by s. 244. Here, television technicians threatened to prevent transmission of the FA Cup Final to South Africa because of the policy of the union to oppose the apartheid regime in South Africa. Counsel for the union submitted that this was a trade dispute about terms and conditions

95 See also *Health Computing Ltd v Meek* [1980] IRLR 437.
96 [1965] AC 269.
97 [1993] IRLR 83.
98 An expansive interpretation of this phrase is favoured. See Lord Diplock in *Hadmor Productions Ltd v Hamilton* [1982] IRLR 102, p. 108.
99 [1977] IRLR 275.

of employment, as the union wished to vary their members' contracts to introduce a term that would allow them to opt out of work that involved broadcasting to South Africa.

The Court of Appeal took the view that this was a straightforward coercive 'political' action unconnected to a trade dispute issue. The contractual device was a mere ruse to give a semblance of legality to the union's actions. However, in the course of the judgment, the Court of Appeal stated *obiter* that if there had been evidence of a previous attempt to renegotiate contracts of employment – to allow employees to opt out of broadcasts they found obnoxious – a trade dispute may well have been in existence on that issue.

This approach to the issue did not find favour with the majority of the House of Lords in *Universe Tankships Inc of Monrovia v ITWF*.[100] Lord Cross made it clear that a dispute that in reality has no connection with terms and conditions of employment cannot suddenly become such a dispute merely on a demand by a union that a term, permitting the employees' action, is incorporated into a contract of employment.[101]

20.6.4 Disputes with government

It is often argued that disputes that involve the government of the day tend to be motivated by political considerations and, therefore, cannot be genuine trade disputes. This is the implication of the decision in *National Sailors' and Firemen's Union v Reed*,[102] where a general strike called by the Trades Union Congress (TUC) in support of workers already taking action did not have the protection of the Trades Disputes Act 1906. Astbury J held that the strike was not in furtherance of a trade dispute as 'no trade dispute does or can exist between the Trades Union Congress on the one hand and the government and the nation on the other'.[103]

Where union members are in dispute with a government department that employs them, then clearly a trade dispute will exist so long as it is on an appropriate subject matter, such as terms and conditions of employment. This is the case no matter what the organiser's motive or whether the action has political ramifications or not.

A trade dispute with government can also occur even where it stems from conflict over wider government economic policy. All that matters is that the political and economic decisions of the government have a direct effect on the terms and conditions of employment of the employees in dispute. This was the essence of the decision in *Sherrard v AUEW*,[104] where a one-day strike was called at the behest of the TUC, in protest at the government's counter-inflation policies which froze pay across industries. This was a trade dispute as the employees in this particular government installation were directly affected by the pay freeze because ministerial authority was required before a pay rise could be authorised.[105]

Conversely, where the industrial action is not aimed at the government as an employer and is not on one or more of the matters listed in s. 244 of the TULR(C)A 1992, but is action taken generally to oppose social and economic policy, there is no trade dispute. This is demonstrated by *Express Newspapers Ltd v Keys*,[106] where strikes were held to protest against government economic

100 [1982] IRLR 200.
101 See also *P v NAS/UWT* [1982] IRLR 102.
102 [1926] Ch 536.
103 Ibid. p. 540.
104 [1973] ICR 421.
105 Note that s.244(2) specifically provides that a dispute between government and workers shall be treated as a trade dispute if the dispute has been referred to a joint body for resolution on which there is ministerial representation or if the dispute cannot be settled without the minister's approval (e.g. see *Wandsworth BC v NAS/UWT* [1993] IRLR 344).
106 [1980] IRLR 247.

policies during a collective 'day of action' called by the TUC. This was classified by the High Court as a political protest strike, the outstanding characteristic of which is that the employer is in no position to do anything about the demands of the union.[107]

The dividing line between industrial relations issues, which fall within the scope of the golden formula, and political issues, which do not, was widened by the 1982 Employment Act. Before this Act, a trade dispute had only to be 'connected with' the list of matters outlined in s. 244. Now the dispute must relate 'wholly or mainly to' one or more of these items. Prior to this change, mixed motives for taking action, partly industrial and partly political, satisfied the test. Now that the industrial nature of the dispute must be predominant, there is a greater danger of trade unions losing their immunity where the dispute is in anyway linked to government policies. This is illustrated by *Mercury Communications v Scott-Garner*.[108] The claimant company was the beneficiary of the liberalisation of the telecommunications industry. The claimant, as a newly licensed operator, planned to establish a digital communications network by using the British Telecom (BT) system. The Post Office Engineering Union supported BT's monopoly and instructed their members employed by BT not to connect Mercury to the system. The union argued that this campaign of industrial action was necessary to avoid redundancies and protect conditions of employment for their members in the industry. Donaldson MR in the Court of Appeal refused to accept this:

> I find it impossible to conclude on the present evidence that the risk to jobs was a major part of what the dispute was about . . . on the other hand there is massive evidence that the union was waging a campaign against the political decisions to liberalise the industry and to privatise BT.[109]

The decision in *Scott-Garner* demonstrates that, where political decision making has a direct effect on terms and conditions of employment (or on other matters included in s. 244(1)), the resulting dispute will only be a trade dispute if the union's main concern is the industrial and employment consequences of the political decision.

❖ THINKING POINT

Does this decision mean that action to prevent the privatisation of public services will always be unprotected industrial action?

The distinction between an ideological objection to government policy and an objection based on that policy's effect on terms and conditions of employment was also the central question in *Wandsworth BC v NAS/UWT*.[110] The Education Reform Act 1988 established a national curriculum for school pupils and required teachers to stage additional tests and assessments. The defendant unions balloted their members to participate in action short of a strike to boycott the tests required under the national curriculum. Neil LJ, delivering the unanimous judgment of the Court of Appeal,

107 See also *Associated Newspapers Ltd v Flynn* [1970] KIR 17.
108 [1983] IRLR 494.
109 Ibid. p. 500.
110 [1993] IRLR 344.

rejected the council's submissions that this was a dispute about opposition to educational policy *per se*, and as such was a dispute with the government. He concluded that, on the evidence, it was clear that the unions believed the reforms increased teachers' workloads excessively and unreasonably and that that issue was the primary impetus for the dispute. The High Court came to a similar decision in *Secretary of State for Education v NUT*[111] where the secretary of state unsuccessfully sought an injunction to halt a proposed strike by teachers working in sixth form colleges where colleges were powerless to improve pay and conditions without further funding from central government. To the court this was not a political strike but a clear trade dispute as the union's primary focus was to improve and protect pay and job security, not to oppose government policy *per se*.[112]

Any action taken to pursue a personal grievance that a union has with an employer will clearly fail the definition of a trade dispute, such as where the union was motivated by a desire merely to suppress criticism of the union's existing dispute with other employers in the area.[113] It should be noted, however, that mere ill will between the employer and the union does not turn what is *prima facie* a trade dispute into an unprotected personal dispute. The dispute may be carried on zealously due to personal animosity between the parties but, so long it is motivated by an issue deriving from the list in s. 244 of the TULR(C)A 1992, it remains a trade dispute.[114]

20.7 The parties to the trade dispute

The trade dispute must involve the correct parties. The form of words defining a trade dispute in the Trade Union and Labour Relations Act 1974 stated that it was 'a dispute between employers and workers, or between workers and workers'. The amendment introduced by the Employment Act 1982 (incorporated into s. 244(1) of the TULR(C)A 1992) provides that the dispute must now be between 'workers and their employer'.[115]

Disputes between unions at the workplace over recognition, recruitment or demarcation matters would previously have been classified as between 'workers and workers'. Thus, where a dispute subsequently damaged an employer, the unions involved would be safeguarded from any legal action. These purely internal disputes are not now protected. However, employers often intervene in internal disputes so as to eliminate or reduce a particular union's influence. Where this happens, the immunities are applicable as the dispute is not a purely internal dispute but one between an employer and their workers.

Under the formula contained in the Trade Union and Labour Relations Act 1974, unions and employer associations *per se* were legitimate parties to a trade dispute. Thus, a union could initiate a dispute purely on its own behalf. This has always been important for unions who start recognition disputes without having members at the workplace. A union now however, cannot engage in a dispute on its own account to recruit members without running the risk of legal action.

Furthermore, as the dispute must solely be driven by the interests of the membership at the workplace, not by the interests of the union *per se*, a union cannot intervene where there is no on-going dispute. In the usual course of events, once a dispute arises, the union is called in by the membership and acts on their behalf. Where this does not happen, a union cannot ignore its members' wishes by calling a dispute of its own accord. This change clearly hampers campaigns

---

111 [2016] IRLR 512.

112 See also *Westminster CC v Unison* [2001] IRLR 524; *University College London Hospitals NHS Trust v Unison* [1999] IRLR 31.

113 See *Torquay Hotel v Cousins* [1969] 2 Ch 106.

114 See *Stewart v AUEW* [1973] IRLR 57.

115 By s. 244(5), this includes former workers whose employment has been terminated in connection with the dispute.

such as the ITWF campaign against 'flags of convenience' ships where employers employ foreign crews on poor conditions and low pay. Before the amendment, the union could raise a dispute with the employers even though there was no evidence that the workers themselves were dissatisfied with their pay and where the employer did not have any union members amongst its staff.[116]

20.7.1 Identity of the employer

It is perhaps self-evident that an employer is the organisation that employs the workers who are taking strike action. However, where employers have complex legal structures, strike organisers may have some difficulty in establishing with some certainty exactly who the correct party is to take action against. For example, several interconnecting companies may exist, so that the real controlling party which has the decision-making power to resolve the dispute is a legal entity that is not technically an employer of the workers who are taking action. If each company is a separate legal entity, the question arises as to whether the courts will lift the 'veil of incorporation' to permit action against the party with the real influence in the decision-making process.

The authorities indicate that, where an employer alters their legal structure with the sole aim of defeating the trade dispute immunities, then the veil of incorporation can be set aside.[117] Where, however, the corporate structure of parent and subsidiary companies has been developed for genuine commercial reasons, the separate legal identities will be honoured by the courts, even though on the face of it the subsidiary companies are controlled by a parent organisation. In these circumstances, a union has to be particularly careful in choosing against which party to take action.[118]

In *University College Hospital NHS Trust v Unison*[119] the hospital trust entered into negotiations with a private consortium under the Private Finance Initiative (PFI) for the consortium to build and run a new hospital. The trust refused the union's request to include a term in the contract to the effect that employees transferred to the new hospital (and any future employees) would receive equivalent terms and conditions to those employees who remained with the trust. The union subsequently balloted for industrial action. The Court of Appeal found that the dispute was about terms and conditions that would apply to workers after their employment with the trust had ceased and about workers not yet identified and not presently employed by the trust. As this was a dispute about the terms and conditions a new or future employer would impose, and so not a dispute between existing employees and their current employer, the requirements of s. 244 had not been satisfied.[120]

20.8 The loss of immunity

The third and final stage is to consider whether, as a consequence of the legislation since 1979, the actions of the organiser of the industrial action cause the removal of the trade dispute immunity, so restoring the original liability for the common law tort.

---

116 See *Camellia Tanker v ITWF* [1976] IRLR 190 and *NWL Ltd v Nelson* [1979] IRLR 478.

117 See *Examite Hire Ltd v Whittaker* [1977] IRLR 312, where the employer formed a new company expressly for the purpose of exacerbating union liability, and *The Marubo Porr* [1979] 2 LR 331 where ship-owners attempted unsuccessfully to outflank the immunities by arranging for an outside agency to contract with the crew of their ship.

118 See *Dimbleby v NUJ* [1984] IRLR 161.

119 [1999] IRLR 31.

120 By contrast, in *Westminster CC v Unison* [2001] IRLR 524, as the identity of the new employer was known, and the transfer of the employment was imminent, the immediate and practical concerns of the employees was the effect of the transfer on their terms and conditions of employment.

The trade dispute immunity is lost in six specific circumstances where:

(1) the industrial action takes place without a valid ballot or without giving appropriate notice of action;
(2) the industrial action consists of prohibited secondary action;
(3) unlawful picketing takes place during the industrial action;
(4) the industrial action is taken to impose a 'closed shop';
(5) the industrial action takes place to enforce recognition of a union or the use of union-only labour;
(6) the industrial action is taken because of the dismissal of unofficial strikers.

20.8.1 Industrial action taken without a ballot or notice

Prior to the passage of the Trade Union Act 1984, the only procedure a trade union had to follow when contemplating industrial action was found by an examination of the provisions of the rule book. This would determine whether there was any requirement for a ballot, and if so, the type of ballot required (for example, workplace or postal) and other matters such as whether any special majorities were necessary. In 1983, the Conservative government, through the Green Paper, *Democracy in Trade Unions*,[121] expressed concern that industrial action was often initiated without a secret ballot and undertaken reluctantly by the majority of 'moderate' and 'sensible' trade unionists, who were obligated to take action against their wishes by trade union shop stewards and leaders. Statutory intervention to ensure secret ballots before industrial action was thus justified as a method of extending trade union members' democratic rights and as a way of providing employers with the power to curtail irresponsible industrial action.[122]

Amendments to the original provisions contained in the Trade Union Act 1984 were made in response to issues that arose from the 1984–1985 miners' strike. Although strike ballots were required under the rule book, the Coal Board was reluctant to initiate legal action when the strike started without a valid ballot. It was left to individual dissident union members to do so. It was argued in the Green Paper, *Trade Unions and Their Members*,[123] that although employers may decline to take action in response to an unlawful strike, unions owed a duty to their members not to initiate action without the legitimacy of a ballot.

As a consequence, the Employment Act 1988 provided a statutory remedy (which supplements the common law remedy of an action under the rule book) for a union member to apply for an order restraining industrial action (employers already had this right under the Trade Union Act 1984) where a ballot had not been held or a majority for action had not been obtained. The Act also granted the Secretary of State the authority to issue a Code of Practice on balloting for industrial action. The first Code was issued in 1989. It was superseded in 1995 by a new Code on Industrial Action Ballots and Notice to Employer which was criticised for unduly elaborating on the provisions contained in the statute. Another Code of Practice (taking into account changes introduced by the Employment Relations Act 1999 and Employment Relations Act 2004) was revised and published in 2005. The latest Code was issued in 2017.

Research, based on the requirement for statutory ballots under the Trade Union Act 1984, has shown that these statutory ballots have often been used as bargaining tools in themselves. A majority vote for industrial action, which shows employee support for the union position, is more effective than a vague threat to call a strike. Thus, strike ballots have often been incorporated into

121 Cmnd 8778, 1983.
122 For an overview of arguments deployed at that time, see Simpson, 1993.
123 Cmnd 95, 1987.

a union's bargaining strategy.[124] Partly to temper the use of ballots in this manner, further amendments to the balloting provisions were introduced by the Trade Union Reform and Employment Rights Act 1993. This Act enforced compulsory postal ballots,[125] the independent scrutiny of ballot procedure, a requirement to give at least seven days' notice of the ballot and of the industrial action to relevant employer(s) and the right for individuals to apply for an injunction to stop unballoted action that interferes with the supply of goods or services. Not surprisingly, the tactical use of ballots became less popular.

Further restrictive reforms were proposed in the Conservative Green Paper, *Industrial Action and Trade Unions*.[126] But before enactment the Conservative administration lost the 1997 General Election. The new Labour government did not abolish these Conservative measures on balloting but introduced significant amendments via Schedule 3 of the Employment Relations Act 1999 and via Schedule 2 of the Employment Relations Act 2004 in order to simplify (but not repeal) some of the more complex and controversial provisions. Most recently, on the election of a majority Conservative government in 2015, further stringent restrictions on the organisation of ballots have been introduced by the Trade Union Act 2016.

It is important to re-iterate that all immunity for industrial action is removed if it is not supported by a ballot that satisfies the detailed and complex provisions of the law. Unions therefore need to take considerable care in preparing the content of the ballot paper, the literature that accompanies it and in adhering to the procedure once the ballot has been completed. Without full compliance with all the fine points of the balloting rules a strike ballot will be nullified and the strike declared unlawful – resulting in an injunction being granted prohibiting the industrial action. Trade unions and academic commentators have been critical of the depth and technical detail of the provisions as trade unions may inadvertently fall foul of the provisions. For example, in *Metrobus Ltd v Unite*[127] the issues concerned the level of information that the trade union must provide to the employer prior to the commencement of industrial action and when this information should be provided – union duties that are outlined by, *inter alia*, ss. 226A, 231A and 234A TULR(C)A 1992.[128]

The union had sent to the employer all the requisite information (relating to the numbers and categories of affected employees who the union believed would be entitled to vote or called out to take strike action) in the necessary notices prior to the ballot and prior to taking action. However, a majority of the Court of Appeal read into these provisions (ss. 226A(2)(c) and 234A(3)(a)) a requirement that the union needed, not just to provide the information, but also explain how the information for non-check of employees had been calculated and where it had been sourced[129] – although arguably this was not strictly justified on a literal reading of the statutory requirements. Additionally, the court held that the union had also failed to notify the employer sufficiently promptly of the result of the ballot. The full result of the ballot had not been sent to the employer immediately it was available as the fax with the results of the ballot sent by the independent scrutineer[130] to the union was delayed in arriving at the union's offices. Even though the union was not at fault for the delay, this was still a technical breach of the provisions as the union could

124 Elgar & Simpson, 1993.

125 Ballots are expensive to hold. Thus, it was a major blow to trade unions when it was announced that the State subsidy for balloting costs, in place since 1980, was to be withdrawn from April 1996 (Funds for Trade Union Ballots (Revocation) Order 1993).

126 Cm 3470, 1996.

127 [2009] IRLR 851.

128 For an analysis of the *Metrobus* decision and its implications, see Barrow, 2011.

129 For check-off employees (those who had their union dues deducted directly from their pay and transferred automatically by the employer to the union) an explanation was not required as that information could be easily determined from the employer's own records.

130 The independent scrutineer has responsibility for supervising the ballot and the counting process – duties outlined in ss. 49–52, 75–78, 100A–100E, 226B and 231B TULR(C)A 1992.

have obtained the information earlier – it had not been sent 'as soon as reasonably practicable' as required by s. 231A and, as a consequence, the industrial action was 'not protected' from action in tort.

This formalistic approach to statutory interpretation was followed by the High Court in *EDF Energy v RMT*,[131] which concerned a pay dispute at EDF installations that supplied electrical power to the London Underground system. Under s. 226A TULR(C)A 1992 the pre-strike notice should contain, *inter alia*, information relating to the 'categories of employees' to be balloted. The union's notice stated that 64 members of the union, working at three designated places of work, were entitled to vote in the ballot, and were all those members of the union employed by the company in the category of 'engineer/technician'. The High Court held that the union had failed to discharge the duty of notification as the category cited was not specific enough for the purposes of s. 226A. EDF described the relevant workforce in a variety of employment categories such as 'fitters, jointers, test room inspectors, day testers, shifter testers and OLBI fitters'. The numbers in each of these sub-categories needed to be disclosed in order to exactly establish which group of employees were to be balloted and to be possibly called out on strike – thus the union's use of such a broad expansive category as 'engineer/technician' was not in compliance with the relevant statutory provision and an injunction prohibiting the action was granted.

During this period there were a number of other cases that caused some alarm amongst trade unionists.[132] More recent case law has acknowledged the complexity of the provisions and their difficulty for trade unions. The Court of Appeal has thus held that a restrictive reading of the legislation was inappropriate and that a more neutral stance in interpretation was required.[133] However, the complexity and the comprehensive nature of the provisions still remains an issue, especially as the requirements for a lawful strike have now been enhanced by the Trade Union Act 2016.

20.8.1.1 The ballot thresholds

Section 2 of the Trade Union Act 2016 (inserting a new s. 226(2)(a)(iia) into the TULR(C)A 1992) introduces a new minimum turnout requirement when a trade union is balloting for industrial action. At least 50 per cent of union members eligible to vote must participate in the ballot, and of those that participate, a majority of those voting must support the call for action. The government's view is that this would enhance the democratic process – that it will ensure that 'industrial action has democratic support and legitimacy within the relevant workforce' and 'avoid great disruption on very old ballots secured by low turnouts'.[134]

In 'important public services' (including the fire service, education (of those under 17) and health services, and the transport, border security and nuclear decommissioning sectors[135]) there is an additional requirement that industrial action will require the support of at least 40 per cent of those entitled to vote.[136] A simple majority (that satisfies the new 50 per cent participation threshold) will not be sufficient in order for action to go ahead in these particular industries and any union member who abstains or forgets to return their ballot paper will effectively be deemed to be opposing the strike.

---

131 [2010] IRLR 114.

132 See for example, *British Airways plc v Unite* [2010] IRLR 423; *Network Rail Infrastructure Ltd v NURMT* [2010] EWHC 1084.

133 *ASLEF v London and Birmingham Railway Ltd* [2011] IRLR 399; applied in *Balfour Beatty Ltd v Unite* [2012] IRLR 452; *London Underground Ltd v ASLEF* [2012] IRLR 196.

134 Trade Union Bill Deb 15 October, col. 162, *per* Nick Boles.

135 Section 3(2) (2D) and (2E) specifies that the details of the exact services affected will be determined by regulations through the Secretary of State's statutory instrument powers.

136 Section 3(2) (2A–2C), amending s. 226 TULR(C)A 1992.

The consequences of requiring a trade union to meet both the 50 per cent threshold and the 40 per cent minimum level of support for public sector disputes will arguably have a serious impact on a trade union's capability in the public services to call for action – one of the few sectors where unions remain strong. It will become difficult for unions to organise and prosecute lawful industrial action in order to protect centralised collective bargaining and these provisions may weaken trade union opposition to the erosion of pay and conditions that are often the corollary to cuts in public services. This provision has also been criticised as a disproportionate and unfair intervention as across all national and municipal elections, an accepted principle is that a simple majority of those who voted is sufficient for a democratic mandate. To many trade unionists this is particularly exasperating as the government has persistently refused in the past to countenance a switch from inefficient postal ballots (that historically produce low turnouts) to secure workplace ballots or electronic balloting – both systems that would be far more likely to yield higher levels of member participation and so guarantee a more democratic decision.[137]

Critics of the threshold requirement have also pointed to academic research that supports trade union concerns. In the period of investigation, between 1997 and 2015, if the 50 per cent criteria was in place, only 85 out of 158 strike ballots would have reached this threshold – a total of 3.3 million workers would have been denied the opportunity to take strike action.[138] It is certainly true that this provision should satisfy the stated objective of ensuring that industrial action has a very high level of democratic validity – nevertheless, in the context of its effect on trade union ability to defend the legitimate interests of their membership, it could be argued that this is not a sufficiently balanced provision, particularly as alternative and less damaging voting methods could have been applied to meet the objective of strengthening the democratic legitimacy of the ballot.

20.8.1.2 The content of the ballot paper

The identity of the person authorised to call the industrial action after a successful ballot must be on the ballot paper,[139] with the name of the independent scrutineer[140] appointed by the union to oversee the conduct of the ballot[141] and the address to where it should be sent and date by which it should be returned.

Before amendments introduced by the Employment Relations Act 1999, all ballot papers had to include a so called 'industrial health warning' – a bare statement which said 'If you take part in a strike or other industrial action, you may be in breach of your contract of employment'. The 1999 Act does not abolish this provision but, by amending s. 229(4) of the TULR(C)A 1992, expands on it, using it as an opportunity to inform employees considering lawful industrial action that a new limited right to protection against dismissal is available. The statement on the ballot paper now reads

> If you take part in a strike or other industrial action, you may be in breach of your contract of employment. However, if you are dismissed for taking part in strike or other industrial action which is called officially and is otherwise lawful, the dismissal will be unfair if it takes place

137 The power to introduce new forms of voting for strike ballots have been available since 2004 through s. 54 Employment Act 2004.

138 Darlington & Dobson, 2015, p. 27.

139 Section 229(3).

140 Section 229(1A).

141 The scrutineer must report to the union within four weeks after the ballot on specific matters, such as whether reasonable grounds exist for believing a contravention of the statute has occurred and whether the balloting arrangements generally were satisfactory (ss. 226B(1), (2) and 231B). The union must not interfere in the scrutineer's functions and must comply with all reasonable requests (s. 226B(3), (4)).

fewer than 12 weeks after you started taking part in the action, and depending on the circumstances may be unfair if it takes place later.

The question to be answered in the ballot must require a 'yes' or 'no' answer. If the union believes members may be called out to take industrial action short of a strike and actual strike action, then two separate questions are required.[142] This ensures the union has approval for both courses of action.[143] The Trade Union Act 2016 section 5 (2C) and (2D)[144] has also introduced the requirement that where unions ask for support for action short of a strike, details of the actual type of action will need to be included on the ballot paper and that the ballot paper must specify the anticipated length of the industrial action.[145] Section 5(2B) also states that the ballot paper must include a summary of the matters in issue in the trade dispute.[146] The designated purpose of these amendments is to enable a trade union member to make an informed decision when deciding how to vote. Employers are also entitled to receive a copy of the ballot paper in advance for the purpose of determining whether the union has complied with these (and existing) requirements and then, where there is an error, to seek an injunction to stay industrial action.

Several issues regarding the framing of the question arose in *London Underground v NUR*.[147] Here, there were originally four matters of dispute between the union and the employers. Before the ballot, the union had failed to publicise to the membership that three of the issues were no longer matters in dispute. Consequently, the employers successfully argued that the resulting ballot was invalid as the members of the union had voted on a single question whether to take strike action, influenced by a belief that all four matters were current. This can be contrasted with a decision of the High Court in *Associated British Ports v TGWU*,[148] where there were other issues in dispute unidentified by the literature sent with the ballot paper. Millett J declined to declare the ballot invalid, as 'what matters is that a majority supported the strike; it does not matter why they did so'.[149]

Both cases illustrate the importance of the provision of accurate information to the membership, either before the ballot or with the ballot paper, so it is clear to the membership what they are voting on. The Code of Practice recommends that background information on the issues to which the dispute relates should be provided.[150]

Another issue that has arisen is how to distinguish between a 'strike' and 'action short of a strike'. In *Connex South Eastern Ltd v RMT*[151] the union successfully balloted for strike action and instructed members to ban overtime and rest day working. The employer argued that the ballot was flawed, as this form of action, was, in reality, action short of a strike that required a separate question on the ballot paper. The Court of Appeal disagreed, holding that this was 'strike action' as it is defined in s. 246 of TULR(C)A 1992 as a 'concerted stoppage of work' – which this was, albeit for a limited period of time. The decision meant that only where a union was balloting for action that does not technically require a stoppage of work – such as a go-slow or work to rule –

---

142 Section 229(2). The union in *The Post Office v UCW* [1990] IRLR 143 fell foul of this provision because a single rolled up question referring to both forms of action was asked.

143 As each question is considered individually, a bare majority only on one question is valid authorisation for the action specified in that question. See *West Midlands Travel Ltd v TGWU* [1994] IRLR 578.

144 Incorporated into TULR(C)A 1992 as s. 229(2D)(2C).

145 On the interpretation of this section, see *Thomas Cook Airlines Ltd v British Airline Pilots Association* [2017] IRLR 1137.

146 Section 229(2B).

147 [1989] IRLR 341.

148 [1989] IRLR 291.

149 Ibid. p. 301.

150 Para. 36

151 [1999] IRLR 249.

will a question on the ballot paper on action short of a strike be required. However, a statutory amendment to s. 229, introduced by the 1999 Act, has overturned this decision. Section 229(2A) now categorically states that for the purposes of the balloting provisions an overtime ban and call out ban both constitute industrial action short of a strike.

20.8.1.3 Entitlement to vote

Entitlement to vote must be accorded equally to all members who it is reasonable at the time of the ballot for the union to believe will be induced to take part in the action. It does not matter that some are not called upon to take action, so long as the union reasonably believed at the time of the ballot that they would be. Where any member who is induced to take part is denied their entitlement to vote, then the ballot is invalid. In the case law, these obligations were read in conjunction with s. 230(2), which qualified the above by providing that a trade union is only under an obligation to provide a ballot paper to those entitled to vote, 'as far as reasonably practicable'.

In *British Rlys Board v NUR*,[152] the question arose as to the validity of a ballot where approximately 200 out of a membership of 70,000 who were called upon to take industrial action had not received ballot papers because of an inadvertent oversight by the union. The Court of Appeal understood this as not being a case of a wilful denial of an entitlement to vote, but rather as a failure to provide an opportunity to vote. As there is no absolute obligation to provide everyone with a ballot paper, and as only a trifling number of voters were affected, the omission did not nullify the ballot.

Since s. 227(1) requires the union to ballot all those employees who are to be called on to strike, the question arises whether the action remains lawful where new employees are called out on strikes, who have not voted, as they were employed after the ballot had been held and before the action started. The Court of Appeal intimated that so long as the numbers are *de minimis* – small enough to have no effect on the result – the validity of the ballot is unaffected.[153]

Alternatively, it may be the case that during the industrial action there is a change in the composition of the workforce. It may then be argued that, if a substantial minority of workers have not voted, the campaign of industrial action has not been legitimised by the ballot. In *The Post Office v UCW*,[154] Donaldson MR indicated that small changes in the composition of the workforce would not necessarily invalidate industrial action taken over a sustained period of time so long as that action is continuous, rather than a series of self-contained actions. However, as regards large, as opposed to *de minimis*, changes in the workforce, the ballot may well be invalidated as any call for industrial action 'should be limited to those employed by the employer who had the opportunity to vote'. However, another Court of Appeal interpretation of the ballot provisions rejected this analysis and held that what is of concern is whether a majority of those voting at the time the action was called have voted in favour.[155]

This realistic approach by the Court of Appeal to the organisation of the ballot was generally welcomed. It would have been virtually impossible for large unions to comply with provisions that made it an absolute necessity to ballot all members without any wastage whatsoever. There will always be a shortfall between the number of members sent ballot papers and those returned, due to the vagaries of the postal service, just as there will always be individuals who have not voted because they have been employed just before or during industrial action.

---

152 [1989] IRLR 349.

153 Ibid. p. 352.

154 [1990] IRLR 143.

155 *London Underground v RMT* [1995] IRLR 636. See also *RJB Mining (UK) Ltd v NUM* [1997] IRLR 621.

In order to clarify the position on ballot failures, Sch. 3, para. 4 of the 1999 Act repealed s. 227(2) replacing it with a similar provision, s. 232A. This repeats the formula of s. 227(2) stating that, where members who are induced to take part in industrial action are denied their entitlement to vote, then the ballot is invalid. However, it also adds the provision that it must be reasonable for the union to believe at the time of the ballot that the member would be induced to take part in the action. Thus, this makes it explicit that the immunity is not lost if the union induces some members to participate in the action who were not included in the balloting process because they were new or transferred employees who only joined the balloted workplace after the ballot had closed. Additionally, a new s. 232B has been introduced affirming the case law that minor accidental failures to comply fully with the provisions on the entitlement to vote[156] and the supply of a ballot paper,[157] that do not affect the result of the ballot, can be disregarded.[158] Issues regarding s. 227 were revisited in *British Airways v Unite (No1)*,[159] where the High Court held that the union had failed to actively investigate and identify those who had taken redundancy and were therefore included in the ballot contrary to s. 227. In that context, this was not an 'accidental' failure.

20.8.1.4 Requirement for balloting separate workplaces

Prior to changes made to these provisions by the 1999 Act, all employees who are likely to be called out on industrial action who had 'different places of work' had to be balloted separately, in respect of each of those places of work. The requirement for a separate ballot at each workplace meant that an immunity would only attach to those workplaces that have obtained a majority 'yes' vote.

The intention behind this requirement was to limit the opportunity for a union to 'gerrymander' the vote by including in the ballot workers at a workplace who have a reputation for militancy to out-vote other more moderate workers at other workplaces. The strictness of this provision outlawing the aggregation of votes was tempered in circumstances of a common claim. Aggregation was permitted where the union reasonably believed members had some factors in common relating either to their terms and conditions of employment or their occupational status and all of those members with common factors were balloted, or where it was reasonable for the union to believe that all balloted members had the same place of work.

This provision took into account the realities of national bargaining. Aggregation is essential where the same union members work in different geographical places for different employers with their terms and conditions of employment negotiated nationally.[160] The operation of these conditions was, however, found to be unworkable due to their complexity. In order to clarify and simplify the law, Sch. 3, para. 5 of the 1999 Act repealed the original sections and substituted new ss. 228 and 228A of the TULR(C)A 1992. Section 228 re-iterates the general principle that in any dispute separate workplace ballots are necessary, subject to the exceptions contained in s. 228A. Section 228A establishes that a union may hold an aggregated ballot across more than one workplace[161] if each workplace contains at least one member who is 'affected by the dispute', or where the union reasonably believes all the members balloted are of a particular occupational description or

---

156 Section 227(1).
157 Section 230(2).
158 See *P v NAS/UWT* [2001] IRLR 532.
159 [2010] IRLR 423.
160 See e.g. *University of Central England v NALGO* [1993] IRLR 81.
161 Section 228(4) describes 'workplace' as the premises from which the employee works or with which the employee has the closest connection. In the original definition, place of work was defined as premises occupied by the employer at which the employees worked or premises with which the employees had the closest connection. On the problems associated with this earlier definition, see *Inter City West Coast Ltd v RMT* [1996] IRLR 583.

descriptions who are employed by an employer or employers with whom the union is in dispute, or where the union ballots all of its members who are employed by the employer or employers with whom the union is in dispute. This now means that unions ought to be free to carry out aggregate ballots in selective workplaces where previously this would not have been permitted. This is particularly the case with regard to the first exception. An aggregate ballot of members across a limited number of workplaces operated by the same employer is now permissible provided that at least one affected member works at each workplace where the balloting is to take place.

20.8.1.5 Notice requirements

The Trade Union Reform and Employment Rights Act 1993 added a new s. 226A to the TULR(C)A 1992 which requires the union to take reasonable steps to ensure all employers whose employees are entitled to vote have seven days' written notice of any ballot. As a consequence of section 8 of the Trade Union Act 2016 (amending this section) this has now been extended to 14 days. The union should also provide a sample voting paper to the employer(s) at least three days before the ballot commences.

This is an attempt to avoid employers being thrown off-guard by quickly organised industrial action. This change gives an employer time to obtain advice on the general legality of the industrial action, whether there are any grounds to object to the ballot and, if so, to prepare an application for an injunction to restrain the action.

The most controversial aspect of this duty was the requirement that the union had to include in the written notice a description, 'so that he can readily ascertain them', of 'the employees of the employer who it is reasonable for the union to believe . . . will be entitled to vote in the ballot'. How controversial it was is illustrated by the practical application of the law in *Blackpool & Fylde College v NATFHE*.[162] The union was engaged in a dispute with the college over the introduction of 'flexible' contracts for newly appointed staff. The union in an attempt to comply with s. 226A, sent the employer a notice that they intended to 'hold a ballot of all our members in the college'. After a successful ballot, a similar second notice was sent to comply with the provisions of s. 234A.

The Court of Appeal held that the reference to members employed at the college in general terms was not a sufficient description as the employer could not 'readily ascertain them', that is, identify who they are. To comply with these provisions, the union must either specify a readily identifiable category of persons who are union members (so the employer can easily find out who they are) or, where that is not possible, the union must provide a full list of individual names.

The union responded to this decision by complaining to the European Human Rights institutions that this amounted to a breach of Arts 8 and 11 of the European Convention. The claim failed at the initial admissibility stage as the European Commission of Human Rights did not consider that the requirement to inform an employer of union names was an unjustified interference with the union's right to protect its members' interests, nor was it a violation of any individual rights.[163] The Labour government, in the White Paper, *Fairness at Work*,[164] subsequently pledged to amend the law so that specific names of union members taking industrial action would not have to be disclosed. The Employment Relations Act 1999 has repealed and replaced the offending provision. After further amendments in the Employment Relations Act 2004, a new s. 226A and s. 226(2A)–(2H) now outline the information an employer is entitled to receive. Although specific names do not need to be disclosed, the level of detail that is required to be disclosed is substantial. For

162 [1990] IRLR 227.
163 *NATFHE v UK*, App No 28910/95.
164 Cmnd 3968, 1998.

example, the section specifies that if the union does possess information as to the number, category or workplace of the relevant employees, then the notice must contain that information.[165]

20.8.1.6 Union participation in the ballot

Section 230(1)(a) makes it clear that the electorate must be permitted to vote without interference from, or have any constraint imposed by, the union, its members or officials.[166] However, the Court of Appeal has held that a union is permitted to be partisan in its views and to campaign for a 'yes' vote in the ballot. What matters is that the union does not induce members to take action before the ballot result is known. There is, however, a thin line between the mere provision of information on the issues and persuasion and inducement.[167]

20.8.1.7 Notice requirements after the ballot

Unions are required to give 14 days' notice to every relevant employer before the start of industrial action.[168] The notice must include (similarly to s. 226A(2)) information about the employees whom the union intends to induce to take part in the industrial action. Furthermore, the union should identify: the starting date of the action, whether the action is intended to be continuous or discontinuous (that is, a series of one day strikes) and, if the action is to be discontinuous, the dates on which the action will be held.[169]

Once the ballot has been held, s. 231 requires the union, as soon as is reasonably practicable, to provide all those entitled to vote with a breakdown of the result. A new s. 231A introduced by the Trade Union Reform and Employment Rights Act 1993 obliges the union to provide the same information to the employers of the employees who were entitled to vote. The scrutineer's report (which deals with the fairness of the ballot) must also be made available to employers and employees for a period of six months after the ballot.[170] Section 6 of the 2016 Trade Union Act (amending s. 231 TULR(C)A 1992) now additionally requires trade unions to specify how many members were entitled to vote and whether the new minimum percentage thresholds have been met.

20.8.1.8 Ballot effective for six months

Prior to changes introduced by the Trade Union Act 2016 industrial action had to take place within four weeks from the date of the ballot result. If the industrial action did not start within the statutory time limit, the union had to either hold a fresh ballot or abandon the planned industrial action. This was partly mitigated by the courts being willing to suspend the time limit once negotiations were initiated.[171] The new provision states that the ballot has validity for six months (or up to nine months with agreement of the employer) and industrial action has therefore to be called within that timeframe.[172] After this period the ballot ceases to be effective and any campaign of action that has been initiated will be interrupted while the union re-ballots.

---

165 See earlier *EDF Energy v RMT* [2010] IRLR 114.

166 Such a restraint is not imposed on employers or any other person unconnected with the dispute. As employers are provided with full details of who is to be induced to take action, employers have an opportunity to contact employees directly to lobby for a 'no' vote.

167 See also s. 233(3)(a) on a 'call' for industrial action.

168 Section 8 Trade Union Act 2016 inserting a new s. 234A (3F)(4)(b) TULR(C)A 1992.

169 Section 234A(3)(b).

170 Section 231B(2).

171 See *Monsanto v TGWU* [1986] IRLR 406.

172 Section 9 Trade Union Act 2016 substituting a new s. 234(1) TULR(C)A 1992.

Should the ballot approve the industrial action, s. 233 holds that the action is only protected if the person specified on the ballot paper calls the action. This specified person provision was enacted so as to avoid the confusion of minor officials initiating action, where the leadership of the union has yet to do so because, for example, they are still engaged in negotiations. It is another provision that puts the responsibility of industrial action on to the leadership of the national union, in an attempt to control the 'hotheads' in local branches. How far the provision permits the delegation of this task was considered in *Tanks & Drums Ltd v TGWU*.[173] Neil LJ in the Court of Appeal accepted that on the construction of the section a conditional authorisation can be given. However, a blanket authority to local officials to call for industrial action could not be permitted as that would subvert the plain meaning of the statutory provision. A conditional authorisation is only lawful where explicit authority is given to named or defined officials.

20.9 Secondary action

Secondary industrial action occurs where employees who are not involved in the primary dispute take action against their own employer, to cut supplies to the employer in that dispute. Such action clearly interferes with the business of a 'secondary' employer who is not a party to the dispute. This form of secondary action has historically been of some importance to employees on strike, enabling them to put tangible pressure on the employer to settle the dispute.

Sympathetic secondary action (action which symbolically demonstrates support for workers in the primary dispute without necessarily having any effect on the dispute in question) was outlawed by the Employment Act 1980. The legality of other types of more effective secondary action was generally not affected by the reforms in the 1980 Act. Thus, coercive secondary action was lawful so long it was organised to disrupt the immediate or primary supplier of goods or services to the employer in the dispute, or was aimed at an associated employer where work had been transferred to that associated employer from the primary employer.

By the late 1980s, the government's position on secondary action had changed. It was argued in the Green Paper, *Removing Barriers to Employment*,[174] that the immunities for secondary action were unjustified and required amendment. The view was expressed that there was 'no good reason' why employers who are not party to a dispute should be subject to disruptive industrial action. It was also stated that secondary action had the effect of deterring new, predominately foreign employers, from investing and setting up new businesses in the UK.[175] The third reason put forward in support of reform was that the law was so complicated that those involved in industrial action would not be able easily to determine whether they were engaged in unlawful action.

As a consequence, the Employment Act 1990 repealed the limited protection deriving from the Employment Act 1980 and has replaced it with what is now s. 224 of the TULR(C)A 1992. By this section, secondary action takes place where a person induces a breach of an employment contract or interferes with its performance and 'the employer under the contract of employment is not the employer party to the dispute'. Thus, a union inducing employees' breach of contract at one employer's geographical site, in support of the dispute at another, will be in danger of losing the trade dispute immunity.[176] It also seems that to organise lawful national action against more than one employer is dependent on showing that there exists a dispute with each individual

173 [1991] IRLR 372.

174 Cmnd 655, 1989.

175 See para. 3.10.

176 This is particularly the case where an employer has several subsidiaries. They may seem to be one and the same legal person but, because of the legal structure employed, they are regarded as technically separate employers.

employer.[177] In addition, the definition of 'contract of employment' has been extended by s. 224(6) to include those who work under a contract for services, thereby allowing for the possibility that secondary action which results in a breach of a contract with an independent contractor is also actionable.

Faced with these provisions, the only alternative for a trade union that wishes to cut off the supply of goods or services to the primary employer would be to engineer a primary dispute at the secondary employer who is providing support to the employer with whom the union is in dispute. However, as we have already seen, the motives and reasons for any dispute will be carefully monitored by the courts to ensure it is a genuine trade dispute.[178]

20.10 Unlawful picketing

Apart from possible criminal offences that pickets may commit, such as public order charges or obstruction, and certain civil wrongs such as nuisance and trespass, picketing may result in the tort of inducing breach of contract. Pickets by their very nature attempt to persuade workers to break their contract of employment by not entering work. They may also attempt to stop supplies entering the workplace by inducing transport workers to refuse to deliver, thereby directly inducing breach of employment contracts and possibly indirectly inducing breach of a commercial contract.

So long as the picketing adheres to the requirements in s. 220 of the TULR(C)A 1992, that is, that it is in contemplation or furtherance of a trade dispute, peaceful, and occurs solely at or near the workers place of work, then pickets are protected from liability.[179] Violent or secondary picketing will result in the immunity being lifted. Section 10 of the Trade Union Act 2016 strengthens these conditions by inserting a new s. 220A into TULR(C)A 1992 Act, introducing several new provisions pickets and unions must meet before the immunity applies. A union must now appoint a 'picket supervisor'[180] who has responsibility for managing the picket line, with the functions of the supervisor outlined in the re-issued Picketing Code of Practice.[181] The union must take reasonable steps to ensure the police are informed of the supervisor's name and contact details and the location of the picket line.[182] The picket supervisor (who must be an official or member of the union) should be present at the picket line or be readily contactable by the police or union to attend the picket at short notice and be in possession of a letter from the union confirming that the picketing is approved by the union.[183] A picket supervisor is under a duty to show the relevant employer or their agent the letter on request 'as soon as reasonably practicable'.[184] When attending the picket the supervisor must wear 'something' (such as a badge or armband) so that they are readily identifiable.[185]

---

177 Section 224(4) states that, 'where more than one employer is in dispute with his workers, the dispute between each employer and his workers shall be treated as a separate dispute'.

178 Note that in *RMT v United Kingdom* [2014] IRLR 467 the union failed in its challenge to these provisions that they were contrary to Article 11 of the European Convention. See Barrow, 2015.

179 Section 219(3).

180 Section 220A(2)(3).

181 The Department for Business, Energy and Industrial Strategy, *Code of Practice on Picketing*, 2017 paras 58–61.

182 Section 220A(4).

183 Section 220A(5)(7).

184 Section 220A(6).

185 Section 220A(8). Originally the Government proposed to legislate in order to limit general protests associated with strike action. The consultation document (Department for Business Innovation and Skills: *Consultation on Tackling Intimidation of Non-Striking Workers*, July 2015), contained proposals to require trade unions to publish a plan of intended action in advance of any protest, to limit their use of social media, to inform the Certification Officer of the picketing and protest activity and the creation of a new criminal offence of intimidation. After widespread criticism this attempt at even tighter statutory control was abandoned.

Should there be a failure to comply with any of these conditions then the protection of the immunities against tort action, for the union and for individual pickets, will be withdrawn. The legal consequences of which is an injunction being granted to stop the picketing and a subsequent damages claim.[186] Some of the conditions may be particularly difficult for unions to follow – the larger the workplace and the greater the number of entrances and exits, the more supervisors will be required. It is highly unlikely that any union could meet such demands solely through their full-time officials. In such circumstances a union may need to recruit ordinary members who, if they are not familiar with the law and the Code of Practice and are not able to be present or to be nearby at all times, may well inadvertently violate the provisions of the statute.

20.11 Action taken to enforce union recognition or the use of union-only labour

The trade dispute immunities are withdrawn where the purpose of the industrial action is to interfere with the supply of goods or services so as to force a supplier to recognise a union or to force the employer to contract only with those who employ union-only labour. This may occur where the purpose of the industrial action is to encourage or compel an employer or other person to impose a union recognition clause into a contract for the supply of goods or services.[187]

The immunities are also withdrawn where a trade union commits an act which induces or attempts to induce another to 'refuse to deal' with a supplier or prospective supplier on the grounds of union membership[188] or union recognition.[189] Finally, protection is removed under s. 225(2) where the union induces employees of an employer to break their employment contracts, resulting in interference with the supply of goods or services to another employer and one of the grounds for this is that the second employer does not, or might not, recognise or consult or negotiate with a union or a particular union.[190]

As the section makes clear, the union recognition issue does not have to be the sole or major reason for the action against the second employer. Furthermore, the section operates even where there is only a belief that there may be a future recognition dispute with that employer.

20.12 Action taken to enforce trade union membership or a closed shop

Under s. 222(1), the statutory immunity does not apply where the reason or one of the reasons industrial action has been taken is the

> fact or belief that a particular employer:
>
> (a) is employing, has employed, or might employ a person who is not a member of a trade union; or
>
> (b) is failing, has failed or might fail to discriminate against such a person.

---

186 For further details of the injunctive process, see Courtouris & Freedland, 2011.
187 Section 225(1)(a).
188 Section 187.
189 Section 186.
190 Contravention of this section and s. 222 is a statutory tort actionable by any person 'adversely affected'.

The provision includes situations where the action is aimed against a person who is a member of any union or branch or section of a union.[191] Thus, inter-union disputes over membership recruitment will be unlawful.

Discrimination for the purposes of s. 222(1)(a), (b) is defined as where a non-union member is treated less favourably than a union member.[192] For example, industrial action organised to force an employer to agree a collective agreement that applies only to union members, or only certain union members, would be unlawful discrimination. This can be contrasted with the provisions permitting an employer to discriminate against union membership in order to encourage union members to leave their trade union to enable a change in bargaining structure.

20.13 Dismissal of unofficial strikers

This is one of many measures passed since 1990 to discourage unofficial action. The protection of the immunities is removed if 'one of the reasons' for the organisation of industrial action is the 'fact or belief' that an employer has dismissed one or more employees who are engaged in unofficial industrial action.[193]

Industrial action is unofficial where the union successfully repudiates the actions of its local officers. In these circumstances, should an employer dismiss workers who are on strike they are not entitled to claim unfair dismissal. Although action on an issue of reinstatement is a trade dispute matter, should the strikers' colleagues organise industrial action on their behalf, as a general protest, or to secure their reinstatement, the immunity they would normally have is withdrawn. It does not matter that this additional industrial action is official, backed by the union leadership and taken in compliance with all other procedures.

20.14 The 'right to strike' and Article 11 ECHR

Article 11(1) of the European Convention on Human Rights provides that 'Everyone has the right . . . to freedom of association with others, including the right to form and to join trade unions for the protection of his interests'. Article 11 case law holds that protection extends beyond a mere right to join a trade union, but also encompasses a number of freedoms including a right of a trade union to make representations to an employer on behalf of the membership[194]; a right for trade union members not to be discriminated against by an employer[195] and a right to engage in collective bargaining.[196] The Strasbourg Court has also now formally accepted that a 'right to strike' is within the scope of trade union rights under Article 11.[197]

The question that now arises is to what extent the severe limitations on the 'right to strike' in the United Kingdom, such as the need of a trade union to comply with the detailed balloting requirements noted above or the picketing provisions, are in violation of Article 11 of the European Convention on Human Rights (ECHR). This issue was litigated domestically in *Metrobus*

191 Section 222(5).
192 Section 222(2).
193 Section 223.
194 *National Union of Belgian Police v Belgium* [1975] 1 EHRR 578; *Swedish Engine Drivers' Union v Sweden* [1976] 1 EHHR 617.
195 *Wilson and Palmer and Others v United Kingdom* [2002] IRLR 568.
196 *Demir and Baykara v Turkey* [2009] 48 EHRR 54.
197 *Enerji Yapi-Yol Sen v Turkey*, App No. 689591 (ECtHR, 21 April 2009); *RMT v United Kingdom* [2015] 60 EHHR 10; *Hrvatski lijecnicki Sindikat v Croatia* [2014] ECHR 1337.

Ltd v Unison.[198] Here an injunction had been granted prohibiting strike action after an inadvertent technical breach of the ballot notice provisions. Lloyd LJ in the Court of Appeal rejected the view that the industrial action balloting requirements were 'disproportionate' and therefore in violation of Article 11 of the Convention, finding them not excessively onerous or unreasonable.

Legal action at the European Court of Human Rights challenging the United Kingdom's strike law as contrary to Convention rights has also yielded little satisfaction for trade unions. The Strasbourg Court has either failed to directly adjudicate on this question, due to the operation of the admissibility criteria,[199] or has not effectively applied Convention principles to the United Kingdom legal framework – acknowledged to be the most restrictive on strike action in Europe.[200] Many commentators have argued that these more recent judgments concerning the United Kingdom have been unduly influenced by domestic political and media pressure.[201] It is arguable that a strict jurisprudential approach taking full account of Strasbourg principles and prior case law would result in United Kingdom strike law being held to be in violation of Article 11. In particular, it is difficult to see how the additional restrictions introduced by the Trade Union Act 2016 are in compliance with Convention principles.

As Convention case law has established there is a 'right to strike', the issue of main concern is whether domestic law complies with the requirements of Article 11(2). Under Article 11(2) the 'right to strike' may be restricted where it is 'necessary in a democratic society . . . for the protection of the rights and freedoms of others'. The terminology 'necessary in a democratic society' has been interpreted to imply that intervention can only be permitted under Article 11(2) if it meets a 'pressing social need' – which involves a balancing of competing interests and an examination as to whether the state's intervention goes no further than is necessary to meet that need – i.e. it is a proportionate response to the legitimate objective pursued.[202] This test is met if the new restrictions are a balanced, measured and proportionate means of securing the policy objectives behind the legislation. As the provisions of the Trade Union Act 2016, amongst others, patently obstruct the 'right to strike', significant reasons would therefore need to be established to justify such measures.

For example, the picketing provisions in the 2016 Act can be criticised as failing the tests in Article 11(2) as described above. Firstly, it is necessary to ascertain the underlying policy objectives for the picketing provisions. They are identified in the Consultation papers published prior to the passage of the statute through Parliament and make it clear that the picket supervisors' role is to encourage responsible behaviour on the picket line and deter intimidation and violent conduct – to safeguard the rights of workers, management and members of the public.[203] Yet, there is little substantive evidence of disorderly picketing,[204] there is already a whole range of criminal and civil

---

198 [2009] IRLR 851.

199 See *RMT v United Kingdom* [2015] 60 EHHR 10; *Roffey v United Kingdom*, App No 1278/11 (ECtHR, 21 May 2013); *POA v United Kingdom*, App No 5925/11 (ECtHR, 21 May 2013).

200 As Tony Blair commented in an interview with *The Times* 31 March 1997, 'Let me state the position clearly, so that no-one is in doubt. The essential elements of the trade union legislation will remain. The changes we propose would leave British law the most restrictive on trade unions in the western world'.

201 See Saul, 2015 and Ewing & Hendy, 2016.

202 See the numerous leading cases on the interpretation of the expression 'necessary in a democratic society' including, *inter alia*, *Handyside v United Kingdom* [1976] 1 EHRR 737; *Sunday Times v United Kingdom* [1979] 2 EHRR 245; *Smith and Grady v United Kingdom* [2000] 29 EHRR 493 and specifically in the industrial context – *Wilson and Palmer v United Kingdom* [2002] IRLR 586 and *ASLEF v United Kingdom* [2007] IRLR 361.

203 Department of Business, Innovation and Skills: *Consultation on Tackling Intimidation of Non-Striking Workers*, July 2015, paras 15–18.

204 The Consultation paper (Department for Business, Innovation and Skills: *Consultation on Tackling Intimidation of Non-Striking Workers*, July 2015, pp. 4–5) cited allegations made in the *Carr Report: The Report of the Independent Review of the Law Governing Industrial Disputes*, 15 October 2014, commissioned by the prime minister to investigate allegations of intimidation during picketing activities at the Grangemouth industrial dispute. The authors of the review themselves admitted there was little empirical evidence for these assertions, apart from anecdotal unsubstantiated commentary.

law actions available to the state or the employer to control unruly picketing and, as noted earlier, picketing has to be peaceful for a union to enjoy the benefit of the immunities. Academic research has also demonstrated there is little need for this level of control. Over a 10-year period from 2005 to 2015, only five applications were made for injunctions in relation to breaches of the picketing provisions of s. 220 TULR(C)A 1992.[205]

It is also necessary to see if the government has balanced the rights of both parties when introducing these restrictions. The consequences for trade unions and their members is not just the inability to picket but also that individual picketers will also lose their protection from unfair dismissal.[206] These substantial penalties for a failure of complying with an organisational regulation (such as forgetting to wear an armband or misplacing a letter of authorisation) arguably offends against the notion of 'proportionality' inherent in the requirements of Article 11(2).

One aspect of the proportionality test outlined in Strasbourg case law is whether the domestic law is consistent with the requirements of relevant international law and contemporary European practice. It is unlikely that legislation that is in violation of international and European standards can be said to be 'proportionate'.[207] The International Labour Organisation (ILO) and European Social Charter (ESC) supervisory bodies recognise that the right to picket is an inherent part of the 'right to strike' and any unreasonable interference is a violation of ILO Convention 87, Article 3 and ESC Article 6(4).[208]

Thus, as there is no clear 'pressing social need' for these new restrictions and as they are disproportionate in their impact it is arguable that these provisions are in violation of the safeguards provided by Article 11. Similar points can be made with regard to the balloting provisions introduced by the Trade Union Act 2016 – that they are disproportionate and therefore potentially in violation of Article 11.[209]

20.15 Further reading

Barrow, 'UK courts, balloting requirements and the right to strike: recent developments' (2011) 45 *The Law Teacher* 132.

Barrow, 'Balloting requirements and the right to strike: the retreat from Metrobus' (2013) 47 *The Law Teacher* 271.

Barrow, '*RMT v United Kingdom*: the European Court of Human Rights intimidated into timidity or merely consistent in in its inconsistency' (2015) 3 *European Human Rights Law Review* 277.

Barrow, 'The Trade Union Act 2016 and balloting for industrial action: is the further restriction on the 'right to strike' a flagrant violation of European Convention standards and a step too far for the courts?' in Smyth & Lang (eds), *The Future of Human Rights in the UK*, Cambridge: Cambridge Scholars Publishing, 2017.

Bogg, 'Beyond Neo-Liberalism: The Trade Union Act 2016 and the authoritarian state' (2016) 45 *Industrial Law Journal* 299.

Courtouris & Freedland, 'Injunctions, Cyanamid and the corrosion of the right to strike in the United Kingdom' (2010) 1 *European Labour Law Journal* 489.

205 Gall, 2016.

206 If there is a breach of s. 220A, picketing will not be 'protected industrial action' for the purposes of a claim for unfair dismissal under s. 238A TULRCA 1992.

207 For example, in concluding that restrictions on collective bargaining were disproportionate, the Grand Chamber in *Demir and Baykara v Turkey* [2009] 48 EHRR 54 made specific reference to ILO Convention 98 (On the Right to Organise and to Bargain Collectively) and 151 (On the Right to Organise in Public Service) and Article 6 of the Council of Europe's 1961 Social Charter.

208 See the Digest of Decisions and Principles of the *Freedom of Association Committee of the Governing Body of the ILO*, 2006, para. 651; On ESC Article 6(4), see *European Trade Union Confederation v Belgium*, (App No. 59/2009) 13 September 2011.

209 See Barrow, 2017.

Darlington & Dobson, *The Conservative Proposed Strike Ballot Thresholds: The Challenge to Trade Unions*, Liverpool: Institute for Employment Rights, 2015.
Duke & Kountouris, 'Pre-strike ballots, picketing and protest: banning industrial action by the back door?' (2016) 45 *Industrial Law Journal* 234.
Ewing & Hendy, 'The Trade Union Act and the failure of human rights' (2016) 45 *Industrial Law Journal* 391.
Ford & Novitz, 'An absence of fairness: restrictions on industrial action and protest in the Trade Union Bill' (2015) 44 *Industrial Law Journal* 522.
Gall, 'Injunctions as a legal weapon in collective industrial disputes in Britain 2005–2014' (2016) 55(1) *British Journal of Industrial Relations* 187.
Saul, 'The European Court of Human Rights margin of appreciation and the process of national Parliaments' (2015) 15 *Human Rights Law Review* 745.
Simpson, 'Strike ballots, the judiciary, government policy and industrial relations' (1993) 22 *Industrial Law Journal* 287.
Simpson, 'Strike ballots and the law: round six' (2005) 34 *Industrial Law Journal* 331.
Simpson, 'Tort liability in labour disputes: the potential impact of the House of Lords' Decision in *OBG Ltd v Allen*' (2007) 36 *Industrial Law Journal* 468.

Index